MILLER'S
ANTIQUES
PRICE GUIDE
1987
(Volume VIII)

Compiled and Edited by
Martin and Judith Miller

ISBN 0-905879-43-0

Typeset in England by The Final Word Limited, Tonbridge, Kent
Printed and bound in Spain by by Graficas Estella, S.A., Navarra, D.L.N.A. 282/1986

PUBLISHED BY M.J.M. PUBLICATIONS LTD.
SISSINGHURST COURT, SISSINGHURST, CRANBROOK, KENT TN17 2JA
Telephone (0580) 713890

There are many pitfalls...

awaiting the novice and experienced buyer alike in the Antique world. The biggest question mark in the mind of the potential container buyer must be "How will they know what to send me and will the quality be right?" In an attempt to answer these and other questions, here follows a typical question and answer session:

BUYER:
"How many items will I get for my money?"

B.A.E.
"A typical 20-foot container will have 75 pieces of furniture and approximately 50 pieces of china-ware packed in it. We can regulate the price of the container with the quantity of small items; the higher the value of the shipment, the higher the number of small pieces. Of course the type and style of furniture, for example period Georgian, Victorian or Edwardian, also regulates the price."

BUYER:
"What type of merchandise will you send me?"

B.A.E.
"We have researched all our markets very thoroughly and know the right merchandise to send to any particular country or region in that country. We also take into consideration the type of outlet e.g. auction, wholesale or retail. We consider the strong preferences for different woods in different areas. We personally visit all our markets several times a year to keep pace with the trends."

BUYER:
"Will we get the bargains?"

B.A.E.
"In the mind of any prospective buyer is the thought that he or she will find the true bargains hidden away in the small forgotten corners of some dusty Antique Shop. It is our Company policy to pass on the benefit of any bargain buying to our client."

BUYER:
"With your overheads, etc., how can you send these things to me at a competitive price?"

B.A.E.
"Our very great purchasing power enables us to buy goods at substantially less than the individual person; this means that we are able to buy, collect and pack the item for substantially less than the shop price."

BUYER:
"Will everything be in good condition and will it arrive undamaged?"

B.A.E.
"We are very proud of the superb condition of all the merchandise leaving our factory. We employ the finest craftsmen to restore each piece into first class saleable condition before departure. We also pack to the highest standards thus ensuring that all items arrive safely."

BUYER:
"What guarantee do I have that you will do a good job for me?"

B.A.E.
"The ultimate guarantee. We are so confident of our ability to provide the right goods at the right price that we offer a full refund, if for any reason you are not satisfied with the shipment."

BUYER:
"This all sounds very satisfactory, how do we do business?"

B.A.E.
"Unlike most Companies, we do not require pre-payment for our containers. When you place your order with us, we require a deposit of £1500 and the balance is payable when the container arrives at its destination."

BRITISH ANTIQUE EXPORTERS LTD

QUEEN ELIZABETH AVENUE
BURGESS HILL
WEST SUSSEX, RH15 9RX, ENGLAND
Telex 87688
Cables BRITISH ANTIQUES BURGESS HILL
Telephone BURGESS HILL (04446) 45577

Member of L.A.P.A.D.A.
Guild of Master Craftsmen

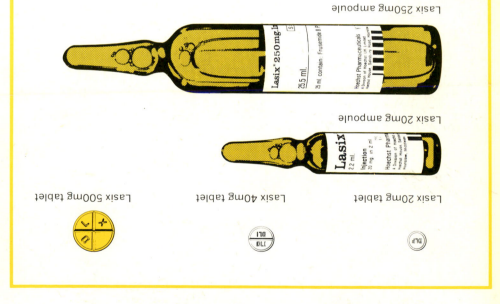

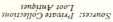

Gilt and painted mirror. Height, 2'. c. 1890. This example gives an idea of how papier mâché was moulded into many different forms. Price approximately £95

Pair of cache pots, c. 1870, gilt round the rim and base, and on both the front and back painted with lily of the valley. Height 11". Price approximately £55 a pair

Two fans, c. 1780, inlaid with mother-of-pearl and hand painted with flowers. The fans have carved wooden handles. Price approximately £12.50 for the pair.

Papier mâché vase, c. 1890, handpainted with flowers. Height 2' 6". Price approximately £160

As one would expect, packing is considered somewhat of an art at B.A.E. and the manager in charge of the works ensures that each piece will reach its final destination in the condition a customer would wish. B.A.E. set a very high standard and, as a further means of improving each container load their customer/ container liaison dept. invites each customer to return detailed information on the saleability of each piece in the container, thereby ensuring successful future shipments. This feedback of information is the all important factor which guarantees the profitability of future containers. "By this method" Mr. Lefton explains, "we have established that an average £7000 container will immediately it is unpacked at its final destination realise in the region of £10000 to £14000 for our clients selling the goods on a quick wholesale turnover basis". When visiting the warehouses various container loads can be seen in the course of completion. The intending buyer can then judge for himself which type of container load would best be suited to his market. In an average 20-foot container B.A.E. put approximately 75 to 150 pieces carefully selected to suit the particular destination. There are always at least 10 outstanding or unusual items in each shipment, but every piece included looks as though it has something special about it.

Based at Burgess Hill 7 miles from Brighton and on a direct rail link with London 39 miles (only 40 minutes journey) the Company is ideally situated to ship containers to all parts of the world. The showrooms, restoration and packing departments are open to overseas buyers and no visit to purchase antiques for re-sale in other countries is complete without a visit to their Burgess Hill premises where a welcome is always found.

BRITISH ANTIQUE EXPORTERS LTD
QUEEN ELIZABETH AVENUE   Member of L.A.P.A.D.A.
BURGESS HILL   Guild of Master Craftsmen
WEST SUSSEX, RH15 9RX, ENGLAND
Telex 87688
Cables BRITISH ANTIQUES BURGESS HILL
Telephone BURGESS HILL (04446) 45577

BRITISH ANTIQUE EXPORTERS LTD

WHOLESALERS, EXPORTERS PACKERS SHIPPERS

HEAD OFFICE: QUEEN ELIZABETH AVENUE, BURGESS HILL, WEST SUSSEX, RH15 9RX ENGLAND

TELEPHONE BURGESS HILL (04446) 45577   TELEX 87688 ANTIQE G

To: Auctioneers, Wholesalers and Retailers of
antique furniture, porcelain and decorative items.

Dear Sirs

We offer the most comprehensive service available in the UK.

As wholesalers we sell 20ft and 40ft container-loads of
antique furniture, porcelain and decorative items of the
Georgian, Victorian, Edwardian and 1930's periods. Our
buyers are strategically placed.throughout the UK in order
to take full advantage of regional pricing.

You can purchase a container from us for as little as £5,000.
This would be filled with mostly 1880's to 1930's furniture.
You could expect to pay approximately £7,000 to £10,000 for
a shipment of Victorian and Edwardian furniture and porcelain.
£10,000 to £25,000 would buy a Georgian, Queen Anne and
Chippendale style container.

Containers can be tailored to your exact requirements - for
example, you may deal only in office furniture and therefore
only buy desks, file cabinets and related office items.

Our terms are £1,500 deposit, the balance at time of arrival
of the container. If the merchandise should not be to your
liking for any reason whatsoever, we offer you your money
back in full, less one-way freight.

We have now opened a large showroom where you can purchase
individual items.

If you wish to visit the UK yourself and purchase individually
from your own sources, we will collect, pack and ship your
merchandise with speed and efficiency. Our rates are competitive and our packing is the finest available anywhere in the
world. Our courier-finder service is second to none and we
have experienced couriers who are equipped with a car and the
knowledge of where to find the best buys.

If your business is buying English antiques, we are your contact.
We assure you of our best attention at all times.

Yours faithfully
BRITISH ANTIQUE EXPORTERS LTD

Norman Lefton
Chairman & Managing Director

DIRECTORS: N. LEFTON (Chairman & Managing),   P. V. LEFTON,   THE RT. HON. THE VISCOUNT EXMOUTH,   A. FIELD, MSC FBOA DCLP FSMC FAAO.
REGISTERED OFFICE: 12/13 SHIP STREET, BRIGHTON   REGISTERED No. 893406 ENGLAND
BANKERS: NATIONAL WESTMINSTER BANK LTD. 155 NORTH STREET, BRIGHTON, SUSSEX   THE CHASE MANHATTAN BANK, N.A., 410 PARK AVENUE, NEW YORK

9

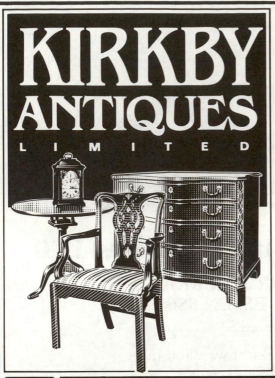

14

PETER SEMUS
Antiques

Established for over 20 years, Peter Semus Antiques deals mainly in a wide range of antique, Victorian and 1920s furniture and accessories. Through our extensive workshop, we specialise in "conversion pieces" such as Bureau Bookcases, Linen Presses, Chests of Drawers, Breakfront Bookcases, Chest on Chests, Secretaire Bookcases, Chest on Stands in a variety of woods. We will also undertake customised pieces to individual requirements.

We are, however, happy to sell unrestored items from either the warehouse or the showroom where we hold an interesting stock of garden statuary and ornaments, in addition to a great variety of furniture. There is no obligation to order a whole container load and we will always welcome your order whatever the size.

Finally, we have our whole container service which specialises in filling your container with your exact requirements whenever possible. Following careful discussion on merchandise and price, we will put together your shipment and handle all aspects of its safe delivery to your door. We can, of course, provide excellent references from current clients.

Please understand that we welcome you as a customer, regardless of whether you use us for shipping or not. We do feel that we can offer one of the most competitive all round packages available, for good quality merchandise and excellent service.

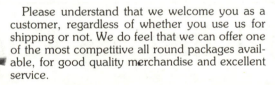

Shipping
LONDON & SOUTHERN
Company

Showroom: 379 Kingsway, Hove, East Sussex BN3 4QD, UK.
Telephone: (0273) 420154 **Telex:** 87323 LASS

Offices & Warehouse: The Warehouse, Gladstone Road, Portslade, East Sussex BN4 1LJ, UK.
Telephone: (0273) 420154 **Telex:** 87323 LASS

19

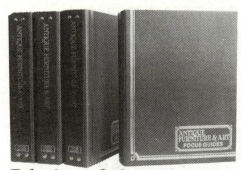

Acknowledgements

The publishers would like to acknowledge the great assistance given by our consultant editors:

POTTERY: **Jonathan Horne,** *66b and c Kensington Church Street, London, W8.*
David Clark, *Elias Clark Antiques Ltd., 1 The Cobbles, High Street, Bletchingley, Surrey.*

PORCELAIN: **Christopher Spencer,** *Greystones, 29 Mostyn Road, Merton Park, London, SW19*
Nicholas Long, *Studio Antiques, Bourton-on-the-Water, Glos.*

WORCESTER: **Henry Sandon,** *11 Perrywood Close, Worcester.*

GOSS & CRESTED WARE: **Nicholas Pine,** *Goss & Crested China Ltd., 62 Murray Road, Horndean, Hants.*

FURNITURE: **John Bly,** *50 High Street, Tring, Herts.*
Richard Davidson, *Richard Davidson Antiques, Lombard Street, Petworth, Sussex.*

   OAK: **Victor Chinnery,** *Bennetts, Oare, Nr. Marlborough, Wilts.*
   COUNTRY: **Mike Golding,** *Huntington Antiques, The Old Forge, Church Street, Stow-on-the-Wold, Glos.*

LONGCASE CLOCKS: **Brian Loomes,** *Calfhaugh, Pateley Bridge, N. Yorks.*

GLASS: **Wing Cdr. G. R. Thomas,** *Somervale Antiques, 6 Radstock Road, Midsomer Norton, Bath, Avon.*

ART NOUVEAU & ART DECO: **Keith Baker,** *Phillips, Blenstock House, 7 Blenheim Street, New Bond Street, London, W1.*
Eric Knowles, *Bonhams, Montpelier Galleries, Montpelier Street, Knightsbridge, London, SW7.*

LALIQUE   **Russell Varney,** *Bonhams, Montpelier Galleries, Montpelier Street, Knightsbridge, London, SW7.*

SILVER: **James Lowe,** *Bonhams, Montpelier Galleries, Montpelier Street, Knightsbridge, London, SW7.*

CARPETS & TEXTILES: **Robert Bailey,** *1 Roll Gardens, Gants Hill, Essex.*

TOYS: **Stuart Cropper,** *Stand L14/15, Grays Mews, 1-7 Davies Mews, London, W1.*

ARMS & ARMOUR: **Roy Butler,** *Wallis & Wallis, West Street, Auction Galleries, Lewes, Sussex.*

PINE FURNITURE & KITCHENALIA: **Ann Lingard,** *Rope Walk Antiques, Rye, Sussex.*

JEWELLERY: **Valerie Howkins,** *Peter Howkins, 39-40 and 135 King Street, Great Yarmouth, Norfolk.*

FISHING: **Nicholas Marchant Lane,** *Salter's Cottage, Bramshott, Liphook, Hants.*

Key to Illustrations

Each illustration and descriptive caption is accompanied by a letter-code. By reference to the following list of Auctioneers (denoted by *) and Dealers (●), the source of any item may be immediately determined. In no way does this constitute or imply a contract or binding offer on the part of any of our contributors to supply or sell the goods illustrated, or similar articles, at the prices stated. Advertisers in this year's directory are denoted by †.

A	*	Aldridges of Bath Ltd., The Auction Galleries, 130-132 Walcot, Bath. Tel: (0225) 62830 & 62839
AAA	●	AAA, Stand 130, Grays Antique Market, 58 Davies Street, London, W1. Tel: 01-629 5130
AF		Albert Forsythe, Mill Hall, 66 Carsonstown Road, Saintfield, Co. Down, Eire. Tel: (0238) 510398
AG	*	Anderson & Garland, Anderson House, Market Street, Newcastle-Upon-Tyne. Tel: (0632) 326278
AGA	●	A. & G., Grays Antique Market, 58 Davies Street, London, W1. Tel: 01-493 7564
AGr	*	Andrew Grant, 59/60 Foregate Street, Worcester. Tel: (0905) 52310
AJ	† *	Arthur Johnson & Sons Ltd., Cattle Market, London Road, Nottingham. Tel: (0602) 869128
AL	†●	Ann Lingard, Ropewalk Antiques, Ropewalk, Rye, Sussex. Tel: (0797) 223486
ALM	*	Allman, Auctioneers, 10 Middle Row, Chipping Norton, Oxon. Tel: (0608) 3087
AP	●	Anthony Preston Antiques Ltd., The Square, Stow-on-the-Wold, Gloucestershire. Tel: (0451) 31586 & 31406
APT	*	Ader Picard Tajan, Commissaires – Priseurs Associes, 12 Rue Favart, 72002 Paris. Tel: 42 61 80 07

AR	●	Armada, 122 Grays Antique Market, London, W1. Tel: 01-499 1087
ARC	●	Arca, Stand 351, Grays Antique Market, 58 Davies Street, London, W1. Tel: 01-629 2729
ARM	●	Armour Antiques, 123 Grays Antique Market, London, W1. Tel: 01-408 0176
ASH	†●	Ashburton Marbles, 6 West Street, Ashburton, Devon. Tel: (0364) 53189
AYL	†*	Aylsham Salerooms, G. A. Key, 8 Market Place, Aylsham. Tel: (0263) 733195
B	*	Boardman, Station Road Corner, Haverhill, Suffolk. Tel: (0440) 703784
BA	*	Bannister & Co., T., Market Place, Haywards Heath, Sussex. Tel: (0444) 412402
BAC	†●	Bacchus Antiques, 27 Grange Avenue, Hale, Nr. Altrincham, Cheshire. Tel: (061) 980 4747
BAD	●	Baddiel & Carlson, B24/25, Grays Mews, 1-7 Davies Mews, London, W1. Tel: 01-408 1239. Home Tel: 01-452 7243
BAL	●	Balcony Antiques, Stand G21, Grays Mews, 1-7 Davies Mews, London, W1. Tel: 01-629 3788
BAG		Bagpuss Grays Antique Market

BD * Burrows & Day, 39/41 Bank Street, Ashford, Kent. Tel: (0233) 24321 (See also CBD – Cobbs, Burrows & Day)

Bea * Bearnes, Rainbow, Avenue Road, Torquay, Devon. Tel: (0803) 26277

BHW †* Butler & Hatch Waterman, 102 High Street, Tenterden, Kent. Tel: (058 06) 3233/2083

BL †● Brian Loomes, Calfhaugh, Pateley Bridge, N. Yorkshire. Tel: (0423) 711163

Bon †* Bonhams, Montpelier Galleries, Montpelier Street, Knightsbridge, London, SW7. Tel: 01-584 9161

BOU ● J. H. Bourdon-Smith, 24 Mason's Yard, Duke Street, St. James', London, SW1. Tel: 01-839 4714

BP †* Bonsor Penningtons, 82 Eden Street, Kingston, London. Tel: 01-546 0022

BRE †● Brenin Porcelain & Pottery (Mr. King), Old Wool Barn, Verity's Court, Cowbridge, South Glamorgan, Wales. Tel: (04463) 3893

BRI ● Britannia, Stand 103, Grays Antique Market, 58 Davies Street, London, W1. Tel: 01-629 6772

BS * Banks & Silvers, 66 Foregate Street, Worcester. Tel: (0905) 23456

BWe †* Biddle & Webb of Birmingham, Ladywood Middleway, Birmingham. Tel: (021) 455 8042

C * Christie, Manson & Woods Ltd., 8 King Street, St. James, London, SW1. Tel: 01-839 9060

CAm * Christie's Amsterdam, Cornelis Schuytstraat 57 1071 JG, Amsterdam, Holland. Tel: (020) 64 20 11

CAS ● Simon Castle, 38B Kensington Church Street, London, W8. Tel: 01-937 2268

CAU * Christie, Manson & Woods (Australia) Ltd., 298 New South Head Road, Double Bay, NSW 2028. Tel: (02) 326 1422

CB †● Christine Bridge Antiques, K10-12, Grays Mews, 1-7 Davies Mews, London, W1. Tel: 01-499 3562

CBB †* Colliers, Bigwood & Bewlay, The Old School, Tiddington, Stratford-upon-Avon, Warks. Tel: (0789) 69415

CBD †* Cobbs, Burrows & Day, 39-41 Bank Street, Ashford, Kent. Tel: (0233) 24321. (See also BD – Burrows & Day)

CBe Collett/Bell, B10/11, Grays Mews, 1-7 Davies Mews, London, W1. Tel: 01-629 2813

CBS * C. B. Sheppard and Son, Auction Galleries, Chatsworth Street, Sutton-in-Ashfield, Notts. Tel: (0773) 872419

CDC * Capes Dunn & Co., The Auction Galleries, 38 Charles Street, off Princess Street, Manchester. Tel: (061) 273 6060

CEd * Christie's & Edmiston's Ltd., 164-166 Bath Street, Glasgow. Tel: (041) 332 8134/7

CG * Christie's (International) S.A., 8 Place de la Taconnerie, 1204 Geneva. Tel: (022) 28 25 44

CGC * Cheffins, Grain & Chalk, Saleroom Dept., 2 Clifton Road (off Cherry Hinton Road), Cambridge. Tel: (0223) 358721/248160

CH * Chancellors Hollingsworths, 31 High Street, Ascot, Berkshire. Tel: (0990) 27101

CKK * Coles, Knapp & Kennedy, Tudor House, High Street, Ross-on-Wye, Herefordshire. Tel: (0989) 63553/4

CLG * Clarke Gammon, 45 High Street, Guildford, Surrey. Tel: (0483) 572266

CM * Christie's (Monaco) S.A.M., Hans Nadelhoffer, Christine de Massy, Park Palace, 98000 Monte Carlo. Tel: 93 25 19 33

CNY * Christie, Manson & Woods International Inc., 502 Park Avenue, New York, N.Y. 10022 USA. Tel: (212) 546 1000 (including Christie's East)

COB †● Cobwebs (P. A. Boyd-Smith), 78 Northam Road, Southampton. Tel: (0703) 227458

CoH * Cooper Hirst, Goldlay House, Parkway, Chelmsford, Essex. Tel: (0245) 58141

CPA * Commissaires-Priseurs Associes, 1 bis, Place du General de Gaulle, 28000, Chartres. Tel: (37) 36 04 33. (see also JPL – Jean-Pierre Lelievre)

CPT ● Crypt Antiques, High Street, Burford, Oxon. Tel: (099 382) 2302

CR * Christie's Roma, Piazza Navona, 114 Roma 00186. Tel: (06) 6564032

Cre ● Croesus, Stand 324, Grays Antiques Market, 58 Davies Street, London, W1. Tel: 01-493 0624

CRO ● Stuart Cropper, L14/15, Grays Mews, 1-7 Davies Mews, London, W1. Tel: 01-499 6600

CRY * Chrystals Auctions, St. James's Chambers, Athol Street, Douglas, Isle of Man. Tel: (0624) 73986

CS ● Connie Speight, 108 Grays Antique Market, 58 Davies Street, London, W1. Tel: 01-629 8624

CSK * Christie's (South Kensington), 85 Old Brompton Road, London, SW7. Tel: 01-581 7611

CW * Cubitt & West, Fine Art Auction Galleries, Millmead, Guildford, Surrey. Tel: (0483) 504030

DA * Dee & Atkinson, The Exchange, Driffield, Yorkshire. Tel: (0377) 43151

DAV ● Barry Davies, E14/17 Grays Mews, 1-7 Davies Mews, London, W1. Tel: 01-408 0207

DDM * Dickinson, Davy & Markham, New Saleroom, Elwes Street, Brigg, South Humberside. Tel: (0652) 53666

DE ● Delomosne & Son Ltd., 4 Campden Hill Road, Kensington, London, W8. Tel: 01-937 1804

DEL †● Marilyn Caron Delion, at Wyllie Gallery, 12 Needham Road, London, W11. Tel: 01-727 0606 01-937 3377 (home)

DF ● Diana Foley, L18-21, Grays Mews, 1-7 Davies Mews, London, W1. Tel: 01-408 1089

DL †● Dunsdale Lodge Antiques, Brasted Road, Westerham, Kent. Tel: (0959) 62160

DM * Diamond, Mills & Co., 117 Hamilton Road, Felixstowe, Suffolk. Tel: (0394) 282281

DON ● Donohoe, L25/27, Grays Mews, 1-7 Davies Mews, London, W1. Tel: 01-629 5633

DSH †● Dacre, Son & Hartley, 1-5 The Grove, Ilkley, West Yorkshire. Tel: (0943) 600655

DV ● Denzil Verey, The Close, Barnsley House, Barnsley, Nr. Cirencester, Gloucestershire. Tel: (0285) 74402

DWB †* Dreweatts, Donnington Priory, Donnington, Newbury, Berks. Tel: (0635) 31234

EA ● Etna Antiques, 81 Kensington Church Street, London, W8. Tel: 01-937 3754

EG * Elliott & Green, The Sale Room, Emsworth Road, Lymington, Hampshire. Tel: (0590) 77225

EH * Edgar Horn, The Auction Galleries, 47 Cornfield Road, Eastbourne, Sussex. Tel: (0323) 22801/2/3

EJ ● Eliza Jay, 319/320 Grays Antique Market, 58 Davies Street, London, W1. Tel: 01-408 0887

ELD ● Eldridge London & Co., 99-101 Farringdon Road, London, EC1. Tel: 01-837 0379 & 0370

ET ● Eugene Tiernan, H18/19, Grays Mews, 1-7 Davies Mews, London, W1. Tel: 01-629 3788

EWS †● E. Watson & Sons, The Market, Burwash Road, Heathfield, Sussex. Tel: (04352) 2132

FA ● Frith Antiques, New Street, Petworth, West Sussex. Tel: (0798) 43155

FF ● Fritz Fryer, 27 Gloucester Road, Ross-on-Wye, Herefordshire. Tel: (0989) 64738/84512

FHF * Frank H. Fellows & Sons, 'Bedford House', 88 Hagley Road, Edgbaston, Birmingham. Tel: (021) 454 1261/1219

FIR ● Jack First, 310/312 Grays Antique Market, 58 Davies Street, London, W1. Tel: 01-629 1307

FM ● Fiandaca-Myers, 386 Grays Antique Market, 58 Davies Street, London, W1. Tel: 01-499 4340

FR * Fryer's Auction Galleries, Terminus Road, Bexhill-on-Sea, Sussex. Tel: (0424) 212994

FRA • Francoise, H24 Grays Mews, 1-7 Davies Mews, London, W1.

GAZ • Gaze, S384, Grays Antique Market, 58 Davies Street, London, W1. Tel: 01-629 3920

GC †* Geering & Colyer, Auctioneers, 22-24 High Street, Tunbridge Wells, Kent. Tel: (0892) 25136

GCA †• Gerald Clark Antiques, 1 High Street, Mill Hill Village, London, NW7. Tel: 01-906 0342

G&CC†• Goss & Crested China Ltd, Nicholas J. Pine, 62 Murray Road, Horndean, Hants. Tel: (0705) 597440

GH * Giles Haywood, The Auction House, St. John's Road, Stourbridge, West Midlands. Tel: (03843) 70891

Gil • The Gilded Lily, 131/43, Grays Antique Market, 58 Davies Street, London, W1. Tel: 01-629 5130

GL • Gloucester House Antiques, Market Place, Fairford, Gloucestershire. Tel: (0285) 712790

GM * George Mealy & Sons, The Square, Castlecomer Co. Kilkenny. Tel: (010 353 56) 41229

GRA • Solveig & Anita Gray, Stand 307/308, Grays Antique Market, 58 Davies Street, London, W1. Tel: 01-408 1638

GRE • Gres, 378 Grays Antique Market, 58 Davies Street, London, W1. Tel: 01-499 3075

GSP * Graves, Son & Pilcher, 71 Church Road, Hove, East Sussex. Tel: (0273) 735266

H †• Huntington Antiques Ltd., The Old Forge, Church Street, Stow-on-the-Wold, Glos. Tel: (0451) 30842

HA • Hallmark Antiques, 360 Grays Antique Market, 58 Davies Street, London, W1. Tel: 01-409 2937

HAL • Hallidays Antiques Ltd, The Old College, Dorchester-on-Thames, Oxon. Tel: (0865) 340028/68

HB * Heathcote Ball & Co., Castle Auction Rooms, 78 St. Nicholas Circle, Leics. Tel: (0533) 536789

HCH †* Hobbs & Chambers, 'At the Sign of the Bell', Market Place, Cirencester, Glos. Tel: (0285) 4736
Also: 15 Royal Crescent, Cheltenham, Glos. Tel: (0242) 513722

HG • Hay Galleries Ltd., 4 High Town, Hay-on-Wye, Hereford. Tel: (0497) 820356

HL • Helen Linfield and Michael Wakelin, 10 New Street, Petworth, Sussex. Tel: (0798) 42417

HOF • Hoffman Antiques, 379 Grays Antique Market, 58 Davies Street, London, W1. Tel: 01-499 4340

HP * Hobbs Parker, Romney House, Ashford Market, Ashford, Kent. Tel: (0233) 22222

HR * Hugo Ruef, Gabelsbergerstrasse 28, D-8000 Munchen 2. Tel: (089) 524084-86

HSS †* Henry Spencer & Sons, 20 The Square, Retford, Notts. Tel: (0777) 708633

HW * H. Wilford Ltd., Midland Road, Wellingborough, Northants. Tel: (0933) 222760 & 222762

JHo * Hall, Wateridge & Owen, Welsh Bridge Salerooms, Shrewsbury, Shropshire. Tel: (0743) 60212

IAT †• It's About Time, 863 London Road, Westcliff-on-Sea, Essex. Tel: (0702) 72574 & 205204

IM * Ibbett Mosely, 125 High Street, Sevenoaks, Kent. Tel: (0732) 452246

JD †* Julian Dawson, Lewes Auction Rooms, 56 High Street, Lewes, East Sussex. Tel: (0273) 478221

JF †* John Francis, 19 King Street, Carmarthen. Tel: (0267) 233456/7

JH * Jacobs & Hunt, Lavant Street, Petersfield, Hants. Tel: (0730) 62744

JHp †• Jonathan Horne, 66c Kensington Church Street, London, W8. Tel: 01-221 5658

JHS †* John Hogbin & Son, 53 High Street, Tenterden, Kent. Tel: (05806) 3200

JIL • Jilliana, 7A Jones Arcade, Westbourne Grove (Portobello Road Market), London, W11. (Also at 164 Kensington Park Road, London, W11)

JJIL • John Jesse and Irina Laski Ltd., 160 Kensington Church Street, London, W8. Tel: 01-229 0312

JMG †• Jamie Maxtone Graham, Nithside, Closeburn, Thornhill, Dumfries, Scotland. Tel: (0848) 31382

JMW * J. M. Welch & Son, The Old Town Hall, Great Dunmow, Essex. Tel: (0371) 2117/2118

JPL * Jean-Pierre Lelievre, 1 bis, pl. General-de-Gaulle, 28000, Chartres, France. Tel: (37) 36 04 33. (See also CPA – Commissaires-Priseurs Associes)

JRB * J. R. Bridgford & Sons, 1 Heyes Lane, Alderley Edge, Cheshire. Tel: (0625) 585347

JRP †* J. R. Parkinson Son & Hamer Auctions, The Auction Rooms, Rochdale Road (Kershaw Street), Bury. Tel: (061 761) 1612 & 7372

JTD * J. T. Davies, 7 Aberdeen Road, Croydon, Surrey. Tel: 01-681 3222

JUD • St. Jude's Antiques, 107 Kensington Church Street, London, W8. Tel: 01-727 8737

KEY †• Key Antiques, 11 Horsefair, Chipping Norton, Oxon. Tel: (0608) 3777

Ksh • K. Shipman, Grays Mews, 1-7 Davies Mews, London, W1.

KSS * K. Stuart Swash FSVA, Stamford House, 2 Waterloo Road, Wolverhampton. Tel: (0902) 710626

L * Lawrence Fine Art of Crewkerne, South Street, Crewkerne, Somerset. Tel: (0460) 73041

LAM †• Penny Lampard, Rectory Farm, Langley, Maidstone, Kent. Tel: (0622) 861377

Lan * Langlois, Westaway Rooms, Don Street, St. Helier, Jersey, C.I. Tel: (0534) 22441

LAY * David Lay, A.S.V.A., 7 Morrab Road, Penzance, Cornwall. Tel: (0736) 61414/5

LAZ • Lazarell, 325 Grays Antique Market, 58 Davies Street, London, W1.

LBA * Lawrence Butler & Co., Butler House, 86 High Street, Hythe, Kent. Tel: (0303) 66022/3

LBP †* Lalonde Bros. & Parham, 71 Oakfield Road, Bristol, Avon. Tel: (0272) 734052

LC †• Luckpenny Antiques, Kilmurray House, Shinrone, County Offaly, Eire. Tel: (010 353 505) 47134

LJ * Louis Johnson, Oswald House, 63 Bridge Street, Morpeth. Tel: (0670) 52210 & 513025

LM • Lilian Middleton, Days Stables, Sheep Street, Stow-on-the-Wold, Glos. Tel: (0451) 30381

LR †• Leonard Russell, 21 King's Avenue, Newhaven, Sussex. Tel: (0273) 515153

LRG †* Lots Road Chelsea Auction Galleries, 71 Lots Road, Chelsea, London, SW10. Tel: 01-352 2349

LT †* Louis Taylor, Percy Street, Hanley, Stoke-on-Trent, Staffs. Tel: (0782) 260222

LUC • Claude Lucbernet, Stand 329/30, Grays Antique Market, 58 Davies Street, London, W1. Tel: 01-493 1219

M * Morphets of Harrogate, 4-6 Albert Street, Harrogate, North Yorkshire. Tel: (0423) 502282

MA • Matthew Adams, A1 Rogers Antique Galleries, 65 Portobello Road, London, W11. Tel: 01-579 5560

MAK • Minoo & Andre Kaae, G22/23 Grays Mews, 1-7 Davies Mews, London, W1. Tel: 01-629 1200

Max • Maxey & Son, 1-3 South Brink, Wisbech, Cambridgeshire. Tel: (0945) 583123

MAY †* May & Son, 18 Bridge Street, Andover, Hants. Tel: (0264) 23417 & 63331

MC †• Margaret Corson, Irstead Manor, Neatishead, Norfolk. Tel: (0692) 630274

McC * McCartneys, 25 Corve Street, Ludlow, Shropshire. Tel: (0584) 2636

MG • Michael C. German, 38B Kensington Church Street, London, W8. Tel: 01-937 2771

MGM †* Michael G. Matthews, A.S.V.A., A.R.V.A., The Devon Fine Art Auction House, Dowell Street, Honiton, Devon. Tel: (0404) 41872 & 3137

MIL †* Millers, Mansion House, Princess Street, Truro, Cornwall. Tel: (0872) 74211. Also: Lemon Quay Auction Rooms, Lemon Quay, Truro, Cornwall.

MN †* Michael Newman, The Central Auction Rooms, Kinterbury House, St. Andrew's Cross, Plymouth, Devon. Tel: (0752) 669298

MOR * Morey & Son, 50 East Street, Bridport, Dorset. Tel: (0308) 22078

MR ● Michael Rooum, Grays Mews, 1-7 Davies Mews, London, W1. Tel: 01-629 2813

MSh †* Michael Shortall, 11 Bayle Parade, Folkestone, Kent. Tel: (0303) 45555 (See also PFo – now Phillips Folkestone)

MW ● Mary Wellard, Stand 164/165, Grays Antique Market, 58 Davies Street, London, W1. Tel: 01-629 5130

N * Neales of Nottingham, 192-194 Mansfield Road, Nottingham. Tel: (0602) 624141

Nes †* D. M. Nesbit & Co., 7 Clarendon Road, Southsea, Hants. Tel: (0705) 820785

NP ● Nick Podmore, 374 Grays Antique Market, 58 Davies Street, London, W1. Tel: 01-408 1550

NSF * Neal Sons & Fletcher, 26 Church Street, Woodbridge, Suffolk. Tel: (03943) 2263/4

O †* Olivers, 23-24 Market Hill, Sudbury, Suffolk. Tel: (0787) 72247

OKM * Osborne King and Megran, 17 Castle Arcade, Belfast. Tel: (0232) 240332

OL * Outhwaite & Litherland, Kingsway Galleries, Fontenoy Street, Liverpool. Tel: (051) 236 6561

ONS * Onslow's. Tel: (0962) 75411

OT * Osmond Tricks, Regent Street Auction Rooms, Clifton, Bristol. Tel: (0272) 737201

P †* Phillips, Blenstock House, 7 Blenheim Street, New Bond Street, London, W1. Tel: 01-629 6602

PB * Phillips Inc. Brooks, 39 Park End Street, Oxford. Tel: (0865) 723524

Pb ● Peter Binks, Stand 331/2, GRays Antique Market, 58 Davies Street, London, W1. Tel: 01-493 1015

PC †* Peter Cheney, Western Road Auction Rooms, Western Road, Littlehampton, West Sussex. Tel: (0903) 722264/713418

Pea * Pearsons, Tower House Sale Rooms, High Street, Winchester. Tel: (0962) 64444. Also: Tower Street, Winchester

PEL * Peter Eley, Western House, 98-100 High Street, Sidmouth, Devon. Tel: (03955) 2552/3

PFo †* Phillips Folkestone, 11 Bayle Parade, Folkestone, Kent. Tel: (0303) 45555. (See also Michael Shortall)

Ph †● Phelps Ltd., 129-135 St. Margaret's Road, Twickenham, Middlesex. Tel: 01-892 1778 & 7129

PHA ● Paul Hopwell Antiques, 30 High Street, West Haddon, Northants. Tel: (078 887) 636

Phi ● Philip, Stand 127, Grays Antique Market, 58 Davies Street, London, W1. Tel: 01-499 4340

PIN †● Pine Finds, The Old Cornmill, Bishop Monkton, Harrogate, N. Yorkshire. Tel: (0765) 87159

PJ ● P. & J., J28/K13, Grays Mews, 1-7 Davies Mews, London, W1. Tel: 01-499 2719

PLJ * Philip Laney & Jolly, 12a Worcester Road, Malvern. Tel: (06845) 61169/63121-2

PMc ● Peter McAskie, D10/12, Grays Mews, 1-7 Davies Mews, London, W1. Tel: 01-629 2813

POT ● Pieces of Time, Stand M17, Grays Mews, 1-7 Davies Mews, London, W1. Tel: 01-629 3272

PR ● Pamela Rowan, High Street, Blockley, Nr. Moreton-in-Marsh, Glos. Tel: (0386) 700280

PSG ● Patrick & Susan Gould, L17, Grays Mews, 1-7 Davies Mews, London, W1. Tel: 01-408 0129

PU ● Penelope Uden, H25, Grays Mews, 1-7 Davies Mews, London, W1. Tel: 01-493 4843

PWC * Parsons, Welch & Cowell, 49 London Road, Sevenoaks, Kent. Tel: (0732) 451211/4

Ram ● Ramsay, 365 Grays Antique Market, 58 Davies Street, London, W1

RAY ● Derek Rayment Antiques, Orchard House, Barton Road, Barton, Nr. Farndon, Cheshire. Tel: (0829) 270429

RBB †* Russell Baldwin & Bright Auctioneers, Ryelands Road, Leominster, Herefordshire. Tel: (0568) 3897

RBE ● Ron Beech, 150 Portland Road, Hove, Sussex. Tel: (0273) 724477

RdeR †● Rogers de Rin, 76 Royal Hospital Road, Paradise Walk, London, SW3. Tel: 01-352 9007

Re * Reeds Rains, Trinity House, 114 Northenden Road, Sale, Cheshire. Tel: (061) 962 9237

Rev ● Reville & Rossiter, L10/12, Grays Mews, 1-7 Davies Mews, London, W1

ROB ● Robinson, Jonathan, Stand C24/25, Grays Mews, 1-7 Davies Mews, London, W1. Tel: 01-493 6692

RP ● Robert Pugh, 6 Goring Road, Llanelli, Dyfed

RPI * Raymond P. Inman, The Auction Galleries, 35 & 40 Temple Street, Brighton, Sussex

RR ● R. & R., Grays Antique Market, 58 Davies Street, London, W1. Tel: 01-629 6467

RT * Richard Turner & Son, Royal Oak Chambers, Main Street, High Bentham. Tel: (0468) 61444

SA ● Studio Antiques Ltd., Bourton-on-the-Water, Glos. Tel: (0451) 20352

SAg ● Sussex Auction Galleries, 59 Perrymount Road, Haywards Heath, Sussex. Tel: (0444) 414935

SAR ● Sarah Baddiel, B24/25, Grays Mews, 1-7 Davies Mews, London, W1. Tel: 01-408 1239 Home Tel: 01-452 7243

SAU ● Saunders, B13, Grays Mews, 1-7 Davies Mews, London, W1

SB ● Stanhope Bowry, Stand 104, Grays Antique Market, 58 Davies Street, London, W1. Tel: 01-629 6194

SBA ● South Barr Antiques, Digbeth Street, Stow-on-the-Wold, Glos. Tel: (0557) 30430

SBO ● Constance Stobo, 31 Holland Street, off Kensington Church Street, London, W8. Tel: 01-937 6282

Sca †● Scallywag, 189 Clapham Road, Stockwell, London, SE5. Tel: 01-274 0300

SCW ● The Sussex Commemorative Ware Centre, 88 Western Road, Hove, Sussex. Tel: (0273) 773911

SD ● Stephen O'Donnell, 156 Grays Antique Market, 58 Davies Street, London, W1. Tel: 01-491 8852

Sei ● Seidler, 120 Grays Antique Market, 58 Davies Street, London, W1. Tel: 01-629 2851

SHa ● Stone House Antiques, St. Mary's Street, Painswick, Glos. Tel: (0452) 813540

SHP ● Shapiro, Stand 380, Grays Antique Market, 58 Davies Street, London, W1. Tel: 01-491 2710

Si ● Simmons & Simmons, K37/38, Grays Mews, 1-7 Davies Mews, London, W1. Tel: 01-629 9321

SL * Simmons & Lawrence, 32 Bell Street, Henley-on-Thames, Oxon. Tel: (0491) 571111

Som †● Somervale Antiques, The Poplars, 6 Radstock Road, Midsomer Norton, Bath. Tel: (0761) 412686

SSD ● Smith & Smith Designs, 58A Middle Street North, Driffield. Tel: (0377) 46321

STE †● A. & P. Steadman, Unit 1, Hatson Industrial Estate, Kirkwall, Orkney. Tel: (0856) 5040

Sto ● Stockspring Antiques, STand J23/24, Grays Mews, 1-7 Davies Mews, London, W1

Stu ● Studium, Stand M20/21, Grays Mews, 1-7 Davies Mews, London, W1. Tel: 01-408 0131

STW ● Stone-Wares, 24 Radford Street, Stone, Staffs. Tel: (0785) 815000

SW †● Shirley Warren, 42 Kingswood Avenue, Sanderstead, Surrey. Tel: 01-657 1751

SYK ● Christopher Sykes, The Old Parsonage, Woburn, Milton Keynes, Beds. Tel: (052 525) 259 and 467

TAL • Talisman, Stand 363, Grays Antique Market, 58 Davies Street, London, W1. Tel: 01-499 4349

TAY * Taylors, Honiton Galleries, 205 High Street, Honiton, Devon. Tel: (0404) 2404/5

TEN †* Tennant's, 26-27 Market Place, Leyburn, North Yorkshire. Tel: (0969) 23451

TG • Thornborough Galleries, 28 Gloucester Street, Cirencester, Glos. Tel: (0285) 2055

THG • Trevor H. Gilbert, Stand 10/11, Grays Mews, 1-7 Davies Mews, London, W1. Tel: 01-408 0028

TKN †* Tiffen King Nicholson, 12 Lowther Street, Carlisle, Cumbria. Tel: (0228) 25259

TLC * Taylor, Lane & Creber, 38 North Hill, Plymouth, Devon. Tel: (0752) 670700

TM * Thos. Mawer & Son, 63 Monks Road, Lincoln. Tel: (0522) 24984

TP • Trevor Philip & Sons Ltd., 2 Prince Albert Street, Brighton, Sussex. Tel: (0273) 202119

TRI • Trianon, Stand 154/155, Grays Antique Market, 58 Davies Street, London, W1

TRi • Trio, L24, Grays Mews, 1-7 Davies Mews, London, W1. Tel: 01-629 1184

TS • Thimble Society of London, Stand 134, Grays Antique Market, 58 Davies Street, London, W1

TW †* Thomas Watson & Son, Northumberland Street, Darlington, Co. Durham. Tel: (0325) 462555 & 462559

V †* Vidler & Co., Rye Auction Galleries, Cinque Ports Street, Rye, East Sussex. Tel: (0797) 222124

VEN †• Venners Antiques, 7 New Cavendish Street, London, W1. Tel: 01-935 0184

Vin • Vintage, Stand 371, Grays Antique Market, 58 Davies Street, London, W1.

VP • Ventura-Pauly, 354/355, Grays Antique Market, 58 Davies Street, London, W1. Tel: 01-408 1057

Wai • Wain Antiques, 45 Long Street, Tetbury, Gloucestershire. Tel: (0666) 52440

WAL †* Wallis & Wallis, West Street Auction Galleries, Lewes, Sussex. Tel: (0273) 473137

WAT * Watsons, 1 Market Street, Saffron Walden, Essex. Tel: (0799) 22058

WBP * Watson Bull & Porter, 79 Regent Street, Shanklin, I.o.W. Tel: (0983) 863441

WD * Weller & Dufty Ltd., 141 Bromsgrove Street, Birmingham. Tel: (021) 692 1414/5

WHA †• Wych House Antiques, Wych Hill, Woking, Surrey. Tel: (04862) 64636

WHB * William H. Brown, Westgate Hall, Westgate, Grantham, Lincs. Tel: (0476) 68861

WHL * W. H. Lane & Son, 64 Morrab Road, Penzance, Cornwall. Tel: (0736) 61447

WIL * Wilson, Peter & Co., Victoria Gallery, Market Street, Nantwich, Cheshire. Tel: (0270) 623878

Wor †* Worsfolds, The Auction Galleries, 40 Station Road West, Canterbury, Kent. Tel: (0227) 68984

WR * Walter & Randall, 7-13 New Road, Chatham, Kent. Tel: (0634) 41233

WSH †* Warner Sheppard & Wade, The Warner Auction Rooms, 16-18 Halford Street, Leicester. Tel: (0533) 21613

WSW * Wyatt & Son (with Whiteheads), 59 East Street, Chichester, West Sussex. Tel: (0243) 786581
Also: Baffins Hall, Baffins Lane, Chichester, West Sussex

WW * Woolley & Wallis, The Castle Auction Mart, Castle Street, Salisbury, Wilts. Tel: (0722) 21711

YES • Yesterday, H20, Grays Mews, 1-7 Davies Street, London, W1. Tel: 01-629 3788

Cover: top two photographs from Bonhams; bottom two photographs from Phillips.

Helmut Hoevelmann & Lloyd Williams

Anglo Am Warehouse
2a Beach Road, Eastbourne, East Sussex BN22 7EX
Tel: England (0323) 648661 · (0892) 36627 Evenings

13,000 sq ft (1,200 sq m) of quality Antique, Victorian, Edwardian & 1920's Shipping Furniture

Particularly suitable for American, German and other European markets.

Container service.

Transport to Germany at very low rates.

**Opening Hours: Monday to Friday 9.30 - 17.00
or by appointment**

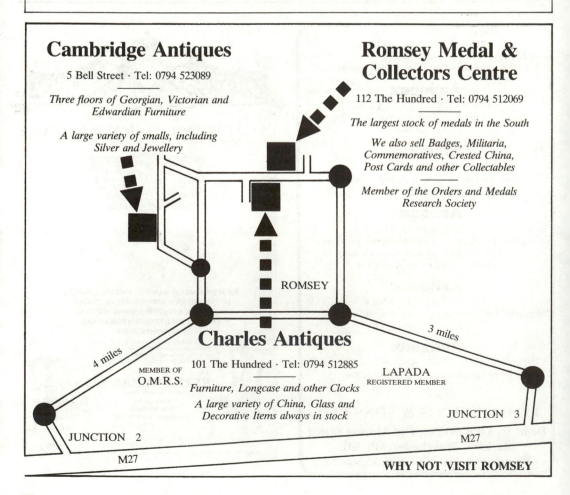

Cambridge Antiques

5 Bell Street · Tel: 0794 523089

Three floors of Georgian, Victorian and Edwardian Furniture

A large variety of smalls, including Silver and Jewellery

Romsey Medal & Collectors Centre

112 The Hundred · Tel: 0794 512069

The largest stock of medals in the South

We also sell Badges, Militaria, Commemoratives, Crested China, Post Cards and other Collectables

Member of the Orders and Medals Research Society

ROMSEY

Charles Antiques

MEMBER OF
O.M.R.S.

101 The Hundred · Tel: 0794 512885

Furniture, Longcase and other Clocks

A large variety of China, Glass and Decorative Items always in stock

LAPADA
REGISTERED MEMBER

3 miles

4 miles

JUNCTION 2

M27

JUNCTION 3

M27

WHY NOT VISIT ROMSEY

Sutton Valence Antiques

(On the A274, near Maidstone, Kent)

**We have
new items
daily**

**Minutes
from the
A20/M20**

FOURTEEN SHOWROOMS OF THE MOST EXTENSIVE STOCK FOR MANY MILES

Our trade and shipping warehouse, for furniture only, is at Unit 4 Haslemere Park Wood Estate, Maidstone, 3 miles from our main premises. Tel. 0622-675332.

Open 10.00–5.30 Mon.–Sat., or ring
0622-843333 or 843499

STOP PRESS....STOP PRESS....STOP PRESS....STOP PRESS....STOP

DATELINE HOUSTON MAY 1986

MARC ROLLINS, 6 YEARS IN BUSINESS IN HOUSTON HAS RAPIDLY BUILT UP TO OVER ONE MILLION DOLLARS RETAIL TRADE TURNOVER. HE HAS ALSO EXPANDED INTO WHOLESALING TO DEPARTMENT STORES, RETAIL SHOPS, DEALERS, AUCTION HOUSES AND VARIOUS OTHER OUTLETS.

Now Marc Rollins announces the formation of a new company — Furniture Classics Incorporated — which will market antique distributorships throughout the U.S.A. and other countries.

Distributors will be required to purchase their beginning stock of antiques, repro furniture and decoratives from the parent company. They will also be provided with a "how to" package consisting of an advertising and marketing manual, computer programme for stock control and record keeping, assistance with their grand opening plus other benefits.

Furniture Classics projects sales of a hundred distributorships in the first year at an average of twenty thousand dollars per distributorship.

Business opportunites like this are one of the hottest new entrepreneurial schemes in the U.S. today. The appeal being that most Americans dream of owning their own business. Also redundancies among middle and upper income executives in the rather depressed oil business have greatly increased the interest in this type of offering. The low initial investment is very attractive to the average prospect.

Exporters with unique lines of Victorian furniture, shipping goods, pine and repro antique furniture, waxes and decorative items are invited to call or write to:

FURNITURE CLASSICS

PO BOX 35101, Houston, Texas 77235
Tel: 0101 713 721 0000 Telex: 6868258
Showrooms: 5426 West Bellfort, Houston, Texas 77035

For UK enquiries contact:
Nigel Gearing,
The Chapel, The Street,
Wittersham, Kent. TN30 7EA.
Tel: 07977 - 684

CONTENTS

A green-glazed model of a tower in three detachable sections, the top section with a ridged and tiled roof, triangular windows and square doors above a larger section fitted with a door moulded with a taotie mask and fixed-ring handle above a pierced galleried stand, supported on a square base with four arched feet (restored), Han Dynasty, 38in (97cm). This piece realised £5,400 at Christie's, London on 21st April 1986.

29

MILLER'S ANTIQUES PRICE GUIDE
£5,000 IN PRIZES
COMPETITION

1st PRIZE

An antique Davenport worth £1,000, plus an Antiques Weekend for two at Chilston Park Hotel; and a copy of **The Antiques Directory – Furniture,** edited by Martin and Judith Miller

2nd PRIZE

A silver tea service worth £500, plus an Antiques Weekend for two at Chilston Park Hotel and a copy of **The Antiques Directory – Furniture**

3rd PRIZE

An 18th-century Chinese porcelain bowl from the Nanking Cargo worth £250, plus an Antiques Weekend for two at Chilston Park Hotel and a copy of **The Antiques Directory – Furniture**

Runners-up will receive a copy of The Antiques Directory – Furniture

What you have to do:

Pictured opposite are three items similar to those offered as prizes in the competition. Answer the questions on each one. Print your answers clearly on a sheet of paper. Then complete the sentence beginning "I always turn first to Miller's because…" in not more than 25 words. Add your name, address and post code and send your entry to **Miller's Antiques Prize Guide 1987** *Competition, The Barn, Sissinghurst Court, Sissinghurst, Cranbrook, Kent TN17 2JA,* to arrive not later than 1 September 1987. Entries must be accompanied by a proof of purchase of **Miller's Antiques Price Guide 1987.**

Chilston Park, home of **Miller's Antiques Price Guide,** is now a country house hotel. The mansion is filled with antiques chosen to complement the style and quality of life in an English Country house. All the bedrooms are luxuriously appointed and have private baths.

    Prize winners will be entitled to 2 nights' stay with dinner, bed and breakfast and Sunday lunch for two people at one of the hotel's Antiques Weekends. Martin and Judith will be their hosts and there will be talks from two of the **Guide's** expert consultants.

1. (i) This Davenport is:
A. Georgian B. Regency C. Victorian?

(ii) It is made from:
A. Rosewood B. Walnut C. Mahogany?

(iii) How many dummy drawers is usual
on the side of a Davenport?

2. (i) Was this silver tea service made in:
A. 1875 B. 1898 C. 1907?

(ii) What shape is it:
A. bullet B. compressed oblong C. baluster?

3. (i) This Chinese bowl is from which Dynasty:
A. Kangxi B. Yongzheng C. Qianlong D. Jiaqing?

(ii) The design is known as:
A. The 'scholar on the bridge' B. The 'leaping boy'
C. The 'blue pine'?

(iii) What is the name of the leader of the
expedition which found the Nanking Cargo:
A. Hatchard B. Hacker C. Hatcher?

Rules of Entry

Entries must bear the entrant's own name and address. All accepted entries will be examined, and the judges will award the first prize to the entrant who has correctly answered the questions and who, in the event of a tie, is judged to have submitted the most compelling, original and best expressed reason for consulting **Miller's Antiques Price Guide.** Remaining prizes will be awarded for next best attempts in order of merit, and no entrant may win more than one award. Prizes must be accepted as offered – there can be no alternative awards, cash or

otherwise.

Entries arriving after the closing date will not be examined and no responsibility can be accepted for entries lost or delayed in the post or elsewhere. Any entries received incomplete, illegible, mutilated, altered or not complying with the instructions and rules will be disqualified. All entries must be accompanied by a proof of purchase of **Miller's Antiques Price Guide 1987.**

Decisions of the judges will be final. No correspondence wil be entered into. Entry implies acceptance of the rules as being

final and legally binding.

The competition is open to all readers aged 18 and over in Great Britain, Northern Ireland and the Republic of Ireland except employees and their families of MJM Publications or associated companies, or anyone else directly involved with the competition.

Winners will be notified. A list of prizewinners can be obtained by sending a stamped, addressed envelope to MJM Publications, The Barn, Sissinghurst Court, Sissinghurst, Cranbrook, Kent TN17 2JA. (Please mark the envelope "Competition Results".)

The Insurance Game
and how to play it

Have you ever had to make an insurance claim after a burglary, fire or flood has deprived you of a prized 18th-century ice-cream goblet or George III bureau? No? You're lucky. Let's hope you're properly insured if and when the times comes. The trouble is, you can't rely on insurance companies to get you the right policy and terms, and point out the pitfalls.

As loss assessor Jeffrey Salmon points out, insurance aims to be a profit-making business, so companies won't necessarily go out of their way to help. Being charitable, one would say that it is 'sins of omission' rather than deliberate deception and concealment, but the effect is the same.

More often than not, the private collector or dealer has to look through the policy his or herself – and be sharp enough to think about valuations, descriptions and photographs of the contents of the shop or house. According to the Ombudsman's Bureau, 99.3% of people do not read their policies properly, and once signed they are never looked at again.

Here's another statistic: 97% of people are underinsured, insurance companies having merely asked their 'client' to give a value to the nearest £50 of the contents – with perhaps a mention of the 'valuables and works of art worth more than £200 each' clause.

Insurance is a negative purchase par excellence, but it has never been more necessary to be insured, and to the full current value. Burglary rates are rising, and premiums have been shooting up in response. But it is false economy to risk a low valuation in order to save the odd hundred pounds. The dreaded 'average value' clause means that if your house contents are insured for £25,000 but there is £50,000 worth of goods in your home, and half the contents are stolen, the insurance company could claim that they were at risk for £50,000 and will only pay out £12,500, not £25,000.

Royal Insurance and the rest of the big five – Guardian Royal Exchange, Commercial Union, Eagle Star, Legal & General – claim not to operate this nasty number, but Lloyds syndicates certainly do.

Valuations may be costly but . . .

Underinsurance is caused by a number of factors: sheer terror at the thought of forking out 2p in the £ for a collection worth £100,000, say; sheer ignorance of the current value of once-inexpensive antiques bought decades ago; the ravages of inflation; and the unexpected and lucrative increase in value of, for example, watercolours.

Inflation was smartly dealt with by the big insurance companies several years ago, when they introduced index-linked automatic updating of sums insured under their household contents policies. They are revised every year, in line with inflation usually.

Once you have 'bitten the bullet' and agreed mentally at least to pay whatever the man asks for, the time comes to seek a valuation. The relevant *Yellow Pages* is sure to have a section on 'antiques' valuers' right after antiques' restorers'. Failing that, most reputable dealers will carry out a valuation of sorts for a fee; and the big auction houses will also make valuations, although they charge somewhat more unless you are a treasured customer.

The big five are in agreement about two things: valuations are essential, and photographs/ detailed descriptions help enormously in recovering lost and stolen items from the police (75% of recovered antiques were recovered via photographs, according to one insurer). Sotheby's and Phillips both charge a scale of fees based on 1½% of valuation up to £10,000, 1% from £10,001 to £100,000 and ½% thereafter. Christies asks for 1½% of the total valuation, with a minimum charge of £50.

Antique valuers tend to charge less than the auction houses, and prices in the country are around 60% less than those in London, for the usual reasons. Valuers in the London area like Andrew Acquier of Godalming and the West End have a scale of fees of 1% for the first £50,000 and ½% thereafter. Some charge on a time basis, like Chancellors Hollingworth – £150 for half a day, £300 for a full day.

Trade associations like LAPADA and BADA will also point one in the general direction of a dealer in the relevant area and willing to undertake valuations. But SKS's Sneath recommends that two valuations are sought. 'It is expensive,' he agrees, 'but their valuations might be thousands of pounds apart.'

None of the big five has special antiques policies

Although Eagle Star subsidiary Star Assurance was set up solely to cater to collectors and dealers. In general, antique furniture is included in the general household contents section of a policy, while jewellery and other 'works of art and valuables' have to be specified. Burglar alarms are advised if not compulsory, especially in London and the Home Counties. 'In an ideal world we would like an accurate valuation, photographs and a full description,' agrees a Commercial Union spokesman. He makes the point that no one item should be insured for more than one third of the total. Royal Insurance concurs with CU on most points, but suggests that individual circumstances dictate what one does – or 'how long is a piece of string?' as a spokesperson puts it.

Red tape and fine print

String aside, what about red tape and fine print, so beloved of institutions. None of the big five (again) admits to clauses which let them out in the event of a claim if (say) a householder has omitted to fit window locks. Logic dictates that policyholders take all elementary precautions, but only Star Assurance offers security advice as part of its service.

Star asks for full burglar alarming, and in some cases connection with the local police station. 'While we do not intend to turn his house into a fortress, adequate security is nevertheless essential' as it dryly puts it. Star claims its representatives are trained in the arts and art markets; its International Fine Art service is headed by former director of the Berlin State Museum Professor Waetzoldt.

Dealers may be naive

One might imagine that dealers in antiques know better than the people to whom they sell the value of insurance, but according to Sneath Kent & Stuart's Geoffrey Sneath, quite a number of the 15,000 or so dealers in Britain are either underinsured or not insured at all.

Only 1,000 or so are members of a trade association, the London and Provincial Antique Dealers' Association or the British Antique Dealers' Association, even though members receive discounts on their premiums if they go through SKS.

'It's especially important for dealers to be adequately insured,' stresses Sneath, especially if they sell to the United States. Product liability insurance is essential – if a dealer sells a chair to someone over there, the leg breaks and the buyer breaks a leg too, the dealer could be sued for $50 million.

'Defective title is also very important – with so many robberies nowadays, it's becoming more and more likely that one will buy in good faith a stolen item.'

He adds that the fidelity clause is interesting; it covers dealers against pilfering by dishonest staff. Dealers can also insure against theft from an unattended vehicle (very careless), but fakes and bounced cheques are not insurable against, as it were.

Sneath, of course, specialises in dealers, but the big five are happy to entertain dealers, too.

Brokers – it pays to shop around

The instinctive reaction of a private person on thinking 'God, I need insurance' is to go to one of the big five – perhaps the company he or she uses to insure the motor car and the house. For specialised service, though, it pays the use an expert.

If your antiques came from a dealer or dealers already insured through a specialist broker, the job is made easier. But brokers should know where to direct a client wherever they are in the country. They all have access to the *Insurance Buyers Guide,* a form of *Yellow Pages* for their profession which details those brokers specialising in the insurance of antiques (or rare birds or . . .). 'The advantage of a specialist broker is that he has built up a knowledge and expertise over the years,' explains SKS's Sneath. 'The big companies don't necessarily know about antiques. The cover will be similar wherever you go – the service you receive is the thing nowadays. Most non-specialist brokers haven't a clue, either. The big companies, too, like banks, are geared up to deal with basic enquiries only.'

Typical specialist brokers include Sneath Kent & Stuart, C. R. Fenton, Harmers and Wingate and Johnston (London area) and Walker Barnett & Hill (Wolverhampton).

They all advertise in specialist magazines such as *Antique Collector.*

Adjusters and assessors

If your claim is more than £500, the insurance company will usually get a loss adjuster (not a loss assessor, who is on the side of the claimant) to interview you about your claim. It is up to you to prove you lost what you said you lost, and that the values were correct – the loss *assessor* will, for a fee, usually 10% of the final settlement, attempt to get the best and fairest settlement.

Jeffrey Salmon of Salmon Adams Hilton has a case history he likes quoting in support of the loss assessor business. An antique dealer client had sent £150,000 worth of goods to a New York auction house, insuring them for cost plus 100% – simple, or so he thought. The insurance company accepted the terms, no ifs and no buts. Unfortunately, some of the goods were damaged in transit, and even more unfortunately the insurance company offered a lower than expected sum because the insured values were greater than the estimated values given in the sale catalogue. The client asked for £25,000, the offer was £9,000.

The company said it would only pay a 'midway' price based on those auction estimates. 'Totally illegal,' says Salmon. 'The contract was simple.' After a year's negotiation the client was paid £34,000.

Salmon adds the general rider that most people only call in assessors when they are in trouble. He thinks they should make the call as soon as they make a claim.

Prevention is better than cure

How does one make it as easy as possible to protect a collection, and identify it in case it does disappear in a big sack marked 'swag' or go up in smoke? Any police station (divisional) will have a crime prevention officer who will carry out a security survey free of charge,

The non-destructive alternative is to have photographs taken in situ by a professional photographer able to capture a panoramic view plus close-ups; or, more and more common nowadays, the video with 'hard copy' available for filing away safely. The police recommend that the scale of each object filmed be shown by placing a ruler or box of matches alongside.

Salmon Adams Hilton will video your property and keep it on file for a fee of £80-£120 (in the London area).

The big insurance companies are not, because of their size, in a position to offer the individual service and advice that antique collectors and dealers need. Brokers are better. And remember – it's a lot easier to prove you own(ed) an object before it is stolen than afterwards!

Martin and Judith Miller

ENGLISH POTTERY TRENDS

'Select the best, reject the rest' has continued to be the motto of pottery collectors. As last year the power of the American dollar has been a strong influence on the market. Collectors increasingly look for pieces in good condition though the interest in unusual items has been sustained and here some damage is acceptable.

Saltglaze, delft and mid-19thC jugs have continued to be popular though not to the extent shown in 1985.

Stonewares have been the subject of renewed interest and prices are rising steadily. Creamware, slipware and early Staffordshire figures have aroused the interest of the market and there have been some exceptionally high prices for unusual animal subjects.

English majolica has gone from strength to strength during the year, reflecting the growing number of collectors.

There has been a particularly healthy market for extensive dinner-services though the level of buyers' enthusiasm is determined by condition and quality of decoration.

CONTINENTAL POTTERY TRENDS

Only exceptional pieces have aroused the enthusiasm of the market though interest has been steady for German stonewares and European faience.

Sales of Dutch Delft in Holland have also generated a steady, rather than ecstatic, response but there are indications of a growing enthusiasm for rare and unusual pieces.

The continuing dearth of good quality maiolica has not depressed the market and the few fine pieces to appear have promoted considerable competition amongst dealers and collectors.

Baskets

A Staffordshire saltglaze basket, the centre applied with a musical trophy flanked by vases of flowers, small hairline crack, c1755, 13 in (32.5 cm) wide. **£1,800-2,500** *CNY*

Saltglaze prices are affected by a strong American interest, particularly for rare pieces in good condition.

A Bayreuth basket, the centre painted with fruit and flowers in colours, the pierced basket work sides with yellow-lined lattice work, minor glaze chips, 2nd half 18thC, 10 in (25 cm) wide. **£1,500-2,000** *C*

The factory was established in 1714 and produced some very finely decorated wares in the mid-18thC.

Bellarmine

A Rhenish stoneware Bellarmine jug, decorated with the English Royal Arms, dated 1594, 16in (40cm). **£4,000-5,000** *JHo*

The English Royal Arms and the date make this a scarce and highly desirable jug.

Bowls

A Bristol delft bowl, the interior painted in iron red, yellow and blue, the exterior painted in blue with a man standing in a field beside a building in a continuous landscape, chip to rim and some glaze flaking, crack to well and chips to foot rim, c1740, 9in (22.5cm) diam. **£2,500-3,000** *C*

◁

A Bristol delft blue and white barber's bowl, the centre painted with a ship at sea, rim restored and chipped, c1740, 10 in (25.5 cm) diam. **£800-1,200** *C*

The decoration, though naive, is interesting and, from a collector's point of view, balances the slight restoration in terms of value. Barbers' bowls are rare. A dated example would fetch three to four times the price.

A Cologne stoneware Bellarmine jug, with hinged pewter cover, late 16thC, 8in (20cm). **£1,200-1,500** *JHo*

Miller's is a price GUIDE not a price LIST

A pair of English delft blue and white bowls, painted in the Oriental style with flowering chrysanthemum and bamboo, within a band of trellis pattern and stylised foliage, the crenellated rims enriched in blue, one with hairline crack, c1750, 9in (23cm) diam.
£500-800 *CNY*

A Liverpool delft bowl, decorated in blue and manganese, the interior reserved a Chinese figure, with prunus blossom border, the exterior decorated 2 Chinese ladies in gardens, 18thC, 10½ in (26 cm) diam. **£400-500** *WW*

A Liverpool creamware bowl, printed and painted with a ship in full sail and inscribed 'Success to the Valentine 1783', and the exterior printed in black with the Sailors Farewell, The Soldiers Farewell and the Triumph of Neptune and Venus, c1783, 11in (27cm) diam. **£300-400** *CSK*

Liverpool 'Ship' bowls were produced in delft, pearlware and porcelain as well as creamware. All types are keenly collected.

A Liverpool creamware bowl, the interior painted in black with a sailing ship, 9in (22cm) diam.
£150-200 *CSK*

Less valuable than a bowl which includes the name of the ship.

An early Staffordshire blue and white transfer ware fruit bowl, with Buffalo pattern, with scalloped edges, c1790, 9in (22cm).
£45-55 *DEL*

A Prattware fish bowl, c1800, 10 in (25 cm) diam. **£600-800** *JHo*

A pearlware blue and white bowl, printed with American Indian figures, a stag and martial trophies and the interior rim with Prince of Wales feathers, c1820, 7 in (17.5 cm) diam. **£80-120** *DEL*

Pearlware was introduced c1780 as a cheap alternative to porcelain. Painted or printed chinoiseries are common. The glaze is often quite blue due to the addition of cobalt. Wares are purchased for their decorative quality rather than their collectability unless bearing unusual decoration including a name, date or political slogan.

A blue and white Delft bowl, decorated with European figures in landscapes, 18thC, 12½ in (31 cm).
£1,000-1,500 *CW*

A rare bowl in good condition made especially collectable by the European landscape decoration.

◁

A George Jones majolica punch bowl, with Mr Punch lying on his back supporting the holly-decorated bowl in his arms, cobalt blue with pale blue interior and naturalistic colouring, impressed with 'G Jones' cypher and monogram, very small chip to one foot, c1875, 14½ in (36 cm) diam. **£2,500-3,200** *C*

A rare and highly collectable piece in spite of the slight damage.

A majolica oval pedestal bowl, with putto handles and suspending floral swags, 21in (52.5cm) wide.
£200-300 *CSK*

A Wedgwood Fairyland Lustre bowl, the interior decorated with mihrab columns, elves, fairies, sailing ships and castles, the exterior decorated with woodland elves at play, painted number Z5340, 8in (20cm) diam.
£400-600 *Re*

Fairy lustre wares remain a popula[r] collecting field.

Busts

A Nevers 'bleu' shallow bowl, painted in white, ochre and yellow with birds and flower-sprays on the blue ground, rim chips, late 17thC, 9½ in (23.5cm) diam. **£300-500** *C*

Cf W B Honey: European Ceramic Art, *pl 79a, for a similar bowl in the Victoria and Albert Museum.*

NEVERS FAIENCE

★ the term Nevers faience refers to a region rather than a single factory

★ Italian potters came to the region after 1565 and by 1600 a flourishing potting industry had developed

★ early products were in the style of Italian faience

★ Nevers bleu grounds became popular after c1625 and were produced in large quantities throughout the 17thC

★ most common form of decoration on Nevers bleu ground is of birds and flower-sprays

★ such wares are sometimes, incorrectly, termed 'Persian' but they have no connection with Persian decoration

---

A good quality Staffordshire library bust of Shakespeare, by Enoch Wood, late 18thC, 17 in (42.5 cm). **£500-800** *JHo*

A Yorkshire pearlware portrait bust of an officer, in bright blue jacket with yellow collar and frogging, chip to side whiskers and epaulette, c1800, 12 in (30 cm). **£800-1,200** *C*

An unusual and collectable figure. Both English and French soldier busts were produced during the period when the two countries were engaged in hostilities.

A Prattware bust of a French ▷ officer, early 19thC, 11½ in (28 cm). **£600-800** *JHo*

A Staffordshire figure of Handel, by Ralph Wood, c1800, 9½ in (23.5 cm). **£300-350** *DL*

A very rare Staffordshire named figure of the Duke of York, c1800, 6 in (15 cm). **£200-250** *DL*

A Yorkshire pearlware portrait bust of an unnamed actor, in blue jacket and ochre, green and blue spotted waistcoat, c1810, 8in (20cm). **£500-600** *C*

Cf John and Griselda Lewis, Pratt Ware, *p.138, where a possible solution to the identity of the sitter is discussed.*

A Staffordshire bust of Rousseau, in coloured enamel finish, mostly blue, green and brown, c1810, 9 in (22.5 cm). **£375-425** *LR*

A bust of Admiral Duncan, decorated in underglaze blue, black and yellow, possibly Yorkshire, c1810, 9 in (22.5 cm). **£375-425** *LR*

A Staffordshire pearlware portrait bust of the Duke of York, named on the reverse, in iron-red jacket with yellow frogging, the socle with lion supporters and the initials GR, enriched in colours, socle restored, c1810, 6 in (15 cm). **£200-300** *C*

A Staffordshire bust of an unknown person, c1815, 8½in (21cm). **£260-300** *DL*

A good English pottery bust of Sir Francis Burdett, 16in (40cm). **£975-1,050** *GCA*

A rare pottery bust depicting Rev William Clowes, Methodist, in enamel colours of black, grey and flesh tones, manufactured by Barker, Sutton & Till, c1835, 11 in (27.5 cm). **£650-750** *LR*

A Robinson and Leadbeater parian bust of Lord Kitchener, on square base, impressed marks, 8½ in (21 cm). **£50-80** *CSK*

A Staffordshire pottery bust, probably by Wood & Caldwell, depicting Tzar Alexander, with iron-red tunic and white sash, on a marbled socle base, 10½ in (26 cm). **£120-150** *Bea*

A Wedgwood terracotta bust of ▷ Locke, some restoration, impressed mark and inscribed on the reverse, c1785, 8½ in (21.5 cm). **£200-300** *C*

This model is taken from the bronze by Michael Rijsbrack.

A rare Wedgwood black basaltes library bust of Lord Byron, 19thC, 14 in (35 cm). **£300-400** *TKN*

Commemorative

A creamware teapot and cover, probably Wedgwood, printed in black, on one side with John Manners, Marquis of Granby and on the other with a battle scene, surrounded with trophies of war, slight damage, late 18thC, 4½ in (11.5 cm). **£300-400** *Bea*

A commemorative Nelson jug, in mint condition, c1790-1800, 5 in (12.5 cm). **£170-220** *DL*

A brown and cream glazed stoneware jug, moulded in relief with scene from Battle of Acre depicting Capt Sir Sydney Smith, 7 in (17 cm). **£40-60** *P*

A Liverpool creamware inscribed and dated armorial jug, transfer printed and enamelled in colours with 'Colonel Tarleton' named below, standing before a cannon, the reverse printed in black with 'The Watchtool Makers Arms' and the motto 'By Hammer and Hand All Arts Do Stand' and with the initials EMH and date 1792 beneath the spout, with green line rim, minor cracks to rim, 1792, 5½ in (14.5 cm). **£600-700** *C*

Colonel Tarleton was a native of Liverpool and a distinguished cavalry officer during the American War of Independence in the 1780s. He was later returned as MP for Liverpool on various occasions from 1790-1807. The print is taken from his portrait by Sir Joshua Reynolds.

CREAMWARE

★ a low fired earthenware first produced c1740
★ Josiah Wedgwood perfected the body in the mid-1760's. This perfected body he named Queen's Ware in honour of Queen Charlotte
★ Wedgwood sold Queen's Ware in the white and with overglaze enamel decoration
★ the body was well suited to overglaze transfer printing
★ other potteries also produced creamware in large quantities, notably Leeds, Melbourne, Cockpit Hill (Derby) and Liverpool

A creamware jug, printed on one side with an interior scene of named people and groups, entitled 'Separation of Louis XVI from his family', on the other an execution scene, inscribed 'Massacre of the French King' and 'La Guillotine or the Modern Beheading Machine at Paris, by which the unfortunate Louis XVI (late King of France) suffered on a Scaffold, Jan 21. 1793', 7½ in (18.5 cm). **£250-350** *Bea*

A pottery jug printed in blue with the ghost of Napoleon before tomb upon St. Helena, 8½ in (21cm). **£40-60** *P*

A pottery jug printed in blue with portrait of Wellington and battle trophies, slight chip, 8½ in (21 cm). **£80-100** *P*

A pearlware blue and white dish, the centre printed with the busts of George III and Queen Caroline, inscribed 'A King Rever'd A Queen Beloved', 'Long May They Live', 7½ in (18.5 cm). **£300-400** *Bea*

A creamware Queen Caroline commemorative jug, printed in black, the reverse side with a political parody based on a popular nursery rhyme, some chips, c1821, 5 in (12 cm). **£180-250** *Bon*

A blue and white transfer printed and band moulded harvest jug, decorated with opposing panels of a View of Shipping in the Avon Gorge, possible Pountneys of Bristol or South Wales Pottery, early 19thC, 11in (27.5cm). **£250-300** *LBP*

A rare portrait jug of Napoleon Bonaparte by Stephen Green of Lambeth, marked to underside 'Stephen Green Lambeth' in an elaborate cartouche, c1830, 7½ in (18.5 cm). **£150-200** *MN*

The verse on this jug refers to supposedly spurious evidence brought against Caroline to support a bill brought forward in 1820 aiming to dissolve her marriage to the Prince Regent on the grounds of adultery. In 1821 she was prevented from attending the coronation and she died later that year. The verse indicates how far public sympathy was on the side of the Queen.

A Staffordshire copper lustre and yellow-ground jug, transfer printed in black on both sides with a portrait of General Jackson, 'The Hero of New Orleans', named above and below, the yellow-ground enriched with foliage, c1830, 8 in (21 cm). **£250-350**   *CNY*

A Swansea Irish commemorative jug of 'Dan O'Connell Esq', and 'The Very Reverend Father Matthew', commemorating the two great regenerators of Ireland, unmarked, c1829, 5in (12.5cm). **£150-200**   *BRE*

A Staffordshire mug printed in puce with a crown above flowering vines, flanked with half-length portraits of William IV and Queen Adelaide, commemorating their Coronation in 1831, 4in (10cm). **£150-250**   *CSK*

A Royal Doulton pottery jug, printed in colours with portrait of George Kinloch Esq, MP and 'Reform' and inscription, 8 in (20 cm). **£40-60**   *P*

A pottery mask jug printed in black with 'The Deliverer', and 'Gratitude' between moulded scrolls and decorated in blue, for the 1851 Exhibition, 8 in (20 cm). **£40-60**   *P*

An Alcock & Co jug with black transfer decoration depicting scenes from the Crimean War, gilt decoration with inscription 'Sam Joinson – Nantwich'. **£100-120**   *WIL*

A Scottish pottery Crimea Peace jug, printed in black with allied servicemen, and a home-coming scene depicting kilted serviceman and inscription, 8½in (21cm). **£50-80**   *P*

A Sunderland lustre frog mug, with a Crimean War illustration, c1860, 5 in (12.5 cm). **£150-200**   *DL*

A Staffordshire pottery Crimean War bowl with heavy foot, printed in blue with a young portrait, naval scenes and inscribed 'Mess No. 56', 6½ in (16 cm) diam. **£80-120**   *P*

A pottery jug, moulded in relief and decorated in colours and lustre with portraits of Sir C Campbell and Sir H Havelock, 8½in (21cm). **£40-60**   *P*

l to r

1 An Alliance pottery jug, printed in black with a military scene entitled 'Light Cavalry Charge at Balaclava', and also 'May England Forever such unity boast', decorated in gilt, 8 in (20cm). **£100-150**

2 A pottery jug, printed with a military scene entitled 'Charge of the Chasseurs D'Afrique, at Balaclava', decorated in gilt, 8 in (20 cm). **£100-150**

3 A white saltglazed pottery water jug, moulded in relief with a scene depicting Florence Nightingale (?) attending the wounded Turk, 11½ in (29 cm). **£100-150**

4 A Staffordshire pottery saltglazed jug moulded in relief with 2 sentimental/military scenes entitled 'Home and Abroad', 7 in (17 cm). **£85-100**

5 A Sunderland lustre pottery jug, printed in black with a naval scene entitled 'Jack's safe return to his True Love' and inscription, chipped, 5 in (12 cm). **£60-80**

6 A brown glazed stoneware jug, in the Gothic style moulded in relief with 4 sentimental 'Home-coming' scenes, 7½ in (19 cm). **£130-180** *P*

An unglazed parian jug with extensively moulded decoration, including portrait of Prince Consort and Royal Arms on blue grounds, wreaths, orders and inscription, 9½ in (23 cm). **£120-180** *P*

A pottery jug, moulded in relief with equestrian portraits of Garibaldi, decorated in blue and cobalt blue, hairline crack to handle, 1864, 8½ in (21cm). **£40-60** *P*

A Disraeli Memorium pottery jug, printed in black and decorated in colours with portrait, inscription and book titles, hairline cracks to base, 1881, 6 in (15 cm). **£80-120** *P*

An 1887 Jubilee pottery plate, the centre printed in brown with portrait arms and inscription, 10 in (25 cm). **£40-60** *P*

STAFFORDSHIRE MOULDED STONEWARE JUGS

★ manufacture commenced c1825
★ increasingly popular with collectors
★ generally made in 3 sizes
★ body can be buff, pale blue, grey, pale green or white
★ manufactured by many Staffordshire potteries
★ marked examples particularly popular
★ value significantly affected by damage and quality of moulding

A pair of Robinson and Leadbetter white parian illumieré busts of Edward VII and Alexandra after W C Lawton, 1902, 16 in (40 cm) high overall. **£150-250** *P*

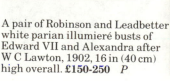

An 1897 Jubilee pottery plate, printed in brown with young and old portraits, Royal Arms and national flora, 9½ in (24cm). **£40-60** *P*

A 12-sided 1902 Coronation porcelain plate, printed in blue with an all-over design including portrait, trophies and details of Empire, and decorated in gilt, the reverse with inscription, 10½ in (26 cm). **£80-120** *P*

A Paragon porcelain 1935 Jubilee plate, the centre printed in brown and decorated in colours with portraits, arms and inscription, 10½ in (26 cm). **£50-80** *P*

A Minton's 1937 Coronation porcelain plate, the centre printed in brown and gilt, and decorated in enamels with profile portraits and inscription, limited edition no. 101/1000, 11 in (28 cm). **£50-80** *P*

A Dudson blue ground stoneware vase, decorated in white with applied moulded portraits of Col Baden Powell and Sir Redvers Buller, between crossed rifles, 7 in (18 cm). **£80-120** *P*

A Ringtons Tea octagonal blue and white pottery biscuit jar and cover, produced for the 1929 North-East Coast Industries Exhibition, Newcastle-on-Tyne, 5½ in (14 cm). **£30-50** *P*

A Gray's pottery plate, printed in brown and decorated in colours with Royal Arms, national crests and inscription, 1939, 11in (27cm). **£30-40** *P*

A rare Staffordshire pottery castle spill vase, c1825, 5½ in (13.5 cm). **£475-525** *GCA*

Cottages

A flower-encrusted pastille burner, in the form of an octagonal house, c1835, 5½in (13.5cm). **£350-400** *LR*

A lilac pastille burner of octagonal form, enriched with gilding, c1835, 7 in (17.5 cm). **£400-500** *LR*

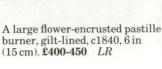

A large flower-encrusted pastille burner, gilt-lined, c1840, 6 in (15 cm). **£400-450** *LR*

An octagonal cottage, with central orange chimney and detachable roof, the gilt-lined base modelled with flowerheads, 4½ in (11 cm). **£250-350** *CSK*

A very unusual Staffordshire blue pottery cottage pastille burner, c1840, 6½ in (16 cm). **£450-500** *DL*

A rare pastille burner modelled as a church, with pierced windows and 3 iron-red doorways, the detachable base modelled with flowerheads and outlined in gilt, 6in (15cm). **£400-600** *CSK*

A pastille burner, with 2-tiered roof, above 5 pierced windows and an iron-red doorway, 5½ in (13.5 cm). **£150-250** *CSK*

An octagonal cottage, with 4 brown doorways below a pierced roof, on separate circular gilt-lined base, 5½ in (13.5 cm). **£250-350** *CSK*

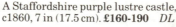

A Staffordshire cottage, c1850, 7½ in (18.5 cm). **£150-180** *DL*

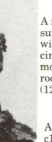

A rare pastille burner, the roof supported by trees, the pierced windows outlined in blue, on circular green and gilt base modelled with flower-sprays, the roof detachable, possibly Spode, 5 in (12.5 cm). **£400-600** *CSK*

A Staffordshire purple lustre castle, c1860, 7 in (17.5 cm). **£160-190** *DL*

Cow Creamers

A Staffordshire cow creamer, 18thC, 5½ in (13.5 cm). **£700-800** *SBO*

A Staffordshire cow creamer, some restoration, 18thC, 6 in (15 cm). **£600-700** *SBO*

A Whieldon type creamware cow creamer, 18thC, 5in (12.5cm). **£675-725** *GCA*

For a well modelled and brightly decorated example in perfect condition.

A Pratt type cow creamer, modelled as a cow with ochre and brown markings, standing before a tree, a calf at its feet, 7in (18cm). **£1,000-2,000** *CSK*

This unusually fine example, in good condition, brightly coloured and with unusual bocage, fetched £2,600 at auction due to fierce competition between two would-be purchasers. An example of how auction rivalry can stimulate price levels particularly in the case of rarities.

A Prattware cow creamer, with hobbled back legs and milkmaid, decorated in yellow, grey and green glazes, lacking cover, c1785, 5½ in (13.5 cm). **£700-750** *LR*

A fine Staffordshire cow creamer and cover, with sponged decoration in yellow and grey-brown, green washed slab base, c1785, 5 in (12.5 cm). **£650-700** *LR*

A pair of early Staffordshire cow creamers, c1790, 6 in (15 cm). **£1,300-1,600** *DL*

A Staffordshire cow creamer, with sponged decoration in yellow and black with green washed base, c1790, 5 in (12.5 cm). **£500-600** *LR*

A Pratt cow creamer, decorated in underglaze ochre and black sponging on a green glazed base, replacement cover, c1790, 5 in (12.5 cm). **£600-675** *LR*

A cow creamer and cover, modelled as a standing cow with pink lustre and brown markings, on shaped rectangular green mound base, 6 in (15 cm). **£200-250** *CSK*

A pottery cow creamer and cover, sponged with brown and ochre, green washed base, c1790, 5½in (13.5cm). **£600-700** *LR*

A fine Prattware cow creamer, sponged and patterned in ochre and grey, with milkmaid in blue and yellow, on a green washed base, c1790, 5 in (12.5 cm). **£700-775** *LR*

A pair of Staffordshire cow creamers, with ochre and brown sponged decoration and milkmaids with green dresses, damage to horns and milkmaid on one creamer, late 18thC, 6in (15cm) long. **£1,200-1,600** *DSH*

It is unusual to find a matching pair of creamers.

A pair of early Staffordshire cow creamers, c1790, 6 in (15 cm). **£1,600-1,900** *DL*

A cow creamer and cover, modelled as a standing cow with copper lustre and pink lustre markings, 5½ in (13.5 cm). **£180-220** *CSK*

A large Staffordshire cow creamer, decorated in brown and blue, on shaped base with green lining, c1830-40, 6in (15cm). **£375-435** *LR*

A Staffordshire cow creamer of scarce type, painted with alternate red and black motifs on a green washed base, restored, c1810, 5 in (12.5 cm). **£450-500** *LR*

A pair of early Staffordshire cow creamers, c1810, 5in (12.5cm). **£1,400-1,600** *DL*

A cow creamer in brown glazed pottery, cover missing, c1840, 4½ in (11 cm). **£350-425** *LR*

Cups

A very rare pottery coloured saltglaze tea bowl and saucer, c1755. **£450-500** *DL*

A Staffordshire pearlware hound head stirrup cup, enamelled in chocolate brown with chestnut detail, the pale brown collar with yellow buckle, early 19thC, 6 in (15 cm) long. **£300-400** *TEN*

A Staffordshire slipware inscribed and dated loving cup, the dark brown body overlaid in cream slip and incised with the initials IBE, the reverse with the date 1763, rim repaired, c1763, 7 in (17.5 cm). **£1,800-2,200** *C*

A Staffordshire dog's head stirrup cup, with black markings and pink muzzle and the rim decorated in solid pink lustre, c1825, 4½ in (11 cm) wide. **£700-800** *CSK*

A Staffordshire stirrup cup, c1825, 4 in (10 cm) long. **£250-300** *DL*

A Staffordshire pug's head stirrup cup, painted in pale brown and the lip decorated in solid pink lustre, c1825, 3½ in (8.5 cm). **£700-900** *CSK*

A pair of Staffordshire pottery fox mask stirrup cups, inscribed inside 'C.P.1858', 19thC, 5 in (12.5 cm). **£350-450** *Re*

Figures – Animals

A Staffordshire pottery cricket mug, 19thC, 5in (12.5cm).
£200-240 *SBO*

A Castleford-type mug, c1810.
£120-160 *JUD*

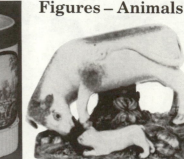

A pottery bull baiting group, by Ralph Wood Jr, the base decorated in overglaze enamels and applied with shredded clay foliage, the beast coloured with large splashes of iron-red, ears and left horn damaged, 5½in (14cm).
£600-700 *Bon*

An Obadiah Sherratt bull baiting group, with male figure and 2 dogs, 13in (32cm) long.
£2,000-3,000 *LT*

An Obadiah Sherratt bull baiting group titled 'Bull Beating', 'Now Captin Lad', much restored, 13½ in (33 cm). **£800-1,200** *DWB*

A rare animal figure which would have been given a much higher price if in better condition.

An early Staffordshire bull baiting group, c1790, 7½in (18.5cm).
£900-1,000 *DL*

A Staffordshire pottery cow and calf bocage group, early 19thC, 5½ in (13.5 cm).
£295-345 *GCA*

A Staffordshire cow group, marked Walton, c1820, 5 in (12.5 cm).
£350-400 *DL*

A Ralph Wood model of a doe, the coat enriched in brown and white, extensively restored, c1770, 6 in (15.5 cm). **£500-600** *C*

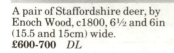

A pair of Staffordshire deer, by Enoch Wood, c1800, 6½ and 6in (15.5 and 15cm) wide.
£600-700 *DL*

A pair of Staffordshire pottery greyhounds, the bases coloured in turquoise enamel, their coats vibrantly splashed in black enamel, enamel flaking, mid-19thC, 10½ and 11½in (26 and 28cm).
£900-1,100 *Bon*

An early Staffordshire figure of Hercules and the Bull, by Enoch Wood, c1800, 5½in (13.5cm). **£400-450** *DL*

A Staffordshire bull baiting group, the red-brown bull engaging a black-patched, white dog, c1815, 5 in (12.5 cm). **£700-800** *LR*

A pair of late spill vases, modelled as cows with brown markings, with calves at their sides, on oval coloured gilt-lined bases, 11 in (27.5 cm). **£150-250** *CSK*

A pair of Staffordshire cows, c1850, 8 in (20 cm). **£250-300** *DL*

A pair of Victorian Staffordshire cow and calf spill vases, c1860, 10½ in (26 cm). **£330-380** *GCA*

An early Staffordshire figure of a doe, of Walton-type, bocage in mint condition, c1820, 6in (15cm). **£450-500** *DL*

An Enoch Wood model of a stag, his coat enriched in ochre with cream spots, the base moulded with a band of berried laurel with leaves at the corners, base, ears and antlers restored, c1800, 11½ in (29 cm). **£1,500-1,800** *C*

A pair of Victorian Staffordshire pottery cows with milkmaids, c1860, 6½in (16cm). **£275-325** *GCA*

A pair of standing greyhounds and hares, one restored, c1860, 10 in (25 cm). **£320-360** *Wai*

A pair of Staffordshire dogs, with free standing front legs, c1850, 9 in (22.5 cm). **£170-200** *DL*

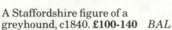

A greyhound on blue base, c1850, 5½ in (13 cm). **£80-120** *RBE*

A Staffordshire figure of a greyhound, c1840. **£100-140** *BAL*

A Staffordshire dog, by Ralph Wood, c1800, 7 in (17.5 cm). **£700-800** *DL*

An early Staffordshire dog, c1800, 6½ in (16 cm) long. **£300-350** *DL*

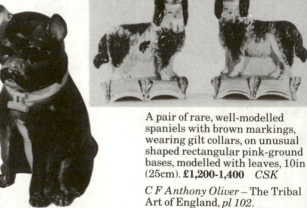

A pair of rare, well-modelled spaniels with brown markings, wearing gilt collars, on unusual shaped rectangular pink-ground bases, modelled with leaves, 10in (25cm). **£1,200-1,400** *CSK*

C F Anthony Oliver – The Tribal Art of England, *pl 102*.

A rare majolica pug, some restoration, c1880, 17 in (42.5 cm). **£500-550** *SBO*

A pair of spaniels with brown markings, wearing gilt collars and chains, 10½in (26cm). **£180-220** *CSK*

A pair of groups of poodles wearing gilt collars, with puppies, on blue and gilt bases, 8in (20cm). **£300-400** *CSK*

A pair of early Staffordshire dogs, in orange and white, c1840-50. **£120-160** *MW*

A Prattware model of a ram, thinly potted and decorated in semi-translucent glazes, mainly green, orange and black, c1785, 5 in (12.5 cm). **£650-700** *LR*

A Ralph Wood model of a ram, on a high mottled yellow base, his body and horns enriched in mottled tones of grey, small chip to base, c1770, 6½ in (16.5 cm). **£800-1,100** *C*

An early Staffordshire group, in mint condition, c1790, 4½ in (11 cm). **£1,000-1,100** *DL*

A Staffordshire pair of Enoch Wood sheep, copied from Derby examples, 5½ in (13.5 cm). **£800-900** *DL*

A pair of early Staffordshire Walton sheep, with bocage, c1830. **£400-500** *BAL*

An Enoch Wood model of a lion, his left paw resting on a yellow ball, his coat and mane enriched in yellow and light brown, the base moulded with stylised foliage and painted in imitation of marble, base cracked, chips to teeth and base, c1790, 11½ in (29 cm) wide. **£800-1,200** *C*

A Yorkshire Prattware figure of a sheep, shepherdess and lambs, 6 in (15 cm). **£900-1,100** *SBO*

A rare model of a lion standing, its left forepaw resting on a yellow ball, on rectangular marbled base, 10 in (25 cm) high. **£700-800** *CSK*

A Staffordshire pair of figures, a ewe and a ram, marked Walton, bocage in mint condition, c1820, 6½ in (16 cm). **£800-900** *DL*

ENOCH WOOD OF BURSLEM

★ one of the most productive potteries of the late 18th early 19thC
★ Enoch Wood started work as an apprentice in the pottery trade in the early 1770's
★ in 1784 commenced a pottery with his cousin Ralph Wood
★ in 1790 established a new firm, Wood and Caldwell
★ in 1818 the firm became Enoch Wood and Sons
★ produced good figure models generally using overglaze colours (earlier Ralph Wood and Whieldon figures used muted in-glaze colours)
★ overglaze colours sometimes produce a matt surface
★ also produced blue-printed wares and exported large quantities to the USA

A rare and unusual pottery figure of a recumbent leopard, its front paw resting on a piece of knarled flesh, decorated in overglaze brightly coloured enamels, damaged, early 19thC, 8½in (21cm) long.
£1,000-1,500 *HSS*

A rare pair of lion and tiger figural groups by Obadiah Sherratt, c1820.
£11,000-13,000 *Bon*

Obadiah Sherratt of Burslem produced some of the most collectable types of Prattware animals and figure groups. His models are often larger than those of contemporary factories. This unusual pair of a lion and tiger attacking a missionary and a native may have been intended to have a satirical content.

A Wood and Caldwell figure of a lion, on a black enamelled rectangular base, wearing a gentle expression and with its tail curled around its body, its coat enamelled in two shades of brown and with brush-stroked mane, some restoration, 5 in (12.5 cm) wide.
£300-400 *Bon*

An early English slip decorated pottery cat, covered in a honey coloured glaze with brown spots, on oval base, one ear repaired, other chipped, c1680, 6in (15cm).
£300-500 *CNY*

A Whieldon type tortoiseshell glazed figure of a seated cat, covered in a manganese tortoiseshell glaze, c1760, 3½in (9.5cm).
£500-800 *CNY*

An Obadiah Sherratt group of a lion attacking a child, the lion with grey mane and yellow coat, on oval marblised base enriched in green, repair to its tail and one leg of child, c1820, 8in (20cm) long.
£1,500-1,800 *CNY*

A pair of spill vases modelled as horses, with foals recumbent at their feet on oval coloured gilt-lined bases, 12½in (31cm).
£250-350 *CSK*

A pair of horse spills, c1880, 13 in (32.5 cm). **£250-300** *RBE*

A pottery figure of a cat, its coat sponged in black and yellow enamel, 3½in (9cm) wide.
£120-150 *Bon*

A Staffordshire pottery horse, finished in chestnut and brown with green shaded base, restored, c1840, 5in (12.5cm). **£180-220** *LR*

A Staffordshire game bird, 18thC, 10½in (26 cm). **£120-150** *SBO*

An early Staffordshire pottery bird, c1790, 3 in (7.5 cm). **£260-300** *DL*

An early Staffordshire pottery bird whistle, c1790, 3in (7.5cm). **£450-500** *DL*

A Ralph Wood model of a polar bear, standing on an oval high green rockwork base, his coat enriched in grey, 2 minute chips to rim, c1770, 3½ in (9.5 cm) wide. **£800-1,200** *C*

A good Ralph Wood model using muted in-glaze colours as opposed to overglaze enamels.

A Staffordshire pottery elephant, c1850, 9½in (23.5cm). **£875-925** *GCA*

A pair of rare figures of goats with brown markings, standing on oval coloured gilt-lined bases, 5 in (12.5 cm). **£250-350** *CSK*

A pottery figure of a giraffe, on a grassy base delineated in gilt, before a palm tree, damage to ears and tree, 4½in (11.5cm). **£120-180** *Bon*

A pair of zebras on oval coloured gilt-lined bases, 8½ in (21 cm). **£150-250** *CSK*

A pair of squirrels, 1890-1910, 6 in (15 cm). **£150-200** *RBE*

A pair of rare figures of rabbits with black markings, recumbent facing right and left, eating lettuce leaves, 5 in (12.5 cm). **£1,500-2,500** *CSK*

Figures – People

An early Staffordshire group of George and the Dragon, by Ralph Wood, some restoration, c1780, 11 in (27.5 cm). **£900-1,000** *DL*

A group depicting St. George and Dragon, some repair, impressed mark Wood & Caldwell, Burslem on rear of base, well coloured in enamels, 1790-1800, 8in (20cm). **£400-800** (Depending on condition) *LR*

A rare English grey stoneware spice dish, 2 figures with repairs to waist, minor chips, 17thC, 9 in (22 cm). **£800-1,200** *CNY*

A Staffordshire white saltglaze figure of Eve, her eyes enriched in brown and her hair and body lightly enriched in blue, c1750, 4½ in (11 cm). **£500-600** *C*

Cf Bernard Rackham: Catalogue of the Glaisher Collection of Pottery & Porcelain, pl 55D.

A Yorkshire figure of the Madonna and Child, she in brown dress and with a blue-edged ochre shawl, the Child in a blue robe, c1790, 9½ in (23.5 cm). **£200-250** *C*

◁ A Yorkshire figure of a man, in brown hat and striped trousers holding a bag and a cudgel, standing before an ochre tree stump, c1790, 5in (12.5cm). **£250-300** *C*

▷ A Yorkshire Prattware figure of a woman with a child, 18thC, 9½ in (23.5 cm). **£450-550** *SBO*

◁ A Yorkshire group of George and the Dragon, c1790, 11 in (27.5 cm). **£900-1,000** *DL*

An early Staffordshire Leeds-type pair of gardeners with urn, 6½ in (16 cm). **£500-600** *DL*

A Ralph Wood Jr, Staffordshire figure group of Vicar & Moses, blue and manganese, cream and green glazes, 1770-95, 9½ in (23 cm). **£800-900** *WIL*

An early Staffordshire figure, sometimes known as The Orator, c1795, 10 in (25 cm). **£500-600** *DL*

A Ralph Wood group, Vicar & Moses, the translucent decoration in mainly brown and grey, base unglazed, untitled, c1785, 9½ in (23 cm). **£700-800** *LR*

An early Staffordshire figure group, possibly by Neale & Co, in good condition, c1800, 8½ in (21 cm). **£700-800** *DL*

An important Lakin & Poole group depicting Cephalus & Procris, with fine detail enamelling to figures and base, c1790, 10½in (26cm). **£950-1,100** *LR*

Locate the source

The source of each illustration in Miller's can be found by checking the code letters below each caption with the list of contributors. In view of the undoubted differences in price structures from region to region, this information could be extremely valuable to everyone who buys and sells antiques.

A Staffordshire figure of Simon, impressed Wedgwood, c1800, 9½ in (23.5 cm). **£400-500** *DL*

A pair of Staffordshire pottery figures of classically draped maidens, on leaf moulded bases, late 18thC, 7in (17.5cm). **£300-400** *DWB*

An early Staffordshire group entitled Vicar & Moses, probably by Enoch Wood, c1800, 12 in (30 cm). **£550-650** *DL*

A pair of early Staffordshire Leeds-type figures, c1800. **£350-400** *DL*

A Staffordshire figure in a chair, c1800, 4 in (9.5 cm). **£300-350** *SBO*

A Staffordshire double Rural Pastimes group, c1810, 11½ in (28.5 cm). **£1,100-1,200** *DL*

A Staffordshire figure, Hurdy Gurdy, impressed mark Enoch Wood, c1800, 8in (20cm). **£150-200** *DL*

An early Staffordshire group of musicians, c1800, 7½ in (18.5 cm). **£500-600** *DL*

A Staffordshire classical figure of a lady holding a baby and attendant child, c1800, 9in (22cm). **£50-60** *CGC*

Two Yorkshire figures of ladies, one dressed in a riding habit, the other in décolleté dress enriched in blue and yellow, standing on high green mound and octagonal bases, both plumes, one hand and one base restored, c1800, 11 and 11½ in (27.5 and 28.5 cm). **£900-1,100** *C*

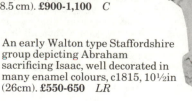

An early Walton type Staffordshire group depicting Abraham sacrificing Isaac, well decorated in many enamel colours, c1815, 10½in (26cm). **£550-650** *LR*

An early Staffordshire group, entitled 'Friendship', in mint condition, 8in (20cm). **£800-900** *DL*

A marked Walton group of 'Songsters' with large bocage support, 1815-25, 9 in (22.5 cm). **£750-850** *LR*

One of this maker's rarer pieces.

A pair of Staffordshire groups depicting Sailors Farewell & Return, c1815, 9½in (24cm). **£550-625** *LR*

Note that the sailor's dress is different in each group which is quite normal on a pair.

A Staffordshire group of musicians, c1815, 9 in (22.5 cm). **£500-550** *DL*

A Staffordshire spill holder, 'Return from Egypt', impressed mark Walton, c1820, 8in (20cm). **£700-800** *DL*

A pair of early Staffordshire figures, 'Widow' and 'Elijah', marked Walton, in excellent condition, c1820, 12 in (30 cm). **£800-900** *DL*

A Staffordshire Gretna Green group, on a rectangular base, with the inscription 'John Macdonald Aged 79 A Scotch esquire run of with a English girl aged 17 to Gratnal Green the old blacksmith to be married' (sic.), restoration to lovers' arms, tree and blacksmith's hammer, c1820, 8in (20cm). **£400-600** *C*

A Walton group of a Sultan and a Sultana, on a grassy mound with 12 resting sheep, marbled serpentine stand with floral border and bracket feet, 8 in (20 cm). **£1,500-2,000** *BD*

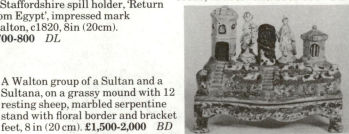

A rare set of Sunderland lustre figures of the Seasons, marked Dixon, Austin, c1820, 9-9½in (22.5-23.5cm). **£1,600-1,800** *SBO*

A pair of Walton-style pottery figures depicting 'Flight' and 'Return', coloured overall in overglaze enamels, damage to limbs of Joseph and donkey, boy's head missing, Joseph's head and the base restuck on 'Return', 10in (25cm). **£400-500** *Bon*

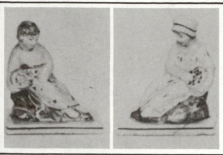

Two Staffordshire pottery figures of small girls, on low rectangular bases delineated in red enamel, both damaged, early 19thC, 3 in (7.5 cm) wide. **£70-100** *Bon*

A Staffordshire pottery figure entitled 'Fruitboys', standing on a blue green mound base, the boy flanked by flowering bocage and wearing blue tunic and wide yellow trousers, base chipped, early 19thC, 5½ in (14 cm). **£250-300** *Bon*

A Walton group of 'Friendship', impressed Walton to reverse, c1820, 7 in (18 cm). **£400-600** *CNY*

A Walton pottery figure of a putto, reverse impressed Walton on a scroll, restored, 6in (15cm). **£80-120** *Bon*

A Staffordshire new Marriage Act group, c1820, 7in (17.5cm). **£700-900** *JHo*

A Staffordshire Walton-type figure of the Shepherd, c1820, 4½ in (11 cm). **£220-260** *DL*

A Staffordshire group of Dandies, wearing brightly coloured costumes, c1820, 7½ in (18.5 cm). **£400-500** *JHo*

A very rare Staffordshire group, The Lovers, of Walton-type, c1820, 5 in (12.5 cm). **£350-400** *DL*

A Staffordshire group of dandies, Walton, enriched in colours, standing on square base, some repairs, c1810, 8½in (21cm). **£300-500** *CNY*

An early Walton-type group of gardeners with implements, decorated in green, red-brown, purple and blue enamels, 1815-20, 7 in (17.5 cm). **£450-500** *LR*

A Walton-type figure of 'St. Peter', backed by large bocage with double flowers, mainly coloured orange and yellow, with green base, c1820, 10 in (25 cm). **£425-475** *LR*

An Obadiah Sherratt figure of
'Venus', naked except for a yellow
and puce drape, slightly damaged,
10 in (25 cm). **£400-600**   *BD*

*Obadiah Sherratt of Burslem was
one amongst a number of makers of
colourful figure groups decorated
overglaze in bright orange, blue,
green and brown. These figures are
sometimes called Prattware figures
after Pratt of Lane Delph who was a
leading manufacturer of such pieces.
Other leading makers were Ralph
Salt of Hanley and John Walton of
Burslem.*

An Obadiah Sherratt group of the
Gretna Green marriage, decorated
in multi-coloured enamels, the lady
figure a replacement, c1825, 7½ in
(18.5 cm). **£650-700**   *LR*

In perfect condition £1,100-1,300.

A rare Obadiah Sherratt figure of
Summer, with typical flower
decoration to dress, c1825, 7 in
(17.5 cm). **£200-250**   *LR*

An Obadiah Sherratt 'Grecian and
Daughter' group, showing the
chained and manacled Cimon being
offered sustenance by his daughter,
c1830, 10in (25cm).
£2,000-3,000   *Bon*

*It is interesting to note that the
actual auction prices of two almost
identical figure groups were £2,100
and £650. This difference cannot
readily be explained by condition,
though the higher priced group was
in slightly better condition and more
pleasingly painted. The more
expensive group was sold in London
some few months before the second
group.*

An Obadiah Sherratt group of The
Courtship, she wearing wide
brimmed bonnet and iron-red
flowered dress, he in green jacket
and puce patterned trousers, the
base enriched in green, iron-red and
grey, the base applied with a
jardinière, minor repair to the rim
of her hat and branches of tree,
c1810, 8in (20cm).
£1,200-1,800   *CNY*

*Cf the example in The Earle
Collection of Early Staffordshire
Pottery, no. 650.*

An Obadiah Sherratt figure entitled
'The Reading Maid', c1825, 11½ in
(28.5 cm). **£550-600**   *DL*

A Staffordshire group entitled
'Rural' by Enoch Wood, with enamel
decoration, 8in (20cm).
£325-375   *LR*

*This is derived from earlier
examples by Ralph Wood Jr.*

A naive Staffordshire group of
musicians with numerous animals,
topped by crude bocage, c1825,
7½ in (18.5 cm). **£425-475**   *LR*

*This is a charming attempt to copy
Walton.*

A Staffordshire group of The
Sacrifice of Isaac, Abraham
standing about to sacrifice his son
seated on an altar applied with an
inscription, enriched in bright
enamels, minor restoration to
dagger, c1830, 10½ in (26.5 cm).
£300-400   *C*

*Cf Reginald G Haggar,
Staffordshire Chimney Ornaments,
pl 79.*

A set of 4 Portobello figures of the Seasons, c1825, 8in (20cm). **£1,300-1,500**   *DL*

A pair of Staffordshire figures, Fire and Water, marked Walton, c1820. **£900-1,000**   *DL*

A fine Obadiah Sherratt 'The New Marriage Act', well decorated in many coloured enamels, c1822, 6 in (15 cm). **£1,250-1,350**   *LR*

A pair of Staffordshire pottery figures, 19thC, 5in (12.5cm). **£120-180**   *DWB*

An Obadiah Sherratt figure entitled 'St. Peter', c1825, 11 in (27.5 cm). **£550-650**   *DL*

Most Obadiah Sherratt items are on bracket feet.

An Obadiah Sherratt figure of The Reading Maid, in iron red flowered dress with 2 dogs by her side, repairs to book, her hat, foliage and neck, c1815, 9in (23cm). **£300-500**   *CNY*

A rare Obadiah Sherratt figure of Hope, with typical bocage support and painting to dress, anchor damaged, c1825, 7 in (17.5 cm). **£200-250**   *LR*

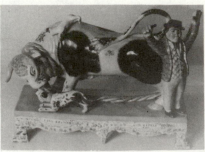

A Staffordshire Obadiah Sherratt Bull Baiting group, c1825, 9½ in (23.5 cm). **£2,300-2,500** *DL*

See other examples in pottery animals section.

A Staffordshire Tithe Pig group showing the farmer's wife offering one of her offspring in lieu of a pig, decorated in underglaze colours, c1830, 6 in (15 cm). **£490-550** *LR*

This has an unusual base.

A pair of Staffordshire figures of a shepherd and shepherdess, modelled by Lloyd Sheldon, c1840, 5½ in (14 cm). **£250-350** *CNY*

A well modelled figure of a man standing wearing a blue neckerchief beside a donkey laden with sticks, the base entitled 'Beesums' in gilt-moulded capitals, 10½ in (26 cm). **£180-220** *CSK*

A Staffordshire pottery figure of a man seated on a tree trunk playing the bagpipes, early 19thC, 6 in (15 cm). **£80-120** *HSS*

A Staffordshire pottery group, The Sacrifice of Isaac, with trunk vase at the rear, on oval base, 12 in (30 cm). **£60-80** *BD*

A large Staffordshire pottery figure of Little Red Riding Hood by Thomas Parr, c1860's, 15 in (37 cm). **£300-400** *Bon*

Modelled after the painting by James Sant.

A Staffordshire pottery figure of a child with a cradle, c1860, 6½ in (16 cm). **£100-130** *BRE*

A later Victorian edition of an Enoch Wood group known as The Drunk Parson and Town Clerk, c1860. **£200-250** *BAL*

A later Victorian edition of a Ralph Wood group known as Vicar & Moses, c1860. **£200-250** *BAL*

A Victorian Staffordshire figure of a kilted Scots hunter with stag and hound, raised on an oval plinth base, 13½in (33.5cm). **£40-60** *CGC*

A Staffordshire figure 'Gipsy Boy' on a dun horse, 19thC, 9 in (23 cm).
£40-60   *CGC*

STAFFORDSHIRE FIGURES

★ period of production c1835 to 1895
★ figures made with 'flat backs' or 'in the round'
★ material used varies from pottery to porcelain type body
★ many figures do not appear in the standard reference book 'Staffordshire Portrait Figures' by P D Gordon Pugh. However, some collectors only buy figures which appear in Pugh
★ many fakes and restored pieces appear on the market
★ value is affected by damage, poorly defined features, flaked overglaze enamel or rubbed gilding
★ unusual animals and theatrical figures particularly collectable

Victorian Staffordshire

A. British & Foreign Royalty

A Staffordshire group of the Prince of Wales and Princess Royal, repair to waist of princess and wheel of carriage, c1845, 7in (17cm) long.
£200-300   *CNY*

Cf Gordon Pugh, Staffordshire Portrait Figures, *pl 47 fig 143.*

A Victorian Staffordshire group of Royal children with bird, c1850, 8in (20cm).
£95-115   *GCA*

A rare well modelled group of Albert and the Princess Royal, the former standing to the left wearing blue jacket and full length iron red ermine edged cloak, on oval gilt lined base, 9in (22.5cm). (A56/172).
£200-250   *CSK*

A rare figure of Victoria and the Princess Royal, the former standing to the right wearing a blue bodice and tartan skirt, 10in (25cm). (A57/179).
£150-200   *CSK*

A Staffordshire pottery figure of the Princess Royal, Empress of Prussia, holding a dog and a bird, on circular base, 17½in (43cm).
£180-220   *BD*

A pair of figures of the Prince and Princess of Wales, 10in (25cm). (A76/225,226).
£100-150   *CSK*

A Staffordshire pottery portrait figure of the Prince of Wales, decorated in colours, on oval base, 18in (45cm).
£80-100   *BD*

A Staffordshire pottery figure of the Prince of Wales, 8in (20cm).
£80-120 *DWB*

A figure of Britannia seated, flanked by a shield and the British Lion, 6in (15cm).
£220-250 *CSK*

A pair of Staffordshire figures of Queen Victoria and Prince Albert, c1848, 8½in (21cm).
£350-400 *DL*

A Staffordshire flat back figure, gilt name to the base 'Empress of France', in underglazed blue and enamel colours, late 19thC, 10in (25cm).
£80-120 *WIL*

A Staffordshire figure of the Prince of Wales with bird, c1848, 5in (12.5cm).
£80-120 *RBE*

A Staffordshire figure of the Princess of Wales with cradle, c1848, 5in (12.5cm).
£100-120 *RBE*

B. Statesmen & Politicians

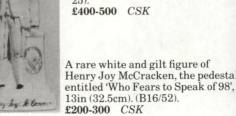

A well modelled figure of Wellington, on raised pink lustre marbled base, 13in (32.5cm). (similar to B2/19).
£200-300 *CSK*

A rare figure of Theobald Wolfe Tone, beside a pedestal entitled 'Who Fears to Speak of 98', the oval base named in gilt script, 13½in (33cm). (B16/51).
£300-400 *CSK*

A well modelled coloured figure of Wellington, wearing a blue jacket and holding a scroll in his right hand, 12in (30cm). (similar to B4/25).
£400-500 *CSK*

A rare white and gilt figure of Lord Edward Fitzgerald, the pedestal entitled 'Who Fears to Speak of 98', 14in (35cm). (B16/53).
£300-400 *CSK*

A rare white and gilt figure of Henry Joy McCracken, the pedestal entitled 'Who Fears to Speak of 98', 13in (32.5cm). (B16/52).
£200-300 *CSK*

A Staffordshire portrait figure, named 'Washington', c1850, 15½in (38.5cm).
£500-600   *DL*

A Staffordshire group of 'Uncle Tom and Eva', Eva's right foot missing, c1852, 8in (20cm).
£300-400   *CNY*

Cf Gordon Pugh, Staffordshire Portrait Figures, *pls 28, 29 figs 87-90.*

A large white and gilt figure of Benjamin Franklin standing before rockwork, the oval base entitled 'General Washington' in gilt script, 16in (40cm). (B23A/70A).
£400-600   *CSK*

A high price because of the American association.

A rare figure of 'Aunt Chloe' standing, holding a basket in her left hand, the circular base named in gilt script, 8in (20cm). (B26/82).
£120-150   *CSK*

C. Naval Military & Exploration

A Staffordshire group from Uncle Tom's Cabin, showing Eva and Uncle Tom, 7in (17.5cm).
£120-150   *WIL*

A rare equestrian figure of Gholab Singh, wearing an iron red jacket and yellow waist sash, holding a scimitar in his left hand, on shaped gilt lined base, 8½in (21cm). (C27/68).
£200-300   *CSK*

A rare group of Topsy and Eva seated, arm in arm on oval scroll moulded base, entitled 'Topsy and Eva', 8in (20cm). (B26/84).
£150-180   *CSK*

A figure of Captain Cook, wearing captain's full dress uniform, holding a manuscript, resting on a tripod table at his side, on shaped gilt lined base, 7½in (18cm). (C5/4).
£1,000-1,300   *CSK*

A rare well modelled figure of Campbell, standing in full military uniform, 10½in (26cm). (C56/144).
£350-400   *CSK*

A Staffordshire pottery fortress, named Sebastopol, Crimean War, c1860, 10in (25cm).
£250-300 *DL*

A Staffordshire figure group of a soldier from the 21st Lancers and a sailor, c1898, 12in (30cm). (C340).
£125-140 *RBE*

A rare equestrian figure of General Simpson, wearing full military uniform, 13in (32.5cm). (C56/150).
£400-500 *CSK*

A Staffordshire figure group of 'Eugenie and Napoleon', c1854, 12½in (31cm). (C80).
£125-150 *RBE*

D. Religious

A Staffordshire figure of Moody, the American evangelist, c1873. (D9a).
£125-150 *RBE*

This figure is one of a pair.

A Staffordshire flat back figure of John Wesley, in enamel colours and gilt, clock face on oval base, c1875, 12in (30cm).
£80-120 *WIL*

Religious figures are amongst the least popular figures in the Staffordshire group. However a rare example will still command a good price.

E. Theatre, Opera, Ballet & Circus

A Staffordshire flat back figure of 'C H Spurgeon', enamel colours, raised name on base, late 19thC, 11½in (28cm).
£80-120 *WIL*

A rare figure of King Henry V, wearing a long tunic, blue ermine-edged jacket and yellow gauntlets, beside a pedestal surmounted by a sceptre, the rectangular base entitled 'Henry V Trying On the Crown', 13½in (33cm). (E12/29).
£2,500-2,750 *RBE*

Cf John Hall, Staffordshire Portrait Figures, pl 27.

A well coloured group of 'Othello and Iago', 11½in (28cm). (E13/31).
£300-500 *CSK*

A figure of John Philip Kemble as Hamlet, standing holding a skull in his left hand, the circular coloured base entitled 'Alas, Poor Yorick', 11in (27.5cm). (E13a/32a).
£150-250 *CSK*

A figure of Madame Alboni as Cinderella, wearing a plumed hat, blue cloak and green skirt in an elaborate pumpkin carriage behind a horse, 8½in (21cm). (E20/43).
£300-400 *CSK*

Cf Antony Oliver, The Victorian Staffordshire Figure, *colour pl 7.*

An unusual hollow Staffordshire figure of Falstaff, c1845, 6in (15cm). (Similar to E25).
£80-100 *RBE*

◁ A rare group of trick riders, probably portraying Andrew Ducrow and his wife, Louisa Woolford, 11in (27.5cm). (E68/131).
£200-300 *CSK*

A rare group of Masaniello and ▷ Fenella, 11in (27.5cm). (E111/221).
£120-180 *CSK*

A rare group of Mr Barton and Miss Rosa Henry as Giaffier and Zuleika, on oval gilt lined base, 12in (30cm). (E28/60).
£350-450 *CSK*

Cf Antony Oliver, The Victorian Staffordshire Figure, *pl 145.*

A rare figure of Mr Pickwick, standing wearing a dark blue tailcoat on shaped gilt scroll moulded base, 7½in (18cm).
£120-180 *CSK*

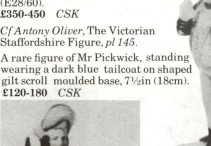

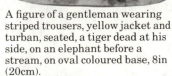

A figure of a gentleman wearing striped trousers, yellow jacket and turban, seated, a tiger dead at his side, on an elephant before a stream, on oval coloured base, 8in (20cm).
£500-600 *CSK*

A figure of Jenny Lind as Marie, her right hand holding a green hat, wearing a blue bodice and striped skirt, the shaped base entitled 'M. Lind', 7½in (18cm). (E83/164).
£400-500 *CSK*

A rare figure of Sarah Eggerton as Helen MacGregor, holding an axe in her right hand, a shield in her left, on oval gilt lined base, 9in (22.5cm). (E74/146).
£220-250 *CSK*

A rare Staffordshire portrait figure of the lion tamer Van Amburgh, titled, the subject standing surrounded by a pride of lions, a leopard on his back, c1840, 6in (15cm).
£3,000-4,000 *TKN*

A Staffordshire group of the Elephant of Siam, enriched in green, iron red, blue and grey, c1840, 6in (15cm) wide. (E156). **£250-350** *RBE*

A Victorian Staffordshire theatrical figure group, c1845, 9in (22.5cm). **£120-150** *GCA*

A Victorian Staffordshire girl mandolin player, c1845, 10in (25cm). **£85-110** *GCA*

F. Sport

An early Staffordshire figure of Tom Cribb, c1830. **£1,000-1,100** *DL*

A pair of Staffordshire figures of the boxers 'Heenan' and 'Sayers', in mint condition, c1850, 9½in (23.5cm). **£400-450** *DL*

A pair of Staffordshire pugilist figures, modelled as the boxers Mollineux and Cribb, both wearing ochre breeches, Cribb's left arm and base restored, c1810, 8in (22cm). **£2,000-3,000** *C*

G. Crime

A figure of George Parr, standing wearing an iron red and blue peaked cap, a cricket ball held in his right hand, flanked by a jacket, stumps and cricket bat, on oval gilt lined base, 13in (32.5cm). (F7/13). **£400-500** *CSK*

Figures depicting cricketers are particularly collectable.

A Staffordshire sporting group, of two pugilists 'Heenan and Sayers', as raised names on base, enamel colours, 10in (25cm). **£200-250** *WIL*

A Victorian Staffordshire pair of figures of Dick Turpin and Tom King, 9½in (23.5cm). **£200-275** *GCA*

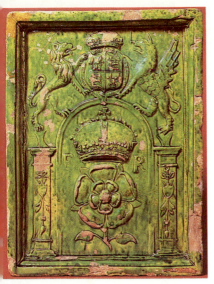

A Staffordshire saltglaze tartan-ground Royalist teapot and cover, with loop handle and faceted spout, painted in sepia with a bust length portrait of Prince Charles Edward Stuart, restored, spout chipped, c1750, 5½in (14cm). **£10,000-12,000** *C*

Above A lead glazed pottery stove tile, moulded in relief with the Royal Coat-of-Arms, mid-16thC, 13½ by 10in (34 by 25cm). **£1,500-2,000** *JHo*

Below A Staffordshire two-handled slipware posset pot, late 17thC, 4in (11cm) high. **£4,000-5,000** *JHo*

A Southwark delft armorial salt, painted in blue, the ends moulded with the arms of the City of London, one foot repaired, chips to rim, second quarter 17thC, 5½in (13cm) wide. **£5,000-6,000** *C*

Very few salts such as this would appear to be recorded.

Right A saltglazed punch bowl, decorated in scratch blue with sprays of flowers, inscribed E. Saddler and dated 1759, 11in (28cm). **£5,000-6,000** *DWB*

Below l. A Yorkshire pearlware oviform jug, with portrait of Lord Nelson, c1800, 5½in (13cm) high. **£400-500**

c. A Yorkshire pearlware oval portrait plaque of Admiral Earl Howe, c1795, 7½in (19cm). **£700-800**

r. A Yorkshire pearlware oviform jug, c1795, 5½in (13cm). **£550-650** *C*

A Staffordshire pottery garniture of 3 figural spill vase groups, in the manner of Ralph Wood, the younger, c1790, 10½ by 9½in (26.5 and 23cm).
£1,500-1,600 *Bon*

A Ralph Wood Toby jug, representing Lord Howe, mould mark '63' impressed under base, c1770, 9½in (24cm).
£1,800-2,200 *LR*

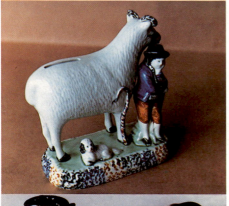

Left A rare Yorkshire money box in the form of a ram, attendant and dog, c1800-20, 6in (15cm).
£1,400-1,600 *LR*

Very few pottery money boxes in this form appear to exist.

A Yorkshire cow group with girl attendant, 6in (15cm). **£1,000-1,250** *LR*
Below A pair of Liverpool delftware candlesticks, c1760, 9½in (44cm).
£10,000-12,000 *JHo*

An Obadiah Sherratt model of Politos Menagerie, impressed 'Menagerie of The Wonderfull Burds and Beasts From Most Parts of the World', c1830, 13in (32.5cm). **£7,000-8,000** *CSK*

Below An Obadiah Sherratt group of Politos Menagerie modelled as a stage, inscribed, restored, one parrot and monkey missing, chips, c1830, 12in (30cm).
£16,000-18,000 *C*

One of the rarest forms of cow creamer, having a large impractical bocage support, unusual acorn-bedecked leaves and large calf, probably from Yorkshire c1780-90, 9in (22.5cm).
£1,600-1,800 *LR*

Above, far left & left Two rare Staffordshire pottery groups of musicians, seated on high graduated grassy bases before flowering bocage, one showing a piper and lute player both wearing feathered bonnets, the other modelled as a flautist and lute player, a stream and swan at their feet, 8¾in (22cm), early 19thC.
£2,000-3,000 *Bon*

Above A Staffordshire pottery figure of Charity in a floral robe and yellow sash on a shaped grassy base before a stump support, with two children at her feet, some paint flaking on base and tree, 7½in (19cm).
£250-350 *Bon*

Above A fine Prattware figure of a cavalry officer, mounted on a prancing horse, wearing a deep blue jacket with yellow sash, yellow breeches and brown boots, his helmet embossed with the cypher GR, on a textured green mound base edged in ochre, 8¾in (22cm).
£2,000-3,000 *P*

Left A rare Staffordshire (Lloyd) group of Isaac Van Amburgh, wearing Roman gladiator dress, with a leopard, a lion, a lioness and a cub, c1830, 5¾in (14cm). (E100/200).
£3,000-4,000 *CSK*

'The new Marriage Act' by Obadiah Sherratt, decorated in typical Sherratt enamel colours, made at the time of the Act, 1822, 6½in (17cm).
£1,300-1,500   *LR*

A Bristol delft blue and white documentary bowl with encircling inscription 'Joseph Springall: whole:sale: potter; in; mattshall: in: the: county: of: Norfolk.' minor chips and restorations, c1735, 14in (35cm).
£6,000-10,000   *C*

A pottery plaque decorated in underglaze colours with unglazed buff earthenware back, Whieldon School, Staffordshire, c1755, 7 by 8½in (17.5 by 21.5cm).
£3,000-4,000   *JHo*

A pair of pottery birds sitting on tree stumps with flowers in relief, decorated in underglaze colours, Whieldon type, Staffordshire, c1755, 7in (18cm).
£12,000-15,000   *JHo*

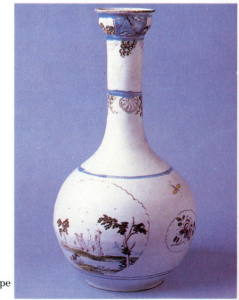

A delftware bottle with finely painted European landscape scenes, Liverpool, c1760, 10in (25cm).
£1,800-2,000   *JHo*

A Wedgwood 3-colour jasper figure of a reclining child modelled by William Hackwood after Della Robbia original, damage, c1785, 5½in (14cm) long.
£10,000-11,000 *C*

A Minton garden fountain, 'Amorini Fountain', modelled as a pair of cherubs sitting on a rock, impressed 'Minton 911' and date code for 1868, 26in (65cm) high.
£4,500-5,000 *C*

Right A Minton urn, with moulded decoration in high relief, impressed Minton 980, date code for 1864, 38½in (96.5cm) high.
£20,000-22,000 *C*

A Minton jardinière and stand, designed by Albert Carrier de Belleuse, naturalistic polychrome colouring on a cobalt blue ground, jardinière impressed 'Minton 990' and date code for 1882, 68in (168cm) high.
£25,000-30,000 *C*

Above right A pair of large Minton two-handled urns, with 2 relief panels below the rim with Bacchanalian scenes, impressed 1359 and date codes for 1872 and 1876, 23½in (59cm) high.
£4,500-5,500 *C*

A large Minton two-handled vase, minor chips, impressed IA, date code for 1859, 28in.
£9,000-10,000 *C*

A Deruta blue and gold lustre a candelieri dish, some glaze repair to centre, rim chips, c1520, 16½in (42cm).
£4,500-6,000   *C*

Above An Hispano Moresque blue and copper lustre deep dish, with central IHS monogram in lustre, Valencia, mid-15thC, 19½in (48cm) diam.
£45,000-50,000   *C*

Below right A Böttger polished brown stoneware baluster coffee pot and domed cover, with scroll handle, minute chip to spout, c1715, 7in (17.5cm).
£10,000-12,000   *C*

Below A Brussels faience boar's head tureen, cover and stand, minor rim chips, traces of S.L.M. mark to base of tureen, mid-18thC, stand 16in (40cm) long.
£5,500-6,000   *C*

The mark of this piece refers presumably to a member of the Mombaers family who were active in Brussels from 1705 until well after 1750.

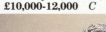

A Safavid tile panel, with a black field and figure of Sagittarius surrounded by palmettes and flowering vine, some repair, framed, 49 by 34in.
£10,000-12,000   *C*

A pair of Luneville lions, in a rich blue glaze, enriched in white, minor repairs, some chips, c1750, 17½in (42cm) long. **£4,500-5,000**   *CNY*

A Bow blue and white ink pot, the top pierced with 4 holes, slight staining, indecipherable mark in blue, perhaps a circle, 1750, 3½in (9cm) diam.
£10,000-12,000 *C*

A Bow circular tureen and cover, the loop handles with incised frowning mask terminals, the cover with twig finial, chips to rim, finial repaired, unglazed base with incised R mark, c1750, 26in (66cm) wide.
£6,500-7,000 *C*

A pair of Bow figures of a cock and hen, the cock with minute chip to tail feathers, the hen with restoration to neck and chips to tail feathers, c1758, 4in (10cm) high.
£4,000-4,500 *C*

A pair of Bow cherubs amidst bocage, c1765.
£600-700 *SA*

A Chelsea 'Hans Sloane' botanical plate painted with hibiscus, with a shaped chocolate line rim, some minute rubbing, red anchor and 43 mark, c1755, 9½in (23.5cm).
£5,000-5,500 *C*

A Chelsea oval sauceboat with scroll handle, painted in the manner of O'Neale with fable subjects, the interior with a bouquet and scattered flower sprays, red anchor mark, c1753, 9in (22cm) wide.
£14,000-15,000 *C*

l. A Chelsea lobed beaker, c1750, 3in (7cm).
£7,000-8,000

Only one other example would appear to be recorded

c. A Chelsea octagonal bowl after a Kakiemon original, c1752, 4in (10.5cm) wide.
£3,000-3,500

r. A Chelsea fluted beaker painted in the Kakiemon palette, rim minutely chipped, c1750, 3in (7.5cm).
£2,500-3,000   *C*

A Chelsea lobed teaplant beaker, minute rim chips, c1745-49, 3in (7.5cm).
£5,000-6,000   *C*

A rare Chaffers Liverpool phosphate mug, decorated in enamels, c1760, 5in (12.5cm) high.
£750-1,000   *WW*

A Derby part dessert service painted with foxhunting scenes, comprising: a two-handled oblong compote, sugar bowl, cover and stand, 4 shell dishes, 12 plates, some minor rubbing to gilt, iron red crown, crossed batons and D marks, c1790.
£12,000-15,000   *CNY*

A rare Chelsea set of 4 cattle, 2 bearing red anchor marks, c1755, 1½ to 3in (3.5 to 7.5cm).
£2,000-4,000   *P*

A Longton Hall grape box and cover, c1755, 5in (12cm) wide.
£8,000-10,000   *C*

A Minton part dessert service, c1878. **£2,000-2,500**   *C*

A Worcester quatrefoil baluster vase, c1758, 6½in (16cm) high. **£8,000-8,500**   *C*

A garniture of 3 Minton vases, painted with flowers and with fine gilding by Thos. Steele, c1820. **£2,500-3,000**   *SA*

A Worcester flared wine funnel, painted in a 'famille verte' palette with an Oriental holding a fan, the interior with a green diaper and flower-head pattern border, minute rim chip and fritting to inside rim, c1755, 5½in (13.5cm) high. **£13,000-14,000**   *C*

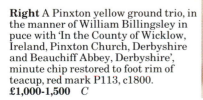

Above A Derby yellow ground tête-à-tête, each piece painted by John Brewer with animals and butterflies, blue crown, crossed baton and D marks, c1800. **£7,500-8,000**   *CNY*

Right A Pinxton yellow ground trio, in the manner of William Billingsley in puce with 'In the County of Wicklow, Ireland, Pinxton Church, Derbyshire and Beauchiff Abbey, Derbyshire', minute chip restored to foot rim of teacup, red mark P113, c1800. **£1,000-1,500**   *C*

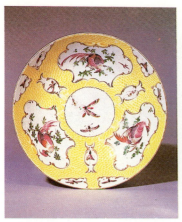

A Worcester yellow-scale saucer-dish, painted with exotic birds and insects within gilt vase- and mirror-shaped cartouches, within gilt line rim, c1765, 7¼in (18.5cm) diam.
£4,000-4,500 C

Two Worcester blue-scale cabbage-leaf moulded mask jugs: One painted with bouquets and flower-sprays within gilt vase and mirror shaped cartouches, on a well-defined blue-scale ground, the handle with pink flowers and 'feuille-de-choux', slight chip to spout and foot rim, c1765, 8in (20cm).
£800-1,200

The other similarly decorated with garlands and flower sprays, slight chip to spout, c1768, 8in (20cm).
£1,000-1,500 C

Left: A pair of Worcester blue-scale oviform vases and covers, 2-handled, painted with phoenix and dragons among flowering plants in Oriental style, in rococo panels within richly gilt scroll borders, the necks with narrow bands of formal flowers in underglaze blue and gilt, floral knops and scroll handles, square seal marks in underglaze blue, c1765, 6½in (16cm).
£2,000-2,500 L

Below: A rare set of 12 Rockingham dessert plates, made to royal order, the centres painted in colours and gilt with the arms of King William IV suspending the Order of St George, puce printed 'Griffin Rockingham Works, Brameld, manufacturers to the King, Queen and Royal family,' within an elaborate cartouche and the date 1832 in gilt, one with repair to rim, 2 with hairline cracks, 9¼in (23.5cm) diam.
£20,000-25,000 CNY

A pair of Worcester circular butter tubs, covers and stands, painted with festoons and sprays of flowers in mirror and vase shaped panels outlined with gilt rococo scrolls on a blue-scale ground, the tubs with scroll handles and the covers with floral knops, square seal marks in underglaze blue, c1765.
£1,900-2,100 L

Left A Worcester quatrefoil two-handled chestnut basket, pierced cover and stand, painted in the atelier of James Giles, the base with blue '8', the cover with blue 'q' mark, some minor repairs to flowers, c1770, the stand 10½in (25.5cm) wide.
£4,500-5,000 *C*

Right An extensive Worcester, Flight, Barr & Barr, dinner service, the borders painted with meandering flowers in underglaze blue, overglaze iron red and pink enriched in gilding, within shaped gilt gadrooned rims, some damage, impressed and printed marks, c1820.
£35,000-40,000 *C*

Left A Worcester yellow-ground honeycomb moulded oval dish, with vinestock and leaf handles, the centre with scattered flower sprays, the border with reeded arcading painted with flowers, c1765, 12½in (30.5cm) wide.
£5,500-6,000 *C*

A Royal Doulton bone china plate, for the Coronation of Edward VII in 1902, with coloured portraits and unusual fluted edge, 8in (20cm).
£60-80 *SCW*

Right A Chamberlain's Worcester porcelain jug, the tapering body with gadroon moulded flutes, painted in sepia with a view of 'Worcester 1798', as seen from the river, the flutes of alternating white and cobalt heightened with gilt leaves, the neck with gilt oval monogram reserves against a ground of cobalt heightened with gilt fleur-de-lys, gilt Chamberlain's Worcester mark on base, body crack, 7in (17.5cm) high.
£150-200 *Bon*

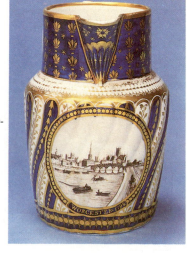

A Fulda figure of a lime seller and a grape seller, standing holding baskets, minor chips to basket of lady, blue cross mark, c1770, 5½in (14.5cm) high.
£9,000-10,000 each *CG*

A pair of Frankenthal figures of Scaramouche and Columbine, modelled by J. W. Lanz, on shaped rococo scroll bases edged in pink and gilt, minute chips to bases, blue rampant lion mark and impressed PH monogram of Paul Hannong and N and 3, 1756-1759, 5½in (14.5cm) high.
£6,000-7,000 *CG*

A Meissen sugar box and cover, painted in the Höroldt workshop, blue KPM and crossed swords mark and gilder's No.38 to each piece, 1723-25, 4in (10.5cm) long.
£9,000-10,000 *C*

An early Meissen chinoiserie coffee pot and cover, painted by J. G. Höroldt, the cover with flowers issuing from rockwork, slight losses to glaze, c1723, 6½in (16.5cm) high.
£8,000-10,000 *CG*

A Meissen teapot and cover, painted with landscapes and river scenes, with horsemen fording a stream, and figures outside a house, in shaped panels outlined with scrolls in lustre and gold, the ground with indianische Blumen in colours, the spout issuing from a mask and the handle with foliage terminals, the cover painted with a coastal scene with shipping, KPM mark and crossed swords in under-glaze blue, both teapot and cover with gilder's numeral 11 in gold, 1725, 4½in (11cm).
£21,000-24,000 *L*

A Meissen bowl, the inside with solid gilding, the outside with 3 groups of chinoiserie figures, in cisélé gold, resting on scrolls and strapwork, with gold borders edged with scrolls, 1725, 7in (17.5cm).
£3,500-4,500 *L*

A Meissen gold-mounted circular bombe snuff box and cover, with gilt base, gold mounts, with the Master's mark of Louis Métayer, c1730–40, 6cm diam. **£22,000-25,000** *CG*

l. A Meissen apple green ground cup and saucer with white and gold shell and scroll handle, blue crossed swords mark, c1740. **£3,500-4,000**

c. A Meissen lime green ground coffee cup and saucer, blue crossed swords and gilt 20, c1740. **£5,500-6,000**

r. A Meissen turquoise ground coffee cup and saucer, blue crossed swords, c1742. **£2,200-2,500** *CG*

Above left A pair of Louis XVI ormolu mounted Meissen figures of a cockerel and hen, naturalistically modelled by J. J. Kändler and coloured on tree stump mound bases applied with coloured flowers, the shaped oval ormolu bases with flutes and acanthus, repair to the cockerel's tail feathers and beak, minor chips, blue crossed swords marks, c1745, the cockerel 12in (30cm) high overall. **£8,000-10,000** *C*

First modelled in 1741.

Above right A Meissen chinoiserie powder box, with 3 vignettes of Chinese figures on 'Laub-und-Bandelwerk' supports in Böttger-lustre, iron-red, puce and gold, with blue crossed swords mark, c1735, 4½in (11.5cm) diam. **£2,500-3,000** *CG*

A Meissen plate from the Christie-Miller Service, with 4 oval quatrefoil panels en camaïeu rose, with scrolls and shells in gold and chocolate, with gilt rim, blue crossed swords mark, Pressnummer 22, c1742, 9in (23cm). **£12,000-15,000** *C*

A Meissen teapot and cover, the mask spout enriched with gilding, the sides painted by P. E. Schindler, blue K.P.M. and crossed swords mark, base and cover with gilder's mark 36, c1723–25, 7in (17cm) wide. **£12,000-15,000** *CG*

A Meissen group of Chinese lovers, modelled by J. J. Kändler and P. Reinicke, some restorations, c1745, 5in (13cm) wide.
£4,000-5,000 *CG*

Right A Meissen figure of a jay by J. J. Kändler, some damage, blue crossed swords mark, c1745, 15in (39cm).
£10,000-15,000 *C*

A Meissen group of lovers with a snuff-box, by J. J. Kändler, minor chips to leaves, blue crossed swords mark under base, c1745, 7in (17cm) high.
£5,000-6,000 *CG*

Two Meissen snuff boxes with gilt metal mounts:

l. Blue crossed swords mark to interior, c1745, 3in (7cm).
£7,000-8,000

r. c1750, 3in (7cm).
£3,000-3,500 *CG*

A Meissen group of Tyrolean or Dutch dancers, modelled by J. J. Kändler, with Louis XV ormolu mounts, his right shoulder repaired, chip to underside of base, blue crossed swords mark, c1745, 8in (19cm).
£9,000-10,000 *CG*

A Nymphenburg Crucifixion group modelled by Franz Anton Bustelli, Christ-figure with repairs to both legs and left arm, impressed Bavarian shield mark to Mater Dolorosa, c1756, 8in (21cm) long, on ebonised wooden base.
£10,000-15,000 *CNY*

A Meissen Papal tea caddy and cover from the Benedict XIV service, bearing the Royal Arms of Saxony, the arms of Lambertini and the Papal tiara and crossed keys of St Peter, Pressnummer 49, c1748, 5in (12cm).
£25,000-30,000 *CG*

l. A Meissen coffee cup and saucer painted after G. P. Rugendas, blue crossed swords mark, c1740. **£4,000-5,000**
c. A Meissen teabowl and saucer, blue crossed swords, gilt 50 mark, c1740. **£4,000-5,000**
r. A pair of Meissen coffee cups and saucers, blue crossed swords, c1740. **£8,000-9,000** *CG*

A Paris, Nast, part tea and coffee service, finely painted with birds, with iron red and gold marks, c1810.
£6,000-9,000 *C*

l. A Vincennes milk jug and cover, marked with blue interlaced Ls enclosing date letter C for 1755, 5in (13cm).
£5,000-6,000

c. A Sèvres cup and saucer, blue interlaced Ls, painter's mark of Evans and date letter M for 1765.
£1,000-1,500

r. A Vincennes sugar bowl and cover, blue Ls, date mark for 1753, 3in (8cm) diam.
£3,000-4,000 *CG*

A Sèvres-pattern garniture with gilt metal mounts, imitation interlaced L marks to covers, c1890, the vases 29in (73cm) high.
£7,000-10,000 *C*

A green-glazed pottery model of a farmhouse tower in three sections, various restorations, Han Dynasty, 23in (59cm).
£18,000-22,000 *C*

A green-glazed red pottery model of a house, one door hinged, interior shelves, some restoration, Han Dynasty, 16in (41cm) wide.
£3,000-5,000 *C*

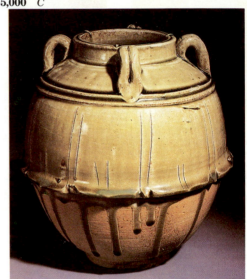

A large Yüeh ware olive-glazed oviform jar, chips restored, 6thC, 10in (26cm).
£6,000-8,000 *C*

A painted red pottery figure of a court lady, minor restorations to extremities, Tang Dynasty, 17in (44cm).
£50,000-80,000 *C*

Dating of this piece confirmed by thermoluminescence test.

A Sancai pottery horse, restorations, Tang Dynasty, 30in (77cm) high.
£230,000+ *C*

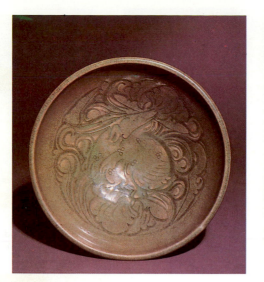

A Northern celadon bowl, borders cracked, Song Dynasty, 8½in (21cm), fitted box.
£3,000-5,000   *C*

An early Sancai glazed pottery warrior figure, with old damage and breaks, Tang Dynasty, 29in (74cm) high.
£6,000-9,000   *CNY*

A Sancai glazed ambrosia bottle, chips to lip, base and foot, Tang Dynasty, 9in (22cm).
£12,000-15,000   *CNY*

A Sancai figure of a court attendant, with restorations to his hat and base, Tang Dynasty, 40in (101cm).
£25,000-30,000   *C*

An early Ming dish, Yongle, 18in (45cm).
£100,000+   *C*

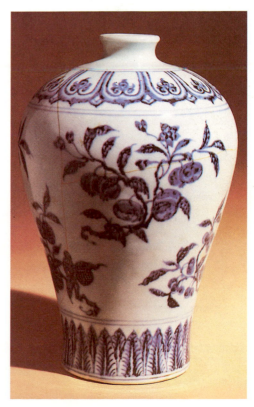

Right An early Ming vase, meiping, extensively repaired, Yongle, 11in (28cm).
£15,000-18,000   *C*

A Jun Yao Bubble Cup, Southern Song Dynasty,
4in (10cm) diam.
£15,000-18,000   *CNY*

A late Ming blue and white figure of
Budai, the God of Happiness, original
firing cracks across the waist, Wanli,
9in (23cm).
£3,000-4,000   *C*

A Guan Yao foliate wine cup, Song Dynasty, 3in (8cm) wide,
with box.
£5,000-8,000   *CNY*

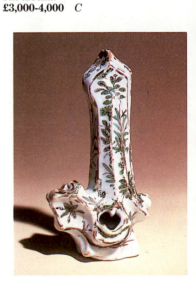

A Ming green and black enamelled
brush rest, fritted, chips to
extremities, late 16thC, 8in (20cm).
£1,200-1,700   *C*

A pair of large 'famille verte' rouleau
vases, minor chips, one with areas over-
fired, Kangxi, 29in (73cm), wood stands.
£10,000-12,000   *C*

A Transitional blue and white
sleeve vase, the shoulder and foot
incised with narrow bands of foliage
and chevrons, mid-17thC, 19in
(46cm).
£4,000-5,000   *C*

A massive blue and white fish-bowl, painted in the manner of the Master of the Rocks, rim fritted, star-shaped body crack, early Kangxi, 24in (60cm) diam.
£4,000-7,000 *C*

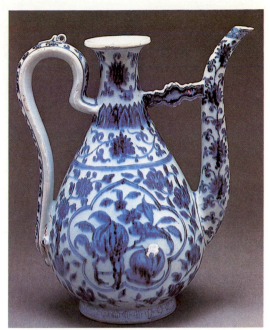

An early Ming ewer, some fritting, first half 15thC, 11in (28cm) high.
£25,000-30,000 *CNY*

A pair of 'famille verte' hexagonal puzzle jugs and covers, one finial and spout restored, Kangxi, 9in (22cm).
£1,000-3,000 *C*

A very rare 'famille rose' plate for the Dutch East India Company, some rim chips and a hair crack, fitted box, Yongzheng, 9in (23cm).
£8,000-12,000 *C*

Three large baluster vases and domed covers, fritted, one vase and cover damaged, another cover with damage to the unglazed inner rim, Kangxi, 22in (57cm) high.
£3,000-5,000 *C*

A 'European Procession' punchbowl painted with mounted figures in late 17thC dress, the interior painted with flowers and central bouquet, Qianlong, 16in (40cm).
£20,000-28,000 *C*

A cylindrical vase, painted in underglaze blue and copper red with spotted deer in a landscape, minor damage, large Qianlong six-character seal mark and of the period, 19in (48cm).
£10,000-12,000 *C*

A pair of Chinese Imari fish bowls, the sides set with biscuit lion-mask handles, one restored, c1750, 24in (60cm).
£20,000-30,000 *C*

A pair of export models of crouching hounds, crisply modelled, ears restored, Qianlong 6in (15cm).
£3,000-5,000 *C*

A pair of green dragon jars and covers, Qianlong six-character marks of the period, 8in (20cm).
£7,000-10,000 *C*

A Kakiemon oviform vase, cracked and riveted, a small hole filled and 2 distinct firing blemishes, c1665, 10in (26cm). **£4,000-6,000** *C*

l. A Kyoto oviform vase, signed Kinkozan zo, late 19thC, 8in (20cm). **£2,500-3,000.**
c. A Kyoto dish, signed, late 19thC, 13in (32cm). **£2,500-3,000.**
r. A Kyoto-Satsuma koro and cover, signed, c1900, 6in (16cm). **£3,000-5,000** *C*

A pair of garden seats, body cracks, late 18th or early 19thC, 18in (47cm). **£1,500-2,500** *C*

A model of a roistering Dutchman, originating from a Dutch Delft design for Bacchus, base of goblet chipped, 18thC, 14in (36cm). **£12,000-15,000** *C*

An Imari ship's plate and cover, Genroku period, 10in (25cm) diam. **£1,000-1,500** *C*

Left A Chinese export punchbowl probably for the American market, the interior painted in sepia and gilt, c1790, 14in (36cm). **£2,000-3,000** *C*

A blue sucrier and
cover, with gilt label and
decoration, c1790, 6½in
(17cm).
£300-500   *Som*

A set of 3 green spirit decanters in papier
mâché stand, each bottle with gilt
simulated wine label, c1790, stand 9in
(23cm) high.
£800-1,000   *Som*

A set of 3 spirit bottles with silver
mounts and stoppers, hallmarked
Birmingham 1845, in a
silver plated stand, with 3 silver
wine labels for port, claret and
madeira, hallmarked London
1822, stand 17in (44cm).
£500-600   *Som*

Right   A cream jug and sugar
basin, the bowl with gilt
inscription 'I Wish you Well',
rubbed inscription on jug, c1820,
jug 5in (13cm) high.
£250-350   *Som*

A roemer-style wine glass on folded conical foot, c1780, 4½in
(11cm).
£150-200   *Som*

Right   A flute-cut decanter with star-cut base, cut mushroom
stopper, c1840, 10in (25cm).
£175-225

A flute-cut claret jug, with strap handle, c1840, 12in (30cm).
£250-300   *Som*

A 'Nailsea' carafe, with crown glass body, c1860, 11½in (29cm).
£220-260 *Som*

Three 'Nailsea' bells, c1860:

l. 12in (30cm).
£120-160

c. 13in (32cm).
£120-160

r. 12in (30cm).
£160-200 *Som*

A Nailsea mug in bottle glass, with applied handle, c1780, 4in (10cm).
£75-100 *Som*

l. A gilt-decorated wine glass on double series opaque twist stem, c1760, 6in (15cm).
£320-360

r. An ogee-bowl wine glass on lace spiral twist stem, c1770, 6in (15cm).
£1,200-1,500 *Som*

A Wrockwardine bonnet glass and hat of bottle glass, the glass with red and white inclusions, the hat with blue inclusions, c1810, 2½in (6cm).
£200-250 *Som*

A set of oval blue glass salts, with star-cut bases, c1780, 4in (10cm) diam.
£180-220 *Som*

A satin glass scent bottle with raised gold floral decorations, silver mount marked Sampson Mordan London, 1885, 4in (10cm).
£250-350   *Som*

Two St Louis weights, **£1,000-3,500**. Three Clichy weights, centre, c1850, **£3,500-5,500** lower, **£2,000-5,000**   *C*

Above   A Bristol or South Staffordshire scent phial, c1770, 3in (7cm).
£250-300   *Som*

Right   A set of 6 wine glasses, marked 'Richardsons Stourbridge' under feet, c1880, 5in (12cm).
£480-580   *Som*

Two unusual potichamanie rolling pins:

l. With amethyst background, c1870, 13in (33cm) long.
£120-150

r. With orange background, c1870, 11in (28cm) long.
£80-100   *Som*

A small Venetian enamelled flask from the atelier of Osvaldo Brussa, mid-18thC, 3½in (9cm) high.
£2,500-3,500   *C*

Flatware

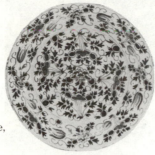

A Bristol delft plate painted in blue, green and red with an insect above a rabbit, c1730, 13in (32.5cm). £200-250 *CSK*

A Bristol delft plate, decorated in iron red, blue and green with stylised flowers, mid-18thC, 5½in (13.5cm). £400-500 *WW*

A rare Bristol delft blue-dash charger, painted central figure of George I dressed in Coronation regalia, standing amongst sponged trees in colours of red, blue, yellow, brown and green polychrome, c1714, 13in (32.5cm). £3,000-4,000 *BS*

A pottery plate printed in black with battle scene and wounded soldier, inscribed 'Caderea Plevlnei. Jsman Pasa ranit se preda prisonier. 28 Noembriu 1877', 8 in (20 cm). £40-60 *P*

A Bristol delft polychrome plate, with bianco-sopra-bianco, 9in (22.5cm). £200-250 *Wai*

A Bristol delft blue and white fluted spoon tray, slight rim chip, c1750, 6in (15cm) wide. £250-350 *C*

A Lambeth delft blue-dash Royalist portrait charger, painted predominantly in blue with King William seated on a rearing horse, enriched in yellow and manganese, flanked by the the initials 'WR', within a yellow line and blue-dash rim, cracks and rim restored, c1690, 13½in (34cm). £2,500-3,000 *C*

A Rogers meat plate, white ground with blue transfer decoration, picture panel to centre depicting a boy with an elephant, impressed mark to base, 19thC, 17in (42.5cm). £100-150 *WIL*

A Lambeth delft blue-dash Royalist portrait charger, the centre painted predominantly in blue with a portrait of Queen Anne, her dress, orb and sceptre enriched in yellow, standing in a green field flanked by sponged trees, within a blue and yellow line cartouche and blue-dash rim, restored, c1705, 14in (35cm).
£3,000-4,000   C

Cf Frank Britton, English Delftware in the Bristol Collection, *pl 3.53.*

A London delft plate, with a Chinaman kneeling with yellow bushes and manganese circle, with floral border, c1740, 9in (22.5cm).
£200-250   *DEL*

A London delft Royalist blue and white plate, painted with the rose and thistle tied with ribbon beneath a crown and the initials 'GR', within concentric blue lines, crack and chips to rim, c1715, 9in (22.5cm).
£800-1,200   C

Cf F H Garner and Michael Archer, English Delftware, *pl 66A.*

A Lambeth delft ballooning plate painted in blue, green, yellow and manganese, within a blue 'feuille-de-choux' rim, minor glaze flaking to rim, c1785, 12in (30cm).
£1,500-2,000   C

See F H Garner and Michael Archer, English Delftware, *pl 119A.*

A Liverpool delft blue and white commemorative dish, the centre painted with The Taking of Portobello beneath a wide border, within an ochre rim, the reverse with blue pennants, slight cracks to well at 1 o'clock, minor chips and glaze flaking to rim, c1741, 12in (30cm).
£1,300-1,600   C

Cf Anthony Ray, op cit pl 10, no 28, also Frank Britton op cit pl 10.48 and Bernard Rackham, Catalogue of the Glaisher Collection of Pottery and Porcelain, *pl 118E.*

A Liverpool delft Fazackerley palette plate, with Flowers and Fence pattern, 9in (22.5cm).
£250-300   *DEL*

Two Liverpool delft plates painted in Fazackerley colours with central flower sprays, c1760, 9in (22.5cm).
£200-250   *CSK*

A London delft blue-dash tulip charger, painted in ochre, yellow and blue within a yellow line and blue-dash rim, the reverse with a pale green glaze, some glaze flaking, c1700, 14in (35cm).
£1,500-2,000   C

A delft dish, painted in green and yellow outlined in manganese, London or Bristol, c1760, 11½in (28.5cm).
£160-200   *CSK*

A pair of Liverpool delft plates, the centres decorated in blue with Chinese peony and rock groups, one hair crack, c1760-75, 13in (33cm).
£250-350 *WW*

A blue and white transfer pottery platter, Chinoiserie Ruins, impressed Stephenson, c1805, 19in (47.5cm) wide.
£250-300 *DEL*

A pottery plate in dark blue and white transfer ware, entitled 'Sheltered Peasants', by R Hall, the title on a branch, 8in (20cm).
£35-40 *DEL*

An English pink lustre plate, c1850.
£15-20 *DEL*

An English delft charger, painted in blue, green and ochre, the border with blue lines and the reverse with an ochre glaze, probably Southwark, a plaster reconstruction riveted to the rim at 10 o'clock, crack, chip and glaze flaking to the rim, mid-17thC, 15in (37cm).
£700-800 *C*

Cf Michael Archer and Brian Morgan, Fair as China Dishes, *pl 8, and Michael Archer,* English Delftware, *pl 17.*

A British Marine pottery soup plate, in blue and white transfer ware, c1830, 10in (25cm).
£35-40 *DEL*

A blue and white pottery plate, transfer printed with the Shipping series, 10in (25cm).
£50-60 *DEL*

Cf Coysh and R K Henry Wood, p 335.

A rare Staffordshire blue and white meat dish, printed with bathing carriages at Monks Rock, Tenby, 18½in (46cm) wide.
£200-300 *CSK*

A rare Staffordshire blue and white meat dish, printed with the Durham Ox pattern, 22in (55cm) wide.
£450-650 *CSK*

A Wedgwood plate, with moulded decoration of 4 standing angels, naturalistic colouring and variegated mottling, chip to one wing, impressed Wedgwood and registration mark for 1861, 12in (30cm).
£500-600 *C*

A Wedgwood charger, the cobalt blue ground with raised polychrome decoration, impressed Wedgwood, 15½in (38.5cm).
£800-1,000 *C*

A Wedgwood fish platter, with moulded decoration in imitation of wickerwork with seaweed and sea shells, polychrome on a white ground, impressed Wedgwood mark, 26in (65cm) long.
£600-700 *C*

A Wedgwood pearlware dish, painted by George Eyre with The Quarrel between Sancho Panza and Don Quixote's Niece and Housekeeper, after Doré, impressed mark, signed in monogram, c1870, 9in (22.5cm).
£180-250 *C*

Eleven Wedgwood creamware shaped plates, painted in colours by William Wagstaff with scenes after John Leech's sketches for Punch, impressed marks and date codes, c1868, 9½in (24cm).
£1,200-1,400 *C*

Cf Maureen Batkin, op cit pl 105.

A rare Dutch majolica pale blue ground dish, painted in colours with a parrot perched on a branch, the border with manganese and ochre dots, Rotterdam or Amsterdam, minor rim chips, early 17thC, 13½in (33.5cm).
£4,000-6,000 *CAm*

A Dutch Delft polychrome plate, restored rim chip, and minor chips, c1700, 7½in (18.5cm).
£250-350 *CAm*

A Dutch Delft polychrome dish, painted with a bird perched on flowers in a yellow vase on rockwork in a landscape, rim chips and repair, early 18thC, 13in (32cm).
£100-150 *CAm*

Dutch Delft tends to make a higher price when sold in Holland.

A Dutch Delft blue and white strawberry dish and stand, the pierced dish on 3 feet, minor rim chips, blue mark of the Porseleyne Klaeuw and 70 mark, early 18thC, 9½in (23.5cm).
£300-500 *CAm*

A Dutch Delft polychrome dish, painted with pagodas and sailing vessels in a river landscape, rim chips, early 18thC, 14in (34.5cm).
£150-200 *CAm*

A Dutch Delft polychrome Royal portrait dish, painted with the head and shoulders of Prince William V, rim chips and repairs, 18thC, 14in (34cm).
£300-500 *CAm*

A Dutch Delft polychrome dish, with yellow and iron red rim, rim chips and repairs, early 18thC, 14½in (36cm).
£150-180 *CAm*

A Dutch Delft polychrome plate, painted with a deer in blue, in a double circle with coloured flowers and insects, rim chips, first half 18thC, 9in (22.5cm).
£120-180 *CAm*

A Dutch Delft polychrome plate, in the Kakiemon manner with prunus issuing from hay bales, minor rim chips, blue P mark of perhaps Johannis Pennis of De Porceleyne Schotel, 18thC, 9in (22cm).
£500-700 *CAm*

A rare example of Dutch Delft in the Japanese style

A Dutch Delft blue and white plate, painted with a deer amongst plants surrounded by foliate and dot-and-dash border at the rim, De Grieksche A factory, rim restored, slight chips, mark of WVDB3, mid-18thC, 10in (24.5cm).
£100-150 *CAm*

A Dutch Delft blue and white dish, painted with a vase of flowers on a border of Oriental figures and flowers, 14in (35cm).
£150-200 *CSK*

A Dutch Delft hunting dish, painted in blue with a huntsman, hound and quarry among sponged foliage, 18thC, 14in (35cm).
£300-500 *TEN*

A pair of Dutch Delft blue and white dishes, painted with vases of flowers within borders of flowerheads and leaves, 13in (32.5cm).
£150-250 *CSK*

A Delft blue and white shaped oval dish, painted with flowering shrubs, 15½in (38.5cm) wide.
£120-180 *CSK*

An Hispano Moresque dish, with raised central boss, painted in copper lustre with a bird with outstretched wings, 14in (35cm).
£400-500 *CSK*

A Bayreuth blue and white armorial plate, blue B.K.C. minor glaze chips to rim, c1735, 9in (22.5cm).
£2,000-2,500 *CNY*

A Rouen bleu Persian shaped dish, decorated in the Gillibaud style in white relief with flowers and insects within borders of scrolls, minute rim glaze chips, c1700, 14½in (36cm).
£400-500 *C*

An Hispano Moresque dish, with raised central boss and leaf moulded border painted in copper lustre and blue with stylised flowers.
£200-250 *CSK*

A Rouen large dish, painted in blue and enriched in manganese, the rim with stylised lappets, small rim chip, 18th C, 16in (40cm).
£400-600 *CNY*

A pair of Castelli dishes painted with the Prodigal at Prayer, the other with Neptune, within borders of putti and scrolling leaves, 9in (23cm).
£1,500-2,000 *CSK*

Make the most of Miller's

For a larger section on Italian maiolica see previous editions of Miller's Guides

A South German blue and white dish, painted with a bird on a flowering branch, the border with symmetrical scrolling flowering foliage, hair crack, minor rim chips, blue S. mark, c1760, 18½in (46cm) long.
£500-600 *C*

An Urbino Istoriato alzata, painted with the Dream of King Astiages, the reverse inscribed in blue 'Dil Vechio Astiage Re L'alta visione 1551', damages to rim, repaired, 9½in (23.5cm).
£5,000-6,000 *C*

The composition on the present dish is very close to the Pesaro dish by Sforza, lost during the Second World War from the Herzog Anton Ulrich Museum but described by Lessmann in her appendix I, pl XXXIV and dated 1576.

An Urbino Istoriato dish, painted with the Rape of Proserpine, the nymph in yellow and ochre dress carried off by Pluto naked and bearded, the reverse inscribed in blue 'Diplutto et Proserpina', in half and repaired, c1555, 10in (25cm).
£3,000-4,000 *C*

Derived from Ludovico Dolce's woodcut in Le trasformazioni di Ovidio *published in Venice in 1553.*

Two Turin (Rossetti) plates, painted with chinoiserie figures in landscapes, rim chips, c1760, 10in (24.5cm).
£1,500-1,800 *C*

Jars

A Lambeth delft blue and white drug jar, for 'U: SAMBUC', c1740, 7in (17.5cm).
£250-300 *C*

A London delft dated blue and white wet drug jar, for 'S. CICHOREI. SYMPI', with fluttering pennants below enclosing the date 1659, with scroll handle, spout lacking, rim chips, 8in (20cm).
£1,000-1,500 *C*

This would appear to be the earliest example recorded of a dated wet drug jar with this angel's head cartouche.

Cf Agnes Lothian, 'Vessels For Apothecaries', Connoisseur Year Book, 1953, where the dating is discussed and also Louis L Lipski and Michael Archer, Dated English Delftware, pl 1600 for the first recorded example of this type dated 1660.

A Turin (Rossetti) saucer dish, painted with a horsedrawn carriage approaching a palazzo, minor rim chips, c1760, 8½in (21.5cm).
£600-700 *C*

A Bristol delft jar of acorn shape, the sides painted in blue, green and iron red, glaze flaking to handles and rim, c1710, 5½in (14cm).
£700-900 *C*

Cf Antony Ray, English Delftware Pottery, pl 66, no 130, for a jar of similar shape.

A Lambeth delft blue and white wet drug jar with scrolling strap handle, for 'S:E: CORALLIIS', chips to foot and some glaze flaking, c1680, 7½in (18cm).
£500-800 *C*

A Staffordshire jar and cover, painted in apple green with the word 'Honey' in gilt, 12in (30cm).
£200-250 *CSK*

A London delftware wet drug jar, with a cherub and shell label, 7½in (18.5cm).
£250-300 *JHo*

A London delft blue and white drug jar, named for 'CONF. DE. OVO', rim flaking, c1680, 7½in (19cm).
£400-600 *C*

A London delftware dry drug jar, with a cherub and shell label, early 18thC, 8in (20cm).
£250-300 *JHo*

A Dutch Delft blue and white tobacco jar for 'SPAANSE', metal cover, rim chips, blue V mark, first half of 18thC, 9½in (23.5cm).
£250-400 *CAm*

A Staffordshire jar with blue and gilt scoll handles, painted in blue and gilt with stylised vines, entitled 'Leeches' in gilt, 7in (17.5cm).
£180-220 *CSK*

A Venice waisted albarello, painted with a saint seated in a C-scroll and foliage cartouche, reserved on a blue ground with sgraffito scrolls and yellow and blue painted mask and trophies, restoration to neck and foot, c1550, 11in (27cm).
£400-600 *CAm*

A Dutch Delft blue and white oviform drug jar, entitled 'SPAANSE', and another similar entitled 'RAPPE', 9in (23cm).
£500-800 *CSK*

An Italian pottery jar and cover, with gold cartouches on a speckled blue ground, the pedestal foot and cover with matching decoration, foot repaired, 39in (97.5cm).
£700-900 *Bea*

A Dutch Delft blue and white large tobacco jar and brass cover, named in blue 'VARINAS', the brass domed cover with ball finial, mark of the claw in blue, 21in (54cm).
£1,200-1,800 *CNY*

A French faience cylindrical tobacco jar, with pewter screw cover, named in manganese 'Tabac' and painted in green, yellow and manganese with tobacco leaves, the screw cover with carrying handle, c1740, 17½in (43.5cm) high overall.
£1,500-2,000 *CNY*

Jugs

A Staffordshire saltglaze bear jug and cover, modelled as a crouching bear, covered in frit and with brown trailed slip collar, his eyes and paws enriched with brown slip, crack to cover, muzzle repaired, both front paws restuck, repair to back right paw, c1740, 10in (25cm).
£1,800-2,200 *C*

These brown bear jugs were traditionally thought to represent performing bears. See A Catalogue of English Brown Stoneware from the 17th and 18th Centuries compiled by Jonathan Horne.

A Staffordshire saltglaze bear jug and cover, covered in frit and enriched with dots of brown slip to its neck, muzzle and cub, cover repaired and with piece lacking, one leg lacking to cub, head and arm of bear repaired, pieces lacking to foot and ear, c1740, 10in (24cm).
£1,600-2,000 *C*

A Nottingham brown stoneware bear jug, with detachable head, holding a dog in his arms, reputedl representing bear baiting, repaired c1740, 9in (22.5cm).
£800-1,000 *JHo*

An English mediaeval globular jug, covered in a greenish ochre iridescent glaze, chips to handle and rim, some glaze degraded, 14thC, 11½in (28.5cm).
£400-500 *JHo*

A solid agate baluster jug, the body formed of marbled white and red clays and covered with a rich glaze, the body with incised line decoration, perhaps Newcastle-under-Lyme, handle, spout and chip to rim restored, c1745, 7in (17cm).
£350-400 *C*

A Wedgwood creamware pear shaped milk jug, painted in colours by James Bakewell with sprays of tulips in puce, yellow and green, with beak spout and entwined stra handle with foliage terminals, impressed mark and potter's marks painter's mark in puce NB, c1770, 7in (18cm).
£1,200-1,500 *CNY*

James Bakewell, enameller at Wedgwood from 1769 to 1773 is bes known for his freely painted flowers in puce monochrome.

A Jackfield black glazed large jug, painted in gilt with a horse and hounds in a landscape, the body with the initials 'I + A' and inscribed 'True Blue', 11in (28cm).
£500-700 *CNY*

A Wedgwood Whieldon cream jug, cauliflower moulded, naturalistically coloured, c1765-70, 3½in (8.5cm).
£600-800 *JHo*

A Staffordshire slip decorated jug, c1765, 6in (15cm).
£500-700 *JHo*

A coloured saltglaze cream jug, c1755, 3in (7.5cm).
£300-350 *DL*

An early Staffordshire Whieldon cream jug, c1770, 5in (12.5cm).
£400-450 *DL*

A fine Prattware jug, depicting Grooms Carousing, the reverse An Offering to Peace, c1790, 6in (15cm).
£250-290 *LR*

A Pratt jug, decorated in the usual underglaze blue, ochre and green, depicting Sailors Farewell and Return, c1790, 6in (15cm).
£200-250 *LR*

A Ralph Wood Bacchus mask jug, cracks to rim and chips to rim and base, c1775, 9½in (23.5cm).
£350-450 *C*

A Pratt jug, depicting field sports, possibly not of Staffordshire make, decorated in brown, green and yellow, c1795, 6in (15cm).
£225-275 *LR*

A Pratt jug, depicting 'Prince Cobourg', the reverse the Duke of York, with coloured underglaze decoration in ochre, yellow, blue and green, c1793, 6in (15cm).
£200-250 *LR*

A Prattware jug, with peacocks in landscapes enriched in blue, brown, green and ochre, the lower part with a band of stiff leaves and bell flowers, the rim with a band of foliage, c1790, 8in (20cm).
£300-400 *CNY*

A pearlware jug, illustrating The Dandies, c1810, 5in (12.5cm).
£250-300 *JUD*

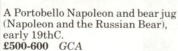

A Portobello Napoleon and bear jug (Napoleon and the Russian Bear), early 19thC.
£500-600 *GCA*

A Liverpool Herculaneum creamware large jug, transfer printed in black with the farmer's arms and inscribed below 'In God our Trust', small chip and star crack to one side, c1800, 13in (33.5cm).
£1,800-2,500 *CNY*

Two Staffordshire blue and silver resist jugs, one transfer printed in blue with a hunting subject after Morland, the other with 'Women grinding Corn' named below, reserved on the silver resist ground, c1810, the larger 5½in (14cm) high.
£400-600 *CNY*

A Staffordshire yellow ground jug and 2 waste bowls, the jug transfer printed in iron red, small hairline crack, 5in (13cm) high, the bowls painted in iron red and green on the yellow ground, the lobed rims in iron red, both with repairs, c1820, 6in (15cm) diam.
£180-250 *CNY*

A rare silver lustre blue and green grape decorated jug, early 19thC.
£225-275 *GCA*

An English earthenware sporting jug, the cream body coloured in copper lustre, pink and turquoise enamel and moulded in relief with 2 sportsmen seated with hounds during a pause in shooting, reversed with sportsmen holding a rabbit surrounded by hounds beneath a band of moulded grapevine, c1810, 6½in (16cm).
£100-150 *Bon*

Two Staffordshire lustre jugs, one enriched in colours and pink lustre with a sporting subject between yellow line borders, the neck with a band of copper lustre, small rim chip to spout, the other boldly painted in pink lustre with flower sprays, small rim chip, repair on spout, c1820, the larger 4½in (11cm).
£60-80 *CNY*

A Sunderland lustre cherubs and goat jug, c1835, 6in (15cm).
£80-110 *GCA*

A Staffordshire pink lustre sporting jug, enriched in green, iron red, brown and black, the neck with a band of foliage reserved on the pink lustre ground, c1810, 6in (15cm).
£200-300 *CNY*

Two Staffordshire pink lustre jugs, one transfer printed in puce with English country houses in landscapes reserved on the pink lustre ground, enriched with foliage, c1820, 5in (13cm).
£200-250 *CNY*

A rare Leeds silver lustre Robin jug, c1815, 5½in (13.5cm).
£600-700 *SBO*

A set of 4 Staffordshire copper lustre jugs, illustrated with Royal coat of arms and animals, c1840, from 4-7in (10-17.5cm).
£650-700   *DL*

A large copper lustre jug, with coloured print, c1840, 11in (27.5cm).
£450-500   *DL*

A Sunderland pink lustre jug, with a Sailor's Farewell scene with inscription and verse, c1840, 7in (17.5cm).
£200-275   *GCA*

A blue and white pottery transfer jug, c1830, 4½in (11cm).
£35-40   *DEL*

A Swansea pottery jug, with lilac transfer design, with mark, c1835, 5in (12.5cm).
£50-60   *BRE*

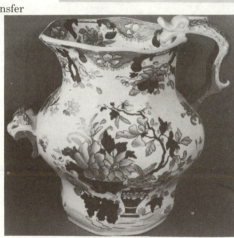

A Mason's Ironstone jug, with dolphin handles, restoration to handle, c1825, 12in (30cm).
£550-650   *SBO*

Two identical transfer printed earthenware jugs, in perfect condition, probably made at Ashby-de-le-Zouche, c1850, 6in (15cm).
Large £40-45, Small £30-38   *DEL*

A Swansea jug, possibly incompletely painted, c1840.
£45-55   *BRE*

A Wedgwood black basalt jug, the body with a band of cherubs watering within borders of engine turned bands and with silver rim, impressed lower case mark, 8in (20cm).
£400-500   *CSK*

A Hanau blue and white pewter mounted enghalskrüg, the strap handle enriched in blue, the hinged pewter cover with ball thumbpiece, hairline crack to handle, c1750, 13in (33cm).
£800-1,200   *CNY*

A Brownfield jug modelled as a goose, the handle modelled as a standing monkey pushing open its beak, with naturalistic polychrome colouring, impressed Brownfield, c1860, 14in (35.5cm).
£300-400   *C*

A Brownfield jug modelled as a cockatoo, with white plumage, yellow crest and naturalistic colouring, impressed Brownfield, small chip to crest, 9½in (24cm).
£400-500   *C*

A Westerwald blue and grey stoneware jug, with contemporary hinged pewter cover and foot rim, moulded with a mask spout and circular flowerheads on a blue ground, hair crack to neck, 17thC, 9in (22.5cm).
£250-350   *CAm*

A dated Rhenish stoneware armorial bartmannkrug, moulded with a bearded mask and 3 oval armorial medallions, each dated 1599, and covered in a mottled brown glaze, crack through base restored, rim chips, 9in (22.5cm).
£250-350   *CAm*

Toby Jugs

A good Ralph Wood Toby Jug, with flaked translucent glaze decoration, 10in (25cm).
£500-700   *LT̂*

An Ewenny pottery jug, inscribed mark, incised Jones Bridgend, c1900, 10in (25cm).
£50-60   *BRE*

'Na werth Nef er benthyg byd' (Don't sell Heaven for things on earth).

A Whieldon Toby Jug, in predominantly brown and green glazes, holding a pear shaped jug, typical of this type of jug, c1770, 9in (22.5cm).
£500-600   *LR*

The shallow base has a 'step' underneath.

A rare Thin Man Toby Jug, possibly made at Leeds, decorated in semi-translucent glazes of green and grey, holding a brown jug, c1765, 9in (22.5cm).
£1,500-2,000   *LR*

A Ralph Wood Toby Jug, c1780, 9½in (23.5cm). **£700-800** *DL*

A Staffordshire Toby Jug of conventional type, in brown hat, green jacket, blue waistcoat and yellow breeches, restoration to hat and jug, c1780, 10in (24.5cm). **£450-550** *C*

A fine Ralph Wood Toby Jug, decorated in typical translucent glazes, 10in (25cm). **£650-750** *LT*

A Whieldon type Toby Jug, known as Admiral Vernon, c1780, 10in (25cm). **£1,300-1,500** *DL*

An early Staffordshire Pratt type Toby Jug, 10in (25cm). **£550-650** *DL*

A Ralph Wood miniature Toby Jug, in mint condition, 6½in (16cm). **£900-1,000** *DL*

A fine Pratt Toby Jug of Whieldon pattern, decorated in underglaze colours, mainly blue and ochre, with brown hat and shoes, c1785, 9in (22.5cm). **£550-600** *LR*

A well decorated Prattware Toby Jug, in blue coat, ochre and brown breeches and stockings, brown hat, with green lined base, c1790, 9½in (23.5cm). **£480-530** *LR*

A Yorkshire Toby Jug, holding jug and glass, in typical Pratt decoration of mainly blue, ochre, brown and black, c1785-90, 8in (20cm). **£400-475** *LR*

A very rare early Staffordshire Toby Jug, c1815, 7in (17.5cm).
£500-600   *DL*

A Prattware Toby Jug, with unusually painted ale jug with flower motif, in ochre coat, brown hat and green breeches, c1790, 9in (22.5cm).
£490-550   *LR*

A Martha Gunn Toby Jug, probably of Portobello manufacture and decorated in raspberry, blue-green and black, heavily and crudely potted, c1830-40, 8in (20cm).
£260-325   *LR*

A Toby Jug marked Walton, c1820, 10½in (26cm).
£500-600   *DL*

A Staffordshire Toby Jug known as The American Sailor, sitting on chest marked 'Dollars', probably by Walton, c1815, 10in (25cm).
£395-495   *LR*

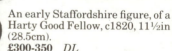

An early Staffordshire figure, of a Harty Good Fellow, c1820, 11½in (28.5cm).
£300-350   *DL*

Locate the source
The source of each illustration in Miller's can be found by checking the code letters below each caption with the list of contributors.

Eight Wilkinson Ltd. First World War Toby Jugs, designed by Sir F Carruthers Gould, brightly coloured caricatures of D Lloyd George, Earl Haig, President Wilson, Marshal Foch, Marshal Joffre, Sir John French, Admiral Beatty and Admiral Jellicoe, 1914-18.
£1,500-2,000   *WIL*

Mugs

A Nottingham stoneware carved mug, the exterior pierced with stylised foliage and flowerheads, the neck with incised concentric lines, with grooved loop handle chips to rims and handle, c1700, 4½in (10.5cm).
£900-1,100   *C*

Cf R G Hughes and Adrian Oswald, 'Nottingham and Derbyshire Stoneware', E.C.C. Transactions, vol 9, pt 2, pl 90a, for a mug dated 1703.

A Staffordshire Toby Jug, with well defined features and partly decorated in underglaze, but coat and hat in brown enamels, c1815, 9in (22.5cm).
£425-485   *LR*

A Staffordshire saltglazed stoneware mug, with applied profile medallion of George II with letters 'GR', scratch blue foliate decorations and banding, hairline crack, c1750, 6in (15cm).
£120-180   *CDC*

A Dutch Delft mug, painted in blue with a stag hunting scene, early 18thC, 3½in (8.5cm).
£600-800   *JHo*

Plaques

A Ralph Wood portrait of The Duke of Cumberland, with yellow edged shirt and green drapery, the border moulded with a band of foliage enriched in green, pierced for hanging, cracked, c1770, 6½in (15.5cm).
£500-600   *C*

A Ralph Wood pearlware plaque, of a Greek philosopher, on a brightly coloured green background, c1780, 12 by 9½in (30 by 23.5cm).
£800-1,200   *JHo*

A Wedgwood & Bentley blue and white portrait medallion of George III, the dipped pale blue ground moulded in white relief, chip to underside, impressed lower case mark, c1775, 2½in (5.5cm).
£200-250   *C*

A Wedgwood & Bentley polished blue jasper oval plaque of Benjamin Franklin, attributed to William Hackwood, impressed Franklin, reverse impressed Wedgwood & Bentley, c1775, 3½in (9.5cm).
£1,600-2,000   *Bon*

A pair of Wedgwood & Bentley black basalt oval portrait plaques of Vespasian and Nero, named 'T. Vespas. Avg' and 'Nero Avg' within self moulded gadrooned and reeded borders, Vespasian with minute rim chip, c1777, 8in (20cm).
£2,000-2,500   *C*

First listed in Wedgwood & Bentley's fourth catalogue in 1777, Class VI, Nos 6 and 10.

A mantel ornament in the form of an architectural clockface plaque by Obadiah Sherratt, base and putto surmount damaged, 2 angels' wings chipped, c1830, 11½in (29.5cm).
£800-1,200   *Bon*

A Spode pottery panel, reverse side impressed with manufacturers mark, indistinctly signed, all mounted in gilt frame, 20 by 13in (50 by 32.5cm).
£450-500   *WIL*

A Wedgwood lilac jasper rectangular plaque, after Flaxman, impressed Wedgwood, 2½ by 7½in (5.5 by 19.5cm).
£180-220 *Bon*

A Castelli plaque, painted in colours in the Grue workshop, minute rim chips, c1720, 10 by 8in (25 by 20cm).
£400-600 *CNY*

A Wedgwood blue and white jasper portrait medallion of William Pitt The Younger, impressed mark, glazed wood frame, c1790, 3½in (9.5cm).
£500-650 *C*

Cf Robin Reilly and George Savage, op. cit., p.276.
This model has been variously attributed to Flaxman, Lochée and Tassie, the original dating to circa 1785, on the evidence of style the Lochée attribution is considered the most likely.

A portrait medallion in blue jasper of Sir Eyre Coote, modelled by Mountstephen from a bust by Nollekeus in 1779, 4 by 3in (10 by 7cm).
£900-1,100 *LT*

See Dictionary of Wedgwood by Reilly and Savage, p 246; also see illustration.

Pots

A Bristol delft blue and white 2-handled posset pot and cover, the handles enriched with blue lines and the spout with whorl pattern, spout, cover and part of rim restored, minor glaze chips, c1730, 9½in (23cm) wide.
£1,400-1,600 *C*

Provenance: S M Taylor.

A Bristol delftware polychrome posset pot, restored, c1730.
£400-600 *JHo*

A yellow lustre chamber pot, made by Deptford or Balls Bros., c1860, 8½in (21cm) diam.
£150-200 *DL*

A rare Wedgwood moonlight lustre pot pourri vase and cover, pierced lid missing, c1815, 12in (30cm).
£400-500 *SBO*

A pearlware bough pot and pierced cover.
£500-800 *Bon*

A Dutch Delft polychrome shaped oval plaque, painted with Chinese figures standing on a terrace before a fence and a screen, restoration to finial and base, early 18thC, 9½in (23.5cm) wide.
£1,500-2,000 *CAm*

Sauceboats

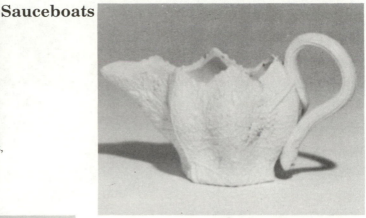

A Staffordshire saltglaze sauceboat, enriched in blue, with 2 snails and winged cherubs' heads beneath the spout, on 3 mask and paw feet, c1750, 8in (20cm) wide.
£1,000-1,300   C

A Staffordshire white saltglaze sauceboat, some restoration, chip to terminal of handle, c1750, 6½in (16cm).
£450-550   C

A Walker pearlware dolphin sauceboat, impressed Walker, late 18thC, 4in (10cm).
£275-325   GCA

A Prattware fox head and swan handle sauceboat, naturalistically modelled as a fox head, enriched in ochre, the handle formed as a swan with incised feather markings, the base enriched in green, minor chips to ears, c1770, 6½in (16cm) long.
£300-400   CNY

Services

A Staffordshire dinner service, decorated in red, blue and yellow comprising: soup tureen, cover and stand, 4 vegetable dishes and covers, salad bowl, 2 sauce tureens, covers and stands, 8 meat dishes in sizes, mazareen, sauceboat, 2 dishes, 16 soup plates, 31 meat plates and 15 pudding plates, printed scroll mark.
£1,800-2,000   L

A Mason's patent ironstone china dessert service, with rich blue glaze and gilt, comprising: comport on foot, 2 shell shape dishes, an oval dish, a rectangular dish and 12 plates, the plates impressed Mason's Patent Ironstone China in one line, c1820.
£180-250   L

See Godden's Mason's China and the Ironstone Wares, *plate 183, for dessert dishes from a similar service.*

A Staffordshire pottery child's tea service, comprising 6 cups and saucers, 1 sugar bowl and 2 plates.
£150-200 *SBO*

An Ashworth's ironstone part dessert service, with dark green ground, comprising: 5 comports and 2 plates, impressed and transfer marks to base, one comport damaged.
£220-280 *WIL*

A Victorian ironstone dinner service decorated in Imari style, comprising: 4 tureens and covers, 1 stand, 8 meat plates/stands, low comport, 12 soup plates, 12 dinner plates, some chips and cracks. Impressed marks BB new stone and pattern No. 6028 in red.
£600-800 *Nes*

A Doulton Lambeth faience coffee service, comprising: coffee pot and cover, sugar bowl and cover and a milk jug, printed Doulton and P.O.D.R. mark for 29th May, 1879, painted 'HH' and 'WJ' monograms, 10½in (26cm) coffee pot.
£250-300 *L*

A black basalt part tea service, comprising: a teapot and cover, spout with minute chips, a milk jug and cover, minute chip to spout, a sugar bowl and cover and a slop basin, c1800.
£250-350 *C*

A Victorian ironstone china part dinner service decorated in iron red, blue, green and gilt, comprising: 12 dinner plates, 12 side plates, 6 soup plates, 3 graduated meat dishes and a similar vegetable tureen and cover.
£800-1,200 *Nes*

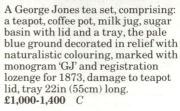

A miniature Wedgwood blue and white printed Willow Pattern dinner service, comprising: 6 dinner and 6 soup plates, tureens and covers, 2 serving plates and a sauceboat and stand, impressed mark, one cover finial damaged, second quarter 19thC.
£220-280   *TW*

A Staffordshire part dinner service printed and painted with iron red foliage on a blue cell pattern ground, comprising: 4 meat dishes, a square shaped bowl, a sauce tureen, 10 soup plates, 15 dinner plates and 11 dessert plates.
£1,000-1,500   *CSK*

A George Jones tea set, comprising: a teapot, coffee pot, milk jug, sugar basin with lid and a tray, the pale blue ground decorated in relief with naturalistic colouring, marked with monogram 'GJ' and registration lozenge for 1873, damage to teapot lid, tray 22in (55cm) long.
£1,000-1,400   *C*

WEDGWOOD BLUE PRINTED POTTERY

★ rapid growth in production by other factories commenced c1780
★ at first Wedgwood bought in printed wares from other factories, e.g. Minton
★ Wedgwood first produced blue and white printed pottery in 1805
★ first pattern was Blue Bamboo
★ series of floral patterns introduced from 1805-11
★ from 1811-21 Chinese landscapes produced
★ products given impressed marks, normally Wedgwood plus numbers, letters or symbols

At present there is a strong market for extensive and reasonably complete services if they are early and decorative. The illustrated service was estimated at only £100-200 but due to fierce competition in the saleroom fetched £2,300.

Tankards

A German faience blue and white tankard, with contemporary hinged pewter cover and foot rim, probably Bayreuth, glaze chips and repair, mid-18thC, 6½in (18.5cm).
£180-250   *C*

A South German small cylindrical tankard, with contemporary hinged pewter cover with ball thumb piece and with pewter foot rim, painted in blue and manganese, hair cracks, minor glaze chips, first half of the 18thC, 6½in (16cm).
£600-700   *C*

A German polychrome faience tankard, the white glazed body decorated with simple green swags, orange and brown lines, pewter mounts and domed cover with knop finial, the cover inscribed 'M.D.4' and with a small medallion, 18thC, 9in (22.5cm).
£200-300   *BD*

A Hannoversch-Münden faience tankard, with contemporary hinged pewter cover with ball thumb piece, the tankard inscribed 'Es liebe mein Mädchen', hair crack, minor rim chips, mid-18thC, 8½in (21.5cm).
£250-350   *C*

A German polychrome faience cylindrical tankard, the white glazed body painted with a man smoking a pipe in a garden with flowering plants, pewter mounts and domed cover with acorn finial, inscribed on lid 'M.G.L.1770', marked on base VX, cover slightly faulty, 18thC, 9½in (23cm).
£600-800   *BD*

Tea Caddies

A Staffordshire square saltglaze tea caddy, minor repair to rim of neck, c1755, 6in (16cm).
£500-700 *CNY*

A Pratt tea caddy, decorated with Macaroni figures, late 18thC, 6in (15cm).
£375-425 *GCA*

Good to find one with its original top.

A Whieldon pottery tea caddy in green and brown glazes, 18thC, 5in (12.5cm).
£435-495 *GCA*

A rare dated and inscribed blue and white Leeds creamware tea caddy and cover, one side inscribed 'Ann Colridge', the reverse with the date '1797', cover and one of the cherub busts to the corners with repair, dated 1797, 6in (16cm).
£800-1,200 *CNY*

A Dutch Delft blue and white tea caddy, minor chips, blue MS marks on base for perhaps Joris Mes, pewter cover, c1680, 7½in (18cm).
£800-1,200 *CAm*

A Leeds creamware square tea canister, the corners enriched in blue with flower sprays, one side inscribed 'Elizh, Hal(istay)', small chip, dated 1798(?), 7½in (19cm).
£500-800 *CNY*

Tea and Coffee Pots

An Astbury redwear coffee pot and domed cover, minute chip to spout, c1750, 9½in (24cm).
£300-400 *CNY*

A saltglaze coloured teapot, c1755, 5in (12.5cm).
£700-775 *DL*

An Astbury armorial cream jug and cover, the rich brown body applied with the Royal coat of arms in white relief, the cover with 3 crowns, cover restored, c1750, 5½in (13cm).
£700-800 *C*

A Whieldon teapot, c1775, 5in (12.5cm).
£550-650 *DL*

An early Staffordshire saltglaze teapot, with bird decoration, c1755, 4in (10cm).
£700-750 *DL*

A Leeds creamware teapot and cover, enriched in blue, green and yellow, the scroll spout moulded with formal foliage, minor chip repair to rim of cover, and tip of spout, c1770, 8in (20cm).
£400-600 CNY

Probably decorated at the Rhodes Enamelling Studio.

A Whieldon type tortoiseshell glazed miniature teapot and cover, splashed in manganese, green and grey blue, minor chip to tip of spout, c1760, 5½in (14cm) wide.
£500-700 CNY

A Whieldon type tortoiseshell glazed teapot and cover, covered in a brown and greyish blue tortoiseshell glaze, minute chip to interior of rim, c1760, 7in (18cm) wide.
£1,200-1,800 CNY

A Whieldon type teapot, shaped like a cauliflower, c1760.
£350-450 JUD

A Whieldon type tortoiseshell glazed teapot and a cover, small chip to tip of spout, finial repaired, c1755, 7in (17cm) wide.
£500-700 CNY

A Rothwell Yorkshire creamware teapot, decorated with mottled translucent glazes, c1700, 6in (15cm).
£400-600 JHo

A Staffordshire yellow ground ▷ teapot and cover, transfer printed in black, c1810, 8in (20cm) wide.
£200-300 CNY

An early Wood creamware teapot, c1800, 6in (15cm).
£425-475 GCA

A Leeds creamware teapot, c1800, 5½in (13.5cm).
£400-475 DL

A Leeds creamware teapot and cover, painted in colours and gilt with Aurora and her chariot, enriched in iron red, puce, green and yellow with flowering foliage in landscape vignettes, minor repair to tip of spout, c1780, 8in (21cm) wide.
£500-800 CNY

A miniature pearlware teapot, c1800, 4½in (11cm).
£140-170 SBO

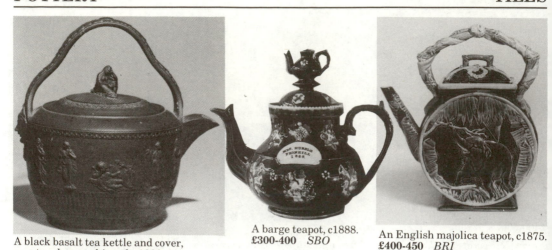

A black basalt tea kettle and cover, spout and cover chipped, c1800, 10in (25cm).
£350-400 *C*

A barge teapot, c1888.
£300-400 *SBO*

An English majolica teapot, c1875.
£400-450 *BRI*

Tiles

Four medieval lead glazed floor tiles, 13th/14thC, 4½in (11cm).
£250-350 *JHo*

A pair of Bristol delft blue and white stove tiles, painted in blue with a statesman in Roman dress, some repairs, c1700, 10in (25cm).
£800-1,200 *CNY*

Possibly intended as candle niches.

A Bristol delft tile, painted in blue, mid-18thC, 5in (12.5cm).
£25-30 *JHo*

A Liverpool delftware tile, 'pencilled' and painted in manganese and purple, c1765, 5½in (13.5cm).
£120-140 *JHo*

Polychrome, chinoiserie and animal subjects are scarce and consequently of greater value than more common biblical or pastoral tiles.

A Bristol delft tile, painted by John Bowen, c1750.
£40-50 *VEN*

A Liverpool delft tile, painted in black by Sadler, c1760, 5in (12.5cm).
£50-70 *JHo*

A Liverpool delft tile, painted in a 'Fazackerley' polychrome palette, c1765, 5in (12.5cm).
£100-120 *JHo*

A Liverpool delftware polychrome tile, c1765, 5in (12.5cm).
£140-160 *JHo*

A Liverpool delftware tile, painted in blue, mid-18thC, 5in (12.5cm).
£15-18 *JHo*

A set of 25 English tinglaze tiles, decorated urns on pedestal feet joined by husk swags, late 18thC.
£350-450 *WW*

A European brown glazed stove tile, covered in a honey brown glaze, chips to rim and glaze, 16th/17thC, 9in (22.5cm).
£300-500 *CNY*

A pair of Rotterdam manganese tile pictures, painted with Abraham dismissing Hagar and Jephta's Return, Aelmis workshop in De Bloempot, damages, c1770, 31 by 26in (78 by 65cm).
£1,200-1,800 *CAm*

Tureens

A tureen with ladle, bat printed in black with rural scenes, factory unknown, early 19thC, 6in (15cm).
£150-200 *BRE*

A pair of Staffordshire bird tureens, naturalistically modelled with incised feather markings enriched in yellow, turquoise, iron red, brown and blue tones, one cover repaired, c1800, 7in (17.5cm) long.
£1,200-1,800 *CNY*

A Rogers pottery tureen and dish, with Zebra pattern, c1820.
£90-100 *DEL*

A Staffordshire dove tureen, the bird with raspberry pink plumage, early 19thC, 4in (10cm).
£350-450 *JHo*

A Staffordshire pigeon tureen, c1840, 6in (15cm).
£280-340 *DL*

A creamware soup tureen, c1780.
£450-550 *JUD*

A John Meir & Son soup tureen and stand, the Italian scenery pale blue with floral borders, mid-19thC, 23in (57.5cm) diam.
£40-60   CDC

With lid £80-120.

A Spode ironstone soup tureen and cover with acorn finial, printed and painted with coloured flower sprays, 13in (32.5cm) wide.
£200-250   CSK

An unusual Staffordshire elephant tureen and cover, with restored base, c1860, 8½in (21cm).
£500-600   SBO

An English Brownfield pottery butter tub, 1868, 4½in (11cm).
£245-275   GCA

A George Jones majolica game dish and cover, the brown ground moulded with dead birds and trophies, the cover with a fox crouching before a swan on bracken, raised cartouche mark, 11½in (27.5cm) wide.
£700-800   C

There has been a great increase in interest in 19thC majolica over the last year.

An Ewenny pottery casserole pot and cover, in brown with cream slipware decoration, some damage, inscribed, dated 1910, 9½in (23.5cm).
£50-60   BRE

A French faience cauliflower tureen, cover and stand, enriched in tones of green, blue and pale yellow, some repairs, firing crack, c1770, the stand 12in (30cm) wide.
£2000-3,000   CNY

Cf Hans Haug, Les Faiences et Porcelaines de Strasburg, Strasburg 1922, pl xxib.

A German faience asparagus tureen and cover, naturally modelled and coloured and tied with a manganese string, minor chips, mid-18thC, 7in (17cm) long.
£1,200-1,500   C

An Erfurt faience cow tureen and cover, naturally modelled as a recumbent cow, with blue markings, blue 3 mark to each piece, repairs to horns and ears, minor chips, mid-18thC, 8in (20.5cm) long.
£800-1,000   C

Vases

A Dutch Delft polychrome butter tub and cover, with bud finial painted with fruit and flowers in panels and garlands within black and yellow lined borders, cover and handles repaired, 18thC, 5in (12.5cm) long.
£80-120   CAm

A Ralph Wood dolphin flower-holder, decorated in translucent glazes, c1770, 7½in (18.5cm).
£500-600   JHo

A pair of sponge-ware vases in blue and ochre, early 19thC, 5in (12.5cm).
£250-350   JHo

A Dublin delft blue and white baluster vase, delicately painted with a fountain in a continuous rocky river landscape with trees and trailing shrubs, beneath 2 swags of flowers and foliage suspended from the rim, c1750, 13in (32cm).
£1,000-1,500 *C*

Cf Castletown Exhibition Catalogue (1971), pl 11 for a wall-cistern with a similar style of painting.

A purple lustre spill vase, impressed mark Sewell & Co, c1815, 8in (20cm).
£280-320 *DL*

A Wedgwood dark blue jasper vase, with pierced domed cover, the side with a band of white reliefs of allegorical figure and shrubs, the everted rim and socle base edged with bands of acanthus leaves, impressed Wedgwood, 13½in (33.5cm).
£450-550 *Bon*

A pair of Wedgwood 3-colour jasper vases and covers, the dipped sage green grounds moulded in white relief, the bodies with dice pattern with yellow flowerheads divided by bands of berried foliage, impressed marks, one rim repaired, one cover cracked, the other with finial restuck, c1860, 13in (33cm).
£1,800-2,200 *C*

A Wedgwood pot pourri vase and cover, the black jasper-dip sides sprigged with a procession of 8 classical dancing women, impressed mark, late 18thC, 10in (25cm).
£200-300 *TEN*

A pair of Wedgwood creamware baluster vases painted by Emile Lessore, the necks, rims and bases with ochre and iron red bands, signed, impressed marks, one with rim chip restored, indistinct date code probably for 1865, 5in (15cm).
£700-800 *C*

A pair of Wedgwood Fairyland Lustre-type vases, painted with river landscapes and trees, printed marks, Z5464, 9in (22.5cm).
£800-900 *CSK*

A Wedgwood & Bentley black basaltes vase, the body moulded in relief with Venus in her Car drawn by mythical birds through clouds, impressed Wedgwood & Bentley, slight damage to left handle, 17in (42cm).
£2,300-2,600 *Bon*

Make the most of Miller's

Unless otherwise stated, any description which refers to 'a set' or 'a pair' includes a valuation for the entire set or the pair, even though the illustration may show only a single item.

A pair of Hicks and Meigh ironstone vases, transfer printed in underglaze brown with a continuous Japonaiserie water garden scene, all painted in underglaze blue, iron red, gilt, green and brown, transfer mark in underglaze brown, Real Stone China, a ribbon below a crown, 20in (50cm).
£2,200-2,400 *HSS*

A pair of large English pottery vases and domed covers, painted on each side with a rustic landscape incorporating buildings and figures within a scroll-moulded panel, upon an overall deep cobalt ground heightened with elaborate gilt scroll, and feathered leaf motifs, 35in (88cm).
£1,500-1,800 *Bon*

These vases appear to be of previously unrecorded form.

A Plichta middle sized pig, painted with roses by Joseph Nekola, 20thC, 8in (20cm).
£150-350 *RdeR*

A Wemyss mug, painted with sweet peas, impressed Thomas Goode, 19thC, 5½in (13.5cm).
£150-250 *RdeR*

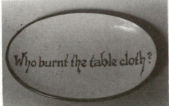

A Wemyss impressed pin tray, c1920, 5in (13cm) long.
£30-50 *RdeR*

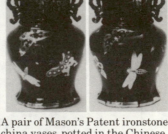

A pair of Mason's Patent ironstone china vases, potted in the Chinese style and decorated in gold with insects on a deep blue ground, 14½in (36.5cm).
£500-600 *Bea*

Wemyss

A large white Scottish Wemyss ware pig, 19thC, 11in (27.5cm).
£300-500 *RdeR*

A Wemyss ware small black and white pig, impressed 'Wemyss' and printed mark of 'T. Goode & Co.', 7in (17.5cm).
£200-300 *WW*

A small plaque, painted with thistles, 20thC, 7 by 4in (17 by 10cm).
£50-75 *RdeR*

A Wemyss heart-shaped tray, impressed, c1930, 12in (30cm).
£75-100 *RdeR*

WEMYSS WARE
c1883-1930

★ Robert Methven Heron introduced a group of continental artists into his Fife pottery in the 1880's. The very characteristic nature of Wemyss derives from their influence although roses, apples and cherries had been stiffly painted before

★ most of the artists returned home but Karel Nekola remained. Wemyss was always wanted by the rich and the ware was well supported by Scottish Lairds

★ Wemyss was fired at low temperatures to produce a biscuit body which would absorb the delicate brush strokes. Then it was dipped in a soft lead glaze and fired again at a low temperature. This accounts for the fragility of Wemyss and the relative rarity of exceptional quality pieces

★ Nekola trained James Sharp, David Grinton, John Brown, Hugh and Christina McKinnon and they were later joined by Nekola's sons Carl and Joseph

★ Karel Nekola tended to paint the large important pieces and also the commemorative pieces from Queen Victoria's Jubilee in 1897 until the Coronation of George V in 1911. He died in 1915

★ Edwin Sandiland became chief decorator in 1916. The change in public taste after the First World War, with the introduction of the Art Deco movement, saw a move away from the traditional Wemyss designs. Various new designs were tried but by the time Edwin Sandiland died in 1928, the end was in sight. The Fife Pottery closed in 1930

★ the Bovey Tracy pottery in Devon bought the rights and moulds of the Fife pottery and gave employment to Joseph Nekola, who continued the familiar decorations to a high standard until his death in 1952. Royal Doulton subsequently acquired the rights

A large 3-handled loving cup, painted with mallard duck, Scottish, impressed Wemyss, c1890, 9½in (23.5cm).
£400-600   *RdeR*

The fluctuation in price and valuation is due to the quality of the painting and the age of the piece.

The early Scottish pieces command a higher price than those made in England.

An unusual Wemyss transfer printed mug, 19thC, 4in (10cm).
£30-50   *RdeR*

A Wemyss cylindrical loving cup, painted pink cabbage roses and leaves with green scalloped borders, impressed mark, 9in (22.5cm).
£350-450   *AG*

A Wemyss Gordon plate, painted with blackberries, 19thC, 8in (20cm) diam.
£100-150   *RdeR*

A Wemyss Gordon plate, painted with roses, 19thC, 8in (20cm) diam.
£100-150   *RdeR*

A Wemyss Gordon plate, painted with irises, 19thC, 8in (20cm) diam.
£200-250   *RdeR*

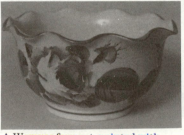

A Wemyss fern pot, painted with roses, 19thC, 5½in (13.5cm) diam.
£40-75   *RdeR*

A Wemyss Gordon plate, painted with a beehive and bees, 19thC, 8in (20cm) diam.
£100-200   *RdeR*

A pair of Wemyss Grosvenor vases, painted with roses, impressed, 19thC, 8in (20cm).
£75-100   *RdeR*

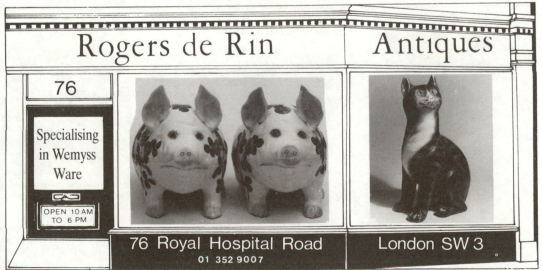
115

A Wemyss bucket with lid, from a washstand set, painted with roses, impressed, 19thC, 11in (27.5cm).
£200-250 *RdeR*

A Scottish Wemyss basket, painted with cherries, 19thC, 12½in (31cm) long.
£250-350 *RdeR*

A large Wemyss bulb bowl, painted with sweet peas, 19thC, 14in (35cm) diam.
£300-500 *RdeR*

A Wemyss matchbox holder, painted with roses, impressed, 19thC, 3in (8cm) long.
◁ **£75-150** *RdeR*

A pair of Wemyss brush vases, painted with roses, impressed, 19thC, 6in (15cm).
£100-200 *RdeR*

A Wemyss preserve pot, painted with strawberries, impressed, 19thC, 6½in (16cm).
£75-100 *RdeR*

A large Wemyss brush vase, ▷ painted with thistles, impressed, 19thC, 11½in (28.5cm).
£200-300 *RdeR*

A small Wemyss brush vase, painted with a pastoral scene with a cow, 19thC, 4in (10cm).
£75-100 *RdeR*

A Wemyss hat pin holder, painted with carnations, 19thC, 6in (15cm).
£75-100 *RdeR*

Carnation paintings are rare.

A Wemyss skep (beehive), painted with bees, Scottish, 19thC, 7½in (18.5cm).
£250-500 *RdeR*

Miscellaneous

A Liverpool delft blue and white cornucopia wall pocket, lightly moulded with a bird on a flowering branch, c1760, 8in (20cm).
£400-500 *CSK*

A Bristol delft bulb pot, with chinoiserie scenes, 5in (12.5cm) square.
£500-700 *JHo*

A Staffordshire pearlware box and cover, modelled as a dog wearing a yellow collar inscribed 'Venture', the cushion lustred in pink with green, yellow and iron red band, the screw cover with the initials 'ET' in black, minor chips, c1815, 2in (5cm).
£1,200-1,400 *C*

Cf W D John and Warren Baker, Old English Lustre Pottery, pl 34B.

A Bristol delft flower brick, with blue chinoiserie scenes, c1760, 3in (7.5cm).
£250-300   *JHo*

A Staffordshire yellow ground oval tobacco box, cover and inner lid, moulded with the Kill and applied with fox head handles, the inner cover with recumbent lamb finial, impressed 2, repair to both finials, chip to foot rim, c1800, 4in (11cm) wide.
£600-800   *CNY*

A rare Bristol delft blue and white brick of unusually small size with ogee feet, c1730, 5in (12.5cm) wide.
£450-550   *VEN*

A Staffordshire cradle, 3½in (8.5cm) wide.
£100-150   *SBO*

A Yorkshire clock group as a money box, on oval grass mound base enriched in ochre, manganese and blue, repair to figure of girl, c1800, 8½in (22cm).
£800-1,200   *CNY*

A Pratt grandfather clock, late 18thC, 6in (15cm).
£475-525   *GCA*

An unusual pearlware bough pot and pierced cover, in the form of a mausoleum, the body painted in pink lustre with three landscape views, cover cracked, early 19thC, 10in (25cm).
£600-800   *Bon*

A Rockingham or Brameld group of bird whistles, c1835, 9in (22.5cm).
£600-700   *DL*

A purple lustre watch holder, with lion at the top, c1815, 8in (20cm).
£650-700   *DL*

An Ewenny money box, with sgrafitto decoration, with cockerel and other birds applied to body, no mark, some damage, c1830, 8in (20cm).
£150-200   *BRE*

An unusual English pottery item, part of a supper set, with high glaze blue and white chrysanthemum transfer, 4in (10cm) wide.
£35-40 DEL

This could be Swansea.

An early Staffordshire Prattware watch holder, c1790, 9½in (23.5cm).
£700-800 DL

A Staffordshire watch holder box, with slip mouldings, 9½in (23.5cm).
£250-300 SBO

A Walton castle spill, depicting bridge and river below, in coloured enamels, Walton mark on back, c1820, 6in (15cm).
£300-350 LR

A rare money box, modelled as a chapel with blue roof and 2 chimneys above 6 windows and 2 doorways outlined in yellow, the rectangular base supported on 4 ball feet, 7in (17.5cm).
£450-550 CSK

Cf Anthony Oliver, The Tribal Art of England, pl 183.

A number of modern fakes have appeared on the market in recent years.

A Staffordshire model of a coiled snake, with a brown and yellow splash glaze covering the green scales, c1800, 2in (5cm) wide.
£160-200 CSK

A Staffordshire puce-printed money box.
£300-400 Bon

An English pottery pocket flask, with classical scenes, 18thC, 6in (15cm).
£335-395 GCA

A Staffordshire blue and white pottery dog's dish, in the Florentine pattern, 19thC, 10in (25cm).
£200-250 McC

A Wedgwood comport, in browns, yellows and greens, impressed Wedgwood and date code for 1884, damage to spout of one dolphin, 17in (42.5cm).
£800-1,000 C

An unusual pottery spirit flask, decorated in dark red, blue and green, with transfers of Dr Franklin on either side, possibly of North-country origin, c1840, 8in (20cm).
£200-250 LR

A Wedgwood & Bentley white stoneware pestle and mortar, impressed lower case marks, minute chip to rim, c1780, the pestle 5½in (14.5cm) long, the mortar 3½in (9cm) wide.
£700-800 C

A Wedgwood black basalt Egyptian inkstand, the exterior moulded with wings and scale pattern, impressed mark, c1810, 12in (30cm) wide.
£2,500-3,000 *C*

A Victorian cheese dish and cover, naturistically modelled and coloured in the form of a straw bee skep, on square rustic pattern stand, unmarked except for Patent Registration Mark, stand chipped on one corner, 13in (32.5cm).
£600-700 *BD*

A pair of Wedgwood majolica wall brackets, modelled as putti supporting drapes on turquoise grounds, 10½in (26cm).
£500-600 *CSK*

MINTON MAJOLICA

★ Joseph-Léon-François Arnoux appointed art director of Minton c1848
★ before 1850 Arnoux introduced a ware imitating 16thC Italian maiolica
★ opaque white glaze over pottery body as surface for polychrome painting in opaque colours
★ in 1851 Mintons displayed wine coolers, flower pots and stands 'coloured in the majolica style'
★ transparent coloured glazes of green, yellow, brown and blue often used over patterns moulded in low relief. These are in imitation of wares produced by Bernard Palissy in the mid-16thC but are sometimes mis-named majolica
★ rival firms copied majolica wares but Minton examples usually bear the name Minton impressed
★ game dishes especially popular with collectors
★ other collectable factories include Wedgwood and George Jones

---

A black Jasperware half stilton dish and cover, second quarter 19thC, 10½in (26.5cm).
£120-180 *TKN*

A George Jones jardinière, cobalt blue with turquoise interior and naturalistic colouring, impressed G. Jones within crescent shape, hair line crack, 13½in (33cm) high.
£600-800 *C*

A George Jones sardine dish and cover, with moulded decoration of a sardine on each side, seaweed and coral reef on the corners, impressed monogram GJ and registration lozenge for 1862, 4½in (10.5cm).
£500-700 *C*

A George Jones ashtray, modelled as a finch on bulrushes, the green ground with naturalistic polychrome colouring, impressed GJ and with registration mark for 1871, beak restored, 7in (17.5cm) long.
£250-300 *C*

A Clews pottery bed pan, transfer-printed in blue with Fonthill Abbey, Wiltshire, impressed Clews, printed title mark, 16in (40cm) long.
£180-220 *Bon*

A Minton pottery salmon dish, with majolica type glaze, the handle in the form of a lemon, coloured predominantly in pale green with salmon coloured highlights, impressed Mintons and numerals, c1860s, 23in (56.5cm) wide.
£900-1,200 *Bon*

A Minton butterdish and stand, in green, brown, blue and white. Dish and stand with impressed marks Minton 485 and date ciphers for '1867', 7½in (18.5cm).
£3,000-4,000 *C*

A Minton majolica game dish and cover, of tapering oval form, the sides brown glazed and moulded to simulate basket weave, interlaced with green oak leaves, the interior turquoise glazed, impressed Minton, date code for '1867', 12½in (32cm).
£500-700 *Bon*

A majolica jardinière in Mintons style, with rams head and cupid mounts on oval base, date code for June 1856 (?), 36in (90cm).
£1,400-1,600 *GSP*

A Mintons jardinière, with moulded relief decoration of stylised flower heads on a turquoise ground surrounding 4 cream panels painted with multi coloured flowers, transfer and impressed factory marks to base, late 19thC, 15in (37.5cm) diam.
£220-250 *WIL*

A large Minton jardinière in the oriental style, with stylised owl masks, pale blue with dark blue bands, yellow and mottled brown, pink interior, impressed Minton 1620 and date code for 1872, 20½in (51cm).
£600-800 *C*

A Minton jardinière on 6 lion feet, with pale blue body, maroon rim, pink interior, and naturalistic colouring, impressed Minton 1023 and date code for '1865', some restoration, 18in (45cm).
£1,000-1,200 *C*

Cf Victoria Cecil, Minton Majolica, 1982, No. 118, illustrated.

A Minton footed jardinière, cobalt blue and naturalistic colouring, pale blue interior, impressed Minton 1429 and with date code for 1884, 14½in (36cm).
£1,800-2,200 *C*

A Minton jardinière, the handles modelled as intertwined snakes, pale blue with pink, yellow, green and white, the snakes naturalistically coloured, impressed Minton 532 and date code for 1876, 18in (45cm) diam.
£1,500-1,800 *C*

Cf Victoria Cecil, Minton Majolica, 1982, No. 50.

A large Minton jardinière, modelled as a giant pale blue nautilus shell with pink interior, the base aubergine with 2 colours of green, impressed Minton 437 and date code for 1867, 18½in (46cm).
£1,000-1,200 *C*

Cf Victoria Cecil, Minton Majolica, 1982, No. 101, illustrated.

A Minton jardinière and underdish, cobalt blue with polychrome naturalistic colouring and pink interior, impressed Minton 1685 and date code for 1874, 16½in (41cm) diam.
£700-800   *C*

A Minton jardinière and underdish, in pink with pale blue interior and yellow rim, the bulrushes naturalistically coloured, square underdish en suite, impressed Minton 1096 and date code for 1865, 9½in (23cm).
£750-850   *C*

A Minton pedestal, with 6 vertical panels and pierced Chinese style decoration, polychrome colouring on a pale blue ground, impressed Minton 451 and date code for 1865, 32½in (80.5cm).
£600-800   *C*

◁ A pair of Minton pedestals, decorated in relief with ribboned swags festooned with fruit and flowers on the upper half and a bank of acanthus leaves below, naturalistic polychrome colouring on a pale blue ground, impressed Minton 891 and with date code for 1872, 37½in (93.5cm).
£2,500-3,000   *C*

▷ A Minton pedestal in the Japanese manner, with pierced decoration of flowers, fish, fans, and tied scrolls, green, mustard colour, pink and white on a cobalt blue ground, impressed Mintons 2081 and with date cipher for 1883, 29½in (74cm).
£1,500-1,800   *C*

A Minton jardinière, with oak and acorn border under the rim, pink with turquoise interior and naturalistic colouring, impressed Minton and with date code for 1867, 11in (27cm).
£800-900   *C*

A Minton majolica stand, painted in bright enamel colours on a dark blue ground between narrow bands of leaves, the top with matching decoration, impressed marks with the date code for 1867, slight damage, 19in (47cm).
£800-1,000   *Bea*

A Minton majolica jardinière upon stand, in green and white, with red, blue and white background, stamped Minton A1007, 19thC, 32 by 43in (80 by 107.5cm).
£2,500-3,000   *B*

A Minton Secessionist majolica stick stand (Robert Pugh), c1902, 16in (40cm).
£120-150   *SBO*

A Minton Secessionist majolica jardinière, c1902-14, 10½in (26cm).
£200-250   *SBO*

A pair of Minton majolica tazzas modelled and painted with flowerheads on yellow, brown and blue grounds, impressed marks, date cipher c1867, 11in (27.5cm).
£1,300-1,700   *CSK*

A Minton bowl, in naturalistic polychrome colours, impressed Minton 874 and with date code for 1863, 13in (32.5cm) diam.
£2,000-2,500 *C*

A pair of Minton full figure Toby Jugs, in naturalistic polychrome colouring, on circular mottled green and brown bases, impressed Minton 1104 and 1140 and with date stamps for 1867, restored, 10½in (28cm) and 11in (28.5cm).
£750-850 *C*

A Minton honeycomb dish, modelled as a beehive with bees crawling on it, naturalistic polychrome colouring, impressed Minton 1499 and date code for 1877, 7½in (18cm).
£2,000-2,500 *C*

Cf Victoria Cecil, Minton Majolica, *1982, No. 119, pattern illustrated.*

A pair of Minton majolica oyster dishes, modelled with turquoise coloured shells, impressed mark, 10in (25cm) diam.
£120-150 *CSK*

A Minton majolica oval dish and cover, the cover modelled as a crab between seaweed, the dish painted with alternating panels of blue and brown, 15½in (38cm).
£2,000-2,500 *CSK*

A miniature Minton majolica amphora, impressed marks, with date code for 1859, 7in (17cm).
£400-500 *Bea*

A Minton majolica ewer, with mask head handle, modelled with drinking figures in white relief on a blue and brown ground, impressed mark date cipher 1874, 14in (35cm).
£650-700 *CSK*

A Minton wall plate, the central boss decorated in relief with a rose and mistletoe, the border with holly leaves separated by 4 panels with cherubs engaged in Christmas pursuits, in naturalistic polychrome colouring, impressed Minton date code for 1859, 16in (40cm) diam.
£1,100-1,300 *C*

A Minton figure of Vintager with Basket in each Hand, base mottled green and brown, the figure with naturalistic polychrome colouring, impressed 'Minton'.
£700-900 *C*

Cf Victoria Cecil, Minton Majolica, *1982, No. 139, illustrated.*

A Minton vase, modelled as a bamboo trunk with leafy bamboo shoots climbing up it, in yellow, green and brown, impressed Minton 1692 and date code for 1873, chip to base and minor glaze chips, 8in (19.5cm).
£1,800-2,200 *C*

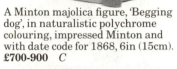

A pair of Minton figures of 'Boy and Girl Resting on Basket', in naturalistic polychrome colouring, each figure impressed Minton the boy with date code for 1865 the girl for 1867, 10in (25cm).
£600-800 *C*

Cf Victoria Cecil, Minton Majolica, *1982, Nos. 23 and 24, illustrated.*

A Minton teapot, the body modelled as a gourd, the cover surmounted by mushrooms forming the finial, pale green body with naturalistic polychrome colouring, impressed Minton 1710 and date code for 1861, 7in (17cm).
£2,000-2,500 *C*

A Minton majolica figure, 'Begging dog', in naturalistic polychrome colouring, impressed Minton and with date code for 1868, 6in (15cm).
£700-900 *C*

Cf Victoria Cecil, Minton Majolica, *1982, No. 55, illustrated.*

A Minton Christmas Jug, the handle modelled as entwined holly branches, blue with green and yellow rim, pink interior and naturalistic polychrome colouring, impressed Minton 580, c1870, 9in (22.5cm).
£800-1,000 *C*

Cf Victoria Cecil, Minton Majolica, *1982, No. 32, illustrated.*

A Minton majolica jug with silver rim, impressed marks, mid-19thC, 9½in (24.5cm).
£400-500 *Bea*

A Minton figural group, 'Lamp Stand', the urn decorated with a band of scrollwork and key pattern border, cobalt blue urn with pale blue interior, mottled green and brown base and naturalistic polychrome colouring, impressed Minton 1517 and with date code for 1881, 14½in (35.5cm).
£1,800-2,200 *C*

Cf Victoria Cecil, Minton Majolica, *1982, No. 67, illustrated.*

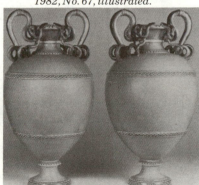

A Minton figural group, modelled as 2 long haired mermaids supporting a large shell, naturalistic polychrome colouring, impressed Minton 1182 and date code for 1868, 17in (43cm) long.
£800-1,000 *C*

Cf Victoria Cecil, Minton Majolica, *1982, No. 69, illustrated.*

A Minton majolica vase, modelled as a trunk of a tree, and with a bird, insects and oak leaves, impressed mark, 7in (17.5cm).
£600-700 *CSK*

A large Minton vase on stand, the turquoise vase with ochre pink interior, blue-black stand, impressed Minton and date code for 1866, 36½in (91cm).
£1,200-1,500 *C*

A pair of large Minton vases, the pale blue body with blue and white ornament, yellow bands and brown snakes, painted marks and indecipherable impressed marks, some restoration, c1870, 25in (62cm).
£4,000-5,000 *C*

Cf Victoria Cecil, Minton Majolica, *1982, No. 139, illustrated.*

ENGLISH PORCELAIN

The demand for early blue and white wares, early figures and rare shapes has, if anything, increased.

Occasionally some freak prices have occurred, notably the £6,000 plus paid at auction for a small and admittedly rare Bow blue and white vase valued by the auctioneers at less than one tenth of that figure. This price was due to the determination of a dealer's runner bidding on an open bid order against a similarly instructed opponent!

Though damage does affect price the number of dealers/collectors willing to accept honest damage appears to have increased.

Some sensational prices have been given for porcelain tureens in the shape of vegetables – an area of keen interest to the American market – and good early white figures have been very popular.

The expected boom in the value of 18thC coloured wares has not yet happened but there are signs that a reappraisal of the market with a consequent steady rise in prices is now under way.

Locate the source

The source of each illustration in Miller's can be found by checking the code letters below each caption with the list of contributors.

CONTINENTAL PORCELAIN

The demand continues to be steady but unspectacular and prices at auction have been fairly predictable.

Meissen flatware of the pre-1745 period, particularly for unusual underglaze blue designs, has created some demand with a consequent slight increase in price levels. The same has been true for Meissen's early armorial wares.

The continued American interest in French porcelain has created a steady growth in prices.

Mennecy, Chantilly and St. Cloud porcelains displaying Chinese or Japanese influences continue to lead the way.

Baskets

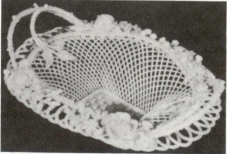

A Belleek basket, 3 strand oval base, lattice sides, intricately modelled with flowers and branches forming two handles, restored, 8in (20cm) diam.
£500-600 *WIL*

A Berlin basket, with pierced decoration, painted and encrusted flower sprays, naturalistic handles, blue sceptre printed orb, 11in (27.5cm).
£200-250 *PWC*

A Meissen (Marcolini) fruit basket, the basketwork sides moulded with gilt-edged shells and scrolls and reserved with panels of flowers, the interior with further flowers and with puce scale border, minor chips, blue crossed swords and star mark, c1785, 15in (37cm) wide.
£500-600 *C*

A very finè Dr Wall Worcester oval basket, with applied and central spray of English flowers, c1770, 8in (20cm) wide.
£1,800-2,000 *SA*

A Meissen basket, the handle and side panel pierced with diapering, the borders profusely encrusted with spring and summer flowers and decorated in colours and gilt on a pale turquoise ground, damaged, Marcoline Meissen mark in underglaze blue, 14in (35cm) wide.
£400-500 *HSS*

A First Period Worcester basket, painted with scattered flower sprays in pink, iron red, yellow and green, the border pierced with circular motifs and with scalloped rims, 7in (17.5cm) diam.
£500-600 *HSS*

A pair of Meissen porcelain chestnut baskets, covers and stands, decorated in colours and gilt, with turquoise chequered banding to the borders, and with chestnut finials, the circular bases pierced with basket weave, scroll and oval motifs, within a border painted with scattered flower sprays and chequered banding in colours and gilt, one stand cracked, crossed swords mark in underglaze blue, baskets 7in (17cm) diam., stands 14in (35.5cm) diam.
£1,100-1,300 *HSS*

Bottles

A Worcester blue and white rosewater bottle, painted with an Oriental figure holding a bird by a pagoda on rockwork and trees, the reverse with children on a bridge, the garlic neck with a band of trellis and hatch pattern enclosing flower sprays, blue crescent mark, c1760, 10in (25cm).
£800-1,200 *CNY*

A pair of Sèvres-pattern square bottles and stoppers, decorated with portraits of Louis XIV and Me. de Lamballe, within gilt line cartouches enriched with ruby enamelled beading, the royal blue grounds enamelled in colours and gilt with elaborate jewelled ornament within turquoise bead borders, the shoulders and stoppers similarly decorated, imitation interlaced L marks, c1880, 6in (15.5cm).
£1,000-1,200 *C*

Bowls

A Bow blue and white flared bowl, the exterior with trailing vine, c1754, 3½in (9cm) diam.
£200-250 *C*

A Longton Hall bowl, painted in bright green, yellow and puce with flowering shrubs issuing from pierced rockwork, rim chips, c1755, 4½in (11.5cm) diam.
£200-300 *C*

A pair of Coalbrookdale bowls and lids, encrusted with flowers, mid-19thC, 5in (12.5cm).
£1,200-1,400 *SA*

A Meissen Kakiemon bowl, painted with chrysanthemum, bamboo and butterflies, the well with a dragon chasing a flaming pearl, his scales picked out in gold, blue crossed swords mark, c1730, 8in (19cm) diam.
£1,000-1,500 *C*

A Meissen pale blue ground bowl, reserved with shaped panels, one with a winter landscape, the other with an Italianate landscape, the interior with a Dutch river landscape en grisaille within a border of puce, gilt and iron red scrolls, restored, mark in blue, gilders number 10 and repairer's mark V, 6in (15cm).
£400-600 *DWB*

n perfect condition, £2,000-3,000.

A Furstenberg bowl, painted with sprays of full blown pink roses below a lightly feathered pink band entwined with a sinuous green foliate chain, the rim edged in gilt, blue F mark and incised numerals, late 18thC, 7in (17cm) diam.
£80-100 *Bon*

A Meissen powdered purple ground slop bowl, the interior with a circular panel of a sailing vessel with gilt rims, blue crossed swords mark, Pressnummer 3 and painter's mark in iron red V, c1740, 7½in (18cm) diam.
£1,500-1,800 *C*

A Pinxton sugar bowl and cover, painted in the Imari style with panels of flowering shrubs within blue edged cartouches divided by iron red trellis pattern on an iron red ground, c1800, 7in (17.5cm) wide.
£300-400 *C*

A Wedgwood Fairyland Lustre bowl, printed in gilt and colours with imps and other little folk darting beneath spreading trees with cobwebs between, upon a ground of brilliant orange, printed Portland vase mark and Made in England, 8½in (20.5cm) diam.
£600-700 *Bon*

A Wedgwood Fairyland Lustre bowl, the exterior with a girl within arcades and bowers, the interior with a continuous scene of pixies and minarets, printed Portland vase mark in gold and pattern No. Z.4968T, c1925, 6½in (16cm) wide.
£800-900 *C*

A Wedgwood Fairyland Lustre circular footed bowl, the exterior with a continuous scene, the interior similarly decorated with pixies in a radiating wooded landscape, the interior rubbed, printed Portland vase mark and pattern No. Z5360/2, c1925, 9½in (23cm).
£500-600 *C*

An early Worcester 'famille verte' bowl, the fluted sides painted with Chinese flowers and a butterfly, faint star crack, c1752-55, 4½in (11cm).
£400-600 *WW*

A First Period Worcester cream jug and slop basin, painted with fruit by the 'Spotted fruit painter' on a ground of butterflies and scrolling tendrils in purple, pink, yellow, puce, red, green and gilt, with turquoise foliate diapered and gilt foliate scrolling borders, open crescent mark in underglaze blue, jug 5in (12cm), basin 6½in (16.5cm) diam.
£300-400 *HSS*

A Worcester small flared bowl, transfer printed in black and coloured with The Red Bull Pattern, c1755, 4in (10.5cm).
£500-600 *C*

An English punch bowl, painted and gilt with a bold pattern of peony branches in colours and foliage and tendrils in dark blue and gilt in Chinese style, within a narrow blue and gilt foliage border, pattern No. 1361, 9in (23cm).
£130-180 *L*

18th-CENTURY WORCESTER

★ founded in 1751
★ soft paste porcelain using soaprock (steatite)
★ c1751-53 a short experimental period. Sometimes difficult to differentiate between Lund's Bristol and Worcester
★ both blue and white and 'famille verte' polychrome wares produced
★ c1752-54 some wares marked with an incised cross or line
★ c1755-60 some finely painted and potted wares produced
★ painters marks, resembling Chinese letters, appear on base of wares
★ the underglaze blue is well controlled and of a good pale colour
★ polychrome decoration is crisp and clean
★ almost all patterns are based on Chinese prototypes
★ transfer printed wares appear c1754
★ from 1760-76 a consistently high standard of potting and decorating achieved though lacking spontaneity of earlier wares
★ most blue and white pieces now marked with a crescent
★ 1776-93 the Davis/Flight period
★ often difficult to differentiate from Caughley where open crescent mark also used

Boxes

A Meissen silver-mounted snuff box, the exterior with blue ribbons with pink roses at intervals, edged in gilding, the interior with a gentleman and 2 ladies standing before an extensive river landscape, with contemporary mount, blue crossed swords mark to the interior, c1755, 3in (7.5cm) wide.
£1,500-2,500 *CG*

A Meissen bombé large snuff box, the interior of the cover with Harlequin and Pierrot beside ladies taking tea in a garden landscape, the gilt-metal mounts with flowers and foliage, c1745, 5in (12cm) wide.
£4,000-6,000 *C*

A Meissen bombé-shaped snuff box, the interior to the cover with further figures beside garden statuary and with contemporary silver mounts, scroll thumbpiece, the silver with French import marks, c1745, 3in (7cm) wide.
£1,500-2,000 *C*

A Volkstedt jagddose, the cover painted with a recumbent stag in an extensive landscape, the hinged silver-gilt mount with waved decoration, blue hayfork and M mark, c1760, 3½in (9cm) diam.
£6,000-7,000 *C*

The mark of the hayfork comes from the Prince of Schwarzburg-Rudolstadt and the M from the founder of the factory Georg Heinrich Macheleid. A soft-paste covered cup similarly marked is in the Kunstundgewerbe Museum, Hamburg.

A Meissen snuff box, the interior of the base gilt, with later English silver-gilt mounts, edge of cover damaged, the porcelain c1745, the silver London 1818, with maker's mark of Charles Rawlings, 3½in (9cm) wide.
£800-1,200 *C*

A Nymphenburg white scallop-shaped casket and cover, with whelk feet and finial naturally modelled and with copper-gilt mount, c1775, 6½in (16.5cm) wide, and another similar cover with copper-gilt mount, 6in (15.5cm) wide.
£1,500-2,000 *C*

A German box and cover, with silver-gilt mounts, possibly Furstenberg, finely painted with battle scenes and encampments in bright enamel colours, each within a gold and puce cartouche, 3in (7cm) wide.
£500-600 *Bea*

A Naples casket, the top and sides modelled in relief with the gods on Olympus, 19thC, 10½in (26.5cm).
£400-600 *L*

A German casket, painted with a group of putti with dead game, the sides with similar figures symbolic of the Seasons, the inside of the lid painted with a lady at her toilet, with numerous attendants, 19thC, 8in (19cm).
£500-600 *L*

An English porcelain snuff box in the form of a cat's head, with hinged brass lid and mount, its eyes in yellow enamel and its muzzle and nose touched in pink, 2in (5cm).
£120-180 *Bon*

Caddies

A Meissen tea caddy, painted in colours with Turkish and European merchants in extensive harbour landscapes, the long sides with iron red and gilt 'Laub und Bandelwerk' enclosing 'Böttger Lustre', blue crossed swords marks, gilder's mark 65, c1735, 3½in (9cm).
£800-1,200   *CNY*

A Meissen yellow ground tea caddy, painted in a Kakiemon palette with flowers issuing from rockwork and a bird in flight within shaped quatrefoil cartouche, blue crossed swords mark and former's mark of Seidel, c1730, 4in (10cm).
£900-1,200   *C*

A Frankenthal tea caddy, painted with peasant figures after Teniers, CT monogram in underglaze blue, incised B2, c1765-70, 4½in (11cm).
£900-1,000   *SA*

A Worcester tea caddy and cover, of Lord Henry Thynne type, with a gilt line and turquoise foliage cartouche, flanked by loose bouquets and butterflies beneath a blue border edged in gilding, minute chips to finial, c1775, 7in (17.5cm).
£800-1,200   *C*

Provenance: A Trapnell.

A Nymphenburg tea caddy and domed cover, painted with wayfarers on paths carrying baskets and bundles in landscape vignettes, cover and finial repaired, blue hexagram mark, impressed Bavarian shield mark and incised mark, the cover with blue alchemical sign with the 4 elements and gilder's mark K, 1763-67, 5½in (14.5cm).
£600-800   *C*

A Kloster Veilsdorf tea caddy, painted with a gallant and companion beneath garden pergola and with gilt bands, traces of blue mark on base, silver gilt cover, c1775, 4½in (11.5cm).
£600-800   *C*

NYMPHENBURG

★ factory founded in the late 1740's but the main production started in 1753
★ J J Ringler was employed as arcanist
★ from 1757 a fine milky-white porcelain was produced
★ the porcelain is of great quality and virtually flawless
★ F A Bustelli modelled some excellent figures from 1754-63 which perfectly expressed the German rococo movement
★ the models are the epitome of movement and crispness and are invariably set on sparingly moulded rococo pad bases
★ note light construction of the slip-cast figures
★ J P Melchior, previously at Frankenthal and Höchst, was chief modeller from 1797-1810
★ on finest pieces the mark is often incorporated as part of the design
★ the factory still exists

Make the most of Miller's

Every care has been taken to ensure the accuracy of descriptions and estimated valuations. Price ranges in this book reflect what one should expect to pay for a similar example. When selling one can obviously expect a figure below. This will fluctuate according to a dealer's stock, saleability at a particular time, etc. It is always advisable to approach a reputable specialist dealer or an auction house which has specialist sales.

A Worcester tea caddy, decorated in gros bleu, with finely painted panels of flowers, cover missing, seal mark, c1765.
£300-350   *PR*

With cover £600-700.

Candelabra

A Chelsea Birds-in-Branches chamber-candlestick group, the birds with yellow and puce plumage on a shaped oval base enriched in puce and applied with a dog, one bird with restoration to tail and wing, the other with minute restoration to one wing, flowers chipped, gold anchor mark, c1758, 7in (17.5cm).
£500-600 *C*

Gold anchor Chelsea is still undervalued by comparison with earlier wares. There are, however, signs of growth in the market for perfect pieces.

A pair of Bow figural and bocage candlesticks, with thick bocage beneath which stands a fox about to devour a chicken, and a spaniel with his bag of 2 partridge, all with decoration in overglaze enamels, both damaged, 11in (28cm).
£1,000-1,300 *HSS*

A pair of Royal Crown Derby candlesticks, on square moulded base supported by 4 gilt fish, painted with panels of iron red, blue and gilt foliage, printed mark, 10in (25cm).
£300-400 *CSK*

A pair of Derby candelabra groups emblematic of Liberty and Matrimony, on pierced scroll-moulded bases enriched in turquoise, puce and gilding, the balustrades supporting the foliage-moulded nozzles, Wm. Duesbury & Co., restorations to nozzles, plumes, his hand and one tree, chipping, c1770, 12in (30cm).
£1,200-1,400 *C*

A pair of Meissen candlesticks, painted in colours with 'deutsche Blumen' and with gilt foliage, tassels and rims, bases of nozzles repaired, blue crossed swords marks, c1745, 9½in (23.5cm).
£500-700 *C*

A pair of Meissen four-light candelabra, painted in colours and enriched with gilding, the shaped square bases painted with exotic birds and insects and moulded with shell scrolls, minor chips and one branch repaired, blue crossed swords marks and incised numerals, c1900, 19in (48cm).
£600-700 *C*

A Meissen five-light candelabrum, enriched in gilding and applied with coloured trailing flowers, restorations and some chipping, blue crossed swords mark, c1880, 19in (47cm).
£500-700 *C*

A pair of Meissen four-light candelabra, encrusted with brightly coloured flowers, minor chips, blue crossed swords mark and incised numerals, c1880, 21½in ((54cm).
£900-1,000 *C*

A Spode candlestick, in the form of a tulip on a vine leaf, c1810-20, 2in (5cm).
£500-550 *SA*

A pair of Meissen candelabra stands, decorated with the figure of Ganymede being carried off by the God Zeus in the form of an eagle, slight chips to one base, incised crossed swords in a triangle, Nos. K49 and K50, 10½in (26.5cm).
£550-650 *Bea*

A Worcester blue and white chamber-candlestick, painted with carnations and trailing flowers within a crisply-moulded C-scroll border, with foliage-moulded nozzle and scroll handle with mask terminal, blue W mark, c1770, 6in (14.5cm).
£1,800-2,200 *C*

18thC English porcelain candlesticks are rare and keenly sought by collectors. Note the mask terminal on the handle.

A Spode taperstick in the form of a recumbent white elephant supporting the gilt sconce, with gilt ears and trunk, painted mark in red, c1815, 4in (10cm).
£150-200 *CSK*

A Royal Worcester chamber candlestick, as a small boy lying on a striped rug, balancing a drum on his right foot, his head resting on a bugle which forms the handle, oval base, impressed mark No. 3/18, 6½in (16cm) long.
£180-220 *HSS*

A Royal Worcester three-light candelabrum by James Hadley, moulded signature, 19in (47.5cm).
£800-1,000 *Re*

Centrepieces

A Meissen table centre, modelled as an oval basket tied with pink ribbon supported on a foliage column, painted with 'deutsche Blumen' and moulded with pink, green and gilt rococo scrolls, minor repairs to foliage, blue crossed swords mark and impressed H, c1750, 18in (45cm) wide.
£1,800-2,000 *C*

A Meissen centrepiece, incised 1931, 42in (105cm).
£1,600-1,800 *FHF*

A Bow blue and white sweetmeat stand, painted in blue with a single large berried leaf against a shaded blue background, 1760's, 5½in (13.5cm).
£550-650 *Bon*

A large Sèvres centrepiece, signed 'Germain', within a border of stylised gilt scrolls and flowering vines on a dark blue ground, the whole with gilt metal mounts, 21in (52.5cm).
£900-1,000 *CSK*

A Royal Worcester 'ivory' mermaid and Nautilus centrepiece, decorated by Callowhill, the Nautilus-shell vase moulded with putti blowing trumpets, among foliage scrolls and gilt with entwined foliage, puce printed marks, c1878.
£1,000-1,200 *C*

A Worcester three-tier centrepiece, edged in pink surmounted by a bird with outstretched wings with predominantly puce and yellow plumage, on a pierced shell and coral encrusted base enriched in colours, some restoration to shells, c1770, 10in (25.5cm).
£1,400-1,800 *C*

An English porcelain and gilt metal table centre, probably Royal Worcester, damaged, c1860, 23in (58cm).
£550-650 *Bea*

A Royal Worcester centrepiece, the bowl supported by 3 Muses, heavily gilt and finely decorated, 9½in (23.5cm).
£450-550 *LT*

A Continental comport encrusted with trailing foliage and roses, in natural colours, 15in (37.5cm).
£300-400 *CBS*

Clock Cases

A Dresden mantel clock, the whole encrusted with flowerheads and leaves, decorated in underglaze blue, black, flesh tones and gilt, some damage, cross swords mark in underglaze blue, 25in (63cm).
£600-800 *HSS*

A Meissen (Teichert) clock case, moulded with foliage heightened in pink and turquoise, with 3 putti emblematic of Winter, Spring and Autumn, chips to flowers, blue Meissen mark, the movement by Lenzkirch, c1900, 20½in (51cm).
£700-900 *C*

A Meissen clock case, enriched with gilding, some minor chipping, blue crossed swords mark and incised numerals, c1880, the eight-day striking movement with enamel dial, chipped, 16½in (41.5cm).
£1,000-1,200 *C*

A Sèvres-pattern porcelain and ormolu-mounted mantel clock, enriched with gilt and enamel spiral berried foliage, glass to circular dial cracked, imitation interlaced L and initial marks, c1880, 24½in (61.5cm).
£2,500-2,800 *C*

Cottages

A Staffordshire porcelain pastille burner, with detached brown roof, the walls painted with flowers and with pierced and gilt windows, on yellow base applied with coloured flowers, probably Spode, c1820, 4½in (11cm).
£650-750 *CSK*

A six-sided cottage pastille burner with pierced windows, probably by Thomas Parr, c1850, 6in (15cm).
£375-425 *GCA*

An English porcelain cottage pastille burner, with detachable roof, c1835, 5½in (13.5cm).
£600-700 *DL*

An English porcelain cottage pastille burner, c1835, 4in (10cm).
£65-95 *GCA*

An English porcelain lilac cottage pastille burner, with detachable base, c1835, 4in (10cm).
£500-550 *DL*

An English porcelain cottage pastille burner, c1835, 5½in (13.5cm).
£600-650 *DL*

A porcelain cottage, with flower-encrusted front and roof, c1840, 4½in (11cm).
£280-320 *LR*

An English porcelain cottage pastille burner, probably Coalport, c1835, 7in (17.5cm).
£900-1,000 *DL*

A large porcelain pastille burner, flower-encrusted and gilt lined, c1835, 5½in (13.5cm).
£450-500 *LR*

An English porcelain two-piece pastille burner in the form of Bladon church, 5in (12.5cm).
£375-450 *GCA*

An English porcelain pastille burner, in the form of a church, c1835, 6in (15cm).
£600-650 *DL*

Cups

An Arras coffee cup and saucer, gilt with birds and floral garlands in scroll foliage cartouches reserved on blue ground and divided by white panels, blue AR marks, c1785.
£400-500 *C*

A Berlin neo-classical cup and saucer, commemorating the Allied entry to Paris on 31 March 1814, the saucer with a map of Paris and inscription, blue sceptre mark, c1814.
£300-500 *CG*

A Berlin cabinet cup and saucer, the cup painted in sepia and with lyres on iron red panels within gilt lozenge-shaped cartouches, reserved on lapis lazuli grounds, with gilt band rims, the centre to the saucer inscribed 'De par L'Amour on fait savoir à tous les coeurs qu'il faut aimer', blue sceptre mark, c1875.
£600-800 *C*

The inscription increases the value of this cup and saucer considerably.

A Berlin neo-classical cup and saucer, painted with pink and white roses, the lilac borders gilt with anthemion between narrow green bands, blue sceptre marks and painter's marks, c1820.
£400-600 *CG*

A Berlin neo-classical cup and saucer, painted with primulas and with gilt lozenge border, blue sceptre marks with painter's mark in puce, c1820
£400-600 *CG*

A Berlin cabinet cup and saucer, painted in sepia with a named view of St. Marienkirche, within a gilt cartouche, the cup with blue sceptre mark, the saucer with blue sceptre and KPM marks, c1860.
£280-320 *C*

BERLIN
★ first factory started by W K Wegely in 1752
★ body hard to distinguish from Meissen
★ particularly close are the Cupids in Disguise and the Commedia dell'Arte figures
★ closed in 1757 at the start of Seven Years War
★ a second factory was started in 1761 by J E Gotzkowsky
★ many artists came from Meissen, including F E Meyer
★ porcelain has a distinctly creamy tone
★ painting was in the restrained rococo manner
★ pieces with puce scale borders and delicate flower painting
★ derived from fashion for Sèvres – in common with most major German factories
★ from 1770 the porcelain has a much colder more brilliant white tone
★ the factory became influenced by the neo-classical movement in common with Fürstenburg and Meissen
★ figure modelling was perfected by the brothers Friedrich Elias Meyer and Wilheim Christian Meyer – note the characteristic small heads and elongated bodies
★ c1775 figure bases became more architectural in design, notably oval and square pedestals
★ in the early 19thC the 'Empire' style of Sèvres and Vienna was copied
★ as the 19thC progressed Berlin tended to follow the prevailing trends

A Berlin neo-classical cup and saucer, painted in colours with hyacinths, the gilt border with scroll motif, the interior gilt, blue sceptre marks and dash in iron red, c1821.
£300-500 *CG*

A Caughley blue and white wine taster with Fisherman pattern decoration, c1785, 1in high by 2in diam. (2.5 by 5cm).
£90-100   *VEN*

A rare Bristol cup and trembleuse saucer, the borders with entwined scroll ornament in green enclosing pink foliage sprays within brown-edged rims, cup and saucer marked B6 in blue enamel.
£600-800   *L*

A Caughley blue and white tea bowl, c1785.
£30-35   *VEN*

A Chelsea teal bowl and saucer, of the raised anchor period, painted in Kakiemon style colours and exotic birds flying above blossoming shrubs issuing from banded hedges, raised anchor pad mark on saucer, c1750.
£2,500-3,000   *Bon*

A Derby stirrup cup, with 'Tally-Ho' on the collar, c1830, 5in (12.5cm) long.
£400-450   *DL*

A Coalport puce ground racing trophy and cover, gilt with the inscription 'Pains Lane Races Sepr. 27th, 1853', within gilt foliage and grass cartouches, the cover gilt with a band of trailing vine and with bunch of grapes finial, minute chip to handle, c1853, 11½in (28.5cm).
£700-800   *C*

A Frankenthal 'bois simulé' cup and saucer, painted 'en grisaille' with landscapes imitating etchings and inscribed 'Braun und Leisser pinxit' and reserved on the simulated wood ground, minor frits to rim of saucer, blue crowned CT monogram mark, c1780.
£300-400   *C*

A Derby cabinet coffee can and saucer, finely painted in the manner of Banford, on a blue ground framed by simulated jewelling, on a ground of cornflowers and gilt stars, minor rubbing to gilding of saucer, crown, crossed batons and D mark and pattern no. 216 in puce, Wm. Duesbury & Co., c1790.
£1,800-2,200   *C*

Cf F Brayshaw Gilhespy, Crown Derby Porcelain, *pl 25, fig 44.*

Two Derby porcelain Named View coffee cans and saucers, the cups painted with views of Devernish Island and Kirkstall Abbey, and the saucers with Lock Gill (sic) and Borrowdale, reserved upon a deep cobalt ground decorated with groups of fronded leaves, all named on the base, 3 pieces with puce crown, crossed batons and D mark, one saucer marked in iron red. **£300-500** *Bon*

A Liverpool coffee cup and saucer, painted in an Imari palette with butterflies among flowering branches within an indented rim, minute chip to underside of saucer, Wm. Ball's Factory, c1764. **£400-500** *C*

LIMEHOUSE (c1747-48)

(a re-attribution of some wares previously attributed to William Reid's Liverpool factory has taken place during the past year)

★ often a crude semi opaque body
★ glaze opacified by the use of tin outside
★ shell dishes and sauceboats are most commonly found
★ mainly blue and white
★ enamel colours are often vibrant and akin to saltglaze
★ some good landscapes, also fruit and roses in underglaze blue
★ identical motifs usually include imitation Chinese decoration – stylised peacock's feathers on handles and spouts
★ body of early phosphatic wares is often grey in colour

LIVERPOOL Brownlow Hill (c1755-68)

(It is now thought that wares previously attributed to William Ball were manufactured at Brownlow Hill, Liverpool, by William Reid, c1755-61, by his successor William Ball c1761-64 and by James Pennington from 1764-68. Ball may have been Reid's factory manager and could have continued in that capacity under James Pennington.)

★ underglaze blue is often bright and the glaze 'wet' and 'sticky' in appearance
★ shapes and style of decoration influenced by the Bow factory
★ decoration often resembles delft
★ paste often shows small turning tears. These show up as lighter flecks when held up to the light
★ polychrome wares are rare and collectable
★ polychrome transfer prints overpainted with enamels are sought after
★ elaborate rococo sauceboats were a factory speciality

A Liverpool blue and white miniature tea bowl and saucer, painted with a flock of birds above 2 wooded river islands, Richard Chaffers' Factory, c1762. **£600-700** *C*

LIVERPOOL Richard Chaffers' Factory (c1754-65)

★ early phosphatic wares have a greyish body
★ some fine polychrome wares are decorated with carefully drawn Chinese figures
★ attractive polychrome mugs are found in the phosphatic body
★ later steatitic wares are noticeably whiter in appearance
★ the underglaze blue of later wares is brighter and less grey
★ the 'Jumping Boy' pattern is particularly collectable
★ later chinoiseries are often peppered with dots. This decorative habit continues on Christians wares
★ potting based on Worcester shapes

A very rare Longton Hall blue and white coffee cup, with split-twig handle, painted with an Oriental gesturing towards a huge vase with a trailing flowering branch, the reverse with a flower spray, minute rim chip, c1755. **£700-900** *C*

Six Meissen tea bowls painted in Augsburg by E Auffenwerth in Eisenrot und Schwarzlot, the interiors with birds and further gilding, one cracked, c1725. **£1,500-1,800** *C*

Derived from prints by J E Ridinger, see S Ducret, Meissener Porzellan Bemalt in Augsburg, figs 100-02.

Cf R Rückert, Meissener Porzellan, no. 110 for a tea bowl with human figures, the interiors similarly decorated. See also Pazaurek Vol 1 Ch 2 for a discussion of this type of painting and gilding. ▷

A fine Meissen tea bowl and saucer, painted with Oriental figures, in the manner of J G Herold, c1725.
£2,200-2,500 *GSP*

A Meissen blue and white tea bowl and saucer, moulded with scrolls and painted in underglaze blue, the reverses similarly decorated, blue crossed swords marks and painter's marks, c1735.
£700-900 *C*

A Meissen blue and white tea bowl and saucer, after a Kangxi original, blue crossed swords marks and K of Kretzschmar, c1735.
£700-900 *C*

MEISSEN

★ in 1709 J F Böttger produced a white hard paste porcelain

★ wares often decorated by outside decorators (Hausmaler)

★ in 1720 kilnmaster Stozel came back to Meissen bringing with him J G Herold

★ from 1720-50 the enamelling on Meissen was unsurpassed – starting with the wares of *Lowenfinck* – bold, flamboyant chinoiserie or Japonnaise subjects, often derived from the engravings of Petruschenk, particularly on Augustus Rex wares, *J G Herold* – specialised in elaborate miniature chinoiserie figure subjects, *C F Herold* – noted for European and Levantine quay scenes

★ crossed swords factory mark started in 1723

★ marks, shapes and styles much copied

★ underside of wares on later body has somewhat greyish chalky appearance

★ in late 1720's a somewhat glassier, harder looking paste was introduced, different from the early ivory tones of the Böttger period

★ finest Meissen figures modelled by J J Kändler from 1731

★ best figures late 1730's and early 1740's – especially the great Commedia dell'Arte figures and groups

★ other distinguished modellers who often worked in association with Kändler were Paul Reinicke and J F Eberlein

★ cut-flower decoration (Schnittblumen) often associated with J G Klinger. The naturalistic flower subjects of the 1740's, epitomised by Klinger, gradually became less realistic and moved towards the so-called 'manier Blumen' of the 1750's and 1760's

★ early models had been mounted on simple flat pad bases, whereas from 1750's bases were lightly moulded rococo scrolls

A Meissen Kakiemon cup and saucer, painted in the Kakiemon palette with birds among flowering chrysanthemum and foliage, with chocolate rims, blue crossed swords marks, c1735.
£200-300 *CNY*

Provence: The Art Exchange.

A pair of Böttger porcelain tea bowls and saucers, with Augsburg Goldmalerei, the interiors to the bowls and the centres of the saucers gilt and engraved in the Seuter Workshop with chinoiserie figures above scrollwork supports, the porcelain 1720-25 and the decoration almost contemporary.
£1,900-2,200 *C*

A Meissen tea bowl and saucer, with powdered purple ground, painted with figures loading boats in harbour scenes, the saucer with quatrefoil lustre, puce and gold 'Laub-und-Bandelwerk' cartouche, blue crossed swords and K mark, c1735.
£800-1,200 *CG*

A Meissen coffee cup and saucer, painted in puce monochrome and gold with 'indianische Blumen', with chocolate rims, blue crossed swords mark, c1735.
£400-600 *CG*

A pair of Meissen powdered purple ground beakers and saucers, with purple cell-pattern and iron red foliage and with gilt scroll rims, 2 handles with minor cracks, blue crossed swords marks and gilder's number 15 to each piece, c1740.
£2,500-2,800 *C*

A pair of Meissen coffee cups and saucers, blue crossed swords marks, Pressnummern 2 and 24, gilder's number 67, c1745.
£1,300-1,600 *C*

A pair of Meissen yellow ground tea bowls and saucers, painted with merchants in river landscapes and wayfarers on horseback within chocolate and gilt quatrefoil cartouches, blue crossed swords marks and gilder's mark B. to each piece, various Pressnummern, c1740.
£1,800-2,500 *C*

A Meissen cabinet cup and cover with pine cone knop, snake handle and set on 3 paw feet, crossed swords mark, 4½in (11.5cm).
£250-300 *Bea*

A Le Nove chinoiserie tea bowl and saucer, painted with Chinese figures in landscape vignettes, iron red star marks, c1790.
£300-400 *C*

A pair of Sèvres tea cups and saucers, painted with birds in landscapes within gilt foliage cartouches on green grounds, tiny chip to footrim of one cup and rim of one saucer, blue interlaced L's enclosing the date letter I for 1761, painter's mark of Aloncle.
£800-1,000 *C*

l. A Meissen cup and saucer, probably painted by C F Herold, painted with shore scene with sailing boats within an elaborate scroll work border, the interior with a quay scene within double red lines, crossed swords mark in underglaze blue and no. 13 in gilt, c1740.
£2,000-2,300

r. A Meissen quatrefoil cup and saucer, painted with flowers, butterflies, dragonflies and other insects, having brown painted borders, crossed swords marked in underglaze blue, c1742.
£750-850   *BS*

A Vincennes 'bleu lapis' coffee cup and saucer, gilt with 'ciselé' bunches of flowers, reserved on the bleu lapis ground and with gilt dentil rims, blue interlaced L marks, the cup enclosing the date letter A for 1753.
£1,000-1,500   *C*

A Sèvres apple green cup and saucer, painted with musical, amatory and floral trophies within 'ciselé' gilt scroll and foliage surrounds, on apple grounds with gilt dentil rims, blue interlaced L marks enclosing the date letter F for 1758, and painter's mark of Buteux aîné.
£1,200-1,400   *C*

SÈVRES

★ most decoration of these early years has a somewhat tentative appearance and few pieces show the sharpness of German contemporaries

★ the vases and other hollow wares including ice pails and flower holders epitomised the rococo style predominant at the court

★ Sèvres plaques were inset into furniture from 1760's

★ Sèvres managed to discover the secret of hard paste porcelain at the same time as Cookworthy at Plymouth in 1768

★ 'jewelled porcelain' was introduced in 1773, using a technique of fusing enamels over gilt or silver foil

---

A Sèvre hop-trellis fluted cup and saucer, painted with blue pilasters with entwined gilt scrolls between berried foliage and pink bands with further gilding and dentil rims, blue interlaced L marks enclosing the date letter L for 1764 and painter's mark of Thevenet, père, various incised marks.
£600-800   *C*

A Sèvres small cylindrical cup and saucer, painted with bands of blue trellis with flowers and bands of roses divided by gilt lines with gilt dentil rims, blue interlaced L marks enclosing date letter S for 1771 and painter's mark of Buteux âiné.
£250-350   *C*

A Sèvres small cylindrical cup and saucer, painted with panels of single roses with gilt cartouches on blue and gilt scale-pattern grounds, blue interlaced L marks enclosing the date letter Z for 1777 and painter's mark EL.
£700-800   *C*

A Sèvres 'bleu nouveau' trembleuse cup, cover and stand, reserved on the 'bleu nouveau' ground, further gilt with bands of C-scrolls enclosing seeding, rim of cover restored, blue interlaced L marks and painter's mark of Le Guay, c1775.
£800-1,000   *C*

A Sèvres 'bleu nouveau' cup and saucer, painted with brightly coloured birds in landscapes within gilt panels reserved on the 'bleu nouveau' ground with gilt 'ciselé' scrolling foliage, blue interlaced L marks enclosing the date letters AA for 1778 and painter's mark of Aloncle, gilder's mark of Chauveaux, the cup incised 27 and 36, the saucer 44.
£650-750   *C*

A Sèvres hard paste coffee cup and saucer, painted with musical trophies in 'ciselé' gilt oval cartouches reserved in a pink ground of 'oeil-de-perdrix', the cartouches joined by floral garlands, minor chip to underside of saucer rim, iron red crowned interlaced marks and painter's mark DR perhaps of Drand and incised marks, c1780.
£600-800   *C*

VIENNA

★ factory founded by C I du Paquier in 1719 with the help of Stolzel and Hunger from Meissen

★ the body of du Paquier wares has a distinctive smoky tone

★ decoration tends to cover much of the body and can be more elaborate than Meissen

★ extensive use of trellis work or 'gitterwerk'

★ the 'State' period of the factory ran from 1744-84

★ the style of this period was 'baroque', with scrollwork and lattice-like gilding

★ plain bases were used from mid-1760's

★ excellent figure modelling was undertaken by J J Niedermayer from 1747-84

★ Konrad von Sorgenthal became director from 1784-1804

★ the style became far less based on rococo and much simpler in taste, but with good strong colours and raised gilding

★ factory closed in 1864

l. A Spode tulip cup with green stalk handle, the overlapping petals striped in pink, the interior with yellow centre with black stamens, on a green octagonal base edged in gilding, 2 slight chips to underside, script mark in red, c1820, 3in (7cm).
£400-600

r. A Spode tulip cup, striped in red, slightly deformed in firing, red mark, c1820, 3in (7cm).
£300-500   *C*

A Vienna Du Paquier chinoiserie beaker and trembleuse stand, painted with Chinamen standing with fans and seated at a table on terraces, with pierced gallery, one handle restored, c1735.
£2,000-2,500   *CG*

A Sèvres yellow ground trembleuse cup and saucer, painted with a band of symmetrical scrolls, ribbons and foliage between the lines, the yellow ground with trailing blue flowers and with gilt rims, blue interlaced L marks and the date letters KK for 1788, painter's mark of André Vincent Viellard, incised 37 to each piece, the cup with 3.
£900-1,100   *C*

A pair of Swansea fluted cups and saucers, probably painted by William Pollard, stencil marks in red, 1813-22 period.
£500-600   *GSP*

139

A Tournai cup and saucer with scroll handle painted 'en camaieu rose' with bouquets of flowers and with chocolate rims, minor rim chip to saucer, c1775.
£250-350   *C*

A Vienna coffee cup and saucer, decorated in imitation of Oriental lacquer, the coral red ground gilt with figures and pagoda buildings in river landscapes, the brown lacquer borders with scrolling branches, saucer and handle restored, blue beehive marks and impressed mark for 1792.
£150-200   *C*

A Vienna Empire cabinet cup and saucer, painted with Cupid fashioning his bow on a ground of gilt stripes, the saucer with the conventional inscription above love, blue beehive marks and impressed mark for 1821, and a blue ground milk jug painted with an en grisaille panel.
£400-600   *C*

A Vienna neo-classical cup and saucer, decorated in silver and pale yellow, the cup with a moonlit and the saucer with a sunlit sky, blue beehive marks and 120 for the painter Bernhardt Rosner, 1823.
£700-900   *CG*

A First Period Worcester tea bowl and saucer, painted with the Japan pattern in underglaze blue, iron red, green and yellow, square mark in underglaze blue.
£170-200   *HSS*

Make the most of Miller's
In Miller's we do NOT just reprint saleroom estimates. We work from realised prices either from an auction room or a dealer. Our consultants then work out a realistic price range for a similar piece. This is to try to avoid repeating freak results – either low or high.

A Worcester yellow scale tea cup and saucer, painted with exotic birds and insects within gilt vase and mirror shaped cartouches, minor rubbing to saucer, blue crossed swords and 9 mark, c1765.
£3,000-4,000   *C*

Prices
The never-ending problem of fixing prices for antiques! A price can be affected by so many factors, for example:
- *condition*
- *desirability*
- *rarity*
- *size*
- *colour*
- *provenance*
- *restoration*
- *the sale of a prestigious collection*
- *collection label*
- *appearance of a new reference book*
- *new specialist sale at major auction house*
- *mentioned on television*
- *the fact that two people present at auction are determined to have the piece*
- *where you buy it*

One also has to contend with the fact that an antique is not only a 'thing of beauty' but a commodity. The price can again be affected by
- *supply and demand*
- *international finance – currency fluctuation*
- *fashion*
- *inflation*
- *the fact that a museum has vast sums of money to spend*

A Worcester blue and white small flared mug, painted with The Tambourine Pattern, crack to top of handle, painter's mark, c1756.
£550-650   *C*

This piece is an excellent example of how damage on a rare hand-painted pattern is totally acceptable to Worcester collectors. A piece in this condition could have been purchased for £40-60 5 years ago.

A fine Worcester coffee cup, the tapering fluted body applied with scroll handle and with a herringbone pattern moulded in shallow relief, painted with sprays of flowers in coloured enamels beneath an underglaze blue floral border, c1760's, 2½in (6cm).
£650-750   *Bon*

A Worcester porcelain tea bowl and saucer, painted with Cannonball pattern, crescent mark, c1760-65.
£140-170   *DEL*

A Worcester cup and saucer, decorated with the Fan pattern, seal mark, c1765.
£350-400   *PR*

A Worcester tea bowl and saucer, decorated in brilliant enamels with panels of exotic birds in landscape, upon a ground of 'wet blue', the rims trimmed with a band of gilt dentil, blue open crescent mark, c1765.
£600-700   *Bon*

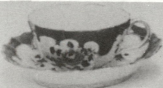

A First Period Worcester cup and saucer, decorated with the Marchioness of Huntley pattern in pink, orange, yellow and blue with apple green borders and gilt line rims, square mark in underglaze blue.
£250-300   *HSS*

A rare Worcester tea bowl and saucer, outside decorated with quails pencilled in sepia, perhaps in the workshop of James Giles, and painted in colourful enamels, the rim trimmed in gilt and iron red with a scroll and dot design, saucer restored, c1760's.
£200-300   *Bon*

A First Period Worcester cup and saucer, decorated outside the factory with panels of leaves and flowerheads in puce, iron red and green, with gilt herringbone and foliate borders, with black beaded bases on a turquoise ground, the borders worn, open crescent mark in gilt.
£100-140   HSS

The condition affects value of coloured Worcester considerably.

A First Period Worcester cup and saucer, painted with cartouche panels of chrysanthemums and other flowers in iron red and green within gilt foliate borders, on a scale blue ground, square mark in underglaze blue.
£250-350   HSS

A Worcester fluted tea bowl, with banded hedge and wheatsheaf pattern, 18thC.
£45-50   DEL

A set of 4 Worcester blue and white tea bowls and saucers, each printed with chinoiserie figures in landscape within a circular or oval panel enclosed by an elaborate scroll, diaper and foliage pattern, one bowl blurred and cracked, one saucer chipped, printed crescent mark.
£200-250   Bon

A Worcester coffee cup and saucer with blue scale ground.
£300-350   DWB

A First Period Worcester trio, of a coffee cup, tea cup and saucer, decorated in the Japan pattern in underglaze blue, iron red, green, turquoise and gilt, square mark in underglaze blue.
£220-280   HSS

A Worcester blue scale Kakiemon coffee cup and saucer.
£300-350   DWB

A First Period Worcester coffee cup and saucer, painted with scattered flower sprays in puce, red, blue and green, with gilt line borders and grooved handle, slight chips to foot rims.
£80-120   HSS

A very rare Dr Wall Worcester trio, Earl of Eley pattern, painted with exotic birds, c1770.
£2,000-2,500   SA

A Dr Wall period Worcester fluted caudle cup and cover and stand, painted with landscape panels within gilt scroll and scale pattern surrounds, reserved upon a deep 'wet blue' ground, knop restuck, the bowl with blue square fret mark, c1770.
£1,000-1,200   Bon

A Worcester cup, decorated in blue and white with floral sprays, blue crescent mark to base, 18thC.
£40-50 *NSF*

A Worcester porcelain tea bowl and saucer, Queen Charlotte's pattern, c1788.
£150-200 *DEL*

A Worcester chocolate cup and saucer, with pierced scroll handles edged in gilding, painted in dry blue with bouquets and scattered flower sprays within a gilt dentil rim, c1770.
£500-600 *C*

A Chamberlain's Worcester cup, cover and stand, with gilt ring handles, painted with named botanical specimens, the cover with chrysanthemum, the body with grape hyacinth and spear leaved geranium, the stand with wild rose, within gilt line rims, some minor rubbing to gilding, script mark in puce, c1800, 4½in (11.5cm).
£250-350 *C*

A Flight, Barr & Barr Worcester trio, comprising 2 tea cups and a saucer, with the Pagoda and Peony pattern, c1813-40.
£150-200 *DEL*

A Flight & Barr Worcester goblet, the grey marbled ground reserved with a shipping scene inscribed 'Dover' on a pale yellow ground within a gilt octagonal cartouche within gilt line rims, script mark and incised B, c1805, 5in (12.5cm).
£800-1,200 *C*

A Royal Worcester cabinet cup and saucer, painted with fruit, by Ricketts, signed.
£100-120 *Re*

An English porcelain tankard, painted with colourful displays of garden flowers, restored, c1800-10, 5½in (13cm).
£80-100 *Bon*

A pair of Royal Worcester coffee cups and saucers painted with highland castle by J Stinton, and 4 other cups and saucers painted with various scenes by various artists in a brush fitted case.
£700-900 *CSK*

A Zurich tea bowl and saucer, painted in Schwarzlot with landscape vignettes and with gilt rims, blue Z marks with 2 dots on the saucer and incised marks, c1775.
£300-400 *CG*

A set of 6 English porcelain coffee cans and saucers, painted with military subjects in coloured enamels illustrating episodes from the life of the Marques de Ponte de Lima, c1818.
£600-800 *Bon*

Tomas Jose de Lima (1779-1822) second Marques de Ponte de Lima was a Colonel in the Legio Portuguesa, and was organised by Junot to fight in the Napoleonic forces. About 1811 he left the French camp and went over to the allies under Wellington. After the victory over Napoleon, it is likely that he visited England and was given a coffee service by an English friend, which would have illustrated his whole military career.

A Grainger miniature cabinet cup and saucer, painted with views of Malvern Link, Wellwalk, Cheltenham, Malvern Church, North Parade, Bath, St. Vincent's Rocks, Bristol and the North West of Worcester.
£300-370 *SA*

Ewers

◁ A Royal Worcester ewer, with serpent handle painted with flowering vines on a white ground outlined in gilt, printed mark, 11½in (28cm).
£120-150 *CSK*

A Royal Worcester ewer, painted in colours with sprays of thistles and other flowers on a blushed ivory ground, printed mark in purple, no. 1144, date code for 1897, 11in (27cm).
£120-150 *HSS* ▷

Fairings

'Some Contributors to Punch'.
£250-300 *P*

'Checkmate'.
£30-50 *P*

'Cancan'.
£80-120 *P*

'To Let'.
£150-180 *P*

'Free and Independent Elector', slight damage and restoration.
£80-120 *P*

'To Epsom', he restuck to his seat.
£400-600 *P*

'Cancan'.
£150-180 *P*

'Cancan'.
£220-250 *P*

'Fair Play Boys'.
£150-180 *P*

'The Organ Boy'.
£150-180 *P*

'Love in Winter', slight damage.
£300-350 *P*

'Master's Winning Ways'.
£180-240 *P*

'No Followers Allowed'.
£350-400 *P*

'A Pleasant Termination to a Happy Evening'.
£120-150 *P*

'Kiss Me Quick', bicycle variety, damaged pedal.
£150-180 *P*

'Return from the Ball', large variety.
£80-100 *P*

'Please Sir, What Would You Charge to Christen My Doll?'.
£120-150 *P*

'Waiting for a Bus', large variety, slight damage.
£200-250 *P*

'Just As It Should Be'.
£220-250 *P*

'Its Only Moustache'.
£250-320 *P*

'Out By Jingo', restored.
£120-150 *P*

'A Long Pull and A Strong Pull'.
£180-220 *P*

'In Chancery'.
£150-180 *P*

'If Youth Knew'.
£220-250 *P*

'If Old Age Could'.
£150-180 *P*

'How's Business?', restored.
£100-130 *P*

'God Save the Queen'.
£80-120 *P*

'The Babes in the Wood'.
£300-400 *P*

'The Attentive Maid'.
£200-220 *P*

'By Appointment – The First of April'.
£180-220 *P*

'All Over', slight damage.
£150-180 *P*

'Animated Spirits'.
£300-400 *P*

'Before Marriage'.
£180-220 *P*

'After Marriage'.
£220-250 *P*

'Mine', 2 pink porkers beside a tub and wrestling with a biscuit.
£60-90 *B*

A pink pig, jumping through a drum, match strike.
£60-90 *B*

Two pigs smooching in the back of an open car, driven by a chauffeur.
£60-90 *B*

Two pink pigs accompanying themselves on a green piano, spill holder.
£60-90 *B*

A pink pig accompanying himself on a green piano.
£60-90 *B*

Figures – Animals

A pair of Bow white figures of a lion and lioness with fierce expressions, prowling on oval mound bases, lioness with crack to back right-hand thigh and left back foot, c1749, the lion 9in (22cm) wide, the lioness 9½in (23cm) wide.
£8,000-10,000 *C*

Cf Anton Gabszewicz and Geoffrey Freeman, op cit pl 251 for the pair in the Freeman Collection.

Lively modelling and early date make these figures highly collectable.

A pair of Bow white models of a lion and lioness, the lion with small firing crack to left forepaw and front of base, the lioness with extended fire crack through base and round her hind quarters, the rear part of the base restuck, some minute chipping to bases, c1750, 11½in (28cm) long.
£2,000-3,000 *C*

Cf George Savage, 18thC English Porcelain, pl 47b and another pair in the British Museum, R L Hobson, Catalogue of the Collection of English Porcelain, fig 4, no.I.11.

◁
A Bow white figure of an owl, his head pierced, perched on a tree stump applied with three flowers, extended firing crack round body, restuck to base, c1754, 7½in (19cm).
£1,200-1,500 *C*

Cf Untermyer Collection Catalogue, pl 78, fig 259 and Frank Stoner, Chelsea, Bow and Derby Porcelain Figures, pl 105 for similar examples.

BOW PORCELAIN
c1745-76

- ★ probably the first porcelain factory in England
- ★ early wares were mostly decorated in overglaze enamel colours
- ★ the body is of the phosphatic soft paste type as Lowestoft, early Chaffers and early Derby
- ★ it is sometimes difficult to differentiate between blue and white wares from Bow, Lowestoft, and Derby
- ★ painters numerals sometimes used on base or inside footrings as the Lowestoft (and occasionally Chaffers, Liverpool)
- ★ body heavy for its size

A Bow white figure of a standing pug, his incised collar with a florette standing on a rectangular mound base moulded with flowers, some minor staining, c1755, 3in (7.5cm) wide.
£800-1,200 *C*

A pair of Derby figures representing Autumn, both seated with baskets of grapes, coloured in pink and puce, with yellow hats, some restoration, c1760, 5in (12.5cm).
£900-1,000 *PR*

A pair of Derby figures as Shepherd and Shepherdess with musical instruments, c1765, 9in (22.5cm).
£800-900 *PR*

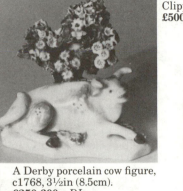

A Derby figure of a woodpecker, with incised feather markings enriched in green, yellow, iron red and puce, chips to flowering foliage, repair to tail and tree stump, c1765, 5in (12.5cm).
£600-800 *CNY*

A Derby group, Father Time Clipping the Wings of Love, c1770.
£500-600 *Sto*

A Derby porcelain pug dog, c1768, 3in (7.5cm).
£250-300 *DL*

A Derby porcelain cow figure, c1768, 3½in (8.5cm).
£250-300 *DL*

A pair of Derby porcelain sheep, c1780, 3½in (8.5cm).
£400-500 *DL*

A Derby porcelain cow and calf group, c1770, 5½in (13.5cm).
£250-300 *DL*

A black cow is unusual.

18th-CENTURY DERBY

★ some early white jugs incised with the letter D have been attributed to the Derby factory under the direction of John Heath and Andrew Planché, believed to start c1750

★ early Derby is soft paste and is generally lighter than Bow and Chelsea

★ very rare to find crazing on early Derby, the glaze was tight fitting and thinner than Chelsea

★ glaze often kept away from the bottom edge or edge was trimmed, hence the term 'dry-edge' (particularly applied to figures)

★ c1755, three (or more) pieces of clay put on bottom of figure to keep it clear of kiln furniture, giving 'patch' or 'pad' marks – which now have darker appearance

★ Duesbury had joined Heath and Planché in 1756

★ Duesbury's early works display quite restrained decoration, with much of the body left plain, following the Meissen style

★ Derby can be regarded as the English Meissen

★ the porcelain of this period has an excellent body, sometimes with faintly bluish appearance

★ 1770-84 known as the Chelsea-Derby period

★ Chelsea-Derby figures almost always made at Derby

★ 1770's saw the introduction of unglazed white biscuit Derby figures

★ this points to the move away from the academic Meissen style towards the more fashionable French taste

★ in 1770's leading exponent of the neo-classical style, and comparable to contemporary wares of Champion's Bristol

★ body of 1770's is frequently of silky appearance and of bluish-white tone

★ 1780's Derby body very smooth and glaze white, the painting on such pieces was superb, particularly landscapes, Jockey Hill and Zachariah Boreman

★ 1780's and 1790's noted for exceptional botanical painting of the period especially by 'Quaker' Pegg and John Brewer

★ around 1800 the body degenerated, was somewhat thicker, the glaze tended to crackle and allow discolouration

A pair of Dresden figures of King Charles Spaniels, blue printed Dresden Potschappel marks, 12in (30cm) long.
£500-800   *CNY*

A matched set of 4 Derby porcelain figures, representing the 4 continents, Africa, Asia, Europe and America, c1780, 9in (22.5cm).
£1,000-1,200   *DL*

A Meissen figure of a rhinoceros, modelled by J J Kändler after Albrecht Dürer, incised decorated in shades of brown with an armour-like skin, chips to ears and tail, 1735-40, 7in (17.5cm) long.
£1,800-2,500   *C*

A Dresden figure of a polar bear, the muzzle, eyes and claws picked out in blue, crossed swords mark in underglaze blue, 10in (25cm).
£800-1,000   *L*

A Derby biscuit group representing Music, c1790, 10in (25cm).
£500-550   *PR*

A Kloster Veilsdorf figure of a crouching leopard, probably modelled by Pfränger Snr, with brown and black markings on brown mound base, c1775, 5in (12cm) long.
£400-600   *C*

A Longton Hall group of 2 putti with a goat, scantily draped in pink and yellow, on a scroll moulded base enriched in puce and green, restoration to goat's horns and base, c1755, 6in (15cm) wide.
£400-500   *C*

A Meissen pipe bowl, modelled as a recumbent sheep dog with hinged neck, incised and brown fur markings, one ear and forepaw restored, blue crossed swords mark on base, c1745, 3½in (8cm) long.
£800-1,200   *C*

A very rare Ludwigsburg figure of an elephant supporting an obelisk, naturally modelled with grey hair markings and pink ears, his puce saddle cloth lined in yellow and edged with gilding, the upper part of the obelisk and the elephant's tusks restored, blue crowned interlaced C mark, c1765, 11in (27cm).
£2,500-3,000   *CG*

The modelling suggests it could possibly be that of Johann Christian Wilhelm Beyer, particularly the presence of the obelisk, a feature which appears in many of his known models.

LUDWIGSBURG

★ porcelain factory was founded in 1758
★ J J Ringler directed the factory from 1759-99
★ best period was from 1765-75
★ porcelain has a distinctly greyish tone which is generally poorer than contemporary German factories
★ specialised in producing figures
★ most desirable are the 'Venetian fair groups' produced by Jean-Jacob Louis
★ in 1770's figures of a more classical nature were produced
★ the later figures were of a much poorer quality
★ quality of the flower painting is of a fairly undistinguished nature
★ the factory closed in 1824

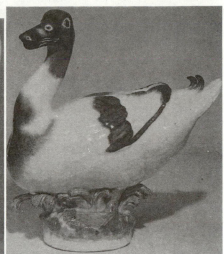

Two Meissen figures of seated cats, modelled by J J Kändler, with yellow, red and black facial markings and eyes and grey fur, on grassy mound bases, minor cracks, restoration to mouse and tail of one cat, blue crossed swords marks on base, c1740, 7in (17.5cm).
£6,000-8,000   *C*

First modelled by Kändler in September 1736 and others in January 1741, and according to Kändler's taxa between 1740-48.

Cf C Albiker: op cit no. 216 where he records the various entries.

A pair of Meissen figures of goldfinches, with incised feather markings enriched in yellow and grey, the tree stump enriched in brown and green, chips to beaks, one with chip to tree stump, blue crossed swords marks, c1745, 5½in (14cm).
£2,200-2,800   *CNY*

A Meissen figure of a mallard duck, with brown head and purple and brown breast, the tips of its wings and tail feathers enriched in black and purple, standing on turquoise water-weeds and on a circular green and yellow mound, cracks and repairs, blue crossed swords mark at back, c1740, 11½in (28cm).
£3,000-3,500   *C*

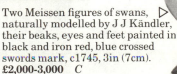

A Meissen bird nesting group, enriched in brown, green, yellow and flesh tints, one tail repaired, minor chips, c1750, 5½in (14cm) wide.
£300-500   *CNY*

Two Meissen figures of swans, ▷ naturally modelled by J J Kändler, their beaks, eyes and feet painted in black and iron red, blue crossed swords mark, c1745, 3in (7cm).
£2,000-3,000   *C*

A pair of Meissen figures of swans, with orange and black beaks, their white feathers with grey markings, firing cracks and some chipping, blue crossed swords marks and incised numerals, c1880, 12½in (30.5cm).
£1,200-1,500   *C*

A pair of Meissen pug dogs, modelled by J J Kändler and P Reinicke with belled orange and pink collars with green and blue ribbon ties, black and brown facial and fur markings, restoration and damages, one with blue crossed swords mark on base, c1745, 6in (15cm).
£3,000-5,000   *C*

First modelled by Kändler in 1741.

Kändler's taxa of June 1744 and December 1744 record the new models.

A Meissen Marcolini figure of a Chaffinch, blue crossed swords and star mark, c1790, 4in (10cm).
£400-500   *C*

> In the Ceramics section if there is only one measurement it refers to the height of the piece.

A large Meissen model of an elephant, naively modelled with large eyes and paw-like feet, some damage to trunk, 19thC, 17in (42.5cm) long.
£500-600 *Bea*

A Meissen figure of a monkey playing the cello, modelled by O Pielz, in white frock, blue jacket, and puce trousers, playing the cello blue crossed swords and dot mark, incised and impressed marks, 8in (20cm).
£600-800 *CNY*

A Meissen group of dogs and a kennel, modelled by J J Kändler, their fur naturally coloured in brown, grey and black, minor chips, blue crossed swords mark, c1750, 5½in (13cm).
£4,500-5,500 *C*

A Meissen figure of a frog, naturalistically modelled, enriched in green, black, yellow and flesh tones, blue crossed swords, impressed marks, 3in (7.5cm) long.
£300-400 *CNY*

A pair of Meissen small figures of pug dogs, after models by J J Kändler, with brown fur markings and black faces and paws, one with blue collar, the other with green, blue crossed swords marks, impressed marks, 3in (8cm) long.
£200-300 *CNY*

A pair of porcelain figures, marked Rockingham, c1830, 5in (12.5cm).
£1,400-1,600 *DL*

A pair of Meissen figures of mice, naturalistically modelled with brown hair markings on oval base, blue crossed swords, impressed ▷ marks, 2in (5cm) long.
£300-500 *CNY*

A Meissen group of 3 dogs, blue crossed swords, impressed and incised marks, 7in (17.5cm) wide.
£250-350 *CNY*

A seated brindled tabby cat with ginger colouring, Sitzendorf mark in underglaze blue, ears restored, c1870, 10in (25cm).
£400-450 *Wai*

A Meissen figure of a squirrel, modelled after Kändler originals with incised hair markings enriched in brown, wearing a violet and gilt collar suspending a chain, blue crossed swords, incised and impressed marks, 8in (20cm).
£250-350 *CNY*

A Staffordshire porcelain eagle, likely to be Lloyd Shelton factory, c1835, 7½in (18.5cm).
£200-250 *DL*

A Samson figure of a partridge perched astride a tree stump applied with blue flowers, the bird's plumage in shades of brown and grey and with orange wattle and comb, blue cross mark, late 19thC, 6in (15cm).
£90-120 *C*

A Samson figure of a white rhinoceros, after the original by J J Kändler, naturally modelled, its nose and ears heightened with flesh tints and with yellow horn, blue cross mark, c1880, 9in (22.5cm) wide.
£500-600 *C*

A fine quality hand painted porcelain figure of a King Charles spaniel, sitting upon a mauve and gilt decorated cushion, early 19thC, 7½in (18cm).
£300-400 *B*

A Staffordshire porcelain dog group, c1835, 3in (7.5cm).
£250-300 *DL*

A white porcelain bear, c1880, 9in (22.5cm).
£200-250 *SBO*

This is a late copy of the stoneware bears.

SAMSON, EDME ET CIE (PARIS)

★ factory opened in Paris in 1845
★ reproduced wares of virtually every other factory (both Continental and Oriental)
★ their fakes of Meissen and Chinese porcelain are excellent
★ their English soft-paste porcelain fakes are easier to detect, as they used a Continental hard-paste body
★ Samson claims that all wares have an S contained within the mark – however this can be easily removed by the unscrupulous
★ more pieces are attributed to Samson than they could possibly have made

---

Figures – People

A rare pair of Belleek female figures, wearing loose classical draperies in shades of iridescent mauve, one with a gold headband and armband, the other with a gold bead necklace, on circular bases, printed mark a hound, a harp and Belleek, 14½in (36cm).
£1,800-2,500 *L*

A Bayeux, Langlois, figure of an Oriental spice-seller, one pot restored, c1835, 7½in (19cm) wide.
£400-600 *C*

Cf George Savage, Dictionary of 19thC Antiques, *col pl pp 84-5.*

A Bow figure of Autumn, a girl sitting with a basket of grapes, square hole at the back, c1755, 4½in (11cm).
£700-800 *PR*

A Bow figure of Spring, with lemon-yellow bodice, white apron and pink skirt, seated beside baskets of flowers on a circular mound base, minor chips, c1754, 5in (12.5cm).
£900-1,100 *C*

A Bow figure representing Smell, from a set of the Five Senses, with marble base, c1760, 10in (25cm).
£600-700 *GSP*

See George Savage, 18thC English Porcelain, *pl 43b.*

A Bow figure of a shepherdess, wearing a yellow bodice and puce decorated dress, slight damage, 18thC, 6½in (16cm).
£600-800 *BS*

BOW FIGURES

★ the earliest Bow figures had simple pad bases in common with Chelsea and Derby
★ many figures left in the white
★ figures tend to be less sophisticated than those from the Chelsea factory
★ from 1750-54 many figures were modelled by the 'Muses modeller'
★ these figures have quite thick glaze and low square bases
★ best period runs from 1750-59
★ the influence of Meissen can be seen in the figures from c1755 on
★ rococo bases appeared in late 1750's, earlier bases of c1760 in common with Chelsea are relatively restrained
★ by 1760 'C & S' scroll decoration was in great demand as were large shell bases, which are often thought of as a trade mark of Bow (although other factories did use them)
★ by 1760's typical colours used are blue, emerald-green, yellow and a good red
★ from c1765 greater use of underglaze blue as a ground colour, like contemporaries at Longton Hall
★ late 1760's figures elevated on more elaborate and pierced bases, generally applied with flowers
★ figures with elaborate bocage are typical
★ figures tend now to copy Chelsea gold anchor groups
★ figures with an underglaze blue crescent tend to be Bow (Worcester produced very few figures)

A pair of Bow figures emblematic of Sight and Smell, wearing pale pink and yellow flowered clothes, Sight with firing crack to sides, some minute chipping, c1756, 6 and 5½in (15 and 13.5cm).
£1,400-1,800 *C*

A Bow figure of Autumn, modelled as a youth in yellow-lined pink jacket, dot-pattern waistcoat and flowered breeches, seated on a tree stump, on a four-footed scroll-moulded base enriched in puce and gilding, some minor chipping, c1762, 6in (15.5cm).
£700-800 *C*

A rare Bow figure of Summer from a set of Seasons taken from Meissen originals, probably modelled by Tebo, decorated in the Giles manner, sconce missing, c1760-65, 9in (22.5cm).
£800-900 *PR*

Locate the source
The source of each illustration in Miller's can be found by checking the code letters below each caption with the list of contributors.

A pair of Bow porcelain figures, The New Dancers, in mint condition, c1765, 10in (25cm).
£1,100-1,300 *DL*

A Bow figure of a shepherd, wearing a colourful costume and green and primrose yellow-lined cape, on rococo base, 9in (22.5cm).
£550-650 *GSP*

A rare Coalbrookdale parian figure of the Duke of Wellington, modelled by G Abbott and issued by Daniell's, impressed Manufactured at Coalbrookdale and the name of sculptor and publisher, c1850, 10½in (26cm).
£250-350 *Bon*

◁ A Copeland parian group of a girl seated on a rock cradling a terrier on her lap, entitled 'Go to Sleep', impressed 'Art Union of London, J Durham Sc 1862', 17in (43cm).
£400-500 *AG*

A Derby white figure of John Wilkes, minute chips to cloak and scroll, Wm. Duesbury & Co., c1765, 12in (29.5cm).
£350-450 *C*

A pair of Derby figures emblematic of Summer, painted in the London studio of William Duesbury, he with restoration to hat and left arm, she to hat, arms and waist, Andrew Planché's period, c1753, 6½in (16.5cm).
£3,000-4,000 *C*

These early standing Seasons are each represented by a pair of contrasting figures for each Season.

William Duesbury's London Account Book refers specifically to Seasons thus:
'Joun 6 (1753) 1 Darbeyshire seson (sic) 1-0
August 3 pr of Darbishire sesons (sic) 0-6-0
and it seems highly likely that they were from this series rather than the seated Seasons of the same date, of which no coloured examples would seem to be recorded.

A Copeland parian group of Cupid and another winged boy struggling for possession of a heart lying at their feet, on oval shaped base, 15½in (38.5cm).
£600-700 *L*

A Derby shepherdess, in yellow-lined pink jacket, the scroll moulded base enriched with turquoise and gilding, chips, Wm. Duesbury & Co., c1765, 10in (24.5cm).
£400-500 *C*

An early Derby figure of a girl with puce bodice and flowered skirt, 6in (15cm).
£500-600 *GSP*

An early Derby figure of a harvester, with pink jacket, gold and orange trousers, c1765, 7½in (18.5cm).
£700-750 *PR*

A pair of Derby figures of a shepherd and shepherdess, both finely decorated in turquoise and yellow, minor chip on hat, c1760.
£1,100-1,300 *PR*

A pair of Derby porcelain Mansion House dwarfs, c1780, 7in (17.5cm).
£800-900 *DL*

A good pair of Bloor Derby figures of Shakespeare and Milton, Shakespeare modelled after the Scheemaker Memorial in Westminster Abbey, Milton probably modelled after John Cheere, both well decorated in bright enamels and gilt, slight chips, Milton with restored scroll, printed crowned banner marks in iron red, incised nos. 291 and 305, 9½in (23.5cm).
£450-550 *N*

A Derby figure of Andromache weeping over the ashes of Hector, c1800, 10½in (26cm).
£250-300 *N*

For the model see J Twitchett, Derby Porcelain, *plt 151. According to the Haslem and Bemrose lists the original cost 'Enamelled and Gilt' was £1.10.0.*

A pair of Derby porcelain figures of Billy Waters and African Sall, c1830, 3½in (8.5cm).
£350-400 *GCA*

A Derby porcelain figure of Edmund Keen as Richard III, c1800, 11in (27.5cm).
£550-650 *DL*

A pair of Bloor Derby figures, c1830, 6in (15cm).
£600-650 *SA*

A pair of Derby porcelain figures of children, raised on scrolled bases, damaged, incised no. 89 and crossed swords mark in underglaze blue, early 19thC, 4½in (11.5cm).
£250-300 *HSS*

A Frankenthal figure of a young woman dancing, modelled by Joh Friedrich Lück, chips and repairs, blue lion rampant mark, and incised JH monogram, c1756-59, 9in (22cm).
£1,200-1,500 *C*

Cf Hoffman, Frankenthaler Porzellan, *Taf 57, no. 258.*

A Frankenthal group of lovers emblematic of Autumn, her dress and apron decorated with puce flower sprigs, on low scroll moulded base picked out in puce and gilt, slight chips to branches and repair, his left hand restuck, blue rampant lion mark, impressed PH, c1750's, 11in (27cm).
£2,500-3,000 *Bon*

A Ludwigsburg miniature group of 3 figures rolling dice, in tricorn hats and coloured clothes, on green and black splashed rectangular base, blue interlaced C mark, c1775, 3in (8cm) wide.
£1,600-1,900 *C*

◁ A pair of Le Nove groups of putti, some repairs and damages, Antonibon's factory, c1780, 6in (14cm).
£250-350 *C*

A Kloster Veilsdorf figure of Harlequin, modelled by Wenzel Neu, holding a yellow hat with black mask and multi-coloured harlequinade costume, on tree stump base, minor damage to his head, base repaired, 1764-65, 6in (14cm).
£2,000-3,000 *CG*

A Kloster Veilsdorf figure of Dr Boloardo, modelled by Wenzel Neu, blue enamel crossed swords mark, 1764-65, 5in (13cm).
£2,000-3,000 *C*

Cf R S Soloweitschik, Thüringer Porzellan, *no. 29.*

FRANKENTHAL

★ Paul A Hannong started producing porcelain in Frankenthal in 1755, under the patronage of the Elector Carl Theodor

★ glaze has a quite distinctive quality as it tends to 'soak in' the enamel colours

★ high quality porcelain produced under Modellmeister J W Lanz, was favoured striped gilt grounds and green and dark puce

★ K G Lück and his brother or cousin J F Lück came to Frankenthal from Meissen in 1758

★ K G Lück's work tends to be quite fussy and often on grassy mounds, with rococo edges picked out in gilding

★ in the late 18thC a fine range of figures produced by J P Melchoir and A Bauer

★ Melchoir also worked at Höchst

★ Frankenthal utility ware is noted for the quality of the painting, particularly flower painting

★ factory closed in 1799

★ moulds from the factory were used in many 19thC German factories

Two Höchst figures of Das Weinende Mädchen and Jammernder Knabe, the girl in black headscarf, pale yellow bodice, grey skirt and puce underskirt, the boy in puce jacket, pale yellow breeches etched in gilding, and iron red shoes, her left hand repaired, blue crowned wheel marks, the boy incised 'Fohler', c1775, 6in (15cm).
£800-1,200 *CNY*

A Höchst figure of a shepherdess, in white cap, chequered bodice and iron red striped skirt, iron red NB monogram and IH incised, c1775, 8in (20cm).
£1,500-2,000 *CG*

A Limbach figure of Europe from the set of the Continents, enriched in puce, repair to his neck, both arms and sceptre, chips to fingers, c1775, 8in (20cm).
£500-700 *CNY*

Cf H Scherf, J Karpinski, Thüringer Porzellan, *fig 233, where the figures of Asia and America in the Anger Museum of Erfurt are illustrated.*

A Ludwigsburg figure of a Chinese musician, modelled by Joseph Weinmuller, his hat and coat lined in puce and edged in green and painted with florettes in iron red and green, on grassy rockwork base, restorations to arm, neck and instrument, c1767, 13in (32cm).
£2,500-3,500 *CG*

HÖCHST

★ factory was founded in 1746 by the painter A F von Löwenfinck from Meissen

★ porcelain was produced from 1750

★ milk-white in colour, almost tin-glazed appearance

★ early wares tended to have poor translucency and be somewhat heavy

★ from 1758-65 the style reminiscent of the French 'Louis Seize' style came into fashion

★ this style was continued and developed by J P Melchior who was chief modeller 1767-79

★ the base of figures from 1765 tends to be in the form of a distinctive grassy mound, executed in dark café-au-lait and green stripes

★ the factory closed in 1796

A pair of Ludwigsburg figures of a river god and goddess, scantily draped in iron red and flowered cloths on grassy mound bases, extensively restored, one with incised FP mark, c1775, both 10in (24cm) long.
£400-500 *C*

A Meissen figure of Harlequin, modelled by J J Kändler, his black hat with red cockade, his jacket with chequer pattern and playing cards and his breeches turquoise, restoration to his hat and instrument, blue crossed swords mark under the base, c1742, 5in (13cm).
£800-1,200 *CG*

A Meissen figure of a Dutch peasant, modelled by P. Reinicke, in pink hat and jerkin and turquoise trousers, hat rim and toe repaired, blue crossed swords mark at the back, c1745, 5½in (13.5cm).
£600-800 *CG*

A Meissen group of Diana and attendants, she in black cape and flowered dress attended by a girl in a pink bodice and yellow dress, a man kissing her hand, and with Cupid seated on a stool in an ermine-lined pink cloak, extensively restored, blue crossed swords mark, c1745, 7½in (18.5cm).
£500-700 *C*

A Meissen group of Count Brühl's Tailor, modelled by J J Kändler, damage and repair to his scissors and one of the goat's horns, blue crossed swords mark, c1740, 10in (25cm).
£3,000-5,000 *C*

There are many later copies of this figure.

A Meissen figure of Harlequin disguised as a sailor, in puce-lined blue cloth cap, yellow jacket, gilt and flowered shirt, damage to his paddle and peak of his cap, blue crossed swords mark and impressed 10, c1750, 5½in (13.5cm).
£600-800 *C*

A Meissen figure of a pilgrim, modelled by J J Kändler, standing in black tricorn hat, black shelled cape, lilac jacket and white breeches, some restoration to hat, hands and extremities, blue crossed swords mark at back, c1745, 12in (29cm).
£800-1,200   *C*

Kändler's taxa of 1740 records that the pair of figures were originally made for Johanne Charlotte, Princess of Anhalt-Dessau who was abbess of the princely abbey of Herford.

A Meissen group of Harlequin beside a young woman, modelled by J J Kändler, Harlequin in harlequinade costume and she in flowered dress, Harlequin damaged through wrist and some damage to table and repairs to the tree, blue crossed swords mark, c1747, 7½in (18.5cm).
£3,000-4,000   *C*

A Meissen chinoiserie figure of a woman, modelled by P Reinicke, in white hat and flowered tunic on square base, blue crossed swords mark on the base, c1750, 5in (12cm).
£700-800   *C*

A Meissen figure of Justice, in white robe puce-lined yellow cloak, some repair to the sword, blue crossed swords mark at the back, c1750, 4½in (11.5cm).
£300-400   *C*

Three Meissen figures emblematic of Spring, Summer and Winter, after the models by J J Kändler, bases enriched with gilding, Spring's left hand lacking, some minor chipping, blue crossed swords marks, c1750, 9in (22.5cm).
£1,200-1,400   *C*

A pair of Meissen sweetmeat figures, painted with 'deutsche Blumen', the shaped bases edged with gilt scrolls, her bowl and left arm repaired, minor chips, blue crossed swords mark, c1750, 7in (18cm) long.
£800-900   *C*

A Meissen figural group of the Arts representing Music, slight damage to fingers and toes, crossed swords Pressnummer 16, c1755, 7½in (19cm).
£600-700   *Bon*

A Meissen figure of a bird-seller, from the cris de Paris series, standing in ermine-lined yellow hat, pale puce frock-coat and green breeches, chips and repairs, blue crossed swords mark at the back and incised 4, c1755, 5in (12cm).
£2,000-3,000   *C*

A Meissen figure of a trinket-seller, from the cris de Paris series, modelled by J J Kändler and P Reinicke, his hat and nose restored, blue crossed swords marks at back, incised no. 8, c1756, 6in (14cm).
£6,000-8,000   *CG*

A Meissen pastoral group of children, minor damage to extremities, blue crossed swords, 19thC, 7in (18cm).
£500-600 *Bon*

A Meissen group of 3 figures under a tree, painted in bright enamel colours, slight chipping, mid-19thC, 10½in (26.5cm).
£500-600 *Bea*

A pair of Meissen groups of Cupid, decorated in colours and enriched with gilding, on oval gilt line bases, slight damage and minor restoration, blue crossed swords marks, c1850, 6½in (16cm).
£650-750 *C*

A Meissen musical group, decorated in colours and enriched with gilding, the shaped base edged with a gilt line, minor chips, blue crossed swords mark and incised numerals, c1860, 6½in (16cm).
£400-500 *C*

A pair of Meissen figures of a marksman and lady archer, both ▷ weapons and his arm and foot damaged, 19thC, 6in (15.5cm).
£150-200 *Bon*

A Meissen group of 2 putti emblematic of the Arts, the base moulded with scrolls and enriched with gilding, slight chip, one putto lacks wing, blue crossed swords mark and incised numerals, c1880, 6in (15.5cm).
£250-300 *C*

A Meissen group of Venus and Cupid, Venus in lavender drapery holding a gilt dish over the flames, Cupid scantily draped in purple, blue crossed swords mark and incised numerals, c1880, 14½in (36.5cm).
£1,000-1,200 *C*

A Meissen group of Europa and 2 nymphs, painted in colours and enriched with gilding, minor chips, blue crossed swords mark and incised numerals, c1880, 9in (22.5cm).
£300-400 *C*

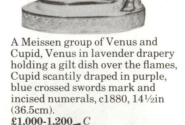

A late Meissen group of 2 freemasons, after the original model by J J Kändler, their blue and iron red jackets enriched with gilding and with black tricorn hats, hilts of swords lacking, chip to corner of one jacket and minor chips to flowers, cancelled blue crossed swords and incised numeral marks, c1880, 9in (22.5cm).
£400-500 *C*

A pair of Meissen figures of a man and woman in 18thC dress, their clothes decorated in colours and enriched with gilding, blue crossed swords marks and incised numerals, c1880, 8in (20cm).
£600-700 *C*

A Meissen group of 2 scantily draped putti counting money, decorated in colours and enriched in gilding, the oval rockwork base moulded with scrolls and similarly gilt, blue crossed swords marks and incised numerals, c1880, 6in (14.5cm).
£300-400 *C*

A Meissen group of 3 children, decorated in colours and enriched with gilding, the fluted circular base with gilt and ochre decoration, chips and some restoration, blue crossed swords and incised numeral mark, early 20thC, 9in (22cm).
£400-500 *C*

A Meissen group of lovers, decorated in colours and enriched with gilding, chips to foliage, blue crossed swords mark and incised numerals, c1880, 6in (15cm).
£350-450 *C*

A Meissen figure of a bass player, probably modelled by Paul Scheurich, blue crossed swords mark, incised P276 early 20thC, 14in (35cm).
£600-800 *CNY*

A Meissen group of Bacchus, the shaped oval base moulded with scrolls and enriched in gilding, minor chip, blue crossed swords mark and incised numerals, early 20thC, 8½in (21cm).
£300-400 *C*

A late Meissen brightly coloured figure, modelled as a young lady, blue crossed swords mark, 6½in (16cm).
£300-400 *CSK*

A late Meissen articulated figure of a seated rotund Chinese woman, 6in (15cm).
£250-300 *CSK*

A Nymphenburg white figure of Capitano Spavento, modelled by Franz Anton Bustelli, chip to his sword, repair to dagger and tip of right foot, impressed Bavarian shield mark, c1765, 8in (19.5cm).
£1,200-1,800 *CNY*

A Nymphenburg white figure of Il Dottore, modelled by Franz Anton Bustelli, repair to his right arm, impressed Bavarian shield mark, c1760, 8in (20cm).
£1,200-1,800 *CNY*

A Minton parian figure of Child's Play, by John Bell, c1840, 14in (35cm).
£350-400 *Wai*

PARIAN WARE

★ first produced by Copeland in 1844
★ it is a white porcelain with a granular surface
★ sometimes called 'statuary' porcelain
★ mainly used for figures and busts
★ in 1845 The Art Union of London commissioned Copeland to make figures taken from the works of contemporary sculptors

A parian bust of a young woman, unmarked, 28in (70cm).
£400-500 *Bon*

A parian standing female figure, probably Belleek but unmarked, 14½in (36.5cm).
£120-180 *L*

Cf C and D Shinn, Victorian Parian China, *pl 16, illustrates a Belleek catalogue of 1904 in which fig 20 shows an identical figure to the above.*

A rare Pfalz-Zweibrucken figure of a peasant woman, wearing white headscarf, lavender blouse, brown skirt and green overskirt, repair to duck, basket and one finger, W mark, incised i, c1770, 9in (23.5cm).
£1,500-2,000 *CNY*

A pair of Plymouth porcelain groups, The Gardener and his Companion, finished in white, slight damage to bocages, 10in (25cm).
£800-1,000 *MN*

A large Royal Dux group with camel and Bedouin seated on its back, on oblong base with attendant, 20in (50cm).
£600-700 *Re*

A rare pair of Rockingham figures of Swiss girls, both with slight damage, one impressed griffin mark, Rockingham Works, Bramald, incised no. 18, the other impressed griffin mark, Rockingham Works, Bramald, incised no. 22, 7in (17.5cm).
£1,800-2,200 *BS*

Cf D G Rice, Rockingham Pottery and Porcelain, *no. 18 'Paysanne du Canton du Zurich', no. 22 'Paysanne de Sagran en Tirol'.*

A pair of Royal Dux figures of a Middle Eastern man and companion, both wearing pink head-dresses and green costumes, dusted overall in gilt, impressed and raised numerals, and pink raised triangle mark, 15in (38cm).
£250-300 *Bon*

A Sèvres white biscuit group of Le Valet de Chien, modelled by Blondeau after Oudry, restoration to his hat, one dog's foreleg, incised interlaced L mark, c1776, 12in (30.5cm) long.
£1,200-1,800 *C*

This is from the Surtout du Groupe des Chasses modelled by Blondeau after Oudry in 1776. There are two valents de chiens listed by Bourgeois but it is impossible to tell which this is.

A pair of Mennecy white figures of a Sultan and Sultana, he repaired at neck, minor chips to both figures, incised D.V. marks on the mount bases, c1740, 9in (23cm).
£2,500-3,500 *C*

A pair of Volkstedt-Rudolstadt figures of a gallant and his lady, on naturalistic mound bases with scroll-mouldings picked out in pink, green and gilt, blue mark for H Greiner, late 19thC, 17in (42cm).
£250-350 *Bon*

A Sèvres bust of Napoleon as First Consul, the bust with green-bronzed patination on spreading green circular socle enriched with gilding, impressed Sèvres mark and incised 'Bonaparte 1. Consul' and with the dating for 1802, 12in (29cm).
£800-1,000 *C*

A Sèvres biscuit group of The Judgement of Paris, damages, incised interlaced L mark and numeral 54, incised modeller's monogram AB and a square, c1781, 16½in (41cm).
£1,500-1,800 *C*

Probably modelled by Alexandre Brachard after the original model by L-S Boizot.

Cf E Bourgeois, Le Biscuit de Sèvres, for the original model, still at Sèvres.

A Sèvres biscuit bust of Napoleon Bonaparte as First Consul, the square marble plinth inscribed 'Bonaparte 1er Consul 1800', the bust inscribed and with impressed Sèvres mark and date numeral 9 for 1802, 14½in (36cm).
£1,600-2,000 *C*

A Sèvres biscuit standing figure of Napoleon in uniform with the badge of the Légion d'Honneur, on later French porcelain base decorated with Napoleon at the Bridge of Arcole, chips to his hat, the figure c1810, 29in (72cm).
£4,000-5,000 *C*

A Thuringian figure of Provender for the monastery, the monk carrying a bundle of wheatsheaves concealing a young lady, chip to the back of his hood, c1775, 4½in (11.5cm).
£600-800 *C*

A Staffordshire porcelain figure of Byron, c1835, 6in (15cm).
£200-250 *DL*

A Staffordshire porcelain figure of
Maria Foote as Arinette, c1860,
6½in (16cm).
£120-160 *CSK*

A pair of Royal Worcester glazed
parian figures of Paul and Virginia,
standing before leaf-moulded tree
stumps, painted in a pale palette,
the rockwork bases applied with
foliage, one with restoration to
foliage, impressed marks, c1865,
13in (33cm).
£400-600 *C*

*Cf Henry Sandon, Royal Worcester
Porcelain, pl 9, for a group of Paul
and Virginia.*

A Strasbourg porcelain group of a
seated young man and woman
before a tree stump, in yellow hat,
lime-green jacket and puce
breeches, his companion in flowered
blue and purple-lined dress on
shaped mound base, his right hand
restuck, other minor chips and
repairs, impressed PH mark, c1755,
9in (23cm).
£2,000-2,500 *CG*

A Royal Worcester figure of Karan
Singh, from the Indian Craftsman
Series, shape 1204, printed mark in
puce and impressed, 1884, 5in
(13cm).
£400-500 *L*

A set of 6 Royal Worcester standing
figures of John Bull, a Swiss man, a
Chinese, an Indian, a Negro and an
American, printed mark in puce for
1881 and impressed factory and
registration marks.
£600-800 *L*

A Royal Worcester figure of a
French fisher girl, by James Hadley,
painted in pale enamel colours and
gold, printed and impressed marks
with the date code for 1888, 17in
(43cm).
£500-600 *Bea*

A Royal Worcester figure of John
Bull, modelled by Hadley, coloured
overall in green, bronze and ivory
with dusted gilt highlights, printed
date code for 1917, 7in (17.5cm).
£150-200 *Bon*

A Royal Worcester figure group of
The Picnic, printed marks, no. 18 of
a limited edition of 250, complete
with certificate.
£300-400 *HSS*

A Royal Worcester standing figure
of a lady, the circular base inscribed
'L'Allegro', printed mark in puce
and impressed, 1890, 16½in
(41.5cm).
£350-400 *L*

A Royal Worcester figural group in
Kate Greenaway style, modelled by
Hadley, coloured predominantly in
shades of ivory and apricot with gilt
highlights, damaged, printed
factory marks and date code for
1892, incised artist's name, 9½in
(24cm).
£250-300 *Bon*

A Royal Worcester standing figure
of Munnasall, in shaded ivory,
painted in soft colours and gilt,
holding a vase, other vases on a low
stool at his side, from the Indian
Craftsman Series, shape 1222,
printed mark in puce and
impressed, 1890, 8in (20.5cm).
£300-400 *L*

An English porcelain Royal Prince on a dog, c1845, 8in (20cm).
£350-400 *GCA*

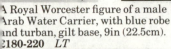

A Royal Worcester figure of a male Arab Water Carrier, with blue robe and turban, gilt base, 9in (22.5cm).
£180-220 *LT*

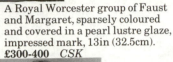

A Royal Worcester group of Faust and Margaret, sparsely coloured and covered in a pearl lustre glaze, impressed mark, 13in (32.5cm).
£300-400 *CSK*

A Zurich figure of a bagpiper, modelled probably by J J Meyer, his cream hat with puce ribbon, his jacket and waistcoat with puce flowers on grasswork base, tip of his pipe missing, blue Z mark, c1767, 7½in (18.5cm).
£5,000-7,000 *CG*

A large pair of Continental biscuit figures of a man and a woman in 18thC dress, one with hair crack to base, one with base repaired, impressed initial marks, probably France, c1900, 27in (68cm).
£800-1,200 *C*

A Victorian Staffordshire English porcelain figure of Zeus and an eagle, early 19thC, 10in (25cm).
£240-290 *GCA*

A French porcelain figure group, 'L'Accordée, du Village' after Greuze, late 19thC, 16in (40cm) wide.
£150-200 *CDC*

A large French ormolu-mounted biscuit equestrian group of Napoleon crossing the Alps, after the painting by David, mid-19thC, 28in (70cm).
£3,000-5,000 *C*

Flatware

A Belleek plate, lightly moulded with initials, printed mark in black, 9in (23cm).
£70-100 *CSK*

Bow polychrome wares

★ early period wares are decorated in vivid and distinctive 'famille rose' colours – pink and aubergine predominate
★ the patterns used usually include chrysanthemum and peony
★ earliest wares have a greyish body but by 1754 a good ivory tone was often achieved
★ on wares after 1760 the colours can appear dull and dirty and this has an adverse effect on value
★ in the late 1750's some attractive botanical plates were produced
★ after 1760 Meissen influenced floral decoration most commonly found

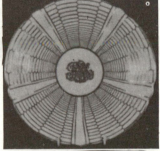

A Bow square dish, painted in a pale Kakiemon palette with The Flaming Tortoise Pattern, within a gilt spearhead pattern border, some minor rubbing, c1754, 7½in (18.5cm).
£400-600 *C*

A Caughley plate, decorated with powder blue ground and hand painted panels, c1775, 8in (20cm).
£160-200   *VEN*

A Chelsea silver shaped plate, finely painted with figures by a moored boat at a quayside, with a ruined turret to the left, the pale blue sky with birds in flight above, small rim restoration at 11 o'clock, c1752, 9in (22.5cm).
£4,000-5,000   *C*

A Chelsea leaf moulded dish, the basket work ground moulded in relief with large foliage enriched tones of green, yellow, puce and turquoise, the rim with brown lin iron red anchor mark, c1760, 10in (25cm).
£1,200-1,800   *CNY*

A very rare Bristol spoon tray, with Meissen-type decoration in puce monochrome, c1775, 6½in (16cm) wide.
£600-700   *VEN*

A pair of Chelsea leaf dishes, moulded as cabbage leaves with puce stalks and veining and painted with bouquets, scattered flower sprays and insects, red anchor marks, c1756, 12in (29.5cm) wide.
£1,500-2,000   *C*

CAUGHLEY

★ factory ran from 1772-99, when it was purchased by the Coalport management
★ painted wares tend to be earlier than printed ones
★ Caughley body of the soapstone type
★ often shows orange to transmitted light, but in some cases can even show slightly greenish which adds to the confusion with Worcester
★ glaze is good and close fitting, although when gathered in pools may have greeny-blue tint
★ from 1780's many pieces heightened in gilding, some blue and white Chinese export wares were similarly gilded in England
★ main marks: impressed 'Salopian', 'S' was painted on hand-painted designs, 'S' was printed in blue printed designs, although an 'X' or an 'O' was sometimes hand-painted beside it, one of the most common marks was the capital C. Hatched crescents never appear on Caughley, they were purely a Worcester mark
★ Caughley is often confused with Worcester; they have many patterns in common, eg. 'The Cormorant and Fisherman' and 'Fence' patterns

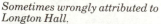

A pair of Bow leaf shaped pickle dishes, c1760, 3½in (8cm).
£600-800   *GSP*

Sometimes wrongly attributed to Longton Hall.

A Chelsea plate, of silver shape, painted with sprays of flowers in green enamel, c1760, 8in (20cm).
£70-80   *DEL*

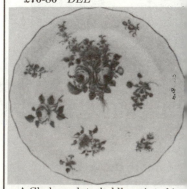

A Chelsea porcelain plate, painted in colours with scattered flower sprays, the border trimmed with feathered scrolls in brown and turquoise, brown anchor mark, c1760, 8½in (21cm).
£200-250   *Bon*

A Chelsea plate, boldly painted in bright enamel colours with sprigs and sprays of garden flowers, red anchor mark, mid 18thC, 8½in (21.5cm).
£200-300   *Bea*

Two Coalport shell shaped dishes, finely painted with exotic birds and the leaf moulded handles picked out in gilt, impressed 6 or 9, 9½in (23.5cm).
£200-250 *DWB*

A Chelsea plate, painted in the centre with an exotic bird with brightly coloured plumage, the background 'en camaïeu rose', gold anchor mark, c1763, 9in (22.5cm).
£600-700 *Bon*

This plate is probably from the service given by Queen Charlotte to the Duke of Mecklenburg Strelitz, as note on reverse of plate.

A Coalport plate, the centre painted with a group of flowers in a lobed panel, the wide border with a basket pattern in turquoise and gold, 9½in (23.5cm). **£120-150** *L*

A Copeland plate, the centre painted with a group of flowers on a shaded brown background, divided by pink and blue oval medallions within a red and gilt border, printed mark in blue, 9½in (24cm).
£200-250 *L*

A pair of Derby botanical plates, some wear, blue crown, crossed batons and D marks, pattern no.142, c1795, 9in (23cm).
£800-1,200 *CNY*

A Derby plate from the Barry service, probably decorated by Robert Brewer, c1802, 9in (22.5cm).
£900-950 *PR*

A Caughley blue and white oval dish with chinoiserie decoration, c1785.
£55-60 *VEN*

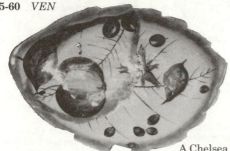

A Chelsea leaf dish, red shaped anchor period.
£700-800 *JUD*

A Coalport square shaped dessert dish, painted with a view of Tantallon Castle by A Perry, signed, on a rich blue ground, outlined with gilt trellis panels and foliage within a gilt gadroon rim, scroll handles, printed mark in green and impressed mark for 1908, 11½in (28.5cm).
£180-220 *L*

An H & R Daniel green ground crested dish from the Shrewsbury Service, the centre with the crest beneath an earl's coronet, c1827, 19½in (48cm) wide.
£600-800 *C*

A Derby botanical plate, patter 141, Scorzeonera Tingitana, blu marking, c1790, 9in (22.5cm).
£600-750 *BRE*

A Derby dish with floral decoration, by the 'cotton-stalk' painter, c1756, 8½in (21cm).
£450-550 *VEN*

A pair of Derby botanical oval dishes, finely painted in colours with specimen flowers named on the reverse, one with 'Annual Lavatera, Large Flowered St. John's Wort & Scarlet Bizzare Carnation', the other with 'Tulip Oculus Solis, Campanula Coronatos & Evergreen Glaucum', with shaped gilt rims, iron red crown, crossed batons and D Marks, c1811-15, 10in (26cm) wide.
£2,000-3,000 *CNY*

A pair of Coalport circular dessert dishes, one painted with a view of Lake Maggiore by C Taylor, signed the other with a view of Naworth Castle by H Perry, signed, on a rich blue ground, gilt with rococo scroll panels, flowers and scrolls, gilt gadroon borders, printed mark in green, 11½in (29.5cm).
£250-300 *L*

A Coalport dessert dish, c1805.
£180-220 *JUD*

A Derby plate, probably painted by William Cotton, hunting scene, red mark, c1810, 9in (22cm).
£900-1,100 *BRE*

A Derby plate, painted by William Billingsley, Love in the Mist, c1790, 8½in (21cm).
£300-400 *BRE*

Ex. Field Collection.

CHELSEA

★ some red anchor marks usually neat and very small and not in prominent position

★ later brown and gold anchor marks are larger and more thickly written

★ paste varies from white to greenish when seen by transmitted light

★ on red anchor ware, look out for 'moons' caused by frit in the kiln, also seen by transmitted light

★ three spur marks often found on the base, left by kiln supports, also a feature of Arita porcelain (not to be confused with Derby pad marks)

★ glaze on early pieces is reasonably opaque, this later becomes clearer and more glassy; later still it becomes thicker when it tends to craze

★ body on later gold anchor wares and figures often has a dry, brownish appearance

A Meissen blue and white plate, painted in the Kang Xi style, minute hairline crack from rim, blue crossed swords mark, c1728, 9in (23cm).
£300-500 *CNY*

A Derby dish, with blue mark, Crown Imperial, c1800.
£450-500 *JUD*

A Frankenthal blue and white plate, painted in underglaze blue with a landscape in the Oriental style, the border with 3 vignettes, hairline crack from rim, blue lion mark, 1756-9, 9in (22cm).
£400-600 *CNY*

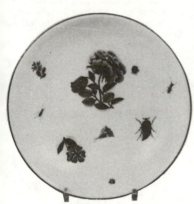

A Meissen saucer dish, painted with 'ombrierte Holzschnitt Blumen' and insects in a manner of Klinger and with gilt rim, blue crossed swords mark, 1735-40, 8in (21cm).
£700-900 *CG*

A small early Meissen dish, painted in colours with European and Turkish merchants in an extensive harbour landscape, in an iron red, puce and gilt, 'Laub und Bandelwerk' cartouche, enriched with Böttger lustre, the reverse with 3 flower sprays in the Kakiemon palette, blue crossed swords mark, gilder's mark 5, c1730, 7in (17.5cm).
£1,000-1,500 *CNY*

A Meissen plate, painted by J E Stadler in bright colours and Böttger lustre, minor rim chip, blue crossed swords mark, c1730, 8½in (21.5cm).
£1,600-2,000 *C*

A Liverpool blue and white shell moulded pickle dish, painted with trailing flowers and scattered insects, minute rim chip, c1755, 4½in (9.5cm) wide.
£600-800 *C*

A Meissen shaped pentagonal teapot stand, painted with figures in a harbour scene within puce and gold 'Laub und Bandelwerk', the border with gilt scroll work, blue crossed swords and gilt 55 marks, c1735, 6in (15cm).
£600-800 *CG*

A Meissen armorial plate from the Sulkowsky service, the large central armorial flanked by scattered Kakiemon flowers within ozier moulded border, blue crossed swords mark, c1738, 9½in (23.5cm).
£3,500-4,000 *C*

The arms are those of Graf Alexander Joseph von Sulkowski and his wife Maria Anna Franziska von Stein zu Jettingen. This is from a large service produced by 1735 and 1738 for Sulkowski who was Augustus III's minister. Numerous pieces from this service are illustrated by Rückert: figs. 487-90.

A Meissen Hausmalerei plate, painted by F F Mayer von Pressnitz, blue crossed swords mark, Pressnummer 14, the porcelain c1740, 9in (22.5cm).
£500-700 *C*

A moulded Derby plate, with red mark, c1820, 10in (25cm).
£130-150 *BRE*

A pair of Meissen Hof service circular dishes, painted with a red dragon in iron red and gold, blue crossed swords mark, Pressnummer 16, puce K H C marks of K G L Hof-Conditorei, c1740, 12in (29.5cm).
£1,800-2,200   *C*

A Meissen Imari plate, painted with 'Brokatdekor' of a vase containing chrysanthemums, painted in underglaze blue and overglaze iron red, black, lustre and gilt, the reverse with trailing flowers, blue crossed swords mark and painter's mark for Kretzschmar, Pressnummer 22, c1740, 9in (22.5cm).
£3,000-3,500   *C*

Cf Rückert, No. 316.

A Meissen dish from the Christie Miller service, the centre painted with hunting figures and dogs, the 'Gitterwerk' well with 4 quatrefoil puce landscape panels, blue crossed swords mark and Pressnummer 22, c1742, 7in (17.5cm).
£7,000-9,000   *C*

A Meissen Marcolini plate from a Jagd service, gilt foliage border, small rim chip retouched, blue crossed swords and 4 mark, c1790, 9½in (24cm).
£300-400   *CG*

A Meissen blue and white oval dish, blue crossed swords mark, Pressnummer 26, c1745, 9in (22.5cm).
£600-800   *CNY*

A Meissen armorial plate, from the St. Andrew service, painted with 'holzschnitt Blumen' and moulded with 'Gotzskowsky erhabene Blumen' and with gilt trellis rim, blue crossed swords mark and Pressnummer 16, red wax Hermitage inventory number, c1745, 9½in (24cm).
£2,500-3,500   *C*

A large Meissen dish from the series of 'Kinder a la Raphael', minor rim chips, blue crossed swords and dot mark, L mark, Pressnummer 95 and impressed Fromer's mark, c1770, 13in (33cm).
£300-500   *CNY*

A Meissen Marcolini dish, the centre painted with an entertainer before a crowd of people beside a tavern door, in gilt scroll borders, 14½in (36cm) wide.
£400-500   *CSK*

Twelve late Meissen pierced bordered plates, on blue, pink, yellow and claret grounds, blue crossed swords mark, 10in (25cm).
£4,000-5,000   *CSK*

A Meissen blue and white plate, painted in underglaze blue with a tiger and a dragon on rockwork with bamboo and prunus within shaped rim, the reverse with scrolling foliage, mock Chinese seal mark and Pressnummer 10, wax inventory number, c1740, 10½in (25.5cm).
£1,200-1,800   *C*

Twelve Minton turquoise ground dessert plates, attributed to Henry Mitchell, the centres reserved and painted in the manner of Landseer, the rims gilt, impressed marks, retailer's mark of A B Daniell and Son, 46 Wigmore Street, London, iron red pattern numbers SG 738, date code for 1873, 10in (25cm).
£1,500-2,500   *C*

A Nantgarw London decorated plate from the Duke of Cambridge service, impressed Nant-Garw C.W. mark, c1820, 9½in (24cm).
£1,500-1,800   *C*

Provenance: from a service of over forty pieces probably purchased from Mortlocks in 1818 by the Prince Regent as a gift for his younger brother, Adolphus, Duke of Cambridge, on the occasion of his marriage to the Princess Augusta of Hesse Cassel.

A pair of Mintons circular dishes, painted by G Taylor, signed and dated 87, gilt borders, impressed mark Mintons, 9½in (24.5cm).
£150-250   *L*

A Nantgarw London decorated plate, painted with a bouquet of garden flowers, within a turquoise wave scroll rim, impressed marks, early 19thC, 9½in (23cm).
£400-600   *Bea*

A Nantgarw topographical plate, painted with 'Bruchmatt bey Lucerne Un Souvenir de Monsr. et Made. Mahler', named in red script on the reverse, impressed Nant-Garw C.W. mark, c1820, 8½in (21.5cm).
£800-1,200   *C*

A Nantgarw dish, painted with a bouquet and bands of pink roses within a gilt moulded flower wreath and C scroll border, impressed Nantgarw C.W. mark, c1820, 9½in (24cm).
£450-550   *C*

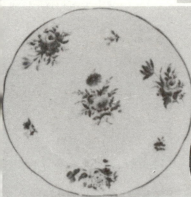

A Nantgarw plate, painted with sprays of flowers, with shaped gold lined rim, impressed marks, early 19thC, 9½in (24cm).
£300-500   *Bea*

A very good Nantgarw plate, painted with the typical Billingsley roses, impressed mark, 8½in (21cm).
£600-700   *SA*

Cf John's Nantgarw Porcelain, *pl 43B.*

A Nantgarw plate, London decoration, impressed mark Nantgarw C.W., c1819, 9½in (23.5cm).
£700–850 *BRE*

A Nantgarw plate, London decoration, elaborate border gilding with central floral bouquet, impressed mark Nantgarw C.W., c1819, 8½in (21cm).
£600-700 *BRE*

A Nantgarw plate, painted by W H Pardoe, impressed mark, c1819.
£150-250 *BRE*

Possibly sold at the last public sale of Nantgarw in 1892.

A very good Nantgarw plate, painted with the typical Billingsley roses, impressed mark, 8½in (21cm) diam.
£600-700 *SA*
Cf John's Nantgarw Porcelain, *pl 43B.*

A pair of Pinxton plates, c1800.
£350-450 *JUD*

A Nymphenburg dish, the centre painted with figures and merchants beside a ruin in a river landscape with sailing boats, impressed Bavarian shield mark and numeral 1, c1770, 9in (22cm).
£300-500 *C*

A Sèvres soup plate from the Madame du Barry service, blue interlaced L marks enclosing the date letter S for 1771, and painter's mark of Bulidon, 9½in (24cm).
£1,500-2,000 *C*

From the service supplied to Madame du Barry on 29 August 1771, which was designed by Auguste de St. Aubin and consisted of 322 pieces.

A Sèvres ecuelle stand, painted with 'bleu lapis' imitation basketwork and interspersed with garlands of coloured garden flowers and with gilt dentil rim, minute rim chip, blue interlaced L mark enclosing the date letter G for 1759 and the painter's mark of Taillandier, 7½in (19.5cm).
£700-900 *C*

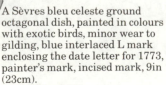

A Sèvres bleu celeste ground octagonal dish, painted in colours with exotic birds, minor wear to gilding, blue interlaced L mark enclosing the date letter for 1773, painter's mark, incised mark, 9in (23cm).
£300-400 *CNY*

A New Hall hard paste porcelain teapot stand, with chinoiserie painting, c1790, 8in (20cm) wide.
£100-120 *DEL*

A Nantgarw shell dish, from the Prince Regent service, central decoration of green urn containing rose, probably by William Billingsley, impressed mark Nantgarw C.W., c1819, 8in (20cm).
£800-950 *BRE*

Forty four Sèvres plates, painted with bouquets of flowers within blue foliage scroll borders and gilt rims, 7 with minor rim chips, blue interlaced L marks enclosing various date letters and with various painter's marks, 18thC, 10in (25cm).
£2,000-3,000 *C*

A Swansea 'duck egg' porcelain plate, from the Lady Seaton service, transfer printed, probably drawn by Henry Morris, unmarked, 10in (25cm).
£100-120 *BRE*

A pair of Sèvres plates with central flower sprays on bleu celeste grounds within gilt wells, wood frames, 9½in (23cm).
£150-200 *CSK*

A pair of Sèvres pattern plates painted with Marie Antoinette and Madame Dubocage, printed date marks, c1837, 9in (22.5cm).
£150-200 *CSK*

A Venice Cozzi plate, painted in the Chinese Imari style, with cell pattern in iron red, the blue ground border with iron red chrysanthemums and gilt scrolling foliage, and four 'famille verte' panels at intervals, iron red anchor mark, c1770, 9in (23cm).
£600-800 *CG*

This pattern is not recorded in Stazzi, but is presumably one of the many replacement pieces for the products of other manufacturers at which Cozzi were so adept.

SWANSEA PORCELAIN

★ factory produced high quality soft-paste porcelain from 1814-22

★ factory started by Dillwyn, Billingsley and Walker

★ superb translucent body, excellent glaze

★ in many ways one of the best porcelain bodies produced in the British Isles

★ also noted for delicacy of flower painting, usually attributed to Billingsley although much was obviously done by other decorators including Pollard and Morris

★ a close study of marked pieces will give one an idea of Billingsley's work but unless actually signed by him pieces should be marked 'possibly by Billingsley'

★ on pieces moulded with the floral cartouches the moulding can be detected on the other side of the rim, unlike the heavier Coalport wares which later utilised same moulds

★ especially notable are figure and bird paintings by T Baxter

★ the Swansea mark often faked, particularly on French porcelain at the end of the 19th, beginning of the 20thC

★ in 1816 Billingsley left to start up again at Nantgarw

★ many pieces were decorated in London studios

A Swansea square dish, with multiple floral decoration, unmarked, c1830, 8in (20cm).
£600-650 *BRE*

A rare pair of Swansea crested shell dishes, Mandarin pattern, painted in polychrome enamels, the borders with coloured bird on branch panels and various designs in rouge de fer, gilt, 8½in (20cm).
£1,400-1,800 *GSP*

A Worcester Blind Earl plate, enriched in green and puce and painted with scattered flower sprays, with scalloped gilt rim, c1765, 7½in (18cm).
£500-700 *CNY*

Three Tournai ornithological plates, painted with brightly coloured birds in landscape vignettes, blue crossed swords and star marks and various incised marks, c1775, 9in (23cm).
£600-800 *C*

A Vienna cabinet plate, painted with a young girl attended by Cupid, inscribed in gilt, impressed mark Colln. Meissen, 9½in (25cm).
£80-120 *HSS*

A Worcester fluted dish, the centre painted with 3 butterflies in colours, the fluted rim with trailing flowering plants divided by blue panels enriched in gilding, blue seal mark, c1760, 10in (25cm).
£600-800 *CNY*

A Worcester blue and white foliage moulded dish, rim chip to underside, c1765, 11in (27.5cm).
£900-1,100 *C*

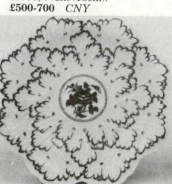

A fine Worcester dessert plate, transfer printed in black, washed in rich coloured enamels with 'Milking Scene No.1' by Robert Hancock, after an engraving by Luke Sullivan, the border enamelled with puce scrolls suspending gilt husks, the rim edged in gold, 7in (17.5cm).
£950-1,200 *TEN*

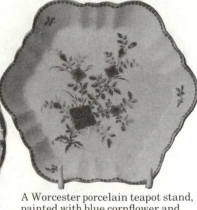

A Worcester blue scale plate painted in the atelier of James Giles in iron red, blue square seal mark, c1770, 8½in (21cm).
£300-400 *C*

A Worcester fluted blue scale dish, minor wear, blue seal mark, museum no.V78, c1765, 12in (30.5cm).
£300-500 *CNY*

A Worcester porcelain teapot stand, painted with blue cornflower and gold, crescent mark, 18thC, 6in (15cm).
£90-130 *DEL*

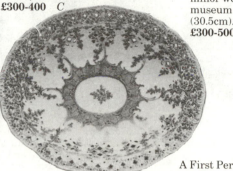

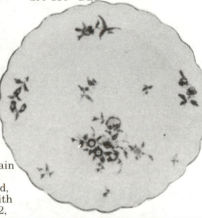

A Worcester pierced oval fruit dish, c1770, 12in (30cm).
£1,000-1,500 *CNY*

A First Period Worcester porcelain small dish of circular form with fluted and scallop rim, in iron red, purple, green and yellow, and with brown painted line border, c1772, 8in (19cm).
£60-80 *HSS*

A Worcester dish from the Duke of Gloucester service, lavishly painted within blue and gilt scroll, minor rim chip restoration, gold crescent mark, c1770, 12in (29.5cm).
£1,500-2,000 *C*

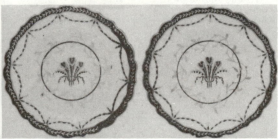

A pair of Flight Period Worcester plates with indented rims, in underglaze blue and gold, late 18thC, 9in (22.5cm).
£300-500 *Bea*

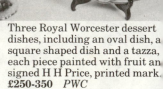

A Worcester apple green ground pierced oval footed dish, painted by the Spotted Fruit Painter, c1770, 12in (30cm).
£800-1,200 *CNY*

Three Royal Worcester dessert dishes, including an oval dish, a square shaped dish and a tazza, each piece painted with fruit an signed H H Price, printed mark.
£250-350 *PWC*

A Royal Worcester plate with pierced white and gilt border with 'jewelled pearls', painted by R F Perling after Herring, inscribed on the back 'after Herring by R F Perling', impressed mark, 9½in (23.5cm).
£80-120 *L*

A Royal Worcester circular dish, painted by C H C Baldwyn, signed, on a sky blue ground, printed mark in green for 1902 and Leadless Glaze, 12in (30cm).
£1,200-1,500 *L*

A Royal Worcester plate, painted, signed on the back 'D Perry', within a gilt dentil rim, mark in gold and Fine Bone China 1965, 11in (27cm).
£80-120 *L*

An English porcelain cabinet plate, with gilt scrolls on a blue ground, pattern 865 in puce, possibly Coalport, early 19thC, 9½in (24cm).
£60-80 *HSS*

A Chamberlain's Worcester two handled tray, finely painted with Buckingham Palace within a border encrusted with coloured shells and seaweed and a moulded gilt scroll rim, cracks to underside, script mark in puce, c1840, 13½in (33.5cm) wide.
£1,000-1,500 *C*

Cf Geoffrey A Godden, Chamberlain Worcester Porcelains, *pls 334 and 335.*

A First Period Worcester porcelain kidney shaped dish, painted in pink, blue, green, iron red and yellow and with gilt line borders, paint slightly worn, 11½in (28.5cm).
£180-220 *HSS*

A Royal Worcester cabinet plate, by E Barker, signed, within a tooled matt gilt border, printed mark, pattern Z1012, date code for 1935, 4½in (10.5cm).
£200-280 *N*

A large plate with cat and dog scene 'Oh Chase Me', signed 'Louis Wain'.
£145-190 *JD*

A Victorian bone china cake stand, in green and gold with pink floral design, 9½in (23.5cm) diam.
£20-50 *DEL*

Three from a set of 7 Spode botanical decorated plates, with a yellow ground, c1810.
£2,300-2,800 *JUD*

A Continental porcelain circular dish, mounted in scrolling-foliate gilt-metal handles and rim, 19½in (48cm).
£150-200 *CSK*

A porcelain teapot stand, with relief moulding, c1825, 7in (17.5cm).
£40-60 *DEL*

Ice Pails

A pair of Berlin two handled ice pails of Antique Zierrath pattern, the angular handles enriched with gilding and with ribbon ties, blue sceptre mark and various impressed numbers, c1780, 6½in (16cm).
£1,500-2,000 *C*

A pair of Meissen ornithological two handled wine coolers, one handle with rim chips, blue crossed swords marks, one with star and numeral 4, mid 18thC, 8in (19.5cm).
£1,500-2,000 *C*

Inkwells

A Paris oviform ice pail, cover and liner, with gilt satyr's mask handles, handles damaged, c1810, 15in (37.5cm).
£250-350 *C*

A Caughley blue and white inkwell, c1780, 2in (5cm).
£500-550 *VEN*

A Sèvres porcelain ormolu mounted inkstand, with ormolu mounts and handle, standing on 3 scroll feet, 9in (23cm) diam.
£250-350 *Bea*

Jardinières

A large Worcester jardinière, with tin liner, slight chipping, printed and impressed marks, pattern no.1233, 20in (49cm) wide.
£700-900 *OT*

A Sèvres pattern gilt bronze oval two handled jardinière of flared form, the gilt bronze mount to the rim joined to the pierced four footed base by berried foliage scroll handles with male mask terminals, c1860, 18in (44.5cm).
£800-1,000 *C*

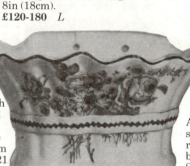

A Royal Worcester circular jardinière, in apricot, outlined with gilding on a basket pattern ground, below a green and gilt basket work border, printed mark in green, 1902, 8in (18cm).
£120-180 *L*

A Royal Worcester jardinière, the handles modelled as gilt flowers on mock giltwood pierced stand, printed and impressed marks, 7in (17.5cm).
£120-180 *CSK*

A Chelsea fluted D shaped bough pot, with a yellow moulded band enriched with puce diamond pattern beneath a chocolate line rim, the top pierced, cracks to rim and base, red anchor mark and 21 c1755, 7½in (18.5cm).
£400-600 *C*

A Spode tub shaped jardinière and stand, with gilt dolphin mask and ring handles, wide gilt borders and bands of dentil pattern, marked Spode 1926 in red, 4½in (12cm).
£120-180 *L*

A large Royal Worcester jardinière painted by W Powell, signed, JH monogram, 10½in (26cm) diam. ▷
£250-350 *Re*

A Belleek lustrous cream ground jardinière of lobed tapering shape, the shoulders with fine applied decoration, black transfer mark to base, 10in (25cm) diam.
£400-600 *WIL*

Jugs

A Caughley blue and white jug with Fisherman pattern decoration, c1785, 8½in (21cm).
£350-425 *VEN* ▷

◁

A lustre jug with Adam Buck decoration in burgundy, c1850, 4in (10cm).
£25-35 *VEN*

A Caughley blue and white jug with floral design, c1780, 6in (15cm).
£200-250   *VEN*

A Swansea 'duck egg' porcelain creamer, with gilded decoration and band of lavender blue surrounding body, unmarked, pattern 649, c1817.
£350-400   *BRE*

A porcelain pitcher, probably by the American China Manufactury, Philadelphia, Pennsylvania, each side enamelled in black with river scene, gilt decoration on rim, spout and handle, firing defect, c1826-38, 9½in (23.5cm).
£800-1,200   *CNY*

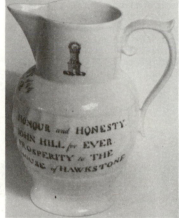

A Meissen octagonal jug and cover, painted in a bright palette, restored, blue caduceus mark and incised cross of J D Rehschuh, c1730, 6in (15cm).
£700-900   *C*

A Coalport Imari pattern jug, c1810, 8in (20cm).
£450-550   *JUD*

A Coalport Election jug, c1796, 9in (22cm).
£1,200-1,600   *SA*

Two brothers, William Hill and John Hill, fought each other in the famous Shropshire election of 1796. John Hill was successful. The family squabble is said to have cost £75,000.

A Philip Christian's Liverpool porcelain helmet shaped cream jug, with flowers and sprigs, c1770, 4in (10cm).
£350-450   *DEL*

A Meissen yellow ground hot milk jug and cover, with contemporary French silver gilt mount, the hinged mount with foliate thumbpiece, blue crossed swords, décharge of Louis Robin, Fermier Général 1738-44, 5in (12.5cm).
£3,000-4,000   *C*

A very large early Worcester sparrow beak jug, with chinoiserie decoration, c1755, 8in (20cm).
£3,000-4,000   *SA*

A Meissen jug with angled scroll handle, the scroll moulded lip and handle heightened in gilt, the rim with gilt fruiting branch design, blue crossed swords and dot mark, c1760's, 5½in (13.5cm).
£250-350   *Bon*

A Sèvres baluster jug and cover with quatrefoil basin, painted with spiralling bands of 'bleu nouveau' and gilt chain pattern with gilt laurel borders, basin cracked, c1780, jug 7½in (19cm).
£400-600 *C*

A Meissen baluster hot milk jug with fluted spout and shell and scroll handle, painted 'en camaïeu rose', blue crossed swords mark and gilder's mark Z, c1740, 5in (12cm).
£600-800 *C*

A Worcester blue and white baluster cream jug, painted with The Peony Pattern, painter's mark, c1758, 3in (7.5cm).
£250-350 *C*

A Grainger Worcester jug, the body superbly painted in the manner of Thomas Steel, unmarked, c1820, 3in (7.5cm).
£200-300 *BS*

A Worcester blue and white cabbage leaf moulded jug, the bulbous body moulded with overlapping cabbage leaves and painted in blue, the cylindrical neck with stylised foliage, with loop handle, c1760, 8in (20cm).
£300-500 *CNY*

A large Dr Wall period Worcester mask head jug, painted with sprays of English flowers, c1770, 9in (23cm).
£4,600-5,000 *SA*

A Royal Worcester jug of flattened form, decorated in high relief with male and female mediaeval heads in iron colour, the spout in the form of an open visor in iron colour and gold, the scroll handle in mauve, green and brown, printed mark in green and 62 for 1862, 10in (25cm).
£200-300 *L*

A First Period Worcester cabbage leaf jug, decorated in coloured enamels, with gilt line border and mask moulded spout, 7in (17.5cm).
£600-800 *HSS*

A Flight & Barr Worcester milk jug with scroll handle, incised B and script mark, c1800, 9in (23cm).
£150-200 *CSK*

Mugs

An English porcelain oviform jug with angular loop handle, inscribed in gilt 'T*WEBSTER 1821', flanked by a mock coat of arms with the inscription 'The Hand that reveals, & the Heart that conceals', the reverse with another coat of arms inscribed 'Success to Trade', some slight rubbing, c1821, 8½in (21.5cm).
£250-350   *C*

A porcelain cabbage leaf moulded mask jug, painted in 'famille rose' palette, with Orientals by a vase in a fenced garden, Baddeley & Fletcher's Factory, c1780, 5in (12cm).
£300-400   *C*

A Bow flared cylindrical mug with moulded loop handle, painted in 'famille rose' palette, c1752, 3½in (9cm).
£500-700   *C*

A Caughley outside decorated cylindrical mug, painted in sepia with the floral initial 'C' in blue and gold, star crack to base, c1795, 5½in (14cm).
£300-400   *C*

A very fine Dr Wall mug, transfer printed in black with a named portrait of Frederick the Great, the print signed 'R.H. Worcester' and dated 1757, known as the King of Prussia mug, 5in (12cm).
£1,000-1,250   *SA*

A Worcester blue and white cylindrical mug, with grooved loop handle, blue crescent mark, c1765, 6in (15cm).
£600-800   *C*

A Worcester baluster mug, gilt with the monogram 'GG' with the motto 'Amity', minute crack to base of handle, c1770, 3½in(9cm).
£700-1,000   *C*

A Worcester Imari pattern armorial mug, painted with vertical panels of flowering shrubs divided by blue bands, gilt with scrolling foliage, reserved with a crest and arms, the interior with a gilt C scroll rim, blue square seal mark, c1770, 3½in (9cm).
£600-800   *C*

A Worcester blue and white cylindrical mug, transfer printed, with loop handle, blue crescent mark, c1765, 6in (15cm).
£250-350   *CNY*

A Worcester blue scale mug, painted with exotic birds among shrubs and trees and with butterflies and insects, between gilt vase and mirror shaped cartouches, between gilt line rims, blue square seal mark, c1770, 3½in (9cm).
£800-1,000   *C*

A Worcester blue scale mug, painted with exotic birds and butterflies, within gilt vase and mirror shaped cartouches, blue crescent mark, c1770, 5in (12cm).
£800-1,200 *C*

A Worcester, Grainger Lee & Co., mug, painted with a view of Worcester Cathedral, within a gilt cartouche, script mark in iron red, c1815, 3in (8cm).
£300-350 *C*

A First Period Worcester mug of tapering cylindrical form, printed in blue with La Promenade Chinoise and La Peche, grooved loop handle, crescent mark in blue, 4½in (12cm).
£180-220 *HSS*

A porcelain bell shaped mug with grooved loop handle, painted in blue with an extensive chinoiserie landscape, diaper and foliate border, disguised numeral mark in blue, Brownlow Hill, c1756.
£700-900 *HSS*

A Worcester mug of Lord Henry Thynne type, blue crescent mark, c1775, 5in (12.5cm).
£1,000-1,500 *C*

A small First Period Worcester mug of cylindrical form, painted in blue and gilt, with grooved loop handle, 3½in (9cm).
£80-120 *HSS*

Plaques

A Berlin rectangular plaque, painted after F Sturm, impressed sceptre and KPM marks, ebonised wood frame, c1880, 12 by 10in (31.5 by 25.5cm).
£500-700 *C*

A KPM porcelain plaque, painted with a portrait of Ruth, named on reverse, impressed KPM and incised numerals, 13 by 8in (32.5 by 19cm).
£700-900 *Bon*

A Berlin rectangular plaque, painted with The Penitent Magdalen after Battoni, by C A Lippold signed, the reverse inscribed in script, Die Magdalena des Battoni, Original copie von C A Lippold 1853, impressed sceptre, KPM and H mark, giltwood frame, 12 by 15in (30 by 38cm).
£1,000-1,500 *C*

An English porcelain plaque painted with a brightly coloured bird perched on a branch in a river landscape, and another plaque painted with a cherub painting a portrait, both in wood frames, 4½in (11cm) and 5in (12.5cm).
£200-300 *CSK*

A Berlin rectangular plaque, painted after P Barthel with The Madonna, seated gazing down at the Infant Child held in her lap, impressed marks and date code for 1904, giltwood frame, 16 by 10in (40 by 25cm).
£3,500-4,500   *C*

A Berlin KPM large rectangular plaque, painted in bluish grey with battleships at war on high seas, inscribed above 'St. Vincent' and below '30 September 1681', impressed sceptre, KPM and incised marks, c1880, 32 by 20in (80 by 50cm).
£2,000-3,000   *CNY*

A Berlin Plaque, The Madonna and Child enthroned, signed 'Wagner', impressed sceptre and KPM, carved gilt frame, 9½ by 6½in (24 by 16cm).
£350-450   *L*

A Berlin porcelain plaque, painted with a draped nymph on a flower strewn headland, with water and cliffs beyond, impressed KPM and sceptre marks, impressed numerals, late 19thC, 9 by 16in (22.5 by 15cm).
£500-700   *DWB*

A Danish porcelain bakeboard, painted in colours with bouquets of summer flowers, within a tied reeded and husk border, impressed and painted marks Rorstrand, NB, made for an exhibition in 1937, 32½in (81cm) long, with a mahogany stand as a table with cabriole legs.
£800-1,000   *HSS*

A Dresden plaque, painted after Gerard Terborch, in carved and gilt frame, crossed swords mark in underglaze blue, 19thC, 17 by 15in (43 by 38cm).
£2,000-2,500 *L*

A pair of English porcelain plaques, c1835, 8½in (21cm).
£700-1,000 *DL*

A Fürstenburg white biscuit oval plaque, modelled with a portrait bust of J H C v Selchow to the left with glazed border inscribed on the reverse with name and F. NO. 1, minor repair at back, c1782, 3in (7.5cm).
£80-120 *C*

A French plaque painted by Lucien Levy with an Eastern scene, signed, carved giltwood frame, late 19thC, 13 by 9in (32 by 22cm).
£400-600 *C*

A German porcelain plaque, painted after Randall with 2 cockatoos and a parrot perched on a knarled tree stump among foliage, c1880, 14½ by 12½in (36 by 30.5cm).
£500-800 *C*

A German porcelain allegorical plaque, painted after Shumann, with 'The Three Fates', framed, impressed numerals and signs of erasure, 12½ by 9½in (31.5 by 24cm) overall.
£400-600 *Bon*

A German porcelain plaque, painted with a classical scene, painted on the base K.P.M. under a star, 9½in (23cm).
£200-300 *Bea*

A Naples porcelain wall plaque, of domed form, the central panel moulded with classical mythological figures in a romantic landscape, within a border moulded with trophies of arms and musical items, heightened in colours and gilt, within moulded ebonised frame, crowned N in underglaze blue, 19½in (48cm).
£400-500 *HSS*

A Vienna pierced bordered rectangular tray, painted with Eleanor & King Edward I, 14½in (35cm).
£400-500 *CSK*

A Continental porcelain oval plaque, painted by Bergler after Rembrandt, with a woman wearing green plumed hat and red dress, with gilt surround, and blue porcelain border heightened with a raised gilt bird and spandrel design, gilt wood frame, porcelain border painted with blue Vienna beehive mark, 13½ by 10½in (33 by 26cm).
£700-1,000 *Bon*

A Royal Worcester oval plaque, painted by John Stinton, signed, with cattle watering at a river, printed mark in puce, 1906, 6½ by 9½in (16 by 24.5cm).
£800-1,200 *CSK*

A Vienna pierced bordered tray, painted with Cleopatra, Mark Antony and attendants, on various coloured grounds, painted blue beehive mark, 14in (35cm).
£300-500 *CSK*

A porcelain plaque, painted with an interior depicting Othello in the presence of the Doge, reserved within a shaped rectangular panel on a stippled gold ground with oval and diamond panels and scrolling foliage, complete with contemporary gold painted and plush frame, 20in (49cm).
£800-1,200 *Bea*

Pots

A pair of Derby D shaped bough pots, painted in the manner of Dodson, with scroll feet and handles, printed crown and circle marks, Robert Bloor & Co., one foot chipped, c1825, 7½in (18.5cm).
£400-600 *C*

A very rare Caughley blue and white artichoke pot and lid, with Fisherman pattern decoration, 3½in (8.5cm).
£110-150 *VEN*

A Doccia armorial pomade pot and cover, painted with accollé coats of arms within puce baroque scroll cartouches beneath a black lined purple mantling and gilt coronet, the reverse with a finely painted bouquet of flowers and with gilt foliage, the cover similarly decorated with flower finial, chips to flower, c1750, 6½in (16.5cm).
£3,000-5,000 *CG*

Sauceboats

A very rare Derby cow creamer jug with floral decoration, slightly damaged, c1764, 3in (7.5cm).
£450-550 *VEN*

A Liverpool helmet shaped cream jug, with bridged scroll handle, the interior with iron red loop, dot and line pattern, on a circular domed foot, Philip Christian's factory, some minute chips and staining to rim, c1770, 4in (10cm).
£250-350 *C*

A rare small size New Hall helmet shaped cream jug with floral decoration, pattern 67, c1785, 4in (10cm).
£150-250 *VEN*

A Bow blue and white double lipped two-handled sauceboat, painted in a bright blue, c1750, 7½in (18cm) wide.
£400-500 *C*

A Bow blue and white peach-shaped butter boat, with tendril handle forming three short feet and painted with insects, flowers and leaves, c1765, 3in (7.5cm) wide.
£250-350 *CSK*

A Bow blue and white fluted oval sauceboat, painted within moulded flower and foliage cartouches, on a fluted oval foot, slight rim chips, crack beneath handle, impressed T mark, c1758, 7½in (18cm) wide.
£150-200 *C*

A Meissen pear-shaped cream pot and cover, with fluted ground and handle set to one side, painted with figures in an extensive harbour landscape, with silver chain attachment to cover, the pine cover finial restuck, blue crossed swords mark, c1740, 5½in (14cm).
£1,200-1,800 *CG*

A Worcester oval sauceboat of small size, painted with a bird in a fenced garden, the oval foot moulded with drapery swags, the interior with a flowering branch within a green diaper border, c1754, 6½in (16.5cm) wide.
£600-800 *C*

A pair of Worcester blue and white sauceboats, of silver shape, the exterior painted in the Oriental style, the interior with a boy fishing by a rock, the flaring rims with flowering foliage and insects, one damaged, c1755, 8in (19.5cm) long.
£400-600 *CNY*

An early Worcester blue and white cream boat, moulded on each side with foliate scroll work enclosing chinoiserie landscape in underglaze blue, workman's mark, c1760, 4½in (11.5cm) wide.
£950-1,500 *TW*

An almost identical cream boat is illustrated in Simon Spero's Price Guide to 18th Century Porcelain, *p. 122.*

A Worcester blue and white faceted oval cream boat, with double scroll handle painted with The Root Pattern, painter's mark, c1758, 4in (10cm) wide.
£600-800 *C*

A Worcester spirally moulded milk jug of flared form, painted in the 'famille rose' style with Orientals, minute blemishes to rim, c1770, 3½in (9cm).
£300-400 *C*

A First Period Worcester porcelain sauceboat, moulded with overlapping leaves, and with rustic loop handle, painted in colours on a white ground with green tinted borders, initialled P in red, c1760, 4in (10cm).
£220-280 *HSS*

A pair of Worcester diaper-moulded oval sauceboats, painted with brightly coloured aggravated birds, the interiors with scattered flower sprays, the gadrooned rims enriched in puce, c1765, 8½in (20.5cm) wide.
£2,500-3,000 *C*

Services

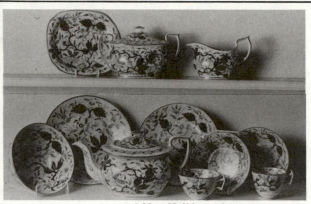

A New Hall bone china 26 piece tea
service, complete and in mint
condition, pattern no. 1542, c1815.
£1,200-1,500 *VEN*

An extensive Spode stone china
dinner service, printed in blue with
the Grasshopper pattern, including
one deep platter, 2 others, 2 smaller,
2 of small size, 2 sauce tureens,
covers and stands, 12 side plates, 24
dinner plates and 12 soup plates,
blue mark Spode Stone China with
pseudo Chinese seal mark, c1815.
£900-1,300 *Bon*

A good Copeland dessert service,
decorated in 18thC Meissen style,
with vignettes of Watteauesque
lovers, including 15 plates, 3 tall
circular tazze, and 5 low dishes, one
plate cracked, one dish cracked, 2
tazze broken, printed green factory
marks, third quarter 19thC.
£700-900 *Bon*

A Belleek white glazed coral
moulded cabaret set, comprising: a
teapot and cover, a milk jug, a sugar
bowl, 3 teacups, 3 saucers, and an
oval tray.   ▷
£500-700 *CSK*

A Coalport yellow ground supper
set, comprising: a circular bowl and
cover with knob finial, 4 trapezoidal
dishes, c1820, 20in (51cm).
£500-700 *CNY*

A Coalport porcelain dessert
service, comprising: 2 comports, 4
low stands and 12 plates, some
damage, printed Salopian mark,
c1875.
£300-500 *Bea*

A Chamberlain's type dessert
service, decorated in Imari style
with flowers, 18 plates, 4 oval dishes
and one other larger, 7 plates
cracked, one dish damaged, 19thC.
£800-1,000 *DWB*

◁ A Chelsea Derby Harlequin tea and
coffee service, of 28 pieces,
comprising: teapot on stand, lidded
sucrier and cream jug, 2 shallow
bowls, 8 teacups, 7 coffee cups and 8
saucers, some pieces damaged, 18
pieces marked with gold anchor and
D mark for 1769-75 and 10 marked
with blue painted Crown and Derby
mark for 1770-82.
£700-900 *MN*

Some pieces as found (a.f.)

A Davenport part dinner service, decorated in Imari colours, comprising: 2 vegetable dishes and 2 covers, a sauce tureen, cover and stand, a fruit dish, 2 oval dishes, 3 medium plates and 12 side plates, printed marks, pattern no. 51, c1850-70.
£700-900   *WW*

A Davenport armorial part dessert service, comprising: 12 plates, 2 low comports, one high comport, 2 rectangular dishes and 2 preserve comports and covers, each raised on a gilded acanthus stem with triform base, 19thC.
£2,000-2,500   *BS*

A Derby dinner service, painted in blue, ochre, green and gilt, comprising: oval soup tureen and cover, 3 square vegetable dishes, one lacking cover, sauce tureen and cover, 10 various oval meat dishes and stands, 25 10in (25cm) plates, 8 soup plates, 12 7in (17.5cm) plates, several pieces oven stained and some cracked, red crown over crossed batons over D mark.
£800-1,200   *PWC*

A Royal Crown Derby service for 12, including cups, saucers, 2 cake plates, teapot, cream jug and covered sugar basin, pattern no. 2451/L/M.
£400-500   *CW*

A Meissen part tea service, comprising: a teapot and cover with silver chain attachment with branch handle and spout, chip to spout, 7½in (19cm) wide, a pear-shaped milk jug and cover, chip to finial, a sugar bowl and cover, a waste bowl, 6½in (16.5cm) diam., an octagonal small dish, 2 shaped oval spoon trays, 12 cups, 12 saucers, blue crossed swords and dot marks, Pressnummer 30, c1765.
£1,500-2,000   *CNY*

A Dresden part dessert service, the
trellis pierced borders finely
moulded with flowers and foliage,
comprising: 13 plates, 4 low
comports and 2 high comports,
19thC.
£1,500-2,000 *BS*

A Meissen ornithological tea and
coffee service, comprising: a pear-
shaped coffee pot and a domed
cover, teapot and cover, finial
restuck, hot milk jug, circular slop
bowl, arched rectangular tea caddy
and cover, 4 coffee cups, 8 tea cups, 2
chipped, 12 saucers, blue crossed
swords marks and blue crossed
swords and star marks, 18thC.
£3,000-5,000 *C*

Three dishes and a pair of sauce
tureens, from a rare marked
Herculaneum porcelain dessert
service, decorated in red and gilt
Lotus pattern, c1805.
£800-1,000 *JUD*

A Royal Worcester dessert service,
painted by T Lockyer and
H H Price, comprising: 2 shaped
oval low stands, 2 shaped square
dishes, one with hair crack, 2 shell
shaped dishes, 12 plates, one
broken, one repaired and 2 with
hair cracks, signed, puce printed
marks and various date codes,
20thC, a pair of shaped rectangular
pickle dishes similarly painted by
A Schuck, 4½in (11cm) wide, 3
oblong octagonal dishes similarly
painted by E Townsend and
C Creese, all signed, puce printed
marks, various date codes, 20thC.
£1,000-1,500 *C*

A Sèvres cabaret set, in fitted
wooden box with red silk interior,
including two handled tray, teapot
and cover, sucrier and cover, milk
jug and cover, 2 cups and saucers,
each piece with panels painted and
signed by individual artists, each
panel outlined in tooled gilt on
overall mazarine blue grounds,
printed marks and date code for
1864.
£500-700 *Bon*

A Paris matt blue ground part coffee service, comprising: an oviform coffee pot and cover, a hot water jug, a sugar bowl and cover, 5 coffee cups, one damaged, one rubbed, and 5 saucers, one damaged, c1815.
£500-700   *C*

A Paris Faubourg St. Denis part tea service with gilt dentil rims, comprising: teapot and cover, a hot milk jug, a circular sugar bowl and cover with cherry finial, 6 cups and saucers, spout of teapot restuck, one cup handle restored, blue H marks of Pierre Antoine Hannong, 1771-6.
£700-900   *C*

A Ridgway pink ground part dessert service, comprising: an oval two-handled centre dish, chip to rim, 2 circular two-handled sauce tureens, covers and fixed stands, 2 oval two-handled dishes, 2 lozenge shaped two-handled dishes, 2 shaped square two-handled dishes, one repaired, 17 plates, 4 cracked, pattern no. 1321, 1825-30.
£1,200-1,800   *C*

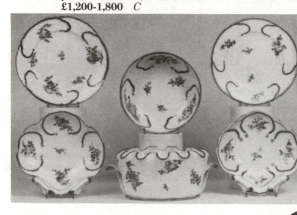

A Sèvres 'feulle de choux' part dinner service, comprising: 3 seaux crenellés, 2 circular deep bowls, 4 shell shaped dishes with scroll handles, 3 shallow circular bowls, 3 slightly smaller shallow bowls, 72 dinner plates, 12 with rim chips, blue interlaced L marks enclosing various painter's and gilder's marks, 18thC.
£8,000-12,000   *C*

A Sèvres pattern royal blue ground part coffee service, comprising: a sugar bowl and cover, finial replaced, and 6 coffee cans and saucers, imitation interlaced L and initial marks, c1860.
£1,000-1,500   *C*

A Sèvres pattern gold ground tête à tête, painted with named French views, on a brilliant gold ground, comprising: an oviform coffee pot and cover, a sugar bowl and cover, a cream jug, 2 flared coffee cups and saucers and a circular tray, mock M. Imple. de Sèvres marks, c1900, the tray 14in (35cm) diam.
£400-600   *C*

A Sèvres dessert service, service fond blue lapis corbeille de fleurs, the 'blue lapis' border speckled with gilt and with gilt rims comprising: an oval sauce tureen, cover and fixed stand, 4 circular pedestal bowls on spreading gilt socles, the interiors with symmetrical trailing grape and vine leaves, 60 plates, blue printed interlacked L marks enclosing a fleur de lys, Sèvres and 23 for 1823, various incised marks, painted inside the foot rim in colours with an exact date, a painter's mark, a gilder's date and some with gilder's marks.
£30,000-50,000 *C*

Provenance: S.E.M. le Vicomte de Chateaubriand. The service was delivered upon the order of The Minister of the King's Household to the Vicomte de Chateaubriand, the Minister for Foreign Affairs on the 21st August 1823. The order was a supplement to the service previously ordered in two different batches whilst Chateaubriand was Ambassador to England. The previous orders were delivered on 15th April 1822 and 2nd May 1822.

A Staffordshire porcelain botanical part dessert service, comprising: a sauce tureen, cover and fixed stand, stained, cover riveted, 2 oval dishes, 2 quatrefoil dishes, 3 trefoil dishes, one cracked, a shaped oval dish, riveted, 17 plates, 7 damaged, each specimen named in iron red in script, perhaps Mayer and Newbold, c1820.
£700-900 *C*

A 'Vienna' gold ground tête à tête, decorated with scenes from Classical mythology reserved on gold ciselé grounds, comprising: a coffee pot and cover on 3 scroll feet, a hot milk jug and cover on 3 scroll feet, minor chip to spout, a circular sugar bowl and cover, finial repaired and chip to rim of cover, and 2 cylindrical cups and saucers, on an oblong octagonal tray, blue beehive marks, c1880, the tray 13in (13.5cm) wide.
£800-1,200 *C*

A Flight and Barr Worcester part tea service, swirl moulded in purple, green and gilt, comprising: a sucrier and cover, a saucer dish, 6 tea bowls, 4 coffee cups and 5 saucers, one saucer repaired, 2 tea bowls chipped, c1792-1800.
£300-500 *WW*

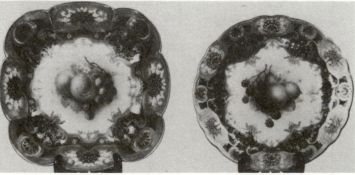

A Royal Worcester dessert service, painted by Shuck, on dark blue and pink grounds, comprising: 2 square shaped dishes, 2 circular dishes, 2 oval shaped dishes and 12 dessert plates, printed marks, c1920.
£2,000-2,500 *CSK*

A Nantgarw part dessert service, painted with pink roses and scattered insects within a moulded border, with gilt dentil rims, comprising: a circular two-handled centre dish with gilt foliage bands to the foot, a pair of cushion-shaped dishes, 3 oval dishes, 21 plates, one riveted, 5 cracked, gilding rubbed, impressed Nant Garw C.W. marks, c1820.
£2,000-3,000 *C*

A First Period Worcester tea and coffee service, painted in Kakiemon style in mirror and vase shape panels with gilt scroll borders on a blue scale pattern ground, square seal mark in underglaze blue, comprising:
a teapot and cover with floral knop, 6½in (16.5cm). **£250-350**
a sugar basin and cover with floral knop, 5½in (13cm). **£200-250**
a bowl, 6½in (16.5cm). **£120-150**
a tea cup, coffee cup and saucer. **£200-250**
a tea cup, coffee cup and saucer. **£200-250** *L*

A quartet of dessert serving dishes, from an important Flight, Barr & Barr Worcester service, with turquoise ground and finely burnished gilding, comprising:
a pair of plates **£350-450**
a square dish **£350-450**
a comport **£450-550** *JUD*

A Chamberlain's Worcester part dessert service, on dark blue and gilt vermicule ground comprising: a sauce tureen, cover and stand, 3 pedestal dishes with pierced handles and 12 dessert plates, the stand with printed mark, c1845.
£500-700 *CSK*

Sucriers

A Sèvres circular sugar bowl and cover, with gilt cherry finial, repair to finial and rim of cover, blue interlaced L marks enclosing date letters MM for 1790 and painter's mark of Fontaine and with gilder's mark Vincent âiné, 4½in (11cm).
£250-350 *C*

A Sèvres circular sugar bowl and cover, with gilt cherry finial, blue interlaced L mark enclosing the date letter aa for 1778 and painter's mark for Jacques Fontaine and gilder's mark of Pierre André Leguay, 4½in (11cm).
£200-300 *C*

This pattern was known at the factory as Rozes et Myrthes.

A Sèvres yellow ground sugar bowl and cover, with gilt berry finial, the borders painted with purple scrolling foliage, blue interlaced L marks, c1770, 4½in (11cm).
£400-500 *C*

Tankards

In the Ceramics section if there is only one measurement it refers to the height of the piece.

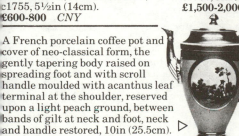

A small Meissen cylindrical tankard with gilt metal cover, the strap handle with scroll terminals enriched in puce, the gilt metal cover embossed with scrolls and flowerheads, with scroll thumbpiece, traces of blue crossed swords mark, Pressnummer 3, c1755, 5½in (14cm).
£600-800 *CNY*

A French porcelain coffee pot and cover of neo-classical form, the gently tapering body raised on spreading foot and with scroll handle moulded with acanthus leaf terminal at the shoulder, reserved upon a light peach ground, between bands of gilt at neck and foot, neck and handle restored, 10in (25.5cm).
£80-120 *Bon*

Tea & Coffee Pots

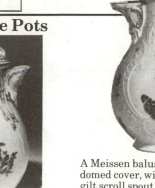

A Berlin baluster coffee pot and domed cover with bud finial, female mask spout and scroll handle painted predominantly in puce, green and gilt, blue sceptre mark, c1780, 9in (22.5cm).
£1,500-2,000 *CG*

A Hausmaler decorated Meissen coffee pot and cover with floral knop, with wish bone handle and scroll moulded spout picked out in gilt, damage, c1750.
£700-900 *DWB*

Cf W B Honey, German Porcelain, pt 11 for a coffee pot of the same shape and with a floral knop.

A Meissen baluster coffee pot and domed cover, with flower finial and gilt scroll spout and handle, cover cracked, blue crossed swords mark, c1745, 9½in (23cm).
£400-600 *C*

191

Two Meissen cockerel teapots and covers, modelled with incised feather markings, enriched in a brilliant palette, blue crossed swords and incised marks, c1860, 6in (15cm) long.
£500-700 *CNY*

A Meissen teapot and cover in the form of a cockerel, modelled as a crouching cockerel, the head forming the spout and the tail feathers the handle, enriched in bright enamels and gilt, the cover with seated dog finial, repair to beak, finial and rim of cover, blue crossed swords mark, c1775, 7in (18.5cm) wide.
£1,000-1,500 *CNY*

Cf Rückert, Meissener Porzellan, *fig. 1127, p. 277.*
Meissen models were repeated over many years. Early examples are almost invariably more valuable.

A Sèvres oviform teapot and cover, with flower finial, the handle gilt with stiff leaves and flowerheads, blue interlaced L marks enclosing the date letter 0 for 1767 and incised I, 6½in (16cm) wide.
£800-1,200 *C*

Tureens & Butter Tubs

A Berlin two-handled oval ornithological soup tureen and domed cover, blue sceptre marks and Pressnummer 35, c1760-70, 14½in (36cm) wide.
£1,500-2,000 *C*

A Chelsea apple tureen and a cover, naturally modelled and coloured in green and russet, the base modelled with a stalk with three green leaves, the cover with puce caterpillar finial, minute chips to two leaves, the base with red 3 mark, c1755, 4½in (10.5cm).
£3,000-5,000 *C*

Cf The Cheyne Book of Chelsea, *pl 15, nos. 307 and 308.*

A pair of Derby pigeon tureens and covers, incised feather markings enriched in tones of brown, puce, green and iron red, seated on basket moulded nests, applied with grasses and feathers, enriched in yellow, puce and green, minor chips, c1765, 8in (20.5cm) long.
£1,800-2,500 *CNY*

A Sèvres écuelle, cover and stand, painted with blue panels encrusté with white dots and gilt cell pattern, the finial modelled as a berried branch, blue interlaced L marks enclosing the date letters, the stand with date letter K for 1763 and the écuelle with small q for 1769 and both with painter's mark S of P A Méreau, the écuelle with incised CZ, 8in (20cm).
£1,500-2,500 *C*

A Meissen partridge tureen, with incised feather markings enriched in tones of grey, brown and iron red, seated on a basket moulded nest, applied with grasses, enriched in green, minor chip to beak, traces of blue crossed swords mark, painter's mark Q to both pieces, c1745, 6½in (16cm) long.
£800-1,200 *CNY*

A Longton Hall cos lettuce tureen and cover, the overlapping leaves enriched in green with cauliflower sprig finial, firing cracks, minor repair to rim of cover, finial reglued, c1755, 9in (22.5cm).
£2,000-3,000 *CNY*

A Meissen blue and white butter tub and cover, with pierced tab handles, rim slightly reduced, Pressnummer 23, c1740.
£350-450 *C*

Cf R Rückert: op. cit., fig. 527.

A Meissen dolphin tureen and cover, with bared teeth, its tail curled over its back with grey scales and coral mouth, minor chip repaired to cover, blue crossed swords mark, c1750, 9½in (24cm) long.
£1,500-2,000 *C*

Vases

A pair of baluster shaped continental porcelain vases and covers, printed on an apple green ground, the shoulders and bases with gilt scale pattern, 18in (45cm).
£300-400 *BWe*

A pair of Berlin two-handled baluster vases and covers, painted in colours with lovers on landscapes after Watteau, with slightly domed covers and berried finials, KPM mark, 13in (32cm).
£300-350 *C*

A Coalport porcelain two-handled pedestal vase and cover of ovoid form, painted with a continuous river landscape at sunset, slight damage, printed mark, 10in (25cm).
£40-60 *HSS*

A garniture of 3 Coalbrookdale vases, painted in colours, on a scroll moulded ground enriched in turquoise and gilt, on scroll and foliage moulded feet and square bases, enriched in green and gilt, some repairs to applied flowerheads and foliage, blue crossed swords mark to one the centre vase with blue C.D. mark, c1820, the centre vase 12in (30cm).
£600-800 *CNY*

A pair of Derby rococo scroll moulded vases of asymmetrical form, painted with peacocks and a magpie in wooded river landscapes, within moulded green and puce foliage cartouches, Wm Duesbury & Co., c1765, 8in (19.5cm).
£400-600 *C*

A Coalport goblet vase, painted with three views of Loch Lomond, with three gilt scroll handles, on baluster stem and circular shaped domed foot, printed mark in green and impressed mark for January 1908, 9in (22cm).
£250-300 *L*

A pair of Derby pink ground pot pourri vases and covers, painted in colours with butterflies and moths, named to the base, within gilt foliage surrounds on the pink ground, the pierced covers, shell moulded handles and flaring feet enriched in gilding with foliage, stars and dots, one cover repaired, part of inner rim broken, blue crown, crossed batons and D marks, impressed No. 2, c1775, 8in (20cm).
£700-900 *CNY*

A Crown Derby porcelain vase and cover, of ovoid form, with pierced scroll handles and pierced knop, painted en grisaille with portrait heads, reserved in oval medallions, with swags of husks in colours, and raised on a square base, printed mark in red, date code for 1890, 9in (22.5cm).
£200-250 *HSS*

A garniture of 3 Derby blue ground tapering oviform vases, with gilt winged swan's neck handles, the bodies richly gilt with a band of trailing oak branches, printed crown and circle marks, Robt Bloor & Co., c1830, 10 to 12in (25 to 30cm).
£600-800 *C*

A Meissen Hausmalerei tall baluster vase, with garlic neck, compressed body and spreading circular foot, painted in the workshop of F F Mayer von Pressnitz, enriched with gilding, blue crossed swords mark and I overgilt with B, the vase c1725, the base and decoration c1745, 12in (29.5cm).
£1,000-1,500 *C*

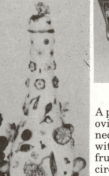

A pair of late Meissen slender oviform vases with tall cylindrical necks and domed covers, modelled with brightly coloured flowers and fruit, and painted with insects, the circular base outlined in gilt, 15in (37.5cm).
£200-300 *CSK*

A pair of Minton flared rectangular spill vases, with gilt fixed ring handles, enamelled and gilt in imitation of Chinese cloisonné, with dark blue, iron red and green geometric pattern cartouches on bright turquoise grounds, the brown glazed lower parts and scroll feet edged with gilding, one with impressed mark, c1880, 12in (30cm).
£1,000-1,500 *C*

A Meissen porcelain figural vase, painted with Watteauesque vignette and festooned with fruiting vine, on a naturalistic pedestal support and base, flanked by two cherubs, slight damage, blue crossed swords, impressed numerals, 19thC, 8½in (21cm).
£300-400 *Bon*

A pair of Meissen vases and covers, 19thC.
£550-650 *FHF*

A Samson copy of a Cantonese baluster vase and cover, in pinks and greens, c1820.
£1,700-2,000   *EA*

A Meissen bullet shaped vase and cover on stand, in blue with decorated panels.
£400-500   *FHF*

A Sèvres pattern and gilt metal-mounted oviform pot pourri vase and cover, one handle partially detached, the decoration signed J Violet, late 19thC, 29½in (74cm).
£1,800-2,200   *C*

A Samson 'famille verte' baluster vase and cover.
£400-600   *Bon*

A Sèvres pattern and gilt metal-mounted garniture, comprising 2 oviform pot pourri vases and covers and an oval centre dish, with gilt metal winged caryatid handles, the royal blue grounds reserved and decorated with pairs of courtiers in 18thC dress, the shaped high domed covers with gilt metal pineapple finials, and on gilt metal circular 4 footed bases, the decoration signed 'Dr Dubuis', late 19thC, 30in (74cm).
£4,000-6,000   *C*

A Sèvres pattern pink ground gilt metal-mounted tapering oviform two-handled vase and cover, painted with a youth and companion in a garden, the flared neck with pendant jewelling and foliage, the circular base cast with berried foliage and with 4 square feet, late 19thC, 17½in (43.5cm).
£300-400   *C*

A massive pair of Sèvres pattern metal-mounted turquoise-ground oviform vases with flared necks, with metal caryatid and foliage scroll handles, the rims with metal mounts, the 4 footed circular bases applied with 2 putti flanking a vase, one with part of rim lacking, the other with damage to the stem, last quarter 19thC, 33½in (84cm).
£4,000-6,000   *C*

A pair of Sèvres pattern ormolu-mounted cylindrical urns, with applied cherub's mask handles, the bodies decorated in colours with equestrian hunting scenes, with ormolu mounts to the rims and lower parts, on shaped stems and square bases, last quarter 19thC, 8in (20cm).
£400-500   *C*

A Swansea ovoid vase,
1813-22, 9in (22.5cm).
£150-200 *GSP*

A pair of Spode urn shaped pot
pourri vases, pierced weights and
covers, with moulded arched
overhandles, painted in an Imari
palette, circular blue feet gilt with
foliage, one with iron red mark and
pattern no. 2214, c1820, 5½in
(13.5cm).
£700-900 *C*

A pair of Sèvres pattern gilt metal
slender oviform vases, the bodies
decorated with scantily draped
maidens and Cupid, imitation
Sèvres and Chateau des Tuileries
marks, c1900, 22½in (56cm).
£800-1,200 *C*

A fine garniture of Spode vases of
trumpet shape, with sprays of
flowers, all on paw feet, marked
Spode pattern no.2575 in iron red,
c1820, 5in and 6in (12.5 and 15cm).
£2,000-2,400 *SA*

A Flight & Barr Worcester blue
ground spill vase, painted with a
band of coloured feathers above a
blue band gilt with foliage and
anthemion, c1805, 5in (12cm).
£350-450 *C*

A fine pair of Sèvres porcelain vases
and covers, the domed covers with
moulded ovoid finials, each with 4
pierced chain moulded handles,
beaded stems, fluted circular and
stepped square pedestal bases, each
painted with a half length portrait
of a lady in 18thC dress, in colours
within richly gilt border on a 'bleu
de ciel' ground, slight chips and
cracks, 18in (45cm).
£800-1,200 *HSS*

A Flight & Barr Worcester canary
yellow ground flared flower pot with
fixed gilt ring handles, painted in
sepia with a view of Worcester
Cathedral flanked by the Royal
China Manufactory, the base
inscribed 'A token of respect to the
Revd Mr Caradec. Barr Worcester
Porcelain Manufacturer to the
King', and with incised B mark,
c1805, 6½in (16cm).
£1,200-1,500 *C*

A pair of Dr Wall Period Worcester
vases, decorated upon a 'gros bleu'
ground with 2 panels enclosing
views of exotic birds in a landscape,
with tall buildings in the distance,
with elaborate gilt outlines, blue
open crescent mark, 6½in (16cm).
£1,600-2,000 *Bon*

A very fine and rare Flight, Barr & Barr vase, on a 'gros bleu' ground, the jewelled neck with cartouche of shells, c1815.
£2,200-2,700 *SA*

A Graingers Worcester slender oviform vase and cover, painted with cattle in a country landscape by John Stinton, 12in (30cm).
£250-350 *CSK*

A Worcester vase, by H Davis, showing sheep in a highland setting, 6in (15cm).
£500-600 *Wai*

A Hadleys Worcester two handled quatrefoil oviform vase, painted with a view of Worcester Rowing Club by W Powell, reverse printed and painted with a coat of arms dated May 4th 1905, printed mark, 4½in (11cm).
£180-220 *CSK*

A Barr, Flight & Barr Worcester vase and cover, on triple dolphin supports, the bowl brightly painted with flowers on a ground of scrolling foliage, the beaded cover with matching decoration, and griffin knop, some damage, printed and impressed marks, early 19thC, 6½in (16cm).
£500-700 *Bea*

A pair of Royal Worcester vases and covers in Sèvres style, with turquoise ground, painted by Josiah Rushton, one inscribed 'Femme de Thebes', signed 'J. Rushton after Ch. Landelle', the other inscribed 'Tsigane Valaque', signed 'J. Rushton after E. Vernet Lecomte', on square bases with incuse corners, on a rich turquoise ground, printed mark in black and date letter for 1870, 16in (39cm).
£1,800-2,200 *L*

Cf Henry Sandon, Royal Worcester Porcelain, pl 56 illustrates a pair of vases with identical panels by Josiah Rushton.

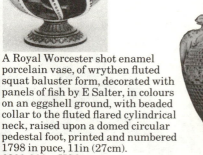

A Royal Worcester shot enamel porcelain vase, of wrythen fluted squat baluster form, decorated with panels of fish by E Salter, in colours on an eggshell ground, with beaded collar to the fluted flared cylindrical neck, raised upon a domed circular pedestal foot, printed and numbered 1798 in puce, 11in (27cm).
£200-300 *HSS*

A Royal Worcester reticulated oviform vase by George Owen, enriched with gilding, incised signature, pattern no.1969, gilt marks and date code for 1912, 7in (17cm).
£1,800-2,200 *C*

A Royal Worcester 'bamboo' vase formed as a section of bamboo, applied with a flowering twig handle, coloured in green and toned ivory, heightened in gilt, date code for 1891, 8in (20cm).
£80-120 *Bon*

A Royal Worcester reticulated globular vase in the manner of George Owen, the sides pierced with a band of pale blue honeycomb decoration within ivory bands of stylised ornament, inscribed in gilt on the base 'January 4th 1895', gilt printed marks and date code for 1895, 4½in (11cm).
£400-600   C

A Royal Worcester large vase and cover, the oviform body painted by C H C Baldwyn, signed, printed mark in green, 1899, 17in (43cm).
£1,200-1,800   L

A Royal Worcester vase and cover, painted by C H C Baldwyn, signed, with scroll handles, printed mark in green for 1900, 8½in (21cm).
£1,200-1,500   L

A Royal Worcester cylindrical vase, with shaded ivory ground, printed mark in puce for 1919, 5½in (14cm).
£60-80   L

A Royal Worcester porcelain vase and cover, the domed cover with acanthus bud knop, painted in colours and gilt with flower sprays on a blushed ivory ground, printed mark in purple, number 2303, date code for 1907, 11in (28cm).
£150-180   HSS

A Royal Worcester two handled slender baluster vase and cover with griffin handles, painted by H Davies, printed marks, c1903, 17in (42.5cm).
£2,200-3,000   CSK

A Royal Worcester porcelain vase and cover, painted in colours and gilt with bouquets of summer flowers on a blushed ivory ground, gilt line borders, damaged, printed mark in purple, number 2249, date code for 1903, 11½in (28.5cm).
£150-200   HSS

A Royal Worcester vase with overhead handle and gilt lion masks in relief, painted by J Stinton, signed, with a pheasant among foliage, printed mark in puce for 1912, 5in (12.5cm).
£100-150   L

A Royal Worcester vase and cover, with pierced neck painted with sheep in a highland landscape by H Davis, printed marks, c1920, 13in (33cm).
£2,200-2,800   CSK

A pair of Royal Worcester vases, with pierced yellow ground handles and flared necks, painted with gilt flowering vines on a blue ground, printed mark, 10in (25cm).
£250-350 *CSK*

A Royal Worcester cylindrical vase, painted with sheep, by H Davis, signed, on pierced and gilt scroll foot, printed mark in puce, 6½in (16cm).
£250-350 *L*

A pair of Royal Worcester vases, painted with flowering vines outlined in gilt on a white ground, printed marks, 12in (30cm).
£200-300 *CSK*

A fine Royal Worcester pot pourri vase and cover, painted with highland cattle by John Stinton, c1930.
£900-1,000 *SA*

An English porcelain pot pourri vase, slight damage, c1815, 12in (30cm).
£800-900 *JUD*

A Royal Worcester vase and cover by George Owen, the body pierced with a wide band of trellis pattern bordered with gilt scroll ornament and festoons, with pierced shoulders, neck, base and cover, griffin head and scroll handles, the square base with incuse corners, incised signature 'G. Owen' and printed mark in gold, 10½in (26.5cm).
£1,500-2,000 *L*

In the Ceramics section if there is only one measurement it refers to the height of the piece.

A pair of English porcelain blue ground campana vases, with gilt serpent handles painted within gilt octagonal cartouches flanked by gilt foliage and anthemion, pattern no.413, perhaps Ridgway, c1820, 6in (15cm).
£300-500 *C*

Lowestoft – *a brief history*

The Lowestoft factory commenced production by 1758 following earlier trials by 4 partners who had taken up the challenge after an earlier attempt by a local landowner, Hewlin Luson. The partners were Philip Walker, a tenant farmer on Luson's land, Obed Aldred, a bricklayer, Robert Browne the local blacksmith and James Richmond, merchant.

The partners converted Aldred's premises in Bell Lane, Lowestoft and ran some trials, apparently with a high failure rate. Browne, the manager of the fledgling factory appears to have taken employment at the Bow factory in order to gain experience and seems to have returned to Lowestoft in 1758 with both experience and a viable porcelain formula very similar to that in use at the Bow factory!

In January 1760 the partnership; trading as Walker and Co, took out their first newspaper advertisement and launched their wares on the open market.

It is possible, because of a number of dated pieces, to be reasonably accurate in dividing the Lowestoft output into various periods.

Early wares, c1759-60 are rare, popular and expensive. All are in blue and white as coloured wares were not introduced into general production until c1766. A similar date is hypothesised for the introduction of printed wares.

By 1761 the range of products had expanded enormously and encompassed most tewares, including rarities such as egg cups, salts and spoon trays. The wares of this first Middle Period, c1761-65, are generally well potted and painted in a crisp inky tone of blue with Chinese-style scenes.

In the latter half of the 1760s the amount of blue and white porcelain produced increased and both polychrome and printed wares were introduced. Again the patterns were usually based on Chinese originals or floral themes.

The period from 1770 to 1799 is known as the late period. The quality of painted blue and white patterns deteriorated and became stylised though some fine quality polychrome wares were produced.

Production ceased in 1799 though stock in hand continued to be sold for a year or 2 before the sale of factory equipment and buildings in 1802.

Specialist works on Lowestoft include: Lowestoft Wares *by Geoffrey Godden, Antique Collectors Club, Woodbridge, £25; and* Early Lowestoft *by Christopher Spencer – Order direct from Greystones, 29 Mostyn Road, Merton Park, London SW19, £9.95.*

An early guglet, decorated in underglaze blue with flowering plants and birds, c1760, 9in (22.5cm).
£1,800-2,500

The only early example recorded. Similar examples were produced in the middle period and these fetch £500-£700 at auction.

A rare basket, decorated in underglaze blue with a Chinese riverscape, some restoration, c1760, 6in (15cm) diam.
£1,200-1,800

One of 4 recorded examples.

A large cider jug, moulded with flowers and leaves and painted with a continuous riverscape, cracked, c1765.
£300-500

l. A blue and white saucer, decorated with a Chinese riverscape, cracked and restored, c1762-64.
£30-50

c. A sparrow beak jug, decorated in runny underglaze blue with rocks and flowers, cracked, c1765.
£120-180

r. A saucer decorated in underglaze blue with the Boy on a Bridge pattern, c1763-65.
Perfect £80-120

The Boy on a Bridge pattern is attractive and popular with collectors. A similar saucer with a different pattern would be less expensive.

A pickle leaf, decorated in underglaze blue with a floral pattern, c1762, 4in (10cm) long.
£150-250

LOWESTOFT

★ late period blue and white teabowls and saucers and other common teawares in painted or printed patterns should still be found at reasonable prices, particularly if damaged

★ coloured wares have been undervalued in recent years and it is still possible to form a collection of extremely interesting pieces without spending a fortune

★ many collectors are interested in unusual shapes – bottles, inkwells, eggcups, salts, eye baths and so on. Even damaged items can be very collectable but tend to be expensive

★ Lowestoft produced quite a large number of inscribed and dated pieces. These are highly collectable even if damaged. Beware of fakes produced by French factories earlier this century which are hard, rather than soft paste

★ early blue and white wares are of great interest to collectors. It is worth consulting a specialist book in order to help identify these pieces correctly as there is a growing tendency to give pieces an inaccurate early date

A Lowestoft square inkwell, painted in colours with a carnation, a tulip, a ranunculus and other flowers, the top with 4 small trellis panels in pink and gold with foliage sprays in ink, the base inscribed in black 'Eliz[th]. Buckle 1775', 2in (5cm).
£2,800-3,500 *L*

An exceptionally rare, perhaps unique, inkwell. Lowestoft made something of a speciality of inscribed and dated wares. Several examples of wares bearing the name Elizabeth Buckle are known. This charming object was decorated by the so-called Tulip Painter.

A Lowestoft blue and white cup and saucer, c1770, 2in (5cm).
£60-70 *VEN*

In the Ceramics section if there is only one measurement it refers to the height of the piece.

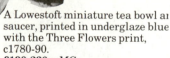

A Lowestoft miniature tea bowl and saucer, printed in underglaze blue with the Three Flowers print, c1780-90.
£190-230 *MC*

A pickle leaf, decorated in pale blue with a fruiting vine, c1765, 4in (9cm).
£120-150

The illustrated leaves show the 2 most common Lowestoft leaf shapes.

A miniature tea bowl and saucer, painted in underglaze blue, 1770-75.
£250-300   *MC*

A rare Lowestoft saucer dish, painted in underglaze blue, cracked, c1775, 7½in (18.5cm) diam.
£180-250   *MC*

A Lowestoft blue and white vase, the tall neck with a flared top, painted with flowering branches and scattered insects beneath a scroll pattern border, crack to shoulder, minute chip to rim, painter's numeral 5(?), c1768, 6in (14.5cm).
£700-900   *C*

Cf Sheena Smith, op. cit. no.647 and Geoffrey A. Godden, Lowestoft Porcelain, *pl.72.*

A rare butter dish, decorated in overglaze polychrome enamels with flower sprays, some restoration, c1768.
£300-400

An early example of polychrome decoration.

A Lowestoft polychrome bowl, decorated in underglaze blue and overglaze iron red and gilt with the Dolls House pattern, unmarked, c1780, 6in (15cm) diam.
£70-100   *TW*

Lowestoft – a guide to identification
Early Period *c1757-61*

Style of Decorations: A limited range of motifs, including flowers, birds, trees, boats and houses in Chinese-style, delicately outlined and shaded in 2 tones of underglaze blue.

Potting: The body often displays a pinkish or pinkish-brown tone and is not always translucent. Wares are thickly potted in the first few years but some very finely potted pieces with white translucency were introduced c1760-61.

Glaze: Before 1760 the glaze is frequently clouded by tin oxide or myriad bubbles. By 1760 a very successful clear 'wet' glaze had been developed.

Underglaze blue: A pale grey-blue is found on some early wares. By 1760 a darker blue was used. Wares were generally marked with a painters number inside the footring. For a fuller consideration of early wares see 'Early Lowestoft' by Christopher Spencer.

A Lowestoft blue and white miniature globular teapot and cover, painted with pagodas on river islands beneath a loop and dot pattern border, painter's numeral 13(?), c1768, 3in (8cm).
£800-1,000   *C*

Cf Sheena Smith, Lowestoft Porcelain in Norwich Castle Museum, *no.572.*

Middle Period *c1761-70*

Style of Decoration: The early decorative themes were soon developed into standard patterns but these can lack the vigour of the early designs. Painters numerals used to mark the base: these are generally from one to 14. Both transfer printing and polychrome decoration were introduced in about 1766. Lowestoft transfer prints are often outlined in a hesitant way, to use a phrase coined by a well known expert, 'as if with a failing ball-point pen'.

Potting: During the early part of the middle period great care was taken with potting. Shapes continued to be well finished. Gradually shapes became simplified and the finish of moulded parts, such as handles, was given less emphasis. After 1765 a more open body showing a yellow, rather than white, translucency was used.

Glaze: Often thick, shiny and more glassy then in the early period. The glaze is prone to bubbling and can show a green hue in gathers around the footrim, under handles or around mouldings.

Underglaze blue: An inky blue was used throughout the period, though sometimes a paler colour is found. Transfer printed pieces are generally dark in tone.

Late Period *c1770-99*

Style of Decoration: The quality of blue and white patterns gradually declines. Chinoiseries tend to be heavily shaded and quickly executed. Floral patterns are highly stylised. By 1775 a brighter blue had been introduced. In contrast some excellent polychrome patterns were introduced and these are highly collectable, particularly those which include Chinese figures or tulips.

Potting: The quality of potting remains robust and utilitarian in concept. A large number of shapes were made and some of these are of great interest to collectors, particularly eye baths, egg cups and other unusual domestic wares. A few figures and animals were made. These are highly popular.

Glaze: A clear glaze which gives the body a creamy appearance was developed about 1775. Polychrome decoration can look particularly pleasing against this warm background.

A Lowestoft blue and white tea caddy, painted with trailing peony, minute chip to shoulder, blue crescent mark, c1775, 4in (10cm).
£180-220   *C*

A moulded cream boat, minor chips, c1770, 3½in (8.5cm).
£150-200

A Lowestoft patty pan, decorated in blue and white with outcurved sides, some damage, c1770, 3in (7.5cm) diam.
£60-90   *NSF*

A Lowestoft blue and white Robert Browne pattern part tea service, comprising: a teapot and cover, handle repaired, finial lacking, a pear-shaped milk jug, minute cracks to lip, a tea caddy, rim chip, a slop basin, 8 tea bowls, 2 cracked, and 8 saucers, one cracked, many pieces with blue crescent marks, some with painter's numeral 17, c1780.
£800-1,200   *C*

Cf Sheena Smith, op. cit. no.589.

A Lowestoft scallop-shaped shell dish, painted with flowers in underglaze blue, c1775, 4½in (11cm) diam.
£160-190   *MC*

A rare Lowestoft blue and white inkwell, inscribed with the owner's name and dated 1798.
£1,200-1,800

A Lowestoft crested coffee cup and saucer from the Ludlow service, c1785.
£800-900   *C*

Cf Geoffrey A. Godden, Lowestoft Porcelain, pl.175 and col. pl. V.

A Lowestoft blue and white eye bath, lightly moulded with scrolls and painted with 2 flower sprays, c1780, 2in (5cm).
£600-700   *CSK*

A rare Lowestoft blue and white inscribed and dated mug, cracked.
£1,000-1,500

A rare Lowestoft milk jug and cover, painted in underglaze blue with the Dragon pattern, c1780-85, 5in (13cm).
£600-700   *MC*

W. H. Goss China

Illustrated in this section are examples of Goss porcelain made by the Goss factory in Stoke-on-Trent between 1858 and 1939. The range is wide and varied, and to indicate age items are numbered (1), (2) or (3):

(1) First period 1858-87
(2) Second period 1881-1934
(3) Third period 1930-39

Throughout the years of manufacture the standards were high, and reproduction of the buildings, Roman urns etc they were modelled after is amazingly accurate. The hand painted coats-of-arms were exact, and the recipes for the brilliant enamels and parian body were developed by Mr William Henry Goss himself. Their quality surpassed that of most other potteries.

Over 1,500 different shapes bearing some 7,000 different decorations and coats-of-arms were produced. For further information, collectors are recommended to *The Price Guide to Goss China* and *Goss China, Arms Decorations and Their Values* by Nicholas Pine, Milestone Publications, Murray Road, Horndean, Hants.

A parian bust of Napoleon, (1/2). **£70** *G&CC*

A selection of large named models, all with inscriptions on their bases, (2).
£8-30 each *G&CC*

A Seaford Roman urn, with butterfly transfer, (1/2).
£35 *G&CC*

A range of models, (2), from smalls at **£4** to the Egyptian Pyramid at **£45**. *G&CC*

'Married Bliss', comedy piece, (3).
£50 *G&CC*

A Weston-Super-Mare clock, in garish coloured surround, (3).
£70 *G&CC*

Cenotaph (2/3) **£28**, Blackpool Tower (2) **£30**, Richmond Market Cross (2) **£35**, Big Ben (3) **£35**. *G&CC*

The Lucerne Lion, (2).
£35 *G&CC*

A Swiss milk pot and lid, (2).
£10 *G&CC*

Windsor Castle, (3).
£50 *G&CC*

GOSS AND CRESTED WARE

Damage considerably affects the value of porcelain. Haircracks, chips and faded crests can halve the values recorded here. Full prices can only be obtained for perfection. Minor firing flaws can be ignored. Goss china shrank up to 10% in the firing processes so manufacturing flaws and minor differences in size are common

A Comedy group on ashtray base, (3).
£55   *G&CC*

WWI flags decorations, (2), **£15-70** and Regimental Badges, (2).
£45-65   *G&CC*

An orange lustre Punch and Judy cruet, (3).
£20 each   *G&CC*

Grinlow Tower, (2).
£150   *G&CC*
This is the rarest tower.

Southampton Bargate, (2).
£45   *G&CC*

A rare Roman vase in orange lustre, (2).
£55   *G&CC*

Ever popular tableware, (2).
Range from £4-15   *G&CC*

Haddon Hall Norman Font, (2).
£45   *G&CC*

Ledbury Market House, (2).
£275   *G&CC*

Goss Oven, (2).
£185   *G&CC*
This is where Goss china was glazed and fired.

Wembley Lion, (2).
£120   *G&CC*

Primroses on a large Exeter vase, (1).
£20   *G&CC*

Isle of Wight Brading Stocks, (2).
£160   *G&CC*

Longships, Lands End, (2) **£26** and Plymouth Eddystone Lighthouse, (2) **£20**.   *G&CC*

Racehorse and Jockey, (2).
£315   *G&CC*

Christchurch Old Court House, (2).
£300   *G&CC*

Wordsworth's Birthplace, Cockermouth, (2).
£200   *G&CC*

Prince Llewellyn's House, Beddgelert, (2).
£120   *G&CC*

A Hereford terra cotta kettle, (2) **£15**, and fairy bagware teapot, (2) **£20**.   *G&CC*

Feather's hotel, Ledbury, (2).
£700   *G&CC*

A bear and ragged staff, (1/2).
£95   *G&CC*

John Knox's House, Edinburgh, (3).
£300   *G&CC*

Two rare Winchester shapes: Cardinal Beaufort's salt cellar **£65** and Warder's horn **£300**, (1/2). *G&CC*

A preserve pot with lid, decorated with coloured poppies, (2).
£65   *G&CC*

Contact Mine League model, (2).
£110   *G&CC*

A Cirencester Roman urn, in lustre, with butterflies, (2).
£87   *G&CC*

This is a scarce model.

Crested China

Collecting crested china is fun and there is a wealth of different shapes made by over a 100 different potteries, mainly based in Staffordshire between 1880 and 1940. The major firms of Arcadian, Carlton, Willow Art, Shelley, Grafton and Corona made the bulk of heraldic ware, complemented by their German counterparts such as Gemma and Saxony. They attracted a different market after initially competing with the Goss factory, the originators of heraldic porcelain. Standards vary and rubbed gilding and firing flaws are to be expected, and do not alter values unless they particularly detract.

The last 5 years have seen a meteoric rise in prices, but certain pieces, once considered rare, have come to light so frequently that their values have fallen. On the other hand, the previously unwanted cheaper domestic cups and saucers, plates and egg cups etc have attracted value during the last year or so. Decorations and transfers have yet to add value to the shape, but this will no doubt happen in the future.

Those interested in learning further about the full range and history of the factories are recommended to *Crested China* by Sandy Andrews, and *The Price Guide to Crested China* by Sandy Andrews and Nicholas Pine, Milestone Publications, Murray Road, Horndean, Hants.

'A Truck of Coal from . . . Skegness' (places vary), Willow Art.
£14   *G&CC*

Unmarked (but Saxony) Swanage Globe, some colouring.
£10   *G&CC*

HMS Lion by Carlton.
£55   *G&CC*

A treadle sewing machine £16 and 14thC spinning wheel £10, both by Carlton.   *G&CC*

Gibbet Cross at Hindhead, by Willow Art.
£10   *G&CC*

Puzzle pieces by Gemma.
£4-10   *G&CC*

Arcadian Maiwand Memorial, Reading.
£13   *G&CC*

Nurse Cavell statue, Arcadian.
£15   *G&CC*

Kitchen Ranges, Carlton £13, Shelley £13 and Carlton £8.   *G&CC*

Willow Art Sun.
£35   *G&CC*

Miniature cheese dishes with lids
£4-8.   *G&CC*

A very popular theme to collect.

Arcadian Marble Arch.
£8   *G&CC*

Grandfather clocks.
£8-13   *G&CC*

Carlton Red Cross van.
£17 *G&CC*

Willow Art Moon.
£12 *G&CC*

Canterbury Cathedral, West Front, by Willow Art.
£20 *G&CC*

Jolly Jugs! from cows, birds, people to the letter S.
£4-16 *G&CC*

A scarce Arcadian Leominster Ducking Stool, 2 hinged pieces.
£85 *G&CC*

Shelley Binoculars.
£14 *G&CC*

Baby, arms outstretched, inscribed 'Cheerio', Willow Art, WWI Mascot.
£16 *G&CC*

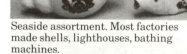

Seaside assortment. Most factories made shells, lighthouses, bathing machines.
£2-20 *G&CC*

Carlton German Incendiary Bomb.
£20 *G&CC*

Arcadian Folkestone Road of Remembrance War Memorial.
£50 *G&CC*

An Arcadian Bactrian camel.
£17 *G&CC*

HMS Humber (Carlton) **£55**, HMS Tiger (Carlton) **£55**, HMS Lion Troup Carrier, liner converted (Willow) **£90**, and HMS Iron Duke (Grafton) **£85**. *G&CC*

DIFFERENTIATING MING AND QING WARES

In order to distinguish Ming porcelain from the later Qing wares it is necessary to appreciate the technical rather than the decorative differences between the 2. The Qing decorators frequently copied ancestral designs with great accuracy and at first sight it is sometimes difficult to attribute certain pieces.

A good example of this is the Doucai (contrasting colours) category. The originals were produced during the Ming reign of Chenghua (1465-87) and the copies were made in the reign of the Qing emperor Kangxi. Were it not for the characteristic smoky ivory appearance of the Ming glaze one might well be at a loss to differentiate early from late.

In the first place, with certain exceptions, Ming porcelain is more heavily glazed and the depth of glaze effects a bluish or greenish tint. The glaze is rarely evenly applied and if carefully examined one can detect runs and dribbles of excess glaze. Most Qing wares are covered in a glaze of uniform thickness. Particularly characteristic is the pure white appearance achieved by the Kangxi potters by only coating the vessel or dish in a thin and even wash. The reigns of Yongzheng and Qianlong did witness some pieces (non-export) which were deliberately covered in a thick glaze in order to emulate the early 15thC porcelains.

As far as potting is concerned there are more obvious idiosyncracies enabling easier identification.

For example, Ming vases if of sufficient size to warrant being made in 2 or more pieces are generally luted horizontally even on vessels which it would appear to be simpler to make in 2 vertical sections, Yongle and Xuande 'moon' or 'pilgrim' bottles are a case in point. Qing pilgrim bottles would invariably be made by joining 2 vertical halves.

The footrims on Ming wares are generally knife-pared and little effort made to remove the facets left by the blade. Most, if not all, Qing pieces are smoothed after the trimming. The feet on Ming dishes or bowls are for the most part higher than Qing examples. They are frequently undercut immediately indicating that they have been thrown by hand and not as many Qing pieces which have been moulded by a mechanical process utilising a profile cutter. A further point concerning the footrim on Ming wares – it will generally manifest a narrow orange zone abutting the edge of the glaze. This is due to the presence of iron in the body of the porcelain which appears to oxidise more strongly in the kiln in the area most closely in contact with the glaze.

This section is alphabetically arranged by object: bowl, box, censer, etc. In each group the wares are firstly divided into Chinese followed by Japanese and then ordered chronologically.

Bowls

A large Jian Yao brown-glazed 'hare's fur' bowl, the mottled and lightly-streaked glaze thinning to matt around the rim and pooling darkly in the well and stopping irregularly around the dark shallowly-cut foot, chip restored, glaze tears around the foot polished, Song Dynasty, 5in (13cm) diam., fitted box.
£550-650   C

A Jun Yao shallow bowl, covered in a pale blue glaze thinning to a pale translucent brown at the rim, small foot chip and minor restoration, Yuan Dynasty, 4½in (11.5cm) diam.
£500-600   C

A bulb bowl covered with a crackled celadon glaze, not reaching the centre, on 3 feet, Ming, 12in (30.5cm).
£400-500   L

A Transitional Wucai fish bowl, painted with 4 fish amongst water weeds below a band of iron red breaking waves, chipped, 17thC, 9in (22.5cm) diam.
£500-600   C

A Chun Yao bowl, with a rich sky blue mottled glaze falling from the brownish rim, with a purple splash, the outside with a deeper shade of mottled blue, Sung, 8in (19.5cm).
£1,000-1,200   L

A dated blue and white small bowl, the exterior with 4 auspicious characters in star-shaped panels against a floral meander below cell pattern at the neck, engraved collectors' marks, the base with an encircled four-character mark including a cyclical date, 4½in (11cm) diam.
£1,300-1,600   C

The cyclical date dingsi year probably corresponds to A.D. 1617.

A blue and white bowl painted on the exterior in a vivid blue, the centre of the interior with a pine in a jardinière reserved on a trellis-pattern ground, below a band of hexagonal cell-pattern reserved with cartouches of pine, prunus, bamboo and peony at the rim, minute rim chips, areas of rim polished, encircled Chenghua six-character mark, Kangxi, 8in (19.5cm) diam.
£750-950   *C*

A pair of bowls decorated in 'famille verte' enamels, the narrow borders of scrolls in iron red, the insides each with a flowerhead medallion, fang-shêng mark, Kangxi, 6in (15cm).
£1,400-1,600   *L*

An ormolu-mounted 'famille rose' bowl, restored, the porcelain Qianlong, the ormolu 19thC, 12½in (31cm) wide.
£300-400   *C*

A 'famille rose' punch bowl, painted with 2 large panels of a family group, on a ground of gilt scrolls reserved with puce monochrome and larger polychrome floral panels, Qianlong, 10in (26cm) diam.
£850-950   *C*

A Chinese export porcelain punch bowl, decorated with European figures in landscapes separated by prunus blossom sprays, 10in (25cm) diam.
£300-350   *LBP*

A 'famille verte' bowl, the interior painted with flowers below a cell-pattern border reserved with cartouches of peach, prunus and finger citrus, the exterior below a cell-pattern border reserved with cartouches of ribboned emblems, chipped, cracked, pieces restuck, Kangxi, 12in (30.5cm) diam.
£650-850   *C*

A pair of Chinese blue and white shallow bowls and domed covers, Kangxi, 7in (17.5cm) wide.
£850-1,150   *CSK*

A Chinese export porcelain bowl, enamelled with figures within a landscape and 4 male figures with a girl at a window, small rim chips, slight wear to enamels, 10in (26cm).
£130-180   *Bon*

A 'famille verte' punch bowl, painted on the exterior with figures below a band of animal cartouches, reserved on a floral seeded green ground at the rim, restored, Kangxi, 14in (35cm) diam.
£1,000-1,200   *C*

A Qianlong bowl, with a red enamel scroll border above 3 cartouches, surrounded by a blue ground, of birds sitting in a peony tree, damaged.
£60-90   *CGC*

A bowl and cover enamelled in 'famille verte' palette, with borders of green 'cracked ice' with flowerheads in iron red, the handles issuing from masks, Kangxi, 8in (19.5cm).
£1,200-1,400   *L*

A Qianlong 'famille rose' barber's bowl painted in colours, 12½in (31cm) wide.
£750-850   *BD*

A Chinese export porcelain bowl, enamelled with a family at a window and with 3 figures with a bird, both groups with colourful leafage and within blue, shaped cartouches, 10in (25.5cm).
£200-300 *Bon*

An unusual large Chinese blue and white circular shallow basin, the inverted rim with wave pattern and the exterior with 4 groups of peony, chrysanthemum, plum and lotus, 1800, 27in (67.5cm) diam.
£3,500-4,000 *CSK*

A Chinese export porcelain bowl, enamelled in the 'famille rose' palette with bouquets and sprigs of large blooms, restored, 12in (29cm).
£300-350 *Bon*

A Cantonese bowl, decorated with panels of flowers and figures, 19thC, 14in (35cm).
£400-500 *CW*

A large Cantonese porcelain punch bowl, in 'famille rose' and 'famille verte' enamels and gilt, 16in (40cm) diam.
£500-600 *HSS*

A fine large Cantonese bowl, painted on the exterior with panels of figures before pavilions, 22in (55cm) diam.
£5,000-6,000 *EH*

A Cantonese fish tank, 19thC, 10in (25cm).
£350-400 *WIL*

A massive blue and white fish bowl, painted with a wide band of 2 four-clawed dragons striding in pursuit of a flaming pearl amongst cloud scrolls above breaking waves and below roundels and cloud scrolls at the rim, cracked, 19thC, 24½in (62cm) wide.
£1,000-1,200 *C*

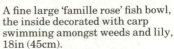

A Chinese circular fish bowl, painted in coloured enamels on a yellow ground, applied with 2 'shi-shi' blue glazed handles, 19thC, 14in (35cm).
£1,200-1,500 *BS*

A fine large 'famille rose' fish bowl, the inside decorated with carp swimming amongst weeds and lily, 18in (45cm).
£1,700-2,000 *EH*

A Raku chawan with mixed black and chestnut brown glaze stopping short of the foot, 18thC, 4½in (11cm) diam., with box.
£1,300-1,500 *C*

The chawan shows the influence of the fourth generation Raku potter Ichinyu (1640-96), who is said to have initiated the addition of a dash of red to the typical black Raku glaze.

An Imari barber's bowl, painted in the interior with flowering and fruiting trees, the border with iron red and gilt scrolling flowers and panels of stylised foliage, early 18thC, 11in (27.5cm) diam.
£500-600 *CSK*

A large deep Imari bowl and domed cover, decorated in iron red, black, green enamels and gilt on underglaze blue, the brass acorn finial of later date, late 17thC, 19½in (48cm).
£1,800-2,000 *C*

A deep Imari bowl and cover, decorated in iron red, enamel and gilt on an underglaze blue ground, Genroku period, 8½in (21.5cm) diam.
£800-1,000 *C*

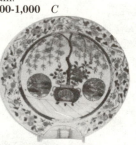

An Imari shaving dish, decorated in underglaze blue, iron red and gilt, a narrow band of underglaze blue and gilt with 4 cartouches containing stylised foliage separating the wide rim decorated with stylised flowers and foliage, the reverse with sprays of plum blossom, gilt rim, repair to rim, Genroku period, 11in (28cm) wide.
£400-500 *C*

A shallow Imari bowl, painted with 'ho-o' among pine and plum, divided by underglaze blue floral lappets, finial chipped, c1700, 8½in (21cm) diam.
£800-900 *CSK*

A Satsuma bowl, 5in (12cm) diam.
£300-400 *Bea*

A pair of earthenware bowls and covers, supported on 3 feet modelled as children, 7in (18cm) diam.
£300-350 *L*

An Imari bowl, the centre painted with a fabulous beast, set with 3 foliate medallions of chrysanthemums, the exterior similarly painted, mid-19thC, 10in (25cm) diam.
£300-350 *L*

A Japanese Imari reeded round bowl, decorated in blue, gilt and iron red flowers, 19thC, 9½in (23.5cm).
£450-550 *CW*

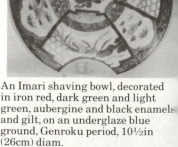

An Imari shaving bowl, decorated in iron red, dark green and light green, aubergine and black enamels and gilt, on an underglaze blue ground, Genroku period, 10½in (26cm) diam.
£500-600 *C*

A Satsuma baluster-shaped bowl, the body enamelled and gilt, with men working in a garden setting, the lid decorated with a sitting figure, mid-19thC, 6in (15cm) diam.
£80-120 *WIL*

An Imari boat-shaped and pierced pedestal stand.
£100-150 *JMW*

A Kyoto chrysanthemum-shaped deep bowl, decorated in colours and gilt, signed on the base 'Kizan kore o tsukuru', late 19thC, 12in (30cm) diam.
£1,000-1,200 *C*

An Imari bowl, 19thC, 13½in (33.5cm) diam.
£400-450 *EWS*

A large Imari bowl, decorated in underglaze blue, iron red, green, yellow enamels and gilt, the exterior with a wide band of flowers and foliage, 19thC, 16in (40cm) diam.
£1,200-1,400 *C*

Bottles

A Chinese blue and white bottle with flared foot, Kangxi, 9in (23cm).
£350-450 *CSK*

A pair of Chinese Imari slender square bottles, Kangxi, 9½in (23.5cm).
£1,200-1,400 *CSK*

A pair of Imari bottles, painted with broad bands of pine, bamboo and plum, early 18thC, 9in (23cm).
£900-1,000 *CSK*

Cups

A pair of Imari slender pear-shaped bottles, the moulded collared shoulders and necks with alternate underglaze blue and gilt bands, early 18thC, 9in (22.5cm).
£1,300-1,500 *CSK*

A Chinese underglaze blue and copper red decorated bottle, painted with a coiled dragon pursuing a flaming pearl among clouds, 18thC, 17½in (44cm).
£600-700 *CSK*

A Kakiemon-type cylindrical sake bottle (tokkuri), decorated in iron red and coloured enamels, fitted with a European gilt metal finial surmounted by a hawk attached to a link chain, 18thC/early 19thC, 9in (23cm).
£3,500-4,000 *C*

A pair of blue and white semi-eggshell beakers and saucers, painted with a design derived from a European print, the interior of the beakers and saucer reverses with 4 fish swimming in mutual pursuit, below leaf-pattern bands at the rims, encircled stork marks, Kangxi.
£450-550 *C*

This is an example of the so-called Cuckoo in the House design.

213

Eight 'famille rose' coffee cups and saucers, each enamelled in colours and gilt, Qianlong.
£600-800 *CNY*

Ewers

A Transitional blue and white silver-mounted oviform ewer, the handle restuck, c1640, 10in (25cm).
£750-900 *C*

The mounts are Dutch bearing the hall marks for 1856.

Figures – Animal

A red-painted grey pottery horse's head, modelled with bulbous eyes, flared nostrils and open mouth, Han Dynasty, 6in (15cm).
£1,200-1,400 *L*

The result of a thermoluminescence test, Oxford, 366L19, is consistent with the dating of this piece.

Six export tea cups and saucers for the American market, each enamelled and gilt with an eagle, 19thC.
£700-900 *CNY*

An Arita blue and white broad oviform ewer, handle cracked, c1670, 10in (24cm).
£400-500 *C*

An unglazed grey pottery figure of a standing caparisoned horse, with areas of green and white pigment remaining under earth encrustation, repaired, 6th/7thC A.D., 11in (27.5cm), with stand, fitted box.
£1,100-1,400 *C*

An export figure of a recumbent dog, its fur painted in brown and gilt and the mouth in pink, the sconce with a band of green below iron red and gold, chipped, sconce reduced, Qianlong, 6½in (16cm) wide.
£500-600 *C*

A 'famille rose' standing duck, with multi-coloured wing feathers, the body primarily painted with sepia plumage, astride a green and blue plinth, neck luting repaired, Qianlong, 7in (17cm).
£1,200-1,400 *C*

An ochre-glazed pottery figure of a recumbent dog, with a vivid glaze, Tang Dynasty, 4in (9.5cm) long.
£2,000-2,500 *C*

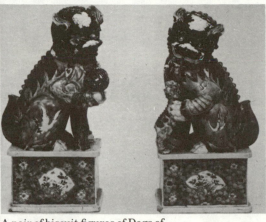

A pair of biscuit figures of Dogs of Fo, seated, their coats green with tufts in yellow and aubergine, Kangxi, 18in (44cm).
£6,500-7,000   *L*

A pair of 'famille rose' figures of standing cranes, the white bodies incised and moulded with feather markings, the eyes, beaks, tail feathers and legs in black and with pink crests, chipped beak, 19thC, 8in (20cm).
£900-1,100   *C*

An export figure of a hound, the eyes and mouth picked out in brown, traces of cold-enamel decoration, fritted, Qianlong, 6in (14.5cm).
£1,500-2,000   *C*

An aubergine and green-glazed cat night light, the body incised with short fur markings and dappled in apple green on the rich aubergine-brown ground, cracked, c1800, 8in (20.5cm) wide, wood stand.
£1,800-2,200   *C*

A pair of Chinese porcelain cockerels decorated with pink, green, blue and yellow plumage on pale green bases, one comb damaged, 19thC, 10½in (26cm).
£1,000-1,200   *DSH*

A Fukagawa white glazed model of a goat, with black-painted eye pupils, Hirado style, signed on the base 'Dai Nihon Imara Fukagawa sei', c1875, 7½in (19cm) long.
£350-450   *C*

A late Japanese Imari recumbent cat, with a blue and gilt bow on its neck, the fur iron red, 8½in (21cm) long.
£500-600   *CNY*

A Ming tilemaker's pottery equestrian group, the ochre-robed dignitary turning to his right, on a green domed base, surface chips and minor repair, 17thC, 16in (39cm).
£600-700   *C*

Figures – People

An unglazed buff pottery figure of a court lady, wearing an orange painted jacket and brown striped dress, Tang Dynasty, 10in (25cm).
£650-750   *L*

The result of a thermoluminescence test, Oxford, 366L22, is consistent with the dating of this piece.

An unglazed red pottery figure of an equestrian lady, restoration to legs and tail, ears chipped, Tang Dynasty, 15in (37cm).
£2,500-3,000 *C*

The result of thermoluminescence test, Oxford, 366h26, is consistent with the dating of this piece.

A blanc-de-Chine Buddhist group, formed as Guanyin, with a small acolyte, repaired at her right wrist, small chips, Kangxi, 10in (25cm).
£400-500 *C*

A 'famille verte' 'egg-and-spinach' figure of Guanyin, wearing a green cowl, white robe and splashed undergarments, chipped, Kangxi, 8in (20cm).
£400-500 *C*

A pair of 'famille verte' figures of the Laughing Twins, Hehe Erxian, painted with iron red aprons over white robes, the bases with 4 large peony heads, one repaired, Kangxi, 11in (27cm).
£800-1,000 *C*

A 'famille verte' figure of Guanyin, wearing a green-ground yellow floral robe, some restoration, Kangxi, 14in (34.5cm).
£450-500 *C*

A Japanese porcelain figure of a standing lady, Kwannon, with painted, enamel and gilt decoration, late 19thC, 22½ (56cm).
£120-150 *TW*

A blanc-de-Chine figure of Pu-Tai, standing on his bag of happiness, Kangxi, 13in (32.5cm).
£350-450 *L*

Flatware

A crackled celadon hexafoil dish of Guan yao type, the pale blue widely crackled glaze pooling in the recesses and stopping around the neatly cut orange-fired foot, slight glaze degradation, Southern Song Dynasty, 6in (15.5cm).
£1,200-1,500 *C*

A blue and white late Ming Kraak porselein dish, hair crack, fritted, early 17thC, 12½in (31.5cm).
£500-600 *C*

A Zhejiang celadon dish, delicately carved with a crane in flight, under an olive glaze pooling on the shallowly-cut grey biscuit foot, Song Dynasty, Li Shui type, 11in (27.5cm).
£800-900 *C*

A large late Ming blue and white Kraak porselein dish, fritted, late 16th/early 17thC, 20in (50.5cm).
£1,000-1,300 *C*

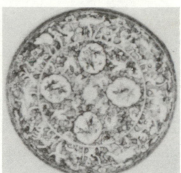

A late Ming blue and white blue-ground saucer dish, 16thC, 12in (30cm).
£300-400 *CSK*

A deep circular dish, decorated in 'famille verte' enamels, shop seal mark, Kangxi, 14½in (36.5cm).
£3,000-3,500 *L*

TRANSITIONAL WARES

★ these wares are readily identifiable both by their form and by their style of decoration
★ Forms: sleeve vases, oviform jars with domed lids, cylindrical brushpots and bottle vases are particularly common
★ the cobalt used is a brilliant purplish blue, rarely misfired
★ the ground colour is of a definite bluish tone, probably because the glaze is slightly thicker than that of the wares produced in the subsequent reigns of Kangxi and Yongzheng
★ the decoration is executed in a rather formal academic style, often with scholars and sages with attendants in idyllic cloud-lapped mountain landscapes
★ other characteristics include the horizontal 'contoured' clouds, banana plantain used to interrupt scenes, and the method of drawing grass by means of short 'V' shaped brush strokes
★ in addition, borders are decorated with narrow bands of scrolling foliage, so lightly incised as to be almost invisible or secret (anhua)
★ these pieces were rarely marked although they sometimes copied earlier Ming marks

A Kraak porselein blue and white dish, the centre painted with deer in a landscape, Transitional, 11in (27cm).
£300-400 *Bea*

A large Kangxi blue and white plate, small chip, Chia Ching mark, c1710, 14in (35cm).
£400-450 *Wai*

A 'famille verte' saucer dish, chipped, encircled Chenghua mark, Kangxi, 14in (34.5cm).
£500-600 *C*

An unusual saucer dish with everted rim, Kangxi, 9½in (23.5cm).
£400-500 *Bea*

A 'famille verte' plate, Kangxi, 8½in (21cm).
£650-750 *CSK*

A 'famille verte' saucer dish, painted with an audience scene around a tented building, small rim chips, 3 patches of blue glaze flaked, Kangxi, 14in (35cm).
£1,600-2,000 *C*

A pair of Chinese blue and white plates, Kangxi six-character marks and of the period, 8in (20cm).
£300-400 *CSK*

A pair of 'famille verte' basins, the exteriors with further birds amongst pine and chrysanthemum, restored, Kangxi, 14in (34.5cm).
£1,100-1,400 *C*

A Qianlong plate, decorated in 'famille rose' enamels with the Judgment of Paris, gilt shell and scroll border, 9in (22.5cm).
£750-850 *GSP*

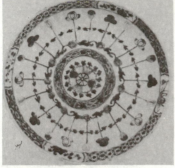

A 'famille verte' fluted saucer dish, Kangxi, 11½in (29cm).
£450-550 *CSK*

A Qianlong 'famille rose' plate, c1740, 9in (22.5cm).
£100-130 *Wai*

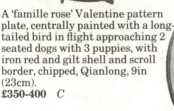

A pair of Chinese saucer dishes, each painted in iron red and gilt, outlined in underglaze blue, Kangxi, 8½in (21cm).
£400-500 *CSK*

A 'famille rose' Valentine pattern plate, centrally painted with a long-tailed bird in flight approaching 2 seated dogs with 3 puppies, with iron red and gilt shell and scroll border, chipped, Qianlong, 9in (23cm).
£350-400 *C*

A set of 3 Chinese 'famille rose' plates, the outer border decorated iron red with dominoes, 2 cracked, Qianlong, 9in (22.5cm).
£250-300 *DWB*

A pair of 'famille rose' plates, the wells with grisaille foliage and blue enamel dragons, the borders with iron red and gilt trailing flowers, Yongzheng/early Qianlong, 9in (22.5cm).
£500-600 *CSK*

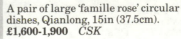

A 'famille rose' ship saucer dish, painted in the centre in iron red, black and green with a full-masted European vessel flying a Scandinavian flag, beneath puce scale panels, c1790, 8in (20cm).
£600-700 *C*

A pair of large 'famille rose' circular dishes, Qianlong, 15in (37.5cm).
£1,600-1,900 *CSK*

A pair of Chinese 'famille rose' plates, one cracked, one chipped, Qianlong, 9in (22.5cm).
£200-250 *DWB*

A pair of blue and white plates, centrally painted with leaping Buddhistic lions above 'lingzhi' sprays within elaborate scroll, pomegranate, cell-pattern and foliage-spray borders, chipped, Qianlong, 10in (24cm).
£450-550 *C*

A Chinese export porcelain plate, the central panel painted with a woman and a boy seated beneath trees on the seashore, in coloured enamels, within a puce diapered border, with pierced rim and gilt outer rim, 8in (20cm).
£250-300 *HSS*

A pair of large 'famille rose' dishes, small hairline, minor chips, Qianlong, 14in (35cm).
£300-400 *CSK*

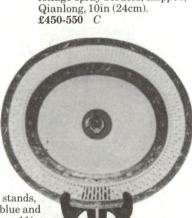

A pair of Chinese export Herculaneum pierced oval stands, painted in iron red, white, blue and green enamels, late Qianlong, 11in (27.5cm) wide.
£800-900 *CSK*

A pair of Chinese Imari dishes, painted with a lady and a child on a fenced terrace, Qianlong, 15in (38cm) wide.
£1,500-2,000 *C*

An Imari dish, 17thC, 17½in (44cm).
£900-1,000 *L*

A rare European subject grisaille plate, painted in shades of grey and flesh tones, grisaille possibly strengthened, small rim chip, mid-Qianlong, 9in (23cm).
£700-800 *C*

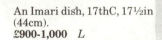

An Imari dish, painted in underglaze blue, yellow, green, turquoise enamels, iron red and gilt, late 17thC, 14in (35cm).
£900-1,100 *CSK*

A set of 4 rare Arita blue and white plates, each painted with The Hall of One Hundred Children, late 17thC, 8in (20cm).
£1,500-1,700 *CSK*

Cf. Catalogue Japanese Blue and White Porcelain Exhibition in Leeuwarden, February 1981.

A large Imari deep dish, with iron red and gilt petals, the border with 4 gold-ground panels of flowers on a ground of scrolling pomegranate, flowers and leaves, c1700, 21½in (54cm).
£1,600-1,800 *CSK*

A Kyoto dish, painted in colours and gilt with 3 ladies at leisure among flowers in a riverside garden, 6in (15cm) wide.
£400-500 *CSK*

A pair of Arita Kakiemon style saucer dishes, the porcelain early 18thC, the decoration later and probably Dutch, 8in (20cm).
£500-600 *CSK*

A pair of Japanese porcelain dishes, finely painted with figures of ladies and actors in extensive landscapes, with elaborate floral borders, 19in (47.5cm).
£850-950 *DWB*

An Imari dish, 18thC, 21in (54cm).
£1,500-1,700 *L*

A Kaga thickly-potted saucer dish, painted in iron red and richly gilt, 14in (35cm).
£350-400 *CSK*

JAPANESE ART PERIODS

★ ***Prehistory and Protohistory***
c7000 B.C. Jomon culture; first recorded pottery with simple design.
c300 B.C. Yayoi culture; bronzes and more sophisticated pottery.
1st to 4thC A.D. Haniwa culture. Bronzes and distinctive red pottery.
A.D. 220; first influence from Korea

★ ***Asuka Period*** – 552-645
★ ***Hahuko Period*** – 672-85
★ ***Nara Period*** – 710-94
★ ***Heian Period*** – 794-1185
★ ***Kamakura Period*** – 1185-1333
★ ***Muromachi (Ahikaga) Period*** – 1338-1573
★ ***Momoyama Period*** – 1573-1615
1598: immigrant Korean potters begin kilns at Kyushu, producing the first glazed pottery
★ ***Edo (Tokugawa) Period*** – 1615-1867
1616: first porcelain made by Ninsei (1596-1666)
1661-73: great age of porcelain; Arita, Nabeshima, Kutani and Kakiemon
1716-36: popularity of lacquering and netsuke as art forms
★ ***Meiji Period*** – (1868-1912)
Strong influence of Western cultures developing and growing. Japanese art appears to decline in many respects. Much trading with the West

---

A large Ao-Kutani saucer dish, decorated in iron red, coloured enamels and gilt, rim repaired, signed on the base 'Dai Nihon Kutani sei, Fukuriken', 19thC, 24in (60cm).
£700-800 *C*

Make the most of Miller's

When a large specialist well-publicised collection comes on the market, it tends to increase prices. Immediately after this, prices can fall slightly due to the main buyers having large stocks and the market being 'flooded'. This is usually temporary and does not affect very high quality items.

A Japanese Imari charger, in underglaze blue, iron red, green and gilt, early 19thC, 13½in (34cm).
£300-350 *HSS*

Garden Seats

A pair of Chinese garden seats, freely painted and enamelled with peony and prunus boughs on a celadon green glazed ground, late 19thC, 19in (48cm).
£900-1,000   *LBP*

A Canton 'famille rose' garden seat, with turquoise grounds enriched with foliage and fruit sprays, early 19thC, 19in (48cm).
£1,300-1,500   *C*

A blue and white barrel-shaped garden seat, painted with birds perched and in flight amongst rockwork and peony within bands of fruit and flower sprays, 19thC, 18½in (46.5cm).
£850-950   *C*

Jardinières

A large Imari jardinière, interior body crack, mid-19thC, 19in (48cm).
£1,500-2,000   *Bea*

A blue and white jardinière, decorated with panels of the Hundred Antiques and Shou characters, Kangxi, 8½in (21cm) diam.
£450-550   *WW*

A Chinese 'famille rose' jardinière, with reserved panels on black ground, early 19thC, 16in (40cm).
£500-600   *O*

A 'famille rose' jardinière, painted with a procession before a pavilion set out for tea, late 19thC, 9½in (23.5cm) wide.
£300-350   *C*

A blue and white jardinière, painted in the 15thC style, 18thC, 9½in (23.5cm).
£600-700   *C*

A 'famille verte' jardinière, rim chip, 19thC, 11in (27.5cm) wide.
£350-400   *C*

A Canton jardinière, the exterior painted in 'famille rose' enamels, cracked, mid-19thC, 10in (25cm).
£450-500   *Bea*

A large Imari jardinière, painted in underglaze blue, iron red, colours and gilt, late 19thC, 21in (53cm) diam.
£2,000-2,500   *C*

Jars

A Yue Yao four-handled jar, the thin translucent glaze stopping above the foot with concave base, restored, 3rd/4thC A.D., 6in (14.5cm) diam.
£250-300 *C*

A Henan black-glazed ribbed jar, the globular body below a short unglazed rim, covered with a fine lustrous glaze, the glaze stopping irregularly around the cut buff stoneware foot, Song Dynasty, 5½in (13.5cm) diam.
£2,000-2,500 *C*

A large Cizhou jar, loosely painted in brown with bands of leaf scrolls on a cream ground, Ming Dynasty, 25in (62.5cm).
£900-1,000 *CSK*

A pair of late Ming blue and white jars and covers, painted in a blackish blue, one rim chipped, early 17thC, 5½in (14cm).
£550-650 *C*

A large late Ming blue and white oviform jar, painted with floral lappets on the shoulder and ruyi above the foot, neck cracked, early 17thC, 17in (42cm).
£1,300-1,600 *C*

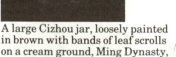

A 'famille verte' broad baluster jar and cover, the neck with a band of cracked-ice and ribboned emblems, restoration to cover and finial, Kangxi, 16in (40cm).
£1,600-2,000 *C*

A potiche and cover, enamelled with 2 dragons, green and yellow, Ming, 16in (40cm).
£1,000-1,200 *L*

A pair of Chinese blue and white square tea jars, one with cover, the shoulders and necks mounted in bronze, minor frits, cover chipped, the porcelain Kangxi, 11½in (29cm).
£1,500-2,000 *CSK*

A Transitional blue and white jar and domed cover, delicately painted in a linear style filled-in with contrasting pale and dark washes, c1643, 12½in (31cm).
£700-900 *C*

A baluster jar, together with similar cover, slight damage, Transitional, 8in (20.5cm).
£800-900 *Bea*

A large Chinese blue and white broad baluster jar and domed cover, Kangxi, 22½in (56cm).
£2,400-3,000 *CSK*

A Chinese jar incised and decorated in underglaze blue, with flowers issuing from celadon rockwork and with copper red peonies and a flying bird in blue and copper red, six-character Kangxi mark and of the period, 8in (20cm) diam.
£550-650 *DWB*

A small Chinese blue and white jar and domed cover, Kangxi, 3½in (9cm).
£180-240 *CSK*

A blue and white jar, small neck chip, c1800, 11in (28cm).
£1,000-1,200 *C*

A Chinese green-dragon jar, pencilled in underglaze blue with 2 dragons in pursuit of flaming pearls, the shoulders with the 'Ba Jixiang' decoration, all picked out in translucent green enamel of pale emerald colour, seal mark and period of Qianlong, 8in (20cm).
£2,500-3,000 *DWB*

A Chinese Imari jar, the top painted with 2 underglaze blue 'qilin', early Qianlong, 25in (62cm).
£750-850 *C*

A 'famille jeune' jar, decorated with birds amongst prunus, 19thC, 9in (22.5cm).
£60-100 *BA*

A Satsuma jar, decorated in coloured enamels and gilt on a finely crackled off-white ground, signed on the base 'Dai Nihon Satsuma yaki Tachibana Yoshinobu Isshuin' below a blue Shimazu 'mon', 19thC, 'sentoku' domed cover with 'kiku' finial, decorated in relief with the 'Takaramono' and flowers, 10in (25cm) high overall.
£2,000-2,500 *C*

A fine Arita blue and white jar, painted with 2 'ho-o' among paulownia, peony and rocks, late 17thC, 21in (53cm), wood cover.
£3,500-4,000 *C*

A Kyoto compressed globular koro, decorated in colours and gilt with figures among buildings and trees in a mountainous river landscape, signed on the base 'Kinzan', Meiji period, 3½in (8.5cm) diam., pierced silvered metal cover.
£900-1,000 *C*

A large Satsuma jar and domed cover, boldly decorated in iron red, colours and gilt with Tokugawa (aoi) 'mon', rim with some restoration, finial with some gilt rubbed off, body with restored crack, signed on the base in a rectangular reserve 'Kintozan', 19thC, 19in (48cm).
£500-700 *C*

Tea & Coffee Pots

A 'famille verte' teapot and cover, painted with birds perched on peony branches, restoration to handle and spout, Kangxi, 8in (20.5cm) wide.
£350-400 *C*

A Chinese export polychrome coffee pot and cover, painted on each side with a pair of European lovers, handle repaired, body crack, Qianlong, 10½in (26cm).
£500-600 *CSK*

A Kakiemon type Mokkogata teapot, vividly decorated in iron red and coloured enamels, handle cracked, spout with gold lacquer repair, cover repaired and chipped, 18th/19thC, 8in (19cm) long.
£1,000-1,200 *C*

An earthenware teapot, with gilt mark, 3½in (9cm) diam.
£100-150 *L*

A Chinese 'famille verte' wine pot and cover, c1700.
£400-450 *ROB*

A Satsuma wine pot and cover, slight chip to spout, 5in (12cm) diam.
£350-400 *Bea*

A blue and white teapot, Qianlong, c1760, 4½in (11cm).
£300-350 *Wai*

A large Cantonese baluster teapot and domed cover, Jiaqing, 9½in (23.5cm).
£450-500 *CSK*

A Chinese part tea set, painted in blue and white with gilding, c1790.
£200-250 *ROB*

Tureens

A Chinese 'famille rose' tureen and cover, the base with iron red animal head handles, star crack to base, crack to lid, Qianlong, 11in (28cm) diam.
£1,100-1,300 *WW*

A pair of 'famille rose' shallow vegetable tureens, covers and stands, within iron red and black cell-pattern bands, the iron red and black trellis-pattern borders reserved with panels of gilt emblems, one tureen restored, late Qianlong, the stands 10in (25cm) long.
£2,500-3,000 *CSK*

Vases

A Yingqing oviform vase, the spreading foot with a band of key pattern, the glaze stopping around the neatly cut concave base, minor chip, Song Dynasty, 4½in (11.5cm).
£350-400 *C*

A 'famille rose' tureen, cover and under-dish, handles chipped, Qianlong, the stand 14in (35.5cm) wide.
£1,200-1,400 *C*

A rare Longquan celadon vase, modelled after a bronze of broad 'gu' shaped form, under a semi-translucent thick glaze filling the interior and the underside of the spreading hollow foot and stopping neatly around the orange-fired grey biscuit foot rim, cracks in foot and small rim crack, Southern Song/Yuan Dynasty, 9½in (23.5cm).
£1,600-1,800 *C*

Two late Ming blue and white vases, meiping, both tops leaning to one side, glaze cracks, Wanli, 10½in (26cm).
£1,200-1,400 *C*

A pair of Chinese blue and white sauce tureens, Qianlong, the stands 7in (17cm) wide.
£850-950 *CSK*

A Transitional blue and white double-gourd vase, c1640, 13½in (33.5cm).
£2,000-2,500 *C*

A late Ming blue and white baluster vase, painted with a Buddhistic lion amongst scrolling peony, reserved on a scale-pattern ground at the shoulder, neck made up, Wanli, 12in (29cm).
£450-550 *C*

A large Ming blue and white slender meiping, painted with 3 pairs of scholars and attendants, neck damaged, long body crack, Wanli six-character mark on the shoulder and of the period, 23in (57.5cm).
£6,000-7,000 *CSK*

A polychrome goose tureen and cover, the webbed feet yellow and the tail feathers in shaded tones of russet, brown, black and grey, extensive restoration and repaint to cover, late Qianlong, c1780, 15in (37cm) long.
£3,500-4,000 *CNY*

A pair of Chinese Transitional period vases, c1650.
£4,600-5,000 *GRA*

A pair of bottle-shaped vases, covered with a rich blue glaze, Kangxi, 20½in (52.5cm).
£2,000-2,500 *L*

A Chinese blue and white tapering sleeve vase, Transitional, 7in (18cm).
£1,300-1,500 *CSK*

A Transitional blue and white sleeve vase, the waisted neck with stiff leaves, the neck and base with incised lines, c1640, 17½in (43.5cm).
£3,300-3,600 *C*

A large Transitional blue and white cylindrical brush pot, painted in a vivid colour with 3 quail, extended firing crack from rim, c1640, 10½in (26.5cm).
£1,200-1,400 *C*

A vase of octagonal baluster form, painted in underglaze blue with figures outside a walled city in a hilly landscape between borders of formal flower branches, Kangxi, 12in (31cm).
£800-1,000 *L*

A large vase of almost cylindrical form with trumpet neck, painted in underglaze blue, artemisia leaf mark, Kangxi, 21in (53cm).
£1,600-1,800 *L*

A blue and white baluster vase, painted in a vivid blue on the panels with birds amongst chrysanthemum, encircled 'lingzhi' mark, Kangxi, 17½in (44cm).
£1,500-1,800 *C*

A Chinese Imari baluster vase and domed cover, painted in iron red, underglaze blue and gilt, cover similarly painted, cover restored and with replacement blanc-de-chine Buddhistic lion finial, late 17th/early 18thC, 25½in (64cm).
£1,500-1,800 *C*

A pair of blue and white baluster vases and covers, painted all over with lotus in dense inky blue leafy scroll, one body and covers with old damage, Kangxi, 16½in (41cm).
£1,100-1,300 *C*

VALUE POINTS FOR CHINESE PORCELAIN

★ condition – this is always an important factor when dealing with porcelain. Some collectors will only buy perfect pieces – this is particularly the case with Far Eastern buyers. They will pay high prices for excellent condition. This affects the price considerably as a very good piece with a hair line crack or small chip can reduce the value by up to two thirds

★ rarity – as with most aspects of antiques, rare items fetch substantially more than common counterparts. This is also important when thinking of damage, as damage to a common piece is much more likely to affect the price dramatically than a similar damage to a rare piece

★ imperial v. export – most of the high prices for Chinese porcelain seem to come from the Hong Kong salerooms. The Far Eastern buyers tend to collect the pieces made by the Chinese potters for their own market rather than exportware. Hence prices are higher

A pair of vases, originally blue and white, now 'clobbered', decorated with jardinières of flowers and circular medallions within borders of petal ornament, on iron red and green grounds, Kangxi, 19in (48cm). **£1,700-2,000**   *L*

A rare 'famille rose' European subject square baluster vase, painted almost certainly after a Dutch special commission, the domed base with a band of turquoise trellis such as one finds on wares decorated after designs by Cornelis Pronk, rim frits, edge and one foot corner chips, c1735, 12in (29.5cm). **£2,000-2,300**   *C*

There is considerable controversy as to whether this design is from the Pronk workshop, or whether it just forms part of the distinctively European 'special commission' range of designs and vessels which have not been attributed to a particular source; see Howard and Ayres, op.cit. p.304, and Jorg, op.cit. The design comes from a Merian source book of botanical drawings.

Two blue and white baluster vases and domed covers, painted with a fisherman steering his craft, scholars playing a board game, restorations to covers and one neck, Qianlong, 17in (43cm). **£1,500-1,800**   *C*

Two blue and white baluster vases, painted in a vivid colour with a phoenix in flight beside hydrangea sprays, Kangxi, 9in (22.5cm), wood covers. **£900-1,100**   *C*

A large 'famille rose' baluster vase and domed cover, with gilt Buddhistic lion finial, cover restored, Qianlong, 20in (50cm). **£1,000-1,200**   *CSK*

A pair of Chinese export porcelain vases and covers, in dark pink palette with brocade borders and rouge-de-fer bases, one cover restored, the other cover with restored lion dog, 12½in (31cm). **£1,700-2,000**   *GSP*

A blue and white 'yen yen', decorated with 2 figures in a river landscape, foot chipped, Kangxi, 18in (45cm), with pierced wood stand. **£1,000-1,200**   *WW*

Two large 'famille verte' vases, one chipped, encircled iron red Wanli four-character mark, late Qing Dynasty, 25in (62.5cm). **£1,700-2,000**   *C*

A pair of gourd-shape blue and white vases, one converted to a lamp, one with silver collar, as tops are missing, c1810, 14in (35cm).
£1,100-1,300   *EA*

A pair of baluster shape vases, enriched with gilt, 17in (42.5cm).
£600-700   *Pea*

A pair of Canton vases, painted in 'famille rose' enamels with figures and panels of text between bands of flowers and insects, mid-19thC, 18in (45cm).
£600-700   *Bea*

An Imari vase, decorated in underglaze blue and overglaze red and gilt, late 19thC, 14½in (36cm).
£250-300   *TW*

A Kyoto slender oviform vase, decorated in coloured enamels and gilt, signed on the base 'Kinkozan zo', late 19thC, 10½in (25.5cm).
£1,700-1,900   *C*

A Kyoto tapering rectangular vase, gilt slightly rubbed, signed in a square reserve 'Nihon Yozan', Meiji period, 5in (12.5cm).
£700-800   *C*

A large Canton vase, complete with carved wood stand, 26½in (66.5cm) high overall.
£500-700   *Bea*

A 'famille rose' butterflies bottle vase vividly painted, Guangxu four-character mark and of the period, 15½in (38.5cm).
£1,800-2,000   *C*

A pair of large Arita slender baluster vases, decorated in iron red, coloured enamels and gilt, on a red lacquered ground decorated in 'hiramakie', both with hairline cracks to neck, 19thC, 33½in (83.5cm).
£1,300-1,500   *C*

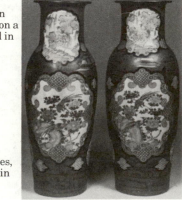

A pair of Imari double gourd vases, one rim chipped, early 19thC, 12in (30.5cm).
£800-900   *Bea*

A pair of Japanese Kutani porcelain vases and covers, with domed covers and 'Fo' dog finials in iron red, green, brown and gilt, 14½in (36cm).
£1,300-1,500 *HSS*

An Imari baluster vase and cover, the jar with an internal lid, 13in (33cm).
£400-500 *L*

A large Japanese Imari vase and cover, with alternating vertical bands of red and blue, 19thC, 19in (47.5cm).
£400-500 *Nes*

A gilded Imari ovoid vase and domed cover with dog of Fo knop, 19thC, 19in (47.5cm).
£500-600 *LBP*

A pair of Satsuma oviform vases, painted in colours and richly gilt, 9½in (23.5cm).
£700-800 *CSK*

Miscellaneous

A pair of Chinese export polychrome candlesticks, painted predominantly in 'famille verte' enamels, Qianlong, 7½in ((18.5cm).
£1,800-2,000 *CSK*

A Transitional blue and white candlestick after a European bronze original, short neck crack, c1640, 13in (32cm).
£3,000-3,500 *C*

A Dehua blanc-de-chine pierced cylindrical brush holder, the sides with an elaborately reticulated design, Kangxi, 5in (13cm).
£700-800 *C*

A gilt-metal mounted 'famille rose' rectangular snuff box and cover, moulded in shallow relief to resemble basketwork, slightly chipped and restoration to base, Qianlong, 3in (7cm) wide.
£1,900-2,100 *C*

A rare 'famille rose' wall sconce, restoration to extremities and hinge section, Qianlong, 8½ by 5½in (21 by 14cm).
£1,500-1,700 *C*

Chinese dynasties and marks

Earlier Dynasties

Shang Yin, c.1532-1027 B.C.
Western Zhou (Chou) 1027-770 B.C.
Spring and Autumn Annals 770-480 B.C.
Warring States 484-221 B.C.
Qin (Ch'in) 221-206 B.C.
Western Han 206 BC-24 AD
Eastern Han 25-220
Three Kingdoms 221-265
Six Dynasties 265-589
Wei 386-557

Sui 589-617
Tang (T'ang) 618-906
Five Dynasties 907-960
Liao 907-1125
Sung 960-1280
Chin 1115-1260
Yüan 1280-1368

Ming Dynasty

洪武年製

Hongwu (Hung Wu)
1368-1398

永樂年製 永樂年製

Yongle (Yung Lo)
1403-1424

大明宣德年製 大明宣德年製

Xuande (Hsüan Té)
1426-1435

大明成化年製 成化年製

Chenghua (Ch'éng Hua)
1465-1487

大明弘治年製

Hongzhi
(Hung Chih)
1488-1505)

大明正德年製

Zhengde
(Chéng Té)
1506-1521

大明嘉靖年製

Jiajing
(Chia Ching)
1522-1566

大明隆慶年製

Longqing
(Lung Ching)
1567-1572

大明萬曆年製

Wanli (Wan Li)
1573-1620

大明天啟年製

Tianqi
(Tien Chi)
1621-1627

崇禎年製

Chongzhen
(Ch'ung Chêng)
1628-1644

Qing (Ch'ing) Dynasty

大清順治年製 大清順治年製

Shunzhi
(Shun Chih)
1644-1661

大清康熙年製 大清康熙年製

Kangxi (K'ang Hsi)
1662-1722

大清雍正年製 大清雍正年製

Yongzheng (Yung Chêng)
1723-1735

大清乾隆年製 大清乾隆年製

Qianlong (Ch'ien Lung)
1736-1795'

嘉慶年製 大清嘉慶年製

Jiaqing (Chia Ch'ing)
1796-1820

大清道光年製 大清道光年製

Daoguang (Tao Kuang)
1821-1850

大清咸豐年製 大清咸豐年製

Xianfeng (Hsien Féng)
1851-1861

大清同治年製 大清同治年製

Tongzhi (T'ung Chih)
1862-1874

大清光緒年製 大清光緒年製

Guangxu (Kuang Hsu)
1875-1908

大清宣統年製

Xuantong
(Hsuan T'ung)
1909-1911

洪憲年製

Hongxian
(Hung Hsien)
1916

BRITISH GLASS – PRICE TRENDS 1985–86
by R G Thomas

Since my review in 1985, little has changed in the field of prices and trends. There is still a general shortage of all glass on the market including what at one time were considered to be mundane items eg jellies, rummers, custard cups etc.

With qualifications, outstanding and good quality glass(es) that have been offered, have done well (but see example 1 below). Other items have advanced much in line with the average year on increase. In a very well-attended London sale, of the 145 lots offered, with many above average items, 52% were either below or within the saleroom's estimates (excluding the 10% buyers premium). Favourites of many collectors; colour twists, whatever their quality, and good engraved glasses, particularly rummers and Jacobites, have done well. The more interesting Beilbys reached a new plateau about three years ago, but haven't advanced much further apart from the rare and unusual items.

Good coloured and Stourbridge glass is hard to find owing to intense American interest, and prices have advanced accordingly. Good 18th and early-19thC cut and table glass has continued to appreciate although certain items such as 'Irish' fruit bowls have faltered, probably because there seems to be sufficient available to meet demand. Good pairs of Georgian, and earlier, decanters go on and on, and one can now expect to pay about £500 for a pair of quite ordinary, but good quality items. Moreover in London, late last year, a pair of early 19thC magnums realised the very high price of £2,970 to a trade buyer against a most unrealistic saleroom estimate of £300-500.

The following three examples of the unpredictable nature of prices in the London salerooms illustrate the difficulty that specialist dealers like myself have in generalising on prices and trends in what is so often stressed in this book, is only a guide to prices.

Last spring a well publicised sale of 18thC Dutch engraved glass was offered. Normally this glass does very well, but at the end of this sale twenty-one of the sixty lots offered (35%) remained unsold. Stipple-engraved glasses (with one notable exception) did very badly; only twelve of the twenty-four sold. Estimates ranged from £800-7,000 and of the eleven glasses attributed to, or "in the manner of David Woolf", four (36%) were unsold. (The notable exception, with a replacement metal foot, made £32,400 against an estimate of £12,000-20,000). Yet, just recently, a stipple Dutch engraved wine glass c1780 with stated mid-19thC stipple engraving made £792 against a very realsistic estimate of £200-300.

Secondly, in 1983 a Beilby with an unusual scene, but very poor execution and damaged enamel, made the very high price of £2,376 against an estimate of £1,400–£1,800. Just recently, in a different London saleroom, a stated similar glass, with the same poor execution and similar damage, was edged up with difficulty to £2,200 against an estimate of £1,800–£2,400. Taking into account the high cost of selling in a saleroom, the loss, if the buyer in the first instance, and the seller in the second had been the same person, would have been considerable.

Lastly, seven months ago, an ordinary balustroid, with unusual bowl decoration, was sold for £286 against a realistic estimate of £200-250. Just recently in the same saleroom, a stated identical glass, of the same quality sold for £660 against an estimate of £300-400. A very high appreciation of approx. 130% in just seven months.

In all aspects of life one likes to have value for money. In the field of collecting this requires knowledge, discrimination and self-imposed discipline.

Beakers

A Bohemian ruby-overlay engraved tumbler, c1860, 5in (12.5cm).
£500-600 *C*

A Bohemian Hyalith goblet, the cylindrical bowl gilt with an Oriental figure, with gilt interior, Count Buquoy's Glassworks, c1835, 5in (12.5cm).
£700-800 *C*

A Bohemian blue-overlay amber-flash waisted beaker, painted with Venus standing naked clasping her long flowing hair, the reverse cut with ovals and drapes outlined in green, 5in (12.5cm).
£300-400 *CSK*

Bowls

A rare glass and ormolu tazza, painted with a wreath of flowers, possibly Irish, c1810.
£350-500 *DE*

FAKES AND FORGERIES
(18th and early 19th Century)
by R G Thomas

Fakes and forgeries may be defined as follows:

Fake – glass that has been altered or later decorated to enhance its value or its intrinsic appeal.

Forgery – old glass that has been copied with the intention to deceive.

Many fakes and forgeries have been produced from the 18thC onwards and time, wear and tear has given some of these examples a superficial appearance of authenticity. Basically, in assessing whether or not an article is genuine, the following factors need to be borne in mind:

Ring – if the example has a good ring, it is probably British lead glass. However, many genuine glasses because of their shape, construction and thickness may not exhibit this attribute.

Pontil Mark – all 18thC glasses, with the exception of a few facet stem examples, should have the rough pontil mark under the foot. It cannot be emphasised too strongly that the presence of a pontil mark does not alone indicate 18thC glass. In the 19thC the pontil mark was invariably ground out. 18thC table ware, such as decanters was similarly treated.

Colour – early 18thC glass often had a straw, then greenish, then dark tint, becoming progressively clearer and brighter as the century progressed.

Striarations – all old glass should show tooling marks in both the bowl and the foot. The bowl should invariably show three or more faint creases running diagonally from the rim down the bowl. The absence of these marks calls for a stringent assessment of the example for age.

Form – knowledge of how glass(es) was made is important in the detection of fakes and forgeries; types of construction and decoration for different groups of glasses, types of feet used and so on.

Test for lead – the ultra violet lamp should show whether or not glass is lead. Lead glass will usually exhibit a blue tint. Other glass a yellow to brown tint or no reaction at all. This test is not infallible, particularly when the glass has developed a film of oxide through constant use.

Engraving – see the 1985 Miller's Guide. Suffice to repeat that many old glasses have been later engraved and cut, particularly Jacobite, Williamite and Sunderland Bridge examples.

Restorations – many glasses (and cut glass) have had their feet and rims ground to remove chips; and feet and bowls replaced, particularly the rarer glasses such as Jacobites, mixed twist and colour twists. A knowledge of how rims were fashioned should enable detection of this restoration. Modern glass glues can defeat the ultra violet lamp.

A patch stand, the shallow bowl set on a bobbin stem, conical folded foot, c1740, 2in (5cm).
£100-120 *SW*

An extremely fine Irish boat-shaped bowl, on square foot, c1790, 13in (32.5cm) wide.
£700-1,000 *DE*

An oval Irish bowl with turnover rim, on moulded foot, c1780-90.
£600-800 *DE*

A rare pair of small Irish turnover bowls, the rims and bodies with geometric and slice cutting, on stems with ball knops, square domed lemon squeezer feet, c1790, 3in (8cm).
£1,300-1,400 *Som*

An Irish bowl of fine colour and unusual form, c1790, 15in (37cm) long.
£700-900   *DE*

A very rare Irish circular glass bowl of double ogee shape, entirely moulded with fine horizontal flutes, on plain stem with centre triple rings and square foot, of fine colour and in extremely fine condition, c1795, 9in (22cm).
£500-700   *DE*

A heavy dark metal, double ogee, circular fruit bowl, with strawberry diamond- and facet-cut bowl, heavy ball knop stem with air-tear, plain conical foot, c1810, 9½in (24cm).
£300-400   *Som*

A cut-crystal punch bowl, on separate base with 11 punch glasses, 6 liquor glasses and ladle.
£150-200   *PC*

A set of 3 English shallow boat-shaped bowls, comprising: a pair and one slightly larger, with scalloped borders and cut swags and stars, on knopped stems and fluted feet, c1800, large bowl 6in (15cm) high.
£1,000-1,200   *DE*

A pair of Georgian glass fruit bowls of rare form, with brilliant diamond and step cutting and silver-plated mounts, c1820, 9in (22.5cm).
£1,400-1,600   *DE*

These were made in two parts in order to take ice.

A group of octagonal step-cut dessert dishes, c1820.
£80-150 each   *DE*

A pink frosted bowl, with frilled and dimpled border painted with flowering foliage, on gilt metal stand, 13in (32.5cm) wide.
£180-240   *CSK*

A sugar basin of opaque white pressed glass, moulded with a portrait head of Benjamin Disraeli, Earl of Beaconsfield, registered by Henry Greener, Wear Flint Glass Works, Sunderland, 31st August 1878, 5½in (14cm).
£45-50   *SW*

Candelabra

A candlestick, the pan-topped sconce with a double collar above a stem with a single cable air-twist, base collar and air-beaded knop, domed plain foot, c1745, 8in (20.5cm).
£450-550 *Som*

A baluster candlestick, the stem with true baluster section above a beaded knop and triple annulated basal knop, on a domed and terraced foot, c1745, 8in (19.5cm).
£650-750 *C*

An air-twist candlestick, the inverted baluster stem filled with spirals and base knop, on a domed and terraced foot, c1750, 8in (20cm).
£600-700 *C*

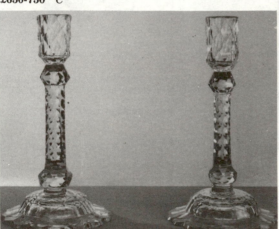

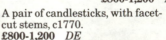

A pair of candlesticks, with moulded pedestal stems, c1750.
£800-1,200 *DE*

A pair of candlesticks, with facet-cut stems, c1770.
£800-1,200 *DE*

A pair of Regency two-light candelabra, with ormolu mounts, hung with icicle drops, c1820.
£2,000-3,000 *DE*

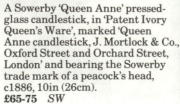

A Sowerby 'Queen Anne' pressed-glass candlestick, in 'Patent Ivory Queen's Ware', marked 'Queen Anne candlestick, J. Mortlock & Co., Oxford Street and Orchard Street, London' and bearing the Sowerby trade mark of a peacock's head, c1886, 10in (26cm).
£65-75 *SW*

A pair of Regency cut-crystal and ormolu table candelabra, 16½in (41cm).
£3,000-4,000 *BS*

A pair of Georgian ormolu-mounted, cut and coloured glass candlesticks, with blue and white jasper porcelain pedestals and beaded spreading bases, 13½in (34cm).
£1,700-2,000 *C*

▷ A pair of Regency diamond-cut candlesticks, with ormolu mounts, hung with icicle drops, c1820.
£800-1,000 *DE*

◁ A pair of brass and glass candelabra, with hanging chains and drops, 19thC, 28in (70cm).
£600-700 *CW*

Decanters

A rare pair of Lynn decanters, the tapered bodies with horizontal moulded bands, cut spire stoppers, c1750, 9in (22.5cm).
£800-900 *Som*

A pair of Victorian pink opaque glass lustres under domes, in white and blue enamel and gilt, hung with 14 crystal drops, c1860, 14in (35cm).
£400-500 *TW*

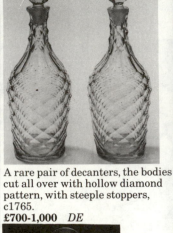

A pair of shouldered decanters and lozenge stoppers, engraved with 'Port' and 'White Wine' in quatrefoil labels, bordered with flowers and fruiting vine, c1755-60, 12in (29.5cm).
£900-1,000   *L*

A rare pair of decanters, the bodies cut all over with hollow diamond pattern, with steeple stoppers, c1765.
£700-1,000   *DE*

A tapered decanter with cut base fluting and lunar-cut lozenge stopper, the body engraved with egg-and-tulip looped band, c1770, 10in (24.5cm).
£200-250   *Som*

An Irish decanter of club shape with base fluting, scale cut neck, engraved with intertwined bands of laurel leaves with cut stars, cut lozenge stopper, c1780, 9in (23cm).
£200-250   *Som*

A Bristol blue carafe, engraved with grapes and vine leaves, with a Sheffield plate stopper, c1830.
£180-230   *SA*

l. A tapered decanter, the body engraved with rose sprays, cut lozenge stopper, c1780, 10in (25cm).
£220-260

r. A fine tapered decanter, the body mould fluted at base, engraved with sunflowers and looped husk decoration, facet-cut neck, cut lozenge stopper, c1780, 10in (24.5cm).
£220-260   *Som*

A pair of Georgian wine decanters, documented as having been the property of William Wordsworth, mallet-shaped and panel-cut with facet-cut ringed-necks with disc stopper and replacement faceted ball stopper and red lacquer coasters, 14½in (36cm).
£280-360   *CDC*

A fine pair of Irish club-shaped decanters, with base and neck fluting, the bodies cut with a band of shallow diamonds, heart-shaped cut lozenge stoppers, c1780, 9½in (23.5cm).
£550-650   *Som*

A good pair of Irish tapered decanters, with base-fluted bodies and scale-cut necks, engraved with looped laurel wreaths, cut lozenge stoppers, c1780, 9½in (23.5cm).
£550-600 *Som*

A pair of George III Irish square-shaped spirit decanters, with cut foliated medallions and cut canted corners.
£300-400 *AG*

▷

A suite of Georgian decanters, of three-quart and two-pint capacity, c1820.
£900-1,200 *DE*

Three cylindrical cut spirit bottles with base fluting and a band of diamonds, cut mushroom stoppers, Sheffield plated trefoil frame, c1810.
£350-400 *Som*

A tapered decanter, the body engraved with 3 bands of floral and leaf scrolling, lozenge stopper, c1790, 10in (24.5cm).
£200-240 *Som*

A tapered plain decanter, the body engraved with initials 'PB' within a heart-shaped cartouche, plain lozenge stopper, c1780, 9½in (23.5cm).
£200-250 *Som*

A pair of amethyst decanters, decorated with silver and gold, probably French, possibly Russian, c1820.
£1,400-1,800 *DE*

GLASS

DECANTERS

A pair of tapering magnum decanters, with hobnail-cut bodies, panelled necks and shallow swag-cut shoulders and star bases, with lozenge stoppers, one neck chipped, late 18thC, 13½in (34cm).
£300-350 *WW*

An Irish Cork decanter, the ovoid body with moulded fluting and cut-star decoration, 3 feathered neck rings, radially-cut lozenge stoppers, marked underneath Cork Glass Co., c1800, 9in (22cm).
£450-500 *Som*

A good tapered decanter, the base and neck flute-cut, band of tulip and printy decoration, cut lunar stopper, c1780, 10in (25cm).
£250-300 *Som*

An amber-tinted wine decanter, with single loop handle, plated mount to neck and matching stopper, 8½in (21cm).
£45-55 *WIL*

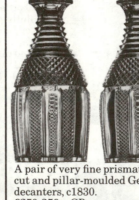

A pair of very fine prismatic step-cut and pillar-moulded Georgian decanters, c1830.
£250-350 *CB*

A pair of very good quality decanters, the ovoid bodies cut with broad flutes and sprig decoration, 3 cut neck rings and cut mushroom stoppers, c1825, 9in (22cm).
£500-600 *Som*

A most unusual heavy baluster glass, the trumpet bowl with pouring lip and folded rim, on a stem with inverted baluster knop with air-tear and base knop, domed folded foot, c1700, 6in (15cm).
£800-900 *Som*

A calligraphic baluster goblet, attributed to Bastiaan Boers or François Crama, engraved in diamond point with the calligraphic inscription 'sine vulnere laedo', the inverted baluster stem enclosing a small tear above a folded conical foot, c1700, 7in (17.5cm).
£6,000-7,000 *C*

A fine quality Victorian cut glass decanter, c1880, 11½in (29.5cm).
£120-130 *SW*

Drinking Glasses

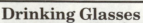

Three 'heavy' baluster wine glasses, c1700-15, 5½in (14cm).
£600-680 each *SW*

An early baluster goblet, the large round funnel bowl with thickened base, set on a wide flattened knop and base knop with tears, conical folded foot, c1690-1700, 8in (19.5cm).
£1,200-1,400 *SW*

A baluster period wine glass, the stem with three-ringed annulated shoulder knop, teared section and base knop, domed and folded foot, c1710, 7in (17cm).
£450-550 *SW*

A heavy baluster wine glass, the bell bowl supported on a five-ringed annulated knop above a true baluster and basal cyst, plain conical foot, c1710, 7in (17cm).
£700-750 *SW*

A baluster wine glass, the funnel bowl with solid lower part enclosing a tear, supported on a ball knop with tear above a true baluster, terminating in a folded conical foot, c1700, 5½in (14cm).
£600-650 *SW*

A baluster goblet, the stem with wide angular knop, short plain section and base knob enclosing an elongated tear, on a folded conical foot, c1715, 6½in (16.5cm).
£300-400 *C*

Three baluster glasses, c1715-25.
£450-750 each *DE*

An armorial baluster goblet, the bucket bowl with everted rim engraved with a coat-of-arms within a scroll-and-strap cartouche, the stem with a wide angular knopped section enclosing a tear above a base knob and folded conical foot, c1760, 6½in (16cm).
£1,300-1,500 *C*

Provenance: R. Vecht Collection, Amsterdam.

A baluster goblet, the funnel bowl with teared and cusped solid lower part, supported on an acorn knop enclosing a tear above a base knob, on a folded conical foot, c1705, 7in (17.5cm).
£1,500-1,700 *C*

A rare green-tinted wine glass, the ovoid bowl set on a hollow stem with shoulder-dropped knop over inverted baluster with base knop, high domed foot, c1750.
£280-300 *SW*

A fine coin goblet, the large flared bucket bowl on a stem with hollow knop with raspberry prunts, containing a silver coin for 1745, a teared inverted baluster knop below, folded conical foot, c1745, 9½in (23.5cm).
£1,400-1,600 *Som*

GLASS

Drinking glasses have been ordered in line with the E Barrington Haynes system (see Pelican Books *Glass Through The Ages* by E Barrington Haynes).

Group I	Baluster Stems	1685-1725
II	Moulded Pedestal Stems	1715-65
III	Balustroid Stems	1725-55
IV	Light (Newcastle) Balusters	1735-65
V	Composite Stems	1740-70
VI	Plain Straight Stems	1740-70
VII	Air Twist Stems	1740-70
VIII	Hollow Stems	1750-60
IX	Incised Twist Stems	1750-65
X	Opaque Twist Stems	1750-80
XI	Mixed and Colour Twist Stems	1755-75
XII	Faceted Stems	1760-1800
XIII	Other glasses with short or rudimentary stems: Dwarf Ales; Jelly Glasses; Rummers; Georgian Ales; wines and drams; 18-19thC.	

A champagne glass with double ogee bowl on a collar, above a star-studded pedestal stem with double coiled collar at base, folded conical foot, c1745, 6½in (16.5cm).
£200-250 *Som*

A pedestal-stemmed Alliance goblet in the manner of Robart, on a triple-annulated knop above an octagonally-moulded pedestal stem with stars at the shoulder, 1735-40, 8in (19cm).
£1,200-1,400 *C*

A pedestal-stemmed wine glass, the straight-sided funnel bowl with solid lower part and tear, set on a six-sided moulded tapering stem enclosing an elongated tear, on an unusual 'petal' moulded domed foot, c1745, 6in (15cm).
£600-650 *SW*

A champagne glass, the double ogee bowl set on an eight-sided pedestal stem with bare collar on a domed and folded foot, c1745, 6½in (16cm).
£300-340 *SW*

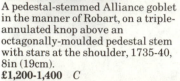

◁
l. A balustroid wine glass, the bell bowl on a stem with an air-beaded centre ball knop, plain domed foot, c1745, 6½in (16.5cm).
£220-260

r. A balustroid wine glass, the bell bowl on a stem with shoulder annulated, inverted baluster and base knops, folded conical foot, c1730, 6in (15cm).
£280-340 *Som*

l. A balustroid wine glass, the trumpet bowl on a drawn stem with air-tears and centre ball knop, plain conical foot, c1740, 7in (17cm).
£320-370

r. A similar glass with folded conical foot, c1740, 7in (17.5cm).
£240-300 *Som*

A balustroid wine glass, the bowl of drawn-trumpet shape set on a knop above a true baluster section, conical folded foot, c1740, 6in (15.5cm).
£180-220 *SW*

A balustroid 'Kit Kat' wine glass, the drawn trumpet bowl on a stem with an air-tear and inverted baluster knop, folded conical foot, c1750, 6in (15.5cm).
£280-320 *Som*

A Williamite wine glass, the trumpet bowl engraved with equestrian portrait of King William, and inscription in a ribbon 'To the Glorious Memory of King William', the reverse 'Boyne, 1st July 1690', on a balustroid stem with shoulder and base collars, folded conical foot, c1780, 6½in (16.5cm).
£950-1,100 *Som*

◁
A light Newcastle baluster glass, with 3 knops followed by slender baluster and base knop, c1735-65.
£450-500 *CB*

l. A mixed-twist wine glass, with bell bowl, c1760.
£280-300

c. A composite-stem wine glass, with domed foot, c1750.
£370-400

r. A double series air-twist wine glass, with bucket bowl, c1750.
£200-250 *SW*

A Royal armorial light baluster goblet, the funnel bowl engraved with the crowned arms of Willem V of Orange within the Garter, above the motto 'JE MAINTAINDRAI' on a double knopped and beaded baluster stem, c1760, 8in (19.5cm).
£1,800-2,200   *C*

l. A wine glass, the trumpet bowl engraved with a band of baroque scrolling, on a drawn stem with multi-spiral air-twist, plain conical foot, c1740, 7in (18cm).
£150-180

r. An unusual wine glass, the bell bowl on a stem with multi-spiral air-twist with unusual conical oval foot, c1745, 4½in (11cm).
£160-190   *Som*

An engraved light baluster goblet, the funnel bowl decorated with a standard-bearer above the mirror monogram 'AFB', inscribed beneath the rim, 'LANG LEVE DEN VAANDRIG VAND COMPAGNIE WYK NO.28', the stem with beaded dumb-bell section, on a conical foot, c1755, 8½in (21cm).
£2,000-2,500   *C*

'Wyk no.28' refers to one of the Amsterdam 'Doelen'.

A composite-stem wine glass, the bell bowl on a stem with beaded cushion knop between plain sections, plain conical foot, c1740, 7in (17.5cm).
£200-350   *Som*

Three 18thC air-twist wine glasses.

l. A rare soda glass wine glass, the bell bowl on a knop above an inverted baluster and base knop, conical foot, a two-piece glass, c1730-40, 6½in (16cm).
£350-380

c. A large bell bowl glass on a multi-spiral air-twist stem with knop below bowl, conical foot, c1750, 7in (17cm).
£180-200

r. A bell bowl glass, the air-twist stem with applied vermicular collar, conical foot, c1750, 6½in (16cm).
£200-230   *SW*

A composite-stemmed wine glass, of drawn-trumpet shape, the stem filled with air-twist spirals set into a beaded inverted baluster section, above a base knop, on a conical foot, c1750, 7in (17.5cm).
£200-250   *C*

A composite-stem Jacobite wine glass, the trumpet bowl engraved with a rose and one bud, on a stem with a beaded knop, central and base ball knops, domed and folded foot, c1750, 7in (17cm).
£800-900 *Som*

An armorial wine glass, by David Wolff, decorated with the crowned arms of Prussia, for Princess Frederika Sophia Wilhelmina, the wild men supporters standing on a broad-rimmed shaped solid base suspending a floral swag, on a plain stem and foot, The Hague, c1790, 6in (15cm).
£2,000-3,000 *C*

Although there are approximately 2 dozen recorded glasses stippled with the arms of the Princess's husband, Prince Willem V, and some 15 Alliance glasses with the arms of both the Prince and Princess, apart from the present example only 3 other glasses are known stipple-engraved with the arms of Princess Wilhelmina.

l. A wine glass, the round funnel bowl with a band of engraved fruiting vine, on a stem with shoulder and base knopped multiple-spiral air-twist stem, plain conical foot, c1745, 5½in (14cm).
£150-170

r. A wine glass, the ogee bowl on a stem with centre cushion knop and multiple-spiral air-twist, plain conical foot, c1745, 6½in (14cm).
£180-220 *Som*

A plain-stemmed landscape wine glass by David Wolff, on a plain stem and conical foot, The Hague, 1790, 6in (15cm).
£6,000-7,000 *C*

The stippled landscape is somewhat reminiscent of an arcadian scene painted by Paulus Constantijn La Fargue in 1778, Rijksmuseum, Amsterdam, depicting the Scheveningsche Boschjes situated between The Hague and the sea, at that time (and still) a very popular recreational area, ideal for promenading. The dunes seen in the distance on the glass would seem to confirm that location.

A rare Jacobite glass with a portrait of the Young Pretender, c1745.
£4,000-6,000 *DE*

This glass has a particularly important inscription and portrait which adds considerably to its value.

A plain-stemmed Jacobite wine glass, the funnel bowl with a seven- petalled rose and a bud, on a conical foot, c1750, 6in (15cm).
£300-400 *C*

A wine glass, with trumpet bowl on a drawn mercury-twist stem and domed foot, c1745, 7in (18cm).
£250-300 *SW*

A green wine glass, the cup-shaped bowl on a plain stem, conical foot, c1760, 5in (12.5cm).
£180-200 *SW*

Three trumpet wine glasses with drawn air-twist stems, the centre glass with folded foot, c1740-50.
£140-180 each *SW*

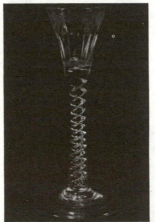

l. A wine glass, the round funnel bowl with base moulding on a stem with cable air-twist, plain conical foot, c1750, 6½in (16cm).
£260-300

r. A wine glass, the round funnel bowl on a stem with single-corkscrew air-twist, plain conical foot, c1740, 6in (15cm).
£130-160 *Som*

A lead wine glass, the round funnel bowl on a stem with a coarse incised twist, c1750, 6½in (16cm).
£380-430 *Som*

This has an extremely rare folded conical foot for this type of glass.

l. A wine glass, the bell bowl on a stem with multiple-spiral air-twist, the twist starting in the base of the bowl, plain conical foot, c1745, 6½in (16cm).
£140-180

r. A wine glass, the waisted bowl on a stem similar to above, but with a vermicular collar round stem, c1745, 6½in (16cm).
£220-250 *Som*

A wine glass, the round funnel bowl on a multiple-spiral air-twist stem with shoulder and central knops, plain conical foot, c1750, 6in (15cm).
£160-200 *Som*

A fine cordial, the small fluted-trumpet bowl engraved with a floral rose band, on a stem with corkscrew mercury air-twist, folded conical foot, c1750, 6½in (16cm).
£460-520 *Som*

A Jacobite wine glass, the bell bowl engraved with a rose, 2 buds and moth, double knopped multi-spiral air-twist stem, conical foot, c1750, 7in (17.5cm).
£500-550 *SW*

Two unusual opaque-twist wine glasses, the ribbed round funnel bowls set on a double series opaque-twist stem, conical foot, c1760, 6in (15cm).
£180-200 each *SW*

A Jacobite wine glass, the bell bowl engraved with Jacobite rose and one bud, on a stem with multiple-spiral air-twist and vermicular collar, plain conical foot, c1750, 7in (17.5cm).
£600-700 *Som*

A good mixed-twist wine glass, the bell bowl on a stem with central air-twist gauze and pair of outer opaque spiralling tapes, very rare folded foot, c1770, 6½in (16.5cm).
£350-400 *Som*

Ex Horridge collection.

A cordial glass, the bowl diamond-engraved by an amateur hand with a sailing ship, churches, a house and a lighthouse, inscribed 'Success to the Ellen Snow Monday Poole drew this glass', English, c1770, 6½in (15.5cm).
£350-400   *L*

An incised-twist wine glass, the generous bell bowl with honeycomb-moulded lower part, on a conical foot, c1760, 7in (17.5cm).
£280-320   *C*

A cordial glass, the small round funnel bowl set on a thick stem enclosing a single series opaque-twist, conical foot, c1760, 7in (16.5cm).
£300-350   *SW*

An ale glass, the extended funnel bowl engraved with hops and barley, on a double series air-twist stem, conical foot, c1750, 8in (19cm).
£300-350   *SW*

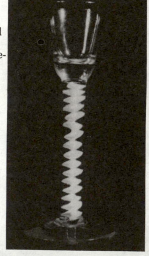

A group of 18thC opaque-twist wine glasses, c1760.
£100-150 each   *SW*

A wine glass, the ogee bowl engraved with a good hunting scene below a band of cross hatching, double series opaque-twist stem, plain conical foot, c1760, 5½in (14cm).
£450-500   *Som*

▷

Two 'Lynn' wine glasses.

l. A Beilby opaque-twist wine, the bowl decorated in white enamel with a border scroll, traces of gilding to rim, c1770, 5½in (14cm).
£1,000-1,200

r. A Beilby opaque-twist wine, the bowl decorated in white enamel with a border of fruiting vine, traces of gilding to rim, c1770, 6in (15cm).
£1,000-1,500   *SW*

l. The rounded funnel bowl with horizontal moulded bands on lower half of bowl, on a double series opaque-twist stem, conical foot, c1760, 6in (15cm).
£350-400

r. The rounded funnel bowl with typical horizontal moulded bands, on a double series opaque-twist stem, conical foot, c1760, 5in (13cm).
£300-350   *SW*

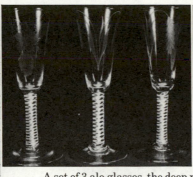

A set of 3 ale glasses, the deep round funnel bowls engraved with hops and barley, on double-series opaque-twist stems, plain conical feet, c1760, 7½in (19cm). **£650-750** *Som*

Three good-quality opaque-twist wine glasses, c1760. **£150-180 each** *SW*

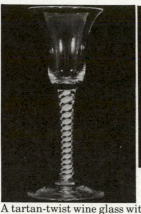

A tartan-twist wine glass with bell bowl, the stem with an opaque corkscrew core, edged with brick red and translucent green threads and entwined by 2 opaque threads, on a conical foot, c1760, 7in (17cm). **£2,000-2,200** *SW*

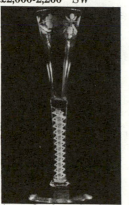

A ratafia glass, the slim funnel bowl engraved with a band of stylised decoration, moulded vertical ribs, on a double-series opaque-twist stem, conical foot, c1765, 8in (19cm). **£500-550** *SW*

A 'Beilby' wine glass, the round funnel bowl enamelled in white with a temple and fir trees, on a stem with a double-series opaque-twist, plain conical foot, c1770, 5½in (14cm). **£450-500** *Som*

This glass has all the stylistic decoration and enamel of a Beilby, but the decoration is on the front only. It may possibly have been a trial piece.

A facet-stemmed portrait wine glass by David Wolff, the ovoid bowl decorated with a portrait of Cornelus de Witt, the stem cut with hexagonal facets and on a conical foot, The Hague, 1780-85, 6in (15cm). **£5,500-6,500** *C*

In Dutch history the year 1672 is known as the disaster year. The plight of the country had become so desperate that finally the populace turned to the young Prince Willem III of Orange, the future King of England, whose talents and courage eventually saved the Republic from the dire effects of gross injustice inflicted by France and England.

There were, however, opponents of Orangist strategy, among whom were two renowned statesmen, the brothers de Witt: Cornelus (1623-72) and Johan (1625-72). At the height of their careers both were most brutally lynched by a pro-Orange mob in The Hague on August 27, 1672.

Memories of these events were stirred in 1755 by the publication of the volume of Wagenaar's Dutch History *in which that era is dealt with. Between the years 1757 and 1758 a 'de Witt's war' on paper ensued between the Orangists and Patriots about the role the brothers de Witt had played in political history. The brothers were again brought to prominence in 1781 when they were hailed as paragons in an inciting Patriotic pamphlet.*

A dram glass, the ogee bowl on a double series opaque-twist stem, c1760, 4in (10cm). **£160-190** *SW*

A sweetmeat, the double ogee bowl with a dentillated rim, on a knopped stem with multiple-spiral opaque-twist, ribbed conical foot, c1760, 3in (7.5cm). **£220-250** *Som*

A green wine glass, the rounded cup-shaped bowl set on a hollow ball, knopped stem and folded foot, c1760, 4in (10cm). **£320-360** *SW*

Four small Georgian wines.

l. A trumpet bowl finely engraved with floral bouquet and monogram 'RR' knopped stem, c1820, 4½in (11cm). **£35-40**

c. Two of a set of 4, with conical bowls, heavily cut with prism and diamond arches, c1820, 4in (10cm). **£100-130 the set**

r. A conical rib-moulded bowl engraved with floral band, knopped, drawn stem, c1810, 4½in (11cm). **£30-35** *Som*

A mammoth pear-shaped goblet, profusely engraved with Masonic emblems, c1810. **£300-450** *DE*

Four dram glasses with firing feet.

l. A trumpet bowl, drawn stem with air-tear, plain conical foot, c1750, 3½in (9cm). **£80-100**

l.c. An ovoid ribbed bowl on a drawn ribbed stem, solid firing foot, c1770, 3½in (9cm). **£70-80**

r.c. A round funnel bowl, with stylised Jacobite rose and bud, plain stem, solid foot, c1780, 4in (10cm). **£55-65**

r. A conical bowl, drawn plain stem, flanged firing foot, c1780, 4in (9.5cm). **£55-65** *Som*

A pair of large goblets of waisted form, the undersides of the bowls faceted, the stems fluted, the domed feet cut and shaped, c1760, 9½in (23cm). **£600-800** *DE*

An ovoid rummer, the bowl engraved with the inscription 'Peace and Plenty' within a shield with a bird in flight at each corner, and flanked by the initials 'CS' and 'FCS', capstan stem, plain conical foot, c1810, 5½in (14cm). **£200-250** *Som*

Three rummers, the ovoid bowls engraved with band of wrigglework and ovals, containing monograms, 'UK' and 'AK', merese, square domed lemon squeezer feet, c1810, 5½in (13.5cm). **£170-200** *Som*

A conical tumbler, the flute-cut body engraved with portcullis and bird above, in a shield, inscribed 'Non Nobis Sed Patria' monogram 'WVC', c1810, 4in (10cm). **£45-55** *Som*

Jugs

An extremely rare covered cream boat, cut with flat geometric patterns, c1765. **£500-700** *DE*

A Richardsons marked water jug, painted with water lilies, c1848. **£400-600** *DE*

A fine claret jug, the body pillar-cut with facet-cut neck, c1830-40, 14in (36.5cm). **£230-260** *SW*

Paperweights

Baccarat garlanded white double-clematis weight, 3in (7.5cm) diam.
£700-800   C

A Clichy swirl weight, with alternate turquoise and white staves radiating from a central claret, green and white cane, 3½in (8.5cm) diam.
£600-700   C

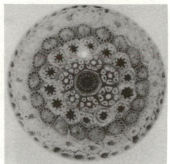

A Bacchus close-concentric-millefiori weight, the central pale pink and white cane enclosed within 4 circles in pale shades of green, white, pink and blue, 4in (9.5cm) diam.
£600-700   C

Scent Bottles

Four clear scent bottles, probably by Apsley Pellatt, 3 with alternate diamond-cut gadrooned panels and plain shoulder, the 4th with plain gadrooning and diamond-cut shoulder, silver-gilt screw mounts, hallmarked 'T & J Phipps', London 1820.
£750-850 set   Som

A cameo glass salts bottle, carved with flowers and ferns in opaque white on a satin ochre ground with silver screw top, in case, 19thC, 4in (10cm) long.
£200-300   CDC   ▷

A Thomas Webb & Son cameo glass swan's-head scent bottle, silver-gilt mount, reg'd mark no.11109, London 1884.
£800-900   WW

pear-shaped apothecaries bottle and stopper, impressed and over-gilt with the name 'Fortnum & Mason Parfumerie Bond Street London, by app to HRM Queen Victoria 1860'.
£140-180   CBS

Vases

pair of Irish urn-shaped vases, with lemon squeezer feet, c1790.
£800-900   DE

An opaque pale blue pressed-glass 'swan' vase, unmarked, c1870, 7in (17.5cm).
£40-50   SW

A pair of French cut-glass vases, with ormolu mounts, c1820.
£800-1,200   DE

A pair of vases in the Venetian style, in mottled blue and white glass, made by Alexander Jenkinson, Norton Park Glass Works, Edinburgh, c1880.
£200-250 *SW*

A Bohemian white-overlay flaring vase, painted with 6 panels of brightly-coloured flower sprays below cusp and angle rims, the circular base cut with ovals gilt with C scrolls, 17in (42.5cm).
£450-500 *CSK*

A pair of Bohemian cased blue glass vases, fitted for electricity, 9in (22cm) high, excluding mounts.
£400-500 *Bon*

A cut-glass flaring cylindrical celery vase, 6½in (16cm).
£60-80 *CSK*

A pair of Bohemian green glass vases, 19thC, 14in (34.5cm).
£130-180 *HSS* ▷

Miscellaneous

A Thomas Webb & Sons Burmese glass ovoid vase of lemon yellow shading to light rose, marked Thomas Webb and Sons Patented Queen's Burmese Ware, c1880s, 10in (24.5cm).
£600-700 *Bon*

An English lead-glass water po[...] and cover, early 18thC, 6½in (16.5cm).
£150-200 *TKN*

A pressed-glass figure of Britannia in frosted glass, by John Derbyshire, Manchester, and registered on 20 November 1874, bearing the Trade mark and design lozenge, 8in (20cm).
£70-80 *SW*

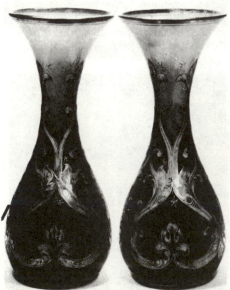

A pair of French blue glass pear-shaped vases, gilt with leaves, 14in (35cm).
£140-180 *CSK*

A pair of oval salts, with cut scalloped decoration, stepped moulded lemon squeezer feet, c1820, 4in (9cm).
£80-90 *Som*

A good oval Irish tea box, with silvered copper mounts, cut with flat geometric patterns, c1790.
£800-1,100 *DE*

This almond-shaped oval is typically Irish.

A baluster gadrooned tankard, with grapes, hops and barley, dated '1785'.
£300-400 *DE*

A French glass tea box, cut with diagonal pillar flutes and fitted ormolu mounts, c1815-20.
£300-600 *DE*

A Victorian pressed-glass dish, with scalloped edge, 6in (15cm).
£12-18 *DEL*

A two-compartment soda glass red and white wine flask, trailed neck decoration, hollow conical folded foot, c1760, 8in (20cm).
£55-65 *Som*

A Sowerby miniature tea caddy, in 'Patent Ivory Queen's Ware', marked with lozenge for 10 March 1879 and Trade Mark, 3½in (8.5cm).
£70-80 *SW*

A cut butter dish, cover and stand, the dish with prism and diamond cutting, the cover with mushroom finial, diamond and star cut stand, c1810, 6½in (16cm).
£350-450 *Som*

A Sowerby 'Patent Ivory Queen's Ware' pressed-glass plate, registration mark for 30 August 1878 and bearing the Sowerby Trade Mark of a peacock's head, 9in (22.5cm).
£30-40 *SW*

TURNED TABLE LEGS OF THE SEVENTEENTH CENTURY

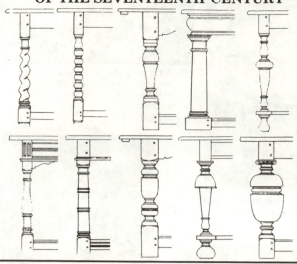

MONARCH CHRONOLOGY

Dates	Monarchs	Period
1558-1603	Elizabeth I	Elizabethan
1603-1625	James I	Jacobean
1625-1649	Charles I	Carolean
1649-1660	Commonwealth	Cromwellian
1660-1685	Charles II	Restoration
1685-1689	James II	Restoration
1689-1694	William & Mary	William & Mary
1694-1702	William III	William III
1702-1714	Anne	Queen Anne
1714-1727	George I	Early Georgian
1727-1760	George II	Georgian
1760-1812	George III	Late Georgian
1812-1820	George III	Regency
1820-1830	George IV	Late Regency
1830-1837	William IV	William IV
1837-1860	Victoria	Early Victorian
1860-1901	Victoria	Late Victorian
1901-1910	Edward VII	Edwardian

Beds

An oak bedstead of Elizabethan design, with plain double arched back and heavily carved border decoration, 72 by 54in (180 by 135cm).
£1,500-2,000   *Pea*

A carved oak tester bed, the whole carved in relief with guilloche and foliate friezes, on 2 turned and bulbous cup and cover supports, on block feet, parts 17thC, 103 by 70in (260 by 175cm).
£3,000-4,000   *P*

An Elizabethan oak full tester bedstead, some carving replaced, 85 by 54in (215 by 135cm).
£7,000-8,000   *B*

A Federal carved maple high post bedstead, with tapering square headposts, and later rails, Massachusetts, c1790-1810, 86 by 57in (218 by 143cm).
£5,500-6,800   *CNY*

An oak tester bed, the footboard carved with panels of foliate strapwork and the motto 'Lord have mercy upon me', part early 17thC, 82 by 62in (208 by 156cm).
£3,000-4,000   *Bon*

A Federal maple high post bedstead, with baluster and ring turned headposts centering a rectangular headboard, the conforming footposts on inverted baluster and ring turned feet, New England c1800-1820, 86 by 54in (218 by 135cm).
£4,000-7,000   *CNY*

Make the most of Miller's

Miller's is completely different each year. Each edition contains completely NEW photographs. This is not an updated publication. We never repeat the same photograph.

late Federal figured maple edstead, with panelled and rolled headboard, 4 old rails and odern tester, probably ennsylvania, 80 by 61in (203 by 53cm).
1,400-2,000   *CNY*

A fine oak and stained pine four poster bed, the bases replacements, late Elizabethan and later, the crewel-work bed cover and valance with bold designs of scrolling foliage, 102 by 74in (257 by 188cm).
£7,000-8,000   *WW*

An oak four poster bed, the panelled headboard dated 1611, with carved canopy and posts, geometric ring-turned collars, boxspring and mattress, 17thC and later, 93 by 64in (235 by 160cm).
£3,000-4,000   *C*

Bookcases

A Chippendale cherrywood secretaire bookcase, rear feet restored, various small patches, Connecticut, c1765-1780, 90 by 38in (229 by 95cm).
£6,800-10,000   *CNY*

A Georgian oak bureau bookcase, with fitted interior and 4 long drawers beneath, with original brass handles and on bracket feet, 87 by 42in (222 by 107cm).
£1,000-1,300   *L*

Victorian carved dark oak ookcase, with 2 glazed doors, 2 awers and cupboards under, 42in 05cm).
00-400   *FR*

A Georgian oak bureau bookcase, with a shaped and fitted interior with well, repairs and some restorations, 80 by 36in (203 by 90cm).
£2,000-3,000   *L*

A Georgian oak bureau bookcase.
£1,000-1,300   *WSW*

Queen Anne oak bookcase, 70 by in (175 by 120cm).
,000-1,250   *B*

A Victorian pollard oak inverted breakfront library bookcase, 108 by 190in (273 by 478cm).
£3,000-4,000   *Bea*

Bureaux

An early Georgian oak bureau, the fall front enclosing a fitted interior, with later bracket feet, with restorations, 38in (97cm).
£1,000-1,400 *L*

A George II oak bureau, with later added inlaid banding and bracket feet, 33in (83cm).
£900-1,200 *CSK*

A Queen Anne oak bureau, the fall flap with book rest, well fitted interior, on bracket feet, 36in (90cm).
£900-1,200 *PWC*

A very small two-part padoukwood bureau, with original carrying handles, stepped interior and well, c1720, 30in (75cm).
£5,000-7,000 *H*

A Queen Anne solid walnut kneehole bureau of fine colour and patina, stepped interior and a well.
£4,000-6,000 *H*

A yew veneered bureau, the fall flap crossbanded, cedar lined, with replacement old pierced brass plate handles and escutcheons, on replacement bracket feet, old restoration, early 18thC, 40in (100cm).
£1,000-1,200 *WW*

A good example with well fitted interior would make substantially more in yew wood.

A fine George I star-inlaid elm bureau of good colour and patina, 36in (90cm).
£2,500-3,500 *H*

A Queen Anne walnut bureau, crossbanded and feather banded, with fitted interior, on later bun feet, 39in (98cm).
£7,000-10,000 *L*

A George II period red walnut bureau, with fitted interior, on replacement bracket feet, 37in (93cm).
£1,500-2,000 *GC*

A small oak bureau, with oak lined interior, 4 long drawers, on bracket feet, 18thC, 36in (90cm).
£600-800 *FR*

A Dutch bombé oak bureau, inlaid with marquetry, with brass grip handles, 18thC, 47in (118cm).
£1,200-1,800 *WW*

small faded oak bureau, with oak
ned interior, mahogany
rossbanded, on bracket feet, 18thC.
1,000-1,400   FR

An oak bureau, with fitted interior
and 3 graduated drawers, on
bracket feet, late 18thC, 35in
(88cm).
£600-800   BA

A good Georgian oak bureau, with
chequered inlay and mahogany
crossbanding, pressed plate
handles, back needing restoration,
c1780, 39in (98cm).
£1,500-1,800   WIL

n oak bureau, crossbanded in
alnut, on bracket feet, 18thC, 34in
5cm).
1,200-1,500   JD

An English oak bureau, c1770, 36in
(90cm).
£1,200-1,500   KEY

A George III oak bureau, with
narrow mahogany crossbandings,
the fall flap enclosing a fitted
interior and with 4 graduated long
drawers, on bracket feet, 36in
(92cm).
£1,200-1,500   L

Cabinets

A Louis XV provincial oak and
walnut side cabinet, with moulded
rounded top and a pair of shaped
panelled cupboard doors, enclosing
a later shelf, on scrolled feet, 41in
(104cm).
£800-1,200   C

good George I oak bureau cabinet
f small proportions.
2,500-4,000   H

George II inlaid oak spice cabinet,
ith boxwood and ebony
erringbone crossbanding, the
elded panel door inlaid with a
ice plant, enclosing a fitted
nterior, top replaced, 28 by 22in (70
y 55cm).
500-600   Re

A Dutch oak display cabinet, 19thC,
90in (228cm) high.
£1,000-1,200   CAm

253

Chairs

A good Stuart period oak wainscot chair.
£1,700-2,500 *WW*

A Charles II oak wainscot chair, Leeds, c1680.
£1,500-2,500 *PHA*

A Charles I style oak armchair with arched scroll crest rail and panelled back, carved with scrolled strapwork, wood seat and on turned front legs and plain stretcher rails.
£550-700 *BD*

A rare beechwood X-framed open armchair, the scrolled shaped back and squab seat covered in fragments of contemporary associated tapestry, 17thC.
£4,000-5,000 *C*

A closely matched set of 8 highback fruitwood, ash and elm wheelback chairs, c1800.
£3,500-4,500 *H*

An English Hepplewhite elm chair, c1780.
£700-900 *PHA*

A set of 6 spindle-back elbow chairs each with a triple row of spindles, rush seat and turned underframe, late 18thC.
£2,500-3,000 *L*

A fine Charles I beech open armchair, stretchers and rails with restorations, the finials later.
£1,500-2,000 *C*

A set of 10 and 2 similar yew and elm smokers bow armchairs.
£6,000-8,000 *Re*

A closely matched set of 6 Macclesfield ladderback chairs, plus 2 armchairs, c1820.
£3,500-4,500 *H*

A massive oak armchair, carved on a stamped ground, the rectangular back with a crenellated top and carved in deep relief with Daniel in the lions' den, inscribed 'My God hath sent his Angel and hath shut the lions' mouths', the open arms formed of scrolling winged beasts, the solid seat carved with flowerheads, on square legs, 19thC.
£550-700   *CSK*

A harlequin set of 6 Cromwellian dining chairs.
£4,800-6,000   *H*

A Queen Anne maple corner chair, with stepped horseshoe-shaped back over 3 tapering columnar supports above a rush seat, the front leg block and baluster-turned with pad foot, the legs joined by double stretchers, New England, 1735-1765, 27½in (68cm).
£830-1,250   *CNY*

A Chippendale period pierced splat chair, English, c1765.
£1,000-1,200   *PHA*

◁

A rare and bold solid yew turners chair, 17thC.
£5,000-7,000   *H*

A set of 4 oak country Chippendale dining chairs, the backs having carved top rail above pierced splat, drop-in seats raised on chamfered square legs, first half 19thC.
£800-1,000   *TW*   ▷

A set of 6 Cromwellian period oak dining chairs, the seats covered in floral Turkey needlework, the turned front legs with bobbin foot rails and stretcher rails, old restoration.
£4,000-6,000   *WW*

A set of 8 George III country oak Hepplewhite chairs, c1800.
£3,000-4,000   *PHA*

A rare matching set of 10 walnut dining chairs, 8 singles and 2 armchairs, c1670
£10,000-12,000   *H*

A set of 6 carved oak dining chairs, 19thC.
£600-800   *JMW*

Eight matching embossed leather dining chairs, Portuguese, late 17thC.
£4,000-5,000   *H*

A set of 4 Swiss oak hall chairs, with pierced shaped moulded backs, carved with wolves heads, with shaped and moulded solid seats.
£500-700   *C*

A pair of William and Mary walnut side chairs, now with Flemish floral verdure tapestry and mustard velvet squab cushions.
£1,500-2,000   *C*

A set of 8 Victorian dark carved oak dining chairs, with red hide seats and barley twist columns.
£1,000-1,500   *FR*

An unusual pair of yew Windsor armchairs, 18thC.
£1,000-1,200   *B*

A closely matched set of 6 Billinge Wigan ladderback chairs, plus 2 armchairs, c1800.
£3,500-4,500   *H*

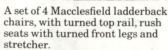

A harlequin set of 10 Derbyshire/South Yorks. oak dining chairs, late 17thC.
£8,000-12,000   *H*

A set of 4 Macclesfield ladderback chairs, with turned top rail, rush seats with turned front legs and stretcher.
£1,500-2,000   *WIL*

A rare set of 5 Charles II side chairs, c1675.
£6,000-7,000   *PHA*

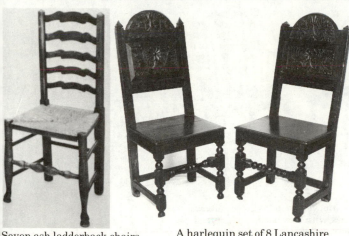

Seven ash ladderback chairs, including one with arms, all with shaped ladderbacks, rush seats and turned underframes, 19thC.
£2,800-3,200   *L*

A harlequin set of 8 Lancashire carved panel back chairs, c1680.
£6,500-8,000   *H*

An elm and beech Windsor armchair with arched toprail and railed splats, the back possibly reduced, 18thC.
£600-800   *C*

A closely matched set of 6 spindleback chairs with Chippendale ears, plus 2 armchairs, c1800.
£2,800-3,800   *H*

A good set of 8 single elm and ash spindleback chairs with unusual spade cresting rails, c1800.
£2,800-3,500   *H*

A William and Mary maple bannister-back side chair, with shaped crest flanked by turned finials above 4 half-baluster supports, minor patch to stile pendants, New England, 1720-40, 41in (103cm) high.
£350-500   *CNY*

A set of 12 ash and elm spindleback chairs, the tops of the uprights stamped P.C. and W.C.
£900-1,100   *Bon*

An oak chair, the back with 2 arched and foliate carved horizontal stretchers, on turned and stretchered legs, restorations, 17thC.
£200-400   *Bon*

Four Lancashire spindle-back chairs, including 2 armchairs, with bun feet and stretchers, 19thC.
£1,200-1,500   *WIL*

An ash spindle back armchair with a pierced splat back, shaped seat, standing on turned supports with hoop form stretcher.
£400-600 *OL*

A pair of yew-wood Windsor elbow chairs, with bow backs and pierced splats, dished elm seats and crinoline stretchers joining the turned supports, early 19thC.
£1,400-1,800 *L*

△ A good composed set of 8 Windsor high-back elbow chairs, in yew and elm, with pierced splats, mid-19thC.
£12,000-15,000 *N*

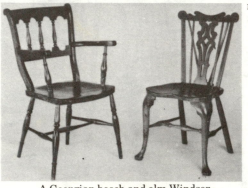

A walnut Windsor armchair, with an arched cresting rail and outscrolled arms with spindle supports, damaged arm, mid-18thC.
£1,000-1,500 *Bea*

A Georgian beech and elm Windsor chair, and a beech and elm Mendlesham chair, with curved arms above a solid seat on turned legs and stretchers, 19thC.
£400-500 each *CSK*

△

A yew and elm Windsor armchair, with pierced vase-shaped splat, first half 19thC, 35in (87.5cm) high.
£600-800 *TEN*

A set of 6 ash and elm Windsor chairs, including 2 armchairs, the arched backs with pierced baluster vertical splat flanked by stick splats, late 18thC.
£3,600-4,000 *Bon*

A rare set of 8 Robert Pryor design yew Windsor armchairs, c1800.
£6,000-8,000 *H* ▷

A fine harlequin set of 8 yew-wood Windsor armchairs, with decorative splats, early 19thC.
£7,000-10,000 *H*

A set of 6 yew wood Windsor style chairs with crinoline stretchers pierced and stick backs.
£6,000-7,000 *BA*

A good matched set of 8 low back yew Windsor armchairs, with standard splats, c1820.
£6,000-8,000   *H*

Two Victorian yew and elm Windsor armchairs, each with an arched pierced splat and spindled rail back, above outscrolled arms on bobbin-turned supports and solid saddle seat.
£1,000-1,500   *CSK*

An elmwood and ash Windsor elbow chair with pierced wheel splat, turned supports with H-stretcher.
£280-400   *CDC*

Six yew, elm and beechwood Windsor armchairs, the bowed rail and pierced splat backs above saddle seats on ring-turned tapering legs, joined with crinoline cross stretchers.
£4,800-6,000   *CSK*

An ash and elm comb back Windsor chair with yoke-shaped crest rail, bowed arm rail with shaped front supports and turned legs, mid-18thC.
£300-500   *DWB*

A child's mahogany rocking chair commode, 24in (60cm) high.
£150-200   *CDC*

A set of 6 fruitwood chairs, the backs with scroll crest rails, turned uprights and balloon splats, rush seats, on turned underframes.
£1,800-2,400   *CBD*

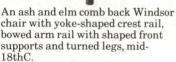

A Windsor open armchair with yew-wood hoop back rails and arms, elm seat, on turned supports with crinoline hoop stretcher.
£900-1,200   *CDC*

Four yew Windsor elbow chairs, slightly different but each with bow backs and pierced central splats, elm seats and crinoline stretchers joining the turned supports.
£3,000-4,000   *L*

A James I oak table chair, c1620.
£4,000-5,000   *PHA*

An oak settle, the base with a row of 2 fine raised fielded panels, the front with 2 long raised and fielded panels, shaped arms on turned baluster supports, previously with end drawers, solid seat, c1700, 66in (165cm).
£500-800   *WIL*

A Gothic Revival oak stall, the solid back filled with tracery with hinged seat and linenfold panelled sides, with silk and metal thread squab cushion, 96 by 26in (242.5 by 65cm).
£1,200-1,500   *C*

A fine roundel carved oak coffer, late 16thC.
£1,800-2,500   *H*

A James I particularly well-carved and moulded oak coffer.
£1,500-2,200   *H*

Chests

A small coffer with unusual carving, late 16thC.
£1,500-2,500   *H*

A late Stuart oak chest faced with ebony and walnut veneers, the upper portion with one narrow and one deep drawer, the lower part with 2 panel doors enclosing 3 drawers, on stile feet, 48in (120cm).
£700-1,000   *L*

An oak coffer with plain cover, with panel sides and front, the central panel also inlaid with 2 small shields with initials AC and date 1604 in vermilion, with moulded stiles and muntins with stop fluting, with repairs, 17thC, 55in (139cm).
£2,000-2,500   *L*

A rare chestnut and walnut coffer with outstanding carving, Spanish origin, 16thC.
£6,000-8,000   *H*

A carved and gadrooned oak coffer, early 17thC.
£1,500-2,000   *H*

A Continental oak coffer, the top a replacement, 16thC, 70in (175cm).
£2,000-2,500   *WW*

A small oak coffer, early 17thC.
£1,200-1,800   *H*

A rare well-carved oak coffer, dated 1627, by repute from the Penn family, initialled I.P.
£2,000-3,000　*H*

A Continental walnut chest with beech top, fitted drawers and cupboards below, all with deeply moulded panels with iron lockplates, the plain panelled sides with iron carrying handles, 17thC, 43in (107.5cm).
£1,400-2,000　*WW*

A small William and Mary oak chest-on-stand, c1695.
£5,000-6,000　*PHA*

A Jacobean walnut chest, fitted with 3 long drawers, with geometric moulded panels, 43in (107.5cm).
£1,500-2,000　*LBP*

A fine Charles I block fronted oak mule chest, c1640.
£1,500-2,000　*PHA*

A William and Mary birch high chest of drawers, in 2 sections, one rear ball foot restored, 44in (110cm).
£8,300-10,500　*CNY*

Provenance: Historic Deerfield Inc.

A Jacobean oak chest with brass oval loop handles and geometric moulded drawer fronts, 41in (102.5cm).
£600-800　*JD*

A fine and unusual William and Mary oak mule chest, crossbanded with end grain oak, c1695.
£1,500-2,000　*PHA*

An English oak carved panelled coffer, good colour and patination, 17thC.
£700-900　*PHA*　▷

A Commonwealth oak coffer, the plank top above a foliate and S-scroll carved frieze flanked by the initials T.D. and dated 1650, the front with a central panel of raised geometric mouldings, 51in (127cm).
£1,000-1,200　*Bon*

A well carved Charles II oak coffer.
£900-1,400　*H*

A Charles II oak chest, the top with moulded edge above 4 long drawers with thin geometrically panelled fronts flanked by split baluster turnings, 40½in (101cm).
£600-800 *Bon*

A William and Mary oyster-veneered chest with oak-lined drawers, the top with small roundel and half-round inlay and crossbanding, standing on 4 bun feet, not original, 37in (92.5cm).
£8,000-12,000 *WSW*

A Chippendale maple chest-on-chest, minor patches, New England, c1770-1785, 38in (95cm).
£3,500-4,800 *CNY*

A West Country painted oak coffer, late 17thC.
£800-1,200 *H*

A William and Mary walnut chest, the moulded top with an oval panel and banding of wavy chevron design in holly and walnut, with brass drop handles, on later turned feet, 37in (92.5cm).
£4,000-5,000 *WW*

A mid-Georgian oak tallboy, crossbanded in fruitwood with fluted pilaster angles, the base with 2 long drawers, chamfered angles and ogee bracket feet, 46in (115cm).
£1,200-1,500 *C*

A cedarwood, fruitwood and oak chest in 2 sections, late 17thC, 41in (102.5cm).
£2,000-2,800 *Bea*

A rare William and Mary burr yew crossbanded chest of drawers, of good colour and patina, 36in (90cm).
£5,000-6,000 *H*

A mid-Georgian oak and mahogany crossbanded mule chest, 58in (145cm).
£500-600 *CSK*

An oak dower chest, the top with thumb mould edge, 3 fielded panels to the front with date, the drawers fitted with brass swan neck loop handles, on ogee bracket supports, 61in (152.5cm).
£400-500 *CDC*

A rare William and Mary solid yew carved coffer with bold carving to the front panels, good moulding, 2 drawers below, fine colour and patina, 50in (125cm).
£3,000-5,000 *H*

A small oak chest of drawers with brushing slide, early 18thC.
£2,000-2,700 H

A good original yellow oak mule chest, the top with slab panel, the ends and front with fielded panels, base mould with bracket feet, interior trinket compartment and secret drawers, mid-18thC, 51in (127.5cm).
£500-700 WIL

A George III mahogany yew wood and ebonised chest of drawers, in the manner of Ince and Mayhew, the sides of yew and kingwood, on bracket feet, c1800, 39½in (100cm).
£4,200-5,500 CNY

A French provincial oak serpentine commode, the moulded top above 3 long shaped panelled drawers with panelled sides, on a shaped apron and moulded feet, 18thC, 49in (122.5cm).
£1,400-2,000 CSK

MAKE THE MOST OF MILLER'S
Price ranges in this book reflect what one should expect to pay for a similar example. When selling one can obviously expect a figure below. This will fluctuate according to a dealer's stock, saleability at a particular time, etc. It is always advisable to approach a reputable specialist dealer or an auction house which has specialist sales.

An oak dower chest, the plank top with re-entrant forecorners, with 4 fielded panels with re-entrant shoulders, with brass swan neck handles and pierced back plates, bracket feet, 18thC, 64in (160cm).
£300-400 CDC

A good Queen Anne oak crossbanded chest on cabriole legged stand, 39in (97.5cm).
£3,000-5,000 H

A George III oak coffer, ▷ crossbanded with mahogany quartered columns, fielded panels, interior fitted with candle box, 49in (122.5cm).
£300-400 WIL

◁ A late George III oak chest-on-chest, with later brass swan neck drop handles and escutcheons, the whole raised upon bracket feet, and crossbanded in mahogany, 38in (95cm).
£1,200-1,500 HSS

Use the Index!
Because certain items might fit easily into any of a number of categories, the quickest and surest method of locating any entry is by reference to the index at the back of the book.
This has been fully cross-referenced for absolute simplicity.

A rare Art Deco oak chest of 2 short and 3 long drawers, by the 'Yorkshire Mouse-Man', signed with carved mouse.
£350-550 FR

Cupboards

A rare small late Elizabethan inlaid oak court cupboard, of very fine colour and patina.
£5,000-7,000 *H*

A painted oak food cupboard, with rectangular top and one cupboard door, flanked by panels with pierced tracery on plank feet, early 16thC, 44in (110cm).
£6,000-8,000 *C*

A late Stuart cupboard, carved with foliate scrolls and strapwork designs, later back and handles, 60 by 58in (150 by 145cm).
£2,000-3,000 *L*

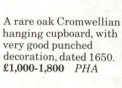

A good small James I three-tier standing or court cupboard, with fine carving, colour and patina.
£8,000-10,000 *H*

A Gothic hutch with pierced tracery, restored and lower door later, 15thC, 44 by 42in (110 by 105cm).
£10,000+ *H*

A rare oak Cromwellian hanging cupboard, with very good punched decoration, dated 1650.
£1,000-1,800 *PHA*

A rare carved and inlaid oak marriage cupboard, late 16th/early 17thC.
£7,000-10,000 *H*

A Flemish oak low cupboard, geometrically moulded and panelled doors inset with rosewood and ebony, flanked by lion mask corbels, on bun feet, c1680, 65in (162cm).
£2,000-3,000 *Bon*

Huntington Antiques Ltd.

Early Period Furniture, Works of Art & Tapestries. Fine Country Furniture, Metalware, Treen & Textiles

The Old Forge, Church Street, Stow-on-the-Wold, Gloucestershire, England.

Tel: Stow-on-the-Wold 01144 451 30842

Very rare and important Early 17th Century Oak Chest of Drawers with Silver Chest Top Section

We offer a substantial stock of fine early oak, walnut and country furniture.

Always a selection of refectory, gateleg and other tables; dressers and court cupboards; wainscots and sets of chairs; and usually some rare examples of gothic and renaissance furniture.

We would always welcome the opportunity to purchase such items.

Open Mon-Sat 9–6 and by appointment

An early Charles II arcaded oak
press cupboard, dated 1665.
£5,000-7,000   *PHA*

An oak hall
cupboard with
pine top and
back, mid-17thC. ▷
£3,000-5,000   *WW*

A rare spindle-fronted wall hutch,
with enclosed stepped cupboard
below, c1680.
£4,000-5,000   *H*

An early Georgian oak court
cupboard, with moulded canopy
with pendant finials above 3
panelled doors, the base with frieze
drawers and panel doors on block
feet, 58in (145cm).
£1,750-2,250   *CSK*
◁

A fine early Georgian oak
double corner cupboard,
of excellent colour and
patina.
£1,800-2,500   *H*

A Flemish oak cupboard in 2
sections, with strapwork carved
doors, on bun feet, constructed
using some 17thC components, 49in
(123cm).
£600-1,000   *Bon*

△

A good William and Mary oak court
cupbord in 2 stages, the upper
having a carved scrollwork frieze
with ownership triad w^{s}i and dated
1689, the lower having carved stiles
and borders, with flute-moulded
panelled doors, the interior having
a single shelf, c1689, 63 by 72in
(157 by 180cm).
£1,600-2,200   *TKN*

*This cupboard now has an added
Victorian lightly-attached egg-and-
dart mould which could be easily
removed to restore the piece to
virtually original condition; the
lower hinges are Georgian
replacements.*

A good small carved oak livery
cupboard, mid-17thC.
£6,000-8,000   *H*

A French Provincial oak
cupboard, with moulded
cornice above a pair
of panelled and carved
cupboard doors, above a
pair of panelled frieze
drawers and a pair of
cupboards, on scrolled
feet, mid-18thC,
94 by 47in
(237.5 by 117.5cm).
£2,000-3,000   *C*

A fine carved oak livery cupboard, early 17thC.
£7,000-10,000 *H*

An oak cupboard with a pair of fielded panelled doors and a pair of drawers under, 17thC, 54in (135cm).
£900-1,400 *JD*

An oak corner wall cupboard, with panelled door and pine interior, 18thC.
£190-260 *FR*

A good small oak court cupboard of fine colour and patina, early 17thC.
£3,000-5,000 *H*

A large Georgian oak standing corner cupboard, the upper section enclosing shelves to the interior, over a single dummy drawer and double panelled cupboard below, all with brass H-shaped hinges, 49in (123cm).
£1,000-1,250 *HSS*

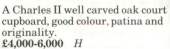

A carved oak food cupboard, on block feet, early 17thC.
£4,000-5,000 *P*

A rare spindle-fronted wall cupboard with spoon rack, 17thC.
£2,000-3,000 *H*

A carved oak livery cupboard, the rectangular top containing a cupboard enclosed by a pair of panelled doors with central fielded panel, on ring-turned baluster front supports united by an undertier with undulating frieze, on block feet, 52½in (131cm).
£1,800-2,200 *P*

A Charles II well carved oak court cupboard, good colour, patina and originality.
£4,000-6,000 *H*

A Georgian oak wall cupboard with 3 drawers below, good colour and patina.
£1,500-1,800 *H*

An oak hanging glass cupboard, the lower section with bobbin-turned spindle cupboards, part 17thC, 56½in (141cm).
£700-1,000 *Bon*

An oak livery cupboard, 18thC, 66in (165cm).
£1,250-1,500 *CDC*

A George II oak tallboy with pierced bracket feet, c1750.
£1,200-1,800 *PHA*

A rare small carved oak standing cupboard of good colour and patina, early 17thC.
£7,000-10,000 *H*

A yew hanging cupboard, 18thC, 78 by 42in (197.5 by 105cm).
£3,500-4,000 *SHa*

An unusual fruitwood corner cupboard of excellent colour and patina, mid-18thC.
£500-800 *H*

An oak cupboard on low stand, with a moulded cornice above 2 doors with arched shaped panels enclosing shelves, the stand with 3 drawers in a waved apron and with moulded block feet, 18thC, later backed, 79 by 51in (200 by 127.5cm).
£600-800 *L*

A good Charles II carved oak court cupboard.
£3,000-4,000 *H*

An oak cupboard, with fall-front and the interior now fitted with pigeon holes and shaped drawers, all with arched panels and mahogany crossbandings throughout, on bracket feet, partly 18thC, 61 by 62in (152.5 by 155cm).
£2,000-3,000 *L*

A two-door oak cupboard, early 18thC, 48 by 52in (120 by 130cm).
£2,000-2,500 *SHa*

A small rare English oak bacon seat and table with drawer, panelled on all sides, 18thC.
£3,000-5,000 *PHA*

A Louis XVI oak armoire with shaped panelled and fielded cupboard doors, on scrolled feet, 89 by 61in (225 by 152.5cm).
£2,000-3,000 *C*

A good small carved oak court cupboard, dated 1704.
£3,000-4,000 *H*

A French oak armoire, the moulded cornice with foliate carved frieze, with 2 similarly carved panelled doors on cabriole legs, Breton, late 18thC, 63in (158cm)
£1,500-2,500 *CSK*

A Federal poplar and cherrywood corner cupboard, mid-Atlantic States, 1790-1810, 85 by 38in (215 by 95cm).
£2,000-3,500 *CNY*

A George II oak hanging cupboard, c1745.
£1,250-1,750 *PHA*

A Louis XV Provincial armoire, on scrolled feet, 95 by 57in (240 by 142.5cm).
£1,800-2,200 *C*

An oak food hutch, 19thC, 36½in (90cm).
£200-400 *BA*

A Federal tiger-maple cupboard, probably Virginia, feet restored, 1800-1810, 85 by 54½in (215 by 136cm).
£3,500-4,800 *CNY*

An oak court cupboard, the top section with a projecting cornice hung with 2 finials above 3 ogee-arched fielded panelled doors, the base fitted with 3 drawers above 2 panelled doors, on block feet, 60in (150cm).
£1,800-2,800 *CSK*

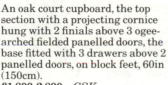

A late George III oak cupboard on base of 4 drawers, c1820.
£1,200-1,700 *PHA*

A Welsh oak deudarn, 2 doors with ogee-arched panels, 3 frieze drawers, 2 panelled doors below and on stile feet, 69 by 53in (172.5 by 132.5cm).
£900-1,400 *Bea*

A rare oak dresser with original lozenge carved panels, well shaped rack, good colour and patina, late 17thC.
£8,000-10,000 *H*

Dressers

A fine oak moulded dresser base of excellent quality, late 17thC, 32 by 102in (80 by 257.5cm).
£7,000-10,000 *H*

A good William and Mary oak dresser with moulded plank top above 4 drawers with moulded facings, shaped frieze on 3 turned front supports, 97in (245cm).
£3,000-4,000 *Re*

An oak and elm dresser, with 3 plate shelves and 2 spice cupboards enclosed by arched doors, the base fitted with 3 drawers on square chamfered legs, 18thC, 80in (202.5cm).
£1,500-2,000 *CSK*

A Georgian oak dresser, with 3 mahogany crossbanded drawers on 4 square supports and 3 open shelves over, 74in (187.5cm).
£1,500-2,000 *WSW*

A rare Charles II dresser base with 3 barley twist front legs, fine colour and patina, 34 by 84in (85 by 212.5cm).
£5,000-6,500 *H* ▷

◁ A Georgian oak dresser with plate rack.
£2,000-2,500 *FHF*

A Charles II oak dresser, ▷ the low raised back with 4 indented panels, fitted 4 drawers with double geometric panel fronts, engraved brass escutcheons and swan neck handles, 108in (272.5cm).
£7,000-10,000 *WW*

A large Georgian oak Welsh dresser, with delft rack and 6 small drawers, 3 deep drawers, all with brass handles and lock escutcheons, shaped frieze, cabriole legs ending in pad feet, parts possibly of later date, 91in (230cm).
£3,000-4,000 *HSS*

A particularly fine oak dresser of excellent colour and patina, early 18thC.
£6,000-8,000 *H*

An unusually small oak canopy dresser, early 18thC, 50in (125cm).
£4,500-5,500 *H*

A small oak dresser base, fitted 3 short drawers with brass bail handles and escutcheons, on rectangular supports with potboard, 18thC, 51½in (128cm).
£2,500-3,500 *GC*

A George I oak dresser base, good colour and patination, original brasses, c1720.
£3,500-4,500 *PHA*

A good oak dresser base of fine colour and patina, North Wales, early 18thC, 74in (187.5cm).
£5,000-7,000 *H*

A fine Queen Anne walnut crossbanded cabriole-legged dresser base.
£4,000-6,000 *H*

A good North Wales oak dresser and rack with raised fielding, fine colour and patina, early 18thC, 72in (180cm).
£5,000-7,000 *H*

An oak Welsh dresser, with 5 baluster turned front legs and pot board, later brass handles and escutcheons, early 18thC, 98in (247.5cm).
£8,000-10,000 *WIL*

A small walnut potboard dresser and rack, early 18thC, 60in (150cm).
£8,000-10,000 *H*

An oak and fruitwood dresser base, with moulded rectangular top and 3 drawers with waved apron on cabriole legs, the drawers partly re-supported, early 18thC, 79in (200cm).
£3,000-4,000 *C*

An early Georgian oak dresser with moulded top, the frieze with 3 drawers and a waved apron on turned tapering legs with pad feet, 73½in (186cm).
£2,500-3,000 *C*

An oak dresser base, with 3 drawers with shaped apron on cabriole front legs with pad feet, 86in (217.5cm).
£3,000-4,000 *BD* ▷

A good potboard dresser and rack, mid-18thC.
£3,000-4,000 *H*

An oak potboard dresser base, North Wales, c1750.
£3,000-4,000 *PHA*

An oak dresser, the plate rack with shaped frieze, shelves and 2 cupboard doors, the base with 3 drawers and shaped apron raised on well shaped cabriole supports, the whole inlaid and crossbanded in mahogany, early 18thC, 74in (187.5cm).
£4,000-5,000 *BS*

An oak 3-drawer dresser, the drawers crossbanded and edged with quadrant mould and period escutcheons, panelled ends and ogee moulding surround, 3 baluster turned front legs, c1700, 75in (190cm).
£3,500-4,500 *WIL*

A solid yew dresser base, mid-18thC, 84in (212.5cm).
£8,000-10,000 *H*

A rare and bold oak dresser of unusual detail, early 18thC.
£6,000-7,000 *H*

◁ An outstanding inlaid and crossbanded oak dresser of very fine form, good colour and patina, mid-18thC.
£8,000-10,000 *H*

A fine George I ▷ crossbanded oak dresser base with breakfront and vertical reeding, 84in (212.5cm).
£7,000-10,000 *H*

A George II oak cupboard dresser, crossbanded with oak, c1740.
£4,000-5,000 *PHA*

An oak dresser with 4 moulded drawers with brass drop handles and escutcheons, shaped beaded apron with turned pendants and turned legs with block feet, one leg broken, handles old replacements, 98in (247.5cm).
£4,000-5,000 *DSH*

An oak dresser with spice drawers, excellent colour and patina, mid-18thC, 74in (187.5cm).
£5,000-6,000 *H* ▷

A fine oak cupboard dresser base, crossbanded in burr elm, c1750.
£4,000-5,000 *PHA*

A good oak cupboard dresser with spice drawers, mid-18thC.
£5,000-7,000 *H*

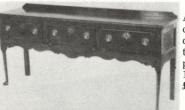

An early George III oak cupboard dresser base, crossbanded with mahogany, c1760.
£4,000-5,000 *PHA*

A French Provincial dresser or buffet a deux corps in oak and chestnut, with original brass hinges and escutcheons, late 18thC, 90 by 54in (228 by 137cm).
£1,600-2,200 *L*

An oak low dresser with a crossbanded top and front with 3 drawers and a shaped apron, on tapering turned legs, with pointed pad feet, 33 by 76½in (82.5 by 193cm).
£2.200-2,800 *Bea*

An oak dresser base with later delft rack, with moulded cornice, shaped frieze and 3 shelves, flanked by 2 cupboards, mid-18thC, 69in (172.5cm).
£1,000-1,500 *DSH*

▷

A fine Montgomery oak dresser and rack of excellent colour and patina, mid-18thC.
£5,000-7,000 *H*

△

A George III low oak dresser with 3 frieze drawers with bevelled panels above 2 cupboard doors, flanking a central panel, on stile feet, with restorations, 35 by 82in (87.5 by 207.5cm).
£1,500-2,000 *L*

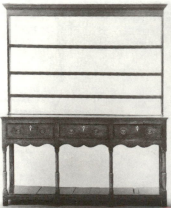

A George III oak dresser with 3 drawers to the base and open shelves above, 63in (157.5cm).
£1,600-2,000   *LRG*

A fine George III oak Montgomeryshire pot boarded dresser, the lower section with 4 cockbeaded and crossbanded drawers, 81½ by 88in (206 by 222cm).
£7,000-8,000   *OT*

A small oak dresser, 18thC.
£950-1,100   *PWC*

An oak dresser with 3 drawers in base and potboard under, the square top fitted with 3 plate shelves, 84 by 45in (212.5 by 112.5cm).
£1,200-1,700   *Wor*

A George III oak low dresser with the stiles forming the feet, some repairs, 32 by 73½in (80 by 186cm).
£3,000-4,000   *L*

An oak and inlaid Welsh dresser, the base having 3 top drawers and 3 dummy drawers, flanked by cupboards, with later moulded glass handles, 76 by 67in (192.5 by 167.5cm).
£1,200-1,600   *OL*   ▷

A George III oak Welsh dresser base, with 4 mahogany crossbanded drawers with brass bail handles, on cabriole legs, 18thC, 29½ by 86½in (73 by 218cm).
£4,000-5,000   *L*

An oak mahogany-banded 9 drawer dresser base, with quarter fluted columns and 4 ogee feet, pierced plate handles and escutcheons, low gallery back, late 18thC, 84in (212.5cm).
£1,600-2,200   *WIL*

Stools

A small oak dresser.
£1,400-1,600   *PWC*

A good bold Charles I oak joint stool, in original order.
£1,800-2,200   *H*

A Charles II oak joint stool, with oblong moulded plank top on bobbin-turned supports and plain stretcher rails, one foot replaced, 16in (40cm).
£800-1,200   *Re*

A good matching pair of oak joint stools, 17thC.
£4,000-5,000 *H*

A rare stool table, the flaps raised on lopers, 17thC.
£2,500-3,500 *H*

A good oak joint stool, the plank top raised above 4 turned legs, united by a stretcher at the base, 17thC.
£800-1,000 *B*

An oak joint stool, with moulded rectangular top and ring-turned legs joined by plain stretchers, with label initialled FMT, 17thC, 17in (42.5cm).
£1,200-1,500 *C*

A good oak box stool, early 17thC.
£3,000-4,000 *H*

l. A fine Charles II bobbin-turned oak joint stool
r. A bold oak joint stool, early 17thC.
£1,250-2,000 each *H*

A William and Mary walnut stool, the padded top upholstered with a fragment of early 17thC tapestry, the scrolled legs with arched front stretchers and bobbin-turned H-shaped stretcher, 17in (42.5cm).
£2,000-3,000 *C*

Tables

A fine Charles II 10-seater oak gateleg table, with exceptional turnings. ▷
£10,000-15,000 *H*

An oak gateleg dining table, with oval twin-flap top on turned spreading knopped legs, joined by moulded stretchers, the top with minor replacements, 17thC, 75in (190cm) open.
£2,000-3,000 *C*

A large 10-seater oak gateleg table, the top French polished but of good originality, 17thC, 74in (187.5cm).
£3,000-4,000 *B*

A bold and fine Charles II oak double gateleg dining table with refined turnings, good colour and patina, seating 10-12.
£15,000-20,000   *H*

A fine walnut 6-seater gateleg table, late 17thC.
£4,000-6,000   *H*

A rare yew lowboy, the burr yew top with crossbanded edge and re-entrant corners above 3 drawers and raised upon turned legs with overlapping knees and pad feet, early 18thC.
£4,000-5,000   *B*

An oak gateleg dining table, with oval twin-flap top and a later frieze drawer with bobbin turned frame, the frame partly reinforced, 17thC, 70in (175cm) open.
£3,000-4,000   *C*

A small oak oval top gateleg table, fitted with a drawer, and flat section gates and turned legs, late 17thC, 36½ by 30in (91 by 75cm).
£1,200-1,500   *WW*

An oak gateleg dining table, 19thC, extending to 60in (150cm).
£1,800-2,200   *TAY*

An important and large oak gateleg table, raised on bobbin and vase-shaped legs, joined by solid square stretchers, 66 by 72in (165 by 180cm) open.
£7,000-10,000   *CBS*

A solid yew 6-seater gateleg table, late 17thC.
£4,000-6,000   *H*

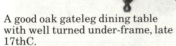

A good oak gateleg dining table with well turned under-frame, late 17thC.
£4,000-6,000   *H*

A yew and cedar gateleg table, fitted with 2 drawers, with baluster turned gates and supports, united by stretchers, late 17thC, 62in (155cm).
£12,000-17,000   *WW*

A George II oak drop-leaf dining table of large size with deep elliptical leaves, on plain turned tapered legs with pad feet, 55 by 67in (138 by 167cm).
£1,400-1,800   *Bon*

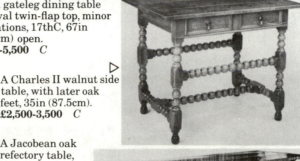

A very bold oak refectory table,
early 17thC.
£12,000-15,000   *H*

A large oak gateleg
dining table, with twin-
flap rectangular top, the
double gateleg action
with spirally turned legs
and stretchers, re-
supported, 66in (165cm)
open.
£3,000-4,000   *C*

An oak 8-seater gateleg table in
sound order, late 17thC.
£3,500-5,000   *H*

An oak gateleg dining table
with oval twin-flap top, minor
restorations, 17thC, 67in
(167.5cm) open.
£4,500-5,500   *C*

A Charles II walnut side
table, with later oak
feet, 35in (87.5cm).
£2,500-3,500   *C*

A Jacobean oak
refectory table,
the triple plank
top with clamped
end, 94½in
(238cm).
£3,000-4,000   *WW*

An oak dining table, the top with
moulded edge, a small drawer one
end and raised on 4 baluster turned
supports, joined by H-stretchers,
added block feet, 18thC, 30 by
70½in (75 by 175cm).
£2,000-2,800   *L*

A Chippendale cherrywood drop-
leaf table, on moulded square legs,
probably New Hampshire, tiny
patch to edge of top, 1770-1790,
48in (120cm).
£1,300-2,000   *CNY*

*Provenance: Josiah Bartlett,
signatory of the Declaration of
Independence from New Hampshire*

An oak refectory table,
dated 1667, good colour
and patina, 102in
(257.5cm).
£6,000-8,000   *H*

An oak lowboy, late 18thC.
£400-500   *BA*

A fruitwood side table with drawer,
17thC, 33in (82.5cm).
£800-1,200   *SL*

A William and Mary oak side or
refectory table, with a 3-plank top,
the front frieze carved with a band
of foliate scrolls and triad initials
GWM and date 1691, on modified
bulbous supports, 30 by 83½in (75
by 211cm).
£2,000-2,800   *L*

A good oak refectory table of bold
proportions, mid-17thC, 150in
(377cm).
£10,000-15,000   *H*

An oak refectory table, 17thC,
156in (392cm).
£10,000-15,000   *H*

A William and Mary side table, the
moulded top parquetry inlaid in
green-dyed ivory and various
woods, raised on barley sugar twist
elm legs with curved cross
stretchers uniting in an oval
parquetry panel, replacement
turned feet, 31in (77.5cm).
£10,000-12,000   *WW*

A particularly fine oak refectory
table of good colour and patina, in
very original order, 17thC, 138in
(345cm).
£12,500-18,000   *H*

A Flemish oak side table, with
rectangular top and one panelled
frieze drawer with waved apron and
bulbous ring-turned tapering legs
with moulded waved stretchers,
with minor restorations, 17thC,
57in (142.5cm).
£2,000-3,000   *C*

A George III oak refectory table, the
four-plank top with cleated ends,
lacking drawer, 115in (290cm).
£1,500-2,200   *Bea*

A Queen Anne cherrywood
candlestand, with a single drawer
over a cylindrical tapering pedestal
with a compressed ball turning, on
arched cabriole legs with shod
slipper feet, Pennsylvania, 1740-60,
17in (42.5cm).
£1,300-2,000   *CNY*

A William and Mary oak side table
with rectangular top on slender
turned baluster and knopped legs,
joined by an X-shaped stretcher,
with bun feet, 18½in (46cm).
£2,500-3,500   *C*

A Charles II oak side table, the top
with moulded edge above a panel
front frieze drawer, on baluster
turned legs, 27in (68cm).
£800-1,200   *Bon*

A rare Flemish oak
side table, the
folding oval top
resting on a split
bobbin turned gate,
61½in (153cm).
£2,500-4,000   *WW*

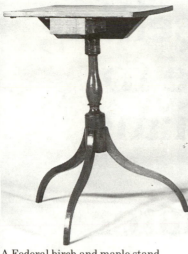

An oak cricket table with an octagonal top, on bobbin-turned legs joined by moulded square stretchers, some restoration, 17thC, 27 by 31½in (67.5 by 77.5cm).
£800-1,200 *Bea*

A Dutch oak rent table, the sliding top enclosing a frieze compartment, on ring-turned columns and dentil-arched apron united by stretchers, bearing an autograph note discussing his acquisition, signed H. Rider-Haggard, 1920, 17thC, 39in (98cm).
£1,000-1,500 *P*

A Federal birch and maple stand, with square top above a through-sliding drawer, New England, 1790-1810, 16in (40cm).
£1,000-1,400 *CNY*

A Charles II oak table settle with pivoting top, the base with hinged lid, carved lunette frieze, indented front and side panels, within moulded stiles, 60in (150cm).
£3,000-4,000 *WW*

A Chippendale cherrywood serpentine-top tea table, Massachusetts, 1760-1790, 33in (82.5cm).
£1,300-2,000 *CNY*

A fine late Elizabethan oak drawleaf table with bold cup and cover legs, gadrooned frieze, in sound order, 168in (422.5cm) open.
£15,000-20,000 *H*

A good oak farmhouse table with well chamfered legs, 18thC, 132in (332cm).
£4,000-6,000 *H*

An unusual early Georgian oak serving table, the hinged rectangular top enclosing a flap with 2 shelves and a lift-out tray beneath, with 3 frieze drawers, the cabriole legs joined by a concave-sided platform with pointed pad feet, 36in (90cm).
£3,000-4,000 *C*

A 3-plank oak trestle table, 79½in (201cm).
£1,200-1,800 *BA*

Miscellaneous

◁ A rare oak bench table in sound original order, late 16thC, 72in (182.5cm).
£5,000-6,000 *H*

▷ An oak dough bin, 45in (112.5cm).
£400-500 *TAY*

bove: A rare small Charles II oak inlaid chest of rawers.
£8,000-10,000 *H*

eft: A rare and unusually small late Elizabethan rved oak 3-tier buffet.
£15,000-20,000 *H*

rovenance: Littlecote House

Above: A fine James I oak refectory table, with 6 well turned baluster legs, moulded stretchers, serpent carved front frieze, 132in (332cm).
£12,000-15,000 *H*

Left: A rare Charles II cushion moulded oak dresser base with 4 barley twist legs and split balusters between the drawers and blind fretwork centres.
£7,000-10,000 *H*

Provenance: Snitterton Hall, Derbyshire

281

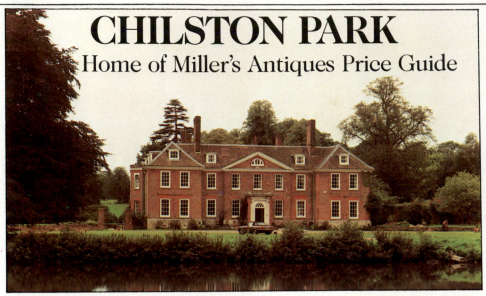

The Private Dining Room...

English cooking and fresh food are the main principles of Chilston's excellent Dining Room. Breakfast, for instance, might include porridge, kidneys, bacon, scrambled and coddled eggs, kippers, kedgeree and muffins. A baron of beef, roast saddle of lamb, game, hams...and a variety of proper puddings feature on the menu.

The Reception Hall...

Atmosphere, warmth and light flickering from chandeliers welcome you to Chilston. Gleaming wood, bright with the patina of age, sets off a gathering of family portraits...dogs doze in front of a blazing log fire...and your hosts wait to receive you.

The Drawing Room...

With an emphasis placed upon comfort, the Drawing Room provides a quiet retreat. Somewhere to rest after a journey or a day's entertainment...to take tea in the afternoon or foregather with friends for a drink before dinner...and to relax completely at the end of the day.

The Bedrooms...

There are 25 bedrooms at Chilston, all of which have private bathrooms en suite. All are luxuriously appointed and delightfully furnished and guests are quite likely to find themselves in a four-poster bed. A special degree of personal comfort is provided by traditional hot-water bottles, complete with hand-knitted woollen covers.

A rare Regency black and gold lacquer side cabinet, decorated in raised gilt, 2 doors enclosing 20 drawers, 92in (234cm). **£35,000-40,000** *C*

Above A Sheraton period satinwood and tortoise-shell cabinet on stand, with tulipwood crossbanding, serpenti apron, on square taper legs ending with brass cappings.
£7,000-8,000 *P*

Left A Charles II blac and gold lacquer cabine on stand, the doors decorated with chased metal, the interior with various-sized drawers, very heavily carved silvered stand, 45in (113cm) wide.
£11,000-15,000 *C*

Above A Queen Anne walnut secretaire cabinet, with brass carrying handles, the upper part fitted with shelves, the fall enclosing a fitted interior, 42in (106cm).
£5,000-7,000 *P*

Below A pair of mid Victorian ormolu mounted and walnut side cabinets, with three-quarter pierced galleries above cupboard doors centred by oval porcelain plaques, 26½in (66cm).
£8,000-10,000 *C*

A William III walnut veneered cabinet on stand w fitted interior, raised on an open stand with 5 barleysugar twist supports, some restoration.
£3,000-4,000 *WW*

An ormolu-mounted scarlet boulle side cabinet, mid-19thC, 51in (129.5cm). **£1,200-1,700**   *C*

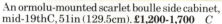

A William and Mary burr-yew bureau, inlaid crossbanded flap, stepped fitted interior with secret drawer, front legs with gateleg action, 32in (80cm).
£3,000-4,000   *C*

Left: A William III mulberry veneered bureau bookcase, sides banded in yewwood, interior with pigeonholes and 17 drawers, doors with yewwood and brass banding, fall flap revealing a well-fitted interior, on later bracket feet, 38in (95cm).
£70,000-75,000   *WW*

Above left: A George III mahogany secretaire-cabinet, centre door enclosing pigeonholes, 11 small drawers, 5 drawers with silver plaques inscribed 'Bills Paid' etc., surrounding 2 doors inlaid with chequered lines, central drawer with baize-lined slide, 43in (109cm).
£80,000-85,000   *C*

Right: A Schleswig Holstein walnut and parcel gilt secretaire cabinet, upper part with shelves and drawers enclosed by a slightly arched door inset with a mirror, the fall to the bombé lower part enclosing fitted interior, late 18thC, 93in (232cm) high.
£6,300-6,800   *P*

Left: A George III mahogany and satinwood cylinder bureau, the solid sliding cylinder enclosing a fitted interior, 45in (114.5cm).
£6,500-7,500   *C*

A Chippendale cherrywood desk and bookcase, the upper part with scrolled pediment and 3 spiral-turned and leaf-carved finials, the lower section with thumb moulded lid, opening to a fitted interior, over 4 long drawers, 41½in (103cm).
£11,000-15,000   *CNY*

A Chippendale mahogany chest on chest, by James Bartram, the upper part moulded with swan's neck pediment, on ogee bracket feet, tip of cartouche missing, Philadelphia, c1750-70, 44½in (110cm).
£75,000-85,000   *CNY*

A Queen Anne walnut bureau cabinet.
£37,000-39,000   *C*

Below A Dutch burr walnut veneered bureau cabinet, with fitted interior, the base with oak lined drawers, 18thC, 50in (126cm).
£9,000-10,000   *WW*

An Italian walnut and ivory marquetry bureau cabinet, inlaid with rosewood, mulberry and fruitwood, 18thC, 49in (122cm).
£10,000-12,000   *P*

Above An important William and Mary seaweed marquetry bureau cabinet, attributable to Gerrit Jensen, decorated overall with geometric panels of stylised foliate and arabesque inlay, the sloping section enclosing a fitted interior and rosewood veneered slide, all on later bracket feet, 39in (97cm).
£11,000-12,000   *P*

Lakeside Antiques

Old Cement Works,
South Heighton
Newhaven · Sussex
England
Tel: 0273 513326

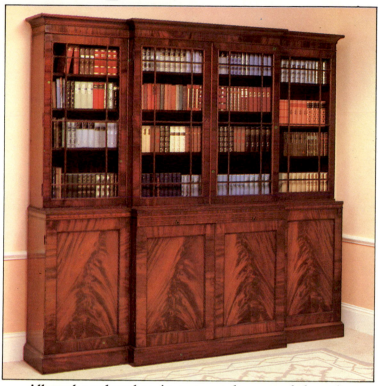

*All work undertaken in our own large workshops by
a group of highly skilled craftsmen.*

Customers commissions gladly undertaken.

*Large stock of good quality, mahogany and
walnut furniture in most popular styles.*

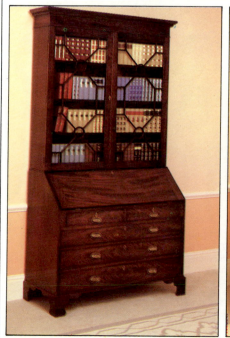

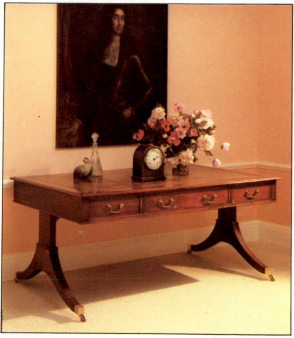

A set of 11 George III mahogany dining chairs, including an open armchair, the panelled solid toprails with fluted tapering splats, turned tapering legs with ribbed collars, later blocks, some replaced seat rails, and a later open armchair.
£15,000-18,000   *C*

A set of 4 George III mahogany dining chairs, a pair of armchairs and a pair of side chairs *en suite*, of later date.
£5,000-6,000   *C*

A pair of mahogany deep seat elbow chairs, with curved backs and moulded frames, scroll arms with ball terminals, padded seats, reeded frames, on sabre legs, English, c1805.
£6,000-8,000   *WW*

A rare set of 6 Queen Anne walnut side chairs, on cabriole legs with pad and disc feet, 3 seat frames original, Annapolis, Maryland, 1740-60, 37½in (92.5cm).
£20,000-22,000   *CNY*

A set of 18 Regency dining side chairs, each with incurved tablet back and horizontal bar splat, stamped Gillows, Lancaster, early 19thC.
£8,000-10,000   *CNY*

A set of 4 Victorian rosewood dining chairs, the moulded pierced balloon backs carved with foliage, ribbon-tied strapwork and flowerheads with grotesque masks, the shaped padded seats with foliate centres to the seat rails on mask and husk cabriole legs with gilt metal rams head sabots.
£3,000-4,000   *C*

An unusual pair of walnut folding chairs, with suede upholstered seats and backs, the frames carved to simulate bamboo, with carrying handles, mid-19thC.
£3,000-4,000   *C*

A pair of Regency painted satinwood open armchairs, with pierced heart-shaped backs, one replaced front rail.
£8,000-9,000   *C*

A fine set of 6 George III painted open armchairs, the pierced shield-shaped backs painted in pastel shades with ribbon-tied feathers and summer flowers, with later caned bowed seats and ivory damask squab cushions, turned tapering legs, with similar decoration.
£19,000-20,000   *C*

A set of 6 Regency simulated rosewood and parcel gilt dining chairs, 3 seat frames inscribed 'Boxall'.
£15,500-16,500   *C*

A set of 12 George IV oak dining chairs in the manner of Morel and Seddon, the backs with octagonal finials and panelled friezes carved with quatrefoils.
£15,500-16,500   *C*

A George IV mahogany reading chair, attributed to Morgan and Saunders, spliced back foot.
£2,500-3,500   *C*

A fine Adam period carved giltwood settee in the manner of John Linnell, with carved and moulded serpentine back, 91in (230cm).
£6,000-7,000   *P*

A Regency brass-mounted mahogany tub bergere, with moulded arm supports.
£5,500-6,500   *C*

A rare pair of William and Mary scarlet and gold lacquer x-frame open armchairs, 26½in (65cm) wide.
£30,000-35,000   *C*

A George III giltwood sofa in the manner of John Linnell, 69in (172.5cm).
£6,000-7,000   *C*

A fine George I mahogany twin-back settee, the back with solid baluster splats with scroll and shell crestings, shepherd's crook arm supports, claw-and-ball feet, 55in (137.5cm).
£28,000-30,000   *C*

A Charles II oak sleeping armchair
£3,000-4,000   *C*

Right A pair of George IV gilt-wood open arm chairs, attributed to Gillows of Lancaster.
£13,000-15,000
C

A set of 6 George II giltwood side chairs, with slightly arched padded backs and upholstered seats, the hipped legs carved with lion masks with bared teeth, 27in (68cm).
£125,000-130,000 *C*

Right A William and Mary walnut armchair, with arched padded back, scrolled arm supports and upholstered seat, the cabriole legs joined by a scrolled stretcher.
£10,000-12,000 *C*

A pair of mid 18thC mahogany library armchairs with padded backs, armrests and seats, on strapwork cabriole legs and pad feet.
£18,000-20,000 *C*

Right A pair of William and Mary walnut and beechwood side chairs, on moulded scrolled shaped legs with X-shaped stretchers.
£5,000-6,000 *C*

A fine Charles II walnut stool with caned seat, on S-scroll legs.
£6,000-8,000 *C*

A George I gilt gesso stool with moulded frame, 24½in (60cm) wide.
£22,000-23,000 *C*

A pair of George II giltwood open armchairs, on imbricated cabriole legs.
£90,000-100,000 *C*

A Regency mahogany window seat of horseshoe shape, with caned seat and leather squab cushion, stamped IF twice, 63in (157.5cm).
£7,000-8,000 *C*

A pair of Regency mahogany metamorphic library armchairs, attributed to Morgan & Saunders, 23in (57.5cm).
£12,000-14,000 *C*

A pair of William IV oak throne armchairs, in the Gothic style, with quatrefoil roundels centred by the Wyndham crest, 53in (132.5cm) high.
£7,000-8,000 *C*

A Queen Anne oyster-veneered walnut chest, with geometric fruitwood stringing.
£5,000-6,000 *C*

A George I burr yew wood, laburnum crossbanded and inlaid coffer on stand, 49in (122cm).
£3,000-4,000 *P*

A George III mahogany secretaire chest, the chamfered top with hinged flap, 60in (150cm).
£4,500-5,500 *C*

A George III satinwood and mahogany serpentine chest, the top inlaid with a batswing oval, 41in (102cm).
£5,000-6,000 *C*

A Queen Anne burr walnut and featherstrung banded secretaire on chest, the crossbanded fall enclosing a fitted interior, on bracket feet.
£4,000-5,000 *P*

Above A Genoese kingwood and tulipwood crossbanded bombé commode surmounted by a serpentine moulded top, with gilt bronze rococo handle pulls and keyplates, 18thC, 54in (135cm).
£5,000-6,000 *P*

Right A walnut and crossbanded tallboy chest, 18thC, 40in (100cm).
£3,000-4,000 *JMW*

A George II mahogany commode, with rocaille handles and lockplates, 42in (105cm).
£15,000-20,000   *CNY*

A William and Mary black and gold lacquer cabinet on chest, 33½in (83cm) wide.
£10,000-11,000   *C*

A Louis XV French Provincial walnut commode of serpentine shape, the 3 drawers with incised moulded lines above a shaped apron carved with leafage design, continuing to hoof feet and with gilt brass handles formed from leafage swags and ribbon bows, 50in (125cm).
£4,500-5,500   *L*

A Louis XVI mahogany, kingwood, ormolu-mounted and inlaid demi-lune commode, with a drawer in the simulated fluted frieze, 2 crossbanded drawers below, with a similarly inlaid enclosed compartment to either side, stamped 'I.P. Dusautoy' and 'JME', 50in (125cm).
£12,000-15,000   *P*

Below A pair of George III satinwood, sycamore and marquetry commodes, cross-banded top with rosewood and inlaid with demi-patera and radiating flutes, the scalloped borders with fan lunettes and foliate scrolls outlined with boxwood lines, 46in (115cm).
£23,000-25,000   *C*

An early Louis XV rosewood, crossbanded and ormolu mounted serpentine commode, applied with rococo cartouche keyplate and foliate handles, pierced scroll sabot bracket feet, marble top defective, 51in (127cm).
£4,000-5,000   *P*

A fine Queen Anne giltwood and blue and gold verre eglomisé overmantel, with bevelled divided plate, 24 by 52½ (60 by 134cm).
£11,000-12,000   *C*

Above A fine George I giltwood mirror with rectangular bevelled plate with scrolling broken pediment, lacking cresting, and imbricated convex frieze, the sides with strapwork and foliate Corinthian pilasters, the pierced apron centred by a shell flanked by flowerheads and profile masks, 35in (87cm).
£10,000-11,000   *C*

Right A fine Charles II carved limewood mirror with later rectangular plate and overlapping foliage slip, the frame crisply carved with Royal arms and motto flanked by foliage and cherubs, the side with putti climbing amid trailing flowerheads and fruit, the base carved with shells, a crab, a lobster and sea serpents, applied to later rounded back with gilt border, some restoration, 64 by 48in (160 by 120cm).
£12,000-13,000   *C*

An Irish George III giltwood overmantel, 59 by 60in (147.5 by 150cm).
£15,000-17,000   *C*

A George II walnut mirror bevelled plate, 60 by 33in (150 by 84cm).
£6,500-7,500   *C*

A Regency burr yew breakfront bookcase, by Marsh & Tatham, inscribed, stencilled and branded with VR monogram, crown and 1866, 74in (188cm) wide.
£150,000-155,000 *C*

A pair of Regency rosewood card tables, the baize-lined tops inlaid with brass bands and dots, on tapering stepped shafts, 36in (90cm).
£4,000-6,000 *C*

Top A George I walnut bureau cabinet, the moulded cornice and later glazed arched cupboard door enclosing a fitted interior, the sloping flap enclosing a fitted interior, the sides with candle slides, the base with hinged writing flap and 4 long drawers, the top fitted with later cedar liners on later bracket feet, 21½in (53cm).
£18,000-20,000 *C*

Above A fine Regency and parcel gilt plum pudding mahogany centre table, the circular top banded and crossbanded in rosewood with fluted frieze on moulded tripartite fluted S-scroll shaft, arched waved, concave side plinth centred by a turned step finial, scrolled claw feet, 50½in (126cm) diam.
£6,000-8,000 *C*

Cf. a table illustrated in R. Edwards and P. Macquoid, The Dictionary of English Furniture, *rev. edn., 1954, Vol III, p. 317, fig 35.*

A Regency rosewood card table with leather and brass inlaid top, 37in (94cm).
£9,000-10,000 *C*

A Victorian satinwood, ebony and marquetry centre table, with waved frieze and a drawer at each end, on quadruple spirally turned shafts, 42in (105cm) wide.
£3,000-4,000 *C*

A fine Italian specimen marble circular table, in a variety of coloured marbles and hardstones, on a carved mahogany base, 19thC, 40in (101cm).
£11,000-12,000 *P*

A William and Mary padoukwood and oak gateleg dining table, 56in (140cm) wide, open.
£3,000-4,000 *C*

A rare Sheraton satinwood and mahogany oval library table with inset green tooled leather top, late 18thC, 72in (182.5cm).
£20,000-22,000 *BS*

A fine George III mahogany four-pedestal dining table, with lion's paw brass casters, early 19thC, 174in (442cm).
£45,000-50,000 *CNY*

Left An early Victorian mahogany dining table, circular top divided into wedges to accommodate 16 leaves, baluster turned stop-fluted stem on quadruped base with lion's paw and scrolled feet, signed 'Johnstone and Jeaves Patentees', mid 19thC, 60in (152cm) diam.
£20,000-25,000 *CNY*

A Regency rosewood occasional table, 31in (77.5cm).
£3,000-3,500 *C*

A Regency mahogany library table with leather-lined swivelling circular top, fitted with 4 drawers, 36in (90cm) diam.
£10,000-11,000 *C*

A George III walnut and mahogany Pembroke table.
£6,500-7,000 *CNY*

A pair of gilt gesso centre tables, each with later inset honey-coloured marble tops, 21in (52.5cm).
£6,000-7,000 *C*

An oak side table, with one frieze drawer, 17thC, 37½in (94cm).
£4,500-5,000 *C*

A fine George II mahogany side table with rounded rectangular Portor marble top, the panelled gadrooned frieze crisply carved with scrolling foliage, 43½in (108cm).
£12,000-13,000 *C*

Left An oak side table, mid-17thC, 28in (70cm). **£12,500-13,500** *C*

Above A pair of mahogany side tables, 78in (198cm) wide. **£11,000-13,000** *C*

A Milanese ebonised and ivory marquetry Blackamoor console table, with D-shaped top, raised on a crouching sculptured figure on a plinth base with bun feet, 19thC, 40in (100cm). **£2,500-3,500** *P*

A George II parcel gilt side table, 80in. **£25,000-30,000** *C*

A Regency rosewood and brass inlaid sofa table, with well figured rectangular twin flap top bordered and inlaid with brass foliate scrolls, the baluster turned stem on outcurved quadruped base, 59in (147.5cm), extended. **£5,000-6,000** *CNY*

A pair of George III satinwood pier tables, with crossbanded D-shaped tops and fluted tapering legs with spade feet, 23in (57.5cm). **£9,000-11,000** *C*

A fine Irish mid-Georgian mahogany gateleg table with oval twin-flap top on cabriole legs, on hairy claw-and-ball feet, 58½in (145cm) wide.
£6,000-8,000 *C*

A Victorian mahogany specimen marble and semi-precious stone centre table, 27in (67.5cm) diam.
£5,000-6,000 *C*

A Regency faded rosewood drum table with crossbanded circular top, 36in (90cm) diam.
£6,500-7,500 *C*

A Regency parcel gilt and burr maple centre table, the circular top inlaid with foliate ebony banding with spreading gadrooned foliate shaft and concave sided tripartite platform base, with scrolled foliate feet, 52in (132.5cm) diam.
£10,000-12,000 *C*

An unusual Regency rosewood card table, with rounded baize-lined top inlaid with scrolling brass lines, on lotus leaf ormolu feet, 36in (90cm).
£8,000-10,000 *C*

A fine William and Mary burr walnut card table, with crossbanded semi-elliptical folding top, fitted with 3 drawers and 2 candle slides, 30in (75cm).
£17,000-19,000 *C*

A George III mahogany writing table with leather-lined top, and 3 frieze drawers either side, on square tapering legs, joined by plain stretchers, 59½in (151cm).
£6,000-8,000   *C*

A George III satinwood and rosewood tripod table, 26½in (67cm).
£9,000-10,000   *C*

A Regency rosewood and gilt metal mounted writing table, with leather inset three-quarter pierced galleried top, on lyre-form trestle ends, brass casters, 19thC, 44in (110cm).
£25,000-35,000   *CNY*

A Federal mahogany and bird's eye maple sewing table.
£35,000-45,000   *CNY*

Above A French kingwood crossbanded ormolu and porcelain mounted bureau plat in Louis XV taste, stamped EHR, 19thC, 38in (95cm).
£6,000-7,000   *P*

Right A Regency brass mounted mahogany wine cooler, 29½in (73cm).
£15,000-16,000   *C*

An early George III mahogany tea and games table,
32½in (80cm).
£7,500-8,500 *C*

A George III mahogany davenport with
carrying handle and pierced gallery,
15½in (38cm).
£6,500-7.500 *C*

A fine William and Mary walnut writing or card
table, the bun feet with restorations, 30in (75cm).
£7,500-8,500 *C*

Left A Regency burr
walnut and giltwood
torchere, with concave-
sided top on tapering
foliate leopard's head
supports, joined by a
circular platform and claw
feet, 17in (42.5cm).
£3,500-4,000 *C*

A Regency mahogany library globe with
Cary's terrestrial globe depicting 'the
tracks and discoveries made by Captain
Cook etc. dated March 1, 1815, additions
and corrections to 1841', the stand with
shaped ribbed tapering legs with foliate
baluster collars joined by plain stretchers,
centred by a glazed compass, 28in (70cm)
diam.
£16,000-17,000 *C*

A pair of George III chinoiserie japanned lacquer pole screens.
£1,000-1,500 *P*

Right A pair of George III mahogany urns and pedestals, the vases with spirally turned shaped lids, the bodies with grotesque masks joined by ribbon-tied drapery swags, the socles with egg-and-oval collars with gadrooned bases and square plinths, 64in (160cm) high.
£18,000-20,000 *C*

A Regency scarlet and gold lacquered papier mâché tray, stamped 'Clay, King Street, Covt. Garden', on later red-painted and gilded bamboo stand, 26in (65cm) wide.
£3,500-4,000 *C*

> **Right** A marquetry boudoir grand piano by Steinway & Sons, the case lid inscribed 'C Mellier of London INV ET FECIT', 57 by 86in (142 by 218cm).
> **£8,000-10,000** *C*

A Regency mahogany three-tier étagère, 24in (60cm) wide.
£9,500-10,500 *C*

A pair of Regency parcel gilt and tôle peinte pole screens, early 19thC, 44in (110cm) high.
£6,000-7,000 *CNY*

One of the more interesting trends within the furniture market, and one that is gaining increasing momentum has, on the surface at least, little to do with furniture.

In recent years, the major auction houses have made genuine and praiseworthy efforts to humanise their image, encouraging members of the general public to seek advice, to sell individual items, and to buy against the bids of dealers. And auctioneers throughout the length and breadth of the country are reporting increasing numbers of private buyers chancing their arms and buying direct from the saleroom instead of seeking the security afforded by buying from the High Street dealer. In

consequence, sales are well-attended, and bidding tends to be vigorous – particularly for middle-range furniture of good, usable quality.

Despite the fact that the quantity of goods passing through the salerooms is not particularly large, quality is normally consistently good. This is a factor which particularly affects the largest pieces of all – the mammoth library bookcases, for example, and massive oak refectory tables. Such pieces, when (and only when) of superb quality continue to rise to astronomical heights despite constant assurances that they have at last reached their limits.

In general terms, Southern buyers favour smaller pieces from the later Georgian and Regency periods, paying particular attention to usability rather than mere decoration, while Scottish salerooms are finding it comparatively easy to sell larger pieces such as partners' desks, breakfront bookcases and large dining tables with sets of eight to twelve chairs – with good repro items fetching notable sums.

In the longer term, such a trend bodes well for a buoyant market in which even the most hardened dealers will find themselves paying higher and higher prices for good, stock pieces, while items in need of restoration are likely to fall still further behind.

Beds

An Irish Chippendale four-poster bedstead, 96 by 54in (240 by 135cm), mid-18thC.
£5,500-6,500 *WW*

This bed has been lengthened to take an interior box spring and mattress.

A walnut four-poster bed, the canopy carved with egg-and-dart ornament, the headboard carved with blind fretwork, with shaped footrest, 82in (208cm) wide.
£2,200-3,000 *C*

A painted four-poster bed, the canopy with pierced foliage, with shaped moulded headboard centred by a scallop and confronting foliate C-scrolls, with 2 moulded pillars, mattress and hangings, 103 by 88in (261.5 by 222.5cm).
£3,000-4,000 *C*

BEDS

Beds have invariably been altered. The most common change being in length – we are simply much taller now. This is regarded as acceptable generally if the bed is to be used. Size can account for considerable differences in price – a good Charles II four poster of, say, 4ft 7in wide by 6ft long might well be less desirable than a less good bed measuring 5ft 6in wide and 7ft long. Most bed buyers *do* want to use their 'fantasy' furniture while retaining 20thC comfort.

A mahogany four-poster bed, with George III carved cluster and baluster posts, lacking canopy with box-spring and mattress, 84 by 61in (213 by 152cm).
£2,200-3,000 *C*

A mahogany four-poster bed, the 2 cluster columns with foliate baluster bases with box-spring and mattress, one distressed leg, George III and later, 93 by 60in (236 by 152.5cm).
£3,000-4,000 *C*

A mahogany cradle, early 19thC,
34in (85cm).
£400-500 *JD*

A Louis XVI, lit a la Polonnaise,
with moulded canopy and waved
fringed hangings, 98½ by 51in (250
by 130cm).
£1,500-2,000 *C*

A mahogany four-poster bed, the
scrolled backboard headed by a
shell and cartouche on reeded
spreading posts, claw-and-ball feet
headed by shells, with flame-
pattern hangings in shades of
brown outlined in beige, 94in
(239cm) wide.
£3,000-5,000 *C*

Bonheur du jour

A George III mahogany bonheur du
jour, the superstructure with 2 oval
inlaid doors, pigeonholes and short
drawers, 36½in (92cm) wide.
£4,000-4,500 *C*

A rare George III mahogany
bonheur du jour the raised
superstructure with bobbin-turned
gallery, the lower part with
secretaire drawer also containing
compartments for inkwells, quills
etc., 30in (75cm).
£2,400-3,000 *HAL*

A Regency mahogany bonheur du
jour, inlaid with geometric ebonised
lines, 33in (82.5cm).
£800-1,200 *CSK*

A Regency calamanderwood
bonheur du jour, the base with
hinged flap enclosing 2 wells,
decorated later with an oval of
summer flowers framed by trailing
foliage above a cedar-lined drawer
and a material-lined work-basket,
on satinwood inlaid tapering legs,
26in (66cm) wide.
£3,000-4,000 *C*

A William IV flamed mahogany
bonheur du jour with writing slope,
set in a secretaire drawer.
£2,000-2,400 *EA*

An Edwardian mahogany and
satinwood crossbanded bonheur du
jour, by T Willson of London, incised
on drawer T Willson, 68 Great
Queen Street, London, 45in
(112.5cm) wide.
£800-1,000 *Re*

A Victorian inlaid walnut bonheur
du jour, in the French style, 43in
(107.5cm) wide.
£1,000-2,000 *WIL*

A Victorian thuyawood and ebonised bonheur du jour, banded in kingwood, inlaid with boxwood and harewood lines, and mounted with gilt-metal and Sèvres style porcelain plaques, 53½in (133.5cm).
£2,500-3,000 *CSK*

A Victorian satinwood bonheur du jour, inlaid with stringing and bands, 42in (105cm).
£1,100-1,400 *GSP*

Breakfront Bookcases

A French boulle bonheur du jour, with brass and red tortoiseshell on an ebonised ground, 19thC, 32in (81cm).
£800-1,000 *L*

◁ A large Regency mahogany breakfront bookcase, in the manner of Gillows, with brass inlaid pediment centred by foliate ormolu plaque, 99½ by 196in (253 by 498cm).
£11,000-13,000 *C*

◁ A small George III mahogany breakfront bookcase, 93½ by 78in (237.5 by 198cm).
£14,000-17,000 *C*

A George IV mahogany breakfront library bookcase, outlined with ebony mouldings, 98 by 112in (247.5 by 282.5cm).
£8,000-10,000 *Bea*

A good mahogany breakfront bookcase.
£3,500-4,000 *Bon*

A Regency mahogany breakfront bookcase, the base fitted with 4 frieze drawers and 2 central cupboard doors, enclosing slides flanked by a pair of doors enclosing drawers on plinth base, 97 by 93in (246.5 by 236cm).
£13,000-15,000 *C*

A breakfront bookcase, veneered throughout in finely figured and well matched walnut veneer, upper part with shaped pediment above 4 glazed doors with plain domed paterae and planted pilasters enclosing 9 adjustable shelves, lower part with 4 blind fielded panelled doors and planted pilasters enclosing 6 adjustable shelves on plain plinth, early 19thC, 93 by 90in (235 by 227.5cm).
£5,500-6,500 *MN*

A George III mahogany breakfront bookcase, the moulded cornice with swan neck centre, the lower part with four-figured panel doors enclosing 3 long drawers in the centre and 3 drawers each side, 94½ by 83in (240 by 210cm).
£8,000-10,000 *L*

A George III mahogany rosewood and boxwood lined breakfront bookcase, with restorations, 90in (225cm) wide.
£14,000-17,000 *CEd*

A Georgian mahogany and boxwood lined breakfront bookcase, adapted, 97½in (243.5cm).
£3,000-3,500 *CEd*

A George III mahogany breakfront library bookcase, the upper part with a moulded and arcaded pendant cornice and fluted and paterae decorated frieze, 189in (472cm) wide.
£30,000-35,000 *P*

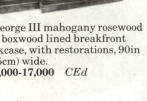

MAKE THE MOST OF MILLER'S

Every care has been taken to ensure the accuracy of descriptions and estimated valuations. Where an attribution is made within inverted commas (e.g. 'Chippendale') or is followed by the word 'style' (e.g. early Georgian style) it is intended to convey that, in the opinion of the publishers, the piece concerned is a later – though probably still antique – reproduction of the style so designated. Unless otherwise stated, any description which refers to 'a set', or 'a pair' includes a valuation for the entire set or the pair, even though the illustration may show only a single item.

A small mahogany breakfront bookcase, the lower part beneath a fluted chair rail with a pair of central fielded panelled doors flanked by glazed doors, on bracket feet, c1840, 92 by 72in (232.5 by 182.5cm).
£6,000-8,000   *HAL*

A Victorian mahogany breakfront bookcase, 94 by 114in (237.5 by 287.5cm).
£2,000-2,500   *AG*

A mahogany breakfront library bookcase, on plinth base, 19thC, 101 by 132in (256 by 336cm).
£3,500-4,000   *L*

A mahogany breakfront bookcase, the moulded cornice above a boxwood inlaid frieze and trellis astragal glazed doors, 85in (215cm) wide.
£1,800-2,200   *Bon*

A Victorian mahogany breakfront three-tier bookcase, 110 by 142in (277.5 by 357.5cm).
£3,000-4,000   *CSK*

A Victorian mahogany breakfront library bookcase, 95 by 77in (240 by 195cm).
£2,200-2,600   *Bea*

Bureau Bookcases

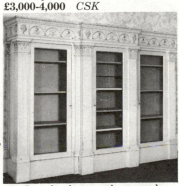

A gilt and pale green lacquered architectural breakfront bookcase, 73 by 100in (185 by 252.5cm).
£1,500-2,000   *GSP*

A George III style breakfront library bookcase, banded and inlaid with boxwood lines, the top section with a dentilled cornice and broken swan-neck pediment applied with satinwood fanned roundels, 100 by 140in (252.5 by 352cm).
£6,000-7,000   *CSK*

It is interesting to note the strong price paid for this later reproduction. This is due to the high quality of the piece.

◁ A walnut bureau cabinet, the fall-flap enclosing a fitted interior above 5 drawers, on later bracket feet, partly early 18thC, 22in (56cm) wide.
£6,000-8,000   *C*

Provenance: by repute Welbeck Abbey.

A late Georgian mahogany bureau bookcase, banded in satinwood and inlaid with boxwood lines, rippled fan ovals and angles, and leafy garlands, 47in (117.5cm).
£2,500-3,000   *CSK*

A walnut and feather banded bureau bookcase, early 18thC, 88 by 38in (222.5 by 95cm).
£4,500-5,500   *CW*

A figured walnut bureau bookcase, early 18thC, 83 by 39in (210 by 97.5cm).
£4,500-5,500 *GSP*

A Georgian mahogany bureau bookcase, 43in (107.5cm).
£2,000-2,500 *JD*

An early George III mahogany bureau bookcase, the bureau with fitted interior above 4 graduated long drawers with original brass handles and escutcheons and side carrying handles (part missing), and on later turned feet, 78 by 40in (198 by 102cm).
£3,000-3,500 *L*

An exceptional Queen Anne period bureau bookcase, in finely figured walnut veneers, the cornice unusually with cushion frieze above a single bevelled mirrored door enclosing an interior with adjustable shelves and small fitted drawers, with good quality replaced brasswork, c1710, 80 by 26½in (202.5 by 66cm).
£16,000-20,000 *HAL*

The plate, brasswork and feet are good early replacements to this fine piece.

A George III mahogany bureau bookcase with associated upper section, the sloping fall front later inlaid with a shell medallion, quadrants and boxwood and ebony stringing, restored, 85 by 39½in (215 by 98.5cm).
£1,500-2,000 *Bea*

An early George III period mahogany bureau bookcase, having finely fret carved broken pediment and cornice, the fall-front enclosing drawers, pigeonholes, central cupboard, and secret compartments, some damage to pediment, 42½in (106cm) wide.
£18,000-20,000 *GC*

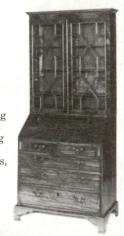

A walnut, crossbanded and featherstrung bureau bookcase, the upper part with rosewood fitted interior with chequerstrung drawers and open compartments, the sloping fall enclosing a similarly decorated interior about an enclosed cupboard with sliding compartment concealing 2 drawers, early 18thC, 41in (102cm).
£10,000-12,000 *P*

A mahogany bureau bookcase, the crossbanded fall enclosing a fitted interior of drawers and pigeonholes the two sections associated, basically late 18thC, 39½in (99cm) wide.
£1,100-1,400 *Bon*

▷ A Georgian mahogany bureau, with later bookcase over, 34in (85cm) wide.
£1,000-1,300 *Pea*

A 'marriage' is perfectly acceptable, especially if well matched, if the price reflects it.

A Queen Anne style bureau bookcase in walnut, the domed top with panelled door enclosing shelves above a candle slide, 66 by 21½in (165 by 53.5cm).
£2,500-3,000 *CW*

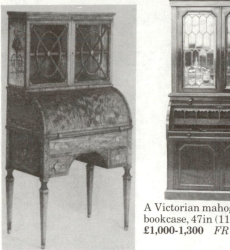

A Victorian mahogany cylinder
bookcase, 47in (117.5cm) wide.
£1,000-1,300 *FR*

A mid-Victorian mahogany bureau
bookcase, 96 by 43in (242.5 by
107.5cm).
£550-650 *DSH*

A neo-classical style cylinder
bureau bookcase, inlaid with
boxwood lines and rosewood bands,
31½in (78.5cm).
£2,800-3,200 *CSK*

A small Italian ebonised bureau
bookcase, extensively decorated
with etched ivory panels in the
classical style, late 18thC, 32in
(80cm) wide.
£1,100-1,400 *A*

Dwarf Bookcases

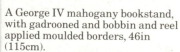

A Regency mahogany open
bookcase, 34½in (87.5cm) wide.
£1,800-2,000 *C*

A pair of George III small open
bookcases, decorated in gilt, grey
and claret, c1800, 49 by 21½in
(122.5 by 53.5cm).
£2,500-3,000 *HAL*

The decoration has been restored.

An Edwardian satinwood bureau
bookcase, banded in rosewood and
inlaid with boxwood and ebony
lines, 31½in (78.5cm) wide.
£1,500-2,000 *CSK*

A George IV mahogany bookstand,
with gadrooned and bobbin and reel
applied moulded borders, 46in
(115cm).
£800-1,000 *CSK*

A late Regency rosewood dwarf
breakfront bookcase, 84in
(212.5cm).
£1,700-1,900 *CSK*

A good pair of George III mahogany
open bookshelves.
£4,000-5,000 *Bon*

A Regency mahogany and gilt metal mounted breakfront dwarf open bookcase, the flowerhead decorated frieze fitted with a central drawer, 85in (215cm).
£3,500-4,000 *P*

A small Regency bookcase, having graduated shelves flanked by original brass carrying handles, with original brass casters, the whole decorated in simulated rosewood with fine gilt stringing, c1815, 46 by 24in (115 by 60cm).
£1,500-2,300 *HAL*

A Victorian breakfront walnut bookcase, decorated with parquetry bands and ormolu mounts, 85in (215cm) wide.
£600-800 *AG*

An Edwardian satinwood revolving bookcase, 56in (140cm) high.
£2,000-2,300 *CSK*

Library Bookcases

An Edwardian mahogany and satinwood banded low bookcase, the crossbanded top above a ribbon and bellflower swag frieze, 50½in (126cm) wide.
£450-550 *Bon*

A George III mahogany bookcase or display cabinet, the upper part with moulded cornice and blind fret frieze, c1780, 74½ by 35in (188.5 by 87.5cm).
£3,000-4,000 *HAL*

A George III mahogany bookcase, 99in (250cm).
£3,000-3,500 *CSK*

BOOKCASES

★ Check that the glazing bars match the rest of the bookcase in quality, timber and age. Breakfront wardrobes of the mid to late 19thC can be turned into bookcases by removing the solid panels to the doors and glazing the frames

★ during the late 19thC many old glazed door cabinets were removed from their bureau or cupboard bases to have feet added and the tops fitted in to make 'Georgian' display or bookcases. This was not an 18thC form; the correct version was much taller and often had drawers to the frieze base. The low 'dwarf' bookcases without doors became popular during the late 18thC

★ the earliest form of adjustable shelf on the better quality bookcases was achieved by cutting rabbets into the sides of the cabinet into which the shelves could slide. Next came a toothed ladder at each side, the removable rungs forming the shelf rests. Finally, by the end of the 18thC, came movable pegs fitting into holes. Regency examples were often made of gilt metal or brass

★ check when a bookcase sits on a bureau or cupboard base that it is slightly smaller than the base, and it is preferable that the retaining moulding is fixed to the base not the top; also, it is unlikely that the top surface to such a base would have been veneered originally

★ a bureau made to take a bookcase on top will have a steeper angle to the fall front to create a greater depth to accommodate the case or cabinet

A George III mahogany bookcase, 79½ by 36½in (202 by 93cm).
£2,800-3,200   *L*

A George III mahogany bookcase, 50in (125cm) wide.
£1,500-2,000   *Bon*

A Georgian mahogany bookcase, 110 by 63½in (277.5 by 158.5cm).
£1,500-1,800   *AG*

A George III mahogany bookcase of Gothic style, designed for an alcove, 82½ by 37in (209.5 by 93.5cm).
£2,000-2,500   *C*

A Regency mahogany library bookcase, with inlaid ebony and boxwood lined doors, 102 by 88in (257.5 by 222.5cm).
£3,800-4,400   *B*

A George III mahogany bookcase, with moulded dentilled cornice, 98 by 59½in (249 by 151cm).
£2,200-2,500   *C*

A George III mahogany bookcase, inlaid with ebony stringing, relined drawers, c1810, 38½in (96cm) wide.
£1,100-1,400   *Bon*

A George III mahogany bookcase-on-stand, the base with blind fretwork frieze and pierced angle brackets on moulded square supports joined by moulded cross stretchers, 47in (117.5cm) wide.
£1,600-1,900   *CEd*

A Regency mahogany library alcove bookcase, with an oak carcase, the mahogany front with a domed moulded cornice above a pair of glazed tracery doors, the sides later infilled, 100 by 87in (252.5 by 220cm).
£3,600-4,000   *WW*

In the Furniture section if there is only one measurement it usually refers to the width of the piece.

An oak book press of the Pepys model.
£4,500-5,500   *C*

The celebrated 12 bookcases commissioned by Samuel Pepys, secretary to the Navy, in the late 1660s from 'Sympson the joyner' were bequeathed to Magdalene College Cambridge. Pepys is credited with the invention of the free standing case book press.

A Regency mahogany bookcase inlaid with ebonised lines, 52½in (131cm).
£2,300-2,600 *CSK*

A bookcase, veneered in walnut with marquetry and ebonised inlay, 19thC, 47in (117.5cm).
£1,500-1,800 *MN*

A Victorian rosewood bookcase, 53in (133cm) wide.
£900-1,100 *Bon*

An early Victorian mahogany bookcase, 45½in (113.5cm).
£750-950 *CSK*

A mahogany bookcase, on matched contemporary base, early 19thC, 51½in (128.5cm) wide.
£1,200-1,400 *LBP*

A pair of George IV mahogany standing pedestal bookcases, 23½in (58.5cm).
£1,700-2,000 *CSK*

A Victorian mahogany and ebonised library bookcase, 90 by 115in (225 by 288cm).
£1,000-1,500 *CDC*

A set of four oak double sided library bookcases, 113 by 102in (285 by 257.5cm).
£7,000-9,000 *CSK*

A Victorian mahogany bookcase, 61in (152.5cm) wide.
£800-1,000 *O*

A large Victorian pollard oak breakfront bookcase cabinet, 108 by 84in (272.5 by 212.5cm).
£2,800-3,200 *TW*

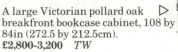

A mahogany bookcase, c1920, 90in (227.5cm) high.
£600-800 *WIL*

314

A large Victorian mahogany
bookcase, 78in (197.5cm).
£850-1,050 *FR*

A mahogany bookcase cupboard,
19thC, 76½ by 43in (194 by 109cm).
£1,800-2,200 *L*

A Victorian mahogany library
bookcase, 98 by 34in (247.5 by
85cm).
£400-500 *CDC*

Secretaire Bookcases

A pair of Edwardian satinwood
bookcases, inlaid in various woods,
the bases banded in coromandel, the
tops centred by ovals inlaid with a
satyr leading a goat, above 2
drawers centred by trophies, on
square tapering legs hung with
pendant bellflowers, 97in (245cm).
£3,000-3,500 *CSK*

A George III mahogany secretaire
bookcase, the pull-out secretaire
drawer below with fall-flap opening
to reveal a fitted interior of
pigeonholes and drawers, 91 by
43in (230 by 107.5cm).
£1,300-1,600 *AG*

An Edwardian bookcase, inlaid
with parquetry and boxwood
stringing, 47in (117.5cm) wide.
£450-500 *FR*

A small George III mahogany
secretaire bookcase, the moulded
coved cornice with satinwood
banding above a pair of doors with
arched astragal glazing bars and
mainly original glass, c1800, 86 by
34in (217.5 by 85cm).
£5,000-6,000 *HAL*

A George III mahogany secretaire
bookcase, 37in (93cm) wide.
£2,600-3,000 *Bon*

A George III breakfront secretaire
library bookcase.
£5,500-6,500 *Re*

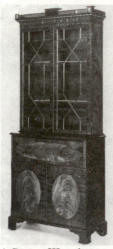

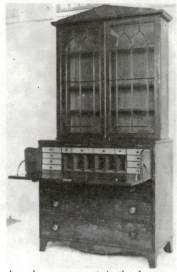

A George III mahogany and satinwood secretaire bookcase, 100 by 39½in (252.5 by 100.5cm).
£2,600-3,000 *C*

A mahogany secretaire bookcase, c1800, 46in (115cm) wide.
£1,000-1,400 *JMW*

A late George III mahogany secretaire bookcase, 92 by 54in (232.5 by 135cm).
£1,200-1,500 *Bea*

A Georgian mahogany secretaire bookcase, the lower section having dummy top drawer, revealing a secretaire base fitted with writing slide concealing 6 filing drawers and 2 secret drawers, 87in (220cm) high.
£4,000-5,000 *OL*

A mahogany secretaire bookcase, the secretaire drawer fitted with satinwood faced small drawers and pigeonholes, early 19thC, 40in (100cm) wide.
£4,500-5,500 *PWC*

A mahogany veneered Sheraton design secretaire bookcase, the moulded cornice with line inlay and a yew veneered frieze, the base with a kingwood banded top, and line inlaid front, the fall-front to an interior with a shell inlaid yew veneered centre door and drawer with pigeonholes, 46in (115cm).
£1,200-1,500 *WW*

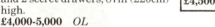

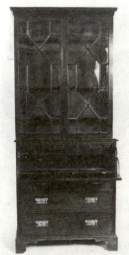

A late George III mahogany secretaire bookcase, the lower section fitted with writing drawer with fully fitted interior of drawers and pigeonholes, 43½in (110.5cm) wide.
£1,800-2,200 *Nes*

A late Georgian mahogany secretaire bookcase, with later handles, 37in (92.5cm) wide.
£1,000-1,300 *Pea*

A Georgian mahogany secretaire bookcase, 45in (112.5cm).
£2,300-2,600 *WSW*

A Regency mahogany secretaire bookcase, 87 by 37½in (221 by 95cm).
£3,200-3,600 *C*

A late George III mahogany secretaire bookcase, decorated with inlaid boxwood stringing, 89 by 43in (225 by 107.5cm).
£3,600-4,000 *AG*

A Regency mahogany secretaire bookcase, the secretaire drawer with satinwood faced small drawers, apron drawers and pigeonholes, 48½in (121cm) wide.
£1,500-1,800 *PWC*

A Regency mahogany secretaire bookcase, the lower part a secretaire with good interior containing a tambour cupboard, small drawers and pigeonholes, c1810, 91 by 42½in (230 by 106cm).
£7,000-8,000 *HAL*

A William IV mahogany secretaire bookcase, applied with ebonised beadings and fitted with brass mounts, 56in (140cm).
£1,500-2,000 *CSK*

A Regency mahogany secretaire bookcase, applied with radial mouldings, 39in (97.5cm).
£2,800-3,200 *CSK*

A late Regency mahogany and ebony moulded secretaire bookcase, 100 by 61in (252 by 152cm).
£3,500-4,500 *P*

A William IV mahogany secretaire bookcase, 52in (130cm).
£1,300-1,600 *CSK*

A William IV mahogany secretaire bookcase, decorated with gadrooned and beaded mouldings, 44in (110cm) wide.
£2,000-2,500 *CSK*

An early Victorian walnut chiffonier bookcase, 83 by 41in (210 by 102.5cm).
£1,400-1,800 *DSH*

A mahogany secretaire bookcase, the front falling to reveal small drawers and pigeonholes, early 19thC, 51½in (129cm).
£800-1,000 *HSS*

An early Victorian mahogany secretaire bookcase, 86 by 48in (217.5 by 120cm).
£1,500-1,800 *TW*

An early Victorian mahogany secretaire bookcase, on bun feet, 48in (120cm).
£1,400-1,700 *CSK*

A Victorian satinwood secretaire bookcase, of neo-classical design, inlaid with masks, amaranth cornucopiae and harewood foliate marquetry arabesques, 44½in (111cm).
£4,000-5,000 *CSK*

A Victorian mahogany secretaire bookcase, 34in (85cm).
£1,000-1,300 *SL*

Bureaux

A William and Mary walnut table bureau, the fall-flap enclosing a fitted interior, 22½in (56cm) wide.
£1,200-1,400 *C*

A Queen Anne walnut bureau, with a quarter veneered flap decorated with feather banding, 40 by 36in (100 by 90cm).
£3,000-3,500 *AG*

A small Queen Anne walnut bureau, the figured herringbone inlaid crossbanded surface with slight gallery, the fall including a book rest opening to reveal a well fitted interior with a well, pigeonholes and small stepped drawers, all with good quality replaced brasswork, the veneers to the feet restored, c1710, 35½ by 30in (88.5 by 75cm).
£13,500–15,000 *HAL*

A George I walnut bureau, the feather and crossbanded fall enclosing a fitted interior of small drawers, flanking a central cupboard door, 40in (100cm) wide.
£4,000-5,000 *B*

It is extremely important with a bureau that it is of good colour and proportion.

A Queen Anne/George I burr walnut bureau, with feather crossbanding, the interior fitted with numerous drawers and pigeonholes, 36in (90cm) wide.
£3,500-4,000 *Pea*

A walnut bureau, crossbanded and feather inlaid with burr veneer to the fall-flap enclosing a fitted interior with 2 sliding panels to the well, small drawers and central cupboard, early 18thC, 39in (97.5cm) wide.
£2,500-3,000 *NSF*

A walnut veneered bureau, inlaid with box stringing, early 18thC, 34in (85cm).
£3,000-4,000 *GSP*

318

An early Georgian walnut bureau, the flap enclosing a stepped and shaped fitted interior, on later bun feet with later back, restored, 37in (94cm) wide.
£5,500-6,000 *C*

A George III mahogany bureau, the flap enclosing a fitted interior, 28in (70cm).
£2,000-2,500 *CSK*

A George III mahogany bureau, the crossbanded fall enclosing a fitted interior, 37in (91cm) wide.
£550-650 *Bon*

A Georgian figured mahogany bureau, inlaid with satinwood stringing, 38in (95cm) wide.
£800-1,000 *LBP*

A George III mahogany and inlaid bureau, the satinwood banded fall inlaid with an oval swagged urn medallion, 45in (112cm) wide.
£1,500-1,800 *Bon*

A mahogany bureau, mid-18thC, 36in (90cm).
£900-1,100 *PC*

BUREAUX

★ Bureaux were not made in this country until after the reign of Charles II
★ this writing box on stand was initially produced in oak and then in walnut
★ these were originally on turned or straight legs but cabriole legs became popular in the last decade of the 17thC
★ note the quality and proportion of the cabriole legs – good carving is another plus factor
★ always more valuable if containing an *original* stepped interior and well
★ also the more complex the interior – the more expensive
★ from about 1680 most bureaux made from walnut, many with beautiful marquetry and inlay
★ from about 1740 mahogany became the most favoured wood, although walnut was still used
★ the 'key' size for a bureau is 3ft 2in, as the width diminishes so the price increases dramatically
★ original patination, colour and original brass handles are obviously important features for assessing any piece of furniture, but these are crucial when valuing bureaux and chests

A George III mahogany bureau, the fall enclosing a well fitted interior of drawers and pigeonholes flanking a star inlaid cupboard with blind fret borders, 36½in (91cm) wide.
£1,300-1,600 *Bon*

A George III mahogany bureau, having fitted interior with 6 small drawers, 6 pigeonholes, 2 secret drawers and centre cupboard, 38in (95cm).
£950-1,150 *WSW*

A George III mahogany bureau, the flame-figured slope front enclosing a well fitted interior, the central cupboard enclosing 2 drawers and a secret sovereign drawer, with original brasses, c1780, 46in (115cm) wide.
£1,700-2,200 *Re*

A walnut bureau, the fall-front enclosing fitted interior, with centre cupboard, secret drawers, small drawers and pigeonholes, 18thC, 35½in (88.5cm).
£800-900 *EWS*

A mahogany bureau, with fitted interior, late 18thC, 36in (90cm) wide.
£700-800 *BA*

BUREAUX
Points to look for:
★ originality and condition
★ good colour and patination
★ good proportions
★ quality of construction
★ original handles and escutcheons
★ original feet
★ small size (3ft is about average)
★ stepped interior and a central cupboard
★ fitted 'well' with a slide
★ oak drawer linings
★ secret compartments

A Georgian mahogany bureau, with fitted interior, 36in (90cm).
£900-1,000 *JD*

An Edwardian mahogany satinwood, boxwood and ebony strung bureau, 29½in (73.5cm) wide.
£450-550 *TM*

A Victorian mahogany cylinder top fitted bureau, 48in (120cm).
£500-600 *PC*

A George III mahogany bureau, with a sloping fall front enclosing drawers and pigeonholes, 32in (80cm) wide.
£1,700-2,000 *Bea*

A William and Mary style walnut bureau-on-stand, 33in (82.5cm).
£950-1,150 *CSK*

An Edwardian mahogany and marquetry bureau of small proportions, the top and sides with satinwood stringing, bearing retailers plaque for Simkin, Upholstery and Furnishing Expert, Colchester, 24in (60cm) wide.
£800-900 *Re*

A late Georgian mahogany bureau, the oak lined drawers with later brass handles, raised on bracket feet, 45in (112.5cm) wide.
£600-700 *TW*

A mahogany child's bureau, 19thC, 22in (55cm).
£400-450 *DA*

An Edwardian Sheraton style rosewood cylinder front bureau.
£750-850 *FR*

A Dutch walnut and marquetry cylinder bureau, with interior pigeonholes and drawers, 19thC, 36in (90cm) wide.
£1,500-1,700 *DSH*

A French mahogany and brass-mounted cylinder bureau, 19thC, 34½in (86cm).
£750-850 *GSP*

A Dutch mahogany and floral marquetry cylinder bureau, reduced, early 19thC, 50in (125cm).
£3,000-4,000 *CSK*

A French bureau, the fall-flap enclosing a fitted interior of tiered short drawers and pigeonhole, late 18thC, 29½in (73.5cm).
£1,500-1,700 *AG*

A French inlaid rosewood bureau-de-dame, with marquetry decorated fall, the fitted interior with well and 2 small drawers, 26in (65cm).
£800-900 *JD*

A Dutch mahogany and rosewood cylinder bureau, the rosewood crossbanded top and fall inlaid with boxwood stringing, enclosing a fitted interior of pigeonholes, c1820, 47½in (118cm) wide.
£850-1,050 *Bon*

NOTES ON DUTCH MARQUETRY BUREAUX

★ beware badly split flaps and sides
★ marquetry on walnut fetches more than marquetry on mahogany, which in turn fetches more than marquetry on oak
★ cylinder bureaux as a general rule fetch less than fall front bureaux
★ always look out for marquetry which includes bone and/or mother-of-pearl
★ marquetry including birds and insects is slightly rarer than the usual floral marquetry

---

An Empire mahogany and ormolu mounted bureau à cylindre, the black fossil marble slab above a superstructure of 3 drawers divided by ormolu lyre mounts, the bird's eye maple interior fitted with 3 drawers above a slide, the kneehole surrounded by an arrangement of drawers and a secure compartment, 58in (144cm) wide.
£3,500-4,500 *Bon*

A Dutch rosewood cylinder bureau, distressed, early 19thC, 48in (120cm) wide.
£1,000-1,200 *Bon*

An Italian walnut bureau, inlaid with ivory, late 17thC, 46in (115cm) wide.
£5,000-6,000 *BS*

Bureau Cabinets

A tulipwood and purple heart Italian cylinder bureau, highly polished and with walnut linings.
£4,000-5,000   *EA*

A Queen Anne walnut bureau cabinet, with later moulded cornice and reduced bracket feet, 81½ by 43in (207 by 109.5cm).
£10,000-12,000   *C*

A Queen Anne cabinet-on-chest, in figured walnut veneers, the moulded cornice with frieze drawer above a pair of herringbone crossbanded doors concealing drawers and a cupboard of similar decoration, with early replaced turned bun feet and brass drawer pulls, c1710.
£8,000-10,000   *HAL*

An early George III mahogany bureau cabinet, 82 by 39in (208 by 98cm).
£3,500-4,000   *Bon*

A Queen Anne walnut cabinet-on-chest, the base with a fitted secretaire drawer and 2 deep long drawers, on later bracket feet, bearing a label inscribed in ink in a 19thC hand '. . . iam Dashwood Bart Kertleton Oxfordshire', 66 by 39½in (167.5 by 100cm).
£6,000-7,000   *C*

A Queen Anne walnut bureau cabinet, the moulded cornice above a pair of later glazed arched bevelled cupboard doors and 2 candle-slides, on later bun feet, 78½ by 39in (199.5 by 99cm).
£5,500-6,500   *C*

An early Georgian walnut bureau cabinet, the associated top with moulded cornice above a pair of glazed cupboard doors, the sloping flap enclosing a fitted interior above 4 graduated long drawers on later bracket feet, later back, 83 by 37½in (211 by 95cm).
£4,000-5,500   *C*

◁ A late George III mahogany secretaire cabinet, 86 by 46in (219 by 117cm).
£1,500-2,000   *L*

A George III mahogany secretaire cabinet, with moulded tear-drop cornice, a fitted secretaire drawer above a pair of panelled doors, enclosing slides, 91½ by 49in (232.5 by 124.5cm).
£4,000-5,000   *C*

A George III mahogany bureau cabinet, the fall enclosing an interior of drawers and pigeonholes flanking a cupboard and blind fret pilaster drawers, 40in (99cm) wide.
1,000-1,200 *Bon*

With a 1945 invoice from Waring & Gillow for £85.

A late George III mahogany cabinet, on chest.
£1,600-1,900 *Bon*

A George III mahogany bureau cabinet, the crossbanded lower section with a fall enclosing an interior of drawers and pigeonholes flanking a cupboard, the 2 sections associated, 40in (100cm) wide.
£1,300-1,600 *Bon*

A walnut, crossbanded and feather-strung bureau cabinet, the lower part with a sloping fall enclosing a fitted interior with a central cupboard, fluted pilaster secret compartments, drawers and pigeonholes having a well with slide below, 18thC, 37in (92cm).
£4,500-5,000 *P*

A mahogany bureau cabinet, a sloping fall-front enclosing a stepped fitted interior with a well, the base 18thC, altered, 77 by 32in (195 by 80cm).
2,500-3,000 *Bea*

A George III mahogany secretaire cabinet, in the Sheraton style, c1800.
£2,800-3,200 *EA*

A George III satinwood and rosewood secretaire cabinet, the baize-lined fall-flap enclosing a fitted interior, 36in (91.5cm).
£10,000-12,000 *C*

A figured mahogany bureau cabinet, the recessed cabinet with concealed sliding pillars enclosed by twin panelled doors crossbanded in walnut, the base having fall-front revealing stepped interior with pigeonholes, drawers, well and concealed section, early 19thC, 38in (95cm).
£2,500-3,000 *JRB*

A mid-Georgian mahogany bureau cabinet, the scrolled pediment with flowerhead ends centred by a shell cartouche, partly re-supported, 97 by 45in (246.5 by 114cm).
£6,500-7,500 *C*

A Regency mahogany cabinet, 65½ by 20½in (166 by 52cm).
£2,200-2,800 *L*

An early Victorian mahogany secretaire cabinet, 42in (105cm) wide.
£1,200-1,500 *CSK*

A Louis XVI tulipwood secretaire abattant.
£3,000-3,500 *EA*

A French kingwood and walnut marquetry inlaid bombé secretaire à abattant, rouge marble top, all with ormolu mounts, 19thC.
£800-900 *Nes*

A fine Victorian walnut dentists cabinet, in Elizabethan taste, with cylinder front and 12 narrow panelled drawers, fitted with 2 veined black marble panels, brass fittings, c1880, 83 by 36½in (210 by 90cm).
£2,500-3,000 *N*

A figured mahogany escritoire in the Biedermeier style, the interior with compartments, drawers and central cupboard, 60 by 40½in (150 by 100cm).
£750-850 *NSF*

Make the most of Miller's

Every care has been taken to ensure the accuracy of descriptions and estimated valuations. Price ranges in this book reflect what one should expect to pay for a similar example. When selling one can obviously expect a figure below. This will fluctuate according to a dealer's stock, saleability at a particular time, etc. It is always advisable to approach a reputable specialist dealer or an auction house which has specialist sales.

A south German walnut bureau cabinet, the upper section with frieze drawer and monogrammed beneath a crown amongst marquetry foliage, inlaid with marquetry, the centre with a queen sitting upon a throne holding a sceptre, the centre section with a marquetry and crossbanded fall, early 18thC, 50in (125cm) wide.
£17,000-19,000 *BS*

A north Italian walnut veneered bureau cabinet, the fall-front revealing 7 drawers, late 18thC, 88 by 52in (222.5 by 130cm).
£4,000-5,000 *WW*

Cabinets-on-stands

A walnut and mahogany writing cabinet-on-stand, the later stand with square tapering legs with carrying handles, the cabinet early 18thC, 20in (50cm) wide.
£2,800-3,200 *C*

A Carolean jewel casket, veneered in walnut with yewwood banding, the front hinging down to reveal 2 secret drawers, the interior lined with rosewood, with brass strapwork bands and hinges, terminating in fleur-de-lis and a fine steel pierced key, the original stand with frieze drawer, casket 18in (45cm) wide, stand 29in (72cm) high.
£8,000-9,000 *WW*

A William and Mary oyster-veneered walnut cabinet-on-stand, the cupboard doors inlaid with concentric circles enclosing 8 various sized drawers and a central cupboard door with 3 further drawers, with later stand, 36½in (93cm) wide.
£4,000-6,000 *C*

An unusual George III mahogany secretaire cabinet, the projecting lower part with a hinged writing surface and 5 crossbanded drawers on turned reeded legs matching the pilasters, c1800, 79 by 31in (200 by 77.5cm).
£4,500-6,500 *HAL*

A William and Mary walnut cabinet-on-stand, on mid-Georgian stand with foliate and bellflower cabriole legs and claw-and-ball feet, 44½in (113cm) wide.
£3,000-3,500 *C*

An Edwards & Roberts Italianate ebonised cabinet-on-stand inlaid with ivory, 70 by 41in (175 by 102.5cm).
£700-800 *Bea*

A good George III satinwood small secretaire cabinet, crossbanded in harewood, the square tapering legs decorated with boxwood lines, 63 by 31in (157.5 by 77.5cm).
£13,000-15,000 *DWB*

A Chinese black and gold lacquer cabinet-on-stand, of Charles II style, 41½in (105.5cm) wide.
£3,500-4,000 *C*

A late Victorian carved black oak cabinet, having 3 leaded stained glass doors enclosing adjustable shelves, 80 by 72in (202.5 by 180cm).
£200-250   *TW*

An ebonised and brass mounted vitrine cabinet, the base in the form of vitrine table with a hinged glaze lid, 36in (90cm).
£1,100-1,300   *CSK*

A Chinese Chippendale Edwardian mahogany Bijouterie cabinet, 30in (75cm) wide.
£200-350   *FR*

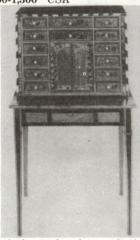

An Edwardian inlaid satinwood Bijouterie cabinet, 24in (60cm) wide.
£850-950   *FR*

A Dutch walnut and marquetry cabinet-on-stand, 65 by 43in (165 by 109cm).
£2,500-3,000   *C*

A Dutch ebonised, walnut and oak 17thC style cabinet-on-stand, inlaid with tortoiseshell panels, tulipwood and rosewood bands in chequer bone borders, enclosing a parquetry and mirror lined interior above a small frieze drawer, on square tapering legs, 27½in (68.5cm).
£1,200-1,500   *CSK*

A Flemish tortoiseshell and ebony cabinet-on-stand, the associated stand with 3 frieze drawers on spirally turned legs, stretchers and squashed bun feet, basically 17thC, 53in (134.5cm) wide.
£3,500-4,000   *C*

In the Furniture section if there is only one measurement it usually refers to the width of the piece.

A French ormolu mounted bombé fronted kingwood cabinet, in 2 sections, all drawers and cupboard door are fronted with Vernis Martin panels, late 19thC, 65 by 36in (162.5 by 90cm).
£3,000-3,500   *CRY*

An Indo-Portuguese cabinet-on-stand, probably in nadum wood, with chased brass mounts, 18th/19thC, 60 by 39in (153 by 99cm).
£900-1,100   *L*

Collectors Cabinets

A George III mahogany collectors cabinet, enclosing a fitted interior with a slide and 30 various sized drawers on ogee bracket feet, 39in (99cm) wide.
£3,500-4,000   *C*

A Regency black japanned breakfront collectors cabinet, decorated throughout with chinoiserie scenes in gilt with red details, 45½ by 64in (113.5 by 160cm).
£3,500-4,000   *Bea*

An unusual Regency maple and ebony collectors cabinet, enclosing 14 various sized drawers on square tapering and spreading shaft, 47½in (120cm) high.
£1,300-1,600   *C*

Display Cabinets

A marquetry display cabinet, inlaid profusely with floral, acanthus, urn and scroll motifs, 18thC, 80 by 38½in (202.5 by 96cm).
£1,800-2,400   *OL*

A George III mahogany display cabinet, 87 by 48in (221 by 122cm).
£6,000-7,000   *C*

A Victorian china cabinet in ebony, decorated with ivory and mother-of-pearl inlays, 37in (92.5cm) wide.
£1,000-1,200   *LT*

A pair of late Victorian satinwood display cabinets, inlaid with fans, marquetry panels, amaranth bands and boxwood lines, 36in (90cm).
£3,000-3,500   *CSK*

A Victorian mahogany display cabinet, 90 by 48in (227.5 by 120cm).
£500-600   *TW*

A walnut inlaid display cabinet with ormolu mounts, 19thC, 96in (242.5cm) high.
£5,500-6,000   *GH*

A mahogany china cabinet in the Chinese Chippendale manner, 63½ by 50½in (158.5 by 125cm).
£3,000-3,500   *PWC*

Locate the source
The source of each illustration in Miller's can be found by checking the code letters below each caption with the list of contributors.

A good late Victorian mahogany display cabinet, with inlaid satinwood panels above a pair of glazed cupboard doors flanked by shelves, on cabriole legs, 55in (138cm).
£450-550 *Bon*

An Edwardian mahogany china display cabinet, with boxwood and ebony chequer banding, on square tapering supports with shaped spandrels, 54in (135cm) wide.
£600-700 *CDC*

An Edwardian mahogany display cabinet, with satinwood stringing and chequered banding, 44in (110cm) wide.
£700-800 *O*

An Edwardian mahogany display cabinet, 64½in (161cm).
£500-600 *GC*

A mahogany Chinese Chippendale design free standing display cabinet, late 19thC, 84in (212.5cm).
£3,500-4,000 *WIL*

A Georgian-style carved mahogany display side cabinet, 78in (197.5cm).
£1,600-1,900 *CDC*

An Edwardian mahogany inlaid display cupboard, 42in (105cm).
£300-400 *WIL*

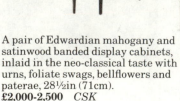

An Edwardian satinwood display cabinet, the whole crossbanded and painted in the classical style and on square tapering supports with block feet, 69 by 42in (176 by 107cm).
£1,000-1,200 *L*

A pair of Edwardian mahogany and satinwood banded display cabinets, inlaid in the neo-classical taste with urns, foliate swags, bellflowers and paterae, 28½in (71cm).
£2,000-2,500 *CSK*

An Edwardian inlaid mahogany display cabinet, the centre panel with marquetry, ribbon and musical trophy inlays on square tapering supports and spade feet, 50in (125cm) wide.
£1,200-1,500 *Re*

A pair of Victorian inlaid walnut pier cabinets with ormolu embellishments, 33in (82.5cm).
£900-1,100   *JD*

A Victorian mahogany display cabinet, decorated with marquetry flowers.
£750-850   *Bon*

A Victorian walnut glazed display cabinet in French style with cast ormolu mounts, 32in (80cm) wide.
£500-600   *FR*

◁

A late Victorian satinwood and mahogany banded breakfront display cabinet, labelled Maple & Company, London and Paris, 48in (120cm).
£2,500-3,000   *CSK*

A Victorian mahogany ornate display cabinet, with shaped bevelled mirror back and fret surround, 48in (120cm).
£450-550   *PC*

A satinwood small cabinet, with boxwood and ebony inlay, late 19thC, 38 by 15in (95 by 37.5cm).
£500-600   *CW*

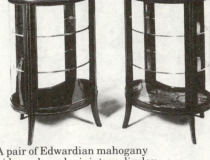

A pair of Edwardian mahogany kidney-shaped miniature display cabinets, inlaid with boxwood and ebonised stringing, on outswept legs, 22½in (56cm) wide.
£1,000-1,200 *Bon*

An Edwardian rosewood, serpentine front display cabinet, bone inlaid.
£1,400-1,600 *EWS*

An Edwardian Sheraton-style inlaid mahogany display cabinet, 36in (90cm).
£1,200-1,400 *SL*

◁ An Edwardian inlaid mahogany display cabinet, 75in (190cm) high.
£600-700 *GH*

▷ An Edwardian inlaid mahogany display cabinet, 41in (102.5cm) wide.
£450-550 *FR*

An Edwardian inlaid mahogany vitrine, inlaid panel doors decorated with musical instruments, sabre supports, 76in (192.5cm) high.
£1,200-1,400 *EWS*

◁ An Edwardian inlaid mahogany display cabinet, 60 by 36in (150 by 90cm).
£450-550 *TW*

An Edwardian ▷ mahogany display cabinet, the shaped apron inlaid with ribbons, urns and scrolls in boxwood and harewood, on square tapered legs, 43in (106cm) wide.
£600-700 *Bon*

An Edwardian ▷ inlaid mahogany display cabinet, with glazed side compartments and bowfront centre section having painted panel.
£280-340 *FR*

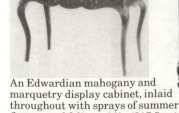

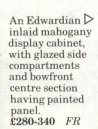

An Edwardian mahogany and marquetry display cabinet, inlaid throughout with sprays of summer flowers and foliage, 86in (217.5cm) high.
£900-1,100 *Bea*

An Edwardian mahogany display cabinet.
£400-500 *MIL*

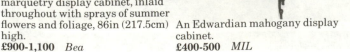

An Edwardian mahogany display cabinet, 38in (95cm) wide.
£450-500   *FR*

A Dutch marquetry shaped domed top display cabinet, some damage, 48½in (121cm) wide.
£2,000-2,500   *GC*

A Dutch oak small cabinet, 18thC, 32 by 32½in (80 by 81cm).
£650-750   *TEN*

A Dutch walnut and marquetry china cabinet, with boxwood and ebony chequer stringing with carved paw feet, late 18thC, 74 by 37in (187.5 by 92.5cm).
£2,500-3,000   *DWB*

A Dutch carved mahogany china cabinet, late 18th/early 19thC, 95in (241cm).
£4,000-5,000   *P*

A Dutch walnut and marquetry veneered display cabinet, 70 by 46in (175 by 115cm).
£2,600-3,000   *BHW*

A Scandinavian satinbirch display cabinet, 39in (97cm) wide.
£550-650   *Bon*

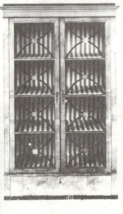

A French kingwood, parquetry and marquetry display cabinet in the Louis XV/XVI transitional taste of bowed outline, 19thC, 65½in (164cm).
£4,000-5,000   *P*

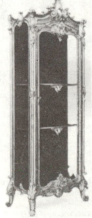

A gilt display cabinet, in the Venetian style, 19thC, 85 by 31in (216 by 79cm).
£1,200-1,400   *L*

A Dutch walnut and marquetry display cabinet, early 19thC, 90 by 68in (227.5 by 170cm).
£2,500-3,000   *GSP*

Side Cabinets – Chiffoniers

A George III mahogany side cabinet, on later turned tapering legs, 68in (170cm).
£2,000-2,500 *CSK*

A Regency mahogany chiffonier, 31½in (78cm).
£1,500-2,000 *CSK*

A Regency chiffonier, in figured rosewood veneers, the lower part a cabinet with brass grillework backed by pleated green satin, c1820, 48 by 30in (120 by 75cm).
£2,300-3,000 *HAL*

A Regency rosewood side cabinet, 48 by 54in (120 by 135cm).
£900-1,000 *L*

A Regency pollard oak and burr yew dwarf cabinet, 26in (65cm) wide.
£3,500-4,000 *C*

A pair of Regency brass bound and inlaid rosewood side cabinets, 29in (72.5cm).
£2,500-3,000 *GSP*

A Regency mahogany secretaire chiffonier, inlaid with chequered bands and applied with gilt metal mounts, 42in (105cm).
£5,500-6,000 *CSK*

A fine Regency rosewood chiffonier, the mirrored superstructure with an urn finial, the whole applied with beaded and bobbin mouldings and with baluster turnings and pierced X-shaped supports to the sides, 22in (55cm) wide.
£2,800-3,200 *Bon*

A Regency satinwood veneered chiffonier, the pair of rosewood veneered solid panel doors with kingwood crossbanding and centred with oval satinwood floret motifs, 36in (90cm) wide.
£1,100-1,300 *LBP*

A Regency inlaid and crossbanded mahogany side cabinet, 41in (102cm).
£1,800-2,200 *JD*

A Regency rosewood chiffonier, 60 by 57in (150 by 142cm).
£1,500-2,000 *AG*

A Regency rosewood chiffonier, 36in (90cm).
£650-850 *Re*

A William IV rosewood breakfront dining room cabinet, 66in (165cm) wide.
£500-700 *Pea*

A Regency mahogany side cabinet, with crossbanded top, the frieze applied with giltmetal anthemions and roundels, 27in (68cm) wide.
£3,200-3,500 *C*

A Regency rosewood chiffonier, 33in (82cm) wide.
£3,000-3,500 *Pea*

A William IV figured mahogany chiffonier, 46in (115cm) wide.
£700-800 *CDC*

A Regency rosewood and maple chiffonier, 45 by 31in (112.5 by 77.5cm).
£1,300-1,600 *AG*

An early Victorian mahogany chiffonier, 41in (102.5cm) wide.
£250-300 *TW*

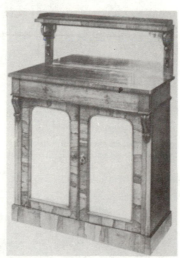

A William IV rosewood chiffonier, 37in (92cm) wide.
£550-650 *Bon*

A mahogany cabinet, 50in (125cm) wide.
£2,200-2,600 *C*

An early Victorian rosewood chiffonier cabinet, fitted with 2 long and 4 short penwork drawers, decorated with classical motifs, above 5 similarly decorated drawers, 36in (90cm).
£1,600-2,000 *CSK*

A Victorian satinwood side cabinet, the top with rosewood banding within satinwood stringing, 73in (182cm) wide.
£1,100-1,300   *O*

A small Victorian mahogany chiffonier.
£180-220   *FR*

A Victorian figured mahogany chiffonier, 47in (117cm) wide.
£400-500   *CDC*

A Victorian boulle dwarf cabinet, with extensive ormolu decoration and single panel door, 34in (85cm).
£650-750   *JD*

A mid-Victorian walnut and inlaid side cabinet with scrolling leaf inlaid frieze, with gilt metal capitals and burr walnut inlay, 43½ by 34½in (108 by 85cm).
£550-650   *DSH*

A William IV carved walnut and marquetry chiffonier, 50in (125cm) wide.
£550-600   *FR*

A Victorian inlaid walnut and gilt metal mounted side cabinet, 32in (80cm) wide.
£500-600   *Re*

A Victorian satinwood white painted and gilt side cabinet, in the gothic taste, 47in (117.5cm).
£1,100-1,300   *CSK*

A Victorian inlaid and marquetry panelled cabinet with fitted ormolu mounts.
£250-300   *FR*

A Victorian rosewood serpentine front marble top chiffonier.
£450-550   *FR*

A Regency small rosewood chiffonier, 49 by 30in (122.5 by 75cm).
£1,200-1,500   *PWC*

A north Italian crossbanded walnut and marquetry inlaid dwarf cabinet, feet probably later, 44in (110cm) wide.
£750-850 *GC*

A French chiffonier, 19thC.
£550-600 *GSP*

A Dutch crossbanded walnut dwarf cabinet, early 19thC, 23in (58cm) wide.
£350-400 *GC*

A French ebonised, ebony, boulle and pewter meuble d'appui, mid-19thC, 34in (85cm).
£850-950 *CSK*

Side Cabinets – Credenzas

A Victorian ebonised and amboyna marquetry breakfront credenza, 72in (180cm).
£450-500 *FR*

A mid-Victorian amboyna, purpleheart and marquetry breakfront side cabinet, 72in (180cm) wide.
£2,000-2,500 *C*

A Victorian burr walnut breakfront side cabinet, inlaid with marquetry and geometric boxwood lines and applied with gilt metal mounts, 60in (150cm).
£1,100-1,300 *CSK*

A Victorian walnut veneered credenza, the polished top with cast floral scroll brass mounts, the front with floral marquetry, 50in (125cm) wide.
£2,000-2,500 *WW*

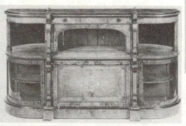

A Victorian burr walnut and ebonised credenza, banded in amboyna and inlaid with bone arabesques and fitted with gilt metal beading, 72in (180cm).
£750-850 *CSK*

A Victorian walnut veneered side cabinet, applied with gilt brass mouldings, 46 by 60in (115 by 150cm).
£800-1,000 *Bea*

A Victorian burr walnut breakfront credenza, decorated with inlaid and marquetry panels having original white marble top and cast ormolu mounts, 78in (195cm) wide.
£1,300-1,600 *FR*

A Victorian ebonised and marquetry side cabinet, applied throughout with gilt brass mounts and caryatids, 43 by 72 (107 by 180cm).
£1,300-1,600 *Bea*

A Victorian marquetry inlaid
walnut credenza, 42 by 88in (105 by
220cm).
£1,500-1,800   *EWS*

A Victorian walnut serpentine front
credenza, 48in (120cm) wide.
£280-340   *FR*

◁
A Victorian walnut and marquetry
inlaid breakfront credenza, 72in
(180cm) wide.
£700-800   *GC*

A mid-Victorian walnut and inlaid
credenza, 42 by 72in (105 by
180cm).
£1,000-1,300   *DSH*

CREDENZAS

★ side cabinets are often
  known as credenzas
★ a credenza normally
  implies the more ornate
  pieces, in the French or
  Italian taste
★ some of these pieces
  display the over elaborate
  decoration and lack of
  craftsmanship which
  would decrease their
  desirability
★ serpentine shaped front
  and sides is always a good
  feature

Canterburies

A George III mahogany canterbury,
20in (49cm) wide.
£850-950   *Bon*

CANTERBURIES

★ name denotes a piece of
  movable equipment
  usually used for sheet
  music
★ first music canterburies
  appeared c1800
★ round tapered legs
  appeared in c1810
★ the canterbury shows
  quite well the stylistic
  development of the 19thC
  – from the quite straight,
  slender severe to the
  bulbous and heavily
  carved later examples
★ many Victorian examples
  with good carving fetch
  more than the earlier
  examples
★ elegance is one of the
  major criteria in this
  small expensive piece of
  furniture
★ note that some are made
  from the base of a whatnot
  or étagère but even more
  are modern reproductions

A George III mahogany canterbury,
18in (45cm) wide.
£850-950   *CSK*

An early Victorian rosewood x-
frame canterbury, with wreath
carved decoration, 20in (50cm)
wide.
£450-500   *Re*

A Regency mahogany canterbury
with 3 dividers headed by turned
finials, on original castors, c1810,
20 by 20½in (50 by 50.5cm).
£1,500-2,200   *HAL*

A late Victorian walnut canterbury,
raised on pierced double C scroll
end standards, 25½in (64cm) wide.
£600-700   *HSS*

Chairs – Open Armchairs

A Victorian rosewood canterbury, raised on spindle supports with fretwork panels, 23in (57.5cm) wide.
£500-600   *AG*

A Victorian figured walnut canterbury, the later two-handled tray top lifting off to reveal 2 divisions, 26in (66cm) wide.
£400-500   *HSS*

A pair of walnut open armchairs, upholstered in gros point foliate needlework, one with reinforced backrail, the other with partly reinforced seat, late 17thC.
£2,300-2,600   *C*

A Queen Anne walnut armchair.
£6,500-7,500   *C*

A George I red walnut library armchair.
£3,500-4,000   *BS*

A George I walnut wing armchair, the front feet spliced.
£2,500-3,000   *C*

An early Georgian walnut open armchair.
£700-900   *C*

A George II walnut armchair, altered from a single chair.
£300-400   *Bon*

A George I walnut open armchair, the bowed drop-in seat with shepherd's crook arms on shell cabriole legs and claw-and-ball feet.
£5,000-6,000   *C*

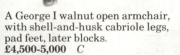

A George I walnut open armchair, with shell-and-husk cabriole legs, pad feet, later blocks.
£4,500-5,000   *C*

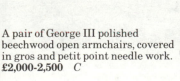

A pair of George III polished beechwood open armchairs, covered in gros and petit point needle work.
£2,000-2,500   *C*

A George III later white-painted and gilt-heightened elbow chair.
£900-1,100   *P*

A pair of George III mahogany open armchairs.
£5,000-6,000 *CSK*

A pair of early George III mahogany open armchairs.
£4,500-5,000 *C*

A fine set of 4 early George III mahogany library armchairs.
£35,000-40,000 *Bon*

A pair of black and gold lacquer open armchairs, the rectangular backs with pierced lyre splats decorated with geometric designs, possible redecorated, late 18thC.
£4,000-5,000 *C*

A George III green-painted open armchair, with shield-shaped back with pierced splat decorated with flowers and foliage.
£400-600 *C*

A fine set of 8 George III paint armchairs.
£20,000-23,000 *Bon*

A pair of George III giltwood open armchairs.
£6,000-7,000 *C*

A mahogany elbow chair, in the French Hepplewhite style, with repairs, late 18thC, 34in (87cm) high.
£550-600 *L*

A set of 6 George III cream-painted open armchairs, with cane-filled backs and seats with moulded frames and later decoration, the seat rails partly replaced and reinforced, with buttoned squab cushions.
£5,500-6,000 *C*

A good pair of George III gilt armchairs.
£4,000-4,500 *Bon*

A George III mahogany library armchair.
£1,800-2,200 *C*

A George III mahogany library armchair, later blocks.
£4,000-5,000   *C*

A George III Gainsborough armchair.
£1,700-2,000   *WW*

A pair of George III mahogany library armchairs, the arm supports applied with later foliate carving, one with additions to the feet.
£3,500-4,000   *C*

A George III mahogany open armchair.
£1,600-1,900   *C*

A George III parcel-gilt and cream-painted open armchair, of Louis XV style, stamped WC, one leg strengthened.
£1,000-1,300   *C*

A pair of George III mahogany open armchairs, later blocks.
£1,300-1,600   *C*

A George III mahogany cockpen open armchair.
£900-1,000   *C*

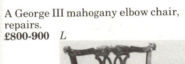

A George III mahogany elbow chair, repairs.
£800-900   *L*

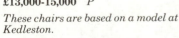

A set of 10 carved mahogany elbow chairs in the Hepplewhite taste, 2 being of slightly larger size.
£13,000-15,000   *P*

These chairs are based on a model at Kedleston.

A George III mahogany open armchair, the drop-in seat on moulded Marlborough legs joined by H-shaped stretchers, mid-18thC.
£800-1,000   *CNY*

A mahogany armchair, some restoration, possibly Colonial, mid-18thC.
£500-600   *Bea*

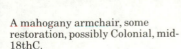

A pair of George III elbow chairs, in the Chinese Chippendale manner, the crest rails carved with C scrolls and pagodas, interlaced fret backs with leaf carving, fret arms and stuffed seats on plain straight legs with stretchers.
£7,500-8,500 *DWB*

A George III mahogany open armchair, early 19thC.
£800-1,000 *CNY*

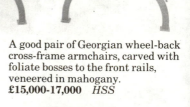

A good pair of Georgian wheel-back cross-frame armchairs, carved with foliate bosses to the front rails, veneered in mahogany.
£15,000-17,000 *HSS*

A Regency beechwood tub armchair.
£1,100-1,300 *C*

A mahogany open armchair in the Regency style, the square tapering sabre legs headed by foliate collars, 19thC.
£4,500-5,500 *C*

Cf. a design for 'Library Fauteuils in Profile' included as pl.48 in George Smith, A Collection of Designs for Household Furniture, *1808.*

A Regency painted and gilt decorated tub-shaped open armchair.
£1,000-1,300 *P*

A pair of Regency simulated rosewood tub bergeres, on sabre legs.
£3,500-4,000 *C*

The continued demand for Regency furniture leads to higher prices.

A fine pair of late Regency mahogany tub armchairs, ending in brass capped feet and castors.
£4,000-5,000 *HSS*

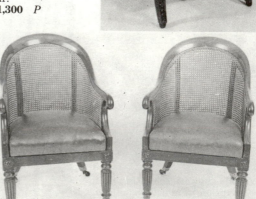

Six Regency painted elbow chairs, the beech frames with rectangular and canted openwork backs, with renewed seat rails and some repairs.
£4,000-5,000   L

A Regency metamorphic library armchair, attributed to Morgan and Saunders, the padded seat opening to reveal 4 baize-lined treads on sabre legs with reinforced seat rails.
£4,000-5,000   C

A metamorphic library armchair of identical design by Morgan and Saunders is at Trinity College, Oxford and is illustrated in R Edwards and P Macquoid, The Dictionary of English Furniture, *rev. ed., 1954, vol. 11., p.291. fig. 15. A chair of this type was published in Ackerman's Repository in July 1811 and was captioned 'This ingenious piece of furniture is manufactured at Messrs. Morgan and Saunders's. Catherine-St Strand' (P Agius,* Ackerman's Regency Furniture & Interior, *1984, fig. 29).*

A mahogany open armchair, the seat rails with pierced X-framed base, early 19thC.
£2,400-2,800   C

A pair of Regency parcel-gilt and black painted open armchairs, repainted, partly re-supported, later blocks.
£4,500-5,000   C

Regency painted and decorated beechwood armchair, on faceted simulated bamboo sabre legs.
£750-950   CSK

A pair of Regency mahogany open armchairs.
£800-1,000   CSK

A pair of Regency mahogany open armchairs, with ribbed top rails and pierced foliate vertical splats, the later caned seats with leather squab cushions.
£5,500-6,000   C

A pair of Regency mahogany armchairs, the broad top rails with brass inlay, reeded arms and turned legs, together with the 2 matching single chairs.
£600-700   NSF

A Regency mahogany floral marquetry carver chair.
£450-500   FR

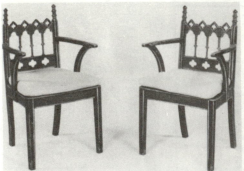

A pair of Regency painted open armchairs, with gothic arcaded backs, pierced with quatrefoils and crocket finials, the later solid seats with squab cushions.
£2,300-2,600 *C*

A pair of Regency ebonized, parcel gilt and caned open armchairs, early 19thC.
£5,500-6,500 *CNY*

An early Victorian mahogany ladies chair.
£150-200 *FR*

A Regency mahogany armchair, with brass inlaid top rail above lyre splat.
£500-600 *TW*

A William IV mahogany armchair.
£2,500-3,000 *C*

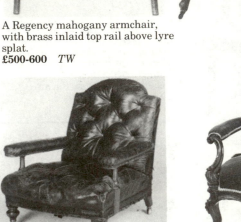

A mid-Victorian mahogany easy armchair.
£2,100-2,500 *C*

A Victorian walnut framed spoon back open arm easy chair, with carved floral cresting.
£700-900 *CBD*

A pair of William IV mahogany armchairs.
£900-1,100 *TEN*

A pair of late Regency mahogany armchairs.
£450-650 *CSK*

A pair of Edwardian inlaid mahogany tub-shape chair.
£100-160 *PC*

A pair of Victorian dining chairs, some damage to seats.
£2,000-2,300 *BHW*

A Victorian rosewood open armchair.
£1,000-1,200 *CSK*

A Victorian walnut open armchair.
£400-600 *CSK*

An Edwardian mahogany bergere chair.
£700-800 *HSS*

An early Louis XV carved giltwood fauteuil.
£3,000-3,500 *P*

A Louis Quinze carved and gilded wood fauteuil, covered in contemporary tapestry.
£600-700 *DSH*

A Louis XV walnut armchair, covered in gros point and petit point needlework.
£4,000-5,000 *WW*

A pair of French Empire mahogany elbow chairs, early 19thC.
£2,200-2,600 *L*

A Flemish walnut open armchair, re-railed, 17thC and later.
£900-1,200 *C*

A walnut armchair, of French design, 19thC.
£1,200-1,500 *CBD*

A pair of Restauration mahogany fauteuils, with scrolling arms terminating in lotuses.
£1,200-1,600 *CSK*

A Dutch walnut and marquetry elbow chair with spoon back, 19thC.
£350-400   *DSH*

A set of 3 Continental carved giltwood and cream-painted elbow chairs, in the Louis XVI taste, late 18thC, probably Dutch.
£2,100-2,400   *P*

A Harlequin set of 10 Spanish walnut open armchairs.
£6,000-7,000   *C*

A Venetian carved giltwood open armchair, in the manner of Bustolon, 18thC.
£1,100-1,300   *P*

A pair of mid-Georgian style mahogany wing armchairs, on cabochon headed cabriole legs and knob feet.
£700-850   *CSK*

A George I walnut wing armchair, the feet with restorations.
£5,000-6,000   *C*

Upholstered Armchairs

A Queen Anne walnut wing armchair, re-railed.
£5,000-6,000   *C*

A Queen Anne walnut armchair, partly re-railed.
£3,000-4,000   *C*

A pair of armchairs on walnut frames, 19thC.
£250-350   *BA*

Prices

The never-ending problem of fixing prices for antiques! A price can be affected by so many factors, for example:
- *condition*
- *desirability*
- *rarity*
- *size*
- *colour*
- *provenance*
- *restoration*
- *the sale of a prestigious collection*
- *collection label*
- *appearance of a new reference book*
- *new specialist sale at major auction house*
- *mentioned on television*
- *the fact that two people present at auction are determined to have the piece*
- *where you buy it*

One also has to contend with the fact that an antique is not only a 'thing of beauty' but a commodity. The price can again be affected by:
- *supply and demand*
- *international finance – currency fluctuation*
- *fashion*
- *inflation*
- *the fact that a museum has vast sums of money to spend*

A George II mahogany wing armchair, raised upon square reeded front legs with outward splayed back legs, united by an H stretcher.
£400-500   *B*

A George II wing back easy chair, on mahogany cabriole legs to front and back.
£2,800-3,400   *JD*

An early Georgian walnut wing armchair, with restorations, later blocks.
£3,500-4,000   *C*

A mid-Georgian mahogany wing armchair with claw-and-ball feet, the rails re-supported, the back rail replaced.
£3,000-4,000   *C*

A George III mahogany wing armchair, on square chamfered legs joined by an H-stretcher and stepped feet, front rail reinforced.
£2,000-2,500   *C*

Two George III stained beechwood bergères of Louis XVI style, with spirally turned arm supports on fluted tapering legs, later blocks.
£8,000-8,700   *C*

A Regency mahogany tub armchair, with fluted frame and ribbed arm supports and sabre legs.
£3,500-4,000   *C*

A pair of George III upholstered armchairs, on 4 cabriole legs moulded with scrolls and ending in scroll feet, 38½in (96cm).
£5,000-5,500   *L*

A mid-Georgian elm wing armchair, outscrolled arms and seat on cabriole legs joined by turned stretchers and pad feet.
£2,300-2,600   *C*

Provenance: by repute Blair Castle, Perthshire.

A Victorian mahogany spoon backed chair, with shaped cabriole legs.
£250-350   *GH*

A pair of Regency mahogany bergères with scrolled backs and reeded arm supports, with distressed upholstery in ribbed frames on ribbed ring turned tapering legs.
£3,500-4,500 *C*

A Victorian mahogany Regency Revival Grecian-style armchair, the close nailed scroll adjustable panel back, seat and armpads, upholstered in leather cloth above graduated leaf and anthemion carved side panels and apron, on lappeted turned tapering front legs.
£350-500 *CSK*

A French blue painted bergère with curved caned back and seat in moulded frame on cabriole legs.
£700-800 *C*

A pair of Louis XVI style bergères, on turned and fluted tapering legs.
£500-700 *Bon*

Miller's is a price Guide not a price List

The price ranges given reflect the average price a purchaser should pay for similar items. Condition, rarity of design or pattern, size, colour, pedigree, restoration and many other factors must be taken into account when assessing values.

A giltwood bergère with shaped back and sides ending in dolphin heads, on club legs and paw feet, c1840.
£2,500-3,000 *C*

A late Regency mahogany bergère, the scoop shaped caned back with lappet carved arms continuing to turned and lobed tapering legs. ▷
£1,000-1,500 *Bon*

A mid-Victorian easy armchair.
£4,000-4,200 *C*

A William IV rosewood armchair, with scrolled arm supports on ring turned ribbed, tapering legs, formerly caned.
£1,800-2,300 *C*

A Victorian walnut framed upholstered armchair. ▷
£300-500 *TW*

A pair of Louis XVI-style cream painted and gilt bergères, on fluted tapering legs headed by scroll capitals, stencilled Jansen, Paris.
£2,000-2,600 *CSK*

Chairs – Dining

A set of 11 early George III mahogany dining chairs, restorations.
£7,000-8,000 *C*

A set of 8 George III stained beechwood dining chairs, the pierced backs filled with trellis-work and pilasters, later blocks, and a set of 4 en suite of a later date with leather seats.
£8,000-9,000 *C*

The form of these chairs is related to some of designs for 'Gothick' and 'Chinese' chairs in Robert Manwaring, The Cabinet and Chair-Maker's Real Friend and Companion, 1765, figs, 10, 12, 14, 15 and 31.

A George II mahogany dining chair, with interlaced gothic pattern and figure-of-eight splat.
£1,500-2,000 *C*

Cf. designs for 'Parlour Chairs' included in Robert Manwaring, The Cabinet and Chair-Maker's Real Friend and Companion, 1765, pl.6.

Cf. also some of the chair designs, almost certainly by Matthew Darly, included in The Chair-Maker's Guide published by Manwaring in 1766 (e.g. plate 41).

A George II walnut chair, in the manner of Grendey.
£1,400-1,800 *C*

Giles Grendey possibly originated the inverted shell design.

A set of 4 Irish George II mahogany chairs, the dished toprails with scroll ears, the vitruvian scroll seat rails on shell and acanthus carved cabriole legs, c1740.
£2,200-2,600 *Bon*

A set of 6 early Georgian walnut and oak dining chairs, later blocks, feet with restorations.
£8,500-9,500 *C*

A set of 14 George III mahogany ladderback dining chairs, including a pair of armchairs with waved backs, some splats replaced, some partly re-railed and with later blocks.
£10,000-12,000 *C*

A pair of walnut veneered dining chairs with drop-in seats, on cabriole legs, early 18thC.
£1,800-2,200 *CW*

A set of 5 early George III mahogany dining chairs, second quarter 18thC.
£5,000-6,000 *CNY*

347

A set of 4 George III mahogany
dining chairs.
£900-1,200 *CSK*

A set of 6 George III mahogany
dining chairs, including two open
armchairs, some re-railed.
£1,600-2,000 *CSK*

A set of 8 ▷
mahogany
dining chairs.
£2,500-3,000 *C*

A set of 6 Irish mid-Georgian dining
chairs, the seat rails replaced.
£2,500-3,000 *C*

A set of 6 George III mahogany
dining chairs, the shaped eared
toprails above pierced vase splats.
£3,000-3,500 *Bon*

A red walnut chair, with pierced
vertical splat back, mid-18thC.
£900-1,000 *CW*

A set of 8 late Georgian
mahogany dining chairs,
including 2 with arms,
with restorations.
£6,000-7,000 *L*

◁
A set of 4 George III
cream and green
painted dining
chairs, the shield
shaped backs with
arched splats with
rush seats.
£1,500-2,000 *C*

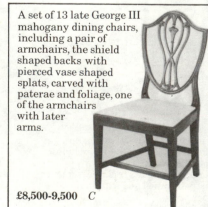

A set of 13 late George III
mahogany dining chairs,
including a pair of
armchairs, the shield
shaped backs with
pierced vase shaped
splats, carved with
paterae and foliage, one
of the armchairs
with later
arms.

A set of 8 George III mahogany
dining chairs, including two
armchairs, 7 with backrails
reinforced, one with reinforced front
and side rails, one armchair with
drop-in seat and later blocks.
£7,000-8,000 *C*

£8,500-9,500 *C*

A set of 6 Georgian mahogany dining chairs, in Hepplewhite style, with pierced vase shaped back splats.
£1,700-2,000 *HSS*

A set of 6 George III mahogany dining chairs, 19thC.
£1,300-1,700 *CSK* ▷

A set of 3 George III walnut dining chairs, including an armchair.
£1,300-1,600 *Bea*

A set of 8 George III mahogany dining chairs, including a pair of armchairs, the shield shaped backs with pierced interlaced splats carved with wheatears and husks and inlaid with fan medallions.
£7,500-8,500 *C*

The design of these chairs is based on a design in George Hepplewhite, The Cabinet Maker's and Upholsterer's Guide, 1788, pl.4.

◁ A set of 6 George III mahogany dining chairs, the shield shape backs with wheatsheaf and husk crestings.
£2,800-3,500 *C*

A set of 6 mid-Georgian mahogany △ dining chairs, the waved toprails and pierced splats carved with flowerheads and foliage, the seatrails reinforced.
£6,500-7,500 *C*

A George III mahogany dining chair, the geometrically pierced splat with conforming rockwork and C-scrolls, later blocks.
£800-1,100 *C*

Three George III mahogany dining chairs, each with a channelled arched back with pierced palmette and waisted splat, later blocks and restorations.
£800-1,000 *CSK*

A set of 8 George III carved mahogany dining chairs, in the Sheraton taste, the backs with reeded curved uprights, satinwood and ebony strung panel backs and horizontal splats with ball ornament, including a pair of elbow chairs.
£4,500-5,000 *P*

A set of 10 George III mahogany
dining chairs, repairs, late 18thC.
£6,500-8,000   *CNY*

A set of 8 Sheraton mahogany
dining chairs, with inlaid rails
within reeded uprights, the carvers
with reeded outswept arms on
turned reeded uprights, upholstery
replaced, c1800.
£5,000-6,000   *HAL*

A set of 8 Sheraton mahogany
dining chairs, including 2 carvers,
the backs with pierced plume splats
and serpentine oval line inlaid
crests.
£3,000-4,000   *WW*

A set of 8 Sheraton mahogany
dining chairs, with bar and lozenge
shaped paterae decorated backs, 2
elbow, 6 standard.
£4,000-5,000   *GC*

A set of 6 Sheraton carved
mahogany dining chairs, including
an elbow chair, the moulded arched
backs with foliate headed Gothic
arched and reeded vertical splats.
£2,600-3,000   *P*

A set of 8 George III Hepplewhite
mahogany dining chairs, including
2 carvers.
£6,000-7,000   *B*

Cf. George Hepplewhite, The
Cabinet Maker and Upholsterers
Guide, *1794, plates 6 and 11.*

A set of 10 late George III
mahogany dining chairs, each with
a curved and incised cresting rail
above an X-shape splat and reeded
uprights, 4 reduced in height.
£3,900-4,500   *L*

A set of 8 Regency dining chairs,
decorated in black and gilt with
reeded frames, with padded seats
and backs, carved in gilt with
leaves, tendrils and patera, on
turned legs with carved gilt leaves
and brass terminals, c1805.
£19,000-20,000   *DWB*

*In the manner of chairs supplied by
Marsh and Tatham for Southill,
Bedfordshire.*

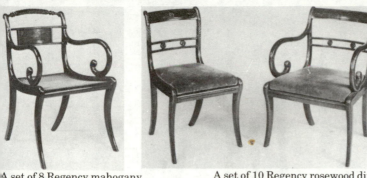

A set of 8 Regency mahogany dining chairs, including a pair of armchairs with curved rope twist toprails, re-caned.
£4,000-5,000   C

A set of 10 Regency rosewood dining chairs, including a pair of armchairs, with curved toprails, centred by rosettes, rope twist supports and bar splats.
£7,500-8,500   C

A set of 4 George III mahogany dining chairs.
£1,000-1,200   L

A set of 12 Regency mahogany dining chairs, including 2 armchairs, some repairs.
£6,500-7,500   DWB

A set of 6 Regency ebonised dining chairs, including a pair of armchairs, with turned shaped toprails and pierced lattice-work splats, 4 stamped SG.
£2,000-3,000   C

A set of 6 Regency mahogany dining chairs.
£1,800-2,200   B

A good set of 8 Regency mahogany dining chairs.
£4,500-5,500   Bon

A set of 9 Regency sabre-leg brass inlaid dining chairs.
£5,500-6,500   B

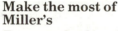

◁
A set of 13 Regency mahogany dining chairs, including a pair of armchairs, with moulded tablet toprails, the horizontal splats filled with balls.
£9,000-10,000   C

A set of 12 Regency mahogany dining chairs, including 2 armchairs, the carved and yoked toprails above anthemions and curved horizontal splats.
£6,000-7,000   CEd

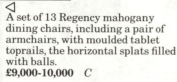

351

A set of 6 Regency mahogany
dining chairs, including one
armchair, with brass inlaid
backrails.
£1,100-1,400 *WBP*

A set of 12 Regency mahogany and
brass inlaid dining chairs, several
with some brass missing.
£6,500-8,500 *L*

A set of 4 Regency
rosewood dining
chairs on sabre legs.
£700-900 *CSK*

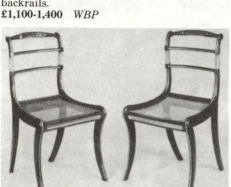

A set of 4 Regency ebonised and gilt
dining chairs, with turned and
reeded toprails on scroll supports
above caned seats, and a similar
open armchair.
£1,200-1,600 *CSK*

A set of 7 Regency mahogany
dining chairs, including 2 elbow
chairs, with panelled oversailing
cresting rails and reeded frames,
one with rails lacking, c1800.
£2,200-2,800 *N*

A set of 6 late Regency simulated
rosewood dining chairs, including a
pair of elbow chairs.
£1,200-1,400 *P*

A set of 6 Georgian mahogany
dining chairs, including an
armchair.
£3,000-3,500 *AG*

A set of 6 Regency simulated
rosewood dining chairs, with
ropetwist cresting rails above drop
in Trafalgar seats, raised on sabre
legs.
£1,000-1,200 *AG*

A set of 6 simulated rosewood
dining chairs, including 2
armchairs, early 19thC.
£1,100-1,400 *DWB*

A set of 6 Regency
mahogany dining
chairs.
£1,200-1,500 *CSK*

A set of 8 Regency mahogany
dining chairs, inlaid with ebonised
lines, including 2 armchairs.
£5,000-6,000 *CSK*

A set of 6 Regency mahogany
dining chairs, including one
armchair.
£1,300-1,600 *Bon*

A set of 11 rosewood grained and
parcel-gilt chairs, including a pair
of armchairs.
£3,500-4,500 *Bon*

A set of 3 Irish Regency oak dining
chairs, including a pair of
armchairs, stamped AH.
£2,500-3,000 *C*

A set of 6 Regency rosewood brass-
inlaid dining chairs, early 19thC.
£2,000-3,000 *CNY*

A set of 6 William IV rosewood
dining chairs.
£950-1,050 *Bea*

A Harlequin set of 11 mahogany
dining chairs, including one
armchair, early 19thC.
£2,000-2,500 *NSF*

A set of 6 William IV dining chairs
in mahogany, c1830.
£1,700-1,900 *EA*

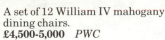

A set of 5 George IV rosewood
dining chairs.
£700-1,000 *CSK*

A set of 12 William IV mahogany
dining chairs.
£4,500-5,000 *PWC*

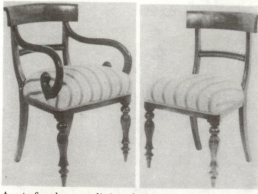

A set of mahogany dining chairs, including 2 armchairs, mid-19thC.
£1,800-2,000 *WIL*

A set of 8 William IV mahogany dining chairs, including 2 armchairs.
£2,500-3,000 *WW*

A set of 6 William IV mahogany dining chairs, with a seventh matching chair which requires restoration.
£1,000-1,200 *TW*

A set of 8 William IV mahogany dining chairs, including one armchair.
£1,000-1,500 *CDC*

A set of 8 William IV rosewood dining chairs.
£1,400-1,700 *Bea*

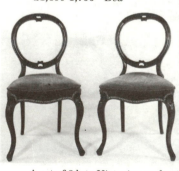

A set of 6 late Victorian walnut framed dining chairs, the hoop backs with carved garlands.
£1,000-1,300 *NSF*

A set of 4 Victorian rosewood chairs.
£500-650 *Bon*

A set of 6 William IV rosewood dining chairs, on ring-turned shaped tapering legs, later blocks.
£2,500-3,000 *C*

A set of 8 rosewood dining chairs, mid-19thC.
£2,500-3,000 *LBP*

A set of 8 rosewood dining chairs, early 19thC.
£1,300-1,600 *MN*

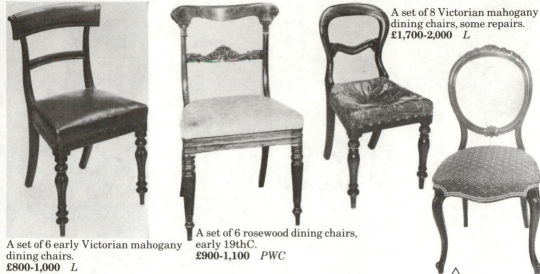

A set of 8 Victorian mahogany
dining chairs, some repairs.
£1,700-2,000 *L*

A set of 6 early Victorian mahogany
dining chairs.
£800-1,000 *L*

A set of 6 rosewood dining chairs,
early 19thC.
£900-1,100 *PWC*

△
A set of 6 Victorian
mahogany
chairs, c1860.
£1,500-2,000 *Ph*

A set of 6 Victorian walnut balloon-
back chairs.
£900-1,100 *CBD*

A set of 6 Victorian balloon-back
rosewood dining chairs.
£1,100-1,300 *WBP*

△
A set of 6 Victorian walnut oval
balloon-back dining chairs, c1860.
£1,100-1,300 *N*

A set of 10 Victorian mahogany
dining chairs.
£1,700-2,000 *L*

A set of 4 Victorian mahogany
dining chairs, c1880.
£700-1,100 *Ph*

A set of 4 Victorian mahogany
chairs, c1870.
£500-700 *Ph*

A set of 6 Victorian mahogany
chairs, c1860.
£900-1,100 *Ph*

A set of 6 Victorian rosewood dining
chairs, carved decoration to vase
splat and shaped fronts.
£1,000-1,300 *EWS*

A set of 6 mahogany Victorian
balloon-back chairs, c1850.
£700-900 *WIL*

A set of 6 Victorian walnut
balloon- back chairs.
£1,000-1,200 *PWC*

A set of 10 Edwardian mahogany
dining chairs, including 2 carvers,
c1910.
£1,200-1,500 *Ph*

A set of 7 early
Victorian rosewood
dining chairs.
£1,200-1,500 *L*

A set of 8 Renaissance style oak
dining chairs, late 19thC.
£700-850 *Bon*

A set of
6 mahogany
Edwardian
dining chairs,
c1910.
£700-900 *Ph*

A set of 6
Victorian
rosewood dining
chairs.
£1,100-1,400 *O*

A set of 6 Edwardian walnut dining
chairs, c1910.
£1,100-1,400 *Ph*

A set of 6 mid-Victorian mahogany
dining chairs.
£700-1,000 *L*

A set of 6 early Victorian
rosewood balloon-back
dining chairs, stamped
Hughes & Co., makers,
47 Bold Street, Liverpool
£950-1,150 *Re*

A set of 6 late Victorian mahogany
dining chairs.
£550-650 *Bon*

A set of 6 Edwardian
walnut chairs, c1910.
£500-700 *Ph*

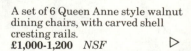

A set of 6 Queen Anne style walnut
dining chairs, with carved shell
cresting rails.
£1,000-1,200 *NSF*

A set of 6 Victorian mahogany
dining chairs, c1850.
£1,200-1,500 *Ph*

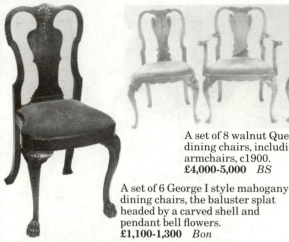

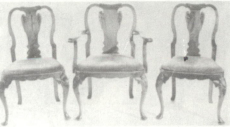

A set of 8 walnut Queen Anne style dining chairs, including 2 armchairs, c1900.
£4,000-5,000   *BS*

A set of 6 George I style mahogany dining chairs, the baluster splat headed by a carved shell and pendant bell flowers.
£1,100-1,300   *Bon*

A set of 8 early George III style ▷ mahogany dining chairs, including 2 armchairs, each back having shaped and pierced splat with simulated interlaced loopings, with ball and claw feet, c1910.
£2,500-3,000   *TW*

The backs of these chairs are not dissimilar to illustration No. 122 page 148, of Edwards Dictionary of English Furniture.

A set of 8 George II style mahogany dining chairs.
£2,000-2,500   *Bea*

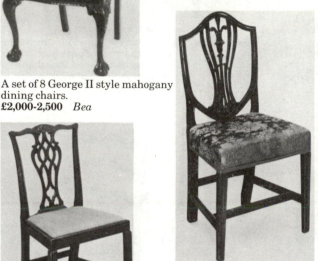

A set of 6 Hepplewhite design mahogany camel-back dining chairs.
£500-700   *Pea*

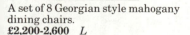

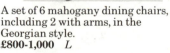

A set of 6 mahogany dining chairs, including 2 with arms, in the Georgian style.
£800-1,000   *L*

A set of 8 Georgian style mahogany dining chairs.
£2,200-2,600   *L*

A set of 8 Chippendale style mahogany dining chairs, including 2 elbow chairs.
£3,000-4,000   *PWC*

A set of 5 Chippendale style mahogany dining chairs, including one armchair, 19thC.
£800-1,000   *DSH*

A set of 8 Chippendale design
mahogany dining chairs, including
2 armchairs, 19thC.
£2,700-3,000 *PWC*

Twelve mahogany Chippendale
style dining chairs, including 2
armchairs.
£4,000-5,000 *JD*

A set of 8 mahogany dining chairs,
including 2 armchairs, in the
Chippendale manner, c1920.
£4,500-5,000 *BS*

A set of 8 George III style
mahogany dining chairs, including
2 armchairs, the serpentine
cresting and pierced vase shaped
splat backs applied with
anthemions.
£3,000-3,500 *CSK*

A set of 8 mahogany Hepplewhite
style shield-back dining chairs,
including 2 armchairs.
£1,600-2,000 *JD*

A set of 12 George III style
mahogany dining chairs.
£2,000-2,500 *Bon*

A set of 6 Chippendale style
mahogany dining chairs, including
2 armchairs, bearing the label of
Hamptons, Pall Mall.
£2,000-2,500 *Bon*

A set of 12 Hepplewhite style
mahogany dining chairs.
£1,500-2,000 *DA*

A pair of
English
provincial
Chippendale
style
ladderback
chairs.
£400-500 *EA*

A set of 8 Chippendale style mahogany dining chairs, including 2 armchairs.
£1,200-1,500 *MIL*

A set of 8 Sheraton style mahogany dining chairs, including 2 carvers.
£1,800-2,200 *WW*

A set of 8 Hepplewhite design mahogany dining chairs, including 2 elbow chairs.
£3,000-3,500 *PWC*

A set of 6 George III style mahogany dining chairs, including 2 armchairs.
£2,500-3,000 *Bea*

A set of 8 mahogany dining chairs, reproduced in the Regency style, including 2 armchairs.
£800-1,000 *WSH*

A set of 6 Hepplewhite style provincial mahogany dining chairs.
£1,300-1,600 *OL*

A set of 4 satinwood and decorated dining chairs, including a pair of elbow chairs, in the Sheraton taste, decorated with trailing husk and pendant floral ornament, late 19thC.
£2,200-2,800 *P*

A matched set of 7 Chippendale design mahogany dining chairs, including one carver.
£850-1,050 *LBP*

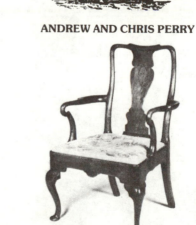

A set of 3 Dutch walnut
and floral marquetry
dining chairs, in the
Queen Anne taste,
18thC.
£1,600-2,000   *P*

A set of 8 Hepplewhite style
mahogany dining chairs, including
2 armchairs, the shield shaped
backs with foliage and drapery
carved pierced splats.
£1,200-1,600   *Bon*

A set of 6 Georgian
mahogany dining
chairs, including
one carver.
£3,000-3,500   *OL*

A pair of Dutch marquetry
veneered single chairs,
late 19thC.
£400-500   *JMW*

Chairs – Hall

A set of 12 late Empire style
mahogany dining chairs, inlaid
with urns, acanthus arabesques and
geometric boxwood lines, one
stamped Newman Gilbey.
£1,600-1,900   *CSK*

A pair of Queen Anne scarlet
painted hall chairs, now lightly
gilded, 44in (110cm) high.
£5,000-6,000   *CNY*

A pair of George III mahogany hall
chairs, the backs with central ovals,
painted with coat-of-arms, repairs.
£1,000-1,200   *CNY*

A set of 4 George III grained hall
chairs.
£1,500-2,000   *C*

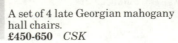

A fine pair of Regency mahogany
hall chairs.
£5,000-6,000   *C*

A set of 6 Regency mahogany hall
chairs, each painted with a lion.
£1,700-2,000   *C*

A set of 4 late Georgian mahogany
hall chairs.
£450-650   *CSK*

Chairs – Side

A set of 7 Gothic style hall chairs with 'bamboo' column supports, 19thC.
£14,500-16,500   *DWB*

A beechwood side chair, late 17thC, re-railed.
£1,200-1,400   *C*

A George III mahogany child's high chair, late 18thC, 36½in (91cm) high.
£500-700   *CNY*

A set of 4 oak framed Gothic chairs, in the manner of Pugin, one damaged, 19thC.
£300-450   *MN*

A mahogany child's miniature rocking commode chair, 18thC.
£400-600   *C*

A Burgomaster chair on 6 cabriole legs, top of the arms surmounted with carved clergymen heads, c1750.
£2,000-2,500   *EA*

A George III mahogany folding campaign chair, the folding frame mounted with brass.
£800-1,000   *C*

A George III painted side chair, with pierced and interlaced oval back and anthemion centre, painted with red and blue harebells on a stone coloured ground, with the trade label of M. Butler Ltd., Dublin.
£1,500-1,800   *C*

A George III mahogany side chair.
£1,100-1,400   *C*   ▷

A walnut   ▷
side chair,
in the manner
of David Marot.
£650-850   *WW*

A set of 4 George III side chairs, with restorations.
£850-1,050 *Bea*

A Regency rosewood music chair, the adjustable seat on reeded and turned tapering splayed legs united by cross stretchers.
£600-800 *CSK*

A Regency mahogany correction chair.
£600-800 *C*

A set of 7 Regency period mahogany side chairs.
£3,500-4,000 *WW*

These could easily come under the heading of dining chairs – these chairs were used as both.

A set of 8 Regency cream painted simulated bamboo side chairs.
£4,000-4,500 *C*

A Regency simulated bamboo side chair in the Brighton Pavilion taste, the panelled divided splat painted with Chinese characters, the cane-filled seat on turned tapering legs joined by conforming stretchers, branded No.139.
£1,800-2,200 *C*

An identical chair, but of black lacquer, is illustrated in the King's bedroom at the Royal Pavilion, Brighton, in M. Jourdain and R. Fastnedge, Regency Furniture, *rev. edn., 1955, pl.1.*

ENGLISH CHAIRS

★ c1630 backs of chairs were like panelled sides from a coffer
★ early 17thC chairs very square and made of oak
★ in Charles II period principal wood walnut – such chairs tend to break as walnut splits easily and is relatively soft
★ chairs have carved top rails, often with a crown, the stretcher will then be similarly carved, the legs are either turned or plain and simple spirals – sometimes called barley sugar twists; the caning in the backs is usually rectangular – any chair with oval caning is highly desirable
★ by the end of the 17thC backs were covered in needlework, the cabriole leg made its appearance, now stretchers have subtle curves
★ the beginning of the 18thC – the Queen Anne spoon back chair – with upright shaped splat, plain cabriole front legs, pad feet
★ George I – carved knees and ball-and-claw feet, solid splats were walnut or veneered, often in burr-walnut
★ William Kent – introduced heavy carved mouldings – greatly influenced by Italian baroque
★ from this time on chairs became lighter in design through the work mainly of Chippendale and Hepplewhite
★ splats now pierced, legs square or tapered
★ the square legs were also much cheaper than the cabriole legs, so they appealed to the large and growing middle class
★ many of the designs came from France
★ Hepplewhite, in particular, developed the chair with tapered legs, no stretchers and very plain splats
★ during the 19thC the taste was once again for heavier more substantial furniture

A Victorian button backed armchair, c1890, 32in (80cm).
£250-300 *Ph*

A late Victorian Prie-dieu mahogany chair, with barley twist sides and front legs, 37in (93cm) high.
£150-200 *Ph*

A pair of Edwardian inlaid mahogany side chairs, c1910, 23in (58cm).
£250-350 *Ph*

A Regency mahogany chair with curved toprail inlaid with flowerheads and ebony lines on reeded uprights, bearing a brass plaque inscribed 'This chair, the last which Napoleon Bonaparte sat on, was at his bedside when he died and was brought home by Gov'nr. Chas. Dallas of St. Helena' with details of an 1883 sale pasted beneath, with 2 authenticating documents.
£8,000-9,000 *C*

A Regency burr maple chair.
£800-1,000 *C*

A pair of German Biedermeier salon chairs, framed in rosewood, early 19thC.
£300-500 *MN*

A set of 4 Victorian walnut side chairs, with acanthus carved top- and back-rails on French cabriole front supports.
£650-750 *Re*

A set of 6 Victorian walnut side chairs.
£1,200-1,400 *WW*

A set of 6 Victorian carved salon chairs.
£1,000-1,200 *GH*

A late Victorian mahogany grandmother chair, with button back.
£350-450 *Ph*

A set of 4 Victorian walnut salon chairs.
£600-700 *Wor*

A pair of Victorian ebonised low chairs.
£1,800-2,000 *C*

A Victorian walnut nursing chair.
£1,800-2,000 *C*

A Victorian button back mahogany nursing chair, c1870, 41in (103cm) high.
£350-450 *Ph*

A Victorian carved walnut nursing chair, with foliate scroll carved and pierced cresting.
£170-200 *CDC*

A Baroque Revival parcel-gilt ceremonial chair or sleigh, with acanthus, scallop shell and scroll carving, seat replaced, 38 by 53½in (95 by 134cm).
£650-750 *OT*

A Victorian rosewood framed nursing chair.
£200-250 *O*

An Edwardian mahogany drawing room suite of 7 pieces, with satinwood panel and boxwood string inlay.
£500-600 *CDC*

Three Edwardian inlaid rosewood chairs.
£90-120 *GH*

A set of 4 Dutch marquetry inlaid dining chairs.
£1,000-1,200 *Wor*

An Anglo Indian padoukwood planter's chair, 2nd quarter of 19thC.
£1,100-1,300 *CSK*

In the Furniture section if there is only one measurement it usually refers to the width of the piece.

A set of 4 Dutch rococo inlaid walnut side chairs, restorations, second quarter 18thC.
£3,000-4,000   *CNY*

A German cowhorn armchair, with twin splat back, late 19thC.
£300-400   *CSK*

A set of 4 Italian walnut and painted side chairs, later blocks, mid-18thC.
£1,100-1,300   *C*

Furniture – Chests

l. An infant's American rocking chair, late 19thC.
£110-150

r. An American rocking chair, late 19thC.
£100-140   *TW*

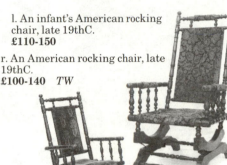

A William and Mary oyster-veneered walnut and olivewood chest, on later bun feet, 34½in (87.5cm).
£6,000-7,000   *C*

A set of 4 Régence painted and carved salon chairs.
£2,200-2,500   *P*

A walnut bachelor's chest, 31½in (79cm).
£15,000-17,000   *C*

A walnut bachelor's chest, with crossbanded hinged top, the sides with carrying handles, 30in (76cm).
£8,000-9,000   *C*

A Queen Anne walnut bachelor's chest, 33½in (85cm).
£12,000-14,000   *C*

A Queen Anne burr walnut chest, the rectangular quartered crossbanded top with re-entrant front corners and a slide, on later bracket feet, 30in (76cm).
£4,500-5,500   *C*

A Queen Anne period walnut chest, the faded top quarter veneered with cross and herringbone banding, 33½in (83.5cm).
£5,500-6,500   *WW*

A small Queen Anne walnut chest on later stand, the top crossbanded and inlaid with geometric stringing, 31in (78cm).
£4,500-5,500 *L*

A Queen Anne chest in figured walnut veneers, of a finely faded colour, the book-matched surface boxwood strung and crossbanded, replacement brasswork, standing on restored feet, c1710, 38in (95cm).
£3,200-4,000 *HAL*

An early Georgian burr yew chest, on reinforced bracket feet, 37in (92.5cm).
£5,000-6,000 *C*

A small George I walnut and herringbone banded chest, with quartered top and 4 long graduated drawers with brass handles on bracket feet, original condition but in need of some restoration, 31 by 29in (77.5 by 72cm).
£17,000-19,000 *DWB*

A walnut chest, with oak top, early 18thC, 38in (95cm).
£900-1,100 *Bon*

A George I chest, in figured walnut veneers, the surface with herringbone inlay and crossbanding, with replaced brasswork, and fretted bracket feet, c1720, 40½in (101cm).
£5,500-6,500 *HAL*

A bachelor's chest, early 18thC.
£2,000-£2,500 *PC*

A mahogany bachelor's chest, with writing slide, 31in (77.5cm).
£2,000-2,500 *C*

Make the most of Miller's

Unless otherwise stated, any description which refers to 'a set' or 'a pair' includes a valuation for the entire set or the pair, even though the illustration may show only a single item.

An early Georgian walnut crossbanded chest, 38in (95cm).
£800-1,000 *CRY*

An early George III mahogany chest, with good quality replaced rocaille brasswork, c1770, 41in (102.5cm).
£2,600-3,300 *HAL*

A figured walnut chest, with later ornate brass handles and escutcheons, early 18thC, 39½in (98.5cm).
£1,400-1,600 *JRB*

An early Georgian walnut chest, on later bracket feet, 40½in (101cm).
£2,200-2,600 *C*

A George III mahogany serpentine front chest of drawers, 47in (117.5cm).
£2,400-2,800 *EWS*

An early George III mahogany serpentine chest, the figured satinwood strung surface with moulded edge, with original lions' mask brasswork, c1760, 42in (105cm).
£4,500-5,200 *HAL*

A George III mahogany serpentine chest, crossbanded and inlaid with stringing, 43in (107.5cm).
£2,500-3,000 *L*

A George III mahogany serpentine front chest, 38in (95cm).
£3,000-3,500 *L*

A George III mahogany chest, with partly replaced ogee bracket feet, the back partly replaced, 42in (105cm).
£4,000-5,000 *C*

A fine George III mahogany serpentine dressing chest.
£5,500-6,000 *Bon*

A walnut and banded chest, in need of restoration, early 18thC, 36in (90cm).
£800-1,000 *CW*

A Georgian walnut veneered dwarf chest, with writing slide, crossbanded and inlaid with ebony and boxwood stringing, 32in (80cm).
£4,500-5,000 *M*

A good George III mahogany and inlaid secretaire chest, c1750.
£2,000-2,500 *Bon*

A George III mahogany serpentine chest, inlaid with stringing, 42½ (105cm).
£900-1,100 *L*

An early George III mahogany chest, of rare small size, the good quality fretted brass drawer-pulls are replacements for the original turned wood examples, c1770, 21in (52.5cm).
£2,000-2,600 *HAL*

A George III mahogany chest of drawers, with a brushing slide, restorations to feet, 31in (77cm).
£900-1,100 *Bon*

A good George III mahogany mule chest, the broadly crossbanded top above a frieze inlaid with shell and ostrich plume medallions, 65in (162cm).
£1,100-1,300 *Bon*

An unusual George III mahogany dressing chest, 49in (123cm).
£1,700-2,000 *Bon*

A George III mahogany dressing and secretaire chest, the uppermost drawer containing sliding baize-covered writing surface and book rest with compartments beneath, the second drawer unusually flanked by supporting lopers, c1770, 36in (90cm).
£2,300-3,000 *HAL*

A George III mahogany serpentine chest, the top banded in satinwood and yew wood and with a central oval fan inlay, 44in (110cm).
£2,800-3,200 *CW*

A George III mahogany serpentine chest, 45in (111cm).
£2,500-3,000 *Bon*

A George III mahogany small chest, 36in (90cm).
£800-1,000 *Bon*

A George III satinwood chest, tulipwood banded, boxwood and ebony inlay, 46in (115cm).
£2800-3400 *CSK*

A George III crossbanded mahogany chest of drawers, the top warped, 36in (90cm).
£800-1,100 *CRY*

Chests

* 17thC oak coffers were made in sufficient numbers to allow a reasonable supply today
* still expect to find original wire or plate hinges; original lock and hasp; original candle box; reasonably tall feet
* the *best* English chest of drawers of the walnut period will be veneered on to pine or other cheaper timber, the drawer linings will be oak, but the interior of the drawer front wil not be; only the top surface visible when the drawer is open will have a slip of oak attached
* an oak drawer front veneered with walnut suggests either Continental provenance or an early oak chest veneered at a later date; check that holes for handles are compatible inside and out for further evidence of this
* feet on William and Mary chests were either formed by the stile continuing down to the floor or by large turned 'buns'. The former were often retained and used as blocks to be encased by the later more fashionable bracket feet; the 'buns' were often removed in the same cause. To ascertain this, remove the bottom drawer and a hole in each front corner will be present, if bun feet were originally used
* by the end of the 18thC, turned wood knobs were fashionable. They were at first fine and small, but soon became the flat bulbous mushrooms so popular on most bedroom and staff quarters furniture. If these are original, it is better to resist the temptation of removing them and applying reproduction brass handles
* accept proper restoration but avoid improvements

A small George III mahogany chest, with a caddy top, one edge with repair, 31½in (78cm).
£1,600-2,000 *WW*

A George III mahogany serpentine chest of drawers, 41in (102cm).
£750-950 *Bon*

A George III mahogany serpentine-fronted chest of drawers, altered, 41in (102.5cm).
£3,000-3,500 *Pea*

A late Georgian mahogany estate writing chest, the top with two lift-up panels revealing one fitted for ink and pen compartments and flanking a central removable section, with pigeonholes and cupboards and folding writing slope, 49in (122.5cm).
£550-650 *L*

A late Georgian mahogany bowfront chest, 42in (105cm).
£300-400 *FR*

A George III mahogany chest of drawers, c1780.
£1,000-1,300 *EA*

A George III mahogany chest, 38in (95cm).
£1,500-1,800 *DWB*

A George III serpentine-fronted chest of drawers, c1810.
£1,500-1,700 *EA*

Locate the source

The source of each illustration in Miller's can be found by checking the code letters below each caption with the list of contributors.

A mahogany dwarf chest, basically late 18thC, 33in (82.5cm).
£1,000-1,200 *CSK*

A George III satinwood chest, with mahogany crossbandings, the centre of each drawer later decorated with swags, 33in (82.5cm).
£1,300-1,600 *L*

A George III mahogany chest, 37in (92.5cm).
£4,500-5,000 *C*

A chest of drawers with kingwood banding, late 18thC, 35in (87.5cm).
£450-550 *FR*

A Georgian inlaid mahogany bowfronted chest, 36in (90cm).
£700-900   *SL*

A fine Regency mahogany military secretaire chest, the top drawer opening to reveal secretaire comprising small cupboard, 3 drawers and pigeonholes, 42in (105cm).
£1,200-1,400   *OL*

A small Regency inlaid satinwood bowfront chest of drawers, 31in (77.5cm).
£650-750   *FR*

A Regency mahogany serpentine chest, the top with banded boxwood line borders, 38in (95cm).
£4,500-5,000   *CSK*

A Regency mahogany chest.
£250-350   *MN*

A mahogany serpentine chest of drawers, with crossbanded front, the top drawer with divided interior, early 19thC, 44in (110cm).
£1,500-2,000   *GSP*

A burr walnut chest of drawers, 19thC, 40in (100cm).
£500-600   *JMW*

An unusual pale oak chest of graduated drawers, below a line of 3 inlaid mahogany faced accessory drawers, c1830.
£1,000-1,200   *ELD*

A Victorian mahogany artists material storage chest, having glazed and sloping lid, 60in (150cm).
£350-450   *TW*

A George IV mahogany secretaire, having boxwood and ebony inlaid decoration, 48in (120cm).
£900-1,000   *Pea*

A mahogany bowfront chest of drawers, early 19thC.
£500-600   *TW*

A pale mahogany campaign chest.
£1,100-1,400   *Wor*

A mahogany secretaire chest, 19thC, 25½in (63.5cm).
£400-500   *BA*

A mid-Georgian style mahogany dwarf serpentine chest, inlaid with satinwood fanned ovals, spandrels and chevron boxwood lined borders, 30in (75cm).
£1,500-2,000   *CSK*

A William and Mary style chest, inlaid with scrolling foliate marquetry, the sides inlaid with ebonised boxwood stars, 39in (97.5cm).
£1,500-2,000   *CSK*

A Dutch walnut veneered chest of drawers, inlaid with elm(?) bands, 18thC, 36in (90cm).
£2,800-3,200   *GSP*

A Dutch floral marquetry bombé chest of drawers, late 18thC, 34in (85cm).
£1,800-2,200   *GSP*

A Dutch walnut and marquetry bombé chest, the serpentine top inlaid, supported by later feet, mid-18thC, 56in (140cm).
£4,500-5,000   *C*

A Colonial rosewood chest of drawers, with parquetry top, c1740.
£2,800-3,200   *EA*

A continental rosewood dressing chest, probably German, mid-19thC, 51in (127.5cm).
£400-500   *Bea*

A Venetian green painted and parcel-gilt chest, late 18th/early 19thC, 49in (122cm).
£2,100-2,400   *P*

Chests-on-Chests

A Queen Anne/George I feather banded walnut chest-on-chest, 39in (97.5cm) wide.
£4,500-5,500   *Pea*

A Queen Anne walnut tallboy, the angles inlaid with lines, on bracket feet, 69 by 44in (172 by 110cm).
£4,000-5,000   *C*

A George II walnut veneered tallboy, some restoration, 76 by 47in (192.5 by 117.5cm).
£3,500-4,000   *Bea*

A Queen Anne cabinet-on-chest, the cornice with later acorn vase finials above a pair of cupboard doors enclosing 11 drawers, below 2 fall-flaps with a slide beneath, the associated base with a fitted secretaire drawer and 3 graduated long drawers on later elongated bun feet, 82 by 41 (207.5 by 102.5cm).
£13,000-15,000 *C*

A walnut and herringbone banded tallboy, early 18thC, 41in (102.5cm) wide.
£4,000-5,000 *CW*

A walnut tallboy, with feather banding, 18thC, 42in (105cm) wide.
£5,500-6,500 *SL*

A Georgian serpentine fronted mahogany tallboy, banded in rosewood, the upper part with hinged concealed compartment at the top, 68 by 46in (170 by 115cm).
£4,000-5,000 *PWC*

A George III mahogany secretaire tallboy, with dentilled broken pediment, 82 by 45 (208 by 112.5cm).
£4,000-6,000 *C*

A George I walnut chest-on-chest, with crossbanded herringbone inlaid drawers, on restored bracket feet, the brasswork an early replacement, c1720, 75 by 42 (190 by 105cm).
£7,000-10,000 *HAL*

◁ A George III mahogany tallboy, the top section with a dentil moulded cornice above a blind fret carved frieze, 44in (110cm) wide.
£1,700-2,000 *CSK*

An early Georgian oak tallboy, of small size, 56½ by 34½in (140 by 86cm).
£4,500-5,500 *GSP*

A George I walnut chest-on-chest, the crossbanded cockbeaded drawers all with fretted brasswork, the feet and back are old replacements, c1720, 67½ by 40in (168 by 100cm).
£7,000-10,000 *HAL*

A George III mahogany tallboy, on ogee bracket feet, c1780.
£2,000-2,300 *EA*

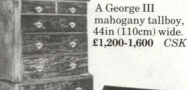

A George III
mahogany tallboy,
44in (110cm) wide.
£1,200-1,600 *CSK*

A George III mahogany tallboy,
with original brass fittings, 44in
(109cm) wide.
£1,000-1,500 *Bon*

A Georgian
walnut inlaid
tallboy, 70 by
39in (175 by
97.5cm).
£2,500-3,000 *DA*

A mahogany chest-on-chest, in the
Chippendale style, the upper
section with acanthus carved
broken swan neck pediment,
pierced with diapering, with blind
fret carved frieze, 18thC.
£10,500-12,000 *HSS*

A late Georgian mahogany
tallboy chest, 42in
(105cm) wide.
£700-900 *JMW*

A fine George III bowfront chest-on-
chest, in flamed mahogany veneers,
the moulded cornice above
cockbeaded drawers with rocaille
brasswork, c1790, 73 by 42½in (185
by 106cm).
£2,500-3,500 *HAL*

A Regency mahogany bowfront
tallboy, the arched cornice inlaid
with geometric ebony lines, 44½in
(111cm) wide.
£1,000-1,400 *CSK*

Chests-on-Stands

A Georgian mahogany tallboy, with
fitted secretaire drawer, 39in
(97.5cm) wide.
£2,500-3,000 *JD*

A William and Mary walnut chest-
on-stand, 61 by 42in (152.5 by
105cm).
£3,500-4,000 *CRY*

A Queen Anne walnut chest-on-
stand, with feather banding and on
later cabriole supports with pointed
pad feet, 68 by 38½in (170 by
96cm).
£3,000-4,000 *L*

A William and Mary walnut and burr yew chest-on-stand, restored, the stand renewed in part, 62½ by 40in (156 by 100cm).
£2,000-2,500 *TEN*

A Queen Anne oyster veneered walnut chest-on-stand, inlaid with concentric roundels above 2 short and 3 graduated long drawers, the stand with partly re-lined drawer and oak bun feet, later back, adapted, 36in (90cm).
£7,500-8,000 *C*

An oak chest-on-stand, the drawers with mahogany crossbanded fronts and brass knob handles, 18thC, 43½in (110cm) wide.
£4,000-5,000 *LBP*

A walnut chest-on-stand, inlaid with stringing, the chest partly 18thC, the stand later, 64 by 41 (160 by 102.5cm).
£1,500-2,000 *L*

△ A carved oak chest-on-stand, 18thC.
£700-800 *FR*

A Georgian oak chest-on-stand, 37in (92cm) wide.
£1,200-1,600 *HSS*

◁

A good George III mahogany tallboy, the upper section with a Greek key cornice above a blind fret frieze, on ogee bracket feet, 44in (110cm) wide.
£2,800-3,400 *Bon*

△ An oyster veneered and birch-banded chest-on-stand, the moulded rectangular top inlaid with geometric boxwood lines in a radiating pattern, basically early 18thC, 41in (100cm).
£7,000-8,000 *CSK*

A William and Mary style walnut chest-on-stand, the quarter veneered rectangular top with feather line bordered inlay, 39½in (99cm).
£2,000-3,000 *CSK*

A Dutch William and Mary style walnut chest-on-stand, the oyster veneer with feather and boxwood line inlay, 37½in (93cm).
£1,500-2,000 *CSK*

A George II red walnut chest-on-stand, 48½in (121cm) wide.
£1,500-2,000 *CSK*

An Italian ebonised cabinet-on-stand, decorated in bone and penwork, supported on a plain stand with ebonised tier below, 24½in (61cm) wide.
£900-1,200 *HSS*

Wellington Chests

Coffers

A walnut four-panelled coffer with mitred decorations, 19thC.
£900-1,100 *BA*

A Victorian burr maplewood wellington chest, with locking bar, 52 by 26in (130 by 65cm).
£900-1,100 *PWC*

A William IV rosewood secretaire wellington chest, the 6 long drawers with beaded edge flanking a central secretaire drawer, 40in (100cm) wide.
£1,000-1,300 *B*

A Queen Anne ▷ walnut coffer, the moulded top inlaid with geometric feather banding, with later bun feet, 38in (96cm) wide.
£4,500-5,000 *C*

An Italian walnut cassone, 17thC, 70in (175cm).
£550-650 *PWC*

A German oak Renaissance chest, 16thC, 46in (115cm).
£2,500-3,000 *B*

◁ A North Italian or South German walnut and marquetry small coffer, the domed top inlaid with a monogram, strapwork, flowers and star motifs, 18thC, 15½ by 31in (37.5 by 77.5cm).
£500-700 *Bea*

△ A North Italian cedarwood chest, 17thC, 22 by 72in (55 by 180cm).
£700-900 *Bea*

An Anglo–Indian green leather covered travelling chest, early 19thC. 37in (92.5cm).
£400-500 *WW*   ▷

A Spanish walnut coffer, 17thC, 66½in (166cm) wide.
£700-1,000 *C*

Commodes

A mahogany pedestal commode, with brass side carrying handles, the locker enclosed by 2 crossbanded doors, the lower pull-out section converted to a drawer, 19in (47.5cm) wide.
£600-700 *WSH*

A George III gentleman's mahogany commode, of serpentine form with cross banded top, the top drawer well fitted with lidded and open compartments, ratchetted mirror and enclosed by a baize-lined slide, 41in (102.5cm).
£1,600-2,000 *GSP*

A George III mahogany tray top
commode, with converted drawer
and cupboard doors.
£1,600-2,000 *EA*

A Hepplewhite style mahogany
commode, serpentine front with
tambour shutter, late 18thC, 28 by
22½in (70 by 55cm).
£500-600 *NSF*

An Italian olivewood and walnut
commode, converted to a cabinet,
the broadly crossbanded top, with a
central panel inlaid with lapping
boxwood circles, the 2 fruitwood-
banded long drawers now forming a
fall-front on short cabriole legs,
41in (102cm) wide.
£450-550 *Bon*

A George III mahogany tray-top
commode, with ebony stringing,
21in (52.5cm) wide.
£500-700 *LBP*

A Georgian bowfront satinwood
commode, decorated with rosewood
crossbanding and painted floral
bands, 45 by 60in (112.5 by 150cm).
£1,800-2,200 *AG*

A mahogany, rosewood, sycamore
and marquetry commode, with
crossbanded serpentine top, with
adapted interior, third quarter
18thC, 33½ by 52in (83 by 130cm).
£2,500-3,000 *C*

*The inlaid decoration on this
commode has possible links with the
work of Swedish marqueteurs
working in England in the 1770s,
particularly for John Linnell. A
commode at Castle Howard made by
Christian Furlohg in 1767 while in
the Linnell's employ is inlaid with
similar urns (H. Hayward and P.
Kirkham,* William and John
Linnell, *1980, vol. II, fig.109).*

An Empire mahogany commode,
with grey fossil marble top, 34½ by
51½in (86 by 128cm).
£2,500-3,000 *C*

A Georgian mahogany bedside
commode, having inlaid decoration,
18in (45cm).
£400-500 *SL*

A Danish rosewood and parcel gilt
commode, with later shaped eared
mottled white marble top,
restorations, mid-18thC, 28in
(70cm).
£2,500-3,000 *C*

An Anglo—Dutch mahogany
serpentine commode, inlaid with
swags and ribbons, the front with a
pair of tambour cupboards flanked
by fluted canted corners, c1800,
40in (101cm) wide.
£1,100-1,500 *Bon*

A Louis XV style serpentine
commode, in kingwood veneers with
moulded rouge marble surface, with
rocaille ormolu mounts, c1870, 32
by 24in (80 by 60cm).
£2,400-2,900 *HAL*

An ormolu mounted kingwood and floral marquetry bombe commode, of Louis XV style, 51½in (128cm) wide.
£2,200-2,800 C

A South German walnut commode, with parquetry decorated serpentine front and sides, 18thC, 46in (115cm).
£2,800-3,200 GSP

A South German walnut and parquetry serpentine commode, 18thC, 51in (128cm).
£2,400-2,800 GSP

Cupboards – Armoires

A high Victorian dark oak court cupboard, 82in (207cm) wide.
£1,100-1,300 HSS

A Flemish rosewood oak ebonised and tortoiseshell cupboard, on later bun feet, minor restorations, 17thC, 67 by 64in (167.5 by 160cm).
£3,000-4,000 C

A fine Dutch walnut and marquetry secretaire armoire.
£11,000-13,000 Bon

A French chestnut armoire, carved with a central basket of flowers and ribbon tied bouquets, Breton, late 18thC, 63in (157.5cm).
£2,500-3,000 CSK ▷

A carved oak, two-door cabinet on cupboard base, 19thC, 45in (112.5cm).
£300-400 CBB

A French red walnut small armoire, with boxwood and ebony inlay.
£2,300-2,600 EA

A Louis XV provincial chestnut armoire, 97 by 60in (245 by 150cm).
£1,200-1,500 L

A German ebonised beech armoire, with classical corner brackets in the form of male guards with tortoiseshell plaques and strung with ebony, c1770.
£5,000-6,000 EA

A Flemish oak buffet, carved throughout with fruit and foliage, 19thC, 125 by 86in (314.5 by 217.5cm).
£1,200-1,400 Bea

A German painted, marblised and parcel-gilt pine armoire, mid-18thC, 70in (175cm).
£2,500-3,000 *CSK*

A Scandinavian walnut armoire, with moulded waved, partly ebonised cornice, 18thC, 87 by 57in (220 by 142.5cm).
£4,000-5,000 *C*

A pair of oak North European cupboards, late 19thC, 46in (115cm).
£550-650 *Nes*

Cupboards – Bedside

A Georgian mahogany pedestal toilet cupboard, 14in (35cm).
£300-350 *DA*

An Empire mahogany cupboard, with an ormolu plaque of Orpheus, 63 by 27in (157.5 by 67.5cm).
£700-800 *C*

A pair of Biedermeier mahogany bedside cupboards, 33 by 22in (82.5 by 55cm).
£18,500-20,500 *C*

Cupboards – Corner

A Queen Anne black japanned corner cupboard, 22½in (56cm).
£600-800 *Bon*

A George III oak two-stage corner cupboard, no back, 86 by 59in (217.5 by 147.5cm).
£1,300-1,600 *DSH*

A George III mahogany bow front corner cupboard, outlined with boxwood stringing, 31in (78cm).
£700-900 *Bon*

CORNER CUPBOARDS

★ these cupboards were made right through the 18thC in various woods including walnut and mahogany, as well as oak

★ examples in oak are usually 'country' versions of the more sophisticated pieces made in walnut or mahogany

★ corner cupboards with glazed doors, that are suitable for the display of porcelain or other objects, are the most sought after type. They are, however, far more difficult to find and are consequently more expensive

★ bow fronted examples are usually considered the most desirable, especially if they are fitted inside with two or three small drawers and the shelves are shaped

★ these cupboards are usually constructed in two parts; 'marriages' do exist and whilst these may be acceptable, it should be reflected in a lower price. Check that the backboards of the two parts match and that the quality of timber and style of construction correspond

A George III mahogany corner cupboard, flanked by canted sides inlaid with boxwood, 34in (85cm).
£400-500   *Bon*

A Georgian red lacquered standing corner cupboard, decorated in chinoiserie, 36in (90cm).
£1,300-1,600   *WSW*

A George III mahogany corner cupboard, c1790, 81 by 44in (205 by 110cm).
£3,500-4,200   *HAL*

A good George III mahogany bow front corner cupboard, 31in (77cm).
£1,100-1,300   *Bon*

An Edwardian rosewood veneered two-tier corner cupboard, 29in (72.5cm).
£950-1,050   *WW*

A mahogany cylinder front corner cupboard with moulded cornice and brass H hinges, 43 by 29in (107.5 by 72.5cm).
£600-700   *WSH*

A Georgian walnut standing corner cupboard, probably veneered, 82 by 44in (207.5 by 110cm).
£1,000-1,200   *L*

A George IV fruitwood corner cupboard, c1820, 85 by 41in (215 by 102.5cm).
£3,000-3,800   *HAL*

A Dutch walnut and marquetry corner cupboard, the top inset with a clock, the painted dial signed A Brugger, 79 High Holborn, London, 99 by 30in (250 by 75cm).
£2,600-3,000   *C*

A mahogany double bow front corner cupboard, 87 by 38in (220 by 95cm).
£850-950   *DA*

A satinwood and rosewood banded standing corner cabinet, inlaid with ebonised lines, basically 19thC, 26in (65cm).
£800-900   *CSK*

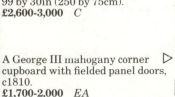

A George III mahogany corner cupboard with fielded panel doors, c1810.
£1,700-2,000   *EA*

379

Cupboards – Linen Presses

A George III mahogany plain clothes press.
£1,000-1,300 *PHA*

A George III mahogany linen press, the dentil cornice above a pair of doors veneered in oval panels with chequer inlay, c1790, 73 by 51½in (185 by 128cm).
£2,600-3,500 *HAL*

A mid-Georgian style serpentine mahogany clothes press, inlaid with ribboned satinwood and harewood fanned ovals, patera and spandrels with chevron geometric lines, 45in (112.5cm).
£3,000-3,500 *CSK*

An early George III secretaire clothes press, 74½ by 45½in (187.5 by 114cm).
£2,000-3,000 *C*

A small Regency mahogany clothes press, 59½ by 36in (147.5 by 90cm).
£5,000-6,000 *Bon*

A George III flamed mahogany press cupboard.
£1,500-1,800 *PHA*

A good George III mahogany bow front linen press, c1810, 50½in (126cm).
£1,200-1,800 *Bon*

A George III design mahogany serpentine fronted linen press, the frieze inlaid with oval shell panels and tied laurel leaves, 48in (120cm).
£2,500-3,000 *Pea*

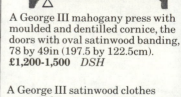

A George III mahogany press with moulded and dentilled cornice, the doors with oval satinwood banding, 78 by 49in (197.5 by 122.5cm).
£1,200-1,500 *DSH*

A George III satinwood clothes press, 82 by 49½in (207.5 by 112.5cm).
£4,000-5,000 *C*

Cupboards – Wardrobes

An Edwardian figured walnut wardrobe chest, 81in (205cm).
£350-400 *PC*

An inlaid mahogany linen press, early 19thC, 50in (125cm).
£1,000-1,500 *JD*

A Sheraton mahogany inlaid gentleman's press cupboard, c1795.
£2,300-2,800 *PHA*

An Italian walnut wardrobe, late 17thC, 69in (172.5cm).
£1,000-1,300 *WW*

A Victorian mahogany wardrobe, inlaid with a marquetry satinwood panel and geometric boxwood lines, 53in (132.5cm).
£600-700 *CSK*

A Regency mahogany linen press, inlaid with ebony stringing and fleurs-de-lys to the corners, 53in (132cm).
£1,200-1,600 *Bon*

A massive walnut cupboard, possibly German, 19thC, 96 by 66in (242.5 by 165cm).
£550-650 *L*

Davenports

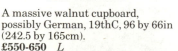

A mahogany davenport, early 19thC, 36 by 20in (90 by 50cm).
£1,200-1,500 *L*

A George IV mahogany davenport, with a pierced brass gallery, 34½ by 21½in (86 by 53cm).
£1,300-1,600 *Bea*

An early Victorian rosewood piano-top davenport, with well fitted interior, pen and ink compartments and slides and with a secret pull button in one of the drawers activating the pop-up document top with pigeon holes and small drawers.
£1,700-2,000 *B*

A Continental oak hanging cupboard, late 17thC, 83in (210cm).
£700-800 *WW*

DAVENPORTS

- ★ the name derives from Gillow's cost book where an illustration of this piece of furniture appeared for the first time. Beside the illustration was written 'Captain Davenport – a desk'
- ★ first examples date from the late 1790s
- ★ they were extremely popular during the Regency and well into Victoria's reign
- ★ there are two quite distinct types of davenport – the quite severe Regency as opposed to the more generous and often highly carved Victorian
- ★ they are bought by a quite different market – at the moment the walnut well carved Victorian can be said to be selling much better than the earlier Regency
- ★ points to look out for: burr-walnut, satinwood, secret drawers or complex interior arrangement, good quality carving and cabriole legs, galleried top
- ★ unless stated all davenports in this section are fitted with 4 real opposed by 4 dummy drawers.

A Victorian rosewood davenport, 22in (55cm).
£700-800 *JD*

A William IV rosewood davenport with gallery to the top, sloping writing surface with leather insert, 33in (82.5cm).
£900-1,100 *NSF*

A Victorian walnut davenport, with hinged stationery compartment, 31in (77.5cm).
£500-600 *AG*

A Victorian walnut davenport, inlaid with foliate marquetry and boxwood lines, 23in (57.5cm).
£1,500-2,000 *CSK*

A Victorian burr walnut davenport, stamped T Willson, 58 Great Queen Street, London.
£1,800-2,200 *CSK*

A Victorian walnut serpentine fronted davenport, with a pierced and carved gallery to the raised stationery compartment, 37 by 23in (92.5 by 57.5cm).
£750-850 *Bea*

A Victorian burr walnut piano-front davenport, with pop-up top section.
£900-1,100 *FR*

A Victorian figured walnut davenport, with boxwood string inlay, on a shaped plateau base, 21in (52.5cm).
£750-850 *CDC*

A mahogany davenport desk, c1920, 32 by 21in (80 by 53cm).
£300-400 *Ph*

Desks

A Queen Anne pollard elm kneehole desk, the top crossbanded with oak herringbone bands, on later turned feet, 33in (83cm).
£4,000-5,000   C

A George II mahogany kneehole desk, the ogee bracket feet carved with foliage, possibly associated at a later date, 33in (82.5cm).
£2,000-3,000   C

A red walnut kneehole desk, 33in (82.5cm).
£1,400-1,800   CSK

An early Georgian walnut and burr walnut kneehole desk, feet partly replaced, 34in (85cm).
£4,500-5,000   C

An unusual George III mahogany kneehole desk, 60in (150cm).
£3,000-3,500   CSK

A George III mahogany kneehole desk, 42½in (106cm).
£5,500-6,500 *C*

A George III mahogany kneehole desk, 38in (95cm).
£1,800-2,400 *Bon*

A mahogany kneehole desk, the whole inlaid with chevron bandings, 37in (93cm).
£850-1,050 *Bon*

A George III mahogany kneehole desk, later added castors and some repairs, 36½in (91cm).
£2,000-2,500 *L*

A George III mahogany kneehole secretaire, in the manner of Gillows, with fitted secretaire drawer, 49½in (123cm).
£3,500-4,500 *C*

A small mahogany and satinwood crossbanded Carlton House desk, 19thC, 48in (120cm).
£1,300-1,600 *DWB*

A walnut and feather banded kneehole desk, 29½in (74cm).
£4,500-5,000 *CSK*

An Edwardian mahogany kneehole pedestal desk, inlaid with satinwood bands and chequered boxwood line borders, 48in (120cm).
£1,000-1,200 *CSK*

A mid-Georgian padouk wood kneehole desk, 43½in (108cm).
£2,500-3,000 *C*

A small Chippendale mahogany kneehole desk, with a small restored patch on the surface, c1770, 29 by 33in (72.5 by 82.5cm).
£4,400-5,000 *HAL*

A George III mahogany desk, the top crossbanded, 33in (82.5cm).
£1,300-1,600 *CSK*

A Hepplewhite style mahogany partners' kneehole pedestal desk 46 by 71in (115 by 177.5cm).
£7,000-8,000 *CSK*

A George III flamed mahogany bow fronted kneehole desk, c1790.
£2,000-2,500 *EA*

A mahogany pedestal desk of serpentine outline, 60in (150cm).
£1,300-1,600 *CSK*

DESKS

- ★ desk correctly describes a piece of furniture on which to read or write and which has the top sloping at an angle. In this form it has medieval origins, but the term now embraces various types, such as bureaux, secretaires and the flat top 'kneehole'
- ★ the davenport desk is highly sought after. Found after the 1790s, the earliest have the upper desk part sliding forward or swivelling to accommodate the knees of the sitter
- ★ later Regency and Victorian models have column supports to the desk and look out for the rising nest of drawers that works on weights and pulleys, when a secret button is depressed. After the 1840s, the 'piano front' became fashionable and is still most in demand. While it matters not if the price is right and the description fair, remember that single sided kneehole desks have been made out of Victorian washstands
- ★ kneehole desks have also been made out of 18thC chests of drawers. Because of cost these are rare and can be detected by incompatible drawer sides
- ★ an original leather top in good condition is desirable, but a fine new one is better than a bad old one
- ★ a bureau made to take a bookcase on top will have a steeper angle to the fall front to accommodate the case or cabinet

An Edwardian Sheraton design kneehole writing desk, in crossbanded and veneered mahogany, 42in (105cm).
£500-600 *LBP*

A partners' desk, with alterations, early 19thC, 65in (162cm).
£2,000-2,500 *Bon*

▽ A mahogany front twin-pedestal desk, 19thC, 48in (120cm).
£650-750 *MN*

A George III Sheraton style cylinder desk, mahogany crossbanded, c1780.
£3,500-4,500 *EA*

A Louis XIV style △ boulle bureau mazarin, the whole inlaid with strapwork and foliate designs incorporating human figures, late 19thC, 31 by 58½in (79 by 146cm).
£3,000-4,000 *Bon*

A mid-Georgian style mahogany pedestal desk, 60in (150cm).
£1,300-1,800 *CSK*

An Edwardian satinwood kidney shaped desk, 54in (135cm).
£750-1,000 *Re*

ANDREW AND CHRIS PERRY

See our main
ADVERTISEMENT
Page: **731**

Wych Hill, Woking, Surrey (04862) 64636

A George III mahogany
partners' desk, 58in
(145cm).
£10,000-12,000 *C*

A George III mahogany
cylinder desk, fitted with
pigeonholes, c1790.
£3,000-3,500 *EA*

A Victorian mahogany cylinder roll
top pedestal desk, with ebonised
bandings and inlaid with radial
lines, applied with brass furniture,
stamped Lamb, Manchester,
No.26106, 44in (110cm).
£3,000-4,000 *CSK*

*James Lamb (1817–1903) opened
premises at Bridge Street,
Manchester, in 1843, moving to 29
John Dawton Street in 1847. In
1888 the firm amalgamated with
Edward Goodall, becoming Goodall,
Lamb and Heyway.*

A George III mahogany partners'
desk, 60in (150cm).
£5,000-6,000 *C*

A late George III mahogany
partners' desk, 38½ by 72½in (96
by 183cm).
£2,800-3,500 *Bon*

A walnut roll
top desk,
enclosing
satin walnut
interior,
19thC, 72in
(180cm).
£3,500-4,500
CDC

A George III
style mahogany
partners' desk,
60in (150cm).
£800-900 *Bea*

A Regency mahogany partners'
desk, 77½in (196cm).
£4,000-5,000 *C*

A George III style mahogany
partners' desk, with replaced
brasses, c1870, 60in (150cm).
£1,600-2,500 *HAL*

A mahogany roll top desk, the S-shape tambour fall enclosing fitted interior, lacking pull-out surface, 50in (125cm).
£750-850 *TW*

A bamboo framed desk, late 19thC, 46 by 27in (115 by 67.5cm).
£450-500 *Bea*

An unusual George III mahogany clerk's desk, the upper part with raised gallery, with lid lifting to reveal simple interior with 2 drawers, c1775, 37 by 23in (92.5 by 57.5cm).
£2,200-2,600 *HAL*

Dressers

A mahogany crossbanded oak dresser, early 19thC, 73in (185cm).
£1,600-2,000 *LBP*

A Victorian walnut writing desk, in the French style, late 19thC, 42 by 32in (105 by 80cm).
£900-1,000 *L*

A Victorian mahogany automatic action cabinet desk, 45in (112.5cm).
£500-600 *FR*

A Flemish oak dresser, 18thC, 62in (155cm).
£800-1,000 *CSK*

An unusual walnut Swiss buffet, on later bun feet, restoration, 18thC, incorporating a complete pewter wall cistern with tray, Swiss, late 18thC, 87in (220cm) high.
£6,000-7,000 *C*

Dumb Waiters

A George III mahogany two-tier dumb waiter, inlaid with brass lines, 36in (90cm).
£6,000-6,500 *C*

A late Georgian mahogany two-tier dumb waiter, 36in (90cm).
£1,300-1,600 *L*

◁

▷

An early Victorian circular three-tier dumb waiter, 40in (100cm).
£650-750 *L*

A George III ▷ mahogany dumb waiter, 24in (60cm) diam.
£1,000-1,400 *CSK*

DUMB WAITERS

★ there is some controversy about when dumb waiters made an appearance
★ they were certainly produced in the 1720s but are rare until the 1750s
★ defined by Sheraton (Cabinet Dictionary 1803) as 'a useful piece of furniture, to serve in some respects the place of a waiter, whence it is so named'
★ 18thC dumb waiters *generally* consist of three tiers
★ made usually from mahogany
★ in Chippendale period supports often carved with foliage, acanthus leaves, broken scrolls, etc
★ Robert Adam's neo-classical style radically changed the design
★ the pillars now tended to become plainly cylindrical with turned collars at top and bottom
★ the late 18thC and early 19thC saw the introduction of pierced galleries often made of brass
★ during the Regency period some dumb waiters made from rosewood
★ marriages are around so beware
  – differing turning on 3 trays
  – two-tier examples (they can be right but are often 'naughty')

A mahogany two-tiered collapsible dumb waiter, c1820.
£2,000-2,200   *EA*

A George III mahogany three-tier dumb waiter, 46in (115cm).
£1,600-2,000   *C*

Fireplaces

A parcel gilt and blue painted fireplace, 53½in (134cm) high.
£1,000-1,600   *C*

An early Victorian cast iron insert, stamped Carron, with a decorative shell design border.
£300-350   *ASH*

A St. Annes Chimneypiece, with full pink columns, c1870, with an arched cast iron interior, c1880.
£900-1,000   *ASH*

A fine George III Carrara marble chimneypiece.
£11,000-13,000   *Bon*

A good George III period mantelpiece in pine with classical gesso decoration, c1780, 54½in (136cm) high.
£2,800-3,600   *HAL*

An Art Nouveau tiled fireplace, with Art Nouveau design to canopy, 38in (95cm) square.
£250-300   *ASH*

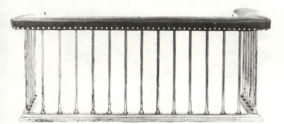

An old brass rail club fender, with green leather seat, 32in (80cm).
£550-650 *LRG*

An Art Nouveau polished brass and steel fire grate, 19thC, 39in (97.5cm).
£1,500-2,000 *HAL*

A statuary marble chimneypiece, with crisply carved corbels c1870, a pierced arched steel plate, c1870, a steel fire basket with a pierced serpentine apron and urn finials, c1850.
£1,200-1,700 *ASH*

A horse-shoe grate, c1870, 36 by 38in (90 by 95cm).
£400-450 *ASH*

An Art Nouveau cast iron and tiled insert, with hobs and continuous pattern, c1900.
£250-300 *ASH*

A Victorian cast iron arched insert, c1860
£280-320
A polished steel fender with studding, c1800.
£150-180 *Ash*

Lowboys

A Queen Anne
walnut lowboy, 30in
(75cm).
£7,000-8,000 *WW*

A Georgian oak lowboy, 30½in
(76cm).
£1,300-1,600 *HSS*

A George II walnut and elm lowboy,
the figured quartered herringbone
inlaid crossbanded surface with
moulded edge, with good quality
replacement brasswork above
fretted apron and 4 legs on pad feet,
c1740, 28 by 32in (70 by 82.5cm).
£2,000-3,000 *HAL*

A small George I lowboy, c1725,
26in (65cm).
£3,000-4,000 *N*

A walnut lowboy, with quarter
veneered top, early 18thC, some
damage, 30 by 19in (75 by 47cm).
£3,500-4,000 *JD*

This piece was painted.

A mahogany lowboy, crossbanded
and satinwood inlaid to the rim,
late 18thC, 29½in (74cm).
£500-600 *NSF*

A George I figured oak lowboy, the
surface unusually crossbanded in
walnut and inlaid with boxwood,
with replaced brasswork, c1720,
29in (72.5cm).
£3,200-4,000 *HAL*

A lowboy, late 19thC, 34½in
(86cm).
£350-400 *BA*

Mirrors

A George I walnut lowboy, the
quartered surface inlaid and
crossbanded, with replaced
brasswork, c1730, 28in (70cm).
£3,800-4,300 *HAL*

A William and Mary walnut, oyster
veneer and marquetry cushion
frame wall mirror, inset with a
later bevelled plate, 45 by 29in (112
by 73cm).
£4,000-5,000 *P*

A George II mahogany and parcel-
gilt mirror, with later rectangular
plate, re-gilded, 37 by 22½in (92.5
by 56cm).
£1,000-1,300 *C*

A pair of George III giltwood mirrors, the shaped partly later plates divided by C scrolls, regilded, 45 by 24½in (112.5 by 61cm).
£16,500-18,500   *C*

An Irish George III giltwood mirror, the slip studded with opaque and blue glass, 32 by 20½in (80 by 51cm).
£3,500-4,000   *C*

A George III carved giltwood wall mirror, with a rectangular quarter divided plate, 44 by 25½in (110 by 64cm).
£5,000-6,000   *P*

A George III pier glass, with rectangular plate within gilt frame pierced and carved with pendant fruit and foliage, c1780, 44 by 23in (110 by 57.5cm).
£3,400-4,000   *HAL*

A carved pine overmantel mirror in the neo-classical taste, the frieze with rinceau and foliate ornament, 47 by 77in (117 by 196cm).
£1,800-2,500   *P*

A George III pier glass, in gilded wood and composition, substantial restorations to this mirror, the plate probably being an old replacement, the urn and swags being substantially restored and replaced in parts, basically c1790, 53 by 27in (132.5 by 67.5cm).
£4,000-5,000   *HAL*

A rococo giltwood wall mirror, 48in (120cm).
£1,350-1,600   *GSP*

A pair of Regency giltwood convex ▷ mirrors, the conforming aprons with sea horses and foliage, 55 by 28in (137.5 by 70cm).
£8,500-9,500   *C*

A Regency giltwood convex mirror, with reeded slip and dolphin entwined frame, supporting 2 candle branches, 31½ by 32in (78 by 80cm).
£4,000-5,000   *C*

391

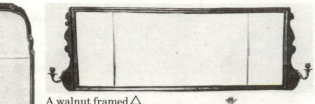

A walnut framed △
landscape mirror,
early 18thC, 53½ by
18in (134 by 45cm).
£1,200-1,400 *PWC*

A George I wall mirror,
54 by 24in (135 by 60cm).
£4,000-5,000 *L*

An early George III painted wood
looking glass, 32 by 25in (80 by
62.5cm).
£3,000-3,500 *Bea*

A George II pier glass, with original
plate, within gilt slip and figured
walnut frame, c1740, 42½in
(106cm).
£2,500-3,500 *HAL*

An English carved giltwood and
painted overmantel frame, 18thC,
54 by 49in (135 by 122.5cm).
£500-600 *Bon*

A George I walnut and parcel-gilt
mirror, 37 by 17in (92.5 by 42.5cm).
£3,500-4,000 *C*

A George III gilt wall mirror, ▷
repairs, 52 by 34in (130 by 85cm).
£5,000-6,000 *L*

A pair of early George III carved
giltwood mirrors, 25 by 30in (62.5
by 75cm).
£17,000-19,000 *BS*

◁ A Chippendale period carved pine
frame, in the manner of Matthias
Locke, inset with a later plate, 83
by 62in (210 by 155cm).
£3,500-4,500 *P*

MIRRORS

★ until 1773, 18thC English
looking glass plates were
produced from blown
cylinders of glass. This
restricted the size and so
large mirrors of the period
were made up of more
than one plate. In 1773, a
new process enabled the
production of the large
single piece mirrors which
became fashionable
thereafter

★ 18thC carved and gilded
mirror frames will be of
wood covered with gesso,
or occasionally of carton
pierre

★ in the 19thC, cheaper and
greater production was
achieved by the use of
plaster 'stucco' or
composition 'carved'
decoration built up on a
wire frame. This has
tended to crack and is
thus detectable. Stucco
work cannot be pierced
with a needle. Carved
wood can

★ do not have the old mirror
plate re-silvered if it has
deteriorated, carefully
remove and store; replace
it with a new specialist
made plate. This
particularly applies to
toilet and dressing
mirrors

★ store original mirror
upright, never flat, using
8 batons slightly larger
than the plate – 6 upright
and 2 across to crate the
mirror around bubble
paper

A William IV giltwood overmantel, with moulded rope twist and concave channelled frame with foliate top corners, branded VR below a crown, 65½ by 42in (162.5 by 105cm).
£4,000-5,000   *C*

Provenance: H.R.H. the late Princess Alice, Countess of Athlone, Kensington Palace.

The overmantel was originally at Claremont, near Esher, rebuilt by Capability Brown and Henry Holland, 1769–72, for Clive of India, near the site of the original Vanbrugh House. In 1816 Parliament purchased the house for the newly wed Princess Charlotte, only child of the Prince of Wales, later George IV, and Prince Leopold. After the 1848 revolution King Louis Philippe lived at Claremont until his death in 1850, his widow died there in 1866. Sixteen years later Queen Victoria settled the estate on her youngest son Leopold Duke of Albany, upon his marriage to Princess Helen of Waldeck, the parents of Princess Alice.

The overmantel bears Queen Victoria's cypher and probably formed part of one of the refurnishings of Claremont, perhaps after the death of Queen Marie-Amelie of France, and may have come from another Royal residence.

A Louis XV carved giltwood pierced and swept frame, 11 by 8in (27.5 by 20cm).
£550-650   *Bon*

A North Italian carved giltwood running pattern frame, 37 by 35in (92.5 by 87.5cm).
£900-1,100   *Bon*

A finely carved Louis XV giltwood frame, 39 by 49in (97.5 by 120cm).
£4,000-5,000   *Bon*

A William and Mary dressing mirror, in figured walnut veneers, the later plate within a moulded frame crested by a pediment fretted in the form of a coronet, the base herringbone inlaid and crossbanded with shaped drawers, c1700, 32½ by 16½in (81 by 41cm).
£1,200-1,800   *HAL*

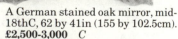

A German stained oak mirror, mid-18thC, 62 by 41in (155 by 102.5cm).
£2,500-3,000   *C*

An Empire giltwood frame, with later rectangular mirror plate, 27½ by 40½in (67.5 by 100cm).
£3,500-4,000   *C*
Provenance: One of a set of 6 frames reputedly presented by Napoleon to Marshal Bernadotte, later King of Sweden.

A George II mahogany toilet mirror, 17in (42.5cm).
£550-650   *Re*

A giltwood toilet mirror, of George II style, 32½in (81cm).
£4,500-5,000   *C*

A Swedish walnut veneered cushion frame wall mirror, early 18thC, 37 by 23in (92.5 by 57.5cm).
£850-1,050   *WW*

An early George III mahogany toilet mirror, 19in (48cm).
£500-600   *Bon*

A Queen Anne walnut toilet mirror, the later spreading supports with acorn finials, on later feet, 18in (45cm).
£1,800-2,200   *C*

A Chippendale mahogany toilet mirror, the serpentine base having reeded canted corners, veneered in the finest figured mahogany, retaining original brass handles, 18thC, 18½in (46cm).
£2,300-3,000   *BS*

A French Empire mahogany cheval mirror, ormolu mounted, c1810.
£2,000-2,500   *EA*

A birchwood toilet mirror, with oval plate in Gothic arched frame, decorated with lines, second quarter 19thC, 29in (72.5cm).
£800-900   *C*

Screens

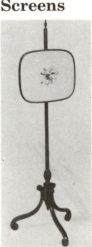

A mahogany needlework pole screen, 19thC.
£200-250   *TAY*

A pair of George III mahogany polescreens, with later silk floral sprays, one slightly reduced, 14½in (36cm).
£350-450   *C*

A painted and gilded cheval firescreen of Empire design, with a panel of early 19thC Lyons cut velvet in shades of purple and gold, 27in (67.5cm).
£3,000-3,500   *C*

A pair of Regency parcel gilt and cream painted firescreens, with later glazed adjustable rectangular panels in moulded beaded frames, 18in (45cm).
£450-550   *C*

A Charles X fruitwood and ebonised firescreen, with glazed needlework panel, 53½in (134cm).
£1,600-2,000 C

A painted three-fold screen in a moulded mahogany frame, the wooden panels painted with exotic birds in flowering branchwork on a turquoise ground in Chinese style, each panel 69½ by 22in (175 by 52.5cm).
£650-750 L

A Dutch painted and gilded leather six-leaf screen, decorated in bright colours in imitation of coromandel lacquer, the leather panels 18thC, each leaf 108 by 21in (272.5 by 52.5cm).
£4,000-4,500 C

A Dutch leather four-fold screen, painted with naive figures, buildings, animals, trees, insects, etc, on yellow ground, early 18thC, 76 by 70in (192.5 by 175cm).
£500-600 WHB

Settees

A George III mahogany small humpback sofa, 63in (157.5cm).
6,500-7,000 C

An early George II mahogany sofa, in the French taste, 61in (152.5cm).
3,500-4,000 C

◁ An early Georgian walnut settee, the seat rail centred by a partly ebonised shell with moulded cabriole legs and pad feet, later blocks, 58in (147cm).
£3,000-4,000 C

A Regency satinwood chaise longue, the scrolled back crossbanded with rosewood and framed by ebonised and boxwood lines, 67in (167.5cm).
£5,000-6,000 C

A Regency black and gilt japanned sofa, the triple chair back with summer flower toprails and pierced trellis-work splats, 60in (150cm).
£6,000-7,000 C

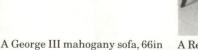

A George III mahogany sofa, 66in (165cm).
£2,500-3,000 C

A pair of George III simulated rosewood window seats, 46in (115cm).
£10,000-12,000 C

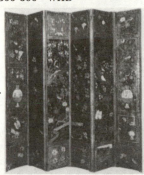

A Regency brass inlaid rosewood sofa, 80in (202.5cm).
£2,200-2,600 GSP

A Regency simulated bamboo sofa, 54in (135cm).
£1,800-2,200 C

A continental sofa with a finely carved solid rosewood frame, original upholstery, c1830.
£1,600-1,900   *ELD*

A Regency simulated rosewood and brass inlaid sofa, 78in (197.5cm).
£600-700   *Bea*

A Regency brass inlaid couch, with simulated rosewood frame, 78in (197.5cm).
£700-900   *L*

A William IV rosewood settee, flanked by shell carved armrests, moulded apron, on turned fluted tapering supports, 79in (200cm).
£900-1,100   *CEd*

An early Victorian rosewood sofa, 72½in (181cm).
£750-850   *CSK*

A Victorian mahogany single ended settee.
£300-350   *FR*

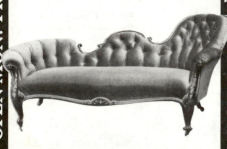

A Victorian rosewood and parcel-gilt sofa, 90½in (228cm).
£2,000-2,500   *C*

A Chippendale style mahogany window seat, on blind fret chamfered square legs, 47in (117.5cm).
£1,000-1,300   *CSK*

A Dutch mahogany chaise longue, inlaid with foliate marquetry trails and boxwood geometric lines, 19thC, 72in (180cm).
£1,100-1,300   *CSK*

A Victorian walnut chaise longue, c1860, 72in (180cm).
£1,400-1,600   *TW*

A Victorian rosewood sofa, 72in (182.5cm).
£800-900   *BWe*

A Biedermeier mahogany sofa, applied with shell and acanthus mouldings, 98in (247.5cm).
£1,600-2,000   *CSK*

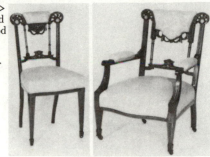

A suite of Edwardian mahogany ▷ seat furniture, inlaid with boxwood and bone arabesques with rosewood plaques, comprising: a two-seat settee, a pair of open armchairs, a pair of occasional chairs and a pair of squat chairs.
£850-1,050   *CSK*

◁ A cream painted wood verandah seat, 60in (150cm).
£500-700   *WW*

A suite of American cast iron garden furniture, partly signed Lister and Fee, Brooklyn, New York, late 19thC, the settees 46in (115cm).
£7,000-8,000   *CNY*

A carved mahogany bergere lounge suite of 5 pieces, comprising a settee, 2 easy arm-chairs and 2 side chairs.
£1,500-1,800   *CDC*

Shelves

A pair of mahogany hanging shelves, of Gothic style, the sides with interlaced trellis-work with cluster columns and scrolling foliate bases, 34in (85cm) high.
£5,000-6,000   *C*

A set of George III mahogany hanging shelves, 36in (90cm).
£4,000-5,000   *C*

A pair of Victorian walnut nanging brackets each with 3 shelves, crossbanded and with satinwood line inlay, 18in (45cm).
£1,000-1,200   *NSF*

Sideboards

A Georgian mahogany serpentine fronted sideboard, with one lead-lined cellaret drawer and 2 others, 66in (165cm).
£5,000-6,000   *JD*

△ A George III mahogany serpentine sideboard, crossbanded and inlaid with narrow bands, flowerheads and stringing, the brass rail missing, 67in (167.5cm).
£8,000-9,000   *L*

A George III mahogany bow front ▷ sideboard, inlaid with satinwood bands and boxwood lines, with cellaret drawer and side fall-flap, 72in (180cm).
£1,800-2,200   *CSK*

A George III mahogany sideboard, the figured overhanging surface with satinwood stringing, the tambour door cupboard flanked on one side by a lead lined cellaret and on the other a pair of drawers, c1800, 74in (187.5cm).
£3,000-4,000   *HAL*

397

A Sheraton period mahogany sideboard, inlaid with satinwood and ebony herringbone stringing, housing a cupboard at each side with a fitted cellaret, 68in (170cm).
£1,400-1,800 *M*

A mahogany inlaid and crossbanded sideboard, with cellaret and 3 drawers, 18thC, 52in (130cm).
£1,700-2,000 *FR*

A George III mahogany sideboard, banded and inlaid with boxwood lines, 76½in (193cm).
£3,200-3,800 *CSK*

A late Georgian mahogany sweep front sideboard, 55in (137.5cm).
£1,600-2,000 *L*

A Georgian mahogany sideboard, with satinwood stringing and inlay, the bowed doors with batswing inlay and satinwood crossbanding, 82in (207.5cm).
£1,300-1,600 *MN*

A George III mahogany serpentine fronted Sheraton sideboard, with 2 drawers on the left and a cellaret on the right, late 18thC, 79in (200cm).
£4,000-5,000 *AGr*

A Georgian inlaid mahogany bowfront sideboard, 48in (120cm).
£1,100-1,300 *JD*

A fine quality George III mahogany sideboard, the upper part with original brass gallery and superstructure with tambour doors, the lower part breaking forward with central crossbanded drawer above a further pair of tambour doors, flanked on both sides by further drawers, cupboards, and a cellaret all of similar decoration on square taper inlaid legs with mahogany collared feet, Scottish, c1780, 66in (165cm).
£5,000-6,000 *HAL*

An Irish mahogany cottage sideboard, c1820, 54in (135cm).
£750-950 *Bon*

An unusual late Georgian mahogany pedestal sideboard, the bow fronted pedestals with 2 cellaret drawers, one fitted for bottles, 75in (190cm).
◁ **£3,500-4,000** *PWC*

A mahogany secretaire serpentine sideboard, early 19thC, 57in (142.5cm).
£1,500-2,000 *CSK*

A Regency Scottish mahogany sideboard, ebony line inlaid, 91in (230cm).
£2,500-3,000 *WW*

A mahogany sideboard, of inverted breakfront outline on front spirally turned legs with paw feet, early 19thC, 85in (215cm).
£350-400 *LRG*

Stands

A Victorian feathered mahogany pedestal sideboard, 84in (212.5cm).
£450-550   *TM*

A George III style mahogany sideboard, the crossbanded top above a central bowed frieze drawer and napery drawer flanked by 2 cupboard doors faced with 4 mock short drawers, inlaid with barber's-pole stringing, 57in (143cm).
£1,000-1,200   *Bon*

A French provincial oak breakfront sideboard, 19thC, 68in (170cm).
£1,300-1,600   *JD*

A Sheraton style mahogany sideboard with satinwood crossbanding and boxwood inlaid.
£3,000-3,500   *EA*

A George III mahogany music stand, with adjustable rounded rectangular top, 18in (45cm).
£1,100-1,500   *C*

◁

A George III mahogany music stand, fitted with a mirror and urn finial, 56in (140cm).
£1,600-1,900   *L*

Two Regency rosewood tripod jardinieres, one bearing the label of Richard Henry Masters, furnishing warerooms no. 1, Pitville Street, Cheltenham, possibly Anglo–Indian, 34in (85cm).
£5,000-6,000   *C*

An unusual pair of mahogany and satinwood urns and pedestals, early 19thC, 52in (130cm).
£3,500-4,000   *C*

A carved Black Forest bear hall/stick stand, 19thC, 84in (212.5cm) high.
£1,300-1,600   *Pea*

A Regency rosewood music stand, with carved double lyre and on adjustable column and platform base, ormolu scroll feet, 15in (37.5cm) wide.
£1,700-2,000   *A*

A Regency rosewood duet music stand.
£750-850   *C*

A pair of Venetian polychrome blackamoors, 19thC, 82in (207.5cm) high.
£4,000-5,000   *GSP*

A carved and ▷
giltwood folio
stand,
mid-19thC.
£120-160 *BA*

△
A pollard oak font, in the Gothic
style, now converted to a
washstand, early 19thC, 23½in
(58cm).
£600-700 *CSK*

An early Victorian mahogany folio
stand, 27in (67.5cm).
£1,600-1,800 *CSK*

Steps

A set of George III mahogany
library steps, 30in (75cm).
£3,000-3,500 *C*

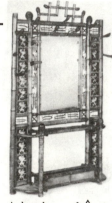

A Japonnaiserie bamboo and △
porcelain hat-and-coat stand,
84in (212.5cm).
£1,400-1,800 *C*

A pair of Spanish scarlet and green
painted parcel-gilt torcheres, with
later bun feet, 18thC, 44in (110cm).
£1,000-1,300 *C*

Stools

A William and Mary stool, 64in
(160cm).
£2,500-3,000 *DWB*

◁ A George II mahogany stool,
possible Irish, 20½in (51cm).
£1,800-2,200 *C*

A George III mahogany library
steps/table, 28in (70cm) wide.
£2,300-2,800 *C*

A pair of George III black lacquer
stools, 24½in (61cm).
£2,500-3,000 *C*

A Regency mahogany hall bench,
the scrolled sabre legs with turned
baluster carrying handles, stamped
James Winter 101 Wardour St, 47in
(117.5cm).
£6,000-7,000 *C*

A pair of Regency beechframed
window seats, 34in (85cm).
£4,500-5,000 *Bea*

A pair of oak stools, possible Liberty & Co., late 19thC, 13½ by 14½in (33 by 36cm).
£500-600 *Bea*

A pair of Regency mahogany music stools.
£2,000-2,500 *Re*

An Edwardian inlaid mahogany kidney shape dressing stool.
£140-180 *TW*

STOOLS

★ until the middle of the 17thC stools were virtually the only form of seat for one person

★ many 17thC 'joint' or 'joyned' stools have been reproduced

★ look for good patination, colour and carving on oak examples. Yew-wood examples with good turning are highly desirable

★ by the end of the 17thC the chair was taking over and the oak stool became less popular, walnut stealing the show from about 1670

★ stools now tend to follow the style of chairs of the period, they also tend to be upholstered

★ many Queen Anne stools have stretchers

★ these have usually disappeared by George I

★ when mahogany was introduced from 1730–40, stools became simpler, the cabriole leg being replaced with the straight leg, often with stretchers

★ mid-18thC the 'drop-in' seat became fashionable

★ some stools made from chairs (this can increase the value of the chair 20 times)

★ check for hessian under the seat – never used until 1840 (often conceals some alterations)

A George III mahogany stool, 36in (90cm).
£2,200-2,500 *C*

An early Victorian mahogany octagonal seat, 21in (52.5cm) wide.
£3,000-3,500 *C*

Tables – Architects

A George II mahogany architect's table, with single ratchet slope and hinged side flaps, c1750.
£2,400-2,800 *EA*

An early George III mahogany architect's table, the rectangular moulded easel top with re-entrant corners, the partly fitted interior including an inkslide to the right, 2 candle sconces, 33in (84cm).
£3,500-4,000 *C*

A George III mahogany artist's table, labelled 'Geo D Pooley, 4 Great Queen Street, Queensway, West Central 2.' 39½in (100cm).
£2,200-2,600 *CSK*

A George III mahogany architect's table, 37½in (94cm).
£3,000-3,500 *L*

Tables – Breakfast

A George III satinwood and rosewood breakfast table, with crossbanded tip-up top, 49½in (125cm).
£8,000-9,000 *C*

A late Regency breakfast table, veneered in pollard oak, the top inlaid with 2 ebonised bands, 53½in (135cm) diam.
£2,800-3,200 *L*

A George III mahogany breakfast table, the surface with broad satinwood crossbanding above a turned pedestal and swept fluted legs terminating in cast brass foliate feet with casters, c1800, 63in (158cm).
£6,000-7,500 *HAL*

A Regency coromandel breakfast table, of large size, c1820, 62in (153cm) diam.
£3,000-3,500 *Bon*

A George III mahogany breakfast table, 64in (160cm).
£3,500-4,000 *CSK*

A fine Regency faded mahogany breakfast table, with rosewood inlay and crossbanding, c1820, 61½in (154cm).
£6,800-7,800 *HAL*

A pollarded oak tilt-top breakfast table, the quartered top with ebony stringing and crossbanding, early 19thC, 48in (122cm) diam.
£1,100-1,400 *Nes*

A late Regency mahogany breakfast table, the crossbanded rectangular tilt-top with rounded ends, line inlay and beaded borders on a rope-carved tapering column, 60½in (151cm).
£1,500-2,000 *CSK*

A twin-flap breakfast table, early 19thC, 48in (120cm).
£650-750 *NSF*

A Regency mahogany breakfast table, crossbanded in rosewood or ring-turned spreading shaft and splayed quadripartite base, 54in (137cm).
£4,500-5,000 *C*

A Regency mahogany snap-top breakfast or dining table.
£1,200-1,400 *PWC*

A William IV mahogany breakfast table, 51in (128cm).
£900-1,000 *Bon*

A Victorian inlaid burr walnut breakfast table, the snap-top raised on turned columns with 4 carved scroll legs, c1875.
£800-1,000 *TW*

A Regency rosewood circular
breakfast table, c1825.
£1,700-2,000 *EA*

A William IV rosewood breakfast
table, the reel-moulded and
crossbanded top above a slight
concave square tapered support,
41in (103cm).
£500-700 *Bon*

An early Victorian mahogany
breakfast table, 57in (143cm).
£450-550 *CDC*

Tables – Card

A George I walnut veneered card
table, with box and ebony line and
crossbanded, folding to a single gate
support, with counter wells fret,
34½in (87cm).
£7,500-8,500 *WW*

A George II walnut card table, the
fold-over top crossbanded and
featherbanded with eared corners
and opening to reveal candle stands
and counter wells with concertina
action, 32½in (83cm).
£10,500-12,000 *L*

A George II mahogany card table,
the baize-lined surface with corner
candle stands and counter wells,
36in (90cm).
£2,500-3,000 *L*

A George II walnut card table, the
cross- and herringbone-banded
folding top with candle stands and
counter wells, 34in (85cm).
£2,000-2,500 *DWB*

A George III satinwood card table,
crossbanded with rosewood and
edged with amaranth, 36in (91cm).
£1,200-1,800 *C*

A George III mahogany and
satinwood card table, the
crossbanded D-shaped top with a
band of trailing berries and foliage,
36in (91cm).
£3,200-3,600 *C*

CARD TABLES

★ the commonest 18thC
form has the fold-over top
supported on one back leg
hinged to wing out at 90
degrees. Better is the
model with both back legs
hinged, each opening to 45
degrees from the frame

★ best of all is the
'concertina' or folding
frame

★ popular during the early
19thC and thereafter was
the swivel top allowing
use of the central column
support

★ the swivel top was also
used on French Revival
models after 1827,
particularly those
decorated with Boulle
marquetry

★ 19thC Boulle work,
revived in 1815 in London
by Le Gaigneur, was
thinner than the 18thC
original. Can be spotted
by the brass being prone
to lift and the tortoiseshell
to bubble. Presence of this
plus a swivel top
eliminates 18thC origin.
The four flap 'envelope' or
bridge table was a
development of the
Edwardian period
Sheraton Revival. The
best examples are of
rosewood with a degree of
fine inlay. In view of
comparatively recent age,
condition should be
excellent to command a
high price

★ many plain Sheraton
period card tables were
inlaid during the
Edwardian period. To
spot, view obliquely
against the light; original
inlays will conform
perfectly with the rest of
the surface; new inlay will
not, unless completely
resurfaced, when shallow
colour and high polish will
be evident

★ all carving to English
cabriole legs should stand
proud of the outline of the
curve; such decoration
within the outline
indicates recarving

An early Georgian mahogany combined tea, card and writing table, the semi-circular top with 3 flaps, the baize-lined card top with guinea wells, the hinged baize-lined writing surface enclosing a mirror-backed compartment with pen slide and inkwell, possibly Irish, 32½in (83cm).
£5,000-6,000 *C*

A George III satinwood, demi-lune card table, with kingwood, partridgewood and boxwood crossbanding.
£1,800-2,200 *CRY*

A fine pair of George III gilt demi-lune side tables, the later Carrara marble slabs above guilloche friezes, centred by an urn of wheatears tablet, 51½in (129cm).
£15,000-20,000 *Bon*

Provenance: The Pepys Cockerell Collection, the most famous piece being the gaming table given by Charles II to Samuel Pepys now in the Victoria and Albert Museum. These tables have been handed down through the Pepys Cockerell family.

A George III satinwood card table, inlaid radially and crossbanded in faded rosewood, with a later baized playing surface, the square tapering ebony-strung legs headed by inlaid panels and terminating in small spade feet, c1790, 36in (91cm).
£2,300-3,000 *HAL*

A Sheraton mahogany card table, with semi-circular folding baize-lined top with wide satinwood bands inlaid with foliage, berries and flowerheads, 39in (98cm).
£1,300-1,600 *GSP*

A George III sycamore and inlaid serpentine card table, the crossbanded top inlaid, 37in (93cm).
£1,500-2,000 *Bon*

A pair of George III mahogany tables, one for cards, the other for tea, the card table having been re-baized, c1800, 38in (95cm).
£4,800-6,800 *HAL*

△

A George III kingwood and satinwood card table, 36½in (92cm).
£1,200-1,500 *C*

A George III mahogany card table, with figured crossbanded surface hinged to reveal re-baized playing surface above boxwood inlaid apron, 2 legs with gate action, c1800, 34in (85cm).
◁
£1,400-2,200 *HAL*

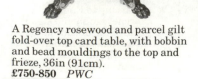

A Regency rosewood and parcel gilt fold-over top card table, with bobbin and bead mouldings to the top and frieze, 36in (91cm).
£750-850 *PWC*

A pair of Regency rosewood folding-top card tables, crossbanded in satinwood, 36in (91cm).
£3,500-4,000 *JD* ▷

A pair of Regency card tables, in figured burr elm veneers, inlaid with ebony stringing and symmetrically placed stars, c1820, 39in (98cm).
£5,500-7,000 *HAL*

An unusual Regency D-shaped card table, banded and inlaid with satinwood lines on ring-turned simulated rosewood legs 35in (89cm). ▷
£2,000-2,500 *C*

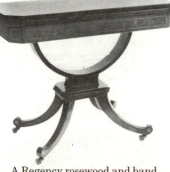

An unusual Regency rosewood brass-inlaid patent card table, the top inlaid with brass line and fleur-de-lys and with dished money wells on the reversed baized side, the mechanical scissor action operated by the push plaques beneath the frieze to extend the legs to take the foldover top, profusely decorated in applied ormolu mounts, lotus leaf feet and brass casters, 36in (91cm).
£6,500-7,500 *B*

There is a pair of similar card tables with the same scissor action in the music room at Buckingham Palace.

A carved rosewood fold-over top card table, early 19thC, 37in (93cm).
£900-1,100 *PC*

A good Regency rosewood and brass-inlaid card table, inlaid with borders of stars and quatrefoils, 36in (91cm).
£1,800-2,200 *Bon*

A Regency rosewood and band inlaid card table, 35½in (88cm).
£1,200-1,500 *GC*

A late Victorian burr walnut and ebonised banded card table, inlaid with amboyna bands, Vitruvian scrolls and boxwood lines, stamped Gillow & Company and numbered 3079, 36in (91cm).
£1,800-2,200 *CSK*

A George II style mahogany card table, 30½in (76cm).
£700-900 *CSK*

A Louis XVI style plum-pudding mahogany card table, 28in (70cm).
£800-900 *CSK*

A George I style walnut card table, with crossbanded top, 32½in (81cm).
£800-900 *Bon*

A Dutch marquetry card table, 32½in (81cm).
£900-1,100 *GSP*

Tables – Centre

A Queen Anne giltwood centre table, 30in (76cm).
£4,000-5,000   *C*

A George III satinwood centre table, the circular tip-up top crossbanded with rosewood, inscribed in ink 'From Drawing Room', 41in (104cm) diam.
£7,500-8,500   *C*

A Regency mahogany centre table, in a pale figured mahogany, the top with coromandel crossbanding, c1815, 45in (113cm).
£5,000-6,000   *HAL*

A gilt-gesso centre table, 32in (81cm).
£1,600-2,000   *C*

A Regency cast-iron, gilt-metal centre table, surmounted by a circular specimen marble top, radiating segments in a variety of coloured marbles and hardstones including lapis lazuli, malachite, porphyry, sarrancolin, brocatelle and poxtor, on a white ground, with a verde antico outer band, 40½in (101cm) diam.
£10,000-12,000   *P*

A Regency rosewood centre table, the top inlaid with brass banding with anthemion spandrels, 45in (114cm).
£2,500-3,000   *C*

A Regency brass-inlaid rosewood centre table, with crossbanded tip-up top and spreading gadrooned shaft, 50½in (128cm) diam.
£3,000-4,000   *C*

A late Regency pollard oak and ebonised centre table, the rectangular crossbanded top above a frieze drawer and pointed arch frieze, c1830, 34½in (86cm).
£900-1,100   *Bon*

A Victorian walnut centre table, the top inlaid in various woods with birds, butterflies, flowers and scrolling foliage on a quartered ground, 53in (133cm).
£2,000-2,300   *CSK*

A Victorian massive giltwood centre table, with marble top.
£5,000-6,000   *EA*

Provenance: His Grace the Duke of Westminster.

A Victorian circular top table, inset in a radiating design with specimen marbles and hardstones including lapis lazuli, malachite and onyx, 34in (86cm) diam.
£6,000-7,000   *L*

A marquetry and parquetry centre table, in the French manner, the top finely inlaid with various trophies, the spandrels inlaid with various woods and ivory in a classical style, attached paper label inscribed 'Howard & Sons, 22 & 26 Berners Street, London', late 19thC, 43in (108cm).
£2,200-2,600   *PWC*

Tables – Console

A walnut and pine centre table, the sliding moulded rectangular top and storage compartment beneath on solid tapering trestle ends and moulded feet, minor restorations, 18thC, 50½in (127cm).
£2,000-2,500 C

An important white marble conservatory table, the circular top with broad Grecian key pattern border and graduated segmented centre, originally inlaid with coloured mosaic, probably Italian, early 19thC, 38in (96cm) high.
£18,000-20,000 WIL

A pair of Regency rosewood and parcel-gilt console tables, with white marble tops, 54in (137cm).
£6,500-7,000 C

An Italian marble topped centre table, the top inlaid in coloured marbles, 18thC, 63in (158cm).
£3,000-4,000 PWC

A grained and parcel-gilt centre table, in the early Georgian style, with massive breche violette top, stamped 'J. Seglie, fecit 1914', 69in (175cm).
£2,800-3,200 C

A pair of Louis XV giltwood console tables, with shaped breccia marble tops, re-gilded, 23½in (60cm).
£3,000-3,500 C

A Dutch walnut centre table, with marquetry inlaid and a frieze drawer, c'790.
£2,200-2,600 EA

A Spanish walnut centre table, with turned iron flying stretchers, 17thC and later, 51in (129cm).
£2,000-2,500 C

A Louis XVI mahogany console desserte, with brass mounts and grey veined marble top, 34in ▷ (85cm).
£1,500-2,000 L

Tables – Dining

A Cuban mahogany twin-flap top dining table, early 18thC, 49in (123cm).
£3,500-4,000 WW

A Regency mahogany dining table, 125in (318cm).
£8,500-9,500 C

A mahogany three-pedestal dining table, the rounded rectangular end sections with fluted borders on ring-turned spreading shaft and quadripartite bases with gilt-metal anthemion feet, 101½in (255cm) including 2 extra leaves.
£7,000-8,000 C

A Louis XVI carved giltwood petite console table, surmounted by a moulded D-shaped marble top, 26in (64cm).
£1,200-1,600 P

An extremely fine George III
mahogany dining table, c1790,
120in (300cm).
£20,000-25,000   *TKN*

A George III mahogany banqueting
table, in 5 parts, of good originality,
brass stamped S. Dobbins & Co.
Patent, Bristol, extending in
various sections up to 192in
(480cm).
£16,000-18,000   *B*

A Regency mahogany D-ended
dining table, with replacement
clips, c1820, 113in (283cm).
£6,500-8,000   *HAL*

A three-pillar mahogany dining
table, part Georgian and part later,
142in (359cm) fully extended.
£6,500-7,000   *L*

A George III mahogany extending
dining table with 5 pillar supports,
2 pillars and 2 leaves probably later
additions, 183in (460cm) wide, fully
extended.
£40,000-45,000   *L*

A fine Regency mahogany
patent Imperial dining table,
in the manner of Gillows,
174½in (449cm) extended.
£11,000-14,000   *C*

A Regency mahogany D-ended
dining table, in 3 sections, the
casters stamped S. Dobbins &
Company, Patent, Bristol, 125in
(313cm) fully extended.
£4,000-5,000   *CSK*

A George III style mahogany 3
pillar dining table, together with a
pair of shallow D-shaped flaps for
use on a pillar as a breakfast table,
51in (128cm) extended.
£3,800-4,200   *WW*

An early Victorian mahogany
extending banqueting table, 176in
(440cm) long, including 7 leaves.
£2,600-3,000   *Bon*

A Victorian mahogany extending
dining table, 166in (422cm)
including 4 various-sized leaves.
£10,000-13,000   *C*

A George IV mahogany   ▷
extending dining table, the
rounded rectangular top
with concertina action, 118in
(295cm) extended, including
3 extra leaves.
£5,500-6,500   *CSK*

◁ A Victorian walnut and marquetry
pedestal dining table, with casters,
52in (130cm).
£1,800-2,200   *PWC*

Locate the source
*The source of each
illustration in Miller's can
be found by checking the
code letters below each
caption with the list of
contributors. In view of
the undoubted differences
in price structures from
region to region, this
information could be
extremely valuable to
everyone who buys and
sells antiques.*

A George IV mahogany twin   △
pedestal dining table, with 2 later
leaves, 91in (228cm) extended.
£2,500-3,000   *TEN*

A late Victorian mahogany extending dining table, with 3 spare leaves, 98in (245cm) extended.
£850-950 *TLC*
The winding mechanism was patented by Joseph Fitter, Birmingham.

A Georgian mahogany dining table, in 3 sections, the D-ended top on square tapering legs, 102in (255cm).
£1,500-2,000 *CSK*

An Edwardian Georgian style three-pillar oval dining table, 138in (345cm).
£2,000-2,500 *JMW*

Tables – Dressing

A Queen Anne walnut kneehole ladies dressing table, the lift-up top quarter-veneered and inlaid with double herringbone, the interior with panel for a mirror, feet missing and in need of restoration, 33in (83cm).
£7,500-8,500 *BS*

A George III mahogany dressing table, the hinged twin-flap top enclosing a fitted interior centred by an oval mirror, 26in (67cm).
£3,200-3,800 *C*

A fine George III mahogany Rudd's table, after a design by George Hepplewhite.
£3,500-4,000 *Bon*

A Regency mahogany dressing table, stamped Gillows of Lancaster, 52in (130cm).
£1,800-2,200 *C*

A satinwood crossbanded kingwood and parquetry wig table, the top in 3 hinged sections revealing centre mirror and compartments to either side, 19thC.
£900-1,100 *CRY*

A Victorian mahogany duchess dressing table, c1890, 62in (155cm) high.
£300-400 *Ph*

Tables – Drop-Leaf

A late George II mahogany two-flap table, 59in (150cm) extended.
£2,000-2,500 *L*

A mahogany drop-leaf table, late 18thC, 36in (91cm).
£450-500 *WIL*

A mid-Georgian mahogany drop-leaf table, 47in (117.5cm) open.
£900-1,100 *CSK*

Tables – Drum

A George III mahogany drum table, with leather-lined revolving circular top and 4 frieze drawers, 2 divided, with the ivory letters A to D, 38½in (98cm) diam.
£5,000-6,000 *C*

A George III mahogany drum table, with revolving top, 44in (110cm).
£9,000-10,000 *C*

A Victorian mahogany drum top table, 47in (120cm) diam.
£600-700 *L*

A George II mahogany demi-lune triple fold-over top tea/games table, having money wells and compartment, 33in (83cm).
£1,000-1,200 *Pea*

Tables – Games

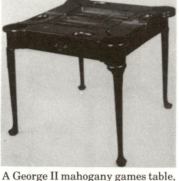

A George II mahogany games table, the top enclosing a backgammon well with candle slides and guinea trays, 36in (91cm).
£2,000-3,000 *C*

A late George II mahogany triple top table, with concertina action, 34in (86cm).
£4,200-5,000 *L*

A Regency mahogany combined games and work table, 19in (48cm).
£4,000-4,500 *C*

A Regency rosewood games table, 35in (89cm).
£2,000-2,500 *C*

In the Furniture section if there is only one measurement it usually refers to the width of the piece.

A parcel-gilt and calamander games table, the instepped top with reversible slide with chess squares and backgammon board, with 2 small drawers enclosing a few ivory chessmen, trestles re-gilded, 28½in (72cm).
£2,200-2,800 *C*

Tables – Gateleg

A George II mahogany gateleg dining table, 59in (150cm) wide, open.
£2,000-3,000   *C*

An unusual mid-Georgian mahogany gateleg table, 48½in (123cm) wide, open.
£3,500-4,000   *C*

An early George III walnut gateleg table, 48½in (123cm).
£800-1,000   *Bon*

Tables – Library

A George IV ormolu-mounted parcel-gilt and fruitwood library table, the top with egg-and-dart border, 56in (142cm) diam.
£10,000-11,000   *C*

A Regency mahogany library table, 32½ by 48in (81 by 120cm).
£3,500-4,000   *P*

A Regency mahogany library table with crossbanded top, one of the drawers fitted with a baize-lined hinged writing surface crossbanded in faded rosewood, 51½in (128cm).
£3,000-4,000   *C*

A George III Chippendale style rectangular library table, with 6 drawers and gadrooned all round, c1770.
£5,000-5,500   *EA*

A William IV mahogany library table, the top with gadrooned border and 4 frieze drawers, flanked by 4 small pivoted drawers on foliate baluster shaft, possibly Irish, 35½in (90cm) diam.
£2,500-3,000   *C*

A William IV pollard oak library table, with inset top and canted panelled corners with brass mounts and satinwood mouldings, the ends and one side with open shelves, the front with 2 doors set with calf tooled book-spines with concealed locking mechanism, on casters, 57in (144cm).
£5,000-5,500   *DWB*

Tables – Loo

A George IV oak library table, with leather-lined top and 2 drawers, on turned baluster stem and tripod base, 42½in (107cm).
£1,500-2,500   *C*

A William IV rosewood library or centre table, fitted with 2 drawers, 54in (138cm).
£500-1,500   *L*

A George IV rosewood library table, the top inset with green leather, on moulded scroll cabriole legs, with scroll feet, 62in (155cm).
£1,500-2,500   *O*

A figured walnut oval loo table, c1850, 58in (145cm).
£1,500-2,000   *JMW*

Tables – Needlework

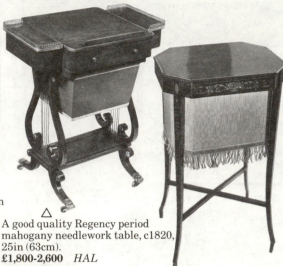

A Victorian inlaid figured walnut loo table, with centre pillar and 4 turned supports and 4 carved feet, 46in (115cm).
£200-300 *PC*

A small Victorian burr walnut oval loo table, on carved quadruped base.
£300-500 *FR*

A good quality Regency period mahogany needlework table, c1820, 25in (63cm).
£1,800-2,600 *HAL*

A Regency period needlework table, with a figured satinwood rosewood crossbanded lid, above an ebonised gilt decorated octagonal frieze, c1810, 17in (43cm).
£1,800-2,300 *HAL*

Nests of Tables

A set of 4 satinwood quartetto tables, the tops with ebony stringings on ring-turned twinned trestle ends and shaped feet, 14in to 19½in (35.5 to 49.5cm).
£3,000-4,000 *C*

A Regency period nest of 3 occasional tables in rosewood veneers, originally a nest of 4 tables, c1820, 19in (48cm).
£2,000-2,400 *HAL*

A nest of 3 rosewood and mahogany quartetto tables, the centre table inlaid with maple and rosewood chessboard, the largest 19½in (49cm).
£800-1,000 *CSK*

Tables – Occasional

A George IV occasional table, made from the willow growing over Napoleon's grave, the rectangular top edged with reed ornament, on ebonised bun feet, 26in (66cm).
£1,000-1,500 *C*

A Queen Anne red walnut pad foot occasional table.
£2,500-3,000 *EA*

A George III satinwood cheveret, the detachable superstructure with carrying handle, the folding cloth-lined writing slide and one frieze drawer formerly with a work basket beneath, on square tapering legs, 22in (56cm).
£2,500-3,500 *C*

A parquetry table, the hexagonal tip-up top on a tapering pillar, inlaid overall in cube patterns, with rosewood, mahogany and satinwood, 19thC, 27in (68cm).
£600-650   *L*

Tables – Pedestal

A Regency rosewood pedestal table, the octagonal top with an Italian inlaid marble panel, framed by specimen marbles, 24½in (62cm).
£1,000-1,500   *C*

A George IV ebonised and gilded pedestal table, the beaded rounded rectangular top with a painting on glass, 24in (61cm).
£800-1,000   *C*

Tables – Pembroke

A George III mahogany Pembroke table, crossbanded in rosewood and ruled in boxwood, with rounded flap top, end drawer, on square tapered supports, 30in (75cm).
£650-750   *Pea*

A George III mahogany Pembroke table, the satinwood crossbanded top with elliptical leaves above a similarly banded bowed drawer, on square tapered legs, 33½in (84cm).
£800-1,200   *Bon*

A George III oval shaped mahogany Pembroke table, on square tapered supports, with brass cup and wheel caster extensions.
£600-800   *CRY*

A George III mahogany Pembroke table, the oval two-flap top crossbanded, inlaid with stringing, with a central large oval fan motif, 39in (99cm) extended.
£1,400-1,600   *L*

A George III period small Pembroke table in mahogany, with figured hinged surface above single cockbeaded drawer and fluted square taper legs, c1800, 33½in (84cm) open.
£2,000-2,800   *HAL*

A George III oval mahogany Pembroke table, on square tapered supports.
£600-800   *CRY*

PEMBROKE TABLES

★ became popular in the mid to late 18thC, possibly designed and ordered by Henry Herbert, the Earl of Pembroke (1693-1751)
★ on early examples the legs were square which are by far the most desirable
★ later tables had turned legs
★ the turned and reeded legs are much less popular
★ those with oval or serpentine tops more desirable
★ flaps should have three hinges
★ rounded flaps and marquetry again increase desirability
★ satinwood was greatly favoured, particularly with much crossbanding and inlay
★ many 18thC Pembroke tables have chamfering on the insides of the legs
★ the Edwardians made many fine Pembroke tables which have been known to appear wrongly catalogued at auction
★ Edwardian tables now in great demand

A George III period Pembroke table in mahogany, with satinwood crossbanding above cockbeaded dummy and working drawers with original brasswork, with good quality replaced brass casters, c1800, 35½in (90cm).
£2,600-3,500   *HAL*

A Regency mahogany Pembroke table, with most unusual banded umbrella understretchers.
£1,000-1,600   *FHF*

A fine quality Irish Regency period mahogany Pembroke table, c1820, 45in (113cm) wide, open.
£1,800-2,400   *HAL*

Tables – Pier

A Regency satinwood Pembroke table of unusual form, with banded rounded rectangular twin-flap top and one frieze drawer opening to each side, on splayed square tapering legs, 44in (112cm) wide, open.
£3,500-4,000   *C*

A late Regency mahogany Pembroke table, with a rosewood crossbanded two-flap top, fitted with 3 drawers opposite 3 dummy drawers, the frieze with stylised ebony inlay, on 4 spiral twist tapering supports, 32in (82cm) extended.
£1,200-1,500   *L*

A painted and gilded pier table, with Portor marble top, the frieze with key-pattern and ram's mask angles on panelled tapering legs moulded with bellflowers, late 18thC, 46in (118cm).
£4,000-5,000   *C*

Tables – Reading

A pair of George III style mahogany pier tables, the eared and concave coffered rectangular tops above 3 frieze drawers, 53½in (133cm).
£500-700   *CSK*

A pair of Regency mahogany pier tables, each with a polished grey slate top, one drawer with brass lion mask ring handle and scroll front supports, joining a shaped base with carved paw feet, 18in (46cm).
£2,500-3,000   *L*

A Georgian mahogany reading table, with lift-up top with adjustable support, 2 drawers in the frieze and 2 candle slides, 19in (48cm).
£2,500-3,000   *JD*

A pair of early Victorian mahogany pedestal reading tables, the adjustable tops on lotus leaf lappeted turned tapering columns, the triform platform base with bun feet, 18in (45cm), and a centre table, en suite, 28in (70cm).
£1,900-2,500   *CSK*

Tables – Serving

A George III mahogany serpentine serving table, with brass rail at the back, the top and frieze crossbanded and inlaid with stringing, with figured panels, 97in (244cm).
£8,500-9,500 L

A George III carved mahogany serpentine serving table, with a bevelled ledge, the fluted frieze with 2 concave drawers, on square tapered legs headed with oval beaded paterae medallions and terminating in block feet, 92in (231cm).
£3,500-4,500 P

A George III mahogany serving table, the serpentine top with a three-quarter gallery centred by a plum-pudding mahogany tablet, the whole inlaid with boxwood stringing, restorations, 46in (115cm).
£2,500-3,000 Bon

Tables – Side

A George III mahogany serpentine front serving table, with plain top above 3 frieze drawers, on 4 square tapering supports, 72in (183cm).
£1,500-2,000 L

A fine George II giltwood side table, with carved rectangular brown jasper-veneered top on fluted shell-centred frieze hung with oak swags, on partly imbricated scrolled legs carved with entrelacs and foliage, 52½in (134cm).
£12,500-15,000 C

A Regency bird's-eye maple and ebonised side table, the top inlaid with a rosewood band above a frieze drawer, on ring-turned tapering legs, 20in (50cm).
£800-900 CSK

An early Georgian walnut side table, on foliate cabriole legs and shaped pad feet, formerly a card table, 33in (84cm).
£900-1,100 C

A George III satinwood, rosewood crossbanded and inlaid elliptical side table, decorated with chequer, boxwood and ebony lines, having a segmental fan veneered top, 49½in (124cm).
£2,500-3,000 P

A Georgian mahogany side table, with a grey and white mottled marble top, 36in (91cm).
£2,000-2,500 L

A Spanish walnut side table with moulded top, on fluted baluster legs with moulded stretchers and bun feet, late 16thC and later, 65in (165cm).
£1,500-2,100 C

A free standing side table in rosewood, profusely inlaid with brass, with 3 frieze drawers, c1830.
£2,500-3,500 ELD

A George III mahogany side table, crossbanded with satinwood, 56in (143cm).
£3,000-4,000 C

A Regency mahogany bow front side table, with arched and moulded three-quarter galleried top, 58in (145cm). **£1,000-1,500** *CEd* ▷

A Georgian mahogany side table, with marble inset top, supported on boldly carved cabriole legs decorated at the knees with acanthus and scrollwork, ending in claw-and-ball feet, 64in (160cm). **£7,000-8,000** *HSS* ▷

A George III mahogany side table, the frieze and square chamfered legs carved with geometric blind fretwork on a pounced ground, possibly later carving, 58in (148cm). **£1,500-2,200** *C*

A simulated mahogany and carved giltwood side table in the style of William Kent, surmounted by a 'rosso antico' moulded rectangular marble top, on cabriole legs with lion masks and terminating in paw feet, 55½in (139cm). **£3,500-4,200** *P*

Tables – Silver

A George III style mahogany silver table, the top with an arcaded and scrolling foliate pierced gallery, 36½in (91cm). **£1,000-1,500** *CSK*

A George III mahogany serpentine silver table, the spindle gallery with shaped corners, on turned column, with birdcage and carved tripod support, 24in (60cm). **£2,500-3,000** *DWB*

Tables – Sofa

A mahogany sofa table, the two-flap top with a wide yewwood band edged with stringing, 60in (152cm) extended. **£1,200-1,600** *L*

A George III mahogany sofa table, the 2 drop leaves above 2 shallow drawers with ebony edge, 51in (128cm) wide, open. **£1,500-2,000** *B*

A late Regency rosewood sofa table, with foliate marquetry panels and crossbanding, 60in (150cm). **£2,000-2,500** *NSF*

A Regency partridgewood sofa table, 47½in (125cm) wide, open. **£2,000-3,000** *C*

SOFA TABLES

★ an elegant feminine writing table, usually with two shallow drawers
★ genuine ones are rarer than it might appear
★ either had two vertical supports or a central pillar
★ many fine examples made in mahogany with satinwood or rosewood stringing and crossbanding
★ rosewood examples can be of exceptional quality
★ examples with stretchers tend to be later
★ lyre end supports, particularly with a brass strip, are likely to increase value
★ many sofa tables have been made from old cheval mirrors
★ if the stretcher rail is turned and has a square block in the centre – it could be from a converted cheval mirror
★ many good sofa tables have been carved with Egyptian heads in the manner of Thomas Hope
★ long drawers are undesirable but many have been cut down

A Regency mahogany sofa table, inlaid with ebonised lines in geometric style, 59in (150cm) extended.
£2,200-3,000   *L*

A Regency fruitwood and mahogany crossbanded sofa table, 60in (150cm) wide, open.
£1,000-1,500   *CDC*

A George IV mahogany sofa table, with rounded rectangular twin-flap top and 2 panelled frieze drawers, with solid scrolled trestle ends, moulded splayed feet and lions paws, bearing the trade label R. Snowdon Cabinet Maker and Appraiser Northallerton, 62in (153cm) wide, open.
£2,000-2,500   *C*

A Regency mahogany sofa table, inlaid with ebony lines, 60in (150cm).
£2,000-3,000   *CSK*

A Regency rosewood and boxwood line inlay sofa table.
£6,300-6,600   *CW*

A Regency rosewood sofa table, extensively inlaid with brass in stylised foliate design and plain lines, 59in (150cm) extended.
£1,500-2,300   *L*

Tables – Sutherland

An Edwardian painted satinwood sofa table, the rounded rectangular twin-flap top painted with rustic scene, the 2 frieze drawers with oval silvered handles, 67½in (170cm) wide, open.
£2,800-3,200   *C*

A Victorian figured walnut oval gateleg Sutherland/occasional table, with fluted bulbous supports, on shaped legs and casters, 42in (105cm) extended.
£450-550   *GH*

Tables – Tea

A George I walnut tea and games table, baize-lined with counter wells and candle stands, enclosing a games board inlaid for backgammon and chess, with easel support and a well, 33in (84cm).
£5,000-5,500   *C*

A George II mahogany tea table with shaped fold-over top, single drawer with brass drop handle and turned tapered legs, on pad feet, 28½in (71cm).
£900-1,400   *DSH*

A mid-Georgian mahogany tea table, with hinged rectangular top and one frieze drawer on lappeted club legs and pad feet, 30in (76cm).
£1,500-2,500   *C*

A Georgian demi-lune mahogany folding top tea table, on square tapering legs, 35in (88cm).
£500-1,000   *JD*

A fine mahogany hinged top tea table of serpentine form, c1770.
£1,000-1,500   *ELD*

An inlaid mahogany half round fold-over tea table, with oval satinwood and marquetry panel, 18thC.
£500-1,000   *FR*

A George III Chippendale style tea table of serpentine form, with egg-and-dart mouldings, small repair or top corner flap, c1790.
£500-1,200   *EA*

A Victorian rosewood fold-over tea table, 38in (95cm).
£700-1,200   *JMW*

A George IV brass-inlaid mahogany tea table, with bold scroll supports and brass casters, 39in (99cm).
£500-1,000   *TEN*

A fine and rare George III mahogany round table, with raised border, attributed to Ince & Mayhew, 22in (55cm) diam.
£22,000-25,000   *DWB*

Tables – Tripod

A George II mahogany tripod table, the moulded circular top with deep pierced fretwork gallery, 15in (38cm) diam.
£1,500-2,500   *C*

A George II mahogany tripod table, with pie-crust top, 10in (25cm) diam.
£1,500-2,500   *C*

△
A George III padoukwood tripod table, with moulded circular tip-up top, birdcage action, 23in (59cm) diam.
£2,500-3,500   *C*

A George II style mahogany circular snap-top tea table, 30in (75cm) diam.
£900-1,400   *Pea*

A mid-Georgian mahogany tripod table, the waved tip-up top re-shaped and carved later with foliate clasps, 32½in (83cm) diam.
£2,500-3,000   *C*

A mid-Georgian mahogany tripod table, with tip-up pie-crust top carved with shells, 27½in (77cm) diam.
£5,000-7,000   *C*

A George III mahogany tripod table, with octagonal tip-up top with lightly raised edge, on an unusual triform support formed as C-scrolls, on a base shaped as opposing C-scrolls, with original leather casters, 28in (71cm).
£10,000-12,000   *L*

The stem and base of this table is most unusual, but compares to an example by John Linnell, illustrated in Ward-Jackson, fig. 191, and another illustration in The Norman Adams Collection, *by Stevens and Whittington, page 297.*

A George III mahogany tripod table, with inlaid octagonal hinging surface above a ring-turned stem and 3 swept legs, c1800, 25in (62.5cm).
£900-1,400   *HAL*

A George III mahogany tripod table, 34in (87cm) diam.
£1,000-1,500   *L*

A circular Regency rosewood tip-up library table, the top inlaid with brass scroll band, 54½in (136cm) diam.
£3,000-4,000   *AGr*

Tables – Wake

A rare George II mahogany double gateleg wake table, with rectangular top on 8 cannon barrel legs linked by powerful mahogany-veneered oak plain stretchers above outset feet, 36 by 58in (90 by 145cm) extended.
£900-1,400   *TEN*

Tables – Wine/Lamp

A Georgian style walnut wine table raised on turned column, with 2 tiers of revolving open book racks raised on tripod supports, 30in (75cm) high.
£400-800   *AG*

A mid-Georgian burr yew tripod table, with circular tray tip-up top and spreading vase-shaped shaft, the arched base with shaped pad feet, 23in (58cm) diam.
£3,000-3,500   *C*

Tables – Work

An unusual George III mahogany work table, with revolving square easel top, the frieze fitted with 4 drawers and 2 candle stands, the panelled pedestal with a cupboard door, 25in (63cm).
£2,500-3,500   *C*

A Regency ebonised lamp table, with rectangular hinged lacquer top on turned stem mounted with stamped giltmetal, 18in (46.5cm).
£900-1,400   *C*

A late Regency rosewood work table, with brass line inlays, 25in (63cm).
£700-1,100   *Re*

A William IV ▷ rosewood work table, the rectangular top with canted corners above a reel-mouled frieze drawer and pleated silk work basket, 23in (56cm).
£250-700 *Bon*

A George III mahogany and inlaid oval work table, the figured top inlaid with musical trophies, 26in (64cm).
£500-1,000 *Bon*

A Regency mahogany sewing table, with 2 graduated and 2 dummy drawers, velvet covered sliding pouch on lyre form supports and leaf carved scroll feet with brass casters, 22 by 19in (55 by 48cm).
£400-900 *NSF*

A Regency ▷ rosewood work table, inlaid with brass lines and foliate motifs, with fitted interior and work bag, 30 by 16in (75 by 40cm).
£2,500-3,500 *Bea*

◁ A small Regency period mahogany work table.
£500-1,000 *M*

A Victorian burr walnut folding top card/work table on twin carved supports with stretcher, having chessboard top, 3 drawers and sliding work box under, 29in (72.5cm).
£600-1,200 *JD*

◁ A George IV rosewood rectangular work table, inlaid with stringings one fitted drawer with compartments and a work-well covered with pleated sateen, 20 by 16in (50 by 40cm).
£400-800 *CBD*

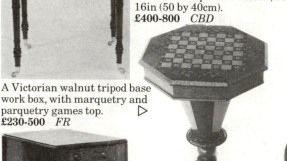

A Victorian mahogany work table, with convex front, the quarter-veneered top enclosing compartments, 19in (48cm).
£400-800 *CBD*

A Victorian walnut tripod base work box, with marquetry and parquetry games top.
£230-500 *FR*

▷

An early Victorian mahogany Pembroke work table, with fall-leaves, 2 drawers and false drawers over a mahogany sliding well, 19in (48cm).
£500-1,000 *CDC*

A Victorian walnut waisted ladies' work table, with lift top lid and fretted sycamore interior and centre well.
£500-1,000 *WIL*

A ladies' work table, in Japanese gold lacquer, the interior with loose centre tray and numerous carved ivory sewing and needlework implements, sliding work bag in red velvet, late 19thC, 25 by 17in (62.5 by 42.5cm).
£500-1,000 *WIL*

Tables – Writing

A George III mahogany writing table, with leather-lined top, the carcase possibly reduced, on square tapering legs, 42in (105.5cm).
£3,500-4,000   *C*

A rare Hepplewhite mahogany kidney-shaped ladies' writing table, the top with a narrow crossbanding and inset tooled leather, 18thC, 54in (135cm).
£21,000-23,000   *BS*

A George III inlaid mahogany secretaire, with shaped tray top, with baize-lined ratchet adjustable writing slope, brass ring handles, concave undertier, on square tapered supports, 17in (42.5cm).
£4,000-5,000   *Pea*

An unusual Regency mahogany writing table, with 2 oval moulded drop leaves, the top fitted for writing, all with ebony line inlay on simulated bamboo turned splay supports and brass castors, 22in (55cm).
£5,000-5,500   *Re*

A fine George III mahogany bookshelf writing table.
£3,500-4,500   *Bon*

An Edwardian satinwood kidney shape writing desk, with gilt-tooled leather panel, 48in (120cm).
£2,700-3,200   *L*

A transitional parquetry kingwood and bois-satiné table à ecrire by J. P. Dusantoy, with leather lined top, stamped 'I.P. Du Sautoy JME', 15in (37.5cm).
£3,700-4,000   *C*

Jean-Pierre Dusantoy, maître in 1779.

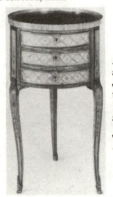

An Italian ebony veneered and pietra dura writing table, the top with inset writing surface within a gilt bronze moulding, 19thC, 43in (107.5cm).
£2,500-3,000   *TLC*

Washstands

Teapoys

A Regency mahogany teapoy, the eared rectangular hinged top enclosing a divided interior with later tin liners, the front and sides with ormolu banding, 20in (51cm).
£2,300-2,600   *C*

Provenance: Quebec House, Westerham, Kent.

◁

A Regency brass inlaid rosewood teapoy, the chamfered top inlaid, enclosing a fitted interior, 2 lidded compartments lacking mixing bowls, with Bramah lock and carrying handles, 18in (45cm).
£2,300-2,700   *C*

A George III mahogany enclosed washstand, inlaid with boxwood stringing and enclosing a later mirror and apertures for bowls, c1800, 24in (61cm).
£400-800   *Bon*

A Georgian mahogany enclosed washstand, with fold-over top, rising mirror and fitted compartments and basin with drainage hole, the front with 2 small cupboard doors, one drawer and the pull-out base with original pewter pot, 18in (46cm).
£600-1,300   *L*

Whatnots

A late Georgian birds'-eye maple four-tier étagère with turned column supports, 24in (61cm).
£2,500-3,500   *C*

A small late Regency mahogany whatnot, c1830, 20in (50cm).
£1,300-1,800   *HAL*

A Regency rosewood whatnot of four tiers, on slender baluster turned columns, the third tier fitted with a drawer, 19in (47cm).
£500-1,000   *Bon*

A rosewood four-tier free standing whatnot, with barley twist supports and fitted drawer, c1840.
£800-1,200   *ELD*

A rare mahogany free standing three-tier dumb waiter, c1830.
£1,250-1,750   *ELD*

A Regency mahogany serving side buffet, on baluster column supports with turned tapering legs, 36in (90cm).
£500-1,000   *CSK*

Wine Coolers

A George III brass-bound mahogany cellaret, the hexagonal top crossbanded in satinwood enclosing lead-lined interior retaining tap beneath, the slightly tapering body with carrying handles, the stand with square tapering legs, 19in (48cm).
£2,800-3,200   *C*

WINE COOLERS

* ★ cisterns for cooling wines were noted back in the 15thC and as objects of furniture became popular after about 1730. The cellaret is basically a cooler with a lid and fitted with a lock
* ★ there are two main types: those made to stand on a pedestal or sideboard and those with legs or separate stands to stand on the floor
* ★ octagonal, hexagonal, round or oval, the commonest form is of coopered construction with a number of brass bands
* ★ a cooler made to stand on a pedestal will often have the lowest brass band as near to the base as possible; a cooler made to fit into a stand will have the band slightly up the body to allow a snug fit
* ★ it is important that all mounts are original and condition should be good, but the absence of the old lead lining is not serious. An octagonal cooler or cellaret on stand may command a slightly higher price than a hexagonal model, but both are much in demand
* ★ after 1800, the sarcophagus shape became popular and later Regency models were made with highly figured mahogany veneers and large carved paw feet
* ★ there were not many new designs after the 1850s

A George III mahogany and brass bound oval wine cooler or jardinière, with brass loop handles and zinc liner, 24 by 18in (60 by 45cm).
£2,300-2,700 *CBD*

A Regency mahogany wine cooler, in the manner of Gillows, with oval tin-liner and slightly tapering body, with giltmetal lion-mask handles, 29in (73cm).
£4,000-5,000 *C*

An Italian parcel-gilt and blue-green painted headboard of scrolled foliate shape, with two putto crestings, 72 by 69in (183 by 175cm).
£800-1,100 *C*

A late George III mahogany wine cooler, with carved decoration, the hinged lid opening to reveal a lead-lined interior, raised on paw feet, 30in (75cm).
£1,500-2,500 *AG*

Miscellaneous

A mahogany waste-paper basket, the slightly tapering octagonal body filled with pierced trellis work with paper liner, on bracket feet, 14in (35cm).
£2,500-3,000 *C*

A set of ▷ William IV style brass fire tools and stand, 27in (68cm) high.
°£380-480 *HAL*

A Regency mahogany oval wine cooler, in the manner of Gillows, with lead-lined interior and tapering body with baluster ribbed pilasters on turned tapering feet, 28in (69cm).
£4,000-4,500 *C*

A pair of Regency painted coal boxes, each with slightly domed lid and tapering body, decorated in blue on a beige ground with trailing foliage, on gilt paw feet, 21in (52cm).
£1,000-1,500 *C*

A mahogany urn table, the waved square top with pierced fretwork gallery, the plain frieze edged with cabochon-and-rosette with a slide, on moulded legs edged with bead-and-reel and joined by an arched pierced cross-stretcher, 13in (33cm) square.
£1,500-2,000 *C*

◁

A Burroughs & Watts full size oak-framed snooker table, raised on 8 supports, each turned and fluted, recently recovered and maintained to a high standard, with white cotton cover, lighting canopy, counter balanced brass fittings and rails for playing billiards.
£3,500-4,500 *WIL*

A Regency mahogany wine cooler, with tapering rectangular body with tin-liner and gadrooned border, 34in (86cm).
£2,200-2,700 *C*

Possibly the most interesting feature of the clocks market at present is the difference in buying trends between northern and southern areas of the country. Although there is a universal demand for high quality and originality throughout – with such virtues being well rewarded in terms of prices – it is in the matter of taste that the divide is seen.

A consensus of Scottish auctioneers and dealers shows the northern trend to be toward simplicity, with soberly-styled English bracket and mantel clocks being in greatest demand along with early mahogany longcase clocks. Boulle, less-than-superb ormolu, painted faces and other embellishments are regarded by many northern and Scottish buyers as minus points.

Buyers in southern parts, conversely, seem universally to be looking for distinctly decorative qualities. That is not to suggest that less emphasis is placed on quality and originality, however, for even relatively minor defects in either department will be found to have a disastrous effect on price.

Still at the low end of the market are the Victorian marble 'lumps', which many people consider to be seriously underpriced through lack of demand. This particularly applies to those with black marble cases. In view of the fact that there are, if anything, fewer clocks appearing on the market than in years past, it is quite possible that these long-ignored pieces will begin to pick up, particularly since many have excellent movements which will give years of reliable use.

In general terms, the clock market is extremely buoyant, with many dealer/restorers finding less time to devote to dealing through pressure of repair work.

Clocks – Longcase

◁ An 8-day painted dial longcase clock, maker Edward Bell, Uttoxeter, in original oak case with mahogany trim, c1785, 92in (232.5cm).
£1,100-1,600   *BL*

An 8-day longcase clock with white dial, maker William Bellman of Broughton, in original oak case with mahogany trim, c1790, 78in (197.5cm).
£900-1,300   *BL*

A chinoiserie black lacquered 8-day longcase clock, the brass dial with silvered chapter ring by John Blake, London, 18thC, 90in (227.5cm).
£1,000-1,200   *GSP*

A George III dark green japanned longcase clock, the dial signed Thomas Allen Deptford, with strike/silent ring above the silvered chapter ring enclosing sunken seconds and calendar aperture, the 5-pillar movement with rack strike and anchor escapement, 90in (230cm).
£2,000-2,500   *C*

A 30-hour longcase ▷ clock, of exceptional quality, maker Matthew Bold of Bold, in original oak case, crossbanded also in oak, c1740, 90in (227.5cm).
£1,000-1,400   *BL*

A mahogany longcase clock by William Barnish of Rochdale, the arch with calendar and lunar aperture painted with faces of the moon and figures in rural and coastal scenes, inscribed 'I am Moving Whilst thou art Sleeping', the 3-train movement with later comb and cylinder strike on 6 graduated bells, and with anchor escapement, late 18thC, 89in (225cm).
£2,200-2,800   *HSS*

◁ A Regency mahogany longcase clock, the 11in (27.5cm) painted dial with subsidiary seconds, signed Barrauds, Cornhill, London 1140, the 5-pillared movement with signed, shaped plates, maintaining power, and deadbeat escapement, the wood rod pendulum with calibrated rating nut, 76in (192cm).
£6,000-7,000   *P*

A mahogany ▷ longcase clock, 13in (32.5cm) dial with painted rolling moon in the arch, signed Nathaniel Brown, Manchester, centre sweep seconds and date pointer, 8-day 4-pillar rack striking movement with dead beat escapement, c1780, 95½in (241cm).
£2,800-3,200 *Re*

A walnut and marquetry longcase clock, the 8-day 5-pillar movement rack striking, signed Claudius de Chesne, Londini, the marquetry door, which is not original, inlaid with panels of flowers and birds, 89in (225cm).
£1,700-2,000 *L*

mahogany
gcase clock, with
n (30cm) brass
l, calendar
erture, seconds
nd, strike and
ent dial, the
rain 8-day
vement with
chor escapement,
John Berry,
ndon, 18thC, 84in
3cm).
300-2,600 *AGr*

0-hour longcase ▷
ck, oak with
hogany
ssbanding, by H.
ke of Appleby,
30.
0-500 *STW*

An 8-day pine longcase clock, the 12in (30cm) brass dial with subsidiary seconds and dated aperture, signed John Carne, Penzance, 84in (212.5cm).
£500-600 *Bon*

An 8-day brass dial longcase clock with moon dial, maker Nathaniel Brown of Manchester, original case in dark Cuban mahogany, c1750, 97in (245cm).
£2,750-3,750 *BL*

PORTANT NOTES TO LOCKS
Brian Loomes

iginality is of paramount portance; any alterations, difications or marriages of y kind cause prices to fall stically. In longcase clocks ginality of the case to the ck is vitally important and en difficult for the xperienced to establish. One uld expect to pay more for ch an item from a specialist ler who will guarantee his ds than when buying at ction where normally no such arantee is given.

ction estimates are useful as ague guide only; actual ces realised may vary widely m the auctioneer's estimates.

A clock in unrestored condition is very difficult for the inexperienced to value as a great deal depends on the amount of restoration needed and, in extreme cases, even whether such restoration can be done. It is very easy to spend £200 or £300 on straightforward cleaning of a clock. Consequently with a clock of low value it is quite possible that restoration could prove more costly than the clock's total worth.

High quality of workmanship in clocks puts such examples at a premium. The beginner may well be unable to distinguish which features are indicative of high quality and which are conventional for the period.

Features of a rare or unusual nature add considerably to the value of a clock, as does greater complexity of the movement. The inexperienced may not be able to recognise an exceptionally rare feature from a commonplace one.

In longcase clocks small height is a very important plus feature, provided the clock has not been shortened in some way or otherwise reduced in size – whether recently or long ago is not important. A very tall clock is often difficult to sell and will usually be held down in price by this feature. Because of this a great many have been reduced in height over the years and the ability to recognise this is vital.

A mahogany veneered longcase clock, the 8-day movement rack striking, subsidiary seconds dial and signed Cottell, Crewkerne, 92½in (233cm).
£700-800   *L*

A mahogany longcase clock, the 12in (30cm) brass dial, signed Thos. Bruton, Bow, Midlx., with subsidiaries for seconds and for date and with strike/ silent in the arch, the 5-pillared movement with anchor escapement, 18thC, 102in (257.5cm).
£4,500-5,000   *P*

A black lacquered and chinoiserie decorated longcase clock, with 12in (30cm) brass dial, recessed subsidiary seconds, and date aperture, signed Joseph Cayre St. Neots, and with strike/silent in the arch, the 5-pillared movement with anchor escapement, 18thC, 99in (250cm).
£1,500-2,000   *P*

A fine month longcase clock with 11in (27.5cm) brass dial, having second and date indicators, by Richard Colston, London (apprenticed 1637, member of the Clockmakers Co. 1646-1697), in walnut veneered and marquetry inlaid case, 86in (217.5cm).
£7,500-8,500   *WSW*

A fine oak and crossbanded longcase clock, by David Collier, Gatley, with paint frieze bearing the initials E.M. 1768, 13in (32.5cm) brass dial, with rolling moon to the arch, 4-pillar 8-day rack striking movemen striking on a bell, late 18thC, 80in (202.5cm).
£1,500-1,900   *Re*

A walnut longcase clock, the 12in (30cm) brass dial signed William Clark, Stalbridge with subsidiary seconds and date aperture, the 5-pillared movement of month duration now with deadbeat escapement striking on a gong, 18thC, 95in (240cm).
£3,000-3,500   *P*

A 30-hour longcase clock with painted dial, prestigious maker Samuel Deacon, with original bill of sale, in original oak case with mahogany trim, c1800, 88in (222.5cm).
£600-900   *BL*

A Victorian mahogany longcase clock, with 8-day movement by J. Galloway, Leeds.
£550-750   *TW*

A walnut longcase clock, the 8-day movement with anchor escapement, rack striking, with 13in (32.5cm) painted dial, subsidiary seconds and calendar dials, signed W. Donald, Glasgow, 85½in (215cm).
£950-1,050   *L*

◁ A George II longcase clock in walnut, herringbone and crossbanded case, by John Ellicott, London, the 8-day striking movement with seconds hand, date and month indicators, plinth reduced, 97in (245cm).
£4,000-5,000   *DWB*

John Ellicott F.R.S. 1706-1772, an eminent maker with examples of his work in many collections. Invented a compensated pendulum in 1752, elected F.R.S. in 1738 and was clockmaker to George III.

A walnut longcase clock, the 12in (30cm) brass dial with silvered chapter ring and date aperture, signed James Drury, London, the 5- ringed pillared movement with anchor escapement, 18thC, 88in (222.5cm).
£2,200-2,600   *P*

A Georgian mahogany longcase clock with 12in (30cm) brass dial, inset seconds subsidiary and date aperture, signed Jeremh Garbett, London, the 5-pillared movement with anchor escapement, 91in (230cm).
£1,800-2,200   *P*

An 8-day clock with painted dial, maker C. Fletcher, Rotherham, in original oak case with mahogany trim, c1790, 87in (220cm).
£800-1,200   *BL*

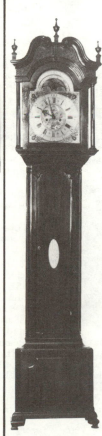

An 8-day clock with painted dial, maker Paul Ganter, Huddersfield, original case veneered in mahogany, c1845, 96in (242.5cm).
£450-750   *BL*

A burr walnut and mahogany crossbanded clock by John Ellicott, London with 12in (30cm) brass dial, the 8-day 2 train movement with dead beat escapement, 5-ringed pillars and striking on bell, 19thC, 90in (227.5cm).
£2,200-2,800   *AGr*

An 8-day longcase clock, with painted dial, maker Hudson, Otley, in original mahogany veneered case, c1850, 96in (242.5cm).
£500-800   *BL*

A 30-hour longcase
clock, maker
Fothergill of
Knaresborough,
original oak case
crossbanded and
trimmed with
mahogany, c1825,
90in (230cm).
£250-500 *BL*

An 8-day painted
dial longcase clock,
with moonwork in
arch, maker Thoma
Holmes, Cheadle, in
original mahogany
case, c1800, 87in
(220cm).
£900-1,200 *BL*

A George III
mahogany and
boxwood strung
longcase clock, the
13in (32.5cm) arched
brass dial with
silvered chapter
ring, centre date (the
hand missing) and
subsidiary seconds,
signed Finney,
Liverpool, the twin-
train movement with
anchor escapement,
94in (237.5cm).
£1,500-1,800 *P*

An oak longcase △
clock, the 8-day
movement rack
striking, with 12in
(30cm) brass dial,
with subsidiary
seconds dial and date
aperture, signed
James Green,
Nantwich, 84in
(212.5cm).
£1,200-1,500 *L*

A walnut, boxwood
and ebony strung
longcase clock, with
12in (30cm) brass
dial, signed Benj.
Heeley, Deptford,
with strike/silent in
the arch the
5-pillared movement
with anchor
escapement, the
pagoda-topped hood
reduced, 18thC, 96in
(244cm).
£2,500-3,000 *P*

◁ A Georgian
mahogany longcase
clock, the 12in
(30cm) painted dial
with subsidiaries for
seconds and for date,
signed C.W. Hooke,
London, the 5-
pillared movement
with anchor
escapement, 92in
(232.5cm).
£3,500-4,000 *P*

◁
An 8-day oak and
mahogany
crossbanded
longcase clock by
Ebenezer Fisler of
Ellesmere, the dial
with rolling moon, by
Wright,
Birmingham, c1835.
£650-750 *STW*

An Irish 8-day ▷
mahogany longcase
clock, the 13in
(32.5cm) brass dial
signed John Knox,
Larne, No. 156, date
aperture, subsidiary
dial for age of the
moon and concentric
tidal dial, the
4-pillar movement
with semi dead beat
escapement and
maintaining power
to the going train,
c1775, 92in
(232.5cm).
£1,700-2,000 *Bon*

An 8-day brass dia
longcase clock,
maker Hampson,
Bolton, in origina
case of dark
mahogany, c1780,
94in (237.5cm).
£2,500-3,250 *BL*

An 8-day brass dial longcase clock, maker Lawson, Bradford, with penny moon feature, in original oak case, c1760, 87in (220cm).
£1,000-1,500 *BL*

A George III ▷ mahogany longcase clock, the brass dial signed Jno. Manley, Chatham the 8-day movement with anchor escapement and rack striking on a bell, 83in (210cm).
£1,400-1,700 *CSK*

A late Stuart ▷ provincial burr walnut longcase clock the 10in (25cm) square dial signed Tho. Power at Weallingborow, the movement with latches to 4 of the 5-ringed pillars, outside countwheel strike and anchor escapement, restorations, 78in (197.5cm).
£3,500-5,000 *C*

n inlaid mahogany uarter chiming ngcase clock, the -train movement ith anchor scapement, with 2in (30cm) brass al, with trade plate, Kemp Brothers, nion St., Bristol, 3in (235cm).
1,300-1,700 *L*

An 8-day brass dial longcase clock, maker J. Lum, ▷ London, in original mahogany case, rocking seesaw in arch, c1760, 90in (227.5cm).
£3,000-4,000 *BL*

oak longcase ck, by Fran tten, Chichester, e 8-day movement iking on a single l, 18thC, 82in 8cm).
300-1,700 *HSS*

◁ A Queen Anne green japanned longcase clock, the hood with later ogee caddy top, figured 12in (30cm) square dial, signed Markwick, London, the movement with 5- ringed pillars, rack strike and anchor escapement, possibly associated, 95in (240cm).
£2,700-3,000 *C*

◁ A George III figured mahogany longcase clock, with 8-day movement by James Lomax of Blackburn, having additional musical movement, 88in (222.5cm).
£1,000-1,400 *CDC*

A carved walnut quarter chiming longcase clock, the movement with massive pillars, anchor escapement, and quarter chiming on 8 bells and 4 gongs, signed Maple & Co., London. ▷
£1,700-2,000 *L*

◁ A Regency mahogany longcase clock, with 8-day chiming movement, anchor escapement by J.A. Paterson, Edinburgh.
£1,000-1,400 *BWe*

◁ An 8-day mahogany longcase clock, the 14in (35cm) brass dial signed William Lawson, Newton, around a rolling moon, the 4-pillar movement with rack striking and anchor escapement, 89in (225cm).
£1,400-1,700 *Bon*

An 8-day brass dial longcase clock with centre calendar and fixed arch landscape scene, dated 1777, maker Thomas Shaw of Lancaster, in original case of bookmatched mahogany, case attributed to Gillow of Lancaster, 90in (227.5cm).
£3,000-4,000 *BL*

◁ A green stained and chinoiserie 8- day longcase clock by Rich Rayment, Bury, early 18thC, 90in (227.5cm).
£1,000-1,200 *PC*

An 8-day painted dial longcase clock with moonwork and centre seconds feature, maker Roberts of Otley, in original mahogany case, c1790, 92in (232.5cm).
£1,200-1,600 *BL*

HINTS TO DATING LONGCASE CLOCKS

Dials

8in square	to c1669	Carolean
10in square	from c1665-1800	
11in square	from 1690-1800	
12in square	from c1700	from Queen Anne
14in square	from c1740	from early Georgi
Broken-arch dial	from c1715	from early Georgi
Round dial	from c1760	from early Georgi
Silvered dial	from c1760	from early Georgi
Painted dial	from c1770	from early Georgi
Hour hand only	to 1820	
Minute hand introduced	c1663	
Second hand	from 1675	post-Restoration
Matching hands	from c1775	George III or later

Case finish

Ebony veneer	up to c1725	Carolean to early Georgian
Walnut veneer	from c1670 to c1770	Carolean to mid-Georgian
Lacquer	from c1700 to c1790	Queen Anne to mid-Georgian
Mahogany	from 1730	from early Georgian
Softwood	from c1690	from mid-Georgian
Mahogany inlay	from c1750	from mid-Georgian
Marquetry	from c1680 to c1760	from Carolean to mid-Georgian
Oak	always	

An 8-day brass dial longcase clock, with moonwork, maker Smith of Chester, in original mahogany case, c1770, 82in (207.5cm).
£2,000-3,000   BL

An 8-day longcase clock with painted dial, maker J. Symonds, Reepham, in original oak case, c1800, 87in (220cm).
£850-1,250   BL

An 8-day longcase clock with painted dial, maker Ward of Evesham, in original oak case with mahogany trim, c1840, 84in (212.5cm).
£600-950   BL

A 30-hour brass dial longcase clock, maker John Woolley of Codnor, a prestigious maker, in original oak case trimmed with mahogany, c1780, 80in (202.5cm).
£800-1,400   BL

A Georgian mahogany longcase clock, the 12in (30cm) brass dial signed Willm. Wasbrough, Bristol, inscribed around arch 'High Water at Bristol Key' (sic), 100in (252.5cm).
£2,000-2,500   P

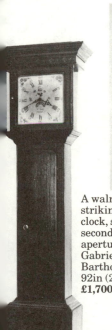

A walnut 8-day striking longcase clock, subsidiary seconds dial and date aperture, inscribed Gabriel Smith, Barthomley, 18thC, 92in (232.5cm).
£1,700-2,000   WW

A 30-hour clock with painted dial, maker William Snow, Padside, in original oak case, c1780, 92in (232.5cm).
£800-1,000   BL

An 8-day longcase clock with painted dial, maker Snowden of Grimsby, in original mahogany case, c1800, 96in (242.5cm).
£1,500-2,000   BL

◁ A Georgian mahogany longcase clock, the 12in (30cm) arched silvered dial with subsidiary seconds and date aperture, signed James Thwaites, London, and with strike/silent subsidiary in the arch, the 5-pillared movement with anchor escapement, 90in (227.5cm). **£1,200-1,400.** *P*

A George III mahogany longcase clock with brass dial, with phases of the moon, the 8-day striking movement with anchor escapement by Standring of Bolton, c1790, 90in (227.5cm). **£3,000-3,500** *AG*

A month longcase clock with 12in (30cm) brass dial, inscribed James West, London, in figured mahogany case, 18thC, trunk 13½in (33cm) wide. **£2,500-3,000** *GSP*

A walnut and floral marquetry longcase clock, the 12in (30cm) brass dial signed John Wainwright, Wellingboro, No. 1132, with subsidiary seconds and date aperture, the 5-pillared movement with anchor escapement, 84in (212.5cm). **£3,000-4,000** *P*

A walnut and marquetry longcase clock, the 12in (30cm) brass dial signed Wm. Wright, Londini Fecit, with subsidiary seconds and date aperture, the 5-ringed pillared movement with latched dial feet and plates, with anchor escapement and inside countwheel strike, the base with replaced skirting, early 18thC, 98in (247.5cm). **£10,000-12,000** *P*

A walnut longcase clock, makers nan Windmills, Londo with 11in (27.5cm brass face, the 8-d 2- train movemen with anchor escapement, with later marquetry, 18thC, 91in (230cm). **£900-1,100** *AGr*

An 8-day brass dial longcase clock with lunar and universal tidal dials in arch, maker prestigious William Stumbels, Totnes, in original oak case with walnut trim, c1740, 96in (242.5cm). **£2,000-3,000** *BL*

▷ A month going 8-day longcase clock, with 14½in (36cm) brass dial, signed 'Samll Young, Nant Wich', the 4-pillar movement with latched plates and anchor escapement, in pollard oak and crossbanded case, case reduced, movement repaired, 85in (214cm). **£2,800-3,200** *Bea*

A George III △ mahogany longcas clock with brass inlaid reeded columns and quart columns, W. Yardl of Bishops Stortfor 96in (242.5cm). **£1,700-1,900** *CR*

△ A 19thC style inlaid mahogany longcase clock with 12in (30cm) brass dial, with Westminster/8 bells dial, the 8-day 3-train movement with anchor escapement, 100in (252.5cm).
£4,000-5,000   *AGr*

A cream lacquer longcase clock, inscribed James Yardley, Bp. Stortford bell striking 8-day movement, 18thC, 86in (217.5cm).
£1,300-1,600   *PWC*

An 8-day painted dial longcase clock, Scottish, in original mahogany case, c1840, 89in (225cm).
£600-900   *BL*

An 8-day longcase clock with painted dial, moonwork in arch, Lincolnshire maker, in original oak case with original brass fittings throughout, late 18thC, 82in (207.5cm).
£1,000-1,500   *BL*

An ornately carved walnut musical clock, with 13in (34cm) symphonium metal discs, 10 discs in total, 89in (225cm).
£5,000-6,000   *AGr*

A Georgian mahogany 8-day striking longcase clock, the arch boss inscribed William Warren, London, 89in (225cm).
£1,300-1,600   *WW*

An 8-day clock with painted dial, unsigned, in original oak case, style suggesting Eastern Scotland, c1825, 82in (207.5cm).
£800-1,200   *BL*

A mahogany 8-day striking longcase clock, c1850.
£600-700   *WIL*

An ebonised mahogany longcase clock, the 14in (35cm) brass dial with chime/silent, strike/silent and Westminster and Whittington, the 8-day 3-train musical movement with anchor escapement, 19thC, 108in (272.5cm).
£4,000-5,000   *AGr*

Clocks – Regulators

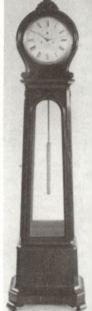

A Federal cherrywood tallcase clock, probably New Jersey, seatboard replaced 1810-30.
£2,000-2,500 *CNY*

Provenance: A brass plate inside the door of the case indicates the first owner was Lieutenant Samuel Cutler, and gives the line of descent in the Cutler family.

A Continental walnut longcase clock and polyphon, with a winding handle to the side, complete with 26 polyphon discs, and original receipt dated 21st March, 1901, for £33. 10s. 0d.
£4,000-5,000 *HSS*

A George III mahogany longcase regulator case, now fitted with a single train movement, the 10in (25cm) square silvered dial signed for Fras. Perigal, Bond Street, the shaped plates with 5 pillars and anchor escapement, stamped on the front I. Thwaites, and numbered with the dial and seatboard 1080, 72in (183cm).
£2,800-3,200 *P*

A Victorian mahogany longcase regulator, with brass glazed bezel to 12in (30cm) dial, signed P.G. Dodd & Son From Cornhill London, dust cover to movement of high count with Harrison's maintaining power, jewelled dead beat escapement and cranked roller crutch, 75in (190cm).
£2,000-2,500 *C*

A rosewood striking longcase regulator, the 12in (30cm) dial signed W. C. Shaw, Glasgow, the going train with dead beat escapement and maintaining power, 83in (210cm).
£2,200-2,800 *Bon*

Clocks – Bracket

A George I ebonised striking bracket clock, the dial signed Ed. Bayley, London, twin fusee movement with verge escapement, the scroll engraved backplate with securing brackets to the case, 19in (48cm).
£1,400-1,800 *C*

An early Georgian bracket clock, with single train movement, anchor escapement by George Elliot, 14in (35cm).
£1,500-2,000 *BWe*

A Regency mahogany longcase regulator, the 11in (27.5cm) dial signed Thwaites & Reed London, high count train with screwed depthed end caps throughout, Harrison's maintaining power, jewelled dead beat escapement with micrometer beat setting to stem of pallet bow and compensated pendulum, now silver plated, 73in (185cm).
£8,500-10,500 *C*

This pendulum compensation presumably a development from that in Ritchie's patent (see Rees, Clocks, Watches and Chronometers, 1819 20, republished extracts 1970, p.343, fig.9.).

An ebonised bracket clock, the brass dial signed John Ellicott, London, with date aperture and subsidiary strike, silent in the arch, the 5-pillared movement originally with verge escapement and pull quarter repeating, now fitted with dead beat escapement, 18thC, 20in (50cm).
£1,200-1,500   *P*

A George II quarter chiming bracket clock, the 7½in (18cm) brass dial with dials for regulation, date and strike/silent and inscribed Daniel Delander, London, 8-day striking 3-train fusee movement with verge escapement, 27in (67.5cm) overall.
£2,500-3,000   *DWB*

Daniel Delander, a famous maker, apprenticed in 1692, free of the Clockmakers Company, 1699, died in 1733, examples in many collections.

A late Stuart ebonised striking bracket clock, the 7in (17.5cm) dial signed John Harris London, the striking movement with 5-ringed pillars, pull quarter repeat on 5 bells and now converted to anchor escapement, 14½in (36cm).
£3,000-3,500   *C*

A tortoiseshell bracket clock by William Ferrer of Pontefract, with transitional arch dated 1707, with brass face, double fusee movement and original verge escapement, 14½in (36cm).
£3,000-5,000   *SBA*

An ebonised bracket clock, signed A. Dunlop, London, with date and mock pendulum apertures, harbored winding holes and strike, the 5-ringed pillared movement originally with pull quarter repeating on 3 bells, now missing, converted to anchor escapement, early 18thC, 16in (40cm).
£2,500-3,000   *P*

A Georgian ebonised bracket clock, signed Chas Howse, London, and with strike-silent in the arch, the twin fusee movement with anchor escapement, striking on a gong, 20in (50cm).
£700-800   *P*

A mid-Georgian ebonised striking bracket clock, the dial signed John Fladgate London, the twin fusee movement with verge escapement and profusely engraved backplate with pendulum hook, 18½in (46cm).
£1,500-2,000 *C*

HINTS TO DATING BRACKET CLOCKS

Dials

Square dial	to c1770	pre-George III
Broken arch dial	from c1720	George I or later
Round/painted/silvered	from c1760	George III or later

Case finish

Ebony veneer	from c1660 to c1850	Carolean to mid-Victorian
Walnut	from c1670 to c1870	Carolean to Victorian
Marquetry	from c1680 to c1740	Carolean to early Georgian
Rosewood	from c1790	from mid-Georgian
Lacquered	from c1700 to c1760	Queen Anne to early Georgian
Mahogany	from c1730	from early Georgian

A double fusee bracket clock, with strike/silent feature, prestigious maker, Frodsham, London, anchor escapement, c1820, 20in (50cm).
£1,100-1,400 *BL*

An ebony bracket clock by Christopher Gould, Little Moorfields, London, with double fusee movement and verge escapement, pull repeat on 6 bell c1720-25, 18½in (46cm).
£8,000-11,000 *SBA*

◁ A walnut cased bracket clock, having brass and silvered dial, inscribed Thomas Harrison, Liverpool, with chain fusee movement.
£650-750 *Pea*

An ebony veneered quarter repeating bracket clock, the 2-train 5-pillar fusee movement with verge escapement, signed Henry Fish, Royal Exchange, London, contained in a bell top case with glazed side panels, 17½in (43cm).
£3,000-3,500 *L*

Henry Fish, 4 Sweetings Alley, Royal Exchange, c1730. Britten says, probably the son of Henri Poisson.

A Charles II ebonised striking transitional bracket clock, twin fusee movement with outside countwheel strike, the backplate signed Henry Jones in the Strand, converted to anchor escapement but retaining original pendulum securing clip, and pull quarter repeat train removed, 12½in (31cm).
£6,000-7,000 *C*

An ebonised bracket timepiece, the 5-pillared movement with verge escapement, signed Jeffery Harris, London, 18thC, 17in (42.5cm).
£1,600-2,000 *P*

A mahogany bracket clock, signed Edwd. Moore, Oxford, the movement converted to anchor escapement with engraved backplate, late 18thC, 20½in (51cm), together with a later mahogany wall bracket.
£1,200-1,600 *P*

A George III mahogany bracket clock, the silvered dial inscribed John Skinner, Exon, 8-day striking fusee movement converted to anchor escapement, 21in (52.5cm) overall.
£1,000-1,200 *DWB*

John Skinner of Exeter, recorded working around 1780, died in 1818.

A rosewood bracket clock by Benjamin Lautier of Bath, the 8-day movement having double fusee, early 19thC, 17½in (43cm).
£2,000-2,500 *AGr*

An ebonised bracket clock, inscribed Philip Lloyd, Bristol, the bell striking repeating movement with anchor escapement, 18thC, 21in (52.5cm).
£800-1,000 *PWC*

A Regency brass mounted mahogany bracket clock, the painted dial signed James Murray, Royal Exchange, London, the movement with anchor escapement, 19½in (49cm).
£1,300-1,600 *P*

A single fusee mahogany bracket clock, maker John Nicholls, London, converted to anchor escapement, c1770, 15in (37.5cm).
£800-1,200 *BL*

An ebony and gilt brass mounted bracket clock, the 7in (17.5cm) brass dial signed J. Mondehare, Londini Fecit, the 5-tulip pillared movement with latched dial and plates, with replaced verge escapement and pull quarter repeating on 3 bells, 18thC, 15in (37.5cm).
£4,000-5,000 *P*

An ebonised bracket clock, with brass dial engraved Jasper Taylor, Holbourn, London, the 5-pillar movement with verge escapement, hour strike and engraved backplate, 18thC, 16in (41cm).
£1,750-2,250 *IAT*

A mahogany and brass decorated Regency bracket clock, the 7in (17.5cm) painted dial signed Thomas Pace, London, unusual twin fusee movement with circular plates, 4-pillar rack striking movement, 19in (47.5cm) overall.
£1,000-1,200 *Re*

A George III ebonised bracket clock, with brass dial, having 3-train movement striking on 2 bells, engraved brass movement by Justin Vulliamy, London, 12in (30cm).
£8,500-9,000 *BWe*

A Victorian bracket clock, with rosewood case and ormolu mountings, chime on bells and Westminster, c1880, 30in (75cm).
£1,000-1,300 *FHF*

A musical ormolu mounted mahogany bracket clock, the 3 train chain fusee movement with anchor escapement and chiming on 9 bells and 9 hammers, signed S. Williams, London, with chime selector in the arch for 'Song', 'Minuet', 'Cotillon' and 'Air', 20in (50cm).
£2,500-3,000 *L*

A mahogany veneered bracket clock, the movement with verge escapement, signed in the arch Richd. Ward, Winchester, with restorations, 18½in (46cm).
£1,800-2,200 *L*

Richard Ward is recorded in Winchester c1795.

A miniature ebony bracket clock by Samuel Watson, London, with pull repeat, 14-day duration, c1680, 13in (33cm).
£17,000-20,000 *SBA*

A large Victorian oak bracket clock, the double chain fusee movement with Westminster chimes striking on 8 bells and 5 gongs, 23in (58cm).
£600-700 *HSS*

A Regency mahogany and brass inlaid bracket clock, the white enamel dial inscribed J. Wells, 15 Hanway St, Oxford St, W.C., wire gong striking movement, 25in (62.5cm).
£900-1,100 *PWC*

A repeater musical bracket clock, fitted 8-day movement chiming on 8 bells and Westminster, late 19thC, 23in (57.5cm).
£1,200-1,600 *BS*

Make the most of Miller's

Every care has been taken to ensure the accuracy of descriptions and estimated valuations. Where an attribution is made within inverted commas (e.g. 'Chippendale') or is followed by the word 'style' (e.g. early Georgian style) it is intended to convey that, in the opinion of the publishers, the piece concerned is a later – though probably still antique – reproduction of the style so designated. Unless otherwise stated, any description which refers to 'a set', or 'a pair' includes a valuation for the entire set or the pair, even though the illustration may show only a single item.

A Regency ebony and brass mounted quarter chiming bracket clock, the painted dial with strike/silent, signed Wm. Wright, Ongar, with triple fusee movement, and anchor escapement striking the quarters on 8 bells, 25½in (64cm).
£1,200-1,800 *P*

A Victorian walnut quarter chiming bracket clock, with subsidiaries at the top for chime/silent, regulation and for Westminster or 8 bells, the triple fusee movement with anchor escapement, 31in (77.5cm).
£750-900 *P*

A brass mounted mahogany table or bracket clock, the French 8-day movement having half-hour striking on gongs, late 19thC, 17½in (43cm).
£300-350 *TKN*

A late Victorian 3-train brass inlaid rosewood clock and matching bracket, the fusee movement chiming the quarters on 8 bells and striking the hours on a gong, with Cambridge/Westminster selector, the clock 30in (75cm), 43in (108cm) overall.
£1,300-1,600 *TEN*

A Neuchatel black lacquered quarter striking bracket clock, the twin-train movement striking on 2 gongs, with enamel dial, with the matching wall bracket, 19thC, 37in (92.5cm).
£850-950 *P*

Clocks – Carriage

A French tortoiseshell, cut brass inlaid and ormolu mounted bracket clock, the 5-tulip pillared movement converted to anchor escapement, with rectangular plates and countwheel strike, with matching wall bracket, 18thC, 48in (122cm) overall.
£1,500-2,000 *P*

A Victorian ormolu mounted mahogany bracket clock, the strike/silent and chime selection with anchor movement, 27in (67.5cm).
£1,300-1,600 *Wor*

A tortoiseshell and silver carriage timepiece, with lever movement, the dial signed for Mappin & Webb, London, the silver marked London 1910, 5in (12.5cm).
£600-750 *P*

439

POINTERS FOR FRENCH CARRIAGE CLOCKS

★ appeared approx. 1850
★ the mechanism in unfinished state made in various French towns and assembled by makers in Paris
★ basic timepieces with various complications e.g. striking, repeating, quarter strike, alarm
★ English Carriage clocks made in French style but often superior in quality with less complex mechanisms
★ the name on the dial is most likely that of the vendor not the maker or assembler
★ best examples produced in the 1870s

A satinwood 'four glass' striking carriage clock, the square gilt dial signed Arnold & Dent London No. 408, the movement with split bi-metallic compensated balance to lever platform, double fusee, strike on gong with signed and numbered backplate, 8½in (22cm).
£3,500-4,500   C

An English carriage timepiece, the fusee movement with lever platform escapement and compensated balance, with maintaining power, signed on the backplate Clarke, London, 19thC, 5½in (14cm), with leather travelling case.
£750-950   P

Clocks

All clock measurements refer to height unless otherwise stated

An early Victorian gilt-metal carriage clock case in the manner of Thos. Cole, with a French carriage clock movement stamped Bolliver a Paris, with lever platform and strike on bell, 11½in (29cm).
£2,500-3,000   C

It is perhaps noteworthy that the earlier cases by Thos. Cole were not numbered.

An Empire ormolu chaise clock, the circular plated movement with curved barrel bridge on top plate, alarm and pull quarter repeat via polished steel hammers on now missing bell, converted to Savage 2-pin lever escapement, with stud feet, one now missing, and ring suspension, in a purpose-made Regency brass inlaid mantel case on ball feet and with carrying handle, 12in (30cm).
£2,000-3,000   C

Provenance: Traditionally bought by an army surgeon on the field after the battle of Waterloo as having been taken from Napoleon's carriage. Though it has no marks of having been in his possession, it is certainly of the quality and type that a leading member of the French staff at the battle might have possessed. With various letters relating to its history.

A champlevé enamel striking carriage clock, with bi-metallic balance to lever platform, strike/repeat on gong, 6½in (16.5cm).
£2,000-2,500   C

Locate the source

The source of each illustration in Miller's can be found by checking the code letters below each caption with the list of contributors.

A repeating carriage clock, with 3in (7.5cm) white enamelled dial signed Müller/Twickenham, the 8-day movement with compensated balance wheel, and lever escapement, 8in (20cm), with carrying case and key.
£400-500 *Bea*

A French repeater carriage clock, retailed by A. E. Halfhide, Wimbledon, 19thC, 7in (17.5cm).
£950-1,050 *BS*

A French gilt brass carriage clock, the lever movement striking on a gong with push repeat, the side panels and dial of pietra dura, 7in (18cm).
£1,500-2,000 *P*

A French brass carriage clock, the lever movement striking on a gong, with alarm and push repeat and bearing the trademark B in a circle, 19thC, 7½in (19cm).
£500-600 *P*

A gilt brass enamel mounted carriage clock, the movement with lever escapement, compensated balance, gong striking and repeating at will, with outer carrying case, 8in (20cm).
£700-900 *L*

A fine French striking and repeating carriage clock, with original lever escapement, by Henri Jacot, Paris, c1880, 7½in (19cm), with travelling case and key.
£1,100-1,300 *THG*

A French carriage clock, by Francois-Arsene Margaine, Paris, with half-hour repeater movement, the dial inscribed Hamilton & Co., Calcutta and Bombay, 6in (15cm), with morocco travelling case and key.
£450-550 *CDC*

A French brass carriage clock, 5in (12cm).
£150-200 *CEd*

A brass carriage clock, the movement with replaced lever escapement, now striking on a gong, with alarm and push repeat, 19thC, 7in (18cm).
£350-400 *P*

A French grande-sonnerie repeating carriage clock, the white enamel dial having numerals replaced by names 'Margaret' and 'Kate', having day, date and alarm subsidiary dials, the backplate stamped 'W.T. & Co.', 19thC, 6in (15cm), with original red morocco leather travelling case and key.
£1,400-1,700 *BS*

A French gilt brass carriage clock, the movement with replaced lever platform, striking on a bell, with push repeat and alarm, 19thC, 6in (15cm).
£550-650 *P*

An engraved oval alarum carriage clock, the enamel dial signed Tiffany & Co., New York, the striking movement with later lever platform, 6in (15cm).
£650-750 *Bon*

A gilt brass striking carriage clock, with uncut bi-metallic balance to silvered lever platform, strike/repeat on gong, stamp of Henri Jacot, 5½in (14cm).
£700-800 *C*

A rare ivory and marquetry panelled timepiece carriage clock, with platform escapement, the top panel signed with monogram FD, Bte, 5in (12cm).
£800-900 *C*

An Austrian gilt metal carriage clock, the lever movement with grande-sonnerie striking on 2 gongs, with alarm and push repeat, 19thC, 6in (15cm).
£550-750 *P*

Clocks – Mantel

A calendar carriage timepiece, the movement with cylinder platform, 5in (12cm).
£400-450 *Bon*

A French repeating alarum carriage clock, with the inscription 'Chedel, Paris', over a subsidiary alarm dial, striking the hours and half-hours on a single bell, with repeat mechanism, 7in (17.5cm), in leather covered carrying case.
£900-1,100 *HSS*

A Regency black slate and gilt bronze mantel timepiece, the fusee movement signed on the backplate Grimalde & Johnson, 431 Strand, London, 11in (28cm).
£1,000-1,200 *P*

A large Victorian black marble 8-day striking clock, with brass commemorative plaque bearing the date 1891.
£100-120   *CBS*

A Georgian ebonised balloon clock, the restored enamel dial signed Leroux, Charing Cross, the fusee movement with shaped plates and anchor escapement, 21in (53cm).
£1,300-1,700   *P*

A Regency ormolu mantel timepiece, the machined gilt metal signed Tupman, London, the single train fusee movement with anchor escapement signed Tupman, Gt Russell Street, London, 8in (21cm).
£450-550   *Bon*

A Regency rosewood timepiece, by Barraud, Cornhill, London, No. 1285, with 8-day fusee movement, 10in (25cm).
£750-850   *DWB*

A Regency mantel clock, with 6in (15cm) white painted dial inscribed Thompson & Shellwell/Manchester, the 8-day movement with anchor escapement and gut fusee going train, 16in (40cm), with pendulum and keys.
£500-600   *Bea*

A terrestrial globe mantel timepiece, the sphere rotating with a fixed 24-hour chapter and signed The Empire Clock, Patent 19460, 11½in (29cm).
£650-750   *P*

A Regency red marble and gilt metal mantel timepiece, by Vulliamy, London 598, the fusee movement with half deadbeat escapement, 12in (31cm).
£1,400-1,700   *C*

A rosewood mantel clock, the 5-pillared fusee movement with anchor escapement, signed on the backplate J. & W. Mitchell, Glasgow, 19thC, 13in (33cm).
£1,000-1,300 *P*

A black slate, bronze and gilt metal mounted mantel timepiece, the fusee movement with anchor escapement and rise and fall regulation, signed Vulliamy, London, 510, 19thC, 12½in (32cm).
£3,500-4,000 *P*

A gilt bronze mantel clock, the twin fusee movement with anchor escapement, signed Payne, 163 New Bond Street, 19thC, 13½in (33cm).
£900-1,000 *P*

A burr walnut mantel timepiece, signed John Walker, London, 3202, the fusee movement with anchor escapement signed on the backplate, 19thC, 9½in (24cm).
£600-700 *P*

A French Louis XV black boule clock, 39in (97.5cm).
£2,000-2,300 *EA*

A slate cased regulator mantel clock, signed Howell & Co., 19thC, 15½in (39cm).
£550-600 *JMW*

A Victorian carved oak mantel clock, 3-train spring driven movement, quarter striking and repeating on 8 gongs, 23in (57.5cm).
£350-400 *Re*

A Louis XVI marble and ormolu mantel clock, the circular movement mounted between two Ionic pilasters, the movement with countwheel strike, 28in (70cm).
£2,600-3,000 *P*

A French boulle mantel clock, the 2-train movement with embossed gilt dial and white enamel numeral reserves, 23in (57.5cm).
£650-750 *Bon*

A French tortoiseshell and cut brass inlaid mantel clock, the gilt dial with enamel numerals, signed Gaudron A Paris, the movement with anchor escapement and square plates signed on the back, 18thC, 20in (50cm).
£1,600-2,000 *P*

An ormolu mantel timepiece, containing a calendar verge watch movement with Continental bridge cock and diamond endstone, 12in (30cm).
£450-500 *Bon*

A French ormolu mantel timepiece, 19thC, 9½in (23cm).
£550-650 *P*

A late Empire bronze, ormolu and griotte marble mantel clock, 31in (77cm).
£1,200-1,700 *C*

A French red marble perpetual calendar mantel clock and barometer, the movement with Brocot type suspension, and bell striking, 2 thermometers, both tubes defective, 18½in (46cm).
£800-900 *L*

A French ormolu mantel clock, the movement with Brocot escapement, perpetual calendar and moon phase, maker Martin Basketh, 19thC, 17in (42.5cm).
£2,600-3,000 *BS*

A French mantel clock, the striking skeleton movement by J. Valery, Paris, 19thC.
£120-180 *MN*

A French Empire striking clock, the 4in (10cm) enamel face having exposed escapement wheel, the movement with outside countwheel, 21in (52.5cm).
£600-700 *AGr*

A French red marble and bronze mantel clock, the case of Louis XVI style, in the form of an urn surmounted by a pineapple finial, 19thC, 33in (82.5cm).
£3,000-3,500 *P*

A French green boulle mantel clock, with ormolu mounts, countwheel striking on a bell, 13in (33cm).
£600-750 *IAT*

A French mantel clock, with 3in (7.5cm) diam. white enamelled dial inscribed Engler à Bordeaux, 8-day movement by Pons (De-Paul) with outside countwheel, striking the hours and half-hours on a bell, dial cracked, glazed door cracked, 16in (40cm).
£450-500 *Bea*

A French mystery clock, 23in (57.5cm).
£1,500-2,000 *CBS*

An ornate metal elephant clock, with 8-day chiming movement, outside countweel, 21in (52.5cm).
£650-700 *AGr*

A gilt metal mantel clock, in the form of an elaborate Gothic tower, the works with outside countwheel and maker Raingo, Paris, mid-19thC, 28in (70cm).
£700-800 *AGr*

A gilt metal striking mantel clock, with outside countwheel in the form of a Gothic arch, mid-19thC, 20½in (51cm).
£750-850 *AGr*

A French alabaster and gilt metal mantel clock, the movement winding through the face and striking on a single bell, numbered 5754, 19thC.
£350-400 *HSS*

A French porcelain mantel clock, with 8-day striking movement, the dial inscribed Raingo Freres, Paris, 19thC, 15in (37.5cm).
£250-300 *CDC*

A French mantel clock, in white marble ormolu mounted case, late 19thC.
£450-550 *MIL*

A South German negro automaton clock, the brass octagonal movement with twin resting bells, basically mid-17thC, 11½in (28cm).
£4,000-5,000 *C*

A Louis XV style mantel clock, with white enamelled dial signed Meunier à Paris, having an 8-day spring-driven striking movement, 19thC, 22½in (56cm).
£1,300-1,600 *TKN*

Clocks – Lantern

A Charles II brass cased lantern clock with 30-hour striking verge movement, inscribed Jos. Norris Abingdon, c1670.
£1,700-2,000 *WW*

An English lantern clock, unsigned, with original verge escapement and original alarmwork, c1700, 16in (40cm).
£800-1,200 *BL*

Clocks – Skeleton

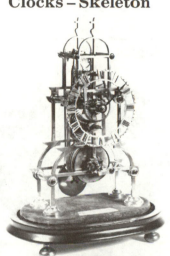

An English skeletonised fusee clock, with anchor escapement.
£450-650 *POT*

l. A brass skeleton timepiece with strike and chain drive under dome, 15in (37.5cm).
£250-300
r. An Orrery clock under glass dome, limited edition numbered 259.
£250-300 *Wor*

A small Victorian brass skeleton clock, with fusee movement.
£450-500 *JD*

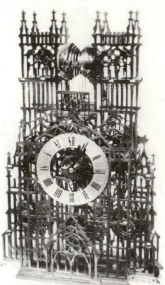

A massive brass 3-train 'Westminster Abbey' skeleton clock, striking on gong and nest of 8 bells having mercury pendulum, by W.F. Evans and Sons, Soho Clock Factory, Handsworth, under oval dome, 24in (60cm).
£4,500-5,000 *AGr*

A brass skeleton clock, the ▷ twin chain and fusee movement with anchor escapement striking on a bell above, with wood rod pendulum, on oval wooden stand and glass dome, 19½in (49cm).
£900-1,100 *CSK*

◁ A brass skeleton clock, 8-day movement with 'one at the hour' strike on a steel bell, 17½in (44cm).
£400-500 *HSS*

Clocks – Wall

A mid-Georgian black japanned tavern or Act of Parliament clock, signed Robert Allam London on the 30in (75cm) dial, the timepiece movement with tapered plates and anchor escapement, 59in (147.5cm).
£4,500-5,000 *C*

An adapted George III brass ▷ mounted mahogany wall clock, with anchor escapement and rack strike to the fusee movement, signed Dutton London 3 on backplate, the 14in (35cm) dial signed Mattw. & Willm. Dutton London, 38in (95cm).
£1,500-2,000 *C*

The cast brass foliate volute mounts have parallels with the mounts on various barometers by Tompion

An Act of Parliament clock, decorated in red and gilt in a chinoiserie landscape, with 8-day movement, 18thC, 54in (134cm).
£650-700 *HSS*

A drop dial wall clock by Birkle ▷ Bros. Commercial Rd, London, with fusee movement, in mahogany case, c1870, 19in (48cm).
£250-350 *IAT*

A George III 8-day wall clock, the verge movement with a dial inscribed Gray and Reynolds, Wimborne, 16in (40cm).
£1,500-2,000   *WW*

A fusee wall dial clock, maker Rhodes & Son, Bradford, with mahogany surround, c1860, 15in (38cm) diam.
£150-300   *BL*

A drop pendulum wall clock, with papier mâché case, inlaid with mother-of-pearl, with 8-day movement, striking on single gong, 28in (70cm).
£200-250   *WIL*

HINTS TO DATING WALL CLOCKS

Dials

Square	to c1755	George II or later
Broken arch	from c1720 to c1805	early to late Georgian
Painted/round	from c1740	George II or later
Silvered	from c1760	George III or later

Case finish

Ebony veneer	from c1690	to William and Mary
Marquetry	from c1680 to c1695	from Carolean to William and Mary
Mahogany	from c1740	from early Georgian
Oak	always	

A German drop dial wall clock, in a walnut case, striking on a gong, c1900, 24in (61cm).
£150-250   *IAT*

A wall clock, having 8-day striking movement, in a floral painted papier mâché case with mother-of-pearl inlay, 19thC.
£280-340   *SL*

A Liverpool wall clock, by Sewill, maker to the Royal Navy, mounted in oak case, 40in (100cm) long.
£150-200   *WIL*

l A walnut and ebonised 8-day weight-driven 2-train Vienna regulator, 'The Farringdon Regulator', 48in (122cm).
£550-650
c A Continental 8-day mahogany weight-driven 2-train Vienna regulator, 58in (145cm).
£350-400
r A walnut and ebonised 8-day weight-driven 2-train Vienna regulator, 42in (107.5cm).
£400-500 *AGr*

A late Biedermeier rosewood Vienna regulator, stamped Crot Berlin 302, with weight-driven movement with deadbeat escapement, 39½in (98cm).
£850-950 *C*

△
A triple-weight Vienna regulator wall clock, in a walnut case, with grande sonnerie striking, c1870, 51in (129cm).
£1,300-1,500 *IAT*

A Dutch walnut Zaanklok, decorated with the motto Nu Elck Syn Sin, the brass movement with decorative 3-spoked wheels, Dutch striking and verge escapement, and alarm, 18thC, 29in (72.5cm).
£2,200-2,800 *P*

◁ An ash and maple double weight Vienna regulator, with architectural pediment, c1840.
£1,500-1,800 *SBA*

A cartel clock in the Louis XV style, the 2-train movement with
▽ countwheel strike on a bell, some damage to chapters, late 19thC, 30in (75cm).
£600-700 *HSS*

A walnut cased Vienna regulator, signed H. Samuel, Manchester, c1860, 48in (120cm).
£450-500 *JMW*

A Louis XVI ormolu cartel timepiece, the movement with pull quarter repeating work, incomplete, the enamel dial signed Hans A Paris, 18in (45cm).
£350-400 *P*

A Black Forest automaton wall clock, an aperture above revealing 3 jacks quarter-chiming on bells, mounted above a red roofed building, the 3-train movement of traditional form, with restorations, 19thC, 20½in (50cm).
£2,000-2,500 *Bon*

A Dutch East Friesland wall clock.
£1,200-1,500 *TAY*

A Continental striking cartel clock, 25½in (63cm).
£650-700 *AGr*

A Dutch marquetry Staartklok, with 11in (27.5cm) painted dial, now fitted with an English 8-day longcase clock movement, case deepened to accommodate movement, 52in (130cm).
£2,000-2,500 *Bon*

Clocks – Garniture

◁ A French gilt brass and enamel clock garniture, the lever movement striking on a gong, numbered 5752, 19thC, 10½in (26cm), together with a matching pair of side urns.
£650-750 *P*

A white marble and gilt metal 3-piece clock set, the French movement chiming on a gong, makers J. Marti and Cie, 23in (57.5cm).
£950-1,200 *AGr*

A French ormolu and bronze clock garniture, 19thC, 17in (42.5cm), with matching pair of side urns.
£1,000-1,300 *P*

An English quarter chiming gilt brass clock garniture, the 3-train chain fusee movement with anchor escapement, chiming the quarters on 8 bells and striking the hours on a coiled steel gong, signed on the backplate J.C. Jennens & Son, 25-26 Great Sutton St. London, 18in (45cm).
£700-800 *L*

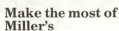

A French porcelain mounted mantel clock garniture, 2-train movement by Japy Freres, 18in (45cm), with a pair of associated gilt metal urns, 13½in (33cm).
£550-650 *Bon*

Make the most of Miller's

Miller's is completely different each year. Each edition contains completely NEW photographs. This is not an updated publication. We never repeat the same photograph.

A French ormolu mounted tortoiseshell clock set of Louis XV design, retailed by R & W Sorley, Paris, the clock 23in (57.5cm).
£1,000-1,200 *CEd*

A pale royal rouge marble and ormolu 3-piece clock set, 34in (85cm).
£6,500-7,000 *AGr*

A French silver plated brass 3-piece clock garniture, 19thC.
£500-600 *PWC*

A French bronze and ormolu 3-piece clock garniture, the bell striking movement inscribed Charpentier, Ft. de Bronzes, 283 à Paris, 19thC, 35½in (88cm), the side pieces inscribed with the initials V.P. beneath a crown, 37in (92.5cm).
£4,000-5,000 *PWC*

Clocks – Table

A gilt brass strut timepiece in the manner of Thomas Cole, the dial signed for Hunt & Roskell, London, the movement with lever escapement and plain gold 3-arm balance, 19thC, 6in (15cm).
£500-600 *P*

A gilt brass strut timepiece, the dial signed for Carrington & Co, 130 Regent St, the movement with lever escapement with compensated balance and overcoil spring, the reverse engraved W.V. (probably Wilhelm Vasel) 19thC, 8in (20cm).
£500-700 *P*

Clocks – Miscellaneous

A German gilt brass octagonal table clock, the movement with chain fusee for the going and resting barrel for the rack strike and repeat, verge escapement with spring balance, eared pierced cock and foot on top plate signed L. Petitot, Berlin, early 18thC, 4in (11cm) diam.
£3,200-3,800 *C*

L. Letitot, a Huguenot émigré to Germany, working 1700-1725 (see Abeler).

A French musical automata clock, the base mounted with a clock movement, containing a Swiss musical movement, 19thC, 34in (85cm).
£1,800-2,200 *P*

A three-dimensional wood model picture clock showing French Chateau, windmill and farmhouse with bridge in centre, complete with music box revolving windmill, 21½in (53cm).
£1,300-1,700 *AGr*

A London and North Western Railways signal box timepiece in mahogany case, 6in (15cm).
£200-250 *ONS*

A British Railways dial clock, with fusee movement, in a mahogany case.
£100-200 *IAT*

A Japanese pillar clock, the weight-driven movement with verge and balance wheel escapement, movement with replacement wheel and case lacking drawer at base of trunk, 20in (50cm).
£600-700 *L*

A George III large turret clock movement by Aynsworth and John Thwaites, London for Lees Court, Kent, with anchor escapement, 3-train, ting tang quarter and hour strike, 2 winding cranks, 4 leading off rods and a box of pulleys, 46in (115cm).
£1,800-2,200 *C*

Originally made for Hon. Lewis Thomas Watson, later 2nd Baron Sondes, Lees Court, Faversham, Kent, with photocopy of Thwaites's day book entry relating to this clock (original deposited at Guildhall Library, London).

An Edwardian novelty timepiece, modelled as a ship's steering wheel, with easel back, Chester, 1909.
£160-200 *P*

A fine rosewood clock, inlaid with various fruitwoods, late 19thC, 18in (45cm).
£500-550 *SD*

An English dial, the 14in (35cm) brass dial signed John Neve, Hingham, the verge escapement in tapering plates, 16½in (41cm) diam.
£1,600-1,900 *Bon*

A French 'Reims' cathedral clock, the movement with Brocot type suspension and gong striking, 21½in (53cm).
£1,600-1,700 *L*

A rare German 'talking clock' movement by Gustav Becker, with plated cast plates and train, the massive spring barrel, train and diaphragm geared to the roller mechanism with fragment of original tape giving the time in German every half hour, the vertically mounted horn of papier mâché.
£650-800 *C*

Stick

A mahogany stick barometer, the silvered brass plate signed J. Patrick, London, mounted with a thermometer the silvered plate with scale engraved Extream Cold/Extream Hot, restored, early 18thC, 39in (97.5cm).
£2,000-2,500 *CSK*

A Georgian mahogany stick barometer, the brass plate signed Wisker York, 36in (90cm).
£450-500 *CSK*

A mahogany ships barometer, the ivory plates unsigned, 36in (90cm).
£850-950 *CSK*

A mahogany wheel barometer, the 12in (30cm) silvered dial engraved with scrolls, with level signed Pastorelli, No. 156 Holborn, London, Timepiece, Thermometer, hygrometer, mid-19thC, 48in (121cm).
£1,000-1,200 *CSK*

A mahogany stick barometer, the silvered brass plate signed Palmer, London, the boxwood and ebony strung case inset with boxwood paterae, the case with hydrometer and swan neck pediment, 19thC, 42in (105cm).
£1,700-2,000 *CSK*

Wheel

A George III mahogany clock barometer, with boxwood edging and inlaid with shell motifs, signed Wm. Ticadell(?) Glasgow, the 10in (25cm) silvered registered dial of 'regulator' pattern, signed W. Cooper Hamilton with subsidiary clock and date of month dials, the clock movement of Sedan type with verge escapement, plain steel balance and signed Jas. Jarvis, London No.709, 44in (110cm).
£3,000-3,500 *CSK*

A rosewood wheel barometer, with unusual 6in (15cm) dial, level signed Limbach, Hull, with thermometer, hygrometer, 19thC, 38½in (96cm).
£350-400 *CSK*

A bird's-eye maple wheel barometer, with silvered 8in (20cm) dial level signed J. Cetta, Stroudwater, mirror, thermometer, and hygrometer, 39in (97.5cm).
£500-600 *CSK*

Chronometers

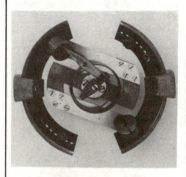

A rare two-day Victorian marine Chronometer with 'Hartnup's Balance', the silvered dial signed Thos. Russell & Son, Makers to the Queen, 30 & 32 Slater Street, Liverpool, No.6626, 10.5cm diam. of dial.
£4,500-5,000 *C*

The Hartnup balance, unique in design and construction, was invented by John Hartnup, the Liverpool Observatory's first director, appointed in 1843. As distinct from the Chronometer Department at Greenwich, primarily concerned with rating and purchase of chronometers for Government service, one of Hartnup's chief tasks was the rating of chronometers for merchant ships and he soon became concerned with the problem of 'middle temperature error'. The

Liverpool maker, William Shepherd, made the prototype of Hartnup's balance probably in 1847. After very successful trials at Liverpool, Hartnup contacted Airy, the Astronomer Royal, at Greenwich. Three Shepherd chronometers with Hartnup's balance were tried there in 1848. The Greenwich trials were not as favourable as those at Liverpool and Hartnup then questioned the mode of testing at Greenwich. Airy, no stranger to disputes, hotly defended Greenwich, enlisting Sheepshanks's aid in the Notices of the R.A.S. Sheepshanks's editorial comments contributed to the commercial failure of Hartnup's balance. As confirmed by Gould, it was never generally used, and therefore extant examples are very rare.

An eight-day Marine Chronometer by Victor Kullberg, the spotted movement with Earnshaw type spring detent escapement, the freesprung balance with Kullberg's auxiliary compensation.
£8,000-9,000 *P*

A two-day Marine Chronometer, the movement with Earnshaw type spring detent escapement, signed William Farquhar, Tower Hill, London, Q/7, in a brass bowl.
£1,200-1,400 *P*

Dials

An unusual Italian brass azimuth compass dial, late 17th/early 18thC, 9in (23cm) square.
£1,200-1,500 *CSK*

A brass universal equinoctial ring dial by R. Glynne, London, 4½in (12cm) diam., in chamois lined leather covered case with gilt tooled decoration to the lid.
£2,700-3,000 *CSK*

A ?German Planispheric Astrolabe, not signed or dated, gilt brass and silver, diam. 6.7cm, ?c1600, The Rete of silver, for 35 stars, two plates, for latitudes 46°, 49°, 52° and 55°, the alidade, rule, bolt and nut appear to be original.
£13,000-16,000 *CSK*

Considering its small size, this astrolabe is well engraved and detailed. It closely resembles a gilt brass and silver astrolabe not signed or dated, in the Museum of the History of Science, Oxford, of which the wider limb increases the diameter to 6.9cm (C.C.A.no.275; see Robert G. Gunther, Astrolabes of the World, 2 vols, Oxford, 1932, repr. London, 1976, vol.II, no.275 & illus.). Both instruments may be attributed to the workshop which produced the astrolabes and other instruments signed by Johann Anton Lynden, a citizen and goldsmith of Heilbronn. The dated instruments signed by Lynden are sun dials and range from 1594 to 1606.

A brass universal equinoctial ring dial, unsigned, late 18thC, 3in (8cm) diam.
£400-450 *CSK*

A brass universal equinoctial ring dial, 3½in (9.2cm) diam., in a gold galloon edged chamois lined leather case, blind stamped with rocaille.
£7,500-8,500 *CSK*

Possibly from the circle of Brander bearing his fleur-de-lys mark and the mark(?) of another maker.

A brass mechanical equinoctial dial, by Thomas Wright, 18thC.
£2,500-3,000 *DWB*

Globes

An 18in (45cm) terrestrial globe, by W. & A. K. Johnson, dated 1888, 26in (66cm) high.
£1,500-2,000 *CSK*

A German 12¾in terrestrial globe, by J. G. Klinger, with engraved brass meridian, globe defective, 18thC.
£850-950 *CSK*

A pair of 18in Dudley Adams terrestrial and celestial globes, signed 'D. Adams, 60 Fleet St., London, 1809', printed with Latin and English names, and the routes of explorers, lacks equatorial zodiac ring, 41½in (107cm) high overall, early-19thC.
£9,000-10,000 *P*

Surveying

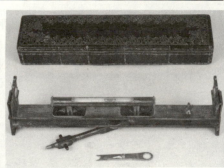

A library 12in terrestrial globe, signed by Bardin, London, with label of Bate, London, pasted over, 1802, the globe bearing a cartouche with the following inscription: 'The new 12in British Terrestrial Globe, representing the accurate positions of the principal known places of the earth, from the discoveries of CAPTAIN COOK and subsequent circumnavigators to the present period, 1802'. The globe is corrected with the additions to the year 1807. 30in (76cm) high, 12in (31cm) diam. of globe, 17in (43cm) diam. of globe with horizon ring.
£2,800-3,200   *TP*

Thomas M. Bardin was a globe maker who flourished between the years 1806–1827. His address is given by E. G. R. Taylor as 16 Salisbury Square, Fleet Street, London. Robert Brettell Bate is listed as being at 20–21 Poultry, London. In 1807 Bate was apprenticed and must have started in business about 1815. Bate was a well-known instrument maker and was famous for his nautical instruments; he made an artificial horizon, which could be attached to any sextant. See E. G. R. Taylor, Mathematical Practitioners of Hanoverian England, *p.355.*

A fine theodolite-stand and compass-table, signed 'G. F. Brander fecit Aug. Vind.', calibrated with three scales for Cathetus, Basis and Gradius, the limb traversing the 360° horizontal scale with vernier scale and micrometer adjustment screw and clamp, 9in (23cm) diam. of table.
£5,000-6,000   *CSK*

No similar theodolite compass-table is recorded in Brachner.

A black enamelled and lacquered brass theodolite, signed 'J. Casartelli Manchester', 13in (34cm) high.
£450-500   *CSK*

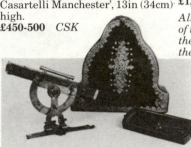

A fine part theodolite, signed 'G.F. Brander fecit Aug.Vind', with rare or unique mahogany barrelled telescope of square section with brass endpieces, mounted with bubble level, and with unusual facility for removing the lens units via latches to one side, 13in (33cm) length of scope.
£7,000-8,000   *CSK*

A surveyor's lacquered brass level attributed to the Brander workshop, unsigned, 11¼in (29cm) wide.
£1,500-2,000   *CSK*

Although unsigned, the construction of this instrument and decoration of the case suggest it being a product of the Brander workshop.

A lacquered brass level, signed 'Hyde, Bristol', with rack and pinion focusing, level and cross bubble, ray shade and dust cap, with trade label for Henry Husband and a mirror in the original mahogany case, 14in (36cm) wide.
£150-200   *CSK*

A rare lacquered brass distance measuring instrument, the drum-type tubular body signed 'G.F. Brander fecit Aug Vind', with a surviving glass micrometer, the eye-piece protected by a red glass shade, in the original fruitwood case, 11¼in (28.5cm) high.
£1,800-2,400   *CSK*

It has been suggested that only one other micrometer glass survives in a distance meter of this type. Although principally a distance finder, this instrument was designed to be used also as a camera obscura and lucida.

An ebony framed octant, with inset ivory scale and unsigned makers cartouche, in mahogany case, early 19thC, index arm radius 9½in (24cm).
£350-400   *CSK*

A brass sextant with telescope, five shades, mirror and detachable rosewood handle, signed 'Northen Hull', 6in (15cm) across the index arm with vernier, lacks magnifier, 3½in (9cm) radius, with one telescope, in mahogany case, early 19thC, 7in (18cm) wide.
£800-1,000   *P*

Microscopes

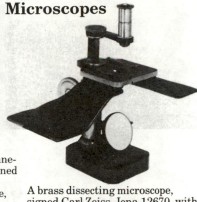

An oxydised brass three circled frame sextant, signed 'Cox & Coombs, Devenport, Plymouth, No.3460', with four index glass and three horizon glass coloured shades, sun inverting and star telescopes, in mahogany box with trade label of George Lee, 33 The Hard, Portsea, index arm radius 6¼in (16cm).
£350-400 *CSK*

A rare surveyors set of brass plane-table triangulation dividers, signed and dated 'I. De Cranendonck M.F.A. 1607', 15½in (39cm) wide, fully opened.
£4,000-5,000 *CSK*

A brass dissecting microscope, signed Carl Zeiss, Jena 12670, with swivel mirror, the stage fitted with 2 leather covered rests, in original case, 19thC, 6¾in (17cm) high.
£180-220 *CSK*

Telescopes

rare lacquered brass miniature refracting telescope, signed Dollond, London', the 1¼in (3cm) lens covered with a screw on dust cap, 4in (9.8cm) long body tube with single graduated draw tube, the eye-piece with rotating wheel of four lens powers, in the original fishskin covered card case, late 18thC, 5in (12.5cm) long.
£1,500-1,800 *CSK*

A brass microscope by Smith, Beck & Beck, complete with lenses, in mahogany case, late 19thC.
£300-350 *RBB*

A lacquered brass 'Martin' type drum microscope, the draw tube signed Gogerty 72 Fleet St. London, with a set of 6 numbered objectives, slides, forceps and bull's-eye condenser, case 11in (28cm) wide.
£250-300 *CSK*

A lacquered brass 3in (7.5cm) refracting telescope by Clarkson's, Holborn, the 36½in (92.5cm) long body tube with rack and pinion focusing, with sighting accessories in the original case, late 19thC, 40in (102cm) wide.
£500-600 *CSK*

A brass simple microscope, unsigned, with 3 objectives, 18thC, the case 5in (13cm) wide.
£220-280 *CSK*

POINTERS FOR TELESCOPES

★ first telescopes developed from 1605 to 1608
★ 17thC refracting models made of vellum with horn binding
★ 1758 Dolland developed lens for day and night vision
★ 18thC has greatest appeal for collectors as everything was hand made
★ 18thC barrels made of mahogany, brass for metal parts
★ 19thC plainer style, machine produced
★ Instruments still widely available. Currently excellent investment potential for 18thC and good 19thC examples

A brass reflecting telescope, in the manner of G.F. Brander, unsigned, the 1¾in (4.5cm) diam. body tube 8¼in (21cm) long, with screw rod focusing, in original walnut case, 11½in (29cm) wide, the interior lined with Augsburg red marbled finished paper as used by G.F. Brander.
£2,700-3,000 *CSK*

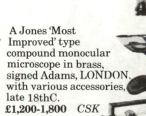

A Jones 'Most Improved' type compound monocular microscope in brass, signed Adams, LONDON, with various accessories, late 18thC.
£1,200-1,800 *CSK*

A 'Culpeper' type microscope, unsigned, early 19thC, base 3¼in (8cm) diam.
£500-600 *TP*

It appears that this small size of 'Culpeper' type microscope was introduced by W. & S. Jones in about 1798. See G. L'E. Turner, Collecting Microscopes, p.42.

A Victorian lacquered brass binocular microscope, probably by Smith and Beck, with the trade plaque of Hesketh Walker, Liverpool, objectives, oculars and live box, in fitted case, c1890, 23in (58cm) high.
£550-600 *Re*

A brass compound monocular microscope, signed J.B. Dancer Optician Manchester, with bull's-eye condenser, 8 objectives, 2 Watson illuminators, 3 eye-pieces, other accessories and items in the original mahogany case, 19thC, 16in (41cm) high.
£450-600 *CSK*

A Victorian brass binocular microscope by C. Coleman, 77 Great Titchfield Street, London, with 2 oculars, 2 object lenses, 2 prismatic attachments, in a fitted mahogany case, 19in (48cm) high overall.
£550-750 *Re*

A pocket monocular microscope, the limb signed Cary, London, with accessories in mahogany case, early 19thC, 3¾in (9.5cm) wide, inset with mounting thread.
£250-300 *P*

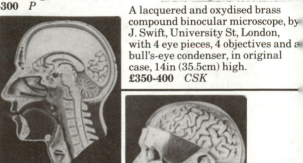

A lacquered and oxydised brass compound binocular microscope, by J. Swift, University St, London, with 4 eye pieces, 4 objectives and a bull's-eye condenser, in original case, 14in (35.5cm) high.
£350-400 *CSK*

Medical Instruments

A Smellie's perforator, signed S. Moore & Son & Thompson, London, c1870, 14in (36cm).
£500-600 *TP*

A plaster relief anatomical model of the head, coloured and with numbered labels for the organs, veins and muscles, 13in (33cm) high, and a companion model similarly mounted.
£500-600 *CSK*

A Georgian mahogany domestic medicine chest, the lid rising to reveal compartments with 4 large jars having brass caps, a pewter double measure and funnel, a spatular, a cautery iron and a balance, the rear door enclosing a poison compartment with 8 glass bottles with stoppers, 10in (26cm) wide.
£550-600 *CSK*

A walnut homoeopathic domestic medicine chest, by Allshorn, 51 Edgware Road, 19thC, the chest 8½in (21cm) wide.
£250-300 *CSK*

A demonstration model head, originally with a glass dome over the model, now lacking, the model consisting of a human cranium with all the vessels, main arteries; nerves being replaced using coloured wax, the eyes made of glass, the teeth natural, the right side of the cranium being hinged in order to allow a view of the blood vessels, the nerves and tissues, the eyes, nose, mouth, etc, Paris, late 19thC, 17in (43cm) high maximum, the base 9in (23cm).
£1,800-2,000 *TP*

A walnut homoeopathic domestic medicine chest, by Thompson & Capper, with 50 medicine bottles, 2 small powder compartments and a copy of Ruddock: Homoeopathic Vade Mecum Medical & Surgical; the 2 drawers below containing a collection of bottles with original labels, late 19thC.
£350-400 *CSK*

A surgeon's travelling instrument case, signed Evans of Old Fish Street, London, with 3 sections of surgeon's instruments, c1855.
£2,300-2,800 *TP*

A pair of Murphy's craniotomy forceps in steel with ebony grips, signed Wood, c1850, 13in (33cm) long.
£450-500 *TP*

A mahogany and brass mounted domestic medicine chest, applied with a label for William R. Hoare, Successor to Squire, 121 Cornwall Rd, Bayswater, 19thC, the chest 10in (26cm) wide.
£850-950 *CSK*

A fine set of surgeon's amputation knives and accessories by Evans & Wormall, 31 Stamford St, Blackfriars, London, with 6 Liston knives, 4 trocar and connulae in fitted case, the lid with a brass plaque engraved B.W. Vince, Saffron Walden, England, late 19thC, 17in (43cm) wide.
£700-800 *CSK*

A monaural stethoscope of ebonised wood, late 19thC. 2⅛in by 6⅜in (5.5 by 16cm).
£200-250 *TP*

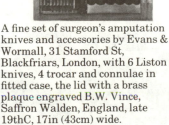

A Staffordshire jar for Leeches, inscribed in gilt over dark pink decoration, 10½in (26cm) high.
£1,400-1,600 *CSK*

An amputation set, including a large Liston's knife and a double-edged Lisfranc's knife, a hook, a saw, a metacarpal saw and Petit's screw tourniquet, each knife stamped Blackwell, of 3 Bedford Court, London, mid-19thC, in a fitted case, 17in (43cm) wide.
£350-400 *P*

An inhaler, with a pressed copper label with the inscription ▷ 'Alformant R.L.P. The Formalin Hygienic Company Limited', c1900, 10in (25cm) high.
£80-100 *TP*

◁

A brass fountain enema, embossed brass maker's plate and coat-of-arms, Salt & Son, Cutlers to the Queen, Surgical Instrument Manufacturers, Birmingham, mid-19thC, 10in (24.5cm) high.
£140-180 *P*

1. An unusual pair of blued steel framed 'D' folding sides clear glass 'railway' spectacles, in a later case. **£120-150**

2. A good pair of tortoiseshell 'D' folding sides spectacles with blue and blue-green shades and silver turnpin sides, in a later case, 19thC. **£350-400**

3. An unusual pair of prismatic reading spectacles, in original case. **£25-35**

4. A pair of Chinese brass rimless spectacles, with ornamental double hinged folding sides, pale brown quartz lenses, in a later case. **£200-250 CSK**

An ear trumpet, signed F.C. Rein & Son Sole Inventor and Patentees 108 Strand, London, the trumpet silver-plated with a turned ivory earpiece, in original leather case with velvet and silk lining, c1860, 4 by 2½in (10 by 6cm). **£800-900 TP**

A cast metal inhaler, together with the original bottle of fluid called Cresolene made by the Vapo-Cresolene Company of 180 Fulton Street, New York, U.S.A., c1900, 7 by 2½in (18 by 7cm). **£80-100 TP**

The front of the bottle bears a label 'POISON' and advises those who have taken an accidental dose to take a large glass of whisky or brandy, vinegar or alcohol. If it falls on the skin, apply the same.

Dental Instruments

A set of dental instruments, signed C. Ash & Sons, England, including a selection of probes and scalers with smooth handles, silver ferrules and steel implements, an ebony-handled mirror, a tooth key, 2 pairs of molar forceps, 3 stump elevators and a pocket knife with various scalpels, c1870. **£1,300-1,600 TP** ▷

A dental scaling kit, comprising 6 steel instruments with tortoiseshell handles, and a pair of scissors in the form of a stork, early 19thC. **£300-350 P**

A selection of demonstration wax teeth in 2 glazed cases, c1900, each measuring 10 by 12in (25 by 30cm). **£800-1,000 TP**

Miscellaneous

A fine lacquered brass gyroscope, ▷ signed Newton & Co Opticians & Globe Makers to the Queen. 3 Fleet St, Temple Bar London, 19thC, 9½in (24cm) wide. **£450-500 CSK**

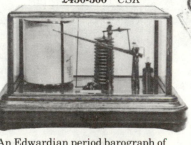

A brass and steel drawing compendium comprising dividers, tripod dividers, double-pen, dividers scale rules, pens, a protractor, square, proportional dividers and sector signed Baradelle A Paris, in original simulated fishskin cover case, 90% complete, 18thC, 9in (23cm) wide. **£1,500-1,800 CSK**

An Edwardian period barograph of unusually large size by J. Hicks, 8, 9 & 10 Hatton Garden London, the card drawer containing cards and correspondence, 22in (56cm) wide. **£1,000-1,200 CSK**

A brass sector, unsigned, 17thC, each arm 12in (30cm) long. **£700-800 CSK**

A rare boxwood plane table frame or ruler, by Henry Sutton, signed H. Sutton fecit 1655, 17in (43cm) wide by 13in (33cm) high extended.
£2,300-2,600 *P*

An electrostatic generator, signed Abraham, Liverpool, with original black silk screens, slightly torn, c1825, 18in (46cm) high.
£2,000-2,500 *TP*

A rare lacquered brass voluter, ▷ signed 'The Voluter H. Johnson's Patent 1857' on the triangular section beam graduated 0-6in, mid-19thC, the case 13in (33cm) wide.
£900-1,000 *CSK*

Invented by Henry Johnson, 39 Crutched Friars, and manufactured by F Hoffmann, 39 Wilmington Square, Clerkenwell, the voluter was designed for tracing spiral curves; deep-sea pressure gauges; for recording the density of sea-water at various depths and deep-sea thermometers.

A rare money scale, by S Henry, London, for weighing a guinea, half and quarter, the brass beam, pans missing, with spring-loaded locking mounted on the oval base, stamped S. Henry Inventor by Royal Patent, in the original fishskin covered case, with instruction label, the lid arranged to hold the scales in 2 grooves when in use, 18thC, the case 5in (13cm) wide.
£450-500 *CSK*

A kaleidoscope demonstration apparatus, late 19thC, 10in (25cm) high.
£450-500 *CSK*

An unusual ophthalmoscope by ▷ Edward Messter, Berlin, late 19thC, the case 10in (26cm) wide.
£600-650 *CSK*

A brass chondrometer, unsigned, with beam engraved 24-80, the weight lbs per Bushel with accessories and instruction label, in fitted mahogany case, 19thC, 11½in (29cm) wide.
£180-220 *CSK*

An acoustic siren, signed Becker, London, the brass wind chest supported on a mahogany circular base, the speed of rotation indicated on 2 dials, one marked 0-100 the other 0-5000, c1910, 8½in (21cm) high.
£400-450 *TP*

A fine money scale, by John William Herberts, the steel beam with brass pans, pillar and weights, 30dram weight missing, contained in the original fitted mahogany case, with original trade label dated 1772 and inscribed JOHN WILLM. HERBERTZ, 18thC, 7½in (19cm) wide.
£600-700 *CSK*

Johann Wilhelm Herbertz (fl 1763-1779) moved from Solingen and took up residence c1763 in Stidwell (Steedwell) St London, later renamed New Compton St. Soho.

A similar instrument is illustrated in Philip Harris & Co, Catalogue of Scientific Instruments, 1905, p383. This type of siren is fully described, with its history, in G. L'E. Turner, 19th Century Scientific Instruments, pp136-7.

A gilt-brass letter balance modelled in the form of a bacchante holding a vine supporting the beam, engraved ¼-16, the counter poise in the manner of 2 baskets of grapes, late 19thC, 6½in (16cm) wide.
£1,200-1,400 *CSK*

461

Cameras

A good Contax III camera outfit, camera No. D.60875 with 3 Sonnar lenses comprising: 5cm.f 1.5 – No. 1909655, 8.5cm. f 2 – No.1493169 and 13.5cm. f 4 – No.2253846, the latter two with hoods and caps, Zeiss Universal viewfinder, Universal sports finder, Contameter set, various filters, Zeiss quick-tilt head, five film cassettes, Zeiss film trimming template, e.r.c., maker's carton.
£300-350 *CSK*

A rare Wide-Angle Rolleiflex twin-lens reflex camera, No.W.2490454 with Distagon 55mm. f 4 lens in Synchro-Compur shutter, standard and pentaprism finders, lens-hood, Rolleinar 2 attachment, spare focusing screen, three filters, pistol grip and carrying case.
£1,100-1,500 *CSK*

A rare Thornton-Pickard F 2 Ruby Speed camera, no.123705, Ermanox-copy with Taylor-Hobson Cooke Anastigmat 3in. Series 0 f 2 lens in helical focusing mount, focal-plane shutter, folding sports finder, three d.d.s. and box of plates, in maker's leather carrying case.
£2,300-3,000 *CSK*

A Houghton's 45mm by 107mm Royal Mail Stereolette camera, with lenses in spring-cocked guillotine shutter, prismatic viewfinder and focusing screen.
£600-700 *CSK*

A 6cm by 13cm Rolleidoscop reflex stereoscope roll-film camera, by Frank Heidecke, No. 3852, with Tessar 7.5cm. f 4.5 lenses in shaped leather case.
£600-700 *CSK*

A Brun's Detective Camera, with luxury varnished wooden body, and Anastigmat lens.
£1,000-1,200 *JPL*

A fine 35mm. mahogany hand crank cine camera, by Zollinger of Turin, Tipo A No.34, with F. Koristka Zeiss Tessar f 3.5 50mm lens, in fitted case.
£600-700 *P*

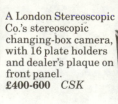

A London Stereoscopic Co.'s stereoscopic changing-box camera, with 16 plate holders and dealer's plaque on front panel.
£400-600 *CSK*

A quarter-plate Redding's Luzo box-form roll-film camera in ever-ready case.
£600-700 *CSK*

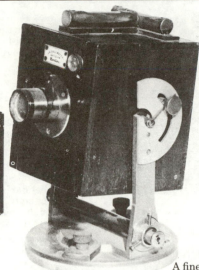

A 4.5cm by 6cm Ernemann Miniature-Ernoflex folding Reflex camera, with Ernon 7.5cm f 3.5 lens in helical mount, film pack adapter, 11 s.m.s., 3 cut film sheaths and French instructions, in maker's leather carrying case.
£500-600 *CSK*

A quarter-plate box-form mahogany survey camera by J.H. Dallmeyer, London.
£450-550 *CSK*

A fine Rolleiflex 2.8 f gold-plated Aurum twin-lens reflex camera, by Rollei Fototechnic GmbH, with Xenotar 8mm f2.8 taking-lens and neck strap.
£900-1,000 *CSK*

A four-lens multiple-exposure camera, probably by J. Lancaster & Sons, taking four 2 by 1½in exposures on one quarter plate, lacking ground glass and plate holders.
£1,300-1,600 *CSK*

A rare 1930s The Ensign 'Sanderson' 'Regular Model' quarter-plate camera, with Aldis-Butcher f6.3 5.25in.lens in Compur shutter, and Dallmeyer f6.5 3¼in wide angle lens, with matching lens cap, with three d.d.s. and film pack back, in Ensign case.
£220-280 *P*

An original-model 9cm by 12cm Goerz Anschutz focal-plane box-form camera, with Goerz, Extra-Rapid Lynkeioskop Serie C. No.1, brass-bound lens and folding sports finder.
£1,000-1,300 *CSK*

A rare Adams & Co. Tropical Vaido mahogany and brass half-plate camera, lacking viewfinder.
£500-600 *P*

l A 15cm by 10cm Ica Tropical folding plate camera in metal reinforced teak casing, with Tessar 13.5cm f 4.5 lens in dial-set Compur shutter, folding sports finder, film pack adapter and three d.d.s.
£120-160

c A quarter-plate Gandolfi hand-and-stand camera in mahogany casing with screw-reinforced joints, with Aldis Anastigmat 5¾in f 6 lens in Universal diaphragm shutter and one d.d.s.
£320-400

r A 9cm by 12cm Tropical Goerz Tenax folding plate camera in brass-reinforced teak casing with Xenar 13.5cm f 4.5 lens in Compur shutter, red leather bellows and film pack adapter, in leather case.
£200-250 *CSK*

A 3¼ by 6½ Lancaster's stereoscopic camera, with matched pair of Dallmeyer landscape lenses nos. 18003 and 18004, stereo roller-blind shutter and one d.d.s.
£300-400   *CSK*

A rare 2¼ by 2¼ Redding's Luzo roll-film camera in brass-reinforced mahogany casing, Patent No.17328, camera no.878, with lens behind spring-activated sector shutter.
£500-600   *CSK*

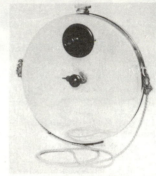

A rare Dickinson's Patent 'The Radial' quarter-plate magazine detective camera, by Marion & Co.
£280-360   *P*

A prototype 2 by 2 miniature changing-magazine camera, apparently by Alexander Rogers, Optician, Croydon.
£70-100   *CSK*

A good Stirn's Waistcoat detective camera, No.5065, in nickel-plated brass casing taking six circular exposures on circular plate with button-hole lens.
£500-600   *CSK*

Viewers

A Murray & Heath, 43 Piccadilly, London, Registered, stereo viewer, with sliding removable eyepiece lens and folding light diffuser, 1850s.
£100-140   *P*

A Cibis hand-cranked 35mm cinematograph projector, with film reels mounted side by side beneath, 35in (89cm) high.
£800-1,000   *CSK*

An unusual rosewood pedestal stereoscope with Knight's Cosmorama-style mirror arrangement, on telescopic brass column with lead-weighted base.
£900-1,200   *CSK*

A rare London Stereoscopic Company's Patent leather-covered Brewster pattern stereoscope, in fitted rosewood box, opening to sectioned compartment containing 17 stereo cards, 13in (33cm) wide.
£400-450   *CSK*

A Claudet-type stereo viewer, the brass eyepieces with assymetric lenses, mid-1850s.
£400-500   *P*

A Zoetrope with revolving metal cylinder, mounted on a turned mahogany base, together with a collection of comic strips, late 19thC, 14in (35.5cm) high.
£180-240   *WIL*

Art Nouveau – Carpets

A wool hanging designed and embroidered by Mary Newill, The Garden of Adonis, 77 by 48in (192 by 121cm).
£1,100-1,600 *C*

The embroidery is one of a set of three commissioned by the architect E. Butler for his own house, the other two now being in the Worcester Museum. This panel was exhibited at the Paris International Exhibition of 1900 and is illustrated in colour in the Studio Special Number 1901.

A large Art Nouveau hand-tufted woollen carpet, designed in the manner of C.F.A. Voysey, woven in rich reds, greens, yellow and blue, with faults, 208 by 146in (519 by 366cm).
£700-800 *P*

Ceramics

A Bretby pottery 'Egyptianesque' jardinière, in the manner of Christopher Dresser, covered overall with an amber glaze shading to olive, impressed marks, 9in (22.5cm).
£120-160 *P*

A Carlton ware lustre china coffee service of 15 pieces, with gilded and enamelled sunflower and hollyhock decoration, comprising: coffee pot and cover, cream jug and sugar basin, 6 cups and saucers, coffee pot 8in (20cm) high.
£300-400 *Re*

A Copeland comport, with green and gilt decoration, printed Copeland, England, late 19thC, 17in (43cm).
£250-300 *CBS*

An unusual Elton pottery ewer, with incised linear decoration beneath a bright blue and green glaze revealing patches of reddish brown, signed 'Elton', 13½in (34cm).
£300-350 *P*

A Foley 'Intarsio' earthenware clock case, with painted underglaze polychrome decoration, printed marks The Foley 'Intarsio' England, Rd.No.337999, c1900, 13in (33cm).
£500-600 *L*

A Della Robbia vase, decorated in coloured slip over a terracotta ground, incised DR mark with sailing ship and painted mark 'ENID', 11in (27cm).
£200-250 *C*

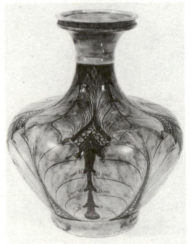

A Della Robbia pottery vase, with incised ship mark and marks of Charles Collis, potter and sgraffito artist and Gertrude Russell, painter, some damage, c1903-06, 11in (28cm).
£80-120 *CDC*

A late Foley Shelley 'Intarsio' ware vase, probably designed by Walter Slater, decorated in green, blue and pink, reserved against a brown ground, printed factory marks No.'3624, 379', 9in (22.5cm).
£120-160 *P*

A pair of Foley 'Intarsio' circular wall plates, designed by Frederick Rhead, printed factory marks and Rd Nos. 330399 for 1898-99, 12in (31cm) diam.
£700-800   *P*

A Gallé yellow ground cat, c1900, 13½in (33.5cm).
£875-950   *GCA*

A terracotta bust of a lady, signed 'Lefevre', c1900.
£250-300   *Phi*

A Gallé cat in tartan garb, c1900, 13in (33cm).
£975-1,050   *GCA*

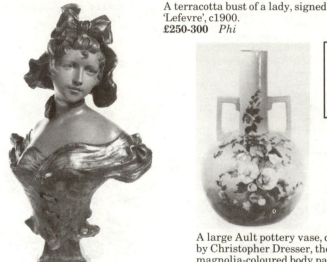

In the Ceramics section if there is only one measurement it usually refers to the height of the piece.

A large Ault pottery vase, designed by Christopher Dresser, the magnolia-coloured body painted in colours possibly by Clarica Ault, impressed facsimile Dresser signature and number '247', 27½in (69.5cm).
£600-700   *P*

A Linthorpe pottery ewer, designed by Christopher Dresser, with linear decoration beneath a streaked honey, green, blue and grey glaze, factory marks, facsimile signature and 'HT' for Henry Tooth, 9in (22cm).
£160-200   *P*

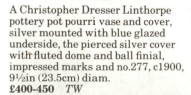

A Christopher Dresser Linthorpe pottery pot pourri vase and cover, silver mounted with blue glazed underside, the pierced silver cover with fluted dome and ball finial, impressed marks and no.277, c1900, 9½in (23.5cm) diam.
£400-450   *TW*

A Linthorpe pottery tobacco jar, the brown glazed body having electro-plated rim and swing handle, impressed mark, Henry Tooth monogram and shape no.913, late 19thC, 5in (12.5cm).
£50-70   *TW*

A globular green glazed bowl, designed by Christopher Dresser, impressed with facsimile signature 'Ch. Dresser', 5½in (14.5cm).
£600-700   *C*

A Christopher Dresser Linthorpe vase, decorated in plum and green crackle effect glaze, impressed marks and shape no.875, late 19thC, 12in (30cm).
£100-130   *TW*

A pair of William de Morgan tiles with Isnik style decoration of stylised flowerheads, green, yellow and purple on a pale green ground, framed together, 8in (20.5cm) square.
£350-400 *C*

A Linthorpe pottery pouring vessel, designed by Christopher Dresser, the brown body streaked milky-green with yellow speckling, 'Linthorpe Chr. Dresser' mark, 'HT' for Henry Tooth and '267', 5½in (14cm).
£450-500 *P*

A Maw & Co. oviform vase, designed by Walter Crane, painted in olive green, signed with designer's device on base, 13in (32.5cm).
£350-450 *P*

A Mintons 'Secessionist' ware garden stool, decorated in raised outline against a printed ground of flowers and foliage, glazed in turquoise, green, brown and yellow against a cream ground, indistinct impressed marks, date code for 1908, 21in (54cm).
£400-450 *P*

A Pilkington 'Royal Lancastrian' oviform vase, by William Salter Mycock, painted in golden and ruby lustres, against a shaded blue ground, impressed rosette mark, incised 'E.T.R.' for E T Radford the potter, artist's monogram and date code for 1933, 8½in (21cm).
£300-350 *P*

A Mintons 'Secessionist' jardinière and stand, probably designed by John Wadsworth and Leon Solon, in pinks, reds and yellows against a ground of block-printed foliage in greens, the cylindrical stand similarly decorated, printed marks and date code for 1902 on stand, 42in (105cm) total height.
£700-800 *P*

A Mintons 'Secessionist' ware jardinière, decorated in green slip-trailing with cream-amber stylised buds on blue stems, reserved against a purple ground, stamped marks and printed mark 'NO.1', 10½in (26.5cm).
£350-400 *P*

A Minton's art studio pottery twin-handled moon flask, the design in the manner of Christopher Dresser, decorated in 2 tones of grey, white and gilt, with leaves against a chocolate-brown ground, circular 'Kensington Gore' marks, impressed 'Minton' with date code for 1872, printed marks 'S.122' and 'K92', 13in (33cm).
£200-250 *P*

Four William de Morgan tiles, ruby lustre on a cream ground, c1890, 6in (15cm) square.
£900-1,100 *C*

A William de Morgan ruby lustre charger, c1900, 14in (36cm).
£600-700 *C*

A set of 10 William de Morgan 'Poppy' tiles, painted with aubergine coloured stylised flowers on green leafy stems, reserved against an off-white ground, impressed 'Merton Abbey' mark, 5in (13cm) square.
£550-600 *P*

A German rectangular tile, in bright colours, 6½ by 11in (16 by 27.5cm).
£400-450 *P*

A Royal Dux conch shell group with 3 water nymphs in relief, on natural ground, 17½in (44cm).
£500-600 *Re*

A Van Briggle baluster vase, 'Despondency', the vessel all beneath a matt turquoise glaze, signed with double 'A' mark and 'Van Briggle Colo Spgs Co.', 16in (40.5cm).
£250-300 *P*

A Sevres stoneware jug, with Gustave Keller gilt metal mounts and cover.
£700-800 *Bon*

Clocks

A Liberty pewter and enamel table clock designed by Archibald Knox, the mottled turquoise enamel face with red enamel decoration and gilt numerals, stamped 'English Pewter made by Liberty and Co. 0608', c1900, 5½in (14.5cm) high.
£1,300-1,600 *C*

Cf. Adrian J. Tilbrook, The Designs of Archibald Knox for Liberty & Co. fig. no. 93.

A 'Jaeger Le Coultre' timepiece, fashioned in gilded metal, marked 'Jaeger Le Coultre', with original fitted box, 8½in (21.5cm) high.
£300-350 *P*

A French inlaid mantel clock, with lever escapement, c1910, 12in (30cm).
£90-110 *IAT*

A Dutch Art Nouveau table pendulum clock, carved walnut with circular copper face and hands, 19in (47.5cm) high.
£300-400 *CAm*

An Arnhem clock set, with hand-painted Art Nouveau stylised plant-form decoration in blues, greens and browns on a cream ground, with painted Arnhem mark with cockerel, c1900, clock 15½in (38.5cm) high.
£1,000-1,200 *CAm*

A Liberty & Co. pewter, copper and turquoise enamel clock, the copper face with embossed Roman numerals set with a round turquoise enamel plaque, the pewter partly hammered, marked 'Tudric 0150', c1900, 13in (33cm) high.
£600-700   *C*

A Liberty pewter and enamel clock, designed by Archibald Knox, the rectangular case incorporating carriage clock movement, the turquoise enamel face with red enamel design, stamped '0608 RD 426015', 5½in (14cm) high.
£1,000-1,200   *C*

A Gallé mahogany and marquetry cabinet, signature 'Gallé Nancy' and cross of Lorraine, c1910, 30in (76cm).
£1,000-1,400   *CAm*

Furniture

An Arts and Crafts oak settle, possibly American, by Stickley, 51in (128cm).
£400-500   *P*

An Art Nouveau mahogany breakfront cabinet, probably made by Liberty's, c1898, 55in (139cm) wide.
£600-700   *L*

See item seven in The Liberty Style, published by Academy Editions, London.

A set of 6 Finmar stained birch chairs, designed by Alvar Aalto, with Finmar Ltd. label.
£450-500   *P*

In the Furniture section if there is only one measurement it usually refers to the width of the piece.

A small Art Nouveau oak cupboard, 12in (30cm).
£50-100   *Ph*

An oak sideboard, by Gustav Stickley, with red decal mark and paper label on reverse, model no.817, c1902, 74½in (187cm).
£1,000-1,500   *CNY*

A Scottish Arts and Crafts oak cabinet, 45½in (114cm).
£1,500-1,800   *C*

An English Arts and Crafts brass-mounted mahogany, sycamore and walnut marquetry partners' desk, 51½in (129.5cm).
£2,500-3,000 *C*

A mahogany, ebonised and marquetry jardinière in the style of Charles Bevan, with 9 marquetry panels inlaid in various fruitwoods, with zinc liner and later burr-walnut chamfered cover, 29in (73.5cm).
£2,800-3,200 *C*

A Glasgow School mahogany and inlaid corner cupboard, 68in (170cm) high.
£750-850 *MN*

A Sidney Barnsley oak bureau with a fitted interior, 34½in (86cm).
£2,200-2,800 *C*

An Emile Gallé oak and marquetry table à deux plateaux, signed in the marquetry 'Gallé', 21in (53cm).
£700-800 *C*

A Wylie and Lochhead mahogany display cabinet designed by E. A. Taylor, inlaid with brass, pewter, mother-of-pearl in a stylised floral motif, mounted with pewter lockplates and drop loop handles on square-sectioned railed trestle ends joined by platform shelf and turned stretchers, 35in (88cm).
£1,800-2,200 *C*

An Emile Gallé walnut and marquetry music stand, 23in (57.5cm).
£1,100-1,300 *C*

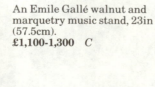

A mirror attributed to Bugatti, decorated with beaten copperwork and copper and pewter inlay, c1900, 26 by 24in (66 by 61cm).
£1,500-1,800 *C*

A Heal's oak linen press designed by Ambrose Heal, c1910, 37in (93cm).
£700-800 *C*

Cf Simple Bedroom Furniture in Oak Chestnut and Colonial Mahogany, designed by Ambrose Heal, Junior, Heal and Son catalogue, no. 432.

An Art Nouveau mahogany plant stand, 46in (115cm) high.
£100-120 *WHA*

Glass

A small Daum Nancy vase, signed in gilt 'Daum/Nancy' with croix de Lorraine, 4in (10cm).
£300-350 *Bon*

A Gallé enamelled and green glass jug, enamelled in white, blue and red, inscribed 'E. Gallé Nancy', 8½in (21cm) high.
£200-300 *CSK*

A D'Argental cameo glass vase, with deep turquoise sides overlaid in navy, signed in cameo 'd'Argental', 6in (15cm) high.
£350-450 *Bon*

A Daum cameo glass vase, the matt streaked yellow ground overlaid in shades of purple, cameo signature 'Daum Nancy France' and with retailer's paper label, 19in (48cm).
£800-1,000 *CAm*

A small Daum cameo glass vase, with pale blue acid-etched body, signed 'Daum Nancy', 6½in (17cm) high.
£400-450 *P*

A good enamelled Gallé enamelled jardinière of green glass, marked on base with acid-etched mushroom and signed 'Emile Gallé delt, Serie C, ft' and 'depose' in fine red script, 13in (33cm) across.
£1,300-1,600 *P*

A green cameo glass vase, etched by De Vez.
£380-450 *PB*

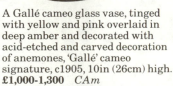

A Gallé oviform vase, overlaid and etched in amber, red and green with daffodils among grasses, cameo signature 'Gallé', bearing label, 13in (33cm) high.
£1,000-1,400 *CAm*

A Gallé cameo glass vase, tinged with yellow and pink overlaid in deep amber and decorated with acid-etched and carved decoration of anemones, 'Gallé' cameo signature, c1905, 10in (26cm) high.
£1,000-1,300 *CAm*

A Gallé cameo glass vase, the frosted white and lemon sides overlaid with deep purple, signed in cameo 'Gallé', 7½in (18.5cm).
£350-450 *Bon*

A fine quality cameo glass vase, by Gallé, with rich brown ochre overlaid on an amber ground with a design of tiger lilies, signed 'Gallé', 8in (20cm) high.
£1,250-1,500 *PSG*

A Gallé cameo footed glass vase, the frosted white and light green sides overlaid with deep purple, signed in cameo 'Gallé', 4in (9.5cm).
£350-450 *Bon*

A Gallé cameo glass vase, overlaid in deep mauve with sprays of laburnum, cameo mark 'Gallé', c1900, 12½in (31.5cm).
£700-800 *L*

A large Gallé enamelled glass vase, the clear sepia glass enamelled in tones of mustard, pink, turquoise and grey, details highlighted in gilt, etched 'Gallé', c1885, 11½in (29cm).
£800-1,200 *Bon*

A small Gallé cameo glass vase, the frosted white sides overlaid in lime green, signed in cameo 'Gallé', 3½in (8.5cm).
£250-300 *Bon*

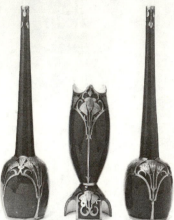

A Legras glass garniture, the 2 oviform vases with tall extended necks, all of white glass cased in a rich red glass and decorated with gilded stylised bell-shaped flowers, gilt mark 'L & Cie St. Denis – Paris', the tall vase 18in (45.5cm) high.
£350-450 *P*

A Gallé glass vase, with overlaid ruby decoration of flowers, signed, 5in (12.5cm).
£400-500 *CW*

A Gallé cameo glass vase, with cameo signature 'Gallé', 14in (34.5cm).
£900-1,100 *C*

A Gallé green ground overlay vase, 12in (30cm) high, with brown floral decoration, and line of verse:
  Béni soit le coin sombre
  où s'isolent nos coeurs
from French symbolist poetess, Marceline Desbordes-Valmore.
£2,200-2,500 *Wor*

A glass dish attributed to Heckart Petersdorfer Glashütte, with enamel painted decoration of a purple clematis bloom, 9½in (23.5cm).
£190-250 *C*

A Gallé cameo glass vase, with amber-tinted body overlaid with 2 tones of ruby glass, signed in cameo 'Gallé', 5½in (14cm) high.
£450-500 *P*

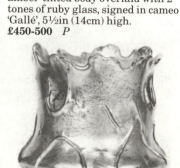

A Loetz vase in iridescent pink and gold glass, c1900, 6in (15.5cm) high.
£800-1,000 *CAm*

A Müller Frères cameo glass vase with mottled orange, ochre and deep violet sides overlaid with turquoise, signed in relief 'Müller Fres/Luneville', 5in (12.5cm).
£1,000-1,200 *Bon*

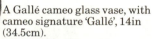

A set of 4 stained glass panels, designed in the Scottish taste, clearly showing the influence of E.A. Taylor and Oscar Paterson, each 46½ by 18in (116 by 46cm) approx.
£700-800 *P*

These were at one time installed in a house belonging to Barratts, the shoe manufacturers in Northampton, the town having obvious Scottish connections with the work of designer Charles Rennie Mackintosh for Bassett-Lowke at Derngate.

A Meyr's Neffe wine goblet, the design attributed to Otto Prutscher, with green over clear glass, c1900, 8in (20cm).
£650-750 *C*

A small Loetz iridescent glass vase, the peacock-blue green lustrous surface applied with a silver spray of flowers with chased detailing and silver collar, 4½in (11.5cm).
£150-200 *P*

A Wiener Werkstätte amethyst glass vase and cover, designed by Josef Hoffmann, etched 'WW' monogram, 7in (17cm) high.
£700-900 *C*

A Muller Croismaire cameo glass vase, the shaded orange and amber ground overlaid with darker orange, cameo mark on the base with butterfly and 'H. Muller Croismaire près Nancy', c1900, 14in (35cm).
£650-850 *C*

A large Müller Frères early glass vase with pale green sides, etched in shades of green and ochre, signed in enamel 'Müller, Croismare', 14in (35cm).
£400-500 *Bon*

A Tiffany Favrile glass bottle, with gilt metal stopper on a chain, the glass iridescent gold, the metal ring with chain attached stamped 'Tiffany & Co.', the glass engraved 'W8565', c1900, 9½in (24cm).
£300-400 *C*

Miller's is a price Guide not a price List

The price ranges given reflect the average price a purchaser should pay for similar items. Condition, rarity of design or pattern, size, colour, pedigree, restoration and many other factors must be taken into account when assessing values.

A Tiffany Favrile iridescent glass dessert set, comprising a large bowl, 11 smaller similar bowls and 10 saucer dishes, en suite, all exhibiting a golden iridescence with shades of blue, red and mauve, signed 'L.C.T.Favrile' or 'L.C.T.', large bowl 8½in (21cm) diam.
£1,500-2,000 *P*

Jewellery

An unusual Argentinian bracelet, stamped 'Axel Giorno'? – 'Buenos Aires', 8in (20cm) long.
£50-100 *P*

An Art Nouveau plique-à-jour brooch, stamped 'Deposé' and '900', 1½in (3cm) wide.
£400-450 *P*

A Boucheron powder compact and 2 lipstick holders, the compact marked 'Boucheron, London, NO.875012. Made in France' and the lipstick holders marked, one – 'Boucheron Paris' and the other – 'Boucheron, London 875012', compact 3 by 2¼in (7.6 by 5.7cm).
£200-300 *C*

An Unger Brothers Art Nouveau brooch, stamped with maker's monogram, 'Sterling' and '925 fine', 2¼in (5.5cm) across.
£200-250 *P*

An Omar Ramsden silver and enamel circular brooch, signed 'Omar Ramsden Me fecit' London silvermarks, 2¼in (5.5cm) diam.
£350-450 *P*

An unusual Arts and Crafts pendant brooch, 2½in (7cm) long.
£250-350 *P*

An Art Nouveau enamelled pendant, the sliding front revealing a mirror, stamped '900', 'Deposé' and dragonfly maker's mark, probably Austrian, 1½in (3.5cm).
£100-150 *P*

An Art Nouveau necklace, 21½in (54cm) long.
£100-150 *P*

An Arts and Crafts enamelled pendant, painted in naturalistic enamelled colours, signed on reverse 'Pegram', 2¼in (5.7cm) across.
£100-200 *P*

A Liberty & Co. 'ship' pendant, designed by Bernard Cuzner, the hull set with a pale blue tourmaline cabochon, unmarked, 2in (4.5cm).
£150-250 *P*

A Liberty & Co. enamelled silver pendant, designed by Jessie M. King, marks for W.H. Haseler and 'Silver', 2in (4.5cm).
£150-200 *P*

A German Art Nouveau pendant of red and green paste, stamped '900' and wolf's head and 'W' maker's mark, 2¼in (5.5cm).
£100-150 *P*

A Murrle Bennett & Co. gold and mother-of-pearl pendant, designed in the manner of Knox, stamped 'MB&Co.' monogram and '15ct', 2¼in (5.5cm).
£150-200 *P*

A Murrle Bennett gold Art Nouveau brooch, enclosing a speckled turquoise-coloured cabochon, marked 'MB&Co' and '15ct', 1¼in (3cm) with fitted box.
£150-200   *P*

A German Art Nouveau pendant necklace, stamped 'sterling silber', 2¼in (5.5cm).
£50-100   *P* ▷

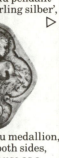

A Lalique Art Nouveau medallion, signed 'R. Lalique' on both sides, partially converted for use as a buckle, 2in (4.75cm).
£400-500   *P*

An Art Nouveau diamond-set pendant on chain spaced with pearls, 2in (5cm).
£400-500   *P*

Lamps

An Art Nouveau bronze oil lamp base with jewelled brass shade and glass funnel, cast after a model by G. Leleu, converted for electricity, signed in the bronze 'G.Leleu', c1900, 23in (57cm) without funnel.
£600-800   *C*

A W.A.S. Benson chandelier.
£1,500-2,500   *Bon*

An unusual figural brass lamp, fitted with lamp fitments, 21½in (54.5cm).
£300-400   *P*

A Tiffany Studios Favrile glass and bronze ten-light lily lamp, some damage, 19½in (48.5cm) high.
£4,800-5,500   *WW*

> *Miller's Antiques Price Guide builds up year by year to form the most comprehensive photo-reference system available. The first six volumes contain over 50,000 completely different photographs.*

A Gallé table lamp in lemon glass, double overlaid with two-tone russet cameo, c1898, 25in (62.5cm) high.
£12,000-15,000   *FF* ▷

An unusual Austrian bronze hanging lampshade, with removable frosted glass oval centre as shade, 26in (65cm) wide.
£350-400   *P*

A Tiffany shade in milk glass on a contemporary base, signed 'L.C.Tiffany', 17in (43cm) high.
£700-850 *FF*

Martin Bros

A Martin Brothers stoneware hanging bowl, painted in white, brown and green with the frieze reserved against a brown ground, the centre incised and heightened in brown and cream and reserved against a buff ground, incised 'R.W.Martin & Brothers, London & Southall', 7.1890, 11½in (28.5cm).
£600-700 *P*

A Martin Brothers stoneware grotesque double faced jug, in brown mottled matt glaze, with white glazed eyes, incised 'Martin Bros. London and Southall 4–1897', 9in (22.5cm) high.
£1,300-1,600 *C*

A Martin Brothers stoneware model of a grotesque bird, its plumage glazed in green, blue, beige and brown, signed 'R.W.Martin & Bros. London and Southall', head dated 15.1.1907, base 19.1.1907, 9in (22.5cm).
£2,500-3,000 *P*

A Martinware gourd pottery jug, the ribs separating vertical bands of dark olive filled incised crescents on a cream ground, incised 'Martin Bros. London, Southall', c1900, 10in (25cm) high.
£380-440 *CSK*

A Martinware jug incised with birds perched on flowering branches, incised marks, 5½in (13.5cm) high.
£250-400 *CSK*

△ A Martin Brothers stoneware vase, glazed in blue and black, reserved against a beige ground, signed 'R.W. Martin, London & Southall, 9.7.81', 9in (22.5cm) high.
£100-150 *P*

A Martin Brothers stoneware tile, incised and decorated in brown, white and green against a stippled brown and cream ground, signed around the edge 'Martin Bros., London, Southall, 3-1895', 6¼in (15.5cm) square.
£50-100 *P*

l. A Martinware grotesque spoon warmer of dragon form, impressed 'R W Martin, London & Southall' and '58', 8in (20cm).
£1,200-1,700

c. A Martinware owl with large beak and sardonic expression, on wood socle, head and base both impressed 'R W Martin & Bros., London & Southall 8.6.1905', 11in (27.5cm).
£2,200-2,600

r. A Martinware grotesque spoon warmer in the form of a bearded animal, impressed '27 R W Martin, London & Southall 11–79', 5½in (13.5cm).
£1,500-2,000 *GSP*

A rare Martinware plaque of the interior of the pottery titled 'Southall Pottery, Middlesex, 1882 R. W. Martin Sc', showing named and identified figures 'Wheel boy, Tom Cox (?)', 'Bench boy, Elvin Kelford' and 'Thrower, Edwin Bruce Martin', 16 by 7in (40 by 17.5cm).
£2,000-2,500 *GSP*

A good Martin Brothers stoneware oviform vase, incised with brown and white detailing reserved against a bronze-coloured metallic ground, signed 'Martin Bros., London & Southall', and dated '4–1899', 7in (18cm) high.
£380-450 *P*

A Martin Brothers stoneware vase, with incised decoration in dark brown glazes over a buff ground, incised 'R.W.Martin Bros. London Southall, 1889', 13in (33cm).
£300-400 *CSK*

A Martin Brothers vase, decorated with sea creatures, signed and dated 1909.
£650-700 *TM*

A Martin Brothers stoneware vase, with incised decoration in green, brown and white tones on a buff coloured ground, incised 'Martin Bros. London & Southall 18.7.84', 8in (20.5cm) high.
£400-500 *C*

Metal

A bronze table lamp in the form of a frog, with red glass eyes, red tasselled fringe, 15in (38cm).
£1,500-2,000 *P*

See Miller's Guide *1981, p.475 for a similar example.*

A bronze bust of the 'Genie of the Dance' by Carpeaux.
£1,600-2,000 *Bon*

A gilt bronze figure of Loie Fuller by Raoul-Francois Larche, with 2 light fittings, base inscribed 'Raoul Larche' numbered K809, stamped founder's mark, Siot Decauville Fondeur, Paris, 18in (45.5cm) high.
£3,000-5,000 *Bon*

A bronze figure of Diana Wounded, by Bertram MacKennal, with good patina but with patches of verdigris across her breasts and right thigh, 16½in (41.5cm).
£9,000-11,000 *Bon*

A bronze figure of a woman by Bertram MacKennal.
£5,200-5,500 *Bon*

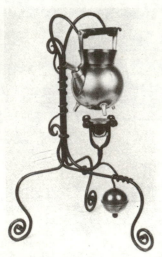

A seven-branch brass candlestick, the design attributed to Bernhard Pankok, raised circular base and central column on which the arms pivot, with cast decoration of concentric rings, 12in (29.5cm) high.
£1,400-1,600 *C*

A Benham and Froud copper and brass kettle on wrought iron and copper stand, designed by Christopher Dresser, stamped 'Benham and Froud' mark, 26in (65.5cm) high.
£350-450 *C*

A bronze bowl with swing-handle, cast after a model by Gustav Gurschner, signed in the bronze 'Gurschner' and stamped with foundry mark K.K.K.F. Wien 1246, c1900, 6in (15.5cm).
£500-600 *C*

A pair of WMF Art Nouveau pewter vases, stamped marks, 14½in (37cm).
£500-600 *P*

A Tiffany Studios bronze and iridescent glass candlestick, with separate pendant snuffer, having overall greeny-brown patination, stamped 'Tiffany Studios New York 1212', 10in (25cm) high.
£500-700 *P*

A Hukin & Heath plated soup tureen and cover, designed by Christopher Dresser, maker's marks, design lozenge for 28th July 1880, numbered '2123' and 'Designed by Dr. C. Dresser', retail mark on cover for 'W. Thornhill & Co. New Bond St. W.', 8½in (21cm) high.
£1,500-2,000 *P*

A Guild of Handicraft Ltd. silver spoon with circular bowl, and ivory handle, the bowl stamped G of H Ltd. with London hallmarks for 1900, 8½in (21cm).
£800-1,000 *P*

An Arts and Crafts plated metal cross, in the manner of Omar Ramsden, engraved with a memorial to Frederic Wilkins, Preist', dated '10th January 1937 22in (56cm) high.
£500-600 *P*

A WMF electroplated pewter drinking set, comprising a lidded decanter, 6 goblets and a tray, all pieces with usual impressed marks, c1900, tray 19 by 13½in (48 by 34cm).
£650-850 *C*

A set of 6 H.M. silver Art Nouveau teaspoons in fitted case, Birmingham 1900.
£170-200 *FHF*

An unusual Liberty & Co. Tudric-Moorcroft cake tray, stamped 'Tudric Pewter 0357', 12in (30cm).
£250-350 *P*

A Liberty pewter and Clutha glass bowl on stand, designed by Archibald Knox, the green glass bowl with milky and aventurine streaks, stamped Tudric 0276, c1900, 6½in (16cm).
£400-600 *C*

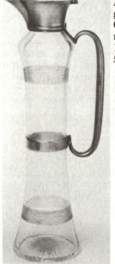

A Barnard Aesthetic Movement silver gilt christening set, comprising: a tankard, a knife, fork and spoon, all engraved and gilded, stamped W.B.J., maker's marks for London 1879, 9oz, in original Goldsmith & Silversmith Company box, tankard 3½in (9.5cm) high.
£500-700 *P*

A Georg Jensen silver tazza, stamped marks, 7½in (19cm).
£750-850 *CSK*

A WMF electroplated pewter tea and coffee set, comprising matching tea and coffee pots, lidded sugar bowl, milk jug and tray, all pieces with usual impressed marks, c1900, 25 by 13in (64 by 33cm).
£900-1,100 *C*

A Heath & Middleton silver and glass claret jug, in the manner of Christopher Dresser, maker's marks JTH/JHM and Birmingham 1892, 15in (38cm).
£250-350 *P*

A Hukin & Heath silver-mounted claret jug, designed by Dr. Christopher Dresser, with ebony handle, stamped with maker's monogram JWH & JTH and London hallmarks for 1884, 9in (23cm).
£800-1,200 *C*

An Art Nouveau bronze on marble base, 'Seagull and Sail' by Guy Edouard.
£450-500 *Ksh*

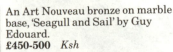

A set of 4 Hukin & Heath silver salts with salt-spoons, decorated in silver, copper and silver gilt, marked H & H and with Birmingham hallmarks for 1879, 6oz 4dwt, 1½in (3.5cm).
£850-950 *C*

An Art Nouveau silver and enamelled garniture of 3 vases by Hutton & Sons, with blue/green enamelled motif, London 1902/3.
£250-350 *TW*

A William Hutton & Sons silver and enamelled picture frame, heightened with blue and green enamelling, fabric backed, maker's marks for London 1905, 5½in (14cm).
£500-600 *P*

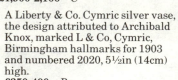

A William Hutton and Co. 5-piece silver tea-set, comprising a teapot, coffee pot, milk jug, sugar basin and sugar tongs, the teapot and coffee-pot with ebony handles, all pieces en suite, each piece stamped with maker's marks WH & Co and London hallmarks for 1904, teapot 6½in (17cm) high, 57ozs 11dwts gross weight.
£1,900-2,100 *C*

A Liberty & Co. Cymric silver vase, the design attributed to Archibald Knox, marked L & Co, Cymric, Birmingham hallmarks for 1903 and numbered 2020, 5½in (14cm) high.
£350-400 *P*

An unusual Tiffany & Co. cup and saucer, embellished against a copper ground, marked Tiffany & Co, Sterling Silver and other metals, pattern numbers 5623, c1879–1880, cup 2½in (6.5cm) high.
£480-550 *P*

A Liberty & Co. silver biscuit box, marked Cymric and L & Co, and with Birmingham hallmarks for 1902, 20oz 14dwt, 5½in (14cm).
£450-650 *C*

A Tiffany & Co. hammered white metal and parcel-gilt 3 piece tea-set, comprising a tea pot, milk jug and sugar bowl, engraved Tiffany & Co maker's mark, sterling silver and other metals and various numbers, c1890, tea pot 6½in (17cm) high.
£3,700-4,200 *C*

A good Tiffany & Co. Japanesque jug, applied with copper and brass, against a 'martele'-textured ground, stamped Tiffany & Co., makers, Sterling silver and other metals, pattern no. 5051, c1878-1879, 8½in (22cm).
£2,700-3,300 *P*

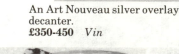

An Art Nouveau silver overlay decanter.
£350-450 *Vin*

An Art Nouveau dressing table tray, maker's mark, R.P., Birmingham 1902, 14in (36cm) long, 13.5ozs (420gms).
£600-700 *Bea*

An Art Nouveau silver condiment set, all with green liners.
£150-250 *Bon*

A silver box, with inserted miniature on ivory, signed, hallmarked 1904.
£150-250 *PJ*

A German four-light candelabra, stamped with crown, crescent and 800, maker's marks for probably Bruckmann and retail mark for M. Stumpf & Sohn, 17½in (44cm).
£800-1,000 *P*

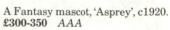

A Perry and Co red enamelled chamber candlestick, designed by Christopher Dresser, the base with brass fitments and curved wooden handle, trade mark for maker, registration mark for 30th October 1883 and Dr. Dresser Design, 5½in (14cm).
£300-400   *P*

A white metal and enamel box with parcel gilt interior, circular shape, the polychrome enamelled decoration depicting a maiden with long hair, in profile, against a background of flowers and leaves, c1900, 4in (10cm).
£600-700   *C*

A Fantasy mascot, 'Asprey', c1920.
£300-350   *AAA*

A David Anderson enamelled oviform vase, in greens, yellow and brown, simulating cloisonné, ground shading from red to violet over engine-turned decoration, with removable pierced domed top, silver-coloured metal with Danish maker's marks and '.925', 8½in (21cm).
£600-800   *P*

A copper Arts and Crafts vase, with pottery inset, c1900.
£50-100   *PJ*

Moorcroft

William Moorcroft Wares

William Moorcroft was born in Burslem in 1872. He studied at the Burslem School of Art, the National Art School (now the Royal College) and in Paris. In 1897 he joined James Macintyre and Co as a designer in their new Art Pottery department. In 1898 Moorcroft designed and produced a range known as Florian Ware. Moorcroft had total control of production and was able to experiment with a variety of glazes and decorating methods. Moorcroft used a white porcellaneous body of great strength. Wares were generally thrown rather than moulded and Moorcroft drew the original designs for every shape and size of pot himself. These were generally taken from nature, particularly plant forms, and were outlined on the pot using a thick slip which also served to prevent the metallic infill glazes from merging during firing.

Macintyre's Art Pottery closed in 1913 and Moorcroft established his own company at Cobridge, continuing with designs produced at Macintyre's as well as developing new ones.
In 1928 Moorcroft gained the Royal Warrant and his company flourished on an international reputation built on the foundations of quality and style. During the late 1930s many Art Potteries were forced to close but Moorcroft soldiered on thanks to the continued support of a thriving American market.
In 1945 William's son Walter took over the Cobridge works and continued to produce a wide range of designs mostly sold to an appreciative American public.

A Moorcroft pottery squat-shaped vase, painted with green trees on yellow to blue ground, impressed marks and signed in blue, 5½in (14cm).
£250-300   *CSK*

A Moorcroft pottery vase, painted in red and purple on a dark blue ground, impressed Burslem mark, signed 'W. Moorcroft' in blue, 13in (31cm).
£200-300   *Bon*

A Moorcroft Claremont vase, decorated in yellows, reds, olive-green and blue against a streaked green-blue ground, marked 'Moorcroft Made in England' and signed 'WM', 7in (17cm).
£250-300   *P*

A Moorcroft bowl, painted with red and green toadstools on a mottled green ground, printed marks and signed in green, 8in (20cm).
£400-600 *CSK*

A Moorcroft Florian ware vase, with black stylised foliage on a white and black ground, printed marks, signed in green, 12½in (32cm).
£250-350 *CSK*

A pair of Moorcroft dawn pattern vases, painted in deep blue against a pale blue sky, between chevron borders of blue and cream, painted initials in blue, impressed Moorcroft, Made in England, 8in (19cm).
£400-500 *L*

An important two-handled trumpet-shaped vase, on matt blue ground, full signature, des., c1898-1900, 10in (25cm).
£230-300 *LT*

MACINTYRE/MOORCROFT

★ first Art Pottery produced in 1897. Early wares marked Macintyre and/or W. Moorcroft des.
★ William Moorcroft established his own works in 1913
★ 1913-21 wares impressed MOORCROFT BURSLEM with painted W.Moorcroft signature
★ after 1916 impressed ENGLAND
★ 1921-1930 impressed MADE IN ENGLAND
★ 1930-1949 paper label, BY APPOINTMENT, POTTER TO H.M. THE QUEEN used
★ 1949-1973 label states BY APPOINTMENT TO THE LATE QUEEN MARY
★ rivals copied patterns and colours

A Moorcroft-Macintyre tobacco jar, decorated in reds, blues, browns and greens and apricot, Macintyre marks and signed 'WM', 4½in (11cm).
£300-400 *P*

A Moorcroft 'Brown Cornflower' vase, decorated in reds, dark blue and orange against a shaded beige-blue ground, impressed 'Moorcroft Burslem' and signed 'W. Moorcroft', 8in (20cm).
£200-300 *P*

A Moorcroft Macintyre vase, Florian-style decoration, full signature, des., c1900, 7in (18cm).
£100-200 *LT*

A Moorcroft Claremont pattern vase, decorated on a greeny-blue ground, base chipped, impressed Moorcroft Burslem England 1440 and with green painted 'W. Moorcroft' signature, 8in (22cm).
£400-500 *C*

A Moorcroft Macintyre baluster vase, decorated in bluey-green and gold against olive green, Macintyre marks signed 'W.M. des.,' and Rd. No. '404017', 12½in (31cm).
£350-400 *P*

A Moorcroft Claremont bowl, decorated in greens, blues, reds and yellows against a shaded olive green and blue ground, 'Made for Liberty' and 'W. Moorcroft', 10in (26cm) diam.
£400-600 *P*

Miscellaneous

A Moorcroft Macintyre two-handled vase, painted with peacock feathers in green and blue, design number 360574, signed in green 'W. Moorcroft, des.', 7½in (19cm).
£300-400 *L*

Alphonse Mucha: 4 unusual menus for Moet & Chandon, lithographic prints, signed in the block, c1900, 8½ by 6in (22 by 15cm).
£250-500 *Bon*

A cartoon for a stained glass window, depicting 'Winter' as an allegorical figure wearing a holly wreath and carrying a bundle of wood, charcoal and gouache on paper, framed, c1890, 48 by 24in (121 by 62cm).
£80-200 *C*

A Moorcroft bulbous pottery jug, painted in cream and pastel shades on a bluish ground, impressed Moorcroft marks, initialled WM in blue, 8in (21cm).
£200-300 *Bon*

A set of 6 Guild of Handicraft Ltd. buttons, each embellished with a heart-shaped leaf on a berried stem, unmarked but in fitted case for Brook St., with the 'works' in Chipping Camden, ½in (1.5cm) diam.
£200-300 *P*

Use the Index!

Because certain items might fit easily into any of a number of categories, the quickest and surest method of locating any entry is by reference to the index at the back of the book.
This has been fully cross-referenced for absolute simplicity.

Posters

A pair of silk-embroidered panels attributed to Morris & Co in coloured silks on a cream ground, 55 by 23in (89 by 59cm).
£300-400 *C*

An unusual walnut and gold-painted 'Puzzle', in a shaped case, the sliding covers emblematic of Yin and Yang, enclosing segments in jig-saw fashion of the entwined bodies, heads and hair of woman, reminiscent of the designs of Jan Toorop, 15½in (39cm) across.
£300-350 *P*

Jessie M. King: 'The Story of Rosalynde' – pen and ink, watercolour and gilding on vellum, signed bottom left 'Jessie M. King. Invt. Del', 9 by 6in (23 by 14cm).
£750-950 *P*

This was designed for the front cover of The Story of Rosalynde by Thomas Lodge with illustrations by Edmund J. Sullivan, of which there were twenty-five copies published by Cedric Chivers Ltd., Bath.

An unusual Austrian figural cigar-cutter by C. Kauba, modelled as the silver-patinated figure of a partially-clad girl, the cutter operated by the movement of her legs (wince!), signed on girl's head, 'C. Kauba', 8½in (22cm).
£270-350 *P*

Doulton

A Doulton siliconware owl by J A Milne.
£350-450 *Bon*

A Doulton Lambeth stoneware Queen Victoria Jubilee commemorative jug, silver mounted neck, 7½in (19cm).
£100-200 *Re*

A pair of Doulton ivory earthenware 'Galleon' jugs, each inverted ovoid body printed with 6 galleons in choppy seas, dolphin lower frieze, c1885, 7in (18cm).
£150-200 *TW*

A group modelled as two frogs attacking two mice, on an oval mound base, entitled 'The Combat', by George Tinworth, 4in (10cm).
£600-1,000 *CSK*

A Doulton Lambeth vase, decorated with leaves and pâte-sur-pâte birds on brown ground, by Florence E. Barlow.
£120-150 *LT*

DOULTON WARES
Doulton marks – abbreviations

o.u.m.	– oval updated mark
o.m.	– oval mark, dated
c.m.	– circular mark
r.m.	– rosette mark
r.m.& e.	– rosette mark and England
d.l.e.	– Doulton Lambeth England
d.s.l.	– Doulton Silicon Lambeth
d.s.p.	– Doulton & Slaters Patent
c.m.l.& c.	– circle mark, lion & crown
c.m.& l.	– circle mark and lion
r.d.e.	– Royal Doulton England
s.c.m.	– slip-cast mark
i.c.f.m.	– impressed circular faience mark
r.d.f.	– Royal Doulton Flambé
b.r.m.& c.	– Burslem rosette mark & crown

A Doulton Lambeth stoneware bowl by Frank A. Butler, in green, pink and blue beneath a beaded band, with gilt metal rim, impressed Doulton mark, incised monogram FAB, dated 1882, 9½in (24cm) diam.
£100-150 *Bon*

A Doulton Lambeth stoneware figure, attributed to John Broad, impressed 'Doulton' on base, 18in (46cm).
£300-400 *P*

l. A pair of inverted baluster form salt-glazed stoneware vases, initials of Florence E. Barlow, assistant Eleaner Tosen, one rim chipped, c1902-5, 10½in (26.5cm).
£200-250

r. A pair of tall salt glazed stoneware vases, coloured grey-green with blue and ochre details, initials of Bessie Newbery, a supervisor at Doultons from 1911, c1912-18, 12in (31cm).
£50-100   CDC

A Lambeth vase, with incised panels of deer, by Hannah Barlow and assistant Annie Jentle, date 1887, 11in (28cm).
£120-180   LT

An unusual Doulton Lambeth stoneware commemorative vase by George Tinworth, glazed in shades of brown, green and blue, incised 'GT' monogram, o.m. 9in (23cm).
£550-650   P

A Lambeth vase finely decorated in Art Nouveau style with mauve flowers on green ground, by Eliza Simmance, 14in (36cm).
£180-220   LT

Royal Doulton – Figures

A set of 'The Four Seasons', 2nd version, 'Spring' HN2085, 'Summer' HN2086, 'Autumn' HN2087, 'Winter' HN2088, designer Margaret Davies, introduced 1952, withdrawn 1959, 6in–8in (15cm–20cm).
£800-1,000   LT

◁ 'Spring flowers', HN1945, designer L. Harradine, introduced 1940, withdrawn by 1949, 7in (18cm).
£200-300   LT

A Royal Doulton china group, 'Afternoon Tea', HN1747, 5½in (14cm).
£100-150   HCH

ROYAL DOULTON FIGURES

★ since 1913 2,000 different models have been produced by the Royal Doulton factory

★ basically thought of as a modern day Staffordshire figure revival

★ since 1920's figures mainly designed by Peggy Davies, Leslie Harradine and Mary Nicoll

★ the HN numbering sequence was introduced with Charles Vyse 'Darling' HN 1 (which is still in production today)

★ since 1938 new figures are introduced only to replace ones which are to be withdrawn and so at any one time there are only 200-300 figures in production

★ any figure which is unsuccessful is withdrawn – and those are the ones most sought after by collectors

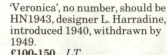

'Veronica', no number, should be HN1943, designer L. Harradine, introduced 1940, withdrawn by 1949.
£100-150 *LT*

'The Awakening', HN1927, 1st version, designer L. Harradine, introduced 1940, withdrawn by 1949.
£1,200-1,600 *LT*

'Top O' The Hill', HN1834, designer L. Harradine, introduced 1937, 7in (18cm).
£60-110 *LT*

◁ 'The Bather', no number, model as HN1708 but with different decoration, with black and white check robe, black costume and blue base, designer L. Harradine, withdrawn 1938, 7½in (19cm).
£200-300 *LT*

◁ 'Mantilla', HN2712, designer E.J. Griffiths, introduced 1974, withdrawn 1979, 12in (30cm).
£150-200 *LT*

'The Mask', HN733, designer L. Harradine, introduced 1925, withdrawn by 1938, 7in (18cm).
£700-1,100 *LT*

A charming pilot Royal Doulton figure of a boy carrying a lantern, in red coat and tricorn, not produced, 6½in (17cm).
£700-1,000 *LT*

◁ 'Sea Sprite', HN2191, designer Margaret Davies, introduced 1958, withdrawn 1962, 7½in (19cm).
£150-200 *LT*

'Ellen Terry as Queen Catherine', HN379, designer C.J. Noke, introduced 1920, withdrawn by 1949, 12½in (32cm).
£600-1,000 *LT*

'Spring', a Doulton figure designed ▷ by Richard Garbe, modelled as a partially draped maiden holding flowers to her bosom as she is swept upwards, her drapery resting on a circular plinth above a stepped square section base, cream-coloured glaze, in two sections with original screw and nut fixing, hand painted signature 'Potted by Doulton & Co. Edition Limited to 100, No. 61 'Spring' by Richard Garbe ARA' and with moulded artist's signature and date 1932 on the plinth, 21½in (54cm) including plinth.
£2,700-3,000 *C*

'Gladys', HN1740, designer L. Harradine, introduced 1935, withdrawn by 1949, 5in (13cm).
£350-400 *LT*

'Carmen', HN1267, designer L. Harradine, introduced 1928, withdrawn 1938, 7in (18cm).
£450-550 *LT*

'Henry Lytton as Jack Point', HN610, designer C.J. Noke, introduced 1924, withdrawn 1949, 6½in (17cm).
£300-400 *LT*

'Angela', HN1204, designer L. Harradine, introduced 1926, withdrawn 1938, hairline crack to base, 7½in (19cm).
£250-350 *LT*

'Coppelia', HN2115, designer Margaret Davies, introduced 1953, withdrawn 1959, 7½in (19cm).
£300-600 *LT*

A Royal Doulton figure, The Mendicant, depicting figure wearing draped costume and turban holding a tambourine and seated on a heap of red bricks, HN1365, printed Doulton mark, withdrawn from production 1969, 8½in (22cm).
£100-150 *TW*

'A Yeoman of the Guard', HN2122, designer L. Harradine, introduced 1954, withdrawn 1959, 6in (15cm).
£450-500 *LT*

'Moorish Piper Minstrel', on plinth, no number, should be HN301, designer C.J. Noke, withdrawn 1938, 13½in (34cm).
£650-750 *LT*

'Lady Jester', HN1222, designer L. Harradine, introduced 1927, withdrawn by 1938.
£1,100-1,500 *LT*

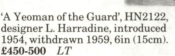

Three rare miniatures, 'One of the Forty', decorated in gilt, no number, should be HN423, designer H. Tittensor, 2½in, 2in, 3in (6cm, 5cm, 8cm).
£950-1,100 *LT*

'Mask Seller', HN1361, designer L. Harradine, introduced 1929, withdrawn by 1938, 8½in (22cm).
£350-400 *LT*

Miscellaneous

A porcelain group of Spooks modelled as two elderly gentlemen wearing long turquoise coloured cloaks and black caps, HN88 by C.J. Noke, printed and painted Royal Doulton, England and Doulton & Co. marks, 7in (18cm).
£1,000-1,100 *CSK*

'Fox in red coat', seated, HN100, 6½in (17cm).
£250-300 *LT*

A Royal Doulton stoneware garden ornament, impressed C.M. & I., 11½in (29cm).
£300-500 *P*

A Royal Doulton Limited Edition loving cup to commemorate the reign of Edward VIII, modelled by H. Fenton, edition No. 699 of 2000, printed inscription and factory mark, and a certificate signed by Charles J. Noke, 10in (25cm).
£200-300   *TW*

A Royal Doulton pottery 'Nelson' loving cup, inscribed 'I Was In Trafalgar Bay' and 'England Expects', decorated in colours and incised Fenton, the base with printed inscription in green, printed mark in green, limited edition number 579 of 600, 10½in (27cm).
£500-600   *HSS*

'Old Charley', a Royal Doulton character teapot and cover, c.m.l. & c., date code for 1939, introduced 1939, withdrawn 1960, 7in (18cm).
£1,100-1,500   *P*

'Mephistopheles', a Royal Doulton character jug, designed by C.J. Noke and H. Fenton, c.m.l. & c., introduced 1937, withdrawn 1948, 6in (15cm).
£900-1,100   *P*

'Sairey Gamp', a Royal Doulton character teapot and cover, c.m.l. & c., date   code for 1939, introduced 1939, withdrawn 1960, 7in (18cm).
£700-1,000   *P*

A Royal Doulton Golfing series ware mug, decorated in relief with figures in period costume, glazed in colours, c.m.l. & c. D5716, 6in (15cm).
£150-200   *P*

A Kingsware whisky flask and stopper, printed Royal Doulton, England Marks, 8in (20cm).
£100-150   *CSK*

A Doulton flambé figure by Noke, with pagoda-like red silk and cream braid shade with metal mounted faceted glass drops, printed Royal Doulton Flambé mark and original printed label, c1930, 22½in (58cm).
£800-1,000   *C*

A pottery character jug modelled as Santa Claus, D6690, printed Royal Doulton England marks, 7½in (19cm).
£50-100   *CSK*

'Santa Claus' and 'Lambeth Walk', a Royal Doulton 'Bunnykins' candleholder with loop handle, designed by Barbara Vernon, made between 1940 and 1949, c.m.l. & c., Bunnykins back stamp, 7in (18cm).
£100-200   *P*

Make the most of Miller's

Every care has been taken to ensure the accuracy of descriptions and estimated valuations. Where an attribution is made within inverted commas (e.g. 'Chippendale') or is followed by the word 'style' (e.g. early Georgian style) it is intended to convey that, in the opinion of the publishers, the piece concerned is a later – though probably still antique – reproduction of the style so designated. Unless otherwise stated, any description which refers to 'a set', or 'a pair' includes a valuation for the entire set or the pair, even though the illustration may show only a single item.

Lalique Glass

RENÉ LALIQUE

The work of René Lalique spans both the Art Nouveau and Art Deco periods. He began his career as a designer of jewellery and was an innovator among goldsmiths in the 1890s, being more concerned with the craftsmanship and decorative elements of the work than its intrinsic value. His pieces of this time are recognised as the finest examples of Art Nouveau jewellery.

By the 1900 Paris Exposition – 'the triumph of Art Nouveau' – the movement was actually on the wane. This, combined with the fact that he had more commissions than he cope with and that numerous imitations of his work were appearing, made him turn elsewhere for inspiration. He found it in glass and exhibited some pieces at the Salon in 1902. In the same year he designed a new studio and set up a workshop where his most notable cire-perdue and glass panels were produced.

He was introduced to commercial glass production around 1907 when François Coty asked him to design labels for perfume bottles. In fact, Lalique designed the bottles as well. These were manufactured by Legras et Cie, until he opened his own small glassworks at Combs in 1909 to cope with the demands of this and other work. After the First World War he opened a larger glassworks which was responsible for the bulk of his output.

Just as Lalique had triumphed at the 1900 Paris Exposition with his Art Nouveau jewellery, so he dominated the 1925 Exposition, establishing him as the leading exponent of mass-produced glassware. His designs by now were in the Art Deco style but the earlier Art Nouveau influence was still apparent in some of the decorative elements.

He was very much concerned with the commercial mass-production of his designs and it is as much as a pioneer of mass-produced art glass that he should be remembered as for his earlier imaginative jewellery.

A frosted glass bottle and domed stopper, 'Enfants', base rim ground and polished, Mk. no. 1, 4in (9cm).
£200-300 *Bon*

A frosted clear and black enamelled box, 'Roger'.
£400-450 *Bon*

A clear scent bottle, 'Imprudence', designed for Worth, formed as a series of graduated discs, including the stopper, Mk. no. 1 with 'France', base with paper label printed with 'Fatice', 3in (7.5cm).
£200-300 *Bon*

This bottle contains its original contents and is sealed.

An opalescent Bruce parfum bottle, 'Papillons', Mk. no. 10, 7½in (19cm).
£500-700 *Bon*

A rare set of 3 Lalique scent bottles, made for D'Orsay, heightened with brown staining, each moulded 'R. Lalique', having paper labels for 'Fleurs de France', 'Charme D'Orsay' and 'La Flambe-D'Orsay', original fitted case, each bottle 3½in (9cm) high.
£300-350 *P*

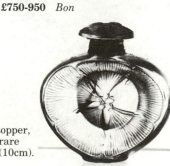

A stylish and rare frosted and enamelled scent bottle, designed for Lucien Lelong, heightened with black enamel, Mk. no. 10 with 'France', with original chromed and enamelled metal case, echoing the design of the bottle, the base with 'Lucien Lelong' in stylish script and 'VDA 1876 1931', 4½in (11.5cm) overall.
£750-950 *Bon*

An opalescent and frosted glass encrier, '4 Sirenes', heightened with turquoise stain, Mk. no. 6, 6½in (16cm).
£700-1,000 *Bon*

A rare perfume bottle and stopper, 'Althea', base moulded with rare 'RL' mark and 'Brevete', 4in (10cm).
£400-500 *Bon*

A clear glass scent bottle, 'Palerme', Mk. no. 10, 5in (12cm).
£200-300 *Bon*

A frosted clear and black-stained hexagonal-sectioned box, 'Saint Nectaire', Mk. no. 10, 3½in (8.5cm).
£300-400 *Bon*

A frosted and clear glass encrier, '3 Papillons', formed as 3 insects, Mk. no. 2, traces of turquoise stain, 4in (10cm).
£350-500 *Bon*

An opalescent circular glass box, 'Cleones', the cover moulded on the underside in relief with beetles upon pinnated foliage, Mk. no. 10, 6½in (17cm).
£450-550 *Bon*

This box has a card from Marlborough House inscribed with 'A gift from Queen Mary, Bazaar at Durham'.

A Lalique blue opalescent circular box and cover, 'Three Dahlias', moulded signature R. Lalique, 8in (21cm).
£300-400 *C*

An opalescent circular glass box, 'Deux Sirens', the cover moulded in relief with two sea nymphs, Mk. no. 10, 10in (25cm).
£1,400-1,600 *Bon*

A fine and rare frosted and siena-stained circular box and cover, Mk. no. 1 with 'France', 5in (12cm).
£1,300-1,600 *Bon*

A frosted, clear and turquoise-stained circular box, 'Amour Assis', the cover formed as a cherub, Mk. no. 6 with 'France' in script, 5in (12cm).
£800-1,000 *Bon*

An opalescent glass vase, Mk. no. 1, 6in (15cm).
£350-550 *Bon*

A green, frosted glass vase, 'Languedoc', of strong hue, Mk. no. 1, two rim chips and fracture to body, 9in (23cm).
£300-500 *Bon*

A good green-cased, frosted glass vase, 'Alicante', Mk. no. 2, with 'France No. 998' in script, 10in (25.5cm).
£6,500-7,000 *Bon*

An opalescent and frosted glass vase, 'Laurier', Mk. no. 3 on side at foot, etched 'No. 947' on base, rim ground, 7in (18cm).
£300-400 *Bon*

A frosted and clear glass vase, 'Pierrefonds', one handle slightly ground on top, Mk. no. 3, 6in (15cm).
£1,000-1,200 *Bon*

A frosted glass vase and stopper, '12 Figurines avec Bouchon', Mk. no. 2 with 'France' in script, 11½in (29.5cm).
£1,000-1,500 *Bon*

A frosted glass statuette, 'Source de la Fontaine', heightened with siena stain, Mk. no. 3 with 'France', 28in (71cm).
£2,800-3,200 *Bon*

A frosted and clear glass vase, 'Bellecour', small internal fissure beneath one bird, Mk. no. 2, with 'France No. 9**', indistinct, 11in (29cm).
£750-1,000 *Bon*

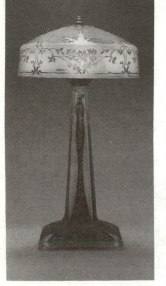

A fine and rare frosted and black-stained glass peacock lamp, Mk. no. 10, 16in (41cm).
£8,500-12,000 *Bon*

A frosted and clear glass bowl, moulded in relief with a design of hounds, Mk. no. 12 with 'France', 9½in (24cm).
£200-250 *Bon*

A grey frosted glass vase and cover, 'Tourterelles', Mk. no. 2, 11½in (29cm).
£2,300-2,600 *Bon*

An opalescent glass bowl, Mk. no. 3 with 'France', 11in (28cm).
£300-600 *Bon*

A Lalique opalescent deep circular bowl, 'Ondine Ouverte', moulded with a frieze of sirens, acid etched R. Lalique, France, 12in (30cm).
£600-700 *CSK*

A frosted, opalescent and turquoise-stained vase, 'Ceylan', Mk. no. 3, and a period lamp fitting with clear celluloid shade painted with similar parakeets, 18½in (47cm) overall.
£1,300-1,500 *Bon*

A Lalique frosted and clear glass oval dish, etched R. Lalique, etched script mark France, slight reduction at rim, 17in (43cm).
£400-800   *Bon*

An R. Lalique car mascot, c1920.
£1,700-2,500   *AAA*

A frosted and blue-stained nightlight, 'Hygenie', Mk. no. 10, with original bronze base, 6½in (16cm).
£700-900   *Bon*

A frosted glass clock, electric movement by ATO, enamelled chapter ring, Mk. no. 3 with 'France', 7in (18cm).
£450-500   *Bon*

A clear and frosted glass car mascot of pale amethyst hue, 'Faucon', Mk. no. 10 with wheel-cut 'France', beak ground, 6½in (16cm).
£400-500   *Bon*

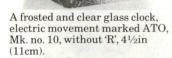

A Lalique car mascot, 'Levrier', clear and satin finished glass moulded in intaglio, moulded signature R. Lalique, France, 2½in (7.5cm).
£1,400-1,700   *C*

Cf Catalogue des Verreries de René Lalique, *1982, pl.77, no. 1141.*

A frosted and clear glass clock, electric movement marked ATO, Mk. no. 10, without 'R', 4½in (11cm).
£400-500   *Bon*

A frosted glass clock, electric movement marked ATO, Mk. no. 3, with 'France', 8½in (22cm).
£400-500   *Bon*

A large frosted glass ceiling dome, 'Charmille', minor chips and a small hole, 13½in (34cm).
£250-300   *Bon*

Miller's is a price Guide not a price List

The price ranges given reflect the average price a purchaser should pay for similar items. Condition, rarity of design or pattern, size, colour, provenance, restoration and many other factors must be taken into account when assessing values.
When buying or selling, it must always be remembered that prices can be greatly affected by the condition of any piece. Unless otherwise stated, all goods shown in Miller's are of good merchantable quality, and the valuations given reflect this fact. Pieces offered for sale in exceptionally fine condition or in poor condition may reasonably be expected to be priced considerably higher or lower respectively than the estimates given herein.

Art Deco – Ceramics

A Foley china part tea service, designed by Paul Nash, comprising: 5 cups and saucers, a milk jug, a slop bowl, 5 side plates and a cake plate, each piece painted in green, brown, yellow and red, factory marks and facsimile signature, cake plate 9in (23cm) diam.
£100-200 *P*

A Foley 'Intarsio' character teapot, designed by Frederick Rhead, no.3359, late Foley mark, Rd. no. 363131, 4½in (11.5cm).
£650-750 *P*

A Foley 'Intarsio' vase, designed by Frederick Rhead, in brown, with 4 yellow 'scaled' panels with mauve irises below against a green ground, factory marks and numbered 3003, 8½in (21.5cm).
£200-300 *P*

A Foley Art China coffee set, designed by George Logan, comprising: 6 cups and saucers, 6 side plates and a sandwich platter, in green and lilac on white ground, printed mark Foley Art China Peacock Pottery.
£400-450 *C*

A Foley china 'Dainty white' shape part teaset comprising: 12 cups and saucers, 12 plates, 2 cake plates, milk jug and slop bowl, each piece decorated in pink, red, green, blue and butterscotch with a white ground, printed factory marks, Rd.no. 272101, 1896.
£200-250 *P*

A Shelley 23 piece tea service, 1930's.
£200-300 *Re*

A Foley 'Intarsio' vase, decorated in blue, white, pink, green and brown, printed factory marks, no 3469, 9in (23cm).
£150-250 *P*

A Shelley 'Mode' shape 'sunray' pattern coffee set, comprising: coffee pot and cover, 6½in (17cm), 6 cups and saucers, milk jug and sugar bowl, each piece decorated in beige, yellow and black against a white ground, printed factory marks, Rd.no. 756533.
£400-500 *P*

A Foley 'Intarsio' tapering cylindrical vase, printed marks, 8½in (21.5cm).
£200-300 *CSK*

A Shelley 'Mode' shape 'Butterfly Wing' pattern part teaset, comprising: 6 cups and saucers, 6 plates, a cake plate, milk jug and sugar bowl, each piece decorated in green, black and grey against a white ground, printed factory marks, Rd. no. 756533.
£500-600 *P*

A Carlton ware coffee service, glazed in pale primrose, comprising: coffee pot, cream jug, covered sugar bowl and 6 cups and saucers, printed marks.
£120-150 *Bon*

A set of 6 Carlton Ware cups and saucers, in mottled red and black lustre, printed marks Carlton Ware Made in England Trade Mark, c1930.
£350-450 *C*

A Shelley 22 piece teaset, comprising: teapot, milk jug, sugar basin, 6 cups, saucers and plates and a cake plate, with orange, silver and black geometric decoration.
£500-600 *TW*

A Carlton ware 'Egyptianesque' ginger jar and cover, decorated in colours and gilding, against a powder-blue ground, factory marks on base, 15½in (39cm).
£1,900-2,100 *P*

A Carlton Ware vase, decorated on mottled purple and white ground, enriched with gilding, marked Carlton Ware, Made in England, 'Trade Mark', c1930, 10½in (26.5cm).
£200-300 *C*

l.` A Carlton Ware rouge royale vase, in enamels and gold, 6in (15.5cm).
£55-80

c. A Carlton Ware rouge royale diamond shaped dish, in enamels and gold, 12in (30.5cm).
£15-25

r. A Carlton Ware rouge royale tulip form vase, in enamels and gold, 5½in (14cm).
£16-25 *CDC*

A pair of Fieldings Crown Devon vases, one damaged, 8in (20cm).
£40-60 *CDC*

A Michael Cardew Winchcombe pottery oviform vase, covered in an amber and brown slip glaze, impressed with pottery seal, and bearing Exhibition label dating the item to 1927 for Retrospective Exhibition in Rotterdam 1976, 7½in (19.5cm).
£90-150 *P*

A large Louis Wain pottery vase, decorated in green, black and red on a cream ground, moulded signature 'Louis Wain', 10in (25.5cm).
£1,100-1,500 *C*

A Pilkington's lustre pottery vase by William S. Mycock, painted in gilt lustre, on a rich ruby ground, indistinct impressed firm's mark, painted lustre galleon on base and WSM monogram, 7in (18cm).
£180-250 *Bon*

A Royal Worcester porcelain horse's head vase, glazed white, 10½in (26.5cm).
£80-120 *CDC*

An English brown glazed stoneware wall mask, modelled as Comedy, 24in (61cm).
£120-170 *CSK*

A Lenci figure of a rooster, painted with black and green spots against a white and black ground, orange painted 'comb', painted marks Lenci, 1936 S.P., 11½in (29cm).
£1,000-1,500 *C*

A Lenci pottery wall mask modelled as a young girl wearing a multi-coloured head scarf, printed marks, 11½in (29cm) wide.
£200-300 *CSK*

A Goldscheider pottery mask of a girl looking down, the polychrome decoration highlighted with vivid orange for wavy hair and lips, printed Goldscheider Wien mark, Made in Austria, and impressed with artist's monogram B, c1925, 9in (23cm).
£300-400 *C*

A Goldscheider terracotta head of a young lady, with orange hair and lips, printed marks, 9½in (24cm).
£150-200 *CSK*

A large Goldscheider terracotta bust, printed marks and incised 'Goebel', 14½in (36.5cm).
£400-500 *P*

A Rosenthal ceramic sculpture by Gerhard Schliepstein, pale buff coloured crackle glaze, with impressed Rosenthal mark and impressed 'Schliepstein', c1930, 19½in (50.5cm).
£1,500-2,000 *C*

A Theodore Haviland porcelain cruet set to a design by Edouard Marcel Sandoz, with factory marks and facsimile of designer's signature, large frog 4in (10.5cm).
£250-350 *P*

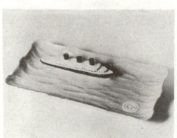

A Lallemant vase, the polychrome hand-painted decoration illustrating the French nursery rhyme, 'Il Pleut, Il Pleut Bergère', painted signature, 'T. Lallemant France', c1925, 11in (28cm).
£500-600 *C*

A Haviland porcelain ashtray, commissioned by the Compagnie Generale Transatlantique for the oceanliner 'Normandie', CGT monogram in relief and printed marks, c1935, 8in (20.5cm) wide.
£150-200 *Bon*

A large Ruskin high-fired transmutation glaze vase and matching circular stepped stand, with cloudy deep purple glaze with green mottling and speckling over a mottled pale grey ground, vase and stand impressed Ruskin England, c1930, 14½in (36cm), including stand.
£250-400 *C*

A KPM white porcelain mask by Hubatsch, blue printed KPM device and moulded signature 'Hubatsch 1930', 9½in (25cm).
£300-400 *C*

A Sèvres porcelain lantern with bronze tassel, designed by Henri Rapin, glazed in dark celadon and amber on a cream ground and embellished with gilding, circular red printed Manufacture Nationale Décoré a Sèvre 1923, and black rectangular S 1923DN marks, 20in (51.5cm).
£500-800 *C*

A Berlin 'KPM' porcelain box and cover, in colours and gilding, and embellished with oval intaglio panels of birds and flowers, sceptre mark and KPM and orb inside cover, SR on base, 8½in (22.5cm).
£150-250 *P*

A vase of cylindrical shape attributed to Venini and the design of Carlo Scarpa, of deep amethyst colour with a random pattern of white dashes, the surface partly iridescent and partly polished, c1958, 8in (20cm).
£500-650 *CAm*

A Rosenthal ginger jar designed by Kurt Wendler, with abstract design in blues, red and green heightened with gilding on a white ground, printed Rosenthal Selb Bavaria mark and artist's signature 'Kurt Wendler', c1925, 8½in (21cm).
£320-400 *CAm*

A Brannan green glazed model of a dragon, with yellow and blue markings, incised marks, 8in (20cm).
£65-120 *CSK*

An Amphora vase, polychrome on a white porcelain ground, enriched with gilding, impressed Amphora and printed Turn Teplitz R. St. K. with maker's device and D.464, c1930, 7½in (18.5cm).
£1,000-1,200 *C*

A Fraureuthporcelain box and cover, blue and white with black and gilt stylised foliate hand-painted decoration, printed mark Fraureuth Kunstabteilung, c1920, 8½in (21cm).
£200-300 *C*

A Limoges porcelain box and cover designed by Sandoz, with white and yellow plumage and blue beak, 6½in (16cm) and another similar 2in (5cm), both with printed marks, signed Sandoz.
£200-300 *CSK*

A Fornasetti porcelain circular rack plate, printed in black against white, 'eye' mark, Tema E. Variazioni, Fornasetti-Milano, Made in Italy, numbered 94, 10½in (26.5cm).
£50-100 *P*

Clarice Cliff

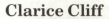

A stoneware tureen and cover, attributed to Reinhold Merkelbach and the design to Richard Riemerschmid, decorated over all with blue and grey design in relief, 13in (33.5cm).
£600-800 *C*

Cf. Kunstgewerbemuseum der Stadt Koln, Meister der Deutschen Keramik, 1978, No.434, p.223, similar example illustrated.

A Clarice Cliff Bizarre hand painted lotus vase with design on blue and white ground, 10½in (26.5cm).
£450-550 *LRG*

A Clarice Cliff Bizarre Fantasque Lotus vase, painted with red, orange and yellow leaves in a coloured landscape, printed marks, 12in (30.5cm).
£600-900 *CSK*

A Clarice Cliff Bizarre vase, painted with orange fruit and purple, blue and green leaves between orange rim and foot borders, printed marks, moulded 370, 6in (15.5cm).
£200-300 *L*

A Zsolnay miniature lustre vase, covered in bronze-brown glaze exhibiting a violet lustrous sheen, circular relief spires mark on base and 'Zsolnay Pecs', 3½in (9cm).
£50-100 *P*

A Clarice Cliff 'Persian' oviform vase, painted in reds, blues, green and brown dissected by a central foliate band, signed 'Persian by Clarice Cliff Newport Pottery Burslem', 8in (20cm).
£130-200 *P*

A Clarice Cliff Lotus shape vase, painted in bright colours, with the Summer House pattern, printed facsimile signature, 'Bizarre', Newport, 9½in (24.5cm).
£400-500 *P*

A Clarice Cliff Bizarre one-person tea service painted in green and black, and sponged green handles, comprising: a teapot and cover, a milk jug, a sugar bowl, a teacup and saucer, all with printed marks.
£250-300 *CSK*

A Clarice Cliff Fantasque Lotus jug, in orange, purple, green and blue, gilt printed on base Lawley's Norfolk Pottery Stoke, and Fantasque by Clarice Cliff, 11½in (29cm).
£300-500 *Bon*

A Clarice Cliff Bizarre oviform jug, painted in yellow and black, printed marks, 7in (18cm).
£350-400 *CSK*

A Clarice Cliff Bizarre Inspiration two-handled vase painted with bands of yellow, blue and turquoise stylised foliage outlined in brown on a turquoise ground, printed marks, 10in (25cm).
£3,000-3,500 *CSK*

A fine example of a Brangwyn plaque, decorated by Clarice Cliff, 17in (43cm) diam.
£2,000-2,500 *LT*

A Clarice Cliff Fantasque single handed Isis vase, painted with blue, purple and orange blossoms amid green and black foliage between yellow rim, printed marks, 9½in (24.5cm).
£300-350 *L*

A Clarice Cliff Bizarre part dinner service, each piece gaily decorated, comprising: 2 tureens and covers, a gravy boat, a pair of graduated oval dishes and 6 plates.
£250-300 *Bea*

A Clarice Cliff Bizarre ginger jar and cover, painted with bright colours, signed with factory marks on base, 8in (20cm).
£300-400 *P*

A Clarice Cliff Lotus shape jug, painted in bright colours, reserved against a cream ground with coloured banded borders, printed facsimile signature, factory marks, Newport, 11½in (29cm).
£400-600 *P*

A Clarice Cliff Fantasque baluster shaped vase, painted with bands of yellow, blue, orange and green, outlined in black between horizontal bands of orange, black, blue and green, printed marks, 16 (40.5cm).
£1,100-1,500 *CSK*

A Clarice Cliff Bizarre crocus pattern tea service, comprising: teapot, milk jug, sugar basin, 2 bread and butter plates, 10 cups, 12 saucers and 12 side plates.
£250-300 *Pea*

A Clarice Cliff Lotus shape jug, painted in bright colours, reserved against a cream ground with orange borders, printed facsimile signature and factory marks, Newport, 11½in (29cm).
£500-700 *P*

A Clarice Cliff Lotus vase with twin handles, painted with yellow trees on tall green trunks, with red buildings, further black and mauve trees against blustery white clouds, printed signature and 'Fantasque' marks, 11½in (28.5cm).
£700-1,000   *P*

A Clarice Cliff Bizarre part breakfast set, painted in bright colours, comprising: a teapot and cover, a milk jug, a sugar bowl, 2 teacups, 2 saucers, a side plate, a two-handled shaped bowl and cover and a rectangular shaped dish, all with printed marks.
£600-800   *CSK*

Bronze figures

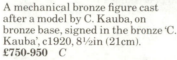

A green painted metal figure by Le Verrier supporting a red glass lamp, adapted for electricity, 23½in (60cm).
£700-800   *CAm*

A mechanical bronze figure cast after a model by C. Kauba, on bronze base, signed in the bronze 'C. Kauba', c1920, 8½in (21cm).
£750-950   *C*

A bronze figure cast after a model by C.J.R. Colinet, on marble base, dull gold patina highlighted with cold-painted colouring, signed in the bronze 'C.J.R. Colinet', c1925, 18½in (47cm).
£1,700-2,000   *C*

A bronze, marble and glass lamp, cast after a model by M. Le Verrier, signed 'M. Le Verrier' in the bronze, c1925, 34in (86cm).
£1,400-1,800   *C*

A bronze figure of a naked maiden, cast after a model by D.H. Chiparus, dull gold patina on black and brown marble base, signed in the marble 'D. H. Chiparus', c1925, 21½in (54.5cm) including base.
£500-700   *C*

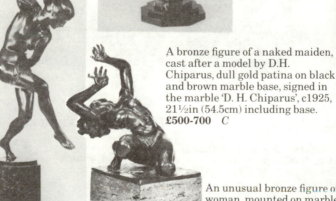

An unusual bronze figure of a naked woman, mounted on marble base, inscribed 'Gergel S', 12½in (31cm).
£300-400   *P*

A bronze figure by Karl Perl, on marble base, inscribed 'Karl Perl', 24½in (61cm).
£1,200-1,500   *CSK*

A bronze figure by Barbara MacDonald, of a young woman standing with naked torso and hands held closely to her body on a tall hexagonal base, inscribed 'Barbara MacDonald, 1936', 27in (68.5cm) overall.
£600-800   *CSK*

A bronze figure, 'Thoughts', cast after a model by M. Geraud Rivière, on marble plinth, c1930, 7in (17.5cm).
£500-700   *C*

A bronze figure, 'Nocturne', cast after a model by Edward-Louis Collet, inscribed in the bronze 'Collet Scpt' stamped foundry mark E Colin & Co. Paris, 18in (45.5cm).
£600-800 *C*

A bronze figure cast after a model by Hugo Lederer, dark brown patina, on stepped circular speckled grey marble base, signed in the bronze 'Hugo Lederer', c1925, 17in (43cm).
£750-950 *C*

A painted bronze figure by Molins, on black marble base, 19in (48cm).
£500-700 *CAm*

A Guiraud Riviere bronze figure, 'Stella', inscribed on star 'Guiraud Riviere', 'Etling Paris' and 'Bronze France', 11½in (28.5cm).
£1,300-1,600 *P*

A cold-painted gilt bronze figure in the style of Bruno Zack, on green onyx base, 12in (30.5cm).
£500-700 *Bon*

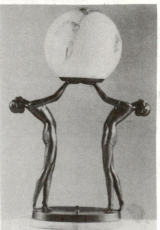

A bronzed electric table lamp with a mottled glass globular shade, on oval base with onyx stand, 20in (51cm).
£300-400 *AG*

A Chiparus bronze figure, 'Dancer of Olynthus', signed on base 'Chiparus', 15in (38cm).
£600-800 *P*

A German gilt bronze figure, by Schmidt-Hofer, inscribed 'Schmidt-Hofer', 16in (41cm).
£400-600 *P*

A Laurel silvered bronze figure, signed 'Pierre Laurel' and stamped 'Marcel Guillemard 14', 17½in (44cm).
£850-1,200 *P*

A silvered bronze figure by Le Faguays, 'Vestal', each hand holding an onyx cup, inscribed 'Le Faguays', 14½in (36.5cm).
£1,100-1,500 *CSK*

A pair of cold painted bronze figural bookends, 'Chinese Students', by H.M. White, on marble bases, signed 'H.M. White', 8½in (22cm).
£300-400 *P*

An amusing bronze candleholder, possibl[y] by Gurschner, 2½in (7cm).
£160-250 *P*

An Ouline green patinated model of a panther, signed on the base 'Ouline', 26½in (67cm) long.
£900-1,100 *P*

A large pewter and gilt metal simulated gem set bust, 'Salammbô', cast from a model by Louis Auguste Moreau, inscribed Salammbô and L. Moreau, 31in (79cm).
£2,200-2,700 *CAm*

A bronze model of a young bull elephant, 'Young Elephant', with short ivory tusks, signed 'C. Wollek Fec', and dated 'MCMXI' (1911), 11in (28cm).
£500-700 *P*

A bronze figure, 'The Skater', c1930, 9in (23cm).
£250-300 *TW*

A bronze figure of a flamingo, cast after a model by Rochard, dull gold patina, on black marble base, the base signed 'Rochard', c1925, 18½in (47.5cm).
£1,300-1,800 *C*

Ceramic Figures

A Goldscheider pottery figure, impressed marks, 14in (34cm).
£350-550 *CSK*

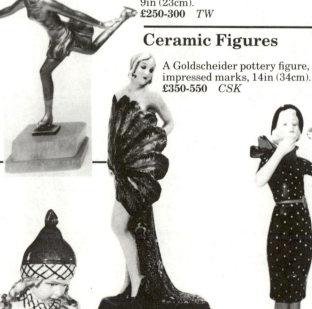

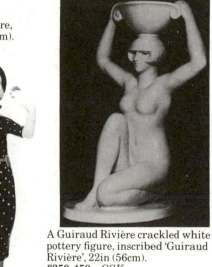

A Guiraud Rivière crackled white pottery figure, inscribed 'Guiraud Rivière', 22in (56cm).
£350-450 *CSK*

◁

An amusing Lenci figure modelled as a girl wearing a black and white dress, a black and red hat and scarf, signed 'Lenci, Made in Italy, Torino', 17in (43.5cm).
£600-800 *P*

A Lenci pottery figure, painted marks, 9½in (24cm).
£450-550 *CSK*

▷

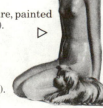

A Royal Dux model of a bathing belle, painted in pale enamel colours and gold, 18½in (47.5cm).
£400-500 *Bea*

Lenci pottery figure, painted marks, 14in (35.5cm).
£450-550 *CSK*

A Goldscheider pottery figure, impressed marks, 14in (34cm).
£400-500   *CSK*
◁

An Ochies pottery figure designed by Dax, printed and painted marks, 13in (33cm).
£100-150   *CSK*

An R. Philippe white glazed pottery group, impressed 'R. Philippe', 15in (38cm).
£50-100   *CSK*
◁

A Lenci figure 'Giovane Negra con Anfore' designed by Scavini, on green circular moulded base, printed marks, 21in (53cm).
£800-1,000   *CSK*

A Rosenthal porcelain figure designed by Gerhard Schliepstein, white and flesh tones, printed mark Rosenthal Germany and impressed 'G. Schliepstein', c1930, 13½in (33.5cm).
£500-700   *C*

A figure of a dancer by Royal Dux, 13in (33cm).
£200-250   *OL*

A Hermann Kähler figure, blue and brown on a cream ground, incised monogram, HAK, c1915, 18½in (47.5cm).
£400-500   *C*

Bronze and Ivory figures

A Preiss painted bronze and ivory figure, 'Champagne Dancer', on red marble base, marked on bronze 'F Preiss', 16½in (42cm).
£2,000-3,000   *P*

An ivory and bronze figure, 'Syrian Dancer', carved and cast from a model by Demêtre Chiparus on a brown striated marble base set with a bronze plaque of a similar figure, and intaglio signed 'D.H. Chiparus', slight restoration, 14in (35cm).
£1,000-2,000   *Bon*
Ref. 'Art Deco and other Figures' by Brian Catley, p.80 for illustration of similar.

A Preiss bronze and ivory figure, 'Con Brio', the young girl wearing silver and green tinted bikini with matching skull cap, on circular green marble dish, 12in (30.5cm) high.
£2,900-3,500   *AG*

A Preiss painted bronze and ivory figure, 'The Torch Dancer', modelled as a girl, naked except for silvered and red flowered bloomers, on black and green onyx base, signed 'F. Preiss', replacement flames, 16in (41.5cm).
£2,500-3,500 *P*

A Preiss painted bronze and ivory figure, 'Little Cricketer', modelled as a young boy wearing pale brown short trousers, a silvered short sleeved shirt, signed 'F. Preiss' on base, 7in (18.5cm).
£750-950 *P*

A bronze and ivory figure by Montini of Henry Fielding playing Dante, robes cold-painted in bronze red, on black marble plinth base, one thumb missing, 1930's, 16in (41cm) overall.
£900-1,100 *HCH*

A bronze and ivory figure by Chiparus, 'The Fan Dancer', the base inscribed 'D. H. Chiparus', 15in (38cm).
£4,500-5,500 *CSK*

A bronze and ivory figure, a dancer, cast and carved from a model by Demêtre Chiparus, inscribed 'D. Chiparus', 21½in (54.5cm).
£2,000-2,500 *CAm*

A gilt bronze and ivory figure, 'Priestess', cast and carved from a model by Demêtre Chiparus, with enamelled blue and green simulated jewellery, inscribed in the bronze 'Chiparus', 17in (43cm).
£3,000-4,000 *C*

A gilt bronze and ivory figure of a girl, 'Innocence', cast and carved from a model by D. H. Chiparus, inscribed, on cream onyx base, 15in (38cm).
£2,500-3,000 *CNY*

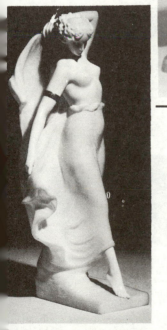

A carved ivory and marble figure, by Ernst Seger, signed 'E. Seger', 11½in (29.5cm).
£1,150-1,350 *P*

Furniture

A wrought iron and zebra wood cabinet, the base with a pair of parquetry cupboard doors, each centred by marquetry cartouches inlaid in various fruitwoods and mother-of-pearl with stylised floral motifs, on plinth base, carved signature 'J. Cayette, Nancy', c1925, 32½in (82cm).
£1,400-1,600 *C*

503

A burr-maple cocktail cabinet of semi-circular section, the upper section enclosing mirrored and fitted interior above overhanging bar fitted with 3 mirrored slides, the lower section enclosing fitted interior on platform base, fitted for electricity, 62in (153.5cm).
£650-750   *C*

A satinwood cabinet on chest, designed by Betty Joel, printed paper label, 'Token' Hand Made Furniture designed by Betty Joel, made by E.O. Miller, H. R. Green, May 1938, 30in (76cm).
£450-650   *C*

A Peter Waals oak bedside cabinet, the rectangular moulded top and panelled frieze drawer with bronze drop handles above plain rectangular shelf on square moulded legs, executed by Peter Waals, assisted by P. Burchett, 1928, 16½in (41.5cm).
£1,200-1,500   *C*

Make the most of Miller's

Unless otherwise stated, any description which refers to 'a set' or 'a pair' includes a valuation for the entire set or the pair, even though the illustration may show only a single item.

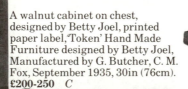

A Hille ash and cream lacquered dining room suite, designed by Robin Day, comprising: a rectangular dining table, 88in (223cm) extended, and 6 cream lacquered chairs with brown and white upholstery, and an ash sideboard raised on cream lacquered supports, 73in (185cm), stamped on drawer 'Hille of London'.
£1,000-1,500   *P*

A pair of mahogany and oak upholstered armchairs, by André Sornay, unsigned, c1935, 25in (63.5cm) wide.
£1,000-1,500   *CNY*

A walnut cabinet on chest, designed by Betty Joel, printed paper label, 'Token' Hand Made Furniture designed by Betty Joel, Manufactured by G. Butcher, C. M. Fox, September 1935, 30in (76cm).
£200-250   *C*

A Heal's sideboard, designed for the Paris Exhibition 1914, this example made 1926.
£1,500-2,000   *Bon*

A sofa designed by Serge Chermayeff, in brown velvet with cream piping on stained wooden platform base.
£1,000-1,500   *C*

This sofa was removed from the Mendelssohn House at 64, Old Church Street, Chelsea, the house for which Serge Chermayeff originally designed it.

Glass

A Décorchment pâte-de-verre bowl, in green and brown marbled glass, with impressed Décorchment mark, c1940, 10in (25.5cm).
£1,600-2,000   *C*

A set of 8 dining chairs and 2 open armchairs en suite, with solid walnut veneered back splats above bowed drop-in brown leather seats, with bronze sabots joined by shaped stretchers.
£1,800-2,300   *C*

Cf. J.C. Rogers, Modern English Furniture, *London, 1930, Country Life, p.40, cabinet and 2 chairs illustrated.*

A large Moser blue glass vase, heightened with gilding, marked on base 'Moser', and 'L.K.M.' linked for Ludwig Moser Karlsbad, 13½in (35.5cm).
£200-300   *P*

A gilt metal mounted deeply engraved and clear glass octagonal lamp, 13½in (34cm).
£500-600   *CSK*

A Daum chandelier, all pieces with deep acid-etched geometric decoration, pale amber glass with aventurine inclusions, engraved signature 'Daum Nancy France', and the cross of Lorraine, c1925, 33in (84cm).
£1,000-1,500   *C*

A Daum glass vase, signed in gilt, 'Daum Nancy France', 7½in (19.5cm).
£250-350   *P*

An Austrian blue glass jar and cover, attributed to Moser of Karlsbad, in the manner of Josef Hoffmann.
£100-150   *P*

A frosted glass figural lamp.
£100-150   *CS*

A decanter and stopper, engraved and decorated in black with triangles and segments of circles, 11in (28cm).
£100-200 *Bea*

A black bakelite and chrome necklace, German.
£40-70 *Stu*

Jewellery

A Lacloche Frères patterned silver and red gold minaudiere, set with 5 sapphires, fitted with compartments inside and mirror inside lid, in suede case, stamped with maker's monogram and silver and gold import marks for 1935, 5 by 3½in (13 by 8.5cm), 13oz. 14 dwt. gross weight.
£1,000-1,500 *C*

An Art Deco style platinum cocktail watch.
£600-800 *DWB*

A two-coloured bracelet, the band formed of basket-weave design, with faceted and buckle design clasp, stamped 750.18ct.
£800-1,200 *C*

A black bakelite and chrome dress clip, French.
£20-50 *Stu*

A brooch, yellow metal set with diamonds and formed as a triple bow, 1940's, 7cm long.
£250-400 *C*

A brooch, fashioned in abstract form as an owl, stamped 'sterling' and mark of 2 R's back-to-back in monogram, 4.5cm, and a 'fish' brooch, silver-coloured metal with 'W.W' and Polish marks, 4cm.
£150-200 *P*

A pair of paste red cabochon dress clips, American.
£30-70 *Stu*

Clocks

A silver and enamel desk clock, enamelled in shades of green on a rich green ground, with easel support, stamped maker's mark C & A. London hallmark for 1930, 9cm high.
£100-150 *Bon*

An Art Deco timepiece, the green marble rectangle centred with a square dial with blue enamelled back, 7½ by 8½in (19.5 by 22cm).
£200-300 *P*

A mottled rouge marble and silvered bronze clock garniture, the clock striking movement by F. Martin, Paris, 24in (61cm) wide, 2 side ornaments en suite with applied silvered bronze geometric decoration, 9in (22.5cm) high.
£650-750 *Bon*

A David Anderson pink-enamelled timepiece, stamped 'David Anderson' and '925S', 13.75cm high
£300-400 *P*

A pair of Arts and Crafts brass hinges, 6½in (16.5cm) long.
£350-400 *C*

A bronze dish, cast after a model by Gazan Chiparus, signed in the bronze 'Gazan Chiparus', c1920, 12½in (31.5cm).
£350-400 *C*

A German cocktail shaker, the multi-coloured vanes being containers for various spirits, the red body containing the shaker and measures, 10½in (27cm) overall.
£200-250 *P*

A Georg Jensen 64-piece Chess pattern table service, stamped Georg Jensen, Sterling, Denmark, comprising: 8 table forks, 8 dessert forks, 8 dessert spoons, 8 tea spoons, 8 table knives with steel blades, 8 cheese knives with steel blades, 59oz 12dwt weight not including knives.
£1,800-2,300 *C*

A set of 10 Ernst Treusch metal, wood and glass modernist tea cups, with flat rounded wooden handles, stamped Ernst Treusch Leipzig and with continental silver marks, c1930, 3in (7.4cm).
£600-800 *C*

A stylised 'Deco' enamelled cigarette case, French.
£50-80 *Stu*

An Art Deco table lighter in the form of a cocktail bar with negro barman, 7in (18cm) high.
£100-150 *LRG*

A Georg Jensen silver tazza, ▷ stamped with maker's marks, Georg Jensen, Denmark, Sterling, 263B and London import marks for 1928, (design introduced 1918), 7½in (18.5cm), 18oz.
£1,000-1,500 *C*

Cf. Georg Jensen Silversmithy, 77 Artists, 75 years, Renwick Gallery, Smithsonian Institution, Washington D.C. 1980, p.168, similar tazza illustrated.

A Dunhill gold and enamelled combined lighter, cigarette case and watch, with black enamelled banding, marked 'AD' and 9ct. hallmarks for London 1929, 4in (10.5cm) wide.
£900-1,200 *P*

A bronze vase, 'Fisherman', cast from a model by J. Öfner, inscribed 'J. Öfner', 7in (18cm).
£550-650 *C*

◁ A Georg Jensen silver teapot and cover, with ivory handle at right angles to it and a domed cover with ivory finial, Danish maker's mark, numbered 80A and with London import marks for 1938, 5½in (13.5cm).
£500-600 *P*

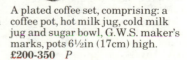

A plated coffee set, comprising: a coffee pot, hot milk jug, cold milk jug and sugar bowl, G.W.S. maker's marks, pots 6½in (17cm) high.
£200-350 *P*

Miscellaneous

A celluloid life-size mask, c1930.
£65-150   COB

An ivory bakelite telephone in working order, c1938.
£85-150   COB

A sheet alabaster leaded ceiling lamp shade, with stylized floral motifs, wreath border, 24in (61cm) diam.
£100-150   CDC

An illustration design showing a group of ladies and gentlemen in evening dress gathered round a Bugatti motor car, 9½ by 12½in (23 by 32.5cm).
£900-1,100   C

A carved wooden panel, 'Speed', partially gilded, with oak frame, 28½ by 45in (73 by 113cm).
£250-500   P

A carved rosewood figure, possibly by Nicholson Babb, 21in (53.5cm).
£300-400   P

A large carved stone circular plaque, by Alan Lydiat Durst, signed 'Alan Durst' and dated '1923', 32in (81cm) diam.
£500-800   P

A J.J. Adnet wool pile carpet, of russet, black, brown and beige, monogram JJA woven into right-hand bottom corner, c1930, 62½ by 57½in (156.5 by 144.5cm).
£900-1,100   C

A James Woolford plaster figure, patina-like grey painted finish, slight restoration and some chips, incised monogram JW, c1930, 23in (59cm) high.
£200-300   C

A stone carving in 2 sections, depicting a bust of a maiden with streaming hair gazing at a sphere held in her hand, c1930, 16in (42cm) high.
£400-800   C

A chromolithograph, Leo Putz, 'Moderne Galerie -Edke Theatiner- u. Maffeistrasse Arcopalais', signed en block centre, left 'Leo Putz', published by Reichhold & Lang Munchen, image area 43½ by 32in (108.5 by 81.5cm) framed and glazed.
£200-300   P

Four cover illustrations for 'Die Dame', 14 by 10½in (35 by 27cm) approx.
£800-1,100   C

Post war

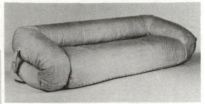

A refrigerator, decorated by Piero Fornasetti, printed in black on white, 37in (94cm) high.
£600-1,200 *C*

A white leather upholstered sofa bed, 'Anfibio', designed by Alessandro Becchi, 95in (240cm) wide.
£600-1,200 *C*

A laminated birchwood chaise longue, designed by Bruno Mathsson, with interlaced russet-coloured webbing, with designer's printed label, rubber stamped, Made in Sweden, 60in (151cm) long.
£500-700 *C*

A KPM modernist teapot, designed by Georg Schutz, white porcelain with a brass handle, with impressed manufacturer's mark and monogram MR, c1960.
£200-300 *C*

An Italian teak and glass executive desk, 1950's, 78in (198cm) wide.
£500-700 *C*

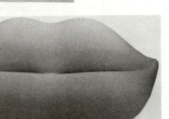

An upholstered chaise longue, 'Djinn series' designed by Olivier Mourgue, c1965, 68in (170cm) long.
£800-1,000 *C*

Cf. Kathryn B. Heisingen/George H. Marcus Design since 1945, *cover illustration.*

A 'Lips' sofa, after a design by Salvador Dali, upholstered in red nylon stretch fabric, 83in (209cm) wide.
£1,500-2,000 *C*

An enamelled oval plaque, converted to brooch, after a design by Salvador Dali, various marks on reverse with '25th Decembre, 1950, New York', 4.5cm high.
£50-100 *P*

A Christofle electro-plated 4-piece modernist tea set, 'Como', designed by Lino Sabattini, comprising: a tea pot, coffee pot, milk jug and sugar basin, each piece stamped Gallia France Pro. Christofle, c1955, teapot 8½in (22cm) high.
£3,500-4,000 *C*

Cf. Museum Villa Stuck, Die Fünfziger, Stilkonturen eines Jahrzehnts 1984, colour pl.14, similar set illustrated.

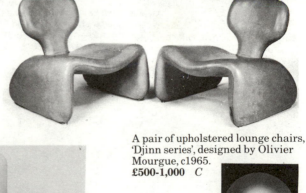

A pair of upholstered lounge chairs, 'Djinn series', designed by Olivier Mourgue, c1965.
£500-1,000 *C*

A Gio Ponti table lamp, in original carton marked with manufacturer's monogram and 'Designer Gio Ponti', 17½in (45cm) high.
£300-400 *C*

An unusual white painted metal lamp, 'Rimorchiatore', designed by Gae Aulenti, with lamp, a night lamp, vase and a vide-poche, 14½in (37cm) high.
£300-400 *P*

Silver – Baskets

A George II oval cake basket, the base engraved with a central coat-of-arms within a rococo cartouche, maker Peter Archambo, London 1742, 11½in (29cm), 52oz 5dwt.
£2,500-3,000 *BS*

A George III swing handle oval sweetmeat basket, maker's mark, probably that of Edward Aldridge, London 1767, 6in (15cm) long, 3.1oz. (97gm).
£200-300 *Bea*

A fine George III shaped oval cake basket by John Houle, London, finely engraved with coat-of-arms superscribed from 'IFF to PP', dated 1815, 15in (38cm) wide.
£7,500-8,500 *SA*

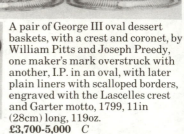

A George II shaped oval cake basket, by Edward Aldridge, two shell feet later replacements, probably 1746, 14½in (36.5cm) long, 56oz.
£2,000-3,000 *C*

A shaped oval swing handle cake basket, engraved at the centre with coat-of-arms, marks worn, maker's mark J.M. Dublin, c1780, 29.9oz (930gm).
£700-1,000 *Bea*

A pair of George III oval dessert baskets, with a crest and coronet, by William Pitts and Joseph Preedy, one maker's mark overstruck with another, I.P. in an oval, with later plain liners with scalloped borders, engraved with the Lascelles crest and Garter motto, 1799, 11in (28cm) long, 119oz.
£3,700-5,000 *C*

A fine George II oval cake basket, by Edward Aldridge, the centre engraved with a coat-of-arms in a rococo cartouche, London 1751, 13½in (34cm), 43.5oz.
£1,900-2,100 *WW*

An early George III basket weave pattern fruit or bread basket, by Parker and Wakelin, the Royal Goldsmiths, 1780, 10½in (26.5cm), 39oz.
£6,000-6,500 *Bou*

An important George III cake basket, belonging to Admiral Lord Nelson and reputedly used by him before the Battle of Trafalgar, by William Summers, London 1798, with accompanying letter written in 1939 by the daughter of Lady Mary Duncan in which she states the cake basket had been handed down through her family from Nicholas Duncan, one of the midshipmen of the 'Victory' in 1805
£1,500-2,500 *Bon*

Exhibited at the Trafalgar Centenary Exhibition, item no. 21426. Exhibited at the Victory Exhibition, 1910.

A George III Irish cake basket, the centre engraved with a crest above script initials, by John Graham, no date letter otherwise fully marked, Dublin c1765, 13in (32.5cm), 38oz.
£2,500-3,000 *L*

A George III sugar basket, engraved with an initial within shield, by Abraham Peterson, 1795, 6½in (17cm) wide.
£350-450 *L*

A large Irish cake basket, centre inscription, Dublin 1801, 15in (38cm), 28oz.
£600-800 *Bon*

A William IV circular panelled cake basket, by Charles Fox, London 1832, 11in (28cm) diam, 27oz.
£400-500   *WW*

A William IV pedestal cake basket by the Barnards, London 1836, 13in (33cm) diam, 934gm.
£450-500   *HSS*

A silver swing handled cake basket by E. J. & W. Barnard, London 1848, 17oz.
£300-400   *TW*

A Victorian pierced sugar basket by Roberts & Briggs, glass liner, London 1866, 7½in (19cm), 6¼oz.
£200-250   *CW*

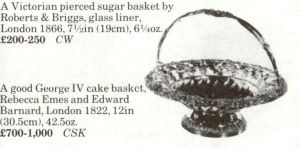

A good George IV cake basket, Rebecca Emes and Edward Barnard, London 1822, 12in (30.5cm), 42.5oz.
£700-1,000   *CSK*

A William Comyns oval cake basket, with pierced scroll and quatrefoil panels, London 1912, 14½in (37cm).
£1,000-1,500   *Bon*

A suite of 3 fine quality bon-bon dessert baskets of boat shape, the centres with engraved crests, comprising: one large basket 11½in (29cm) wide and a smaller pair, 9in (23cm) wide, maker W. Comyns, London 1890, 41¾oz.
£650-700   *NSF*

A pair of Victorian swing handled shaped oval baskets, in 18thC style, on pierced bases, C.S. Harris, London 1900, 9½in (24cm), 23.1oz (721gm).
£450-500   *Bea*

Beakers

A silver chalice, No. 172 of a limited edition, the gilded column moulded in the form of a lion, London 1977, 7in (18cm), 13oz.
£50-150   *WIL*

A pair of Daniel Pontifex goblets, the rims engraved 'As a Token of Gratitude, John Crickitt, Marshall of the Admiralty to James Henry Arnold LLD for his disinterested Assistance as Counsel', London 1797, 6¾in (17cm), 16oz.
£600-800   *Bon*

A set of 6 George III small silver gilt cylindrical beakers, engraved with a crest, by William Burwash and Richard Sibley, 1809, 2in (5cm), 8oz 13dwt.
£1,800-2,100   *C*

Bowls

A large Portuguese bowl, scalloped and lobed with heavily chased leafage, late 17thC.
£1,300-1,600   *Bon*

A Dutch two-handled octagonal brandy bowl, engraved with initials and a later crest and coronet, Bolsward, handles repaired, maker's mark indistinct, c1685, 8oz 12dwt.
£3,200-3,700 *C*

An Indian circular sugar bowl and cover, engraved twice with a crest, By David Hare, Calcutta, c1820, 6½in (16.5cm), 21oz.
£2,500-3,000 *C* ▷

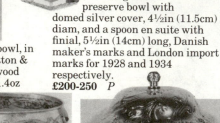

◁ A Georg Jensen preserve bowl with domed silver cover, 4½in (11.5cm) diam, and a spoon en suite with finial, 5½in (14cm) long, Danish maker's marks and London import marks for 1928 and 1934 respectively.
£200-250 *P*

A Victorian circular punch bowl, in monteith style, William Hutton & Sons Ltd., London 1896, on wood base, 12½in (32cm) diam, 61.4oz (1,911gm).
£650-750 *Bea*

A Queen Anne two-handled circular monteith, with a scrolling foliage and scalework cartouche enclosing a later coat-of-arms, the detachable rim chased with matting and with applied cherubs mask and scroll border, by Richard Syng, 1705, 11in (28cm) diam, 69oz.
£11,000-15,000 *C*

An Arts and Crafts silver rose bowl, supported on 4 heavily wrought and chased scrollwork feet, maker's mark 'F.S.G' London 1910, 7in (18cm) diam, 24oz.
£300-500 *P*

A George III pedestal sugar vase with domed cover, by George Cowes, London 1766, 6in (15cm) high, 9¾oz.
£400-600 *HCH*

A Queen Anne two-handled porringer by Seth Lofthouse, makers mark L.O., London 1708, 5½in (13cm), 380gm.
£600-800 *HSS*

A large late Victorian pedestal two-handled punch bowl, London 1897, 15½in (40cm) diam, 3,100gm.
£2,200-2,500 *HSS*

A small bowl, engraved 'Omar Ramsden Me Fecit' on base, by Omar Ramsden, London, 1936, 4½in (11.5cm), 4½oz.
£250-300 *DWB*

A Victorian circular punch bowl, engraved with a crest, by Martin Hall & Co. Ltd., Sheffield, 1898, 12in (30cm) diam, 75oz.
£1,500-2,000 *C*

A punch bowl, maker's mark indistinct, probably that of Charles Stuart Harris and Sons, 1929, 11½in (28cm) diam, 37.5oz.
£500-700 *L*

A Russian bowl and cover, Moscow, 1874, by M.H., assayers mark for Victor Savinkoy.
£250-300 *DWB*

A bowl by Georg Jensen, London 1937, 4in (10cm), 5½oz.
£250-300 *DWB*

A set of 8 George V circular fruit bowls with frosted glass liners, on spreading bases, in fitted case, with 8 spoons, Mappin and Webb, Sheffield, 1926–8, extensive damage to glass liners, bowls 4½in (11.5cm) diam, 42.9oz (1,336gm). **£500-700** *Bea*

Boxes

A George IV hunting scene snuff box, the cover cast and chased with 'The Kill', by John Jones III, 1824, 3½in (8.8cm). **£500-600** *L*

A George III 'goldstone' mounted vinaigrette, with a panel of 'goldstone' (aventurine glass), by John Shaw, Birmingham 1809, 2.9cm. **£90-120** *L*

A George III oblong vinaigrette, engraved with a border of oak leaves around the name 'M.G. Binnie', by Samuel Pemberton, Birmingham 1810. **£120-160** *P*

A George IV silver gilt oblong vinaigrette, by Lawrence & Co., Birmingham 1826. **£300-600** *P*

A William IV silver gilt vinaigrette, the cover engraved on a matted ground, pierced grille, by Taylor and Perry, Birmingham 1833, 2.1cm. **£50-100** *L*

A Victorian silver gilt shaped oblong vinaigrette, engraved with foliate scrolls and flowers, by Eliezer Nash, 1853. **£250-300** *P*

An unusual George III flat oblong vinaigrette, engraved with a tiger, by Thropp & Taylor, Birmingham 1812. **£200-300** *P*

A George IV vinaigrette in the form of a purse, with gilt interior and pierced scroll foliage grille, by Lawrence & Co., Birmingham 1821, 3cm. **£200-250** *L*

A George IV rectangular vinaigrette, the cover engraved with script initials, with gilt interior, by John Bettridge, Birmingham 1825, 3cm. **£50-100** *L*

A George IV rectangular vinaigrette, the cover chased with roses on a matted ground, with gilt interior, by Thomas Newbold, Birmingham 1821, 3.2cm. **£150-250** *L*

A George IV rectangular vinaigrette, the cover engraved with script initials, with gilt interior, by John Bettridge, Birmingham 1825, 3cm.

A George III silver mounted cowrie shell snuff box, the lid engraved with a crest, inscribed 'E.N. Parole Jevis' and with a leaf scroll monogram, by Phipps & Robinson, c1800, 3 by 2in (7.5 by 5cm). **£200-250** *BD*

A George IV silver snuff box, London 1825, 3in (8cm) wide, 5oz. **£300-350** *HCH*

A Victorian serpentine vinaigrette with engraved decoration, by Nathanial Mills, Birmingham 1845, 1¾in. **£200-300** *CW*

A Victorian oblong table snuff box with chased floral borders, engine-turned surfaces and vacant reserve, by Edward Edwards 1846, 3½in (9cm) long, 6oz.
£250-300   *P*

A Victorian silver tobacco box, Birmingham 1900, 3½in (8.5cm) high, 10oz.
£300-350   *HCH*

A George III oval nutmeg grater, by Phipps & Robinson, 1793, 5.4cm long.
£200-250   *P*

An unusual Edwardian commemorative vesta case, the cover enamelled in green with an inscription in yellow beneath a white panel, the inscription reading 'Inauguration of the New Shortest & Quickest route from New York to London, via Fishguard, by the Great Western Railway, August 30th, 1909', the interior of the cover inscribed with facsimile signature, 'From Churchill, Xmas 1909', by Sampson Mordan & Co., 1909, 5.5 by 4.5cm.
£450-500   *P*

A cigar case, initialled G.K. Moscow 1879, assayer's mark AK.
£200-250   *DWB*

An Austrian cigarette and match case combined, with 2 hinged lids, each with a cabochon sapphire clasp, end strike, maker's mark J.R. for Scharwg and Steiner, 3½ by 2in (9 by 5cm), 3oz.
£80-120   *CDC*

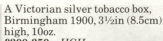

A George III oval nutmeg grater engraved with cartouche and floral swags and with chased borders, by Phipps & Robinson, London 1800, 2 by 1in (5 by 2.5cm).
£150-200   *BD*

An engraved cigarette case, 1924.
£120-180   *P*

A George IV gadrooned nutmeg grater, with shell and foliate handle, engraved with a monogram, I.R. London 1825, 4in (10cm).
£400-450   *CSK*

A George IV silver gilt engine-turned rectangular toothpick box, engraved with an earl's coronet above a unicorn crest, by Mary & Charles Reily, 1827, 3½in (8.5cm).
£200-250   *P*

A Victorian litmus paper case engraved with foliate scrolls and inscribed on an oval cartouche, 'Dr. Barton', by Hilliard & Thomason, Birmingham 1889.
£150-200   *P*

A Queen Anne oval tobacco box, the cover elaborately engraved, at a slightly later date, engraved with EB monogram above the date 1736, Britannia Standard 1708 maker's mark rubbed, possibly AS, 4in (10cm).
£400-500   *L*

The only new standard maker's mark AS recorded is that of Thomas Ash, though an attribution to Ash seems unlikely as there is evidence that Ash was a specialist maker of candlesticks.

An Edwardian trinket box, with piquet work hinged lid, guilloche border, raised on pierced trefoil feet, 4in (10cm) wide.
£170-230   *CDC*

A George III rectangular toothpick box, the base with rayed prick dot decoration, by Samuel Pemberton, Birmingham 1795.
£100-150   *P*

A George III silver tobacco box, marks rubbed, 4½in (11.5cm) wide, 4oz.
£180-250   *HCH*

A Continental box, presumably to hold a small pack of cards, the panel signed 'Hovander', one mark only on the rim, rubbed, mid 19thC.
£200-250   *P*

An American vesta case, chased with a coiled cobra, c1900.
£70-100 P

A George IV silver gilt oblong snuff box, the cover chased in relief with a scene from the life of Alexander the Great, inside of cover inscribed 'Presented to John Atkinson by I.H. Anderson as a mark of his friendship', by Thomas Shaw, Birmingham 1827, 3in (7.5cm) long, 4.25oz.
£400-450 P

A William IV castle top rectangular snuff box, the cover chased with a view of Abbotsford Castle, Edwin Jones, 1835, 2in (5.5cm), 1.3oz (41gm).
£300-350 Bea

An Edwardian vesta case, enamelled with a red and white shipping pennant with black motif in centre, Birmingham 1901.
£50-80 P

A William IV rectangular silver gilt snuff box, with hinged cover, Thomas Elerton, London 1836, 3½in (9cm), 4.9oz (154gm).
£600-700 Bea

A Victorian sentry box vesta case, enamelled on the front with a trooper of the 3rd (Prince of Wales' Own) Dragoon Guards in full dress, by Sampson Mordan, 1886, 2½in (6cm) high.
£500-550 P

An Edwardian vesta case enamelled with armorials, a white shield with a blue lion, with yellow label above with the name 'Emmanuel', Chester, 1902.
£50-80 P

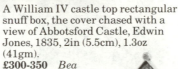

A Continental silver gilt snuff box of cartouche shape, engraved on incurved sides and base, the cover similarly chased in relief and set with an oval coral panel carved in high relief, unmarked, 19thC.
£500-600 P

A metal vesta case of rectangular shape, cover enamelled in off-white with a French train return ticket, Monte Carlo–Nice, c1900.
£100-120 P

A George IV snuff box, makers Adey & Joseph Savory, London 1839, 3in (8cm) long, 4oz.
£80-120 CDC

A Victorian snuff box in the form of a lady's shoe, with a polished bloodstone, maker's mark T.J., London 1876, 3½in (9cm) long, 1.3oz (41gm).
£500-600 Bea

An Edwardian vesta case, by Liberty & Co., in green and blue enamel, Birmingham 1906.
£120-160 P

A Victorian large silver snuff box, engraved on the cover with a view of Wricklemarsh, Blackheath, Kent, by Yapp & Woodward, Birmingham 1845, 4½in (12cm) long.
£1,400-1,600 C

A Victorian novelty box modelled as a valise with two buckled straps, by William Summers, 1875, 2in (5cm) long.
£100-150 *P*

A George III rectangular toothpick box with rounded ends engraved on cover with rayed prick dot decoration, the base with navette cartouche, by Samuel Pemberton, Birmingham 1796, 7.3cm long.
£150-250 *P*

A decorative combined purse and note pad with pencil, by Davis, Moss & Co., Birmingham 1911.
£200-300 *P*

A Dutch toilet box, with engraved decoration, the cover with English armorials, by Jesayas Engouw, The Hague, 1725, 5½ by 4½in (14 by 10.5cm), 15oz.
£800-1,000 *P*

An unusual Victorian silver mounted octagonal oak jewel casket, heavily carved, the domed hinged cover with two applied shield-shaped cartouches, one engraved with a coat-of-arms, two inlaid monograms, and a crest finial in the form of a whelk on seaweed base, the mounts by John S Hunt, 1856, 10in (25.5cm) high.
£1,000-1,300 *C*

The arms are those of Shelley.

A George III ivory toothpick box, with Highland scene in ivory on a blue background, behind glass panel in a gold frame, c1800.
£150-200 *P*

A George III circular patch box with bright-cut borders and monogram, by Joseph Taylor, Birmingham 1799, ¾in (2cm) diam.
£50-100 *BD*

A silver and silver-gilt Freedom casket, 'City of Bristol', with enamelled City of Bristol crest, makers Walker and Hall, Sheffield 1921, approx 116oz.
£800-900 *EH*

A Victorian card case chased in relief with the Scott Memorial, by Nathaniel Mills, Birmingham, date letter unclear.
£150-200 *P*

Candelabra

A contemporary silver three-branch candelabrum, No. 159 of a limited edition of 250, London 1977, 11in (28cm), 25oz.
£150-200 *WIL*

Four important Louis XV four-light candelabra, femier-general Hubert Louvet, maker's mark perhaps PH for Pierre Hannier, Paris, 1732, 13½in (34cm), 217oz.
£50,000-70,000 *C*

A pair of German two-light candelabra, the branches date letter 'L', the columns date letter 'G' by a different maker to the branches, Augsburg, c1820, 15½in (40cm), 51.5oz.
£900-1,100 *P*

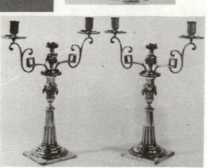

A Victorian cast four-light candelabrum, by the Barnards, 1873, 25½in (65cm), 90oz.
£1,300-1,800 *P*

Two George IV three-light candelabra, the central light with flame finial, by John Watson, Sheffield, 1823, one branch 1820, one nozzle defective, 25½in (64.5cm), weight of branches 99oz.
£3,200-4,000 *C*

A pair of German five-light candelabra, by Johann Georg Christoph Neuss, Augsburg, c1830, date letter 'O', 28in (71cm), loaded, weight of branches 107.5oz.
£3,200-4,000 *P*

A pair of Victorian five-light Corinthian column candelabra, engraved with inscription dated 1886, maker's mark, 26½in (67cm) high overall, weight of branches 116oz.
£5,000-6,000 *C*

A Victorian cast six-light candelabrum centrepiece, by E & J Barnard, 1852, 27½in (70cm) high, 194oz.
£3,200-4,000 *P*

A set of 4 candlesticks and matching candelabrum, Sheffield 1898–1900, weight of branches 64oz.
£3,200-3,800 *DWB*

A pair of silver gilt three-light candelabra, in the style of the 1730's, by the Goldsmiths and Silversmiths Company Ltd., 1911, 33.2oz.
£1,700-2,000 *L*

Candlesticks

A pair of early George I cast candlesticks, maker Thomas Ash, London, 1714, 6½in (16.5cm), 25oz 7dwt.
£5,000-6,000 *BS*

A pair of George II cast table candlesticks, John Cafe, London, 1754, nozzles apparently unmarked, 9in (23cm), 36.3oz (1,131gm).
£1,200-1,600 *Bea*

A set of 4 Queen Anne silver candlesticks, maker's mark M.E. probably Lewis Mettayer, 1711, 7½in (19cm), about 78oz.
£100,000+ *RPI*

A pair of George II cast silver candlesticks with detachable nozzles, maker John Cafe London, 1752, 8½in (22cm), 37oz.
£1,200-1,500 *NSF*

A pair of shell-cornered candlesticks, by Samuel Courtauld, London 1751, 9in (23cm), 44oz.
£3,500-4,000 *Bou*

A pair of German cast table candlesticks, maker's mark IWV, Osnabrück, c1750, 6½in (16.5cm), 12oz.
£3,500-4,000 *N*

A pair of early George III cast table candlesticks, by William Cafe, the sockets with standard marks, one nozzle only with standard mark, 1760, 8½in (22.5cm), 30oz.
£1,000-1,300 *L*

A pair of Frederick Kandler candlesticks, the cast shaped hexafoil bases with gadroon borders, London, 1765, 10½in (26.5cm), 44oz.
£2,200-2,600 *Bon*

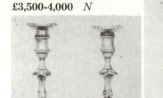

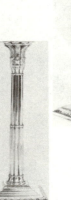

A pair of George II cast silver candlesticks, with detachable nozzles, maker William Cafe, London, 1758, 10in (25.5cm), 41½oz.
£3,000-3,500 *NSF*

A pair of George II cast table candlesticks, with detachable nozzles, by John Preist, 1754, the nozzles unmarked, 8in (20cm), 27.3oz.
£1,300-1,600 *L*

A set of 4 George III cluster-column candlesticks, engraved with crests, by Ebenezer Coker, 1766, 12in (30.5cm).
£3,500-4,000 *C*

A set of 4 early George III cast candlesticks, by William Cafe, the detachable nozzles marked with a French control mark, London, 1761, 10½in (25.5cm), 76.5oz.
£9,000-10,000 *WW*

A matched pair of George II cast table candlesticks, with detachable conforming nozzles, 1758 by William Gould and 1760 maker's mark indistinct, perhaps that of John Cafe, the sockets with standard marks and the nozzles unmarked, 9in (22.5cm), 34oz.
£1,000-1,500 *L*

A matched pair of early George III cast table candlesticks, 1762 maker's mark DM over a star and 1763 by Ebenezer Coker, the sockets with standard marks and the nozzles unmarked, 10½in (26cm), 42oz.
£1,500-2,000 *L*

A pair of George III candlesticks, with detachable circular nozzles, engraved with a coat-of-arms and a crest, by John Scofield, 1792, 11in (28.5cm), 41oz.
£3,200-3,800 *C*

A pair of George III coffee house candlesticks, each engraved New Hummums Coffee House, with detachable nozzles engraved with a crest, 1765 by Ebenezer Coker, one candlestick with maker's mark only, 11½in (28.6cm), 29oz.
£1,200-1,600 *L*

Tavern Anecdotes, a work published c1825, mentions two houses so named, The Old and The New, both situated in Covent Garden 'affording excellent accommodation to gentlemen and families and where there are commodious hot and cold baths'. Hummums being a corruption of Hammum, the Arabic term for bath or bagnio.

A pair of early George III cast candlesticks, with detachable nozzles, the bases engraved with a contemporary coat-of-arms, Ebenezer Coker, London 1766, 10in (25cm), 38.5oz.
£4,500-5,000   *WW*

A pair of Regency chamber candlesticks, by William Burwash, marked on bases and extinguishers, London 1818, 6in (15cm) long, 27oz.
£2,000-2,500   *CNY*

A Victorian silver gilt cast Harlequin taperstick, by S Crespell, 1838, 7in (17.5cm), 10oz.
£600-700   *P*

A pair of George III table candlesticks, by John Green & Co., Sheffield 1804, 13in (32cm), loaded bases, scratch weight 30oz 16dwt.
£1,600-1,900   *Re*

A matched set of 5 George IV and William IV rococo style candlesticks, maker John Watson, Sheffield 1824, 1827 and 1836, and a matched plated three-branch candelabrum insert with snuffer, 17½in (45cm) wide overall.
£1,500-2,000   *LBP*

An early Victorian chamber candlestick, by Charles T and George Fox, crested, London 1842, 7in (18cm), 10.5oz.
£1,000-1,200   *WW*

A pair of George III table candlesticks, John Rowbotham & Co., Sheffield 1814, 7in (18cm), loaded.
£700-900   *Bea*

A pair of Victorian embossed table candlesticks, on square bases, Sheffield 1844, 9½in (24cm).
£750-850   *HCH*

A set of 4 Portuguese cast candlesticks, maker's mark FIF or PIF, Lisbon, c1830, 18in (46cm) high, 239.25oz.
£3,500-4,000   *P*

A pair of William IV circular table candlesticks, Mathew Boulton, Birmingham 1830, 9in (23cm) high, loaded.
£700-800   *Bea*

A set of 4 late Victorian cast table candlesticks, in the style of the mid-18thC, by W Gibson and J Langman of The Goldsmiths and Silversmiths Company Ltd., 1896, 11in (27cm), 95oz.
£4,500-5,000   *L*

A pair of Victorian Corinthian column candlesticks, by Heath & Middleton, 1898, 16½in (42cm).
£1,200-1,600   *C*

A pair of late Victorian candlesticks, maker's mark HW, Sheffield 1899, 8½in (21.5cm), loaded.
£400-500   *HSS*

A set of 4 William IV candlesticks, makers T J and N Creswick, Sheffield 1832, 11in (28cm) loaded.
£1,200-1,600   *WW*

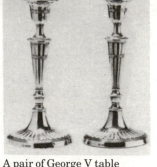

A pair of George V table candlesticks in 18thC style, Mappin & Webb, Sheffield 1908, 9in (23cm), loaded.
£450-500   *Bea*

A pair of late Victorian table candlesticks, with a pair of plated three-light candelabra branches en suite, maker's mark J & T, Sheffield 1894, 18in (46cm), loaded.
£600-700   *L*

A pair of George V table candlesticks in 18thC style, J. Round and Son, Sheffield 1919, 11in (28cm), loaded.
£450-500   *Bea*

Casters

A Warwick cruet, comprising 3 shakers and 2 full height faceted clear glass bottles with caps, with a matched stand with central carrying handle and 4 scrolled legs with scallop shell feet, bottles probably by Mordecai Fox, 1754, stand probably by Samuel Wood, 1759, 8½in (21cm), 40oz.
£1,600-1,900   *OT*

A Victorian pepperette in the form of a lighthouse, Henry Wilkinson & Co., Sheffield 1887, 3in (7cm).
£100-140   *Bea*

A George III vase shaped pepperette, Robert Hennell, London 1793, 3in (7cm).
£80-100   *Bea*

A George I octagonal vase shaped sugar caster, by Charles Adam, London 1714, 7½in (19cm).
£1,000-1,400   *DWB*

A silver lighthouse sugar caster, by Elkington & Co., Birmingham 1913, 7in (18cm), 10½oz.
£220-250   *THG*

Centrepieces

A George III centrepiece, pierced and shaped with leaf, floral and fruit decoration, comprising central four-footed stand with shaped oval basket surrounded by 4 similar smaller baskets on detachable scroll supports, William Pitts, London 1764, 10½in (26.5cm) high, 17in (43cm) wide, 81oz.
£4,500-5000   *HCH*

A table centrepiece, the base with lion mask and claw corners, cut glass bowl on a contemporary old Sheffield plate mirrored plateau base, Sheffield 1818.
£2,500-3,000   *Bon*

A Victorian oval-shaped centrepiece, in the Egyptian taste, by Elkington & Co., Birmingham 1884, 11½in (29cm) high overall, 122oz net, together with a similarly bordered Victorian oval shaped mirror plateau, by Elkington & Co., Birmingham 1889, 21½in (54cm) wide.
£3,000-3,500   *N*

Provenance: Charles Littlewood Hill Collection.

A pair of Victorian comports, by Smith & Nicholson, one glass liner missing, 1864, 12in (30.5cm), weighable silver 74.5oz.
£1,000-1,200   *P*

An Edwardian epergne, London 1907, 13in (33cm), 46oz gross, weighted.
£180-240   *CDC*

Coffee Pots

A Queen Anne coffee pot, engraved with a later coat-of-arms, by Simon Pantin, 1705, 10in (26cm), 29oz gross.
£2,600-3,000   *C*

A Queen Anne coffee pot, engraved with a coat-of-arms, by Augustin Courtauld 1710, 10in (25.5cm), 27oz gross.
£4,500-5,000   *C*

The arms are those of Bell Co, Norfolk.

A George II coffee pot, by Thomas Farren, 1727, 9½in (24cm), 21oz gross.
£1,800-2,200   *C*

◁ A George I coffee pot and stand, by John East, 1714, 10in (25cm), 33oz gross.
£26,000-29,000   *C*

A Queen Anne coffee pot, engraved with a baroque cartouche enclosing a later coat-of-arms, by Edward Yorke, 1711, 9in (23cm), 20oz gross.
£2,500-3,000   *C*

The arms are those of Forbes.

A George II baluster silver coffee pot.
£850-950   *PWC*

▷ A George II coffee pot and cover, engraved with an armorial shield, by Peter Archambo, London 1732, 838gm gross.
£1,400-1,800   *HSS*

A George II pear shaped coffee pot, with stepped cover, by Jas. Morrison, London 1746, 22oz.
£1,300-1,600   *AGr*

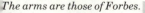

A George I coffee pot, by Simon Pantin, 1714, 10½in (26cm), 29oz.
£3,500-4,500   *P*

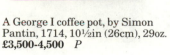

A George II chocolate pot, maker's mark IB coronet above, probably a variation of John Burdon's mark, Exeter, 1736, 10in (25cm), 28oz gross.
£3,500-4,000   *C*

A George II coffee pot, with a contemporary engraved crest within a baroque cartouche, maker Edward Feline, London 1740, 9in (23cm), 26oz 10dwt.
£1,400-1,800   *BS*

A George II coffee pot, engraved with a crest, by John Cafe, c1750, 9in (23cm), 25oz gross.
£1,700-2,000   *C*

A George V coffee pot, Birmingham 1922, 847gm gross.
£260-320   *HSS*

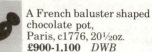

A French baluster shaped chocolate pot, Paris, c1776, 20½oz.
£900-1,100   *DWB*

A George II pear-shaped coffee pot, engraved with a coat-of-arms and crest within chased rococo cartouches, by Isaac Cookson, Newcastle 1748, 9in (23cm), 26oz gross.
£1,500-2,000   *C*

A George II coffee pot, chased in the contemporary rocaille manner, by John Swift, 1748, 10in (25cm), 30oz.
£2,500-3,000   *P*

A George III baluster coffee pot by Hester Bateman, London 1781, 12½in (32cm), 857gm gross.
£2,000-2,500   *HSS*

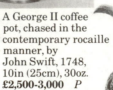

A George IV coffee jug, by William Eaton, London 1824, 30oz.
£450-550   *Re*

An early George III Irish coffee pot, with embossed ornament of later date, fruitwood handle, repair to body, Dublin hallmarks indistinct, 12in (30.5cm), 37oz.
£650-750   *CBD*

A George II baluster coffee pot, engraved with a contemporary coat-of-arms in a rococo cartouche, maker John Berthelot, London 1752, 9½in (24cm), 20oz gross.
£1,200-1,500   *WW*

An Empire coffee pot, by Thomas-Michel Bary, Paris, 1798–1809, 8½in (21.5cm), 15oz gross.
£1,500-2,000   *CNY*

A coffee biggin, part fluted, shaped gadroon edge, crested, on heavy leaf and claw feet, Joseph Angell, London 1815, 41oz.
£750-850   *Bon*

A Victorian baluster coffee pot, by & G Fox, London 1847, 9½in (24cm), 31.1oz (968gm).
£450-500   *Bea*

A George V baluster coffee pot with matching hot water jug, in Queen Anne style, London 1910–14, 8in (21cm), 43.1oz (1,341gm) gross.
£400-500   *Bea*

A George III cup and cover, by William Holmes, 1789, 12½in (32cm), 32oz.
£500-600   *L*

Cups

A rare Queen Anne Exeter chalice and paten, of customary form, engraved with contemporary arms in scroll cartouche, by John Elston, 1713.
£1,800-2,200   *Bon*

A Channel Islands wine cup, engraved with initials MFL, by Guillaume Henry, Guernsey, c1740, 5½in (14cm), 6oz.
£1,200-1,600   *C*

A George III trophy cup and cover, raised on a circular foot, slightly damaged cover with canopic finial, maker John Emes, London 1803, 1,873gm.
£550-650   *HSS*

A French two-handled chocolate cup, cover and trembleuse stand, maker Francois Joubert, Paris 1772 hallmarks, also later Paris hallmark for 950 quality silver, 13oz.
£450-600   *PWC*

A silver cup trophy and cover, the body inscribed 'The Greyhound Racing Association 1933, The Greyhound Derby . . .', maker Sebastian Garrard of Garrard & Co., London 1933, 16in (40.5cm), 62oz.
£400-500   *PWC*

A William IV campana shape cup and cover, by E, E J and W Barnard, with Jack Tar finial with rope and anchor, cast leaf border, London 1834, 13in (33cm), 40oz.
£700-800   *WW*

A matching pair of Victorian parcel gilt covered cups in the Gothic style, by D & C Hands, one 1862, the other 1860, with cover 1874, 10½in (27cm), 36oz.
£600-700   *P*

A William IV silver gilt pedestal cup, with a cartouche panel inscribed 'Robin Hood Rifles Evocatus Paratus', with detached rim, makers Robinson, Edkins and Aston, Birmingham 1836, 1,677gm.
£800-900   *HSS*

A Chinese export cup, inscribed Shanghai Regatta April 25th, 1848, The Ladies Cup for Wherries pulling a pair of oars', by Wongshing of Canton, c1848, 9½in (24.5cm), 22oz.
£950-1,050   *P*

A two-handled sporting trophy, 'Destroyer flotilla football cup', with embossed decoration, maker Goldsmiths & Silversmiths Company, London 1901, 32oz.
£150-200   *Nes*

A French silver cup of inverted bell shape, maker's mark I.B., early 19thC.
£45-55   *PWC*

A Victorian floral embossed and chased two-handled Theseus cup, Sheffield 1898, 35oz.
£250-300   *Nes*

A lidded trophy cup, inscribed 'The Gift of Mrs. Cordeux In Memory of Lt. E.H.N. Cordeux Killed In Action at The Bluff, Ypres. September 1915', maker John Marshall for Messrs. Spink, London 1911, 1,033gm.
£300-350　*HSS*

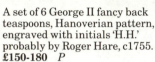

A Victorian yachting trophy, with a presentation inscription, by Stephen Smith, 1867, 16in (41cm), 77oz.
£1,200-1,500　*P*

The inscription relates to the 'Royal Cornwall Yacht Club'.

An M.T.E. Rosyth Adam design two-handled boxing trophy and cover, Birmingham 1920, 13½oz.
£75-100　*Nes*

A Charles Boyton regatta trophy and cover, London, 1937, 7oz.
£45-65　*Nes*

Cutlery

cl). A William III Provincial ascribed Norwich trefid, the back of the cleft terminal pricked SS/SA/1703 with below later initials B.B., by Elizabeth Haselwood, Norwich, 1697, 8in (20cm).
£550-600

l). A rare William III Provincial ascribed Hull trefid, part lace back, cut with the initials AH, punched twice with the Hull mark (the treble crowns) and the maker's mark TH three pellets above and one below for Thomas Hebden, c1690.
£300-350

cr). A Charles II Provincial unascribed trefid, struck with 3 marks, a leopard's head, the second indistinguishable, and a third resembling a figure, c1680, 8in (20cm).
£120-160

There are various attributions to the leopard's head, outside London. Ellis, p69 suggests possibly Great Yarmouth(?), Jackson, pp.446–447 illustrates and states Shrewsbury.

r. A Charles II Provincial ascribed Plymouth (Exeter) trefid, the back of the pronounced cleft terminal pricked FY/P/TE/1687, punched twice with the Exeter crowned 'X', the third overstamped with script R for Row of Plymouth, 8½in (21cm).
£200-250　*P*

A William III trefid, the back of the cleft terminal prick-dotted 1709/LS, maker's mark NG in a heart-shaped shield, possibly for Nathaniel Greene(?), 1695, 8in (20.5cm).
£200-250　*P*

A set of 6 George II fancy back teaspoons, Hanoverian pattern, engraved with initials 'H.H.' probably by Roger Hare, c1755.
£150-180　*P*

A George III cheese scoop, the blade crested, with green stained ivory handle, maker's mark obliterated, 1790.
£250-300　*P*

A rare George II Irish soup ladle, engraved with a crest, initial and Baron's coronet, date letter and maker's mark lacking, Dublin, c1745, 15in (38cm), 12oz 19dwt, on fitted wooden stand.
£900-1,100　*C*

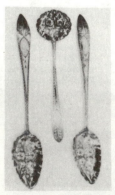

A pair of George III Irish table spoons, now converted to berry spoons and a sifter spoon, of Celtic taper pattern, by John Nicolson, Cork c1790, 182gm total, cased.
£180-220　*HSS*

A large part service of George III Old English and Thread pattern cutlery, comprising: 20 table forks, 12 table spoons, 12 dessert forks, 12 dessert spoons, 13 teaspoons, a gravy spoon, a salad fork and an Old English pattern gravy spoon, 1784, 1790 and 1795 by Richard Crossley, except the table forks and salad fork, 1776, 1777 and 1781 by William Sumner I and Richard Crossley, the teaspoons 1804 by George Creak and the gravy spoon 1767 by Paul Crespin, 139oz.
£3,000-3,500　*L*

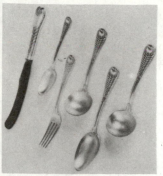

A set of Regency Coburg pattern cutlery, comprising: 6 table spoons, 12 table forks, 12 dessert spoons and a pair of sauce ladles, makers William Eley and William Fearn, London 1819, 88oz, and a set of 12 steel blade dinner knives, maker George W. Adams, London 1864.
£900-1,100 *WW*

A Queens pattern table service, comprising: 42 table spoons, 48 table forks, 36 dessert spoons, 24 dessert forks, 14 teaspoons, 4 sauce ladles, a soup ladle, 3 condiment spoons, 2 sifting spoons, a pickle fork, a butter knife and a fish slice and fork, c1830, 445oz.
£5,000-6,000 *C*

A French Christening set, comprising: a beaker, an egg cup, a napkin ring, a rattle with whistle, a table knife, fork and spoon, and an egg spoon, French post 1838 guarantee and purity 950/1000 marks for large items, and with maker's mark of Veyrat of Paris, 8.8oz weighable silver.
£400-500 *L*

A Victorian 3 piece Christening set, George Adams, London 1859–61, 4.6oz (144gm.) gross.
£160-200 *Bea*

A composite table service, Georgian and Victorian, mostly Irish, various dates and makers, comprising: 28 table spoons, 74 table forks, 30 dessert spoons, 15 dessert forks, 29 teaspoons, 6 egg spoons, 4 sugar shovels, a pair of sugar tongs, a sauce ladle, a soup ladle, 4 basting spoons, a strainer spoon, 34 table knives with steel blades, 12 fruit knives with silver blades, 352oz.
£3,500-4,000 *CNY*

△ A Victorian silver gilt Christening set, the terminals cast with a Russian double eagle displaying the Moscow Imperial arms, the spoon by George Adams, 1845, the fork and knife by Nikols Karland Plinke, St. Petersburg, 1847, 5.25oz weighable silver.
£220-280 *P*

A set of 6 Victorian cast salt spoons, silver gilt, by Francis Higgins 1880, 4½in (10.5cm).
£180-220 *P*

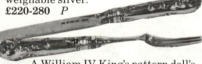

A William IV King's pattern doll's knife with silver blade, Birmingham 1835, 4in (10cm), and a matching three-pronged fork, 4in (9.5cm), unmarked.
£50-60 *BD*

A set of 6 pairs of Russian silver gilt and niello fruit knives and forks, by Antip Kusmitshev, Moscow, 1886, 26oz gross.
£800-900 *P*

A gilt Bacchanalian pattern dessert service, comprising: 18 dessert forks, 18 dessert knives, 18 dessert spoons, 6 serving spoons, a pair of grape scissors, a pair of sifter spoons, a serving knife and fork, London 1888. ▷
£5,000-5,500 *Bon*

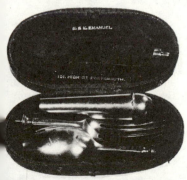

A Victorian silver gilt travelling canteen of cutlery, W.W. & F.D., London 1867.
£500-600 *CSK*

A 12 piece setting of Victorian cutlery, consisting of 12 table forks, 12 table spoons, 12 dessert forks, 6 dessert spoons, London 1850, 6 dessert spoons, London 1874, maker George Angell, engraved with lion rampant crest, 117oz.
£2,200-2,500 *TEN*

Spoons – Caddy

A canteen of cutlery, the mahogany box fitted with 2 trays containing various Old English pattern flatware including: 6 soup spoons, 7 table spoons, one soup ladle, 2 sauce ladles, sugar tongs, 12 table knives, 9 dessert knives, carving set, 12 teaspoons, 12 dessert forks, 12 table forks, 103oz approx.
£600-1,000 *WIL*

A service of Hanoverian pattern cutlery for 12 place settings, comprising: 12 table forks, 6 table spoons, 12 dessert forks, 12 dessert spoons, 12 soup spoons, 12 tea spoons, 12 coffee spoons, a pair of sauce ladles, 12 pairs of fish knives and forks, a pair of fish servers, and the following with stainless steel blades, 12 table knives, 12 cheese knives and a 5-piece carving set, all contained in a floor standing bow front mahogany veneered canteen, with trade label of Harrods Ltd., Knightsbridge, SW., maker's mark G & H, Sheffield 1960–63, 169oz excluding steel-mounted items.
£3,400-3,600 *L*

◁A Victorian Adelaide pattern table service, mostly by George Adams, comprising: 23 table forks, 12 table spoons, 22 dessert forks, 24 dessert spoons, 18 teaspoons, 4 sauce ladles, a pair of basting spoons, 2 meat skewers, 7 condiment spoons, a soup ladle, a sifting spoon, a butter knife and a pair of sugar tongs, 1858, 273oz.
£8,000-9,000 *C*

A George III feather edge caddy spoon, with scalloped bowl, maker's mark T(?), c1770.
£50-70 *P*

A George III caddy spoon, with scalloped bowl and short handle engraved with petal motifs, no maker's mark, 1791.
£50-80 *P*

A Continental caddy spoon, with ribbed back to oval bowl and with bifurcated volute handle, engraved with owl crest, possibly Italian, late 18th or early 19thC.
£50-80 *P*

A good George III caddy spoon, the stem and oval bowl engraved with Greek key decoration, the centre of the bowl pierced with an oval filigree panel, by Samuel Pemberton, Birmingham, 1807.
£100-150 *P*

An extensive service of Kings pattern cutlery for 12 place settings, with diamond point heels, comprising: table forks, 6 table spoons, dessert forks, dessert spoons, soup spoons, pastry forks, tea spoons, coffee spoons, a pair of sauce ladles, soup ladle, pastry slice, fish knives and forks, pair of fish servers, hors-d'oeuvre knives and forks, fruit knives and forks, table knives, cheese knives, tea knives and a 5-piece carving set, by Harrison Brothers and Howson, Sheffield 1948, 4 dessert forks 1946, the steel blades etched Asprey, Bond Street, 190oz weighable silver.
£2,400-2,600 *L*

A George III shovel caddy spoon, the fiddle pattern handle with canted corners, by Joseph Taylor, Birmingham, 1807.
£50-70 *P*

A George IV caddy spoon, by Joseph Taylor, Birmingham, 1826.
£100-140 *P*

Four various foreign silver caddy spoons.
£180-210 *RBB*

l). A George III leaf caddy spoon, the bowl chased with veins, and with coiled tendril handle, King's head and sterling lion marks only, c1810. **£80-120**

c). A George IV fiddle pattern caddy spoon with oval bowl engraved with acorns, by William Traies, 1825. **£50-100**

r). A Victorian Irish fiddle pattern caddy spoon, with scalloped bowl, maker's mark J.S., Dublin, 1884. **£60-100**   *P*

Dishes

A rare George I Plymouth tazza by Pentecost Symonds, with an elaborate contemporary coat-of-arms, either Nanphant, Cornwall or Penpons, Treswithian, Cornwall, raised on a plain trumpet foot, fully marked to top and foot, Exeter 1721, 8in (20cm) diam, 10oz. **£875-950**   *MN*

An American parcel gilt fancy spoon, by Tiffany & Co., c1890, 4½in (12cm). **£50-100**   *P*

A Victorian covered dish, by J. Mortimer & S. Hunt, 1840, 8in (20cm) high, 69oz. **£1,300-1,600**   *P*

Four George III silver gilt shell shaped butter dishes, three engraved with crests, by John Foskett and John Stewart, 1810, one engraved with a coat-of-arms, by William Burwash and Richard Sibley, 1810, 24oz. **£2,000-2,500**   *C*

A fine set of 12 George II plates by Edward Feline, engraved contemporary coat-of-arms, within gadroon borders, London 1747, 9½in (24cm) diam, 227oz. **£13,500-14,500**   *WW*

Four George II circular strawberry dishes, engraved with a coat-of-arms in a rococo cartouche, three by Charles F. Kandler, 1747, one by S. Herbert & Co., 1753, 10in (25.5cm), 81oz. **£15,000-16,000**   *C*

A set of 6 Timothy Renou dinner plates, with engraved leaf of Arms and motto, London 1800, 9½in (24cm), 114oz. **£1,800-2,000**   *Bon*

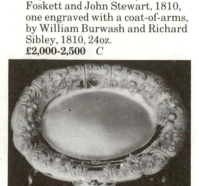

A set of 4 George IV silver gilt oval dessert dishes, each raised on elegant electroplated stand, maker's mark TB, London 1822, 50oz. **£650-750**   *TW*

A pair of George III oval meat dishes, with armorial bearings, possibly Thomas Heming, London 1763, 12in (30.5cm), 38oz. **£700-800**   *HCH*

A late Victorian silver shell shape dish, raised on 3 shell feet, Sheffield 1898, 10in (25.5cm) diam. 10oz. **£150-200**   *TW*

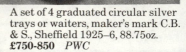

A pair of Victorian shaped circular
entree dishes and covers and
matching serving dish and cover,
London 1895, 5,750gm weighable
silver.
£2,200-2,500 *Bea*

A set of 4 graduated circular silver
trays or waiters, maker's mark C.B.
& S., Sheffield 1925–6, 88.75oz.
£750-850 *PWC*

A George V shaped oval dish
with matching smaller dish,
Birmingham 1913, 14in (36cm)
and 10in (26cm) long, 56.3oz
(1,754gm).
£500-1,000 *Bea*

A pair of Edward VII rococo style
oval fruit dishes, with presentation
inscription dated 1908,
Birmingham 1906, 12in (30.5cm)
wide, 31oz.
£350-400 *LBP*

◁ A set of 4 William IV butter shells,
on cast whelk feet, by Richard
Sibley, London 1831.
£1,500-2,000 *Bon*

Inkstands

A George III oval inkstand with
French gadroon mounts to the rim,
on 4 reeded panel feet, with oval
lidded box at centre, by John Emes,
London 1804, 9 by 4in (23 by 10cm)
with cut glass and silver mounted
pounce pot and a later inkwell for
same, 10oz weighable silver.
£400-500 *BD*

A George IV rectangular inkstand,
fitted central taperstick and
snuffer, and two cut glass ink
bottles, maker Matthew Boulton,
Birmingham 1826, 11in (28cm)
wide, 33oz 10dwt weighable silver.
£1,200-1,600 *BS*

A large George IV inkstand with ▷
three cut glass cubic fittings, with
silver covers, the centre with fitted
taperstick and snuffer, engraved
with crest and inscribed 'Presented
by my friend Thomas Roberts Esqr,
Novr 1 1823', by William Elliott,
1821, 13in (33cm) wide, 60oz
weighable silver.
£2,500-3,000 *P*

A rectangular late
Victorian double
inkstand, by W J Barnard,
London 1894, 11in (28cm),
25oz.
£500-600 *WW*

An early
Victorian
portrait bust
inkstand
on plinth
of The Duke of
Wellington, by Charles T. & George
Fox, interior with a glass liner and
pierced cover, London 1846, 8in
(20.5cm), loaded.
£1,000-1,500 *WW*

A Victorian foliate pierced gadrooned oblong gallery inkstand on scroll feet, E & J Barnard, London 1853, 28.75oz, free.
£800-1,200   *CSK*

An early George III pear shaped silver cream jug, with scroll handle and foot, by James Waters, London 1763.
£60-120   *PWC*

Jugs

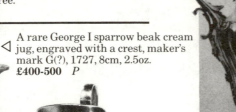

◁ A rare George I sparrow beak cream jug, engraved with a crest, maker's mark G(?), 1727, 8cm, 2.5oz.
£400-500   *P*

A George III claret or hot water jug, engraved with a shield of arms, and on the other side script initials below a crest, by Henry Chawner, 1791, 12½in (31cm), 23oz gross.
£1,300-1,600   *L*

A William IV fluted inverted pear shaped claret jug with domed hinged cover, with presentation inscription, Messrs. Barnard, London 1836, 12in (30.5cm), 29.25oz.
£600-800   *CSK*

A George II sparrow beak cream jug, engraved with armorials, the underbase with the contemporary inscription, 'Mrs Elizth Edwards at Ye King & Queen', by Benjamin Sanders, 1737, 3½in (9cm), 3oz.
£500-600   *P*

An unusual Victorian cream jug formed as a nanny goat, with hinged cover, gilt lined, Joseph and John Angell, London 1840, 5in (12.5cm), 8.25oz.
£2,000-2,500   *CSK*

A George IV claret jug, maker's mark rubbed, but probably that of Joseph Angell, 1829, 11½in (29cm), 31oz.
£1,600-1,800   *L*

A Victorian glass claret jug, the tapering body etched on oval panel of monkeys imbibing, with a bead drape border, maker W.E., London 1873, 12in (30.5cm).
£1,200-1,500   *WW*

An American jug, chased with water lilies, made by the Moore Company for Tiffany & Co., c1853, 9½in (24cm), 27.25oz.
£1,500-2,000   *P*

Marks as page 247, No.5, Tiffany Silver by C.H. & M.G. Carpenter.

Models

A French silver gilt statuette of an angel, loop on back for attachment, hands possibly replaced, reddish marble base, 15thC, 8.3cm.
£1,600-1,800   *C*

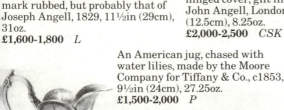

A statuette of a knight, with shield and sword, ivory carved head, his belt set with semi-precious stones, import marked, 14in (35.5cm) high.
£1,300-1,600   *Bon*

A French silver gilt statuette of Napoleon, standing in uniform with his right hand tucked inside his coat, 19thC, 12in (30.5cm).
£700-800   *C*

A Continental model of a coach and horses, the coach with detachable cover, import mark for London 1902, 11in (28cm) long, 11.7oz (365gm).
£550-650 *Bea*

A pair of silver pheasants, 1970, about 23oz, and a pair of chicks, about 5oz.
£450-550 *RPI*

A silver gilt statuette of an angel holding a reliquary, in the Gothic manner, the wings separately attached, standing on an octagonal base, 19in (48cm) high.
£1,800-2,100 *C*

Mugs

An early Victorian silver goblet, presentation inscription dated 1866, maker's mark I.H. and R.R. surmounted by a crown, Hunt & Roskell, London 1865, 8oz 15dwt.
£400-500 *GC*

A George II silver half pint mug, with engraved armorial, maker possibly Thomas Whipham, London 1744, 5in (12cm), 12oz.
£300-400 *NSF*

An early George II mug, the tapering body engraved with script initials below the everted moulded rim and on a tuck-in base, with a spreading foot rim, scroll handle, the underside engraved with initials, by Francis Spilsbury I, 1735, 4½in (11cm).
£500-600 *L*

A George II silver mug, the scroll handle with initials I.H., maker John Langlands, Newcastle 1756, 5in (12.5cm), 9½oz.
£300-500 *NSF*

◁

A George II mug, by Richard Bayley, London 1747, 4in (10cm), 7oz.
£260-300 *DWB*

A large Chinese Export mug, by Hung Chong of Canton & Shanghai, c1880, 5½in (14cm), 13.5oz.
£450-650 *P*

Salts

A pair of George II circular silver salt cellars, each with 3 feet, maker's mark I.M., London 1757.
£100-200 *PWC*

A set of 4 George III plain circular salt cellars, by Paul Storr, 1798, 3in (8cm), 15oz 5dwt.
£1,300-1,600 *C*

The crest and coronet are those of the Dukes of Bedford.

A set of 4 George III silver two-handled boat shaped salts, on rectangular bases, maker's mark J.W. (John Wren), London 1791, one 1790, 14oz 12dwt.
£300-500 *GC*

A pair of William IV circular fluted salts, crested, maker William Eaton, London 1837, 4in (10cm) diam, 12oz.
£250-500 *LBP*

A William IV circular mustard pot, with blue glass liner, by Charles Fox, London 1837, 9oz, and a cast salt spoon, London 1831.
£450-550 *WW*

A pair of George I plain circular salvers, each on central spreading foot, with moulded borders, engraved with a coat-of-arms in a baroque cartouche, by Robert Timbrell and Joseph Bell I, 1714, 10in (25cm) diam, 33oz.
£6,000-7,000 *C*

The arms are those of Winston impaling another.

A fine and heavy pair of French salt cellars, the well chased and gilded shell bowls supported on two fighting dragons, by Lebrun, Paris, c1860.
£1,800-2,000 *Bon*

A Victorian H.M. silver matching set of 6 open salt cellars and spoons in fitted case, maker Richard Sibley, London 1868.
£150-200 *FHF*

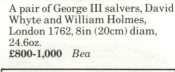

A George II waiter, monogrammed, maker probably William Justus, London 1752, 6in (15cm) diam, 6½oz.
£200-250 *LBP*

Salvers

A George II circular salver, initialled to reverse, maker Francis Pages, London 1736, 9in (23cm) diam, 15oz.
£400-600 *LBP*

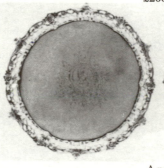

A pair of George III salvers, David Whyte and William Holmes, London 1762, 8in (20cm) diam, 24.6oz.
£800-1,000 *Bea*

A George I rare silver gilt fifteen-sided salver, on 3 cast pad feet, with moulded border, engraved with a coat-of-arms in a baroque cartouche, by Augustin Courtauld, 1723, 11in (28cm), 35oz.
£30,000-35,000 *C*

The arms are those of Willmot of Stodham, Co. Oxford, impaling Mann.

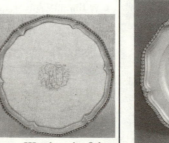

An early George III salver, by John Crouch, 1772, 12in (30.5cm), 30oz.
£700-800 *L*

Twelve George III shaped circular dinner plates, by Paul De Lamerie, 1741, 9½in (24cm) diam, 233oz.
£30,000-40,000 *C*

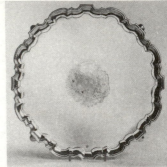

A fine pair of George II salvers, London 1730, 5½in (14.5cm), 443gm gross, and a fine pair of George II salvers, London 1735 and 1736, 6½in (17cm), 567gm gross.
£500-600 each pair   *HSS*

A George II plain octafoil salver, by John Robinson II, 1738, 13½in (34cm) diam, 30oz.
£2,200-2,500   *C*

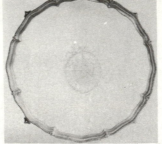

A large Ebenezer Coker waiter, on well cast shell feet, engraved full coat-of-arms in floral cartouche, London 1772, 14in (35.5cm).
£1,500-2,000   *Bon*

A George III salver, on 4 claw and ball feet, by Richard Rugg, 1775, 14in (35.5cm) diam, 42oz.
£1,800-2,200   *C*

A George II shaped circular salver, engraved with a coat-of-arms and a motto in a rococo cartouche, by Sarah Holaday, 1740, 17in (42cm) diam, 70oz.
£3,100-3,500   *C*

A George III salver, on 4 ball and claw supports, the underside engraved with triad initials, by John Crouch, 1774, 13½in (34.5cm), 42oz.
£850-950   *L*

While there is no record of Crouch's mark alone, only in partnership with Thomas Hannam, it is known he worked alone between 1774 and 1784.

A George III salver, on 4 tapering cast panel feet, by William Fountain and Daniel Pontifax, London 1793, 13in (33cm) diam, 34oz.
£700-800   *WW*

A George IV silver salver, the borders cast with rococo shells, flowers and foliage, makers Waterhouse, Hodson & Co., Sheffield 1824, 11in (28cm), 25.25oz.
£450-500   *PWC*

A pair of George III salvers, by William Bruce, 1817, 12in (30.5cm), 52oz.
£2,500-3,000   *L*

A William IV salver, on 3 leaf scroll feet, makers Samuel Roberts & Co., Sheffield 1833, 18in (46cm) diam, 70oz.
£1,000-1,500   *WW*

A silver salver, maker's mark W.B., London 1824, 9in (23cm), 18.75oz.
£220-280   *PWC*

A pair of George III Irish salvers, on 3 anthemion and paw supports, by John Laughlin Jnr, Dublin 1782, 8½in (21.5cm), 26oz.
£800-900 *L*

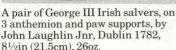

A late Victorian silver salver, maker's mark W.J.B. (Messrs. Barnard), London 1894, 27oz approx.
£400-500 *GC*

A salver, with shaped and moulded border embossed with scrolled foliage, Sheffield 1943, 14½in (37cm) diam, 45oz.
£400-450 *CDC*

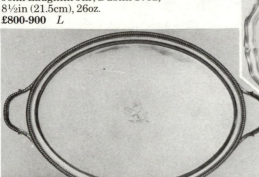

A George III tray, by Thomas Hannam and John Crouch, 1800, 21in (52cm), 53oz.
£2,000-2,500 *C*

A salver, with cast Chippendale style border, Sheffield 1973, 15in (38cm) diam, 54oz.
£600-650 *WIL*

Sauceboats

An early Victorian salver, maker William K. Reid, London mark 1837, 19½in (49cm), 98oz.
£900-1,100 *AG*

A George II style silver sauceboat, mark rubbed.
£85-115 *RPI*

A George II silver sauceboat, 1755, 5oz.
£400-450 *RPI*

A pair of George II plain sauceboats, with serpent scroll handles, by Robert Brown, 1743, 24oz.
£2,300-2,800 *C*

A rare pair of side-handled sauceboats, by Samuel Blachford, Exeter 1732, 4½in (35cm), 11oz.
£6,000-6,500 *Bou*

A pair of George II sauceboats, by John Pollock, London 1749, 7in (18cm) long, 21oz 10dwt.
£1,500-2,000 *CNY*

A George II silver sauceboat, maker's mark W.S., probably William Sheen, 1755, 8½oz.
£450-500 *RPI*

A pair of George II sauceboats, by
William Robertson, London 1755,
808gm.
£1,500-2,000 *HSS*

A pair of Georgian oval
sauceboats, rubbed
marks, London 1759,
22oz.
£600-700 *Wor*

An early George III
sauceboat, maker's mark
G.S., London 1764,
6oz 10dwt.
£450-500 *GC*

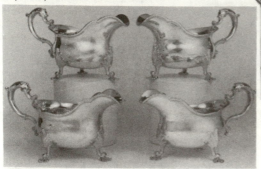

Four George II plain sauceboats, by
Edward Wakelin, 1757, 74oz.
£5,000-5,500 *C*

A matched pair of George III/IV cast
sauceboats, one by Paul Storr, 1812,
the other by Robert Garrard, 1825,
59oz.
£11,000-13,000 *P*

A pair of large George IV
sauceboats, by I.H. and G. Lias,
London 1824, 28oz.
£1,300-1,500 *WW*

A pair of George III helmet shaped
pedestal sauceboats, by William
Pitts, London 1784, 710gm.
£1,500-2,000 *HSS*

A set of 4 mint condition
sauceboats, by Edward, Edward,
James and William Barnard,
London 1835, 9in (22.5cm) 79oz.
£9,000-11,000 *Bou*

Scent bottles

A Victorian silver gilt
double-ended scent flask,
maker E.M.S. London
1884, 5in (12.5cm).
£700-800 *NSF*

A George IV silver gilt scent bottle
stand, hexagonal, William Eaton,
London 1829, 10oz, and cut glass
scent bottle.
£350-400 *HCH*

A Victorian silver gilt and ruby
glass scent bottle and vinaigrette,
by S. Mordan, London 1866, 4in
(10cm).
£200-250 *BD*

A scent bottle with silver collar,
1937.
£250-300 *FM*

◁
A Victorian cut glass perfume
bottle, with a silver top,
Birmingham 1892.
£100-130 *Tri*

A Victorian silver scent phial,
Birmingham 1892, 8in (20cm) long,
5oz, in case.
£250-300 *HCH*

Services

A George III tea service, by Henry Chawner, 1792, hot water jug on shaped foot, 1794, and a helmet shaped cream jug, maker's mark ID perhaps for James Darquits Jnr, 1791, 89oz gross.
£3,200-3,800 *C*

A George III silver gilt partly fluted tea and coffee service, by Samuel Hennell, 1800, coffee pot 10in (25cm) high, 102oz gross, in fitted wood box.
£8,500-9,000 *C*

A George III five-piece tea and coffee service, by John Emes, London 1799, handle to coffee biggin broken, height of biggin on lampstand 13in (33cm), 68oz 10dwt.
£1,800-2,200 *CNY*

A George IV silver tea service.
£1,300-1,500 *MIL*

A George III silver teapot, maker C.P., London 1817, 21oz.
£250-300

A George IV silver sugar bowl, maker Edward John and William Barnard, London 1829, and a matching William IV cream jug, London 1830, 23½oz.
£300-350 *NSF*

A George IV and William IV three-piece tea service, maker R. Pearce and G. Burrows, London 1828 and Joseph and John Angell, London 1833, 43oz gross.
£500-600 *WW*

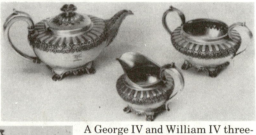

A Victorian four-piece tea and coffee service, Dublin 1845–6, 82oz.
£1,500-2,000 *RBB*

A William IV tea and coffee service, by Charles Fox, London 1835, 90oz gross.
£3,200-3,800 *WW*

A Victorian tea service, Louis XV pattern, by Joseph and Albert Savory, London 1850, 41oz.
£500-600 *WW*

◁ A William IV silver tea and coffee set, makers E.J. and E.W. Barnard, 1833–4, 77oz.
£2,200-2,600 *GSP*

A George III three-piece silver teaset, maker's mark W.H., London 1818–19, 41oz.
£600-700 *PWC*

An early Victorian tea and coffee service, by William Eaton, 1838 and 1839, coffee pot 8½in (21.5cm) high, 75oz.
£1,400-1,800 *L*

A Victorian four-piece silver tea service, Sheffield 1883, 118oz 16dwt.
£1,200-1,500

A Victorian eight-sided silver tray to match, Sheffield 1884, 24in (61cm) wide, 147oz.
£1,200-1,500 *DSH*

A William IV coffee pot, teapot and milk jug, by Henry Wilkinson & Co., Sheffield 1832, coffee pot 9½in (24cm) high, 62oz.
£800-900 *L*

A Victorian tea and ▷ coffee service, by J. Whipple & Co., Exeter, 1877 and 1879, 90oz gross.
£2,000-2,500 *C*

◁A Victorian four-piece engraved tea set, maker's mark J D & S, 1867, 71.75oz.
£2,000-2,500 *RPI*

A Victorian three-piece teaset and coffee ewer, by Martin & Hall, Sheffield 1868, the ewer London 1879, 75.5oz weighable silver, cream jug loaded.
£1,800-2,300 *P*

A Victorian tea and coffee service, by John Edward Terrey, 1844, coffee pot 10½in (26.5cm) high, 73oz.
£1,300-1,700 *L*

A Victorian five-piece tea and coffee service, with tray, Holland, Son and Slater, London 1881–2, 127.7oz.
£1,400-1,900 *Bea*

A silver tea service, Birmingham 1902, 15oz.
£140-180 *CDC*

An Edward VII tea and coffee service, Mappin & Webb Sheffield 1901, and a pair of sugar tongs, 65.5oz.
£900-1,100 *Bea*

A Victorian tea and coffee service,
by Thomas Smiley, 1865, coffee pot
8½in (21.5cm) high, 68oz.
£1,200-1,400 *L*

A South American four-piece teaset
on tray, 113oz.
£600-700 *Bon* ▷

A Danish silver coffee service by
Georg Jensen,   23oz.
£1,000-1,400 *SL* ▽

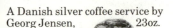

A Victorian silver tea/coffee service,
makers Martin Hall & Co., London
1869–70, 110oz, in a fitted oak case.
£2,500-3,000 *Pea*

An Edward VII three-piece coffee
set, in the neo-classical style,
Sheffield 1909, 1,400gm gross.
£500-600 *HSS*

An Edward VII five-piece tea and
coffee service, Birmingham 1902,
81oz 4dwt.
£600-700 *BS*

An oriental
three-piece silver
teaset, 44oz.
£450-500 *JMW*

A William IV tea service, the teapot
and milk jug by Marshall & Sons,
Edinburgh 1836, the sugar basin by
George Hunter II, London 1835,
48oz gross.
£450-550 *WW*

A four-piece silver tea set.
£400-500 *PWC*

A modern five-piece tea and coffee
service, maker's mark C.J.V Ltd.,
London, 1961, 127.3oz (3,960gm).
£1,300-1,800 *Bea*

A Victorian four-piece silver tea
and coffee set, maker's mark
F.B.M., London 1886, 57.25oz.
£700-800 *PWC*

Tankards

A Charles II tankard and cover, maker's mark EG, 1671, 6½in (16.5cm), 21oz.
£3,500-4,000 *C*

A James II tankard and cover, maker's mark IO a device between, perhaps for John Oliver, York 1686, 7in (18cm), 21oz.
£3,500-4,000 *C*

A William III tankard, engraved with later armorials, 1730, the handle with contemporary initials R*I, by John Gibbons, 1701, 7½in (18.5cm), 26oz.
£1,800-2,200 *P*

A Queen Anne tankard, by Humphrey Payne, 1708, 7in (18cm), 24oz.
£1,600-1,900 *P*

A Queen Anne silver tankard by S. Holaday, London 1709, 7in (18cm)
£4,000-4,500 *SA*

A George I tankard, by Christopher Canner II, fully marked Britannia Standard 1719, 6½in (17cm), 22oz.
£1,500-1,800 *L*

A George II silver tankard, maker's mark I.S., Joseph Smith, 1730, 8oz.
£350-400 *RPI*

A George II tankard, by Thomas Whipham, 1745, 8in (20cm), 31oz.
£1,200-1,600 *C*

A George II silver engraved tankard, maker's mark J.P., John Payne, 1754, 7oz.
£280-340 *RPI*

A George II tankard, by Francis Crump, London 1755.
£1,000-1,300 *Bon*

A George II silver tankard, London 1759, 5in (12.5cm), 10oz 12dwt.
£280-340 *DSH*

A George III tankard, maker Thomas Watson, Newcastle 1795, 5in (12.5cm), 10.25oz.
£120-160 *PWC*

A George III tankard, by John Payne, 1768, the handle with maker's mark, 8in (20cm), 26oz.
£1,200-1,500 *L*

A George II silver tankard, maker's mark F.S., 1740, 11oz.
£400-450 *RPI*

A late Victorian large tankard trophy, the base inscribed 'The Gift of Her Most Gracious Majesty Queen Victoria, Cowes Regatta, 1888', by Robert Allan Roskell & John Mortimer Hunt, 1887, 14in (35cm) high, 96oz.
£4,000-4,500 *P*

A Scandinavian silver gilt tankard, maker's mark P.K.I., possibly for Peder Knudsen of Oslo, c1660.
£5,500-6,000 *C*

A German tankard, inscribed around the rim 'Ludwich Pruszycky Anno 1677', by Abraham Wilde, Königsberg, Prussia, c1675, 8½in (22cm), 32.5oz.
£2,500-3,000 *P*

A Norwegian peg tankard, dated 1666, 9in (23cm), 26oz 12dwt.
£3,500-4,000 *BS*

An Indian tankard, with inscription 'AMA, shot for at the Maroon Club of H.M. 14th Regiment, Berhampore 1813–14. Won by Lieut. Colnl. Watson', by Robert Hamilton, Calcutta, c1812, 6in (15cm), 19oz 8dwt.
£2,500-3,000 *C*

Tea Caddies

A pair of George III tea caddies, oval, straight sides, reeded upper mount, pull-off covers, London 1783.
£550-650 *Bon*

A George III tea caddy, by John Denziloe, London 1787, 6in (15cm), 13oz.
£900-1,100 *CW*

A Queen Anne tea caddy, by Thomas Ash, London 1702, 4½in (11.5cm), 5.75oz.
£450-500 *DWB*

A set of George II tea caddies and ▷ sugar box, by Peze Pilleau, 1743, in a fitted velvet lined shagreen box, with lockplate, key and handle, 4in (10cm), 38oz.
£3,000-3,500 *C*

◁ A pair of caddies, chased with leaves, flowers and shells, by Joseph Angell, London 1821, 4½in (11cm), 34.75oz.
£2,000-2,400 *Bou*

Three Pierre Gillois tea caddies, London 1760-65, 33oz.
£1,700-2,000 *Bon*

A George III tea caddy, maker Hester Bateman, London 1788, 6in (15cm) wide, 14oz gross.
£450-500 *AG*

A gilt tea urn with royal associations, the pyriform body on square pedestal base and cast shell feet, and floral garlands, the body engraved with the Royal Cypher, by Lewis Herne and Francis Butty, London 1763.
2,500-3,000 *Bon*

A French silver gilt tea urn by Jean-Baptiste-Claude Odiot, Paris, c1830, 20in (51cm), 139oz.
£7,500-8,500 *P*

A George III tea caddy, by John Robins, 1790, 6in (15cm), 16oz.
£3,000-3,500 *Bou*

Tea Kettles

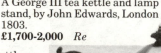

A George III tea urn on stand by John Emes, London 1805, 97oz gross.
£1,500-2,000 *WW*

A George III tea kettle and lamp stand, by John Edwards, London 1803.
£1,700-2,000 *Re*

A George II baluster tea kettle on stand, maker John Payne, London 1754, 15in (38cm).
£2,500-3,000 *RBB*

Teapots

A George III teapot on stand, by Henry Chawner, 1796, the stand 1795, teapot 10½in (26cm) wide, 19.2oz gross.
£850-950 *L*

A George III teapot, by John Emes, 1801, 10½in (27cm) wide, 16.7oz gross.
£180-220 *L*

A 'bright cut' teapot and stand, the former by Robert Hennell, London 1791, the latter by Edward Jay, 1792, both engraved with the letter 'B' for Luke Baker of Roxbury of Connecticut, whose name is engraved on the base of the stand, 18oz.
£1,800-2,200 *Bou*

A George III biggin, stand and lamp, engraved with armorials, by William Frisbee, 1802, 12½in (31cm) high overall, 59oz.
£1,500-2,000 *P*

A George IV small coffee pot, by William Bateman, 1827, 7½in (19.5cm) high, 34oz.
£600-700 *L*

A George IV teapot and a similar cream jug.
£550-600 *RBB*

A William IV teapot, by Paul Storr, 1833, 5½in (14cm) high, 24oz.
£1,200-1,600   *P*

A pair of early Victorian flared cylindrical teapots, by Robert Garrard, London 1844, 46oz gross.
£1,100-1,400   *WW*

An early Victorian teapot by John S. Hunt, to a design by Paul Storr, inscribed Hunt and Roskell, late Storr Mortimer and Hunt, London 1847, lip with repair, 25oz gross.
£250-300   *WW*

A William IV naturalistic melon-shape teapot, by E.J. & W. Barnard, the root loop handle a Victorian replacement, portcullis crest, London 1835, 6in (15cm), 17oz gross.
£400-500   *WW*

An Indian Colonial silver pear-shaped teapot, by Hamilton & Co., Calcutta, c1830, 5½in (14cm) high, 18.5oz.
£300-350   *P*

A George V bullet-shaped teapot, in 18thC style, Edward Barnard and Sons Ltd., London 1913, 5in (12.5cm) high, 19.2oz.
£550-600   *Bea*

Trays

A tea tray by William Stroud, London 1802, 23in (58cm) overall, 84oz.
£2,200-2,400   *Bon*

An Indian oval teapot, by Hamilton & Co., Calcutta, c1822, 7in (17.5cm), 29oz gross.
£1,800-2,200   *C*

A tea tray, maker's mark rubbed, 1906, 27in (70cm), 145oz.
£1,200-1,400   *L*

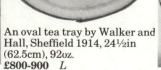

An oval tea tray by Walker and Hall, Sheffield 1914, 24½in (62.5cm), 92oz.
£800-900   *L*

A George III tray by John Crouch, 1807, 26in (66cm) long, 102oz.
£4,000-4,500   *C*

A tea tray by Walker and Hall, Sheffield 1910, 29in (74cm) across handles, 131oz.
£1,200-1,400   *L*

A William IV card tray, London 1833, 8½in (21.5cm) diam, 11.5oz.
£200-250   *LBP*

A tea tray, maker's mark JS, Sheffield 1927, 26in (66cm) across handles, 104oz.
£900-1,000   *L*

Tureens

Four George III boat-shaped sauce tureens and covers, by John Emes, 1798, 10in (25cm) long, 72oz.
£4,500-5,000   *C*

A George IV tray by William Elliot, 1822, 24½in (62cm) long, 138oz.
£2,000-2,500   *C*

A George III tureen, maker's mark rubbed, London 1816, 3,325gm.
£1,000-1,300   *HSS*

A George III soup tureen, by Paul Storr, 1807, 18in (45cm) long, 207.5oz.
£16,000-19,000   *P*

A pair of George III Regency two-handled oval sauce tureens and covers, by Thomas Robins, 1810, 9in (23cm), 74oz.
£3,300-4,000   *C*

A set of four George III sauce tureens and covers, by R. Sibley and W. Burwash, 1807–1808, 8¼in (21cm), 112oz.
£3,500-4,000   *P*

A pair of Swedish covered sauce tureens, in the early 19thC style, by C.G. Hallberg, 1892, 41oz.
£700-800   *P*

A pair of oval entrée dishes, covers and detachable handles, by Walker and Hall, Sheffield 1911, 11in (27.5cm), 108oz.
£650-750   *L*

A Victorian soup tureen and cover, by T.W.H. and H. Dobson, 1880, 12in (30cm) across handles, 46.5oz.
£1,200-1,500   *L*

Wine Antiques

An unmarked folding corkscrew, with fluted torpedo-shaped handle, late 18thC, 2in (5cm).
£650-750   *CSK*

A Dutch silver-handled steel corkscrew, engraved 'T.Y.V.G.' in cursive upper case, 18thC, 4¼in (10.5cm).
£600-700   *TKN*

A sheathed corkscrew, with faceted loop, 18thC.
£100-130   *BAC*

The sheath which protects the worm doubles as a handle, fitting through the loop at the top of the shank.

A Thomason 1802 type of brass double action corkscrew, with bone handle.
£170-190   *SYK*

A Thomason 1802 type brass, steel and bone corkscrew, with Royal coat-of-arms.
£170-200   *SYK*

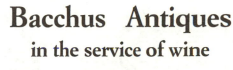

A Kings screw with a turned bone handle, brush missing, metal side handle and helix screw, with tablet marked 'Heeley & Sons' and royal coat-of-arms.
£450-550   *BAC*

A James Heeley's 1890 patent corkscrew, 'The Empire'.
£280-320   *BAC*

An all steel corkscrew named 'The Pullezi', stamped with Heeley Original Patent and 4307, perfect helical worm, traces of original gilt/bronze finish, 10in (25cm) long fully extended.
£90-100   *SYK*

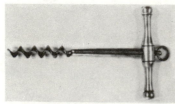

A brass and steel bladed worm corkscrew.
£35-40　*SYK*

A peg and worm or serpentine corkscrew, 4½in (11.4cm) long when closed.
£90-100　*BAC*

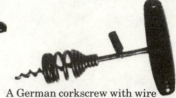

A German corkscrew with wire spring barrel and hinged flange to assist in the removal of the cork.
£75-85　*BAC*

A rare George III Provincial cartouche wine label, by Richard Richardson, Chester, c1765.
£150-180　*P*

A George III wine label, by Hester Bateman, c1765.
£140-180　*P*

RUM

Four George III wine labels, by Matthew Boulton and John Fothergill, Birmingham, two with replaced chains, two 1774 and two 1776, 2oz.
£600-700　*CNY*

A George III scroll wine label, pierced 'Claret', by Susanna Barker, c1785.
£300-350　*P*

A George III wine label, incised 'Claret', by John Steward, c1790, 2in (5cm) long.
£80-100　*P*

A George III Scottish Provincial plain eye-shaped wine label, incised 'Gin', by John Ewen, Aberdeen, c1790.
£70-100　*P*

A rare George III Provincial wine label, incised 'Lisbon', by Langlands & Robertson, Newcastle, c1790.
£300-350　*P*

A George III wine label, maker's mark overstruck by that of Richard Evans of Shrewsbury, 1791.
£250-300　*P*

A George III disc wine label, by Robert Barker, 1794, 1½in (3.5cm).
£200-250　*P*

A George III crescent-shaped wine label, probably by Crespin Fuller, 1800.
£180-220　*P*

A very rare George III fouled anchor wine label, incised 'Madeira', by Phipps & Robinson, 1799, 2in (5cm) high.
£1,200-1,400　*P*

A George IV Irish wine label, in the late 18thC style, incised 'Burgundy' by James Fray, Dublin, c1820, also bearing retailer's name of West, and a similar label incised 'White', by Susanna Barker, 1784–5.
£60-80　*P*

A George IV oval wine label, by John Reily, 1824, 2½in (6.5cm) long.
£250-300　*P*

A George III/IV Scottish wine label, incised 'Cape-Madeira', by Francis Howden, Edinburgh, c1820.
£70-90　*P*

This design is unusual for a Scottish label.

A George IV wine label, pierced 'Calcavella' by Emes & Barnard, 1825.
£120-180 *P*

A rare Irish wine label, incised 'Ennishowen', maker's mark only H.F., untraced, but almost certainly an alternative mark of Henry Flavelle of Dublin, c1825.
£280-340 *P*

A George IV Scottish vine leaf wine label, pierced 'Madeira', maker's mark Edinburgh, c1825, 3½in (9.5cm) long.
£40-50 *P*

A George IV Provincial wine label, with a disc surmount engraved with a Blackamoor's head crest within a garter, inscribed 'Gang Forward', the crest of Stirling, incised 'Rum', by Joseph Hicks, Exeter, 1825.
£130-160 *P*

A rare George IV armorial wine label, a dragon's head raised between two wings, by I.E. Terry, 1828.
£500-600 *P*

A George IV Irish wine label, incised 'Port', by Henry Flavelle, Dublin, 1829, 2in (5cm) long.
£80-100 *P*

A George IV cast wine label, pierced 'Sherry' and surmounted by the coronet of the Earl of Eglington, by Rawlings & Summers, c1829.
£450-500 *P*

An early Victorian architectural wine label, on an unusual chain, by Robert Garrard, 1839, 2½in (6cm) long.
£260-320 *P*

A rare and large Victorian fern leaf wine label, with applied title 'Port', apparently no maker's mark, 1845, 3½in (9cm).
£800-900 *P*

A Victorian cast cartouche shaped label, with border of raised scrolls, pierced 'Madeira', by John S. Hunt, 1849.
£160-200 *P*

A pair of Victorian pierced wine labels, enamelled in blue and red, 'Burgundy' and 'Sherry', W.S. London, 1886.
£280-340 *CSK*

A Victorian silver gilt label, in the Gothic style, incised 'Maraschino', by Robert Garrard, 1846.
£130-160 *P*

A cast silver gilt decanter label, hallmarked London.
£190-210 *SYK*

A Victorian electroplated wine label, chased with a 'flying fox', 3½in (8cm) long.
£60-80 *P*

A composite set of 6 cast bacchanalian wine labels, some unmarked.
£300-350 *CSK*

An Indian silver wine label or bottle ticket, marked 'Orr' on the reverse.
£60-70 *SYK*

A pair of George III coasters, with wood bases and silver buttons, by S. C. Younge & Co., Sheffield 1817, 6in (15cm).
£800-900   *CW*

Two early Victorian decanter stands, by Charles Fox and Charles T and George Fox, London 1839–41.
£1,300-1,600   *WW*

A pair of Sheffield plate coasters, 7½in (18.5cm).
£150-180   *Bea*

An unusual pair of George IV brass bound mahogany wine coasters, 12½in (31.5cm) high.
£2,200-2,500   *C*

A pair of Sheffield plate coasters, 6in (15cm) diam.
£200-250   *Bea*

A pair of double coasters as carriages, with turned wooden bases, and turned ivory handles.
£350-450   *HSS*

A pair of plated circular bottle stands, 4½in (11.5cm).
£100-150   *Bea*

A George III silver wine funnel, maker's mark P.B.A.B, Peter and Ann Bateman, London 1793, approx 4oz 10dwt.
£350-450   *GC*

A George III H.M. silver wine funnel and stand, no date letter, but marks for Ann Robertson, Newcastle 1801.
£350-450   *FHF*

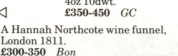

A Hannah Northcote wine funnel, London 1811.
£300-350   *Bon*

A pair of Sheffield wine coolers by James and Thomas Settle, 1817, 10in (25cm), 136oz.
£10,000-15,000   *Bou*

A fine pair of Victorian wine coolers, engraved with armorials and presentation inscription, by Messrs. Barnard, 1838, 10½in (26.5cm), 237oz.
£13,000-16,000   *P*

The inscription reads: 'To Sir James Gibson Craig Baronet, from his Countrymen and Fellow Citizens, December 1838'.

An American ovoid wine ewer, the body chased overall in the Chinese style, by Samuel Kirk, Baltimore, c1830, 16in (41cm) high, 48oz.
£1,700-2,000   *C*

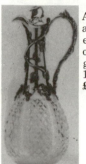

A Victorian electroplate and cut glass claret jug, engraved with coat of arms and inscription, glass foot damaged, 12in (31cm).
£170-250   *Bea*

An Epping Forest Centenary flagon, London 1978, 41oz.
£250-300   *WIL*

Accompanied by certificate signed by the Lord Mayor of London.

A Victorian baluster wine ewer, E & J Barnard, London 1865, 12in (30cm), 22.8oz.
£450-550   *Bea*

A Victorian vase shape wine ewer, C. F. Hancock & Co. London 1892, 12in (30.5cm), 26oz.
£400-600   *Bea*

A wine bottle carrier/coaster of steel mesh with brass edges, stamped with maker's initials in an oval *B*, c1860, 12½in (31cm) long.
£400-450   *SYK*

A rare George III double barrel cup, the two halves with gilt interiors combining to form a coopered cask, probably Peter Bateman, London 1813.
£600-700   *Re*

A late Victorian novelty port bottle carrier, maker H.T. London 1890, 13in (33cm) long, 27oz.
£950-1,000   *WW*

An unusual tole peinte double wine bottle carrier, the red ground decorated with oval landscape panels and gilt vine decoration, 19thC, 17in (43cm).
£350-400   *DWB*

A Channel Islands wine cup, engraved with initials, maker's mark RB, a fleur-de-lys and coronet above, struck also with a coronet and with an A with coronet above, Guernsey, c1695, 6in (14cm), 7oz 3dwt.
£1,500-2,000   *C*

See Richard H. Mayne, Old Channel Islands Silver, *Plate 7, for similar marks.*

A Russian gilt wine service, comprising: a circular waiter, 7in (18cm), and 6 stem cups, 3in (8cm) high, Moscow marks 1887, contained in original silk lined case.
£200-250   *AG*

Make the most of Miller's

Every care has been taken to ensure the accuracy of descriptions and estimated valuations. Where an attribution is made within inverted commas (e.g. 'Chippendale') or is followed by the word 'style' (e.g. early Georgian style) it is intended to convey that, in the opinion of the publishers, the piece concerned is a later – though probably still antique – reproduction of the style so designated. Unless otherwise stated, any description which refers to 'a set', or 'a pair' includes a valuation for the entire set or the pair, even though the illustration may show only a single item.

Miscellaneous

An Edwardian silver animal pincushion, in the shape of a hedgehog, Birmingham 1904.
£100-120 *EJ*

A glass and silver hip flask, Asprey, 1906.
£160-250 *HA*

A pair of Italian polychrome and giltwood dishes, supported on dancing goblins, late 19th/early 20thC, 9in (23cm).
£300-400 *CSK*

A sterling silver pincushion, by Tiffany & Co., 4in (10cm).
£350-400 *RBB*

A silver hip flask, 1873.
£250-300 *HA*

A George III hot water jug, by Benjamin West, London 1772.
£300-400 *HOF*

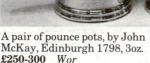

A pair of pounce pots, by John McKay, Edinburgh 1798, 3oz.
£250-300 *Wor*

A Victorian cigar lighter, the rim engraved with a presentation inscription, by J.S. Hunt, stamped Hunt & Roskell late Storr, Mortimer & Hunt, on circular ebonised plinth, 1851, 5in (13cm), 18oz 17dwt.
£1,300-1,700 *C*

A rare French ivory and silver snuff rasp, engraved with a portrait of Mary Queen of Scots, the legend Maria Scotorum Regina 1567, early 18thC, 7½in (19cm).
£2,000-2,500 *WW*

By descent to the present owner from William Forrester Cochrane, Factor to the Earl of Mar d.1792.

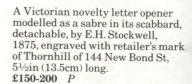

A pair of George IV silver gilt grape scissors, by Charles Rawlings, 1828, cased, 5oz.
£250-300 *P*

A Victorian novelty cigar cutter, modelled as a monkey, unmarked, c1880, 5in (13cm) long.
£150-200 *P*

A Victorian novelty letter opener modelled as a sabre in its scabbard, detachable, by E.H. Stockwell, 1875, engraved with retailer's mark of Thornhill of 144 New Bond St, 5½in (13.5cm) long.
£150-200 *P*

A Victorian novelty propelling pencil, by Sampson Mordan, modelled as an owl with coloured glass eyes, engraved with maker's name only 'S. Mordan & Co.,', c1880.
£100-150 *P*

A Victorian silver centrepiece
stand.
£300-350 *MGM*

An Irish silver dish ring by E.
Johnson, Dublin, in late 18thC
style, dated 1896, 8in (20cm) diam.
£600-800 *SA*

A George III dish ring, the pierced
collar frame finely chased and
engraved with a frieze, Dublin,
c1780, 8½in (21cm) diam., 18oz.
£850-950 *P*

An ivory box, the cover set with a
compass in a gold frame, the
interior containing a small ivory
barometer and two small brushes,
c1810, 7cm long.
£200-250 *P*

A rattle, formed as a jester, 2 bells,
mother-of-pearl handle, stamped
W.H.G., Chester.
£150-200 *CAm*

A gilt rattle with a whistle, the
mouth piece decorated with a castle,
4 gilt and one silver bell, coral
mouth piece, maker's mark GU,
England, 19thC.
£200-250 *CAm*

A small rattle shaped as a bear, 2
decorated bells, maker's mark C &
N, Birmingham.
£100-150 *CAm*

A George III pocket cheese scoop or
apple corer, with plain handle and
reversible screw-in blade, marks
rubbed, 5in (12.5cm).
£100-150 *BD*

A George IV silver mounted cut
glass condiment jar on stand, by
Paul Storr, London, 1825, together
with another stand and mount,
1829, 5in (12.5cm) high, 2 stands
14oz.
£2,000-2,500 *CNY*

A German condiment with English
import marks, modelled as a lady in
16thC costume, possibly Mary of
Guise, import marks for 1913, 3½in
(9.5cm) high.
£120-180 *P*

A George III mustard pot, by
Crispin Fuller, London 1795, 3in
(7.5cm), and spoon, London 1803 5oz.
£160-220 *DWB*

A Victorian composite silver gilt
dressing table set, by Charles
Stuart Harris, William Comyns,
Sampson Mordan, Rosenthal and
Jacobs, etc., the rectangular box
Dutch silver gilt coloured metal,
1885–1889.
£950-1,100 *L*

A four-piece silver and enamel dressing table set, 1909.
£300-350 *Ram*

A Louis Vuitton travelling case with silver gilt and tortoiseshell fittings, c1925.
£4,000-5,000 *Rev*

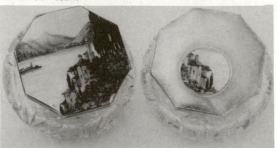

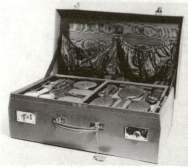

l. A cut glass dressing table tidy with H.M. silver and enamel lid, monogram by artist.
£80-120

r. A cut glass dressing table tidy with H.M. silver and enamel panelled lid.
£60-100 *FHF*

A pigskin beauty case by Mappin and Webb, with silver, gilt and crystal fittings, contained in a separate removable case, hallmarked 1943.
£850-950 *SB*

An interesting Victorian novelty pepperette as Benjamin Disraeli, with sphinx shaped helmet, knee breeches and tail coat, standing beside a pyramid, maker H.W.D., London 1878, 155gm.
£1,700-2,000 *HSS*

A pair of Victorian cast novelty frog pepperettes, one bearing traces of gilding, each with realistically textured skin, A.C. London 1881, 2in (5cm).
£350-400 *CSK*

A fine Victorian silver stand with 3 glass bottles, and with rope border.
£300-350 *MGM*

A George III lyre shape toast rack, the oval base engraved initials, maker Nathaniel Smith & Co., Sheffield, 1798, 5oz.
£255-300 *WW*

A George III oval boat shape 6-division toast rack, with crested initialled ring handle, by John Emes, London 1805, 7.5oz.
£160-220 *WW*

l. A George III oval silver cruet stand.
£220-260

c. A heavy quality silver sugar box and scoop.
£400-450

r. A Victorian circular and footed silver dessert basket, 12in (30cm).
£200-250 *PWC*

A silver toast rack, spelling 'Toast', c1935.
£200-220 *SA*

A Regency rectangular egg cruet, by William Eley, with a set of 6 matching egg cups, bulls head crest, London 1820, together with a set of 6 George IV fiddle thread pattern eggspoons, makers Eley and Fearn, London 1824, 32oz.
£800-1,000 *WW*

A Victorian rectangular basket design egg cruet, with 6 egg cups and a stand, presentation inscription and crested, by Robert Hennell III, London 1856, 9½in (24cm), 28oz.
£480-550 *WW*

A George III Scottish butter pail, engraved with a crest below a motto between reeded bands, the interior gilt, maker's mark GMH in monogram, Edinburgh 1814, 5½in (14.5cm) across handles.
£600-700 *L*

A Continental cow creamer, probably Dutch, 19thC, 7in (18cm) long, 7oz.
£290-350 *TEN*

◁ An Edwardian table bell, formed as a lady with spreading skirts, 1905, 5½in (14cm), 15.5oz.
£350-450 *P*

◁ A snuff box whistle, in the form of a boar's head, London 1975, 1½in (4cm).
£100-150 *Bea*

A pair of Victorian presentation silver riding spurs, each inscribed 'Presented by Mr. H. Clayton to the Winner of the Salford Cup, 1887', hallmarked Birmingham 1846, maker's mark J.B., with fitted morocco leather covered case.
£280-350 *PWC*

An early George I cast candle snuffer and stand, maker Roger Kempton, London 1714, 7½in (19cm), 10oz 6dwt.
£2,250-2,500 *BS*

A George IV silver strainer, maker's mark J.B., London 1828, 4in (10cm) diam., 4oz.
£200-250 *PWC*

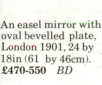

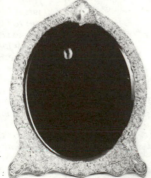

An easel mirror with oval bevelled plate, London 1901, 24 by 18in (61 by 46cm).
£470-550 *BD*

An Austrian cane handle modelled as a greyhound's head, by Georg Adam Scheid, also bearing German duty marks, mounted on wood cane, c1890.
£400-500 *P*

A George III silver pastry slice with wooden handle, 1767.
£500-550   *RPI*

An easel dressing table mirror, with vacant cartouche, embossed 4 panels of angels heads after Reynolds, makers T. May & Co., Birmingham 1904, 17½ by 18in (44 by 46cm).
£900-1,000   *WW*

A George III gadrooned square cruet on lion's paw feet, by Matthew Boulton, Birmingham 1817, 7in (18cm), 16.5oz free.
£280-320   *CSK*

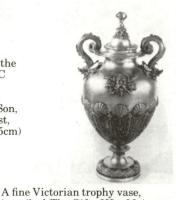

A pair of Victorian urn shaped silver vases, London 1882, 54oz.
£750-850   *RBB*

A Victorian silver gilt model canoe, Birmingham 1900, 7in (18cm) long, and a pair of Edwardian silver gilt model canoes, Chester 1910, 9½oz.
£270-320   *HCH*

A Victorian 6 bottle tantalus, the case in the form of a late 18thC Dutch mahogany and floral marquetry bureau, inset with makers' label, Watherston & Son, Silversmiths, 12 Pall Mall East, London, London 1887, 10in (25cm) wide.
£1,400-1,600   *BS*

Toys and Miniature Pieces

A fine Victorian trophy vase, inscribed 'The Gift of Her Majesty the Queen, Cowes Regatta Jubilee 1887', by James Garrard, 1887, 22in (56cm) high, 147oz.
£3,000-4,000   *P*

A Dutch toy table embossed and chased with figures in a garden, 2 by 1½in (5 by 4cm), and a similar armchair, import marks for London 1903.
£100-150   *BD*

A George III oval epergne on 4 lion's paw feet with openwork foliage and berries above with arcaded gallery, maker's mark IP, probably for Joseph Preedy, 1802, with cut glass bowl, 10in (25.5cm) high, 38oz.
£1,500-1,600   *C*

A Japanese miniature four-fold table screen, signed, 3½ by 6in (9 by 15cm).
£120-160   *BD*

Candlesticks

A pair of Sheffield plate candlesticks, by M. Fenton & Co., c1779, 11½in (29cm).
£700-800 *P*

An early Sheffield plated taperstick, c1770, 7in (17.5cm).
£250-290 *SA*

A pair of plated on copper table candlesticks, in the George II style, 9½in (23.5cm).
£130-170 *HSS*

A pair of Old Sheffield plate candlesticks, 10½in (26cm).
£80-100 *HSS*

A Victorian Sheffield plate table candelabrum, 28in (71cm).
£350-400 *Re*

A pair of plated candelabra with sconces, 22in (56cm).
£250-300 *Wor*

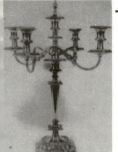

Services

A pair of Sheffield plate candelabra, 21in (53cm) high.
£550-600 *WIL*

A Victorian electroplated four-piece tea and coffee service.
£250-300 *Bea*

A Victorian plated tea or coffee set.
£350-400 *PWC*

Make the most of Miller's

When a large, specialist, well-publicised collection comes on the market, it tends to increase prices. Immediately after this, prices can fall slightly due to the main buyers having large stocks and the market being 'flooded'. This is usually temporary and does not affect very high quality items.

An electroplated four-piece tea and coffee service, Henry Wilkinson & Co., late 19thC.
£250-300 *Bea*

An electroplated four-piece tea and
coffee service.
£200-250   *Bea*

An electroplated four-piece tea
service.
£200-250   *Bea*

A plated tea and coffee service.
£150-200   *BD*

l. A Victorian lozenge-shaped
plated biscuit box.
£85-105

c. A Victorian pear-shaped cut
glass claret jug.
£145-180

r. A three-piece plated teaset,
19thC.
£120-150   *PWC*

Tureens

A Sheffield plate part dinner
service, comprising: 4 entrée dishes
and covers, a two-handled warming
stand, and a pair of sauce tureens,
crested, two detachable handles
broken.
£3,500-4,000   *Bea*

A Sheffield plated soup tureen and
cover, 16in (41cm) across handles.
£900-1,100   *L*

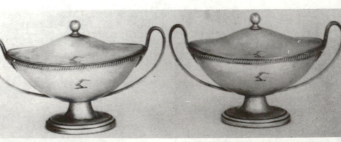

A pair of Sheffield plated sauce
tureens and covers, 9½in (23.5cm)
across handles.
£500-600   *L*

An early Victorian Sheffield plated
rococo style scalloped oblong entree
dish, 15in (38cm).
£350-400   *LBP*

Miscellaneous

An Elkington plate shell shaped spoon warmer, 8in (20cm) diam.
£90-110 *WIL*

An Elkington & Co., electrotype ink standish, 7½in (19cm) diam.
£150-200 *CDC*

An Elkington electrotype wedding scene from Much Ado About Nothing, engraved by Leonard Morel-Ladeuil, 1884, 16 by 22in (41 by 56cm).
£300-350 *Wor*

A Victorian Sheffield plate centrepiece, c1860, 21in (53cm) high.
£400-500 *Re*

A Regency Sheffield plate meat dish and matching dish cover, 18in (46cm).
£350-400 *WW*

A Victorian spoon warmer, in the form of a 16thC mortar, c1870, 6½in (16cm).
£200-250 *P*

A Sheffield plate Argyle, with beaded rim and water reservoir below, 19thC, 6½in (16cm) high.
£100-130 *Re*

A large silver plated centrepiece and stand, by Elkington & Co., dated April 1851, and with original iron bound oak carrying case.
£2,200-2,600 *HSS*

A table-centre candelabrum, 28½in (72cm) high.
£450-500 *CBD*

A Victorian plated table centrepiece.
£300-350 *PWC*

A George III Sheffield plate tea caddy, 5in (13cm).
£300-350 *WW*

A wall mirror, plated, late 19thC, 25 by 16in (64 by 41cm).
£500-600 *DWB*

A travelling coffee set of cylindrical form, with reeded girdles comprising: coffee pot on stand, cream jug and sugar bowl, by Hukin and Heath, c1885.
£140-180   *P*

An E.P.B.M. tea urn, late 19thC, 18in (46cm) high.
£130-160   *TW*

A silver plated tea urn, 19thC.
£220-280   *MGM*

A pair of large silver plated hearse lamps, 43in (110cm) high.
£1,800-2,200   *BS*

A late Victorian chamber pot.
£500-550   *WW*

An old Sheffield plate wire-work sugar basket.
£150-200   *HSS*

A Sheffield plate kettle, c1850–60.
£80-90   *YES*

A plated cruet stand with 8 bottles.
£120-180   *Wor*

An old Sheffield plate box, depicting Frederick the Great in profile wearing armour, c1765.
£180-220   *P*

A Victorian novelty brandy warmer, modelled as a witch's cauldron, 13in (33.5cm) high.
£150-200   *P*

An old Sheffield plate fruit basket, 11in (28cm) wide.
£60-80   *CDC*

A Sheffield plate cake basket, 19thC, 15in (38cm) wide.
£70-100 *PWC*

A Sheffield plate tea tray, early 19thC, 29in (74cm).
£250-300 *PWC*

An old Sheffield plate wine cooler, by Matthew Boulton & Co., 9in (23cm) high.
£250-300 *CDC*

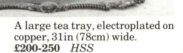

A Victorian novelty condiment set, moulded as a bird perched on a branch, 5½in (14.5cm) high.
£150-200 *P*

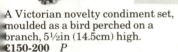

A large tea tray, electroplated on copper, 31in (78cm) wide.
£200-250 *HSS*

A pair of novelty biscuit boxes, formed as melons, the three segments each with their own pierced cover, 13in (33cm) high.
£700-800 *P*

A Continental electroplated cigarette case, c1900.
£220-260 *P*

A Victorian novelty condiment set, modelled as a drayman standing behind 3 condiments shaped as barrels, 5½in (14cm) high.
£130-160 *P*

A Victorian electroplated meat press, by Elkington & Co., 17½in (44cm) screwed down, excluding wood base.
1,500-2,000 *L*

An Australian decoratively plated mounted two-handled emu egg trinket box, some damage, 19thC, 7in (18cm) high.
£1,000-1,300 *GC*

A Continental electroplated cigarette case, c1900.
£200-250 *P*

Gold

A late Victorian 15ct gold presentation key, decorated and enamelled with the arms of the Borough of Huddersfield, Birmingham, 1898.
£350-400   *P*

A French gold and enamel 'memento mori' model of Napoleon's sarcophagus, c1821, 1¼in (3.5cm) long.
£450-500   *P*

A gold mounted oval seal, inset with a bloodstone, 1⅛in (3cm), in original fitted case.
£800-900   *BS*

A two-colour gold calendar of book form, c1811.
£300-350   *P*

A four-colour gold calendar of book form chased with flowers and set with turquoise, c1820.
£400-450   *P*

A French blue enamel and two-colour gold spy glass, applied with a diamond-set monogram on either side, lacking catch, c1770.
£1,800-2,000   *P*

A Scottish gold mounted vinaigrette, opening to reveal a three-quarter hinged pierced grille, the body with 12 coloured agate stones, 19thC, 3in (7cm) overall.
£1,400-1,700   *BS*

A Continental gold perfume box, probably Dutch, c1770.
£400-450   *P*

A Continental gold compact, the cover decorated with a Limoges enamel panel, with red and blue cloisonné enamel decoration, unmarked, probably Austrian, c1890, 2in (5.5cm).
£750-850   *P*

A George II gold snuff box, unmarked, c1735, 3in (7.5cm) lon[g] 5oz.
£2,500-3,000   *P*

An Irish gold and silver-gilt Masonic snuff box, maker's initials E.(?), with retailer's mark of Matthew West, Dublin, 1819, 3½in (9cm) long.
£1,300-1,600   *C*

A gold snuff box, with agate pane[l] in cover and base, unmarked, possibly English, c1790.
£1,000-1,300   *P*

Tortoiseshell

A Jacobite tortoiseshell snuff box, the lid inset with a painted miniature portrait on glass of The Young Pretender, Charles Edward Stuart, gilt metal rims, 3½in (9cm).
£600-700 *WW*

A gold mounted and gem set tortoiseshell parasol handle, late 19thC, 11½in (29cm) long, in fitted case.
£450-500 *Re*

A French tortoiseshell and silver egg, 19thC.
£250-300 *ARC*

Three tortoiseshell and silver frames, c1890.
Pair **£200-250**
Singles **£85-100** *FRA*

A late Victorian heart-shaped tortoiseshell/silver frame.
£350-400 *ARC*

Metal Brass

A pierced brass fender, 34in (86cm).
£70-80 *LRG*

A brass door porter, 16in (41cm) high.
£200-250 *L*

c. A copper and brass grape hod, 18thC, 30in (76cm) high.
£300-350

l. and r. A pair of cast brass and wrought iron firedogs, 26in (66cm) high.
£400-450 *PWC*

An Edwardian brass coal box and shovel.
£100-120 *ASH*

A Dinanderie gilt brass recumbent lion, 15thC, 3in (8cm) high.
£1,200-1,400 *C*

A pair of Regency gilt brass and bronze three-light candelabra, 20in (51cm) high.
£1,300-1,600 *Re*

A gilt brass chandelier, fitted for electricity, 19thC, 35in (90cm) high.
£2,200-2,600 *Bea*

A Louis XV style brass, polished steel and cast iron fender, with 3 brass and steel implements.
£500-550 *PWC*

559

A Queen Anne brass candlestick, c1710, 6½in (16cm).
£280-330 *SA*

A brass chamber candlestick, c1820.
£60-80 *KEY*

Two brass peppers, English, c1780, 4½ and 3in (11 and 7.5cm) high.
£130-160 each *KEY*

A brass candle snuffer and stand, c1740.
£350-400 *KEY*

A collection of brass candlesticks, six pairs, ten singles and three candelabra, 18th and 19thC.
£1,800-2,200 *TW*

A brass warming pan, 18thC, 44in (111cm).
£200-250 *HSS*

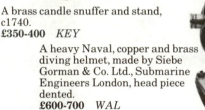

A heavy Naval, copper and brass diving helmet, made by Siebe Gorman & Co. Ltd., Submarine Engineers London, head piece dented.
£600-700 *WAL*

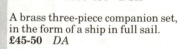

A brass warming pan, the wrought iron handle with turned brass finial, early 18thC, 41in (103cm) long.
£400-450 *DSH*

A brass three-piece companion set, in the form of a ship in full sail.
£45-50 *DA*

A teak Naval binnacle, containing heavy brass compass dated 1950, 52in (130cm) high overall.
£400-450 *WAL*

A heavy pre-W.W.II brass ship's bell, engraved 'H.M.S. Barlow 1938', 11in (28cm) high.
£160-200 *WAL*

A brass skimmer, with a wrought iron handle, c1780, 24in (61cm).
£120-140 *KEY*

A German brass tobacco box, c1770, 6in (15cm).
£140-160 *KEY*

Three brass ladles with wrought iron handles, c1790.
£100-130 each *KEY*

PACE SETTER

"Orilla", this painted bronze and ivory figure by Chiparus, tip-toed to £6,300 in a Phillips sale of Art Nouveau and Deco, despite having mislaid a left hand while dancing through the six decades from the Roaring Twenties.

Phillips conducted over 1,300 sales last year, incorporating art nouveau, studio ceramics, books, pictures, furniture, stamps, furs, silver, jewellery, ceramics – in total over 60 specialist categories. If you have any item which you wish to sell or have valued, you can rest assured that, at Phillips, our very high standards of service and attention to detail will apply whether we are handling a single item or a whole collection.

For further information regarding the services offered by Phillips, please contact Nicholas Fortescue (UK) or Richard Madley (USA) at the relevant address.

Phillips
FINE ART AUCTIONEERS & VALUERS SINCE 1796.

7 Blenheim Street, New Bond Street, London W1Y 0AS. Tel: 01-629 6602.
406 East 79th Street, New York, NY10021, USA. Tel: 010 1 212 570 4830.

LONDON · NEW YORK · PARIS · GENEVA · BRUSSELS
Eighteen salerooms throughout the United Kingdom. Members of the Society of Fine Art Auctioneers.

A James II ebonised striking bracket clock of phase III type, the finely engraved backplate signed 'Joseph Knibb Londini fecit', restorations, 12in (30cm). **£10,000-12,000** *C*

Above left A mid-Georgian walnut clock by Jno Melling Chester, 89in (225cm).
£10,000-15,000 *C*
Above right A seven day clock, dial signed Geo. Graham London, some restorations, 92in (232cm).
£30,000-40,000 *C*
Below A green-japanned clock, signed Newman Cartwright, early 18thC, 105in (265cm).
£4,000-6,000 *C*

An ebony veneered bracket clock, with glazed sides and solid back, signed 'Henricus Jones in the Temple, Fecit', late 17thC, 17in (43cm).
£18,000-22,000 *P*

A Royal presentation grande sonnerie spring clock by Thomas Tompion, c1700, 28in (71cm).
£250,000+ *C*
Presented, c1700 by William III of England to Cosimo III de Medici Grand Duke of Tuscany, and still not paid for at the time of the King's death, on the evidence of a petition in 1703 from the maker to Queen Anne.

A small George II ebonised grand sonnerie bracket clock, the moulded arched case with gilt brass mouldings, door fronting, the enamel dial signed Thos. Hughes London between strike/silent and calendar rings in the arch, the 7-pillar movement with triple fusee and chain, quarter strike on 6 bells, now with lever platform and signed engraved backplate, and a brass bound mahogany box, 10in (25cm) high.
£5,500-6,500   C

A George III scarlet and gold japanned bracket clock, made for the Turkish market, signed William Dunant London, 22½in (56cm) high.
£9,000-10,000   C

Left A French engraved brass carriage clock with porcelain dial, 8-day hour and half-hour striking and repeating movement, by Margaine, Paris, No.11506, late 19thC, 7in (17.5cm) high, in leather travelling case.
£2,500-3,500   CW

An early George III ebonised striking bracket clock, the enamel mounted dial signed Robt. & Peter Higgs London, 17½in (43cm).
£7,500-8,500   C

A George III satinwood 'balloon' bracket clock, signed Richd. Webster Exchange Alley London, 24in (60cm).
£4,500-5,500   C

A lady's boudoir timepiece, 6½in (17cm).
£800-1,000

An 18ct gold open faced key wind watch.
£300-400 *L*

Left A French gilt brass and white marble perpetual calendar 4-glass mantel clock, the circular enamel dial with visible 'coup perdu' escapement and centre seconds, signed Breveté, Le Roy & Fils, Paris, the enamel calendar dial showing month, date, and in the centre day and phases of the moon, in a chased gilt mask, 19thC, 16½in (42cm) high.
£2,500-3,000 *P*

Below A rare month-going Vienna regulator with perpetual calendar, signed Meisterstück Des Ludwig Deffner in Wien, c1820, 61in (152cm).
£14,000-15,000 *CG*

A George III ormolu, marble and biscuit porcelain mantel clock, the movement with a circlet of Roman numerals within an astrolabe on a plinth, inscribed Vulliamy, London 235, 12½in (32cm) high.
£7,500-8,500 *C*

Right An Austrian or Swiss Biedermeier ormolu mounted walnut and parquetry automaton table clock with organ, stamped HLR within a lozenge, restoration, 22in (55cm) high.
£16,000-18,000 *C*

l. A South German giltmetal tabernacle clock or Turmuhr, restorations, early 17thC, 19½in (48cm) high.
£11,000-14,000

r. A South German silver-fronted Telleruhr, the circular movement signed Matthias Geill on backplate, 14in (35cm) high, excluding stand.
£7,000-8,000   *C*

A Louis XIV tortoiseshell and gilt brass mounted 'Pendule de Voyage', the shaped case arched at the top, on 4 bun feet, signed along the base 'Duchesne A Paris', the gilt chapter ring mounted with enamel numerals and subsidiary regulating dial above, with pull quarter repeating on 2 bells, outside count-wheel strike, tulip pillars and signed shaped plates, 11in (28cm) high.
£4,500-5,500   *P*

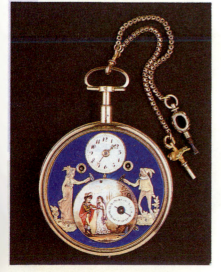

A gold cased repeating watch with Robin escapement, signed on the gold cuvette, Breguet No.2187, case No.2790/B 2187, with chain and key, 4.4cm diam, in a morocco fitted case by Dessoutter.
£26,000-30,000   *CG*

Above and right A fine and rare Swiss gold and enamel double-dial automaton watch, with quarter repeating on 'real bell', gold chain and two keys attached, c1800, 6cm.
£30,000-35,000   *CG*

A gold and diamond-set clock watch for the Turkish market, signed 'by Daniel de St Leu, Wtchmar to Her Majesty, London', in tortoiseshell veneered gilt metal protecting case, c1790, 2½in (6cm).
£26,000-30,000   *CG*

A Swiss gold, hunter-cased, one-minute chronometer tourbillon watch, by F. William Dubois Locle, in leather case, c1840, 2in (5cm).
£30,000-32,000   *CG*

A gold pocket chronometer, signed 'John Arnold & Son Inv. et fec. London No.357/658', maker's mark TH, London, 1788, 2in (5cm).
£5,000-8,000   *C*

A Swiss, gold and enamel, musical automaton verge watch, the unsigned bridge cock movement with diamond endstone, c1820, 2½in (6cm).
£10,000-15,000   *C*

Left   A gentleman's size perpetual calendar gold chronograph watch by Patek Philippe, Geneve, plain 18ct case, no. 1518/674143, 3.5cm diam, on 18ct gold Rolex flexible bracelet.
£22,000-25,000   *CG*

Above A gold and enamel, pair-cased watch with 3 outer cases, and gilt-metal chatelaine, the movement signed 'Geo. Musgrave, Taunton', the inner and outer cases hallmarked 1784, all in a later glazed display case, slight chip to bezel, 4.8cm diam.
£6,000-8,000 *L*

Left Top, a slim gold and enamel open faced key-wind watch.
£800-1,000

Below, an open faced keyless cylinder fob watch, the bar movement stamped Savoye Freres & Cie, and signed on the cuvette 'Faucard à Dinard', 3cm.
£140-180 *L*

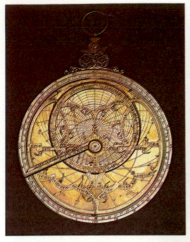

Left A brass astrolabe comprising mater, rete, 3 latitude plates, pivoted alidade, pivoted rule for stellar co-ordinates and axis pin, signed 'GEORGIVS HARTMAN NORENBERGE FACIEBAT ANNO MD XXXII', 5in (13cm).
£17,000-18,000 *CNY*

Right A gilt and silvered brass astrolabe comprising mater, rete, latitude plate pin with nut and alidade, probably German, late 16thC, 7in (17cm) diam.
£7,000-10,000 *CNY*

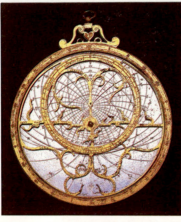

Left An English brass nocturnal, calculated for latitude 50° 30′ N, unsigned, but bearing monogram *F*, index arm 5in (12.5cm).
£8,000-12,000 *CSK*

A fruitwood, Gunter-type honary quadrant, unsigned, early 18thC, 5in (13cm) radius.
£1,000-1,400 *CSK*

A gilt brass compendium, German, mid-16thC.
£10,000-12,000 *CNY*

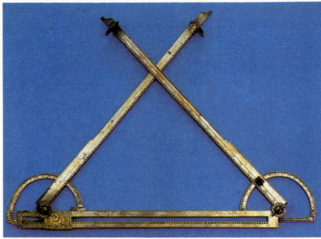

A rare brass trigonometer, the base rule with a linear scale 10-210 fitted with a slide secured by two screws, the reverse with miniature plumb bob and protractor, damaged, signed Philipus Danfrie, F, late 16thC, 15in (38cm) folded.
£35,000-40,000 *CSK*

Philipe Danfrie, described as an outstanding maker, fully described and illustrated his Trigonometre in Usage du graphomètre, published in Paris in 1597

A brass geared universal ring dial, probably from the workshop of Thomas Heath, London, the circular base with levelling screws, the geared meridian ring within annular support mounted on scroll brackets engraved with flowers, the base inset with compass and spirit levels (lacking needle and glass), engraved with degree scale graduated from 0° to 90° in each quadrant, and an outer scale graduated from 0° to 360°; the base engraved with table of the Equation of Time and reading to the nearest 5 minutes of arc by means of vernier on rim, English, mid-18thC, 14in (36cm).
£20,000-25,000 *CNY*

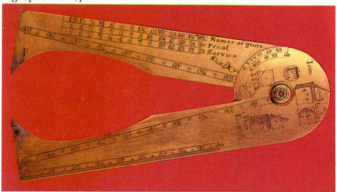

A gunner's caliper, one arm engraved with scale, the Weight of the cube Foot in, with symbols and owner's monogram, the other arm with gunner's scale, the reverse with pictorial representation of geometric solids, various scales, the tips of both arms with hardened steel points, signed I Rowley fecit, in original fishskin covered case, 7in (18cm) long.
£2,000-2,500 *CSK*

An unsigned armillary sphere demonstrating the apparent motion of the planets, the outer Zodiac calendar ring supporting 2 circles showing the position of fixed stars, the Pole Arctique and Pole Le 1'Eclipque, possibly French, 16in (40cm) high.
£800-1,000 *CSK*

A cabinet of geological specimens in 2 trays, each specimen with printed paper label, the accompanying pamphlet entitled 'Catalog de la Nouvelle Collection des Roches du Mont-Blanc', Classe par M. le Professeur Jurine et M. Brard, early 19thC.
£1,000-1,500 *CNY*

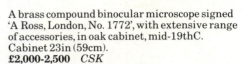

A brass compound binocular microscope signed
'A Ross, London, No. 1772', with extensive range
of accessories, in oak cabinet, mid-19thC.
Cabinet 23in (59cm).
£2,000-2,500   *CSK*

A 2in (5cm) reflecting telescope, signed
John Cuff, London, with 13½in (33cm)
long body tube, in original oak case.
£2,000-3,000   *CSK*

A lacquered brass
compound binocular
microscope, by R&J
Beck, London &
Philadelphia, with oak
case of accessories, late
19thC, 19in (48cm).
£2,000-2,500   *CSK*

A brass 'Grand Model'
compound binocular
microscope, with a collection
of accessories and eyepieces,
by W. Watson & Sons Ltd, in
fitted mahogany case, 19in
(47cm) high.
£2,000-2,500   *CSK*

A Tiffany 'peacock' table lamp, the base impressed TIFFANY STUDIOS NEW YORK 23923, 26in (65cm).
£22,000-25,000   CNY

A magnolia leaded glass and bronze floor lamp, the shade impressed TIFFANY STUDIOS NEW YORK 1599, the base cast with a band of leaves and impressed TIFFANY STUDIOS NEW YORK 379, 80in (203cm) high to top of pig-tail finial.
£80,000-90,000   CNY

A Tiffany 'peony' leaded glass and bronze table lamp, the shade and base impressed with maker's marks and numbered 1505 and 550 respectively, 31in (79cm) high.
£27,000-30,000   CNY

A Tiffany 'apple blossom' leaded glass and bronze table lamp, shade and base impressed with maker's marks, the base numbered 7806, 26in (66cm) high.
£14,000-16,000   CNY

A Gallé triple overlay cameo glass lamp, shade and base signed Gallé, 28in (71cm).
£11,000-15,000 *CM*

A Gallé double overlay cameo glass lamp, Gallé cameo signature to base and shade, c1900, 13in (32cm).
£7,000-9,000 *C*

Below Five Gallé cameo vases, all with signature.

Back row: 14in (35cm).
£500-700
12in (29cm).
£450-550

Front row: 7in (18cm).
£400-450
9in (23cm).
£1,000-1,250
7in (18cm).
£450-650 *C*

A Gallé 'blowout' lamp with bronze mount, base and shade signed Gallé, c1900, 18in (45cm).
£35,000-45,000 *C*

A Gallé marqueterie-de-verre vase, with incised chinoiserie signature, c1900, 14in (35cm)
£8,000-10,000 *C*

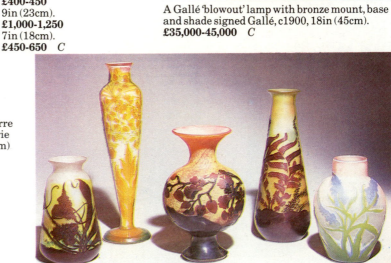

Five Tiffany Favrile vases, all inscribed, l.-r.:
**£2,000-3,000, £6,000-7,000, £2,000-3,000,
£2,000-3,000, £1,500-2,000**   *CNY*

A plique à jour and metal lantern 13in (34cm).
£1,500-2,000   *C*

l. to r. Galle vase 19in (48cm).   **£4,000-5,000**
Galle vase 22in (56cm).   **£3,500-4,500**
Daum vase 20in (51cm).   **£2,000-3,000**   *C*

A pâte-de-verre liquor service by G. Argy-Rousseau.
£2,000-3,000   *C*

A glass and brass vase attributed to
Loetz, in the manner of Hans
Christiansen, c1900, 15in (37cm).
£750-1,200   *C*

l. A vase designed by Kolomon Moser, 7in (17cm).
£1,200-1,600
c. A Loetz vase 8in (21cm).
£600-800
r. A Ferdinand Poschinger Glasshütten vase, engraved signature and 'Bayern No. 189', 10in (25cm).
£1,000-1,250 *C*

A Daum cameo glass vase 9in (22cm).
£700-1,000 *PSG*

A Gallé cameo glass vase 10in (25cm).
£1,500-2,000 *PSG*

A Gallé cameo glass vase 12in (30cm).
£800-1,200 *PSG*

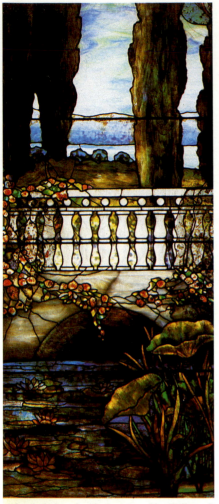

A bronze lamp, 'L'Ombellifère' signed Leo Laporte-Blairsy, c1900, 20in (50cm).
£9,000-10,000 *CAm*

A leaded glass landscape panel by Tiffany Studios, 69 by 30in (179 by 78cm) excluding frame.
£25,000-30,000 *CNY*

Originally one of 10 panels commissioned as a window, and dispersed upon demolition of the house. The whereabouts of 4 of the panels unknown.

A collection of 11 Art Nouveau drinking glasses, few minor chips, 8in (21cm) and smaller.
£400-500 *C*

A pair of Orrefors mirrored doors by Simon Gate, inscribed Simon Gate Orrefors 1936, 84in (214cm) high.
£7,000-10,000 *C*

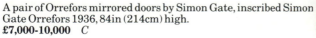

A mahogany display cabinet, designed by Carl Davis Richter, 65in (163cm).
£2,500-3,500 *C*

An Ernest Gimson bureau, with elaborately fitted interior, barber's-pole inlay, executed by Sidney Barnsley, 33in (83cm).
£12,000-18,000 *C*

A Sidney Barnsley walnut dresser with diamond pattern moulding, 75in (190cm) wide.
£3,500-5,500 *C*

Right An oak daybed by Charles Eastlake, with panelled sides, the headrest carved with daisies, and a gothic roundel, upholstered in green velvet on turned legs, 73in (185cm) long.
£3,500-4,500 *C*

A walnut extending dining table, with barber's pole inlay and plain octagonal moulded legs, and a set of 6 dining chairs with leather drop-in seats, by Ernest Gimson, executed by Sidney Barnsley, the table 114in (283.5cm) extended.
£10,000-15,000 *C*

A German teak desk, the rectangular top with rounded corners, covered in beige leather, the drawers oak-lined, with brass handles, stamped on one drawer Otto Fritzsche, Munchen, 45in (112cm) wide.
£800-1,200 *P*

A Martin Brothers stoneware tobacco jar and cover modelled as a grotesque cat, inscribed R. W. Martin & Brothers, London & Southall 5.1885.
£7,000-9,000 *C*

A Royal Doulton polychrome glazed stoneware, fountain figure, the 'Lily-Maid', inscribed Gilbert Bayes, 24in (61.5cm) high.
£8,000-10,000 *C*

A Rozenburg eggshell glazed vase, decorated by Sam Schellinck, crowned Rozenburg Den Haag and stork mark, painter's monogram and work order no. 459, c1902, 10½in (26.5cm).
£6,000-9,000 *CAm*

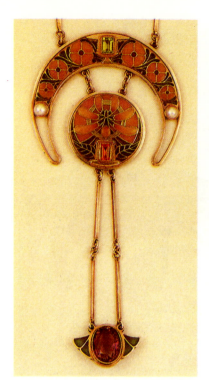

A Concord Watch Co. ladies' watch, yellow metal set with peridots, topaz, diamonds and pearls, and with diamond and pearl clasp.
£2,000-2,500 *C*

An unusual and elaborate plique-à-jour pendant necklace, unmarked but probably German, on baton chain, total length of pendant 6½in (15.5cm).
£2,000-2,200 *P*

A gold, diamond and plique-à-jour enamelled pendant.
£3,000-4,000 *CNY*

Right A pair of gold, diamond and plique-à-jour enamelled ear pendants.
£1,000-1,500 *CNY*

578

A baluster ewer, stamped 'Tiffany & Co makers', and 'Sterling Silver, 925-1000', pattern No. '14106', 1899-1900, 19in (48cm).
£1,100-1,400 *P*

A liqueur set comprising decanter and 6 cups, stamped with 935 German silver mark and PH, for Patriz Huber, c1900, decanter 7in (18cm).
£3,000-4,000 *C*

A bronze group of mermaid and fisherman, signed 'Ed.Lanteri' and dated '1898', 24in (60cm).
£1,500-2,000 *P*

A silver and enamelled picture frame stamped 'W.H.H.', for W. H. Haseler, Birmingham 1899, 11in (27cm).
£1,000-1,500 *P*

A white metal and enamel inkwell attributed
to C. R. Ashbee, seven-sided on ball feet, 4in
(11cm) high.
£2,000-3,000   *C*

An early William De Morgan tile panel consisting of 16
squares, painted on blanks from the 'Architectural
Pottery, Poole, Dorset', 24in (61cm) square.
£600-800   *P*

A Tiffany Favrile oviform glass vase,
signed 'LCT' and 'F183', 9in (24cm)
high.
£1,200-1,500   *P*

A bronze and ivory figure, Bat Dancer, cold painted in green and yellow, inscribed signature on base F. Preiss, 9½in (24cm) high.
£3,500-4,000 *C*

An ivory figure, 'Nude', carved after a model by Ferdinand Preiss, 17½in (44cm) high.
£8,000-10,000 *C*

An Art Deco jade, lapis lazuli and mother-of-pearl table clock, signed by Cartier, 1216, base repaired.
£11,000-15,000 *CNY*

Three gilt bronze and ivory figures after models by A. Gori:

l. 'Exotic Dancer', inscribed in the bronze A. Gori, 15in (37.5cm).
£1,500-2,000

c. 'Flower Girl', inscribed A. Gory Salon Des Beaux Arts Paris, 14in (35cm).
£650-850

r. 'Flower Seller', inscribed A. Gori, 15in (38cm).
£2,500-3,500 *C*

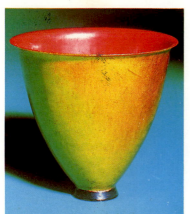

A lacquered metal bowl on small raised circular foot, with rounded flaring body and everted rim, distressed gold body and coral red interior, signed in red lacquer Jean Dunand, c1925, 4in (10cm).
£800-1,200 *C*

A Carlton Ware oviform ginger jar and cover enriched with gilt decoration, printed marks Carlton Ware, Made in England 'Trade Mark', 12in (31.5cm).
£1,000-1,500 *C*

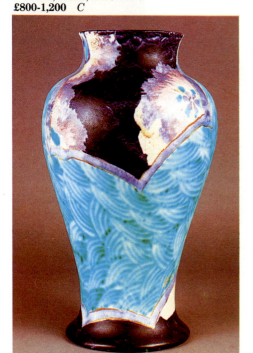

A Clarice Cliff vase, hand painted marks Inspiration by Clarice Cliff New Pottery Burslem England, hand painted signature Clarice Cliff, c1930, 16in (40cm).
£3,000-4,000 *C*

A pâte-de-verre vase with stylised moulded decoration of fish swimming through waves, moulded signature G. Argy-Rousseau, c1925, 6in (15cm).
£2,500-3,000 *C*

A Lalique butterscotch glass statuette, 'Thais', inscribed R. Lalique, 9in (22cm).
£3,500-4,000 *CSK*

Three Fauré vases, silver and thick enamel, with geometric abstract designs, signed C. Fauré Limoges, c1925.
£1,500-2,000 each *CAm*

A white metal and enamel cigarette case, enamel signed F Zwichl, stamped marks 'made in Austria', c1920.
£500-1,000   C

A covered jug modelled as George Robey, 10in (25cm).
£3,500-4,500   P

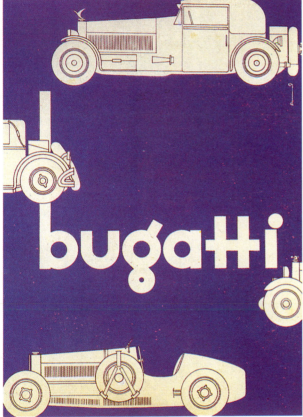

A poster design showing 4 different Bugatti models, signed with the artist's monogram, 21½ by 16in (53 by 39cm).
£4,000-5,000   C

Right An enamelled minaudiere caricaturing Enrico Caruso, enclosing compartments, a mirror, aides memoire and pencil, maker's marks 'Lacloche Freres Paris' and facsimile of Caruso's signature, 5in (12cm) long.
£2,500-3,000   P

It is thought that Caruso probably did his own caricature.

583

A silver and rosewood tea and coffee service by Charles Boynton, maker's and London marks for 1947, 77oz 17dwts.
£3,000-5,000 *C*

A bronze figure, 'Anagke', after a model by Gilbert Bayes, signed and dated 1918, 23in (59cm).
£10,000-15,000   *C*

A 78-piece silver table service by Charles Boynton, maker's and London marks for 1947, 154oz 11dwts.
£4,000-6,000   *C*

A complete Art Deco burr walnut bedroom suite, attributed to Jules Leleu, including telephone and cigarette case.
£10,000-15,000   *C*

Below A mahogany and satinwood baby grand piano by Eavestaff, inlaid metal inscription Healey, c1930, 56in (143cm) long.
£2,000-3,000   *C*

An illustration design dated 1926, 21in (42cm).
£600-800   *C*

A brass tobacco box, Dutch, c1740,
5in (12.5cm).
£140-160   *KEY*

An unusual nickel plated brass
solder testing balance, the support
signed 'W. Butterworth, maker,
Tutbury', with 9 cone solder
samples in a glazed wall cabinet,
20in (51cm) wide, and an Austrian
postal balance.
£150-200   *CSK*

A brass tavern tobacco box, c1830.
£350-450   *KEY*

A brass alms dish, German, c1550,
15in (38cm).
£400-450   *KEY*

A Regency brass music stand, with
blue-painted and gilded rest, 60½in
(153cm) high, fully extended.
£1,200-1,500   *C*

A pair of Anglo-Indian brass
jardinières, 41in (102.5cm) high.
£2,000-2,500   *C*

A rare Volta brass pistol, with brass
combustion cylinder conical reducer
and brass electrode in a bone ivory
collar, 19thC.   ▷
£160-200   *CSK*

A pair of W & T Avery Ltd. snuff
scales, to weigh 1lb. Class B. No.
A189, with brass pans, together
with a set of 5 weights.
£130-160   *OT*

A pair of early Victorian lacquered
brass postal scales, inscribed R. W.
Winfield, Birmingham, 10½in
(26.5cm).
£150-200   *WW*

A pair of brass and steel sovereign
weighing scales, 8 brass weights to
weigh from 5–300 sovereigns, the
latter and the scales stamped with
the makers' name Vandome & Co.,
London, 27in (69.5cm) high, the oak
box with makers' label.
£280-320   *PWC*

Make the most of Miller's

*In Miller's we do NOT just
reprint saleroom
estimates. We work from
realised prices either from
an auction room or a
dealer. Our consultants
then work out a realistic
price range for a similar
piece. This is to try to
avoid repeating freak
results – either low or
high.*

A Spanish gilt brass relief of the
Young St. John The Baptist with
his lamb in a wood, two nicks on
edges and drilled at corners, the
reverse bearing the inscription
'Divan. Unes.' 5½ by 4in (14 by
10cm).
£500-600   *C*

A pair of brass andirons, early 18thC, 29½in (77cm) high.
£3,000-3,500 *C*

A large brass mounted lodestone, 8in (20.5cm) high.
£2,500-3,000 *CNY*

A pair of German brass reliefs of the Judgement of Solomon, and David Anointed by Samuel, after the Master H.G., polished surfaces, 6½in (16.7cm), a copper electrotype relief of Darius's family before Alexander, after Charles Le Brun, late 16th/early 17thC, 3 by 4½in (8cm by 11.5cm).
£350-450 *C*

Bronze

An English bronze bust of a jester, in the style of John Cheere, ebonized wood pedestal and stand, early 18thC, 14in (36cm), with painted wood column, 19thC, 54½in (136cm) high.
£7,500-8,000 *C*

A parcel-silvered bronze figure of a trained seal, cast from a model by Marcel Bouraine, French, lower rear of base drilled, ball missing, early 20thC, 19in (48cm) high.
£700-800 *CNY*

A bronze figure of a Crusader, after E. Fremiet, inscribed 'Credo', signed, red marble plinth, 14½in (37cm) high.
£180-230 *L*

A French bronze statue of a lute player, known as 'Vendangeur Improvisant', cast from a model by Francisque Joseph Duret, patina slightly rubbed, 19thC, 36½in (92.5cm).
£1,600-2,000 *C*

A large copper kettle, complete with spirit lamp, the carrying handles of white glass, 13in (33cm) high.
£100-150 *WIL*

A Louchet gilt bronze picture frame, stamped on the metal 'Louchet' and on the leather back 'Louchet, Ciseleur, 3 Rue Auber, Paris', 8½in (21cm) high.
£350-450 *P*

An Arts and Crafts brass desk set by Margaret Gilmour, comprising: table blotter, 12 by 18in (30 by 45cm), pen tray, inkwell, stamp box and picture frame, stamped with 'GM' monogram.
£150-200 *P*

A Japanese bronze model of a prowling tiger, signed with a seal, 19thC, 10in (25.5cm) high.
£450-500 *LRG*

A Florentine bronze model of a frog, from the workshop of Giambologna and Pietro Tacca, hollow cast and probably having served as a fountain spout, shaped wooden base simulated porphyry, both sides of mouth worn, late 16th/early 17thC, 5in (14cm) high.
£5,000-6,000 *C*

A bronze figure, 'Cat Lapping', cast from a model by Rembrandt Bugatti, Italian, inscribed 'R. Bugatti (7)' and stamped with the Hébrard foundry cire perdue seal, rich dark brown patina, early 20thC, 6in (15cm) high.
£12,000-14,000 *CNY*

A pair of bronze dogs, modelled by A Dubucand, 19thC., 4½ by 5in (11.5 by 12.5cm).
£550-600 *CRY*

A painted Vienna bronze model of a young dog, 7in (18cm) long.
£350-400 *CSK*

Two bronze deer with antlers, 48in (122cm) high, including base.
£1,000-1,500 *LRG*

An animalier bronze of stallion and mare, P.J. Mene.
£1,700-1,900 *MGM*

A French bronze cockerel and farmyard scene, signed 'Arson', 19thC, 8½in (21cm) wide.
£250-350 *RdeR*

A green-patinated bronze group, unsigned, 15½in (39cm).
£500-600 *P*

An English bronze group of 2 sleeping lovers, late 19thC, 4½ by 7½in (11 by 18.5cm).
£400-450 *C*

A bronzed head and shoulder bust of a young Roman, with impressed marks and signed B.S. Asche, 19thC, 27in (68.5cm).
£350-400 *BWe*

A bronze allegorical figure, after Emile Louis Picault, titled 'La Source Du Pactole', c1880, 24in (61cm).
£2,200-2,800 *TW*

A French bronze statuette of the Neapolitan fisherboy, after Jean Baptiste Carpeaux, signed 'J.B. Carpeaux', and inscribed Susse Fres. Edt. Paris and stamped with the foundry seal flanked by P & B, late 19thC, 24in (61cm) high.
£3,500-4,000 *C*

A bronze figure of a man, signed 'Jobbagy' and stamped F. Dunn & Co., oars damaged, 19thC, 25in (63cm).
£500-600 *DSH*

A bronze figure of a labourer with sledge hammer, entitled 'Pax Et Labor', signed on base Picault, 19thC, 28in (71cm).
£600-700 *BWe*

A bronze figure of Mercury, on ebonised socle, early 19thC, 14in (35.5cm).
£9,000-10,000 *Re*

A pair of bronze figures of Mercury and Fame, 19thC, 32½in (82.5cm) and 31½in (80.5cm).
£550-600 *TKN*

A bronze figure of the ballerina 'Nattova' by S. Yourievitch, early 20thC, 29in (73cm) high overall.
£1,000-1,300 *McC*

◁

A Coalbrookdale bronze group, stamped 'Bell Fecit, Coalbrookdale' and bearing inscription 'A Gift from Mrs. Abraham Darby to Frederick Monks 1898', polished patination, 19thC, 32in (94cm).
£600-700 *Re*

A pair of bronze figures, signed Felix Joubert, Sculpt, 1937, 112in (284cm) overall.
£5,500-6,500 *PWC*

A pair of bronze figures, by Kessler, 9in (23cm) high.
£200-250 *Wor*

An important cast bronze figure of Hercules and the Erymanthian boar, 19thC, 31in (78.5cm).
£700-800 *FR*

An Italian bronze study, signed 'P. Chiapparelli, Fe Roma', on veined green marble plinth, 19thC, 24in (61cm) wide.
£800-900 *Pea*

A bronze statue 'Diana the Huntress', 19thC, 34in (86cm)
£900-1,000 *JMW*

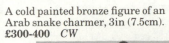

A cold painted bronze figure of an Arab snake charmer, 3in (7.5cm).
£300-400   CW

A Japanese bronze figure on stand.
£1,600-1,800   FHF

A bronze group of a fox hunt, cast from a model by Isidore Jules Bonheur, French, inscribed 'I. Bonheur', stamped Fabr. Francais D'Art J. D'Estray, and */*, blackish brown patina, late 19thC, 19in (48cm) high.
£4,000-5,000   CNY

A pair of French ormolu and bronze candleholders, 19thC, 12½in (31.5cm) high.
£500-600   Pea

An Austrian cold painted bronze figure of a bearded Arabian warrior sitting on a horse, 9in (23cm).
£350-400   Re

Two fragments from a Hispano-Visigothic bronze sword handle or terminal of a cross, set with malachite, almandines, other stones and gold, gemset and with a centre section of similar form, 6th or 7th Century A.D., 4½in (10.5cm) and 2½in (6.5cm).
£700-900   C

A bronze figure of a rider upon a runaway horse, Santa Coloma, signed, 19thC, 15in (38cm) high.
£1,300-1,600   B

A bronze plaque depicting the flagellation, 4 armed soldiers scourging the haloed Christ, reeded edge with shell pendant, 16thC, 5½ by 4½in (14.5 by 11cm).
£150-250   P

A Paduan bronze triangular sandbox, in the style of Andrea Briosco, called Riccio, early 16thC, 3½in (8.5cm) high.
£2,200-2,500   C

An English bronze mortar, dated 1708, 6in (15cm) high.
£400-500   KEY

A collection of 12 Henth bronze weights, some bearing verification marks.
£160-200   CSK

An English bronze cauldron on hoof feet, c1650.
£350-400   KEY

A Regency bronze and ormolu inkstand, with blue glass liner, 3½in (9cm) wide.
£650-750   *C*

A pair of Chinese bronze vases, decorated with hens and foliage in low relief, 16in (40.5cm).
£250-350   *FR*

A bronze cigarette box, cold painted bronze on brass base, 4in (10cm) high.
£400-500   *CDC*

A Shan bronze drum, cast with a ▷ star motif and numerous concentric bands, applied strap handles, 28in (71cm) diam.
£600-700   *Bea*

An English bronze posnet cooking pot, c1590, 6in (15cm) high.
£450-550   *KEY*

A green patinated bronze inkstand, with 2 square wells, matching letter rack and blotter, 19thC.
£300-400   *LRG*

An Italian uniface bronze medal of Lorenzo the Magnificent De' Medici, after Niccolo Fiorentino, 3½in (8.5cm) diam, another of Lorenzo di Piero de Medici, Duke of Urbino, after Francesco da Sangallo, 3in (8cm) diam, and two after Selvi, of Lorenzo the Magnificent and Christina of Lorraine, 3in (8cm) diam.
£200-250   *C*

Copper

A small English copper kettle, c1840, 6in (15cm)
£150-200   *KEY*

A copper kettle with swing handle, c1790.
£150-200   *KEY*

A copper kettle with fixed brass and copper handle, acorn finial, late 19thC, 13in (33cm).
£50-70   *WIL*

◁ A Georgian copper kettle, c1800, 11in (28cm).
£150-200   *KEY*

△ A copper kettle on original brass stand, c1800, 12in (30.5cm).
£300-350   *KEY*

A Victorian copper tea kettle on stand with spirit burner, 7½in (19cm).
£100-150 *PC*

A George IV copper samovar, warranted best London Manufacture No.29, 15in (38cm).
£150-200 *WW*

A set of 4 Victorian copper baluster measures on flared feet, 1 pint to 1 gill.
£300-350 *WW*

An English copper spirit measure, ½ pint size, c1840, 4in (10cm) high.
£100-150 *KEY*

A late Georgian copper tea urn, with brass tap, c1830, 15in (38cm) high.
£100-150 *WIL*

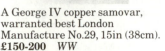

A set of 10 graduated copper pans with steel handles and copper lids, some engraved initials NGC by Benham & Sons, Wigmore Street, London and Temple & Crook, Motcomb Street, S.W., 19thC, 14in (35.5cm) to 5in (12.5cm) diam.
£600-700 *AG*

A copper coal scuttle.
£50-120 *Ph*

A set of 3 European gilded and copper dishes, early 19thC, two 20in (51cm) and one 25in (63.5cm).
£500-550 *DWB*

A copper urn with elephant handles, 24in (61cm).
£200-250 *TAY*

Two English gilt copper processional crucifixes, with applied Corpora Christi and enamelled terminals of the symbols of the Four Evangelists, one slightly damaged around top edge, mourning Virgin and St. John missing, late 15th/early 16thC, 15in and 16½in (37.5 and 42cm) high.
£1,200-1,500 *C*

A Victorian copper and steel basket grate and fender en suite, bearing the registration number 75774, 34in (86cm) and 60½in (151cm) wide.
£600-700 *Bon*

A gilt copper electrotype frame housing a Limoges enamel plaque of the Virgin and Child Enthroned, after Bellini, the frame with an applied Holy Water stoup, top left hand corner of plaque damaged, traces of verdigris around stoup, 19thC, 25½ by 12in (64.5 by 30.5cm).
£1,000-1,500 *C*

A copper crucifix, the Corpus Christi applied separately, the foot with a peg for attachment, with traces of gilding, 12thC, 9½in (23.5cm) high, perspex stand.
£1,700-2,000 *C*

A brass and copper jardinière, with a detachable liner, with a border of husk swags centred by cows' skulls, on 3 monopodiae supports headed with sphinxes, united by scrolling foliate cross stretchers and with honeysuckle and Babylonian mask ornament, 19thC, 36in (92cm) high.
£2,000-2,500 *P*

Based on the example excavated from Pompeii and now in Naples Museum.

Ormolu

A copper electrotype model of the Vendôme Column, cast with a continuous spiralling relief of military manoeuvres inscribed 'Neapolio . Imp . Aug . Monumentum Belli Germanici Anno MDCCCV Trimestri Spatio Ductu Suo Proflugati Ex Aere Capto Gloriae Exercitus Maximi Dicavit', mid-19thC, 52in (132cm) high.
£11,000-13,000 *C*

A pair of Louis XVI ormolu figures of scantily-clad Bacchantes, 28in (71cm) high overall.
£2,500-3,000 *CSK*

A pair of ormolu ostrich candlesticks, 12in (31cm) high.
£700-800 *EA*

A pair of Regency ormolu twelve-light candelabra, 24½in (62cm) high.
£3,500-4,000 *C*

A George III ormolu hall lantern, with arched glazed cylindrical body in waved frame, 30in (76cm) high, excluding chain suspension.
£5,200-5,600 *C*

A Russian ormolu and serpentine marble desk set, 18½in (47cm) wide.
£3,500-4,000 *C*

An Hungarian onyx and ormolu desk set.
£200-250 *EA*

◁

An Empire ormolu cut-glass twelve-light chandelier, the nozzles fitted for electricity, 36in (92cm) high.
£3,500-4,000 *C*

A set of 4 ormolu candlesticks with shaped drip-pans, nozzles, shafts and swirling bases with rockwork and chased berried foliage, 11in (28cm) high.
£1,500-2,000   *C*

A Regency ormolu inkstand, with a pair of cut-glass bottles and 2 pentrays, 13in (33cm) wide.
£3,500-4,000   *C*

A pair of Regency ormolu urns, 10½in (27cm) high.
£4,200-4,600   *C*   ▷

Iron

A set of 4 cast-iron garden urns, 20in (51cm) high.
£600-650   *Bea*

A pair of wrought iron lancet shaped gates in the manner of A.W.N. Pugin, c1840–45, 108in (275cm) high.
£1,200-1,500   *Re*

A pair of gilt painted wrought iron and brass Communion rail gates, attributed to Augustus Pugin, 19thC, 28in (71cm) high, with letter of attribution.
£300-350   *CDC*

A Continental tall iron strong box, the lid and sides riveted with straps and twin handles, the front with a cartouche, 17th/18thC, 14in (36cm) wide.
£500-550   *P*

A cast-iron statue of a blackamoor, holding a snake on his left arm with a base for a lamp, early 19thC.
£5,000-5,500   *WW*

Said to have been purchased from the Duke of Cumberland's Lodge, Windsor Great Park.

▷

A rare pair of iron candle snuffers on stand, maker's mark Dowler, 18thC, 6in (15cm) high.
£800-1,200   *TKN*

A pair of enamelled cast-iron door stops in the form of a classical Punch with Toby and Judy with the baby, 7½ by 12in (19 by 31cm).
£150-200   *P*

A pair of Regency cast-iron campana shaped garden urns, 20in (51cm).
£400-500   *WW*

A large wrought iron and painted metal screen, possibly designed by Skidmore, c1840–45, 90in (228cm) high.
£300-500   *Re*

A cast-iron garden seat, in the Coalbrookdale style.
£500-700 *MN*

A George III polished steel and cast-iron basket grate, 35in (89cm) wide, and a fender en suite, 46in (117cm) wide.
£2,500-3,500 *C*

A wrought iron weather vane, 18thC, 14in (36cm) high.
£300-350 *KEY*

A pair of Victorian iron door stops, cast as a lion and unicorn, 28 and 22in (71 and 56cm).
£250-350 *P*

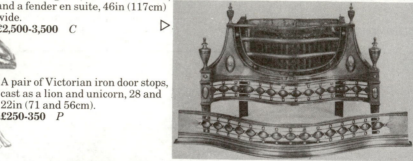

Pewter

A quart-size pewter tankard, c1790, 7½in (19cm) high.
£250-350 *KEY*

A Scottish pewter chopin measure, c1790, 8½in (22cm) high
£500-600 *KEY*

An English quart-size barrel-shaped tankard, c1820, 6½in (16cm) high.
£200-300 *KEY*

An English half-pint pewter double volute lidded measure, c1780.
£150-200 *KEY*

A Normandy pewter measure, c1800, 10in (25cm) high.
£250-300 *KEY*

A set of 5 West Country pewter measures, 19thC, ½gall–½gill.
£800-900 *WW*

A set of 6 graduated haystack measures, by Austen & Son, Cork, with loop handles, 19thC, ½gall–½noggin.
£1,000-1,500 *WW*

A pewter plate, inscribed 'Thomas's Chop House Cornhill', c1800, 9in (23cm) diam.
£850-950 *KEY*

A pewter charger, 17thC, 22in (51cm) diam.
£500-600 *WW*

A pair of broad rimmed English chargers, stamped with 'hallmarks', touch of SB with fleur-de-lys (ad) verso, c1670, 20½in (51.5cm) diam., the rim 4in (10cm).
£1,250-1,500 *P*

A pair of pewter candlesticks, c1830, 8in (20cm) high.
£120-160 *KEY*

An English pewter salt and pepper set, with engraved crown over 'B' monogram, c1790, pepper 4½in (11.5cm) high.
£150-200 *KEY*

A Dutch pewter chalice, c1620, 9in (23cm) high.
£500-550 *KEY*

l. An English latten trefid spoon, c1710, 6in (15cm).
£75-100

c. An English pewter slip-top spoon, c1650, 5½in (15cm).
£125-175

r. An English latten seal-top spoon, c1630, 5½in (15cm).
£125-175 *KEY*

Locks and Keys

A group of Gothic keys, 3 to 6in (7.5 to 15cm),
top: iron, c1500 **£100-150**
l. bronze, c1300 **£230-300**
c. iron, c1400 **£100-125**
r. bronze, c1400 **£200-225**
bottom: iron, c1500 **£100-150** *KEY*

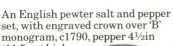

A group of keys, all c1680:–
l. A French steel key, 3½in (9cm).
£150-175

lc. An English steel key.
£150-175

rc. An English steel key.
£125-150

r. A French steel key.
£100-125 *KEY*

Five steel keys, 19thC, 4in (10cm) approx.
l, lc, and r. **£50-75**
c, and cr. **£10-15** *KEY*

Lead

An Italian lead metal of Niccolo Piccinino, possibly late 15thC after Pisanello, 3½in (8.8cm).
£100-150 *C*

A pair of English lead urns, one slightly sunken on its foot and bowl splitting at corners, late 17th/early 18thC, 43in (107cm).
£5,500-6,000 *C*

A pair of lead urns, the fluted baluster bodies applied with trailing foliage and hirsute mask heads, on tapering stands with circular naturalistic bases, slight damage, 18thC, 16in (40cm).
£150-250 *P*

A tôleware miniature tray, with hand painted scene, c1830, 9in (22.5cm) diam.
£100-150 *DEL*

A cold painted lead Arab group.
£75-125 *WW*

A good Chinese export card case, chased in relief with people taking tea, the front applied with a cartouche inscribed 'Hilda, 1905', the reverse chased with birds amidst bamboo, by Luen Hing of Shanghai, c1905.
£150-200 *P*

A Victorian Pontypool coal scuttle, with picture of dog on glass panel to lid.
£600-700 *JD*

Miscellaneous

An English tin horn lantern, c1800, 10in (25.5cm).
£150-200 *KEY*

A large pair of French spelter figures of children, by Miroy Freres, bearing metal labels numbered 4 and 5, late 19thC, 39in (99cm).
£700-750 *TEN*

A pair of Pontypool urns and covers, with gilt decoration and lion mask ring handles, 13in (33cm).
£1,500-2,000 *CW*

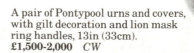

An Indian chased white metal ink stand, with 2 glass bottles, ivory inlaid border to stand, 10½in (26.5cm) wide.
£150-200 *HCH*

A Victorian tôle coal box, the glazed lid decorated with a winter scene with tapering body and iron tripartite base, 19½in (49cm) wide.
£1,000-1,500 *C*

A cold painted spelter figure of a Middle Eastern girl dancer, after Louis Hottot, 31in (79cm).
£700-800 *Bea*

An unusual tôle peinte tea urn, the pierced quatrefoil base with a drawer for cinders, decorated overall with painted flowers and gilt sprays, 19thC.
£500-600   *P*

A gilt metal shaped oval casket and hinged cover, surmounted by a putto and with scroll handles and feet, printed with cherubs and flowers, 14in (35.5cm) wide.
£500-600   *CSK*

A National Fire Brigade's Union Chief Officer's plated helmet, with dragon and scroll cresting, crowned sunburst pattern badge, original lining and chin strap.
£500-600   *CBD*

A pair of lead-coloured metal figures of harvesters, 27in (68.5cm).
£300-400   *LRG*

A pair of Regency ormolu-mounted Pontypool chestnut urns, painted on a cream ground, 10½in (26.5cm) wide.
£6,000-7,000   *C*

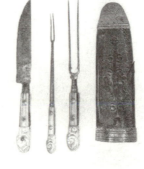

An English tin candle mould, c1830, 9in (23cm).
£75-125   *KEY*

A patinated spelter bust of a young woman, entitled 'Time is Money', set with a clock with striking movement and enamelled chapter segments, slight damage to rear of base, 26in (66cm).
£350-450   *Bon*

A Trousse, comprising knife, and long and short fork, all with ivory handles bound with engraved brass, the leather sheath with tooled decoration, 17th/18thC.
£300-500   *P*

Two French or Italian uniface medals of Roman Empresses, one inscribed 'Albia Terentia Othonis Mater', the other 'Petronia AV: Vitellii Vxor', 17thC, 3½in (8.5cm) diam, and 7 French oval bronze plaquettes of Roman Emperors, 18thC, 2 by 1½in (5 by 4cm), and a bronze cast of a Renaissance cameo, 2½ by 1½in (6 by 4cm).
£150-250   *C*

An English tin wall sconce, c1800, 10in (25.5cm).
£100-150   *KEY*

Locate the source

The source of each illustration in Miller's can be found by checking the code letters below each caption with the list of contributors. In view of the undoubted differences in price structures from region to region, this information could be extremely valuable to everyone who buys and sells antiques.

Ivory/Shell

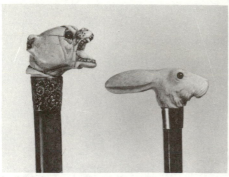

l. A Malacca cane with ivory dog's head, silver collar.
£300-350

r. An ebony walking stick with ivory rabbit's head, gold collar.
£350-400   *ARC*

A pair of Shib decorated ivory tusks, 19thC, 14in (35.5cm).
£300-350   *LRG*

From l–r.
A German turned ivory ball of concentric spheres and spiked stars, minor damage, late 17th/early 18thC, 2½in (6cm) diam.
£500-600

An English turned ivory Auctioneer's gavel, 4½in (11.5cm).
£200-300

A mother-of-pearl vase and cover, minor losses, possibly 17thC German, 10½in (26.5cm) high.
£500-800

An ivory concentric ball novelty, 19thC, 18½in (47cm) high.
£700-800   *BWe*

A carved Dieppe ivory and silver gilt fork and spoon, 19thC.
£3,000-3,500   *DON*

A German silver-mounted shell spoon, the handle formed from the spiral centre, 18th or early 19thC, 12½in (31cm).
£600-800

An English ivory gaming ball, in a turned wood box, the ball with numerous roundels (for painted numbers?), the box in 2 halves with a screw thread, minor chips to box, 18th/early 19thC, 4in (10cm) diam.
£1,000-1,500   *C*

A French ivory diptych of the Nativity, Adoration of the Magi, Crucifixion and Coronation of the Virgin, arranged in 2 tiers beneath Gothic arches, Virgin's finger missing, overpainted and with new hinges, mid to late 14thC, 7 by 3½in (18 by 8.5cm) each panel.
£7,200-8,000   *C*

An ivory and ebony elephant thermometer, 1880.
£200-250   *GRE*

A fine Swiss 'Bears of Berne' chess set carved in ivory, one side natural, one brown stained, tiny defects to 2 weapons, 19thC, 3½in (9cm) height of kings, 2½in (6.5cm) height of pawns.
£7,500-8,500   *C*

A pair of Austrian fruitwood and ivory statuettes of 2 beggars, in the style of Simon Troger, minor defects, 18thC, 8in (20cm).
£900-1,200   *C*

A Japanese carved ivory figure of a female deity playing a stringed instrument and seated upon a dragon, on oval base, 11in (28cm).
£600-700   *DSH*

A buffalo horn dinner gong, the two horn supports with plated mounts on wood plinth.
£200-250   *Bon*

A German ivory mirror case of Hercules and the Nemean Lion and Samson and the Lion, the central roundels within frames of vines which interlock, some cracks, probably early 16thC, 4½in (11.5cm), four parts.
£1,000-2,500   *C*

A Scottish horn table snuff mill, engraved 'May we never forget a Friend at a Pinch'.
£500-600   *DWB*

A good whales tooth scrimshaw, decorated in polychrome fashion with a three-masted sailing ship and a coconut tree, early 19thC, 5½in (14cm) long.
£200-250   *Re*

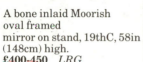

A bone inlaid Moorish oval framed mirror on stand, 19thC, 58in (148cm) high.
£400-450   *LRG*

A Portuguese rhinoceros horn group of Orpheus charming the animals, carved and pierced with numerous animals, on an ivory mounted black-stained horn foliate plinth, 9in (23cm).
£600-700   *L*

A French ivory Dieppe figure of Napoleon, his chest opening to reveal a triptych depicting scenes from his campaigns, 12in (31cm).
£900-1,000   *CSK*

A group of 7 German bone panels of Salvator Mundi, the Virgin and Five Apostles, with stained wood frame, 17thC, 4½in (12cm).
£1,000-1,200   *C*

Marble

An Italian marble bust of the Fate Lachesis, sometimes ascribed to Michelangelo, late 16th/17thC, 29in (73cm).
£7,000-10,000   *C*

This amazing bust of one of three Fates was popular, judging from the existence of 3 other examples, 2 in marble and one in bronze.

A fine Roman white marble bust of the head of Laocöon, on a waisted grey marble pedestal inscribed 'Laocoon', late 17th/early 18thC, 27in (68.5cm).
£8,000-9,000   *C*

A French marble bust of a cherubic boy, clutching a doll of Punch inside his garment, marble socle; minor chips, late 18thC, 12in (30cm).
£1,500-2,000 *C*

A pair of carved marble figures of Mars and Minerva, each seated with shield and helmet, early 19thC, 22½ and 16in (57 and 41cm) high.
£1,200-1,700 *GSP*

A white marble portrait bust of a young lady, on veined yellow marble base, early 19thC, 16in (41cm).
£200-250 *TKN*

A French white marble statue of Antinous, left thumb cracked, 18thC, 25in (63cm).
£2,000-2,500 *C*

An English marble bust of Mercury, wearing the petasus and with curly hair, on marble socle, late 18th/early 19thC, 17in (43cm).
£600-800 *C*

A pair of white statuary marble busts of Grecian semi-clad young ladies, each standing on mottled brown and grey fluted plinths, Marshall Wood, signed and dated 1869, 27in (68.5cm) and 25½in (65cm) height of busts.
£2,800-3,200 *BS*

A carved verte marble figure of a lion, late 18thC, 11in (28cm).
£250-300 *CBD*

A white marble sculpture of a standing naked Venus, her arms outstretched within a carved shell, 26in (66cm) high.
£450-500 *LRG*

A German ivory model of a recumbent dog, in the style of Loenhard Kern, on a wooden plinth veneered with tortoiseshell, end panels missing, possibly 17thC, 2 by 4½in (5 by 11cm).
£1,200-1,500 *C*

An English marble relief of Napoleon fleeing from the field of Waterloo, by Sir Richard Westmacott, R.A., carved in 3 sections with irregular joints, minor abrasions, early 19thC, 68 by 189in (173 by 480cm).
£50,000-70,000 *C*

Provenance: The Manor of Littleton, Shepperton, Middx.

A marble statuette of a maiden in classical dress, signed P. Barzanti Florence, 44in (110cm).
£2,000-2,500 *Wor*

A Roman marble fragment.
£400-450 *Bon*

A marble relief of a Roman Emperor, on a blue ground in giltwood frame, 8½ by 7in (21.5 by 18cm), and another similar, 7½ by 6in (19 by 15cm).
£2,000-2,500   C

A sculpture, Wise Owl, in figured grey marble, perching upon 3 books, 19thC, 13in (33cm).
£400-600   B

A pair of Watcombe terracotta jars and covers, each brightly painted between turquoise bands, slight damage, printed mark, c1880, 18in (46cm).
£300-350   Bea

Terracotta/Stone

A pair of French terracotta busts of a Satyr and a Bacchante, by Louis Delaville, signed on the reverses 'Delaville', on waisted square socles, marble plinths, late 18thC, 9in (23cm).
£3,800-4,000   C

Louis Delaville, 1763–1841, was a pupil of Boizot.

A pair of carved stone figures of Summer and Autumn, both damaged, late 17th/early 18thC, 37in (94cm).
£1,500-1,700   DWB

A Belgian terracotta bust of Socrates, by Charles Malaise, signed on the back, in the opening, 'Malaise', traces of paint, chipped around edges, late 18th/early 19thC, 12½in (31cm).
£1,200-1,500   C

A William IV green porphyry pedestal, 15½in (40cm) wide.
£500-550   Bon

Charles Malaise, 1775–1836, came from Brussels and was a pupil of Godecharle.

A French terracotta bust of an 18thC lady with dressed hair, 16in (40.5cm).
£1,800-2,200   C

A painted terracotta model of a pug with red and gold collar, 14½in (36.5cm) wide.
£2,500-2,700   C

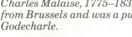

A terracotta bust of a young lady, signed by the French sculptor 'Henri Alphonse Nelson', 19thC.
£300-350   Phi

A French terracotta bust of an 8thC boy with wig and cravat, on urned socle, 18in (46cm).
2,400-2,700   C

A fine terracotta figure of an Indian musician, 19thC, 43in (107.5cm).
£800-900   BWe

A pair of terracotta Berber musicians, 18in (46cm).
£750-1,000   EA

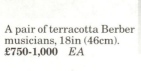

A German limewood high relief of the Virgin of the Immaculate Conception, several fingers damaged or missing, minor cracks and repairs, supported on a wooden post on a velvet-covered base, 15½in (40cm) high.
£3,000-5,000   *C*

An oak panel, 16thC.
£300-350   *KEY*

A larger than life-size terracotta pug dog.
£200-225   *Wor*

Woodcarvings

An oak panel, 16thC.
£400-450   *KEY*

A pair of German polychrome wood reliefs of gambolling putti amidst foliage, paint flaking and minor defects, 17thC, 20 by 9in (51 by 23cm).
£800-1,200   *C*

A fine carved limewood oval mirror, late 17thC.
£3,500-3,700   *PWC*

A carved wooden figure of a long eared owl, 19thC, 22in (56cm).
£700-800   *JD*

A chip carved casket, English, c1680, 5in (13cm) high.
£300-350   *KEY*

A German wood palmesel, 15thC, ridden by a 19thC wooden figure of Christ, surface distressed, some damages and restoration, mounted on a wooden trolley, 44½in (111cm) high overall.
£4,500-5,000   *C*

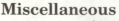

A large wooden model of a seated camel, naturalistically and finely carved, 19thC, 27½in (70cm) high.
£14,000-15,000   *C*

A pair of Italian parcel gilt and painted brackets, partly redecorated, 20in (51cm) wide.
£700-800   *C*

Miscellaneous

A carved wood relief picture of a tropical port, in Georgian ebonised frame, 14 by 18½in (35.5 by 47cm).
£500-700   *C*

A Flemish oak statuette of the mourning Virgin, her hands clasped in prayer, chips on base, early 16thC, 33½in (85cm) high.
£800-1,200   *C*

An Italian mosaic picture panel, with 4 pigeons drinking from a bronze bowl, 19thC, 5½ by 4in (14 by 10cm).
£300-350   *WIL*

An Italian alabaster bust of a little girl, wearing an embroidered bib and bonnet, minor chips, grimy, 17thC, 13½in (34cm) high.
£1,300-1,600 *C*

A Nottingham alabaster relief of the Resurrection, top edge missing, repaired crack, 14th or 15thC, 14½ by 11½in (36 by 29cm).
£4,500-5,000 *C*

A pair of Georgian straw-work pictures, of the Church and Parsonage at Chilton, Wiltshire, in giltwood frames, 7 by 9½in (18 by 24cm).
£1,000-1,200 *C*

A large Flemish alabaster relief of the Entombment, minor chips and repairs, 16thC, 39½ by 31½in (101 by 79.5cm).
£3,500-4,000 *C*

A Campanian neck amphora, from the Cassandra-Parrish Workshop, 350-340 B.C., 11½in (29cm).
£400-600 *C*

An Attic black figure neck amphora, by the Red Line painter, late 6th Century B.C., 10in (25cm).
£2,000-2,500 *C*

An Attic black figure olpe, repaired and restored, late 6th Century B.C., 9in (22.5cm).
£300-500 *C*

Pottery

A predynastic painted pottery jar, with reddish-brown concentric spirals and wavy bands, rim chipped, Naqada II, 6in (15cm) high.
£1,300-1,600 *C*

A Jemdat Nasr bichrome pottery jar, the upper half painted with red and brown panels, 5in (13cm).
£1,000-1,200 *C*

An Apulian hydria, associated with the Darius/Underworld Painter, c330 B.C., 12in (30.5cm) high.
£900-1,000 *C*

A glazed frit cosmetic jar and lid, the swivel lid attached with modern bronze pin, 9th-8th Century B.C., 2in (5cm) high.
£500-600 *C*

An Attic black figure Siana cup, by the C Painter, 2nd quarter of 6th Century B.C., 13½in (34cm) diam. across handles.
£5,000-6,000 *C*

A terracotta figure of Horus, 1st/2nd Century A.D., 7½in (18.5cm).
£100-150 *P*

An early Lucanian red figure squat lekythos, early 4th Century B.C., 5in (13cm).
£500-600 *C*

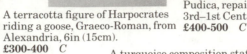

A cream glazed composition shabti for the King's Son of Kush, Hori, in dark brown glaze, Dynasty XX, Seth-nakht-Rameses III, from Tell Basta, 4in (11cm).
£300-400 *C*

A Cypriot terracotta stylised figure of a female idol, Middle Bronze Age, 7in (18cm).
£200-300 *C*

A terracotta figure of Harpocrates riding a goose, Graeco-Roman, from Alexandria, 6in (15cm).
£300-400 *C*

A painted terracotta figure of Venus Pudica, repaired, Hellenistic, 3rd–1st Century B.C., 8in (20cm).
£400-500 *C*

A turquoise composition statuette of Bastet, an inscription down the back in brown glaze reading 'Recitation by Bastet, Mistress of Bubastis: Eye of Re', Lord of all the gods', Graeco-Roman, 6in (15cm) high.
£2,500-3,500 *C*

A turquoise glazed composition shabti for Lieutenant, In-t3y, repaired, Dynasty XIX/XX, 5½in (14cm).
£1,000-1,200 *C*

A terracotta figure of a female musician, 1st/2nd Century A.D., 7½in (19cm).
£100-150 *P*

A green glazed composition shabti of the Chancellor of the Exchequer, Psamtek, called Ahmose, Dynasty XXVI, 7in (18.5cm) high.
£1,200-1,400 *C*

A predynastic slate turtle palette, in the form of a stylised turtle, the head inlaid with shell eyes, one missing, Naqada II, 5in (12cm) diam.
£2,500-3,000 *C*

A Syrian pottery model wheeled wagon, 2nd–1st Millennium B.C., 10in (25.5cm).
£1,300-1,600 *C*

Metalware

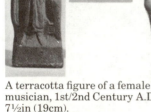

A baked clay cuneiform tablet, an administrative document, 3rd Millennium B.C., 3 by 2½in (7.5 by 7cm).
£4,000-4,500 *C*

An Egyptian predynastic stone vase, encased in additional gold sheet, Naqada II, c3100 B.C., 2in (6cm) high.
£3,000-3,500 *C*

A collection of turquoise glazed composition gaming pieces, mainly New Kingdom, Dynasty XVIII, ½in (1.5cm) high average.
£1,000-1,200 *C*

A Coptic steatite oil lamp, in the form of a bird, 6th-7th Century A.D., 3½in (9.5cm) long.
£700-900 *C*

A bronze head of a leopard, mounted on marble, Hellenistic, 3rd–1st Century B.C., 2in (5cm) long.
£600-700 *C*

A bronze terminal in the form of a panther's head, early 1st Millennium B.C., 1½in (3cm) high.
£400-500 *C*

A rare Romano-British solid bronze figure of a standing stag, the eyes recessed for inlay, now missing, three legs damaged, 6½in (16.5cm) high, and a bronze stamped patera handle fragment, 1st Century A.D., from Southern England, 3½in (8.5cm) long.
£20,000-21,500 *C*

A bronze seated figure of the ram-headed God Khnum, 3in (7.5cm), another of a seated cat 2½in (6cm), a standing figure of Hathor, 3½in (9cm), a crouching figure of Harpocrates, 3½in (9cm), and a figure of a writhing crocodile, 4in (10cm) long, 4th–1st Century B.C.
£1,100-1,500 *C*

An Egyptian bronze head of a cat, broken away from a statue, 6th–4th Century B.C., 1½in (4cm).
£500-700 *C*

A bronze figure of a seated ibis, Ptolemaic Period, 3½in (9cm).
£500-600 *P*

A Canaanite bronze female votary, mid 2nd Millennium B.C., 3½in (9cm).
£1,300-1,500 *C*

A Greek cast bronze applique, late 5th/early 4th Century B.C., 1½in (3.5cm).
£3,000-4,000 *C*

A bronze figure of Osiris, Late Period, 13in (32cm).
£2,000-2,500 *C*

A gold and garnet ring, convex garnet intaglio, a crab, the sign of Cancer, 1st Century B.C./A.D.
£500-700 *C*

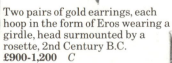

A bronze rein-guide in the form of an eagle's head above a naked youth wearing Phrygian cap, 5in (13cm) high, and another with square-shaped handles and spherical top, 5½in (14cm) high, East Roman, 2nd–3rd Century A.D.
£600-700 *C*

Two pairs of gold earrings, each hoop in the form of Eros wearing a girdle, head surmounted by a rosette, 2nd Century B.C.
£900-1,200 *C*

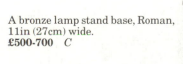

A Hellenistic gold ring, with mottled pink stone intaglio bearing robed youth holding staff, 1st Century B.C.
£400-500 *C*

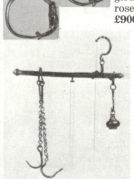

A bronze lamp stand base, Roman, 11in (27cm) wide.
£500-700 *C*

A bronze steelyard, mounted on perspex, 2nd–3rd Century A.D., 20in (51cm) high, 540gm.
£600-700 *C*

A fine Coptic bronze oil lamp, 5th Century A.D., 8in (20cm) long.
£2,000-2,500 *C*

A bronze lion-headed mask appliqué, probably from a chest, perspex mounted, 2nd–3rd Century A.D., 4½in (11.5cm) diam.
£200-250 *C*

A bronze mirror with 'Hathor' handle, Dynasty XVIII, 10in (25cm) high.
£5,000-5,500 *C*

A Villanovan bronze boat-shaped fibula, 7th Century B.C., 2in (5cm) long, an Anglo-Saxon bronze and enamel triangular brooch, 5th–6th Century A.D., 2in (6cm) long, and an Anglo-Saxon bronze key, 5th–6th Century A.D., 3½in (8.5cm).
£400-500 *C*

Marble

A large marble head of Venus, right eyebrow, nose and chin restored, 1st–2nd Century A.D., 17½in (44.5cm).
£9,000-10,000 *C*

An East Roman marble architectural relief of a female mask, mounted, 2nd Century A.D., 10½in (26.5cm).
£4,000-5,000 *C*

A marble portrait head, possibly the Emperor Commodus, eyes with articulated pupils, mounted, late 2nd Century A.D., 9in (23cm).
£4,000-5,000 *C*

◁ A marble head and torso of a sleeping Eros, mounted, 2nd–3rd Century A.D., 12in (31cm).
£3,000-3,500 *C*

A Greek marble female head, mounted, Hellenistic, 3rd Century B.C.
£1,200-1,400 *C*

▷

A marble statue of Diana, restored, Roman, 2nd Century A.D. in the main, 37½in (95cm).
£7,000-9,000 *C*

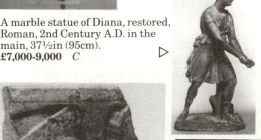

▷

◁ A marble statue of Aphrodite and Cupid, repaired at neck and right arm, late 3rd Century A.D., 11½in (29cm).
£2,000-3,000 *C*

Miscellaneous

A translucent bluish-green glass beaker, 4in (10cm), and an almost colourless glass bowl, 3in (7.5cm), both 1st Century A.D.
£400-500 *C*

A Roman marble fragment from a relief in Greek style, 5in (13cm) high.
£400-450 *Bon*

A twin-handled green glass ungentarium, Romano-Syrian, 3rd-4th Century A.D., 5½in (13cm).
£200-300 *Bon*

A limestone head of a female votary, late 6th Century B.C., 6in (15cm).
£400-500 *C*

A translucent green glass bowl, 4in (10cm), a similar beaker, 3in (7.5cm), both 1st–2nd Century A.D., and a flask, with white swirling pattern, 3rd–4th Century A.D., 5½in (14cm).
£200-300 *C*

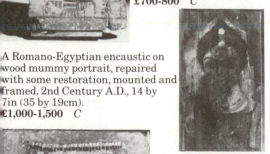

A fragmentary painted limestone erotic figurine, traces of red, brown and black pigment, 5th Century B.C., 3in (8cm) long.
£2,500-3,000 *C*

A limestone torso fragment of a female votary, late 6th Century B.C., 10in (25cm) high.
£400-500 *C*

A South Arabian limestone figure of a seated woman, mounted on perspex, 3rd–1st Century B.C., 8in (20cm).
£300-400 *C*

A gesso-painted linen mummy cloth, and another inscribed strip of mummy cloth, mounted behind glass and framed, Ptolemaic, 4th–1st Century B.C., 17 by 12in (43 by 31cm).
£500-600 *C*

A limestone relief fragment, from Sakkara, Old Kingdom, 8 by 5½in (20 by 14cm).
£200-300 *P*

A gesso-painted wooden foot end from an anthropoid coffin, Late New Kingdom, c1000–700 B.C., 11 by 10½in (28 by 26.5cm).
£700-800 *C*

Rugs & Carpets

A Romano-Egyptian encaustic on wood mummy portrait, repaired with some restoration, mounted and framed, 2nd Century A.D., 14 by 7in (35 by 19cm).
£1,000-1,500 *C*

An Agra mat, c1870, 36 by 36in (91 by 91cm).
£550-600 *TG*

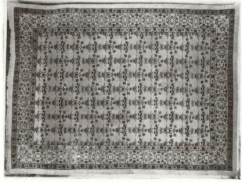

An Amritzar carpet, c1850, 144 by 106in (365 by 269cm).
£4,000-4,500 *TG*

A triangular mosaic fragment, grotesque mask ornament, red, black, greenish grey and cream tesserae, set in concrete, Roman, 3rd–4th Century A.D., 16 by 15½in (41 by 39cm).
£300-500 *C*

An Aubusson rug, c1850, 84 by 48in
(212.5 by 120cm).
£2,000-2,500   *TG*

A Charles X Aubusson carpet,
woven in pastel shades, the olive
coloured ground with a pattern, the
borders in pale blue on an ochre
coloured ground, areas of
restoration, 128 by 113in (325 by
287cm).
£2,000-3,000   *C*

A Belouch rug, the camel field
woven with 4 brown and red
rectangular medallions, enriched
with silk, the kelim ends woven
with 3 rows of scroll work, pile
slightly low, 64 by 37in (160 by
92.5cm).
£400-500   *L*

A Bergama rug, c1850, 54 by 42in
(135 by 105cm).
£1,700-1,900   *TG*

A Baktiari nomadic rug, with 15
square panels of flowers and 3
borders, 71 by 55in (177.5 by
137.5cm).
£500-600   *DWB*

A Bessarabian kelim, the mottled
ivory field with sprays in a pale
raspberry red border, one tiny hole,
78 by 60in (197.5 by 150cm).
£400-500   *C*

A Bessarabian kelim, c1900, 108 by
72in (272.5 by 182.5cm).
£3,000-4,000   *TG*   ▷

A Chinese rug, the royal blue field
with clouds and Buddhist emblems
around an Imperial five-clawed
dragon, 109 by 67in (275 by 168cm).
£2,800-3,400   *C*   ▷

A Caucasian rug, the centre with
blue field, with a yellow shaped
border, red and ivory multiple
borders with stylised animal
figures, 71 by 47in (177.5 by
117.5cm).
£500-600   *NSF*

A Caucasian Khila Shirvan-Baku
rug, with red and floral hexagonal
medallion on midnight blue field, 56
by 37in (140 by 92.5cm).
£140-180   *CDC*

A Kirman carpet, the burgundy
field with a stellar floral medallion
with pendant mosque lamps, in a
royal blue medallion and flowering
vine border, areas of very slight
wear, 202 by 139in (513 by 352cm).
£1,000-1,500   *C*

An Isfahan prayer rug, 88 by 56in
(222.5 by 140cm).
£1,200-1,600   *CSK*

A Caucasian Kelim, c1850, 76 by 54in (193 by 135cm).
£2,500-3,000 *TG*

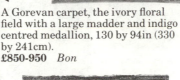

An Isfahan rug, with ivory field, 89 by 60in (225 by 149cm).
£2,300-2,800 *Bon*

◁
A Gorevan carpet, the ivory floral field with a large madder and indigo centred medallion, 130 by 94in (330 by 241cm).
£850-950 *Bon*

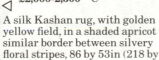

A Kirman carpet, the shaded ice blue field with large cusped indigo floral radiating medallion, in a multiple ivory, burgundy and blue palmette and flowering vine border, 185 by 122in (469 by 309cm).
◁ **£2,000-2,500** *C*

A silk Kashan rug, with golden yellow field, in a shaded apricot similar border between silvery floral stripes, 86 by 53in (218 by 135cm).
£5,000-6,000 *C*

A Caucasian rug, c1870, 96 by 54in (242.5 by 135cm).
£4,500-5,000 *TG* ▷

A Karabagh rug, the terracotta field with Chelaberd medallions, 95 by 58in (241 by 145cm).
£1,800-2,400 *Bon*

A Muslagham rug, Hamadan area, 78 by 54in (197.5 by 135cm).
£1,250-1,500 *TG*

GLOSSARY

Abrash	Variations of density in a colour seen in a carpet by irregular horizontal washes, can greatly add to the value.
Aniline	Chemical dye, a derivative of coal-tar, first produced in the 1860's, most common in the red-blue-purple range, colours tend to fade (orange-pink, for instance can fade to walnut-brown).
Boteh	Widespread pattern of Persian origin (original meaning 'cluster of leaves'), used in Europe in the Paisley pattern.
Ch'ang	Chinese endless knot, the inextricable knot of destiny.
Chrome dye	A fast synthetic dye now used in all the major rug weaving areas, colours do not fade.
Gol Henai Pattern	Floral pattern associated with Persian rugs, mainly found on Hamadan rugs.
Hejira (or Hijra)	The beginning of the Muhammedan calendar, 16 July, A.D. 622.
Herati Pattern	Also called the mahi or fish pattern. This common pattern originated in East Persia.
Jufti	'False' knot, either Turkish or Persian, whereby the knots are tied to four, not two, warp threads.
Kelim	Also spelled kilim, gilim, gelim. Principally from Anatolia.
Madder	Deep red-brown dye.
Palas	Caucasian name for kelim.
Palmette	A flowerhead of heart-shape with many radiating lobes or petals.
Sileh	A corruption of a now lost Caucasian place name. A form of Soumak, sileh pieces tend to be woven with rows of large S-motifs.
Soumak	Sumak, Summak, Sumacq, Sumakh, thought to be a corruption of Shemaka, town in south east Caucasus.
Spandrels	Architectural term for the space between the curve of an arch and the enclosing mouldings.
Swastika	A hooked cross. Chinese symbol for 10,000 (wan) and happiness.
Tiraz	Official weaving factory usually set up under Royal patronage.

A Kurdish carpet, c1830, 144 by 72in (365 by 182.5cm). £3,500-4,000 *TG*

A Kazak rug. £350-400 *PWC*

A Kashan silk embossed and metal thread rug of vase design, 79 by 54in (200 by 134cm). £6,000-7,000 *P*

A large Senneh corridor Kelim, the royal blue field with diagonal rows of multi-coloured stepped lozenge medallions in a triple blue, yellow and indigo flowering vine border, one area of slight repair, 222 by 61in (562 by 155cm). £650-750 *C*

A Kashan rug, the red ground corners on a blue field with one main red ground border, 80 by 54in (202.5 by 135cm). £1,000-1,400 *DWB*

A Qashqai Kelim, the field divided into blood red, green and mustard yellow serrated panels in a light blue hooked lozenge border, 101 by 60in (255 by 152cm). £800-1,000 *C*

A Kuba rug, c1870, 72 by 50in (180 by 125cm). £2,500-3,000 *TG*

A needlepoint rug, in crimson wools on a cream ground, lined, late 19thC, 70 by 49in (175 by 122cm). £550-650 *P*

A needlepoint carpet, Continental, with khaki, black and multi-coloured variations, shows slight wear, repairs and backed, comprised of numerous panels sewn together, 19thC, 102 by 99in (259 by 250cm). £2,000-2,500 *CNY*

A pair of fine Qum rugs, the ivory field around a scalloped blue floral medallion, surrounded by fluted columns, in an ivory palmette and vine border, a signature cartouche at one end, 86 by 54in (217.5 by 137cm). £5,000-6,000 *C*

An antique Rescht panel, the indigo ground with 6 columns of burgundy scalloped floral medallions, a broad outer tomato red boteh stripe, backed, areas of splitting along seams, 138 by 85in (350 by 215cm). £600-800 *C*

A silk Qum rug, the ivory field with 3 radiating open medallions surrounded by stylised vine, in an ivory serrated lozenge border between mock kufic stripes, 85 by 52in (215 by 132cm).
£3,000-4,000   *C*

A Turkoman Juval, woven in shades of rose and brown, with diagonal rows of small medallions, enriched with silk, deep fringe, in excellent condition, 12 by 43in (30 by 108cm).
£600-700   *L*

An antique Senneh rug, the ivory field with a central indigo herati pole medallion, the spandrels similar, in a yellow floral border between ivory similar stripes, 40 by 28in (102 by 72cm).
£1,800-2,200   *C*

A pair of antique Serapi runners, the field of each with a blood red lozenge with flowering plants around an indigo lozenge medallion, one dated AH 1300 (AD1883), 143 by 36in (360 by 90cm).
£1,700-2,000   *C*

A Shirvan rug, the indigo polychrome floral motif field enclosed by an ivory motif border, 58 by 44in (145 by 110cm).
£550-750   *Bon*

A Talish runner, the dark blue field woven with small red florets, the cream main border with bold florets, some wear, 93 by 39in (236 by 98cm).
£1,800-2,200   *L*

◁ A Tabriz rug, the madder field with a sky blue poled medallion and matching spandrels enclosed by a triple meander border, 68 by 48in (170 by 120cm).
£750-850   *Bon*

An antique Talish runner, the   ▷ shaded light blue field, in an ivory border of cusped lozenges, areas of slight wear, one small repaired cut, 141 by 41in (356 by 103cm).
£1,500-1,800   *C*

An antique Yomut flatweave, the brick red field with columns of blue double hooked motifs divided by split lozenges, 120 by 74in (304 by 189cm).
£1,800-2,200   *C*

A Shirvan rug with multiple floral decoration on an indigo field, ivory multi-coloured star border and twin guard stripes, 78 by 49in (197.5 by 122.5cm).
£550-650   *Re*

A Tabriz style carpet, the mustard yellow field with scrolling vine around large ivory cusped palmette medallions, in a broad peppermint green border, very slight staining, slightly dry, 159 by 142in (409 by 360cm).
£2,000-2,500   *C*

A Yugoslav Kelim, the raspberry red field with two stylised floral sprays in an ivory floral border, 109 by 69in (275 by 174cm).
£650-750   *C*

Textiles – Costume

An antique Tekke Turkoman carpet, the brick red field with 6 columns of linked Tekke guls divided by secondary linked cruciform guls, 155 by 104in (394 by 262cm).
£1,000-1,200 *C*

A pair of North West American or Canadian Woodlands Indian moccasins, 19thC, 10in (25cm).
£500-600 *TKN*

A pair of yellow silk shoes, embroidered in blue silk, lined, c1700.
£1,000-1,300 *P*

A fine and rare gentleman's banyan or dressing gown, of crimson silk damask, lined with emerald green silk, mid-18thC.
£6,000-7,000 *CSK*

A pair of green damask silk shoes, with ivory silk brocade, c1780.
£350-400 *P*

A Yomut carpet, the fox brown field with interlocking rows of guls, 139 by 91in (355 by 230cm).
£1,200-1,500 *Bon*

A pair of lady's shoes of mainly blue, orange and ivory silk brocade, c1700.
£1,000-1,200 *P*

A pair of braces of pale blue grosgrain, embroidered with trailing flowers, c1840.
£250-300 *P*

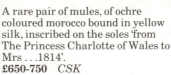

A rare pair of mules, of ochre coloured morocco bound in yellow silk, inscribed on the soles 'from The Princess Charlotte of Wales to Mrs . . .1814'.
£650-750 *CSK*

A fine calash of emerald green silk with 12 wired arches, late 18thC.
£650-700 *CSK*

l. A trilby hat of grey felt, trimmed with coral pink and black velvet, with traces of label, c1865.
£100-150

c. A bonnet of ivory satin and coral pink velvet, labelled Mrs. Seale, Milliner, 80 Oxford Street, c1865, and a bentwood hat box labelled William Whitley, Westbourne Grove.
£150-200

A Zejwa corridor carpet, the blue field woven with 4 large sunburst medallions, in shaded brown or cream, generally good condition but pile low, 125 by 53in (318 by 138cm).
£950-1,050 *L*

r. A young man's cap, of black wool with patent leather peak, lined with green and telescopic upper part, mid-19thC.
£100-150 *CSK*

A pair of lady's shoes of cornflower blue watered silk, c1850.
£150-200 *P*

A rare crinoline hoop of blue, pink, and grey striped cotton, with 4 whale bone hoops, c1760.
£4,500-5,500 *CSK*

A dress of pale pink silk, c1815.
£400-500 *CSK*

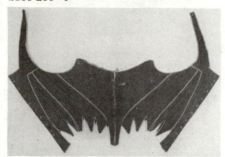

A corset of brown linen, stiffened with whale bones and bound with pale linen braid, c1770.
£1,100-1,500 *CSK*

An open robe of pale yellow silk ▷ lustre, woven with garlands of flowers, the neckline edged with 18thC Binche lace, the front of the bodice slightly altered.
£2,000-2,500 *CSK*

◁ An open robe and petticoat of green and white striped silk, trimmed with pinking, slightly altered, c1780.
£3,500-4,000 *CSK*

A suit of rust coloured wool, with deep cuffs and wide skirts and gilt buttons, comprising: coat, waistcoat with detached sleeves and breeches, c1760.
£5,500-6,000 *CSK*

A gentleman's waistcoat of cream silk, with 22 embroidered jacket buttons, late 18thC, and a garter.
£150-200 *P*

A Chinese Imperial robe, altered, 19thC.
£2,200-2,500 *P*

A mink chiffon dress, with front and back panels of lace, a silk imitation snakeskin belt and neckline trim, lined, bearing the maker's label Lucile Ltd., 11 rue de Penthièvre, Paris, c1910.
£600-700 *P*

A red silk dress, with chiné print of flowers in black, and accompanying jacket, lined, bearing the maker's label Christian Dior, Paris, Automne-Hiver 1958.
£500-600 *P*

An evening mantle or burnouse, by Liberty, made from an Indian embroidered shawl, fastened at the front with multi-coloured tassels and an Art Nouveau pewter clasp set with pink hardstone, lined with blue silk and labelled Liberty & Co., London and Paris, late 1880's.
£850-950 *CSK*

Believed to have belonged to the mother of Sir Edward Mortimer Archibald, a British Consul General in America, 1857–93.

An iridescent green silk taffeta dress bound in yellow silk, lined, bearing the maker's label Lucile Ltd., 11 rue de Penthièvre, Paris, c1910.
£800-900 *P*

Lucile (Lucy Wallace Duff Gordon) b1870, d1935 was the first London based designer to attain world celebrity and had ateliers in London, Paris and New York.

A cream gauze dress with black spot print, lined, bearing the maker's label Jeanne Lanuin Paris, Castillo, late 1950s, and accompanying petticoat.
£80-100 *P*

A cream gauze coat, probably silk and alpaca, with matching dress sprinkled with diamanté, each lined, bearing the maker's label Balenciaga, 10 Avenue George V, Paris, late 1950s.
£1,000-1,200 *P*

A picture of blue felt with silk and wool embroidered and applique, c1790, 12in (30cm) diam. framed and glazed.
£280-340 *P*

An embroidered picture, the linen ground worked in crimson wools and silks with mainly stem, buttonhole and running stitches, c1650, 19 by 22½in (48.5 by 57.5cm) framed and glazed.
£1,400-1,700 *P*

A petit point picture, worked in coloured wools and silks, c1770, 9in (23cm) square, framed and glazed.
£1,700-2,000 *P*

Embroidery

A needlework picture, the ivory silk ground embroidered and applied with coloured silks, metal thread and spangles with raised work, mid-17thC, 10½ by 14½in (27 by 37cm) framed and glazed.
£1,000-1,300 *P*

A silk work picture, worked in coloured silks on an ivory silk ground, late 18thC, framed and glazed, 18½in (47.5cm).
£350-400 *P*

A silk work picture, some damage, early 19thC, 19 by 25in (49 by 64.5cm).
£300-350 *DWB*

A needlework picture, inscribed 'Elijah Arise and eat', 1 Kings Chap 19 SR, the linen ground embroidered in metal thread and coloured silks, c1720s, 6½ by 7½in (16.5 by 19cm) framed and glazed.
£1,000-1,300 *P*

A pair of Georgian silk work pictures, embroidered in black thread on cream silk, in the manner of an engraving, in later gilt surround, 12½ by 10in (31 by 25cm) framed and glazed.
£450-500 *Bon*

Lace

A stumpwork picture, embroidered and applied in coloured silks and coiled metal thread with mainly tent, eye and satin stitches, c1660, 17 by 21in (43 by 53cm) framed and glazed.
£4,000-5,000   *P*

A length of reticella, early 17thC, 4½ by 46in (12 by 114cm).
£400-450   *P*

A petit point panel, 18thC, 20 by 25½in (51 by 64cm), now framed as a firescreen.
£1,600-1,900   *HSS*

A bertha of Brussels bobbin and needlepoint lace, a collar and a handkerchief with similar surround.
£80-120   *P*

A Brussels bobbin and needlepoint bertha collar, 19thC, and another.
£250-300   *P*

A silk needlework picture, 'The Moralist', 17in (43cm) square, in gilt frame, with a note on the back which records that the picture was worked by Mary Callaghan, and was finished in 1800.
£1,900-2,200   *L*

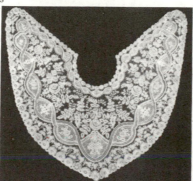

A Brussels point-de-gaze collar, late 19thC.
£180-220   *P*

A deep Youghal needlepoint flounce, 31½ by 160in (80 by 400cm).
£450-500   *P*

A pair of Brussels bobbin lace lappets, c1730, 21½in (54cm) long.
£250-300   *P*

A woolwork ship's picture, of a British frigate in full sail, with embroidered label H.M.S. Emerald, 19thC, 16½ by 12½in (42 by 32cm), framed and glazed.
£400-500   *P*

A pair of joined Brussels bobbin lace lappets, c1750, mounted with seal inscribed Elise & Co., 170 Regent St, London, Antique & Modern Lace Warehouse, 41½in (104cm), and a similar edging, 2½ by 38½in (7 by 98cm).
£130-180   *P*

A length of Mechlin edging, designed with sailing boats, cherubs, birds and flowers, c1740, 3 by 67in (8 by 168cm).
£300-350   *P*

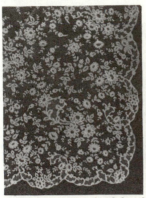

A Carrickmacross bridal veil, with scalloped border, 19thC.
£160-240 *P*

Samplers

A needlework sampler, inscribed 'Margaret Neilsons sampler sewed in her tenth year taught by Mrs. Henderson, Miss Macredies School 1831. The rev. William Woodrow Minister of Dreghorn', early 19thC, 17 by 14in (43 by 37cm), mounted.
£1,100-1,300 *P*

A woolwork sampler by Elizabeth Shufflebottoms, 1832, 24in (61cm) square, in contemporary maple frame.
£300-500 *Re*

A drawnthread and needlepoint lace linen sampler, late 17thC, 12½ by 7½in (31 by 19cm).
£250-300 *P*

A sampler worked by Rebekah Danford dated March 31st, 1788, 18 by 14in (46 by 37cm).
£250-300 *Bon*

A sampler by Peggy Kellbrick, dated 5th February 1836, 23 by 23in (58.5 by 58.5cm).
£1,300-1,600 *DWB*

A needlework sampler, decorated in coloured silks, holed, 18thC, 17 by 12½in (43 by 32cm).
£550-600 *GSP*

A sampler, c1842, 19 by 21in (47.5 by 52.5cm).
£450-500 *SBO*

A needlework sampler, by 'Mary Ann Hunter aged 14 years 1844', 26 by 16½in (66 by 42cm) in stained wood frame.
£350-400 *AG*

A sampler worked in brightly coloured silks, in red, yellow, blue and green, with initials D.A. and D.G. and the date 1784, Dutch, 19 by 11in (48 by 28cm).
£450-550 *CSK*

A George IV needlework sampler, by E.H., slight holing, 1826, 17 by 12½in (43 by 32cm).
£400-500 *GSP*

A needlework sampler by Jane Brannan, age 9, 1829, the wool ground embroidered with coloured silks in mainly cross stitch, early 19thC, 16 by 12in (40.5 by 30cm), framed and glazed.
£350-400 *P*

A needlework sampler by 'Elizabeth Mawdsley, 1807', the wool ground embroidered mainly in cross stitch with coloured silks, early 19thC, 22½ by 16½in (56.5 by 42cm).
£750-850 *P*

A needlework sampler by Hannah Ransome, 1795, the wool ground embroidered in coloured silks, late 18thC, 14 by 11½in (35.5 by 28.5cm), framed and glazed.
£400-500 *P*

A Brussels verdure tapestry, borders now lacking, 17thC, 164 by 72in (416 by 182cm).
£8,500-9,500 *WW*

A Brussels tapestry, woven in silk and wool with the triumph of Mars, the sky partially rewoven, mid-18thC, 194 by 155 (492 by 393cm).
£6,000-7,000 *C*

A panel of Brussels tapestry, woven mainly in blue, green and ivory wool, 17thC, 60 by 66in (150 by 166cm).
£550-600 *P*

A Flemish verdure tapestry, restorations, 17thC, 101 by 115in (255 by 290cm).
£2,500-3,000 *C*

Tapestries

A Flemish tapestry, depicting Athena, repairs, late 17th/early 18thC, 108 by 55in (272.5 by 137.5cm).
£1,000-1,300 *WW*

A pair of woven tapestry panels of pastoral scenes, in muted colours of blue, crimson, green and brown, 18thC, each 31 by 22in (79 by 56cm).
£600-700 *DWB*

An Aubusson tapestry, on a beige ground with shaped olive green borders, 90 by 56in (227.5 by 140cm).
£2,500-3,000 *C*

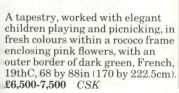

A tapestry, worked with elegant children playing and picnicking, in fresh colours within a rococo frame enclosing pink flowers, with an outer border of dark green, French, 19thC, 68 by 88in (170 by 222.5cm).
£6,500-7,500 *CSK*

A tapestry of Diana, guild mark, D.T.W., 19thC, 76 by 81in (192.5 by 205cm).
£3,500-4,000 *GSP*

A tapestry woven in muted colours, with a Mannerist cartouche with a coat of arms, Spanish or Italian, 17thC, 94 by 99in (237.5 by 250cm).
£5,000-6,000 *C*

Curtains & Covers

A Persian cover, the cotton ground printed in indigo and madder, lined, early 19thC, 81 by 48in (204 by 120cm).
£90-120 *P*

A joined panel of green satin, embroidered in silver thread, with pairs of initials crowned and similar monograms at each corner, possibly a bed tester or coverlet, late 17th/early 18thC, 48 by 54in (120 by 135cm), framed.
£850-1,050 *CSK*

A cream cotton coverlet, printed in green, blue and red, with stylised tulips and anemones, padded and quilted, the reverse printed in red, late 19thC, 82 by 73in (208 by 186cm).
£180-220 *P*

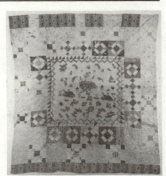

A patchwork coverlet, quilted, early 19thC, 99 by 87in (250 by 220cm).
£200-250 *P*

An American patchwork coverlet, worked in squares of plain, printed and chiné silk and brocades, in a squared design bordered in pale yellow, inscribed with names including: Mary Blair, Blairville South Carolina, Mrs. C. E. Kennedy, William Blair Brigaley, Mary S. Bryan 1846, Lancaster Theodore Bagaley aged 3 year, lined in glazed blue cotton and quilted, made in Pennsylvania, mid-19thC, 107 by 111in (270 by 280cm).
£500-600 *P*

A coverlet of filet squares, linked with lawn and having vandyked, fringed filet border, probably Italian, joined, c1900, 79 by 60in (200 by 150cm).
£85-105 *P*

A 'mosaic' patchwork cover composed of white, Turkey red and printed cottons, including dark ground and lilac, the cottons dating from 1800–45, 95 by 100in (240 by 252.5cm), unfinished with papers intact.
£170-200 *CSK*

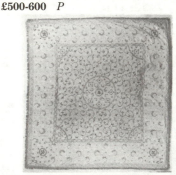

A linen coverlet, embroidered in chain stitch with mainly brown and pink wools, lined, the reverse embroidered with the initials, D.H. 1779, 100in (252cm) square.
£300-350 *P*

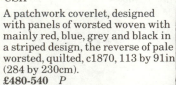

A patchwork coverlet, designed with panels of worsted woven with mainly red, blue, grey and black in a striped design, the reverse of pale worsted, quilted, c1870, 113 by 91in (284 by 230cm).
£480-540 *P*

A Greek cover of undyed linen, embroidered in coloured silks, 17thC, 22½ by 46in (57 by 114cm), and another similar piece, probably Epirus, 20½in (52cm) square.
£400-500 *P*

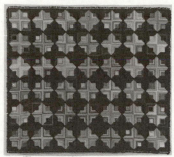

A patchwork quilt of log cabin design, worked with coloured, corded silks and brocades, lined, late 19thC, 99 by 83in (250 by 210cm).
£250-300 *P*

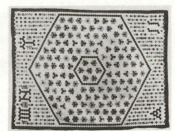

A patchwork coverlet, with hexagonal pieces of printed and plain cotton, c1860, 113 by 83in (286 by 210cm).
£250-300 *P*

A crewel work bedspread, embroidered with scrolling foliage in dark and light blue wool on linen ground, holed.
£520-600 *WW*

A patchwork coverlet, of red and white embroidered squares, embroidered with the date 1892, lined, 101 by 83in (256 by 210cm).
£220-280 *P*

A Durham quilt, worked in a waved feather pattern with alternating stripes of pink and white cotton, late 19thC, 90 by 80in (228 by 202cm).
£80-100 *P*

An Eastern quilted cream damask coverlet with tufted border, possibly Indian or Chinese in origin and made for the European market, late 17thC, 60 by 38in (150 by 95cm) and matching pillow cover with self covered wood buttons, 19 by 27in (47.5 by 67.5cm).
£2,200-2,800 *DWB*

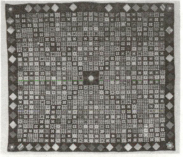

A patchwork cover, worked with diamond-shaped pieces of plain and printed silks, brocades and velvets, mid-19thC, 93 by 79in (236 by 200cm).
£250-300 *P*

A large wool and silk challis shawl, printed all over in scarlet, aquamarine, shades of brown and cream with an elaborate floral and Paisley pattern, c1860, 128 by 63in (325 by 160cm).
£400-500 *C*

A Mexican saltillo, worked mainly in red, blue and cream wools, 19thC, 48 by 79in (120 by 200cm).
£1,000-1,300 *P*

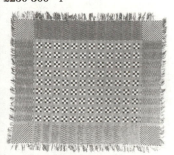

A Welsh coverlet, double woven in black, blue and cream wools, late 19thC, 84 by 71in (212 by 178cm).
£180-220 *P*

Woven in 1891 by the two sisters who lived at Maesgwyn House, Maesgwyn, Carmarthenshire, Wales, and who were mentioned in Under Milkwood by Dylan Thomas: 'Who milks the cows now at Maesgwyn'.

A Hanoi wall hanging of ivory silk embroidered in pastel silks, 48 by 53in (120 by 134cm).
£120-140 *P*

An altar cloth, finely embroidered with gold and silver thread, dated 1615 in English and Latin on each side, 26 by 26½in (66 by 67cm).
£500-600 *AGr*

A panel of linen and cotton, worked in coloured wools with crewel and tambour stitch, early 18thC, 70 by 87in (175 by 220cm) and the companion, and another 2, 89 by 32in (226 by 80cm).
£3,500-4,000 *P*

A set of three Aubusson portieres, with twisting blue ribbon on a sand coloured ground with pale eau-de-nil border, 19thC, 108in (274cm) drop.
£2,500-3,000 *C*

An altar frontal of crimson damask silk, the upper part and two falling panels of 17thC Italian cream silk applique, part fringed, lined, 41 by 66in (102 by 164cm).
£250-300 *P*

An Aubusson tapestry portiere pelmet, woven mainly in green, red and blue, 19thC, 44 by 114in (110 by 299cm) wide.
£700-800 *P*

A large hanging, formerly of cream velvet, worked in silver thread and sequins, Indian, late 19thC, 104 by 60in (264 by 150cm).
£250-300 *C*

A Victorian embroidered pelmet, worked in coloured wools, highlighted in silk, on a black ground, edged with twisted silk cord, 10½in (26.5cm) deep.
£650-700 *CSK*

A pair of linen curtains, embroidered in crewel work, with two pelmets en suite, Indian for the European market, 19thC, 104 by 59in (262.5 by 147.5cm).
£3,200-4,000 *CSK*

▷ A Schleswig–Holstein wall hanging, of double woven blue wool and undyed linen, late 18thC, 65 by 37in (164 by 92cm).
£1,300-1,600 *P*

A rare wall hanging or valance, worked in coloured wools and silks, some repairs and re-working and overpainting, 16thC, 88in (222.5cm) wide.
£3,200-3,500 *CSK*

It is very unusual to find secular wall hangings of this period.

A fine set of bed hangings, comprising one large panel, a pair of narrow curtains and a valance, of linen embroidered in brightly coloured red, blue, yellow and green wools, with flowering trees growing from rocky hillocks, English, 18thC, curtain 88 by 92in (222.5 by 232.5cm).
£5,500-6,000 *CSK*

A long panel of Victorian beadwork densely worked in coloured beads with flowers, 9in (23cm) deep.
£180-240 *CSK*

Handkerchiefs

A satirical printed handkerchief, 'The Reformers attack on the Old Rotten Tree – of the Foul Nests of our Morants in Danger', printed in colour on silk, c1830, fragile.
£250-300   *CSK*

A silk handkerchief, commemorating the Peace of Rysbach, published by Charles Weston at the Nag's Head in Bishop's Gate Street, near Leaden Hall, 1713, fragile.
£300-350   *CSK*

Fans

A French fan with carved, pierced and gilded ivory sticks, c1770s, 11in (28cm) long, in a shaped framed and glazed case.
£250-300   *P*

A Chinese ivory brisé fan, c1790s, 10½in (27cm) long, and a box.
£600-700   *P*

A fan with black wood sticks and gauze leaf, applied with a velvet and lace mask, with cut-out eyes and nose, one guard inset with looking glass, the other with silvered metal container for scissors, buttonhook and pencil, the handle with attached powder puff, c1880s, 14in (36cm) long.
£300-350   *P*

A French fan with carved, pierced, silvered and gilt ivory sticks, the silk leaf painted with a central panel of Mars, Venus and Cupid, c1780s, 11in (28cm) long.
£350-400   *P*

A fan, the silk leaf painted with a military scene, probably the surrender of Fort St. Philip in Minorca by the English to the Spaniards, the ivory sticks pierced and silvered, French for the Spanish market, 1756, 10½in (26.5cm).
£550-600   *CSK*

Lord Blakeney (1672–1761) after seventy days' defence of an almost indefensible fortress, surrendered on the honourable terms, whereby his garrison was transported to Gibraltar and not made prisoners of war. He was 84 and had not gone to bed throughout the siege.

A fan with tortoiseshell sticks, c1880s, 12in (31cm) long, in a silk lined velvet box.
£120-180   *P*

A French fan with carved, pierced, silvered and gilt mother-of-pearl sticks, c1750s, 11½in (29cm) long.
£120-180   *P*

A fan with chinoiserie sticks of carved and pierced ivory, probably French, c1760s, 8½in (22cm) long.
£220-280   *P*

A French fan with carved and pierced ivory sticks, c1760s, 10½in (26cm) long.
£650-700   *P*

A French fan, with mother-of-pearl sticks, the leaf painted with an 18thC pastiche, signed 'B. Bisson de Récy', c1890s, 10½in (27cm) long.
£150-200   *P*

A fan with carved, pierced silvered and gilt mother-of-pearl sticks, the leaf of Brussels point-de-gaze, c1870s, 14½in (37cm) long, in original box.
£450-500 *P*

A Canton carved ivory Hundred Faces fan.
£180-220 *Bon*

A Japanese tortoiseshell fan, with gilt lacquered decoration.
£120-160 *HSS*

An Italian fan with pierced ivory sticks, mainly in terracotta and yellow, c1770s, 11in (28cm) long.
£250-300 *P*

A Chinese mother-of-pearl brisé fan, c1840s, 7½in (18.5cm) long.
£300-350 *P*

A painted fan, the leaf decorated with the Virgin and Child, the ivory and mother-of-pearl inlaid sticks with silver pique point, probably Italian, mid-18thC, 10½in (27cm).
£90-110 *Bon*

A fan, the chickenskin leaf painted with classical vignettes, with plain ivory sticks, Italian, c1780, 10½in (27cm), in contemporary pink paper-covered box, lacking lid.
£450-550 *CSK*

A Japanese fan, the stiffened cream cloth leaf printed and painted with figures.
£80-110 *HSS*

A fan, the leaf a hand-coloured etching with detailed Almanack for the year 1794, published 1st January, 1794, by John Cox and J. P. Crowder, Wood Street, with plain wooden sticks, damaged, 11in (28cm).
£200-250 *CSK*

A bone brisé fan, probably Dutch, c1730s, 8in (20cm) long.
£180-220 *P*

A pair of lacquered fans.
£250-300 *CW*

A fan with wood sticks and carved guards, the printed hand-coloured leaf inscribed 'Vaughan's Quadrille Fan', c1790s, 11½in (29cm) long.
£450-500 *P*

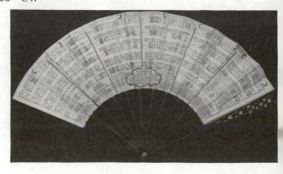

An unusual Jamaican fan, the leaf composed of leaf-shaped panels of lace barke (Lagetta Lintearea), edged with cabbage barke (Orodoza Oleracea), and fringed with French cotton (Colotropie Procera), the sticks of tortoiseshell and trimmed with a tassel of penguin fibres, c1880, 15in (38cm).
£120-150 *CSK*

An autograph fan, the chickenskin leaf painted with a cat and signed by various members of European Royal Families, signed 'Karl' twice 'Thyra', 'Albert', etc with simulated blond tortoiseshell sticks, gilt and clouté with steel, 1903, 9in (23cm).
£600-700 *CSK*

A church printed fan, 1776, the leaf a hand-coloured etching with pious verses and quotations from the Scriptures, published by I. French, 47 Holborn Hill, June 1, 1776, inscribed 'Beauty like Flowers soon fades away, the charms of virtue ne'er decay', with bone sticks, 12in (31cm).
£400-500 *CSK*

A fan with carved, pierced and gilded mother-of-pearl sticks, the printed leaf after the painting of 'George III, Queen Charlotte and their six eldest children', by Johann Zoffany, c1860s, 10½in (27cm) long.
£110-150 *P*

A painted Spanish fan, the leaf decorated with mythological figures in a landscape, ivory red lacquer and cut steel guards, 18thC.
£100-120 *Bon*

A shaped handscreen of catgut stained blue appliqué with featherwork birds holding sprays of flowers, with white metal handle, probably made in the Northern half of South America for the European market, 13in (33cm).
£3,000-3,500 *CSK*

This fan closely resembles the famous handscreen in the Messel/Rosse collection at the Fitzwilliam Museum. As to date, it is very difficult to pronounce – the fan in the Fitzwilliam has always been called 17thC – no portraits are known of ladies carrying such fans and until now no other such fan has been found. The colours of the feathers are as delicate as watercolour. They fade fast in the light. This fan is very fresh and is mounted on what appears to be catgut. Examples of English folding fans of catgut dating from the mid-18thC have been found. The provenance of this fan could point to an early 19thC date, the silver handle is probably not European and could date from as late as 1840.

Shawls

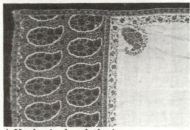

A Kashmir shawl, the centre panel of blue pashmina, the border worked in coloured wools and silks, c1860, 76 by 67in (192 by 168cm).
£600-700 *P*

A Kashmir shawl, the ivory pashmina centre with boteh to either end woven in madder and indigo, c1800, 51 by 122in (128 by 310cm).
£400-450 *P*

A Kashmir shawl, the indigo pashmina ground woven with boteh to either end in mainly green, red and yellow, c1820, 53 by 103in (132 by 260cm).
£400-500 *P*

A shawl, with cream cashmere ground woven with cones and florets to the border and each corner in mainly red, blue, yellow and green, probably French, c1850, 66in (165cm) square.
£220-300 *P*

A Sumatra shawl, the ikat centre woven in red, black and ivory silks and gold thread in a striped design.
£400-450 *P*

Dolls – Wooden

A carved and turned painted wooden doll with carved ears, inset enamel eyes, pink cheeks, stitched brows and lashes with the remains of nailed-on wig, c1790–1810, 18½in (46cm) high.
£1,200-1,500   *CSK*

A fine and rare George II wooden doll, painted gesso-covered face, black enamelled eyes with red dots at each corner, painted eyelashes and line eyebrows with short brush strokes above and below, and stitched nailed wig, elongated 'fork' fingers, tip of nose and upper lip rubbed, slight damage to three fingers on one hand, re-dressed, 22in (56cm).
£10,000-12,000   *P*

A group of painted wooden headed dolls, 'There was an old woman who lived in a shoe', with silk clothing and shoe, early 19thC, 5in (13cm) long.
£140-180   *DSH*

A carved and painted wood figurehead in the form of a French Cantinière, 39½in (100cm) high.
£500-600   *L*

A turned and carved painted wooden doll, with inset blue enamel eyes, remains of wig base nailed to the head, with painted wooden legs and pink kid arms, wearing contemporary linen under-bodice, c1830, 12½in (31cm) high.
£650-700   *CSK*

Wax

A rare beeswax shoulder headed doll, the brown eyes wired between the legs, the stuffed body in original white dress, underclothes including pantalettes, with blue kid slippers, c1810, 17in (43cm) high.
£500-600   *CSK*

A doll with wax head, arms and feet, natural brown hair, 19thC, 19in (47cm).
£140-180   *BD*

A wax over composition shoulder headed doll, the blue eyes wired from the waist, with original wig, the stuffed body with wax over composition limbs, in contemporary petticoat and straw bonnet and necklace.
£350-400   *CSK*

A wax composition doll, with closed mouth, sleeping blue eyes, fair wig, stuffed cloth body, voice box, with waxed composition lower limbs, in original white cotton and lace dress and coat and underclothes, 14in (35cm).
£300-350   *L*

A wax headed pedlar doll modelled as an old crone, carrying a basket of wares including gloves, a brush, bellows, toasting fork, skeins of wool, fans, nutmeg grater, book and a purse, 19thC, 9½in (24cm) high, under dome.
£600-700   *CSK*

A Victorian display case containing a wax head doll, standing among stuffed songbirds, butterflies and artificial flowers, larger birds below, mid-19thC, 31 by 34in (79 by 86cm).
£350-400   *TEN*

A wax over composition headed doll, with fixed pale blue eyes, the stuffed body with blue arms, wearing contemporary organdie dress, mid-19thC, 22in (56cm) high.
£180-240   *CSK*

A wax over composition shoulder headed doll, the stuffed body with yellow kid arms and separated fingers, in contemporary sprigged muslin dress, 1810–1815, 14in (36cm) high.
£280-340 *CSK*

A brown wax over composition headed doll, the stuffed body with brown wax over composition limbs, in original clothes, late 19thC, 10½in (27cm) high.
£220-280 *CSK*

Bru

Gebruder Heubach

A bisque headed character doll, with blue intaglio eyes and blonde wig, the jointed composition body wearing blue tucked frock and petticoat, marked 14676 24 and stamped in green 43, by Heubach, 16in (41cm) high.
£1,000-1,300 *CSK*

An all bisque child doll, the open/closed mouth showing two upper teeth, the moulded blonde hair with three glazed blue bows, jointed at the shoulder and hip, marked 10490 3 and stamped 23, probably by Heubach, 9in (23cm) high.
£500-600 *CSK*

An unusual black Bru bisque head doll, with mohair wig, cork pate, fixed paperweight eyes, pierced ears and open/closed mouth, marked Bru Jne, 13in (33cm).
£3,000-3,500 *P*

◁

A bisque headed character doll, with closed water melon mouth, blue googlie eyes and with tubby rigid limb composition body wearing a yellow striped tunic, marked 9578 2/0 and the Heubach square mark, 8½in (21.5cm).
£500-600 *CSK*

A bisque head doll on a bent limbed body, made in Germany by Ernst Heubach, 1865–1925, moulded 300–2.
£220-280 *LM* ▷

Jumeau

A Dep Tete Jumeau bisque headed doll, impressed Dep 8, and marked 'Tete Jumeau' in red, with open mouth and moulded upper teeth, fingers, feet and body chipped, 19in (49cm).
£400-450 *L*

A French bisque head closed mouth doll, on a jointed body, in original dress, by Jumeau, Paris, 1850–1899, marked 'Tete Jumeau', 26in (66cm) high.
£4,000-4,500 *LM*

A bisque headed bébé, with closed mouth, fixed bulbous brown eyes, pierced applied ears and with jointed fixed wrist composition and wood body, marked EHJ and stamped on the body 'Jumeau Medaille D'or Paris', containing non-functioning voice box, 18½in (46cm) high.
£2,500-3,000 *CSK*

A French bisque head doll by Jumeau, with wig, with Mama/Papa voice box, inoperative, 24in (61cm).
£850-950 *P*

J. D. Kestner

A bisque headed character baby doll, with open closed mouth, brown sleeping eyes, short blonde wig and composition baby's body, with upturned big toes, contemporary clothes, marked 211 JDK, 15½in (39cm) high.
£600-700 *CSK*

l. A bisque headed character baby doll, with open closed mouth, brown sleeping eyes, short brown wig and composition baby's body, marked 211 JDK, 17in (43cm) high.
£400-500

r. A bisque headed character child doll, with closed mouth, blue sleeping eyes, later blonde hair wig and composition jointed toddler body, original socks and shoes, marked K*R SH115/A 42, 16½in (42cm) high.
£2,500-3,000   *CSK*

Armand Marseille

l. A bisque headed doll with moving glass eyes, open mouth, jointed composition body, marked 'Armand Marseille, Germany, A9M', 24in (61cm) high.
£200-250

r. A bisque headed doll with moving glass eyes, trembling tongue and composition body, marked 'Porzellan Fabrik Burggrub Daslachende Baby, 1930/3/ Made in Germany DRGM', 18in (45cm) high.
£450-500   *DSH*

An Armand Marseille musical/dancing bisque headed puppet doll, impressed 70.20,5, lower limbs stuffed, forearms wood.
£550-650   *L*

An Armand Marseille bisque headed doll, with open and shut eyes, composition body and limbs, marked 980, 22in (56cm) high.
£200-250   *Re*

An Armand Marseille bisque heade googlie eyed doll, the straight limbed composition body dressed i printed cotton with matching hat, marked 323 A 11/0, 6½in (17cm).
£450-550   *P*

A bisque headed bent-limbed character bébé, by Armand Marseille, Kollesdorf, 1880–1925, moulded 996, 20in (51cm) high.
£220-280   *LM*

S.F.B.J.

l. A bisque headed doll with glass eyes, kid covered body and bisque hands, impressed mark on shoulder 501, 12in (31cm) high.
£280-340

r. A bisque headed doll with moving glass eyes, open mouth and composition body, marked S.F.B.J.60 Paris, 18in (45cm) high.
£130-160   *DSH*

A bisque headed child doll, with blue lashed sleeping eyes, pierced ears, blonde wig and jointed composition body wearing contemporary clothes, marked 'SFBJ Paris 14', also 'Bébé Français', 32in (81cm) high, in original box.
£850-950   *CSK*

A S.F.B.J. boy doll, with articulated limbs, some damage to hands, model 237, 18in (45cm).
£250-300   *JPL*

A bisque headed bent-limbed character bébé, by S.F.B.J. in Paris, 1899–1925, moulded 301, 8in (20cm) high.
£100-120   *LM*

Simon & Halbig/ Kammer & Reinhardt

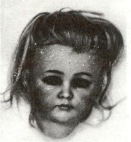

A bisque headed character doll, with closed mouth, brown lashed sleeping eyes, blonde wig and composition jointed body, marked 'K*R Simon and Halbig 117/A 39', the head 4¼in (11cm) high.
£1,700-2,000   *CSK*

A bisque headed character baby doll, the open mouth showing two glazed teeth and cardboard tongue, composition baby's body, marked 'K*R Simon and Halbig 122 42', 17in (43cm) high.
£450-500   *CSK*

A clockwork toy of a bisque headed doll, in original Scottish outfit, pulling a two-wheeled cart, marked '1079 Halbig S & H 7½', by Roullet Decamps.
£600-700   *CSK*

A small bisque headed doll, on a 1920s five-piece body, by Simon & Halbig, Grofenhain, 1870–1925, moulded 1079, 9in (23cm) high.
£250-300   *LM*

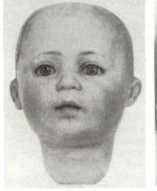

A Simon & Halbig bisque headed doll with long brown mohair wig, fixed blue eyes, pierced ears, open mouth with upper teeth and jointed composition body dressed in original undergarments, marked SH 1079 2½, 11in (28cm).
£450-500   *P*

A bisque character doll's head, with closed mouth, blue sleeping eyes and with remains of body, marked '1488 Simon & Halbig 6', the head 4in (10cm) high.
£1,500-1,800   *CSK*

Miscellaneous

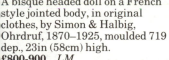

A bisque headed doll on a French style jointed body, in original clothes, by Simon & Halbig, Ohrdruf, 1870–1925, moulded 719 dep., 23in (58cm) high.
£800-900   *LM*

A bisque headed jointed doll, made by Theo Recknagel in Alexandrinentan, 1886–1925, marked RA, 11in (29cm) high.
£140-170   *LM*

CHARACTER DOLLS

★ in 1909 Kammer & Reinhardt introduced a large number of character dolls

★ these were modelled from life, showing all the nuances of childish temperament

★ a model was made and then a mould taken, which was used about fifty times

★ Simon and Halbig cast and painted the heads for many other manufacturers, including Kammer & Reinhardt, such heads are marked K & R, Simon & Halbig, or K & R, S & H and the model number

★ early K & R character dolls are of exceptional quality

★ the French had remained supreme in the manufacture of dolls, in the 19thC, with Jumeau one of the main exponents

★ however, from the 1890's the Germans had perfected equal skills

★ after K & R introduced their characters many other makers followed: Heubach, Armand Marseille, Bruno Schmidt, Kestner, and S.F.B.J. (the Societe Francaise de Fabrication de Bebes et Jouets)

★ obviously these dolls were expensive and so they were hardly produced in large quantities

★ K & R Model 117 is usually considered to be one of the most desirable, in fact any 'pouty' doll is highly collectable

★ the most common is model 126

★ there are more Heubach characters than any other

★ as one gets nearer to the First World War quality tends to decrease and character dolls produced after the war are in many cases, poor quality.

A bisque headed closed mouth doll on a kid leather body, with its original Scottish outfit, made in Germany, c1885–1900, 7in (18cm) high.
£140-170 *LM*

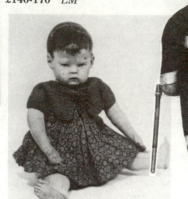

A printed cloth rag doll, modelled as a wounded First World War soldier, printed on the foot 'specially made for Boots, by Deans Rag Book Co Ltd, Hygienic stuffing, guaranteed British manufactured', 10½in (27cm) high.
£300-350 *CSK*

A painted cloth doll, with brown painted hair, the stuffed body jointed at hip and shoulder, wearing cotton frock and cardigan, by Kathe Kruse, 17in (43cm) high.
£400-500 *CSK*

A cloth doll painted in oils, with attached cloth ears with cloth jointing at shoulder, elbow, thigh and knee, marked under the right arm 'Chase Stockingnet doll Trademark, made in the U.S.A.', 23in (58cm) high.
£220-250 *CSK*

A doll in original clothes, made in Germany by Kathe Kruse, at Bad Kosen, 1910–1925, 18in (45cm) high.
£370-420 *LM*

A bisque headed bent-limbed ▷ character bébé, in original clothes, made in Germany by Otto Reinecke in Moschendorf, 1878–1925, marked P.M.914, 14in (36cm) high.
£240-290 *LM*

Miller's Antiques Price Guide builds up year by year to form the most comprehensive photo-reference system available. The first six volumes contain over 50,000 completely different photographs.

A bisque headed bébé, with pierced ears, animal skin wig and fixed wrists, jointed composition body, wearing contemporary home-made dark blue sailor suit, marked '0 by Jules Nicholas Steiner', 13in (33cm) high.
£1,800-2,200 *CSK*

△

A bisque shoulder headed poupard, with turned white wood handle, and original skirt and streamers, marked 3200 AM 10/OX DEP, 13in (33cm) high.
£300-350 *CSK*

A Steiff Infantryman, marked with Steiff button in the left ear, 9in (23cm).
£350-400 *P*

A rare china headed doll, the neck swivelling inside the carton body portion, with squeaker in the centre of the body and with carton lower body portion and china limbs, thumb and feet damaged, c1860, 12½in (31cm) high.
£1,000-1,300 *CSK*

◁

A bisque headed character boy doll, frowning brows, large ears, short blonde wig and jointed toddler body wearing white sailor suit, marked 'K*RS & H 115/A 42', 16in (41cm) high.
£2,000-2,400 *CSK*

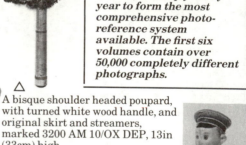

A French fashion doll, the bisque head with swivel neck, cork pate, fair mohair wig, the gusseted kid body with stitched fingers, dressed in original undergarments, 18in (46cm).
£1,600-1,800 *P*

A bisque headed doll, the unusual composition body with stuffed central body portion and upper legs, with jointed arms and fixed wrists, marked DEP, 13in (33cm) high.
£400-500 *CSK*

A boxed effigy of a queen, possibly Queen Elizabeth I, her composition hands and face finely modelled and painted, English, probably late 17thC, 12in (30.5cm) diam.
£550-650 *TKN*

l. A bisque headed doll with moving glass eyes, open mouth, jointed composition body, marked on head 'A.M.4DEP, Made in Germany', 19in (47cm) high.
£200-250

r. A bisque headed doll with tinted complexion, moving glass eyes, open mouth, kid covered body and bisque hands, marked 370 AM DEP, 21in (53cm) high.
£280-340 *DSH*

This figure may perhaps be a form of May Day 'Lady Doll', a floral decorated doll, with early pagan origins, which was traditionally carried in procession on May Day in some country districts – see Pollock's Dictionary of English Dolls, Robert Hale, 1982.

A crudely carved wood doll, with blue enamel and nail eyes and jointed limbs, early 19thC, 15½in (39cm).
£180-230 *AG*

A shoulder china doll of an Irish gentleman, gusseted kid body and china lower limbs, 13in (33cm), with blue and white spotted kerchief tied to a stick, containing 2 lace handkerchiefs, a yellow flower, a bag of Irish gold, a watch, a locket, 2 miniature books, one of Occasional Pieces by Lord Byron, and a miniature envelope containing a letter to 'Dearest Emy' dated Sept.1904.
£140-180 *L*

A composition headed ventriloquist dummy, contained in a collapsing painted wooden box, with articulated levers to the eyes, arms, upper and lower limbs, upper and lower lips, and the head, 10in (25cm) high.
£300-350 *CSK*

A bisque headed character doll, modelled as a laughing boy, with fixed wrist jointed composition body, wearing grey suit with red socks and black shoes, marked H128, 14in (36cm) high.
£350-400 *CSK*

Automata

An automaton mandolin player, the composition headed figure with movement to the neck, forearm and leg, with musical movement in base, stamped 'G. Vichy, Paris', 25½in (65cm) high.
£1,600-1,900 *CSK*

A bisque headed jester, hand-operated mechanical figure, the wire covered body with wooden hands and feet, in original alternate coloured blue and white costume, as the handle is turned, the music plays and he hits a ball, bearing shop label, 11in (29cm) high.
£750-850 *CSK*

An automaton picture of a negro boy.
£900-1,000 *FHF*

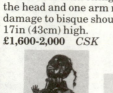

An automaton doll mandolin player, with bisque Jumeau head, bisque forearms and original clothes, automaton movements, with 2 rods controlling movement of the head and one arm respectively, damage to bisque shoulder section, 17in (43cm) high.
£1,600-2,000 *CSK*

A fine musical automaton, of a clown turning a somersault on the back of a chair, with two cam movement and musical movement concealed in the chair, 25in (64cm) high.
£4,500-5,000 *CSK*

A composition headed automaton, in original white silk trousers under a long red brocade coat, as he puffs his pipe moving it towards his mouth, his lower jaw moves and his eyes open and close as he moves his head, French, 1880, 30in (76cm) high.
£6,500-7,500 *CSK*

A musical automaton banjo player, the composition headed negro figure seated on a chair, with musical and automaton movements, in dilapidated condition, 22in (56cm) high.
£350-450 *CSK*

An automaton negro flute-player, with composition body and bisque head, the body containing musical and automaton movements, lacks flute, 24in (61cm) high.
£2,700-3,000 *CSK*

A French bisque head doll with swivel neck from The Waltzers Automation, one bisque arm damaged, 16½in (42cm).
£400-500 *P* ▷

An automaton doll negro flute-player, with bisque head and painted forearms, in original clothes, with musical and automaton movements, with two cams controlling vertical and horizontal head movements, head cracked behind ear, 17½in (44cm) high.
£1,600-2,000 *CSK*

A printed paper-on-wood dolls' house, opening at the front to reveal four rooms, with contemporary papers, German, late 19thC, 28in (71cm) wide.
£400-500 *CSK*

Dolls Houses

A folding dolls' house, by J.C. Russley of Hull, the front opening to reveal a two-roomed interior and stair-well, 23½in (60cm) wide, with a quantity of Art Deco furniture.
£900-1,000 *P*

A painted wood dolls' house, by G. & J. Lines, the front opening to reveal a six-roomed interior with central stair-well, fitted with electricity, 33in (84cm) wide.
£500-600 *P*

A French painted wood dolls' house, the front opening to reveal a four-roomed interior with original wallpapers, one room with fireplace and piano, 19½in (49cm) wide.
£350-450 *P*

A Georgian style baby house, the back opening in three sections to reveal one upper and two lower rooms, May 1830, 28in (71cm) wide
£750-850 *P*

A papered brick and painted wood dolls' house, the back opening to reveal a four-roomed interior with stair-well, 31½in (80cm) wide.
£300-350 *P*

A German toy milliner's shop, with four free-standing paper dolls and a similar table centrepiece, displaying four hats, in original box with pictorial label, in good condition.
£1,300-1,600   *P*

A late Victorian pine dolls' house, the back with removable panels, 23in (58cm) wide, complete with a small quantity of dolls' furniture.
£700-800   *HSS*

A selection of dolls' bedroom furniture.
£50-80   *JPL*

A group of dolls' house tinplate items including a stove, saucepan, oval kettle, food warmer, etc.
£50-60

A quantity of dolls' house pewter and tinplate utensils.
£140-200

A large quantity of dolls' house furniture.
£320-380

Two Victorian carved wooden dolls, 1½ and 6½in (4 and 17cm), and six miniature dolls with porcelain heads.
£250-300   *Bea*

An English colonial dolls' house, opening at the back to reveal three floors, 16in (40cm) wide, with some furniture.
£300-350   *JPL*

A set of pale wood dolls' house furniture.
£120-160   *CSK*

Teddy Bears

A Steiff pale plush teddy bear, the straw stuffed body with elongated arms, back hump and felt pads, marked with Steiff button in the left ear, 17in (43cm).
£800-1,000   *P*

A Steiff blond plush teddy bear, marked with Steiff button in the left ear, 20in (51cm).
£1,000-1,200   *P*

A Steiff yellow plush teddy bear, marked with Steiff button in the left ear, 24in (60cm).
£1,200-1,600   *P*

A gold plush teddy bear, probably by Steiff, pads worn, 16in (40cm).
£350-400   *P*

A golden plush covered teddy bear, with button eyes and hump, long felt pads, the front unhooking to reveal a metal hot water bottle, contained in the body of the bear, by Steiff, 17in (43cm) high.
£1,200-1,500   *CSK*

Known as Admiral Beattie, this bear was illustrated in Therle Hughes Edwardiana for Collectors.

l. A plush covered teddy bear, with leather muzzle and collar, by Steiff, 13in (33cm) high.
£450-500

c. A golden curly plush covered bear, 'Nigel', with pronounced hump, 27in (69cm) high.
£250-300

r. A plush covered bear, with long cut snout, bearing Chad Valley button in right eye, marked Chad Valley Hygienic Toys, British.
£100-150 *CSK*

A good Steiff blond plush teddy bear, with growler, straw stuffed body with swivel joints, elongated arms and large feet, moth holes in felt pads, plush worn in patches, 17in (43cm).
£1,000-1,200 *L*

This teddy bear is called Sebastian.

A pale gold plush covered bear, square manufacturer's mark, possibly Deans, 19in (47cm) high.
£120-160 *CSK*

l. A dark plush teddy bear, probably by Steiff, 16in (40cm).
£450-500

c. A dark plush teddy bear with wide apart rounded ears, probably by Steiff, forepads worn, 13½in (34cm).
£420-480

r. A fine Steiff pale plush teddy bear, with a leather muzzle and lead, marked with Steiff button in the left ear, 13in (33cm).
£550-600 *P*

A short golden plush covered teddy bear, with brown eyes, felt pads, growler defective, c1910.
£250-300 *CSK*

Lead soldiers

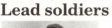

Heyde large scale model of King George V, damaged, 1911, 10cm.
£120-150 *P*

Elastolin 30/16 Goering in party uniform, arm loose, 1938, 7cm.
£25-35 *P*

Three early Britains model Lifeguards and the Officer, damaged.
£25-30 *HCH*

Britains rare set 2124, Welsh Fusiliers at attention with mascot some damage, 1957.
£280-340 *P*

Britains set No. 2076, 12th Royal Lancers, Prince of Wales' Officer on grey with sword, in original box.
£100-130 *CSK*

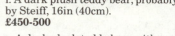

Heyde, 23 Prussian guards, damage, c1740.
£130-160 *CSK*

Britains Set No. 212, Royal Scots with piper.
£50-60 *P*

Britains Set No. 315, five 10th
Royal Hussars, Prince of Wales'
Own, in original box.
£150-180 *CSK*

A set of 9 Britains camels, with 8
Indian soldiers with drawn swords,
camels with some fatigue, the
Indian chiefs with broken swords.
£150-180 *CSK*

Britains Mountain Artillery, with 4
mules, disassembled gun, 7 gunners
and a mounted officer.
£70-90 *L*

Britains Set No. 1613, British
Infantry in gas masks, with officer,
in original box, 1937.
£60-70 *P*

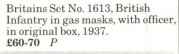

Britains Set No. 35, Royal Marines
at the slope, 1947.
£80-100 *P*

Britains Set No. 82, Colours
and Pioneers of the Scots
Guards, 1953.
£60-70 *P*

Britains farmers gig
No. F28, with horse and
Britains Fordson tractor,
both unboxed.
£35-40 *HCH*

Britains, 4 Imperial Yeomanry,
with Boer Cavalry officer, 2 CIV's
with paper labels, and a Devon,
some damage.
£70-90 *P*

Britains from a set of Infantry of the
Line Band, and a set of Drums and
Bugler, damaged, 1933.
£65-75 *P*

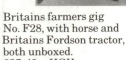

Britains Set No. 1254, Royal
Engineers pontoon section, 1937.
£350-400 *P*

DIE-CAST MODELS

★ 1870-1900 flat and semi-
  flat soldiers made by
  Germans
★ Britains invented the
  hollow cast technique
★ this led to wide range of
  military figures
★ earliest had oval bases
  and paper labels – now
  rare
★ farm items gaining
  popularity, but soldiers
  still most desirable, zoo
  animals still not so
  desirable
★ original box adds
  substantially to value

Britains Set No. 28, Mountain Artillery with mule team and quick firing gun, early version, in original Whisstock box.
£200-250 *CSK*

Britains assorted footballers with goalie, 2 linesmen, one arm missing, referee, arm missing, 1938.
£120-150 *P*

Britains Salvation Army, 1938.
£460-500 *P*

Britains model hunt, 18 pieces, unboxed.
£55-65 *HCH*

Britains Salvation Army, 1938.
£300-350 *P*

Britains Set No. 50, types of the British Army, including the First Life Guard, in original box.
£150-180 *CSK*

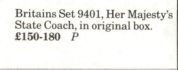

Britains Set No. 144, Royal Field Artillery, early version, in original box.
£380-420 *CSK*

Britains Set 9401, Her Majesty's State Coach, in original box.
£150-180 *P*

Britains Eastern People, repainted in the Britains style, 1953.
£75-85 *P*

Make the most of Miller's

Unless otherwise stated, any description which refers to 'a set' or 'a pair' includes a valuation for the entire set or the pair, even though the illustration may show only a single item.

Britains, a specially moulded and painted Band of the Royal Fusiliers, originally commissioned from Britains by Mr. Poitier-Smith, c1937, in excellent condition.
£1,500-1,800 *P*

Tinplate

A printed and painted tinplate toy, 'Dancing Sailor', EPL 535, fitted with clockwork mechanism causing the sailor to sway from side to side, by Lehmann, c1920, 7½in (19.5cm).
£160-190   *CSK*

l. A printed and painted tinplate toy of a single engine wing monoplane, 'Heinkel-Kampfflugzeug He 70', No. 819B, by Lehmann, c1936, in original box.
£150-200

r. A printed and painted toy of a single engine low wing monoplane, 'Fchenellverkehrfflugzeug, Heinkel-Blitz, He 70', by Lehmann, c1936, in original box.
£180-240   *CSK*

A Lehmann tinplate clockwork auto bus, complete with bus driver, No. 590, one wheel missing, 8in (20cm) long.
£550-600   *HSS*

A Lehmann tinplate clockwork delivery van, No. 550 and inscribed 'A.H.A.', damaged, 5½in (13cm) long.
£140-160   *HSS*

A painted tinplate model of a gentleman, 'Heavy Swell', EPL 525, with clockwork mechanism causing the gentleman to advance, by Lehmann, c1912, 9in (23cm).
£750-850   *CSK*

A printed and painted tinplate toy, 'Bulky Mule, The Stubborn Donkey', EPL 425, of a donkey and cart with clown driver, fitted with clockwork mechanism, causing the cart to advance and reverse erratically, by Lehmann, c1910, 7½in (20cm), in original box.
£160-190   *CSK*

A printed and painted tinplate toy of Gustav the Miller, 'Mill and Miller', EPL No. 230, by Lehmann, weight in bag missing, c1920, 16½in (42cm).
£150-180   *CSK*

A painted and felt covered tinplate dancing pig with a clown rider, 'Paddy and the Pig' EPL No. 500, with clockwork mechanism, by Lehmann, some damage, c1910, 5½in (14cm) long.
£350-400   *CSK*

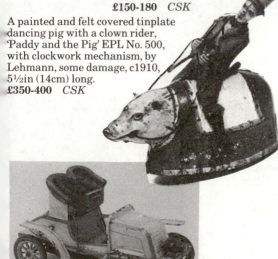

A Bing tinplate clockwork Mercedes automobile, complete with key, 8½in (21cm) long.
£1,400-1,800   *HSS*

A printed and painted tinplate cable car, 'Rigi', EPL No. 795, 2 printed tinplate gentlemen passengers, by Lehmann, c1930, 4in (10.5cm) long.
£150-200 *CSK*

A Triang tinplate and bakelite clockwork toy cyclist, c1930, 8in (20cm) long.
£70-90 *TKN*

A printed and painted tinplate toy of a butterfly, with clockwork mechanism causing the insect to advance and flap its wings, by Fischer & Co, c1910, 7in (18cm) wingspan.
£130-160 *CSK*

A printed and tinplate model of a limousine, with driver, by Bing, fitted with clockwork motor, c1925, 10½in (27cm).
£480-560 *ONS*

A printed and painted tinplate woman, 'Busy Lizzy' fitted with clockwork mechanism causing the woman to rapidly polish a floor, possibly by Fischer & Co, mop missing, c1920, 7½in (19cm).
£160-200 *CSK*

A printed and painted tinplate 4-door limousine, with clockwork mechanism, by Tipp, c1928, 8in (20cm) long.
£300-350 *CSK*

A painted tinplate bear, by F. Martin, with clockwork mechanism, causing the bear to shuffle forward, French, the bear's central rod in its back broken, c1905, 8½in (22cm).
£160-200 *CSK*

A fine Bing hand enamelled tinplate 4-door saloon car, with a clockwork mechanism with operating hand brake, in claret with red lining, black cab with gold lining and red lined windows, red seats, German, lacks chauffeur, c1912.
£4,000-4,500 *CSK*

l. A Crawford's printed tinplate motor car biscuit box, with original box, 11½in (29cm) long.
£400-450

c. A German tinplate char-a-banc, clockwork drive, stamped 'P.W.', windscreen broken off and one headlamp missing, c1920, 10½in (26.5cm) long.
£450-500

r. A Hudson Scott & Sons Carlisle tinplate motor car biscuit box, in red, 6½in (16.5cm) long.
£350-400 *McC*

A printed tinplate model of a lorry, with clockwork motor, by Mettoy, c1950, 6½in (17cm) long, in original box.
£40-60 *ONS*

TOYS

- ★ musical automata were produced from the 18thC
- ★ some of the first were the singing birds
- ★ 18thC birds were enamelled with no feathers
- ★ there has been a glut of reproductions in the last year
- ★ 19thC clockwork nursery pictures are now highly desirable – always more so if in working order
- ★ many made in the 1880's and 1890's in tin
- ★ wooden arks have been made from the middle of the 18thC
- ★ mass produced arks arrived in 1800
- ★ the best period for the collector of arks is 1860's and 1870's
- ★ German arks always the best
- ★ many wooden, iron and papier-mache pull-along toys made especially in the 19thC
- ★ in the 19thC many cheap wind-up toys were produced – the most collectable by Fernand Martin
- ★ mechanical toy banks appeared in the 1870's mainly from America
- ★ the most desirable being in cast iron with moving parts, worked by the coin
- ★ many have a patent number

A Bing painted tinplate beer wagon.
£160-200   *P*

A fine printed and painted tinplate early fire engine, with clockwork mechanism, with 2 firemen, 3 missing, by Tipp, lacks bell, c1925, 11in (28cm) long.
£130-160   *CSK*

A printed tinplate model of Captain Campbell's Bluebird, by Gunther-man, c1930, 20in (51cm), in original box.
£500-600   *ONS*

A fine printed and painted tinplate model of a 4-door limousine, with clockwork mechanism and operating handbrake, by Tipp & Co, c1928, 12in (30cm) long.
£1,300-1,600   *CSK*

A German lithograph tinplate clockwork racing car, the tyres printed Dunlop Cord, number plate TC 959, printed monogram T.C.O.
£250-300   *HSS*

A German pre-First World War tinplate Sedan clockwork motor car, with driver and passenger, rusting, lacking steering column and one mud guard, 6½in (16.5cm).
£300-350   *Re*

A Crawford's tinplate biscuit box, lid with grocer's scale, 8in (20cm) high.
£40-60   *McC*

A fine painted tinplate bear standing on an early 3-wheel carriage, with fly wheel mechanism, German, c1905, 6in (15cm).
£450-500   *CSK*

A printed tinplate push along model of a two-door Coupe, German, c1930, 17in (43cm) long.
£280-340   *ONS*

A tinplate friction drive Cadillac 300 Saloon, Gama, mid-1950s, 12in (30cm).
£280-340   *P*

A rare 22d 'Meccano' delivery van, finished in yellow paintwork.
£500-600   *CSK*

A KKK, battery operated tinplate Million Bus, boxed.
£150-200   *P*

A remote control printed tinplate Sonicon Patrol Car, boxed.
£60-70   *P*

A printed and painted tinplate toy of 'Popeye the Sailor', No. 268, with clockwork mechanism, some very slight rusting, some paint peeled inside boat, some slight chipped paintwork, by the Hoge Mfg. Co. Inc., U.S.A., c1935, 14in (36cm).
£1,400-1,600   *CSK*

A German painted tinplate floor toy paddle boat, Starlight, finished in blue, red and yellow, 11½in (29cm).
£1,800-2,000 *P*

A German tinplate clockwork open limousine, the bodywork in yellow, brown and black, early 20thC, 10½in (27cm) long.
£600-700 *HSS*

An early painted tinplate toy of a roller skater, with clockwork mechanism, possibly French, some chipping of paintwork, c1903.
£400-450 *CSK*

A French tinplate clockwork toy, in the form of an acrobat, 14in (35cm).
£450-500 *Bea*

An early German painted tinplate floor toy paddle boat, marked 'Douglas' with the national symbol for the Isle of Man below, finished in green, yellow, red and orange, 14½in (36cm).
£2,000-2,200 *P*

A Kiddyphone tinplate toy gramophone by Bing, with circular case and conical horn.
£50-100 *CSK*

A rare painted tinplate Bleriot monoplane, with painted tin pilot, German, c1903, 5½in (14cm) wingspan.
£500-600 *CSK*

An Arnold printed and painted tinplate motor bike with rider, with clockwork mechanism, in red and silver, inscribed 'M.A.C.700', W. German, c1950, 7½in (18cm) long.
£500-550 *CSK*

A German tinplate diver, with rubber tube, 5in (12.5cm).
£50-75 *McC*

A Kico printed and painted tinplate toy of a gentleman pool player, with clockwork mechanism housed underneath pool table, German, ball missing, c1912, 6in (15cm) long, in part original box.
£450-500 *CSK*

A German tin toy, for connection to steam engine water or sand wheel, 10in (25.5cm) high.
£80-100 *WHA*

A painted single funnel tinplate model of a liner, 'Cruise Liner', No. 856, finished in brown, red, white, grey and green, by Fleischmann, c1955, 21in (53cm).
£700-750 *CSK*

A tinplate clockwork car, British made, mid-1930s, 12in (30cm) long.
£70-100 *COB*

An English tinplate airliner, late 1930s.
£50-70 *MR*

A German tinplate clockwork toy, in the form of a man seated on a barrel-shaped cart drawn by a pig, 8in (20cm) long.
£200-250 *Bea*

A Spot-On, London Transport Route Master bus, boxed.
£400-450 *P*

A 4-door limousine, with clockwork mechanism and operating handbrake, finished in light green and green, yellow and black linino, by Karl Bub, lacks glazed windscreen, c1928, 15½in (39cm).
£1,200-1,600 *CSK*

A pre-war tin toy station in mint condition, 10in (25.5cm).
£160-180 *WHA*

Miscellaneous

A Huntley & Palmer's 'Double Decker Biscuit Tin Bus', with clockwork mechanism, British, c1928, 9½in (24cm) long.
£1,300-1,500 *CSK*

A Chevrolet Station Wagon, friction motor, boxed.
£25-50 *P*

A Crescent, Scammell Scarab mechanical horse and Shell B.P. tanker, slight fatigue to cab, boxed.
£150-200 *P*

A Marusan, clockwork tinplate NYC Police Car, boxed.
£100-150 *P*

A Carette lithograph limousine, with clockwork mechanism, in red and white, finished in cream, turquoise and gold lining, German, some rust and 2 front headlamps missing, c1911, 8½in (21cm) long.
£750-800 *CSK*

A Levy, clockwork motorcycle rider with lady passenger, 6in (15cm).
£1,500-1,600 *P*

Above. A clockwork saloon with driver, and automatic brake mechanism operated by the small 5th wheel, finished in blue and black with red detail, S. Gunthermann, roof missing, some damage, 9½in (24cm).
£1,300-1,400
Below. A Lehmann, Mars tricycle, No. 471.
£500-520 *P*

A Friction drive Ford Ambulance with siren, and Ford Highway Patrol car and a San, battery operated Fire Chief's car.
£50-75 each *P*

A Tasoy, friction Ford Fairlane 500, boxed.
£25-50 *P*

An Opel, made in Japan, by Yonezawa, c1960.
£300-350 *BAD*

Three boxed Dinky toys.
£80-120 *P*

A circus lorry, 23in (58.5cm) long.
£25-45 *AL*

A Lesney Yesteryear model No. 9, Fowler showman's engine, unboxed.
£30-40 *HCH*

A double decker bus by 'Minerva' English, c1925.
£350-400 *BAD*

A rare Dinky 28n 'Marsh's Sausages' delivery van, with metal mounts, tinplate radiator, finished in green paintwork.
£450-550 *CSK*

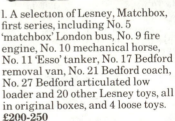

A Dinky pre-war No. 22b yellow and green sports Coupé, with painted gold metal wheels.
£400-450 *CSK*

A rare Dinky No. 22A red over cream sports car, with blue metal wheels.
£350-450 *CSK*

l. A selection of Lesney, Matchbox, first series, including No. 5 'matchbox' London bus, No. 9 fire engine, No. 10 mechanical horse, No. 11 'Esso' tanker, No. 17 Bedford removal van, No. 21 Bedford coach, No. 27 Bedford articulated low loader and 20 other Lesney toys, all in original boxes, and 4 loose toys.
£200-250

r. Lesney, 'Models of Yesteryear', including Y-1 Allchine traction engine, Y-2 1911 'B', Y-3 1907 'E' class tramcar and 2 others, all in original boxes.
£150-200 *CSK*

A collection of Dinky commercial vehicles, including 957 turntable fire engine escape, 955 fire engine with extending ladder, 60 Royal Mail van, 442 tanker 'Esso', 421 electric articulated lorry, 290 cream and green double decker bus, 414 rear tipping wagon, all in original boxes; Corgi 119 HDL Hovercraft SR-N1 in original box, and a Daimler ambulance box.
£150-200 *CSK*

A Dinky model Guy van with upright radiator grille, unboxed.
£50-75 *HCH*

A Dinky 265 Plymouth USA taxi, and a 448 Chevrolet pick-up and trailer, boxed.
£80-120 *P*

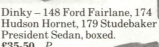

A selection of Dinky toys, most with slight fatigue.
£350-400 *P*

Dinky – 148 Ford Fairlane, 174 Hudson Hornet, 179 Studebaker President Sedan, boxed.
£35-50 *P*

A Victorian painted Noah's Ark, with 107 stained wood and carved animals and people, including Mr and Mrs Noah, German, slight damage, c1870, 18in (46cm) long.
£400-500 *CSK*

A painted wood Noah's Ark, with flat bottom and roof opening to reveal a hollow interior, with approx. 140 painted animals and figures, mid-19thC, 12in (30cm).
£600-700 *P*

A brightly painted wood Noah's Ark, with hollow interior, and approx. 700 painted animals and figures, early 19thC, 17½in (45cm) high.
£2,800-3,800 *P*

A Victorian skewbald toy pony, covered in horse hide with grey hair mane and tail, with leather bridle and breast plate, on a green painted wooden base and metal wheels, one missing, 19½in (49cm) high; and a ginger straw filled polar bear with glass eyes, stitched nose and mouth, on 4 metal wheels, 9½in (24cm) high.
£350-450 *HSS*

An early Lines Bros. pedal car, the wooden body painted suede grey with sprung chassis, some underparts cast G & JL, 39in (99cm) centrewheel to centrewheel.
£600-700 *L*

A pedal car, c1930.
£60-120 *AL*

A selection of boxed Dinky toys.
£150-175 *P*

A selection of boxed Dinky toys.
£150-200 *P*

A wooden rocking horse, c1930, 34in (86cm) high.
£200-250 *AL*

A velocipede, with front wheel mounted pedals and wood handles, the horse of painted wood, 35in (89cm).
£400-500 *P*

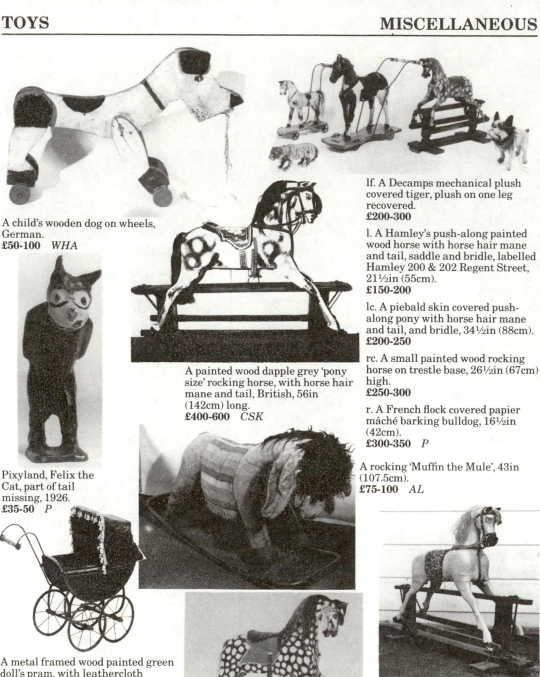

A child's wooden dog on wheels, German.
£50-100 *WHA*

Pixyland, Felix the Cat, part of tail missing, 1926.
£35-50 *P*

A metal framed wood painted green doll's pram, with leathercloth interior, folding hood, wood handle and rubber tyred wheels, c1900, 28½in (73cm).
£150-250 *P*

A painted wood dapple grey 'pony size' rocking horse, with horse hair mane and tail, British, 56in (142cm) long.
£400-600 *CSK*

lf. A Decamps mechanical plush covered tiger, plush on one leg recovered.
£200-300

l. A Hamley's push-along painted wood horse with horse hair mane and tail, saddle and bridle, labelled Hamley 200 & 202 Regent Street, 21½in (55cm).
£150-200

lc. A piebald skin covered push-along pony with horse hair mane and tail, and bridle, 34½in (88cm).
£200-250

rc. A small painted wood rocking horse on trestle base, 26½in (67cm) high.
£250-300

r. A French flock covered papier mâché barking bulldog, 16½in (42cm).
£300-350 *P*

A rocking 'Muffin the Mule', 43in (107.5cm).
£75-100 *AL*

An early Victorian wood and plaster rocking horse on wooden stand, 42in (105cm) high.
£450-550 *GH*

A large dappled rocking horse, with red draylon padded saddle, repainted and some replacement parts, ear chipped, 51½in (131cm), height of head to ground.
£150-200 *L*

A toy wooden pony cart, the base pale green with green and black shaft, 35in (89cm) long.
£100-150 *CSK*

Churchers model fairground: hand built and constructed in wood, brass and cloth, resembling a real fairground in 1/12in scale, finished by hand in coloured enamels, complete with mains, driving motors and lights by a 12 volt transformer.
£3,000-3,500 *P*

A German Heinkel, made by Lehmann, in mint condition and boxed, late 1930s.
£300-350 *BAD*

A painted carved wood set of a fair, probably Erzebirge, Germany, late 19thC, in original wood box.
£1,000-1,500 *CSK*

A rare Heyde circus, some damage.
£250-350 *CSK*

A Victorian doll's pram, with wickerwork frame lined with canvas, and fitted collapsible hood, with South African makers tab, i.e. 'Handy House, Grand Hotel, Cape Town', two small tears to canvas.
£200-300 *MN*

A French singing bird and cage, c1860, 12in (30cm).
£1,000-1,500 *RdeR*

A painted wooden 3-wheeled perambulator, upholstered in black American cloth with wire frame for a hood, 3rd quarter 19thC, 52in (130cm).
£150-300 *CSK*

An American aeroplane by Kingsbury, c1920.
£200-250 *BAD*

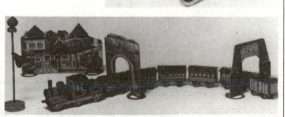

A penny toy train, Japanese, c1920.
£100-150 *PMc*

A painted metal early 2-funnel gunboat, with clockwork mechanism, finished in grey, red and green, by G. Carette, hull chipped and dented, lacking flag on rear of boat, c1904, 8in (20cm).
£100-150 *CSK*

An early painted metal 4-wheel carriage, with lady rider on a grey horse, German, c1890, some chipping to paintwork, 8in (20cm) long.
£600-650 *CSK*

A Japanese battery operated robot, mid-1960s.
£400-500 *CBe*

A rare metal headed bicycling toy modelled as a boy with blonde moulded hair, French, lacks clockwork central pivot mechanism, c1880, 8in (20cm) long.
£500-800 *CSK*

Two Sharps toffee men, and 3 cocoa cubs, kangaroo, duck and pig.
£200-250 *P*

A rare character figure, 'Felix the Cat'.
£300-350 *P*

A fine hand carved and stained wood clockwork toy of two animated dancers, The 'Juba' Dancers, the mechanism concealed in wood base causing the dancers to shuffle, U.S.A., c1874, 10in (25.5cm), in original wood box.
£600-700 *CSK*

Nineteen various model road signs, 9 Dinky petrol pumps, 3 street lamps, 7 various figures, etc. 40, unboxed.
£50-70 *HCH*

A very rare French double magic lantern, called a Lampadorama, c1882.
£500-800 *JIL*

A German street scene, The Leipsic Fair, with lithographed free-standing props of buildings and figures, in original box in excellent condition, complete with story booklet, mid-19thC.
£1,400-1,800 *P*

A French polychrome boule lampascope, by Lapierre, c1880.
£80-150 *JIL*
▷

A Bavarian clockwork tinplate game of Baker St. Station, with 5 trains travelling between 2 terminii, BUU Series, boxed.
£260-300 *P*

◁

A small German magic box with chromolitho label on the lid, c1880.
£60-100 *JIL*

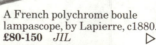

A rare French mahogany box with painted tin apparatus, hand painted, c1870-80.
£200-400 *JIL*

A French magic box, c1880.
£150-300 *JIL*

A mechanical music moire screen, 'Ombro-Cinema', French, c1920.
£150-250 *JIL*

A Taylor & Barratt Zoo Series, 'Chimpanzees' Tea Party', 1938, in original box.
£100-150 *P*

A rare Charbens set 519, Hikers Camp, comprising metal tent, 4 hikers, 2 cups and 2 saucers, 1938, in original box.
£400-450 *P*

◁ A rare Taylor & Barratt Zoo Series 'Visitors at Tea', 1938, in original box.
£200-250 *P*

Models

A fine painted metal model of a 2-funnel ship, 'Columbia', with clockwork mechanism, by Bing, slightly rusting, lacking flags. c1904, 26½in (67cm) long.
£3,500-4,000 *CSK*

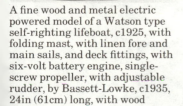

A half-model boat, TSS Glenomera, by Napier & Miller, Glasgow, in glazed oak case with mirrored back, 83 by 25in (208 by 62cm).
£1,000-1,200 *JD*

A wooden model of 'Queen Mary', with electric motor, British made, c1936, 36in (91cm) long.
£150-200 *COB*

▷

A fine wood and metal electric powered model of a Watson type self-righting lifeboat, c1925, with folding mast, with linen fore and main sails, and deck fittings, with six-volt battery engine, single-screw propeller, with adjustable rudder, by Bassett-Lowke, c1935, 24in (61cm) long, with wood carrying case.
£350-450 *CSK*

A model of RMS Titanic in glass case, built by L. Osborne, 18in (45cm) long.
£400-450 *COB*

A fine large half-section shipbuilders model of the Tramp Steamer 'Great City' completed by Roper & Sons Ltd. the shipbuilders, and Blair & Co Ltd the engineers, at Stockton-upon-Tees in 1914 for the Great Steam Ship Co Ltd, Cardiff, in glazed mahogany case with mirrored back, boat 110in (278cm) long, case 124in (310cm) long.
£2,000-2,500   *P*

A half-model of a steam trawler 'Good Luck', built by Cook, Welton & Gemmel Ltd, Beverley, 1912, in mahogany mirror back case, 41 by 17in (103 by 43cm).
£1,200-1,500   *DA*

A Victorian sailing model of a 'J' class yacht 'Valiant', built by P. McQuade, restored, with original masts, spars and sails, 1895, 109in (276cm) high by 103in (258cm) long overall, on mahogany stand.
£500-550   *Bea*

A painted wood model of 'The Victory', with rigging, lifeboats, deck detail and cannon, 37in (93cm), in glazed case.
£250-300   *AG*

A model of a pond yacht.
£750-850   *Bon*

A long model of SS Queen Mary, complete with Stewart & Turner steam engine and illustrated magazine, 60in (150cm).
£50-100   *FR*

A shipbuilders model of a freighter 'St. Catherine', with full detail to rigging, winching, lifeboats, all of wooden construction, finished predominantly in pink and grey, mounted, on wooden plinth 50in (126cm) long overall.
£1,800-2,200   *P*

A prisoner-of-war bone ship model, with a carved figurehead, and flying an ensign at the stern, rigged at the stern with pull cords to 'secure' and 'run-out' the guns, 11½in (29cm) long overall, on stand, in ebonised glazed case.
£1,300-2,000   *Bea*

A fine Gebrüder Bing electric tram-car, with a staircase at either end, finished in red, yellow and black, 9in (23cm).
£900-1,000   *P*

A Bassett-Lowke 2-6-4 tank engine No. 2524 LMS.
£600-650   *AG*

A spirit-fired 4-4-0 tank locomotive No. 88, by Bing, in wooden box.
£900-1,000   *P*

A modern cased model of the training ship 'Danmark'.
£400-450   *TAY*

A Bing engine for Bassett-Lowke, gauge 1, London and North Western Railway, c1920.
£700-800 *BAD*

A gauge 0 clockwork model of the London Midland and Scottish Railway 4-4-0 No. 2 tank locomotive No. 2107, in original claret livery, by Hornby, in original box.
£200-250 *CSK*

A very rare gauge 1 clockwork model of the London and North Western Railway 4-6-2 'Bowen-Cooke' tank locomotive No. 2663, in black livery, with three front lanterns, by Marklin for Bassett-Lowke, c1913.
£900-1,200 *CSK*

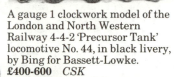

A gauge 1 clockwork model of the London and North Western Railway 4-4-2 'Precursor Tank' locomotive No. 44, in black livery, by Bing for Bassett-Lowke.
£400-600 *CSK*

A 3½in (9cm) gauge live steam coal-fired 0-4-0 tank locomotive, 'Juliet', together with a trailer with wooden seat, 20in (50cm) overall length of locomotive.
£300-350 *L*

A 3RE 0-4-0 German Railways pattern locomotive and tender No. 2990, by Bing, finished in black with red lining.
£200-250 *P*

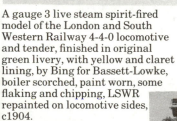

A gauge 3 live steam spirit-fired model of the London and South Western Railway 4-4-0 locomotive and tender, finished in original green livery, with yellow and claret lining, by Bing for Bassett-Lowke, boiler scorched, paint worn, some flaking and chipping, LSWR repainted on locomotive sides, c1904.
£2,900-3,200 *CSK*

Bing for Bassett-Lowke: A fine c/w 4-4-0 GWR locomotive and six-wheeler 'Sydney', re-named Cape Town and re-numbered to 3397, tender marked Lowko, c1904.
£600-650 *P*

A scarce Bing gauge 1 live steam spirit-fired model of an early 2-2-0 'single' locomotive and tender, in original green and black livery with red lining, boiler badly scorched, paintwork worn and chipped, some parts missing, c1902.
£300-500 *CSK*

A 3½in (9cm) gauge 'Caledonian Tank' live model steam engine, 0-6-0, in blue livery with brass dome and tender.
£450-550 *HCH*

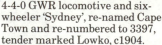

A model of an American 'Virginia' type steam locomotive and tender, 'The Rio Grande', maroon colour, with brass fittings throughout, '1865' painted on side of locomotive, 'Denver & Rio Grande Western 3517' painted on side of tender, 51in (128cm) long overall.
£400-500 *WAL*

Marklin: A 3RE 20 volts 4-4-0 LMS locomotive and 4-wheeler tender, with first/third class carriages and brake van, Bing controller.
£500-600 *P*

Bing: a spirit-fired 0-4-0 LNWR locomotive and tender No. 1942 with separated lamps, and a Bing gauge 1 signal.
£300-400 *P*

A 7¼in (18cm) gauge live steam powered 4-4-0 locomotive and tender, in LNER livery, locomotive 55in (138cm) long, tender 38in (95cm) long.
£1,400-1,800 *Bea*

A gauge 0 3-rail electric model of the SNCF Autorail, finished in cream over red and blue, in original box, by Hornby.
£300-350 *CSK*

A Marklin working model tinplate horizontal steam engine, in original box.
£200-250 *AG*

Three gauge 1 Midland Railway twin-bogie passenger cars, including two first class coaches, both lacking corridor connectors, in original red livery, with grey roofs, and a third class brake car, No. 2783, in original livery, all by Bing for Bassett-Lowke, c1927.
£400-500 *CSK*

A model six column rotative beam engine, painted in green, with oak block base and panel, under glass case, c1850, 16 by 12in (40 by 30cm).
£200-250 *CBS*

A gauge 1 London and North Western Railway twin-bogie third class brake car, in original cream and brown livery, with white roof, side opening doors, by Bing for Bassett-Lowke, lacking corridor connectors, some slight chipping to paintwork, c1922.
£150-250 *CSK*

An English wooden model of an open-top bus, c1912, 24in (61cm) long.
£300-350 *CRO*

l. A gauge 0 Pots wagon No. 1914, with brake man's cabin, one lid missing, by Marklin, c1930.
£300-350

c. A rare gauge 0 bogie flat car, with early single propeller monoplane, with pilot, collapsible wings, by Marklin, c1930.
£300-350

r. A gauge 0 model of a Bordeaux No. 416 'Wagons Foudres' vat container wagon No. 1940, by Marklin, c1930.
£250-300 *CSK*

Two gauge 1 Great Northern Railway twin-bogie, teak, first/third class passenger cars, Nos. 2875, in original paintwork, with grey roofs, by Marklin, c1925.
£300-350 *CSK*

A Tipp & Co limousine, possibly a Rolls Royce, German, c1930.
£700-900 *BAD*

A Hornby '0' gauge clockwork model railway set and track, 17 pieces in all.
£900-1,000 *RBB*

A well-detailed upright model mountaineers steam engine, with brass, copper and wood fittings, with chain drive to the 5in (13cm) gauge undercarriage.
£400-450 *CBS*

A painted metal model of an Austin A40 roadster pedal car, with operating headlamps and horn, finished in light blue with chrome trim, British, one glass missing in lamp, no battery, c1950, 64in (160cm) long.
£900-1,200 *CSK*

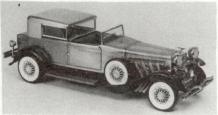

A 1960s radio model of a 1934 Dussenberg.
£150-200 *AAA*

Chess Sets

A Meissen chess set, each modelled as sea animals, enriched in iron red and brownish-grey, all on circular bases with gilt line, blue crossed swords and impressed marks, from ¾in to 3½in (2 to 8.5cm) high.
£1,500-2,000 *CNY*

A 1/11th scale scratch built model of a Centaur multi-role military vehicle, half-track Land Rover, fitted with a 3.5cc glow-plug engine with full radio-control, complete with radio controller, 20in (51cm) long overall.
£800-1,000 *P*

An Anglo-Indian ivory chess set, in the mediaeval style, 19thC.
£10,000-11,000 *Wor*

A scale model of a milk float, 'Express Dairy – College Farm Finchley', well finished with brass lamps, churn and accessories, ceramic driver, and Norwich Pottery cart horse, 21½in (54cm) long overall, with wood stand.
£500-600 *P*

A carved ivory chess set with one set stained red, carved as officials and warriors, the white bishops probably replacements, one castle and some of the small figures restored, late Qing Dynasty, highest figure 5in (12cm) high, rectangular glass cover.
£350-400 *C*

A carved ivory chess set, one set stained brown, all in a silk-lined box opening to form the chess board, incised with seal marks on the base, box 24in (61cm) wide.
£700-800 *C*

A scale model of a Ferguson TE20 tractor and plough, tyres stamped 'Goodyear', with the Ferguson plough safety attachment, 16in (40cm) long overall.
£300-350 *L*

An Indian miniature ivory chess set with table stand, the octagonal stand mounted with ivory, late 19thC, the stand 10in (26cm) wide, the chessmen 1¼in (3cm) high.
£700-800 *L*

Games

An Anglo-Indian Vizagapatam ivory and ebony games box, the exterior inlaid with chess squares, the sandalwood interior inlaid with a backgammon board, with 30 ivory and ebony draughts counters in a ribbed ebony box, early 19thC, 18in (46cm) wide.
£1,400-1,600 *C*

Britains Set 1400, Bluebird Land Speed Record car, in original box (G, box G), 1938.
£120-150 *P*

Musical-Instruments

A silver mounted violoncello bow, by W.E. Hill & Sons, branded W.E. Hill & Sons, 72gm.
£900-1,000 *C*

A Strocello acoustic 'cello with 4 strings sounding through a diaphragm and horn, the diaphragm 7in (18cm) diam, 48in (120cm) high overall.
£1,000-1,200 *CSK*

An 8-keyed boxwood clarinet, stamped 'Astor & Co, 79 Cornhill, London' and marked with a unicorn's head, with ivory mounts and brass keys with square covers, ebony mouthpiece, 23½in (59.5cm) long.
£200-300 *HSS*

A rare ivory recorder, by Thomas Stanesby Junior, branded 'Stanesby/Junior/6'; the body piqué in gilt, the gold mounts chased with miniature hunting scenes, 12½in (31cm) long.
£28,000-30,000 *C*

A Black Forest organ clock, the 22-key 8-air barrel movement with 2 ranks of wood pipes controlled by manual stops, with 2-train clock movement striking on a bell, 93in (235cm).
£2,000-2,200 *CSK*

A gold-mounted violin bow, by Albert Nurnberger, branded Albert Nurnberger, an ivory face mounted with a gold and ebony frog with pearl eye and gold and ebony adjuster, 59gm.
£1,300-1,600 *C*

A Bechstein baby grand piano, No. 240150, the mahogany case on tapering square legs with brass casters, 56in (140cm).
£2,000-2,500 *Bea*

An Edwardian concertina, leather covered with gilt tooling, and metal pierced fret ends with keys, inscribed 'C. Jeffries, Maker, 12 Aldershot Road, Kilburn N.W.6', in a leather case.
£100-150 *WW*

A portable street reed barrel organ, by Chiappa, playing 7 tunes, on 31 notes, with part rosewood veneered case, inlaid front panel, later fret and oak lid, 22in (56cm) wide.
£3,000-3,500 *CSK*

A Spanish 32-note miniature barrel piano with castanet and triangle, playing 6 tunes, in grained case with label of Enrique Salva Mane, Barcelona, 24in (61cm) wide, on wood handcart.
£500-600 *CSK*

A good overstrung baby grand piano, by Archibald Ramsden, Leeds, with steel frame and mahogany case, 48in (120cm).
£1,500-2,000 *WIL*

A Victorian grand piano in burr walnut case, by John Broadwood & Sons, 83in (210cm) long.
£700-1,000 *O*

An 'Autoplayer' pianola, the upright mahogany case with hinged top, the iron frame stamped 35160, 63in (157cm) wide, with a quantity of pianola rolls and a beech two-handled piano stool.
£400-600 *HSS*

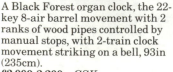

A Weber boudoir grand piano, the mahogany case on 3 pairs of fluted tapering square legs with brass casters, 66in (165cm).
£600-800 *Bea*

A pochette (kit violin), bearing a manuscript label, London 1766, 14½in (37cm) long overall, in wood box.
£800-900 *P*

A fine English walnut case spinet, by John Langshaw, Wigan, early 18thC.
£9,000-10,000 *TKN*

With a Victorian receipt for the instrument dated 1888.

A French violin, the one-piece back of almost horizontal flame, with grained table, ebony finger board and scroll finial with rosewood turners, complete with bow, c1900, length of back 14in (36cm), contained in a fitted case.
£150-200 *HSS*

A French violin by Joseph Hel, labelled 'Fait par Hel . . . Lille 1878' and branded 'J. Hel' on the inside back, length of back 14½in (36.5cm), in case.
£3,500-4,000 *C*

A French viola, labelled 'Bennettini . . . Milano 1881', the varnish of a gold-red colour, length of back 16in (40cm), in case.
£1,900-2,000 *C*

An English spinet, by Thomas Hitchcock, inscribed 'Thomas Hitchcock, Londini fecit No. 1102' in Virginia walnut case, with ebony and ivory keys, c1725, 74in (187.5cm) wide, on later oak stand.
£6,000-7,000 *C*

Compass: 5 octaves, GG-g³.

The upper and lower keys are inscribed H, and the reverse of the nameboard is inscribed H/1102/1725.

A violin by Honoré Derazey, bearing the maker's script brand on the inner back and labelled 'Joseph Guarnerius', c1870, length of back 14in (35cm).
£3,800-4,000 *P*

Varnish of a clear red-brown colour on a yellow ground.

A good viola by Frank H. Howard, bearing the maker's label in London, signed and dated 1928, L.O.B. 17in (43cm), in a fitted rectangular case, lined green velvet, with waterproof cover.
£1,800-2,000 *P*

A good English violin by William E. Hill & Sons, with one-piece back, label inscribed 'William E. Hill & Sons, makers, 38 New Bond Street, London 1895, No. 92', 14in (35cm), with oak case.
£3,900-4,000 *PWC*

A fine violin by Arthur Richardson, bearing the maker's label in Crediton, Devon, dated 1932, dated and numbered 208 on the centre inner back, L.O.B. 14in (35cm), with a bow in shaped blackwood case.
£2,000-2,500 *P*

The oil varnish of a clear rich red-brown colour on a yellow ground.

A fine French violin by Jean Baptiste Vuillaume, labelled 'Jean-Baptiste Vuillaume à Paris/Rue Croix des Petits Champs'; the length of back 14½in (36cm), in case.
£11,000-12,000 *C*

◁ A violoncello, unlabelled, with two-piece back, early 20thC, L.O.B. 30in (76cm), with 2 nickel mounted violoncello bows, in a cloth carrying case.
£400-500 *Re*

An interesting violin, possibly Neapolitan school, faintly labelled, the varnish of a golden-brown colour, length of back 14½in (36.5cm), in case.
£2,000-3,000   *C*

A violoncello by John Betts, London, unlabelled, c1790, L.O.B. 30in (76cm), in a wood case by W. E. Hill & Sons.
£4,000-6,000   *P*

A fine English violin, by John Lott, unlabelled, the varnish of a red colour over a golden ground, length of back 14in (35.5cm), in case.
£17,000-18,000   *C*

Boxes

A 12in (30cm) symphonion disc musical box with 'Sublime Harmony' combs, in walnut case with monochrome print in lid and disc storage drawer in base, with 35 discs.
£950-1,100   *CSK*

A 19in (48cm) upright symphonion disc musical box with 'Sublime Harmony' combs, coin-slot mechanism and walnut case of conventional design, lacks pediment, and 6 discs.
£1,900-2,200   *CSK*

A 16in (40cm) table polyphon disc musical box, with double combs and panelled walnut case with monochrome print in lid, with 20 discs.
£1,900-2,000   *CSK*

◁ A walnut cased musical box, the cylinder and comb movement marked B.H.A., with butterfly hammers striking on 3 bells, 19thC, 19in (48cm) wide.
£500-550   *HSS*

A rare changeable cylinder overture box, by Nicole Freres, with 5 cylinders, 3 overtures, one operatic airs and one dance, each playing 4 tunes, in crossbanded burr walnut case, 38in (96cm) wide, the cylinders 13 by 3in (33 by 7.5cm).
£4,000-6,000   *CSK*

A French singing bird box, the feathered songbird with ivory beak, in enamelled case, No. 3771, with original key, late 19thC, 4½in (12cm).
£1,000-1,100   *P*

◁ A 24½in (62cm) upright polyphon disc musical box with coin mechanism, side-wind motor and walnut case of typical form, with flat cornice, on disc-bin stand, 74½in (187cm) high, with 24 discs.
£3,500-4,500   *CSK*

l. A 7½in (19cm) symphonion disc musical box, with single comb, in walnut case with monochrome print in lid, with 8 discs.
£250-300

c. A Pearl & Pearl crystal set, in mahogany box, with headphones, and two other items.
£50-75

r. A 7½in (19cm) symphonion table disc musical box, with single comb, in mahogany case with monochrome print inside lid and transfer decoration to top, with 24 discs.
£270-300   *ONS*

An early keywound Swiss cylinder music box, the movement with segmented comb, playing 4 airs, stamped 3568, cylinder 8½in (21cm), in mahogany case, 12in (30cm) wide.
£500-700 *P*

A bells-in-sight musical box, with 13in (33cm) cylinder playing 10 airs, with 9 bells with insect and bird strikers, in walnut case, 23in (58cm) long.
£800-1,000 *Bea*

A small automaton disc musical box, the single comb playing 5½in (14cm) discs and activating an automaton see-saw with cats in a glazed compartment, slight woodworm, 7½in (19cm), together with 12 discs.
£350-400 *L*

A 30in (75cm) cylinder music box, rosewood inlaid, with 10 airs, 6 bells and drum-in-sight, WO, mid-19thC, 19½in (49.5cm) cylinder.
£1,100-1,300 *GH*

A square section bird cage of wire and turned wood construction containing automata bird in flight and one other pecking at a nut, box case containing musical box, 19thC, 17in (43cm) high.
£200-300 *WIL*

A small fairground organ with 58-note paper roll reed-organ action, in covered trolley on casters, 100in (250cm) wide, with 63 Angelus/Symphony rolls.
£2,000-2,250 *CSK*

A French key wound singing bird automaton, the tortoiseshell case with oval silver and parcel gilt engraved cover, late 19thC, 4in (10cm) wide, in original leather travelling case.
£450-500 *Re*

A good symphonion table musical box, the case carved in rococo style, late 19thC, 19in (48cm) wide, with a quantity of discs.
£1,600-1,800 *N*

An automaton monkey violinist on a snuff box, the musical movement playing 2 airs, 20in (50cm) high overall.
£2,500-3,000 *CSK*

Phonographs

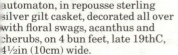

A Continental singing bird automaton, in repousse sterling silver gilt casket, decorated all over with floral swags, acanthus and cherubs, on 4 bun feet, late 19thC, 4½in (10cm) wide.
£600-800 *Re*

A gilt metal singing bird musical box, 4in (10.5cm).
£600-800 *P*

An Edison Gem phonograph, with large horn, c1903.
£200-250 *WHL*

A rare Edison Diamond Disc phonograph, with nickel diamond reproducer, gilt fittings and lateral cut soundbox adapter, 50in (125cm), and 46 Edison discs.
£1,000-1,300   *CSK*

An Edison Opera phonograph, No. 3574, with Model L reproducer, some restoration, with 90 Edison Blue Amberol cylinders, in original cases.
£1,900-2,000   *P*

An Edison standard phonograph, patented November 17th, 1903, serial No. S268942, with a brass horn, complete with carrying case and a quantity of cylinders in a fitted case.
£250-300   *HSS*

An Edison Triumph phonograph, Model E, in oak case, with Model O reproducer.
£700-800   *P*

An Edison standard phonograph, Model C, No. 660275.
£280-360   *ONS*

An Edison Gem phonograph, Model A, No. G134126, with B reproducer.
£220-260   *ONS*

An Edison fireside combination type phonograph, Model B, No. 89443, with C reproducer and Cygnet No. 10 horn with crane.
£500-600   *ONS*

A Columbia Type BS coin-operated phonograph, with floating reproducer.
£900-1,000   *CSK*

Gramophones

A horn gramophone with mahogany case of HMV Model 7 design, double-spring motor and brass flower horn.
£400-450   *CSK*

A horn gramophone with oak case, Big Ben No. 1 soundbox and blue flower horn of early Morning Glory pattern.
£200-250   *CSK*

An oak cased EMG concert hand-made acoustic horn gramophone, with EMG soundbox, and papier mâché horn, 19½in (50cm) diam.
£350-400   *P*

An early Kammer & Reinhardt Berliner gramophone, with iron travelling arm, rusted, papier mâché elbow, disintegrating, and part of maker's wood box with printed label, lacks horn.
£500-600   *CSK*

Although this model is sometimes considered to be earlier than the wood-based version with belt drive, the fact that the box label illustrates the latter type suggests that the two were made concurrently.

An HMV Monarch gramophone, with double spring motor, Exhibition soundbox and fluted oak horn, c1911.
£900-1,000   *CSK*

An oak HMV Monarch gramophone, 1911 model, with double spring motor, gooseneck tone arm and fluted oak horn, soundbox replaced.
£500-600   *CSK*

A German walking stick violin, mid-19thC, 34in (86cm).
£1,500-1,800 *C*

A Gramophone & Typewriter Ltd, New Style No. 3 gramophone, with 7in (18cm) turntable and concert soundbox, c1904.
£600-800 *ONS*

A modified version of the original Trade-Mark Gramophone of 1898, with a larger main spring and combined brake and speed regulator. The latter was necessitated by the 10in (25.5cm) record, which prevented the previous bolt brake from being operated on the rim of the 7in (18cm) turntable.

A Viel-O-Phone horn gramophone, the case applied with company transfer, Imperial soundbox, Swiss made double spring motor stamped 30B and fluted brass horn.
£350-400 *ONS*

Miscellaneous

A metronome by Theadore Charles Bates, minor mechanical restoration required, 12in (30cm) high.
£1,500-1,700 *P*

An AMI 200 jukebox, Model JAH 200, with 200 selections, Serial No. 370904, 1957, the records mainly early 1970s.
£700-800 *ONS*

Boxes

A casket, the lower front doors ▷ opening to reveal 3 small and one long drawer and a panel hiding 3 other drawers, mid-17thC, 12½ by 11in (31 by 28cm).
£650-750 *P*

◁ A mother-of-pearl inlaid hardwood cosmetic box, 19thC, 15in (38cm) long.
£250-300 *C*

A rosewood fitted toilet case, with brass stringing, 8 glass bottles and boxes, 5 having Sheffield plated lids, 19thC, 12½in (31.5cm) wide.
£60-80 *CDC*

An oak Bible box, with small interior compartment, early 18thC, 31 by 18in (77.5 by 45.5cm).
£150-180 *WIL*

A Victorian silver gilt mounted dressing table set, maker's marks FBT; GB/GWB/JR; WJ; and JA/TS,
London 1884/5, 968g.
£4,000-5,000 *Bea*

A Continental painted alms box, c1700, 13in (33cm).
£160-200 *KEY*

A Bible box, with fitted interior, 18thC.
£170-200 *DA*

A cased set of 3 scent bottles with ormolu mounts and painted porcelain stoppers, in kingwood case, 19thC.
£170-220 *Wor*

A Victorian maplewood brass inlaid vanity case, the interior fitted with 11 silver topped glass bottles and boxes, the majority hallmarked London 1842, maker's mark G.R., mother-of-pearl and cut steel instruments, with base drawer, 13in (33cm).
£400-500 *PWC*

A companion set, veneered in tortoiseshell with pique work decoration, some instruments missing.
£100-130 *WIL*

A pair of George III mahogany vase-shaped cutlery boxes, 26in high.
£3,000-3,500 *C*

An oak inkstand with horseshoe pen rack and 2 cut glass inkwells.
£130-160 *PC*

A Regency mahogany decanter box, the interior with 6 small and 6 large decanters, 2 tumblers and 3 liqueur glasses with gilt decoration, 19in (48cm) wide.
£1,100-1,300 *C*

A pair of Regency mahogany knife boxes.
£2,600-3,000 *C*

An oak inkstand, early 20thC.
£90-110 *WIL*

A Victorian brass mounted oak tantalus, the front with cigar drawer and compartments for playing cards, etc.
£400-500 *PWC*

A pair of George III mahogany cutlery boxes, the sloping shaped lids inlaid with batswing oval, with fitted interiors, 9in (23cm) wide.
£2,200-2,600 *C*

A George III mahogany cutlery box, the top inlaid with the Prince of Wales's feathers, enclosing a later fitted interior, 9in (23cm), and another similar, the shaped chamfered front with trompe l'oeil fruitwood inlay, 9½in (25cm).
£1,300-1,600 *C*

A George III mahogany decanter box, the hinged lid inlaid with a shell, with 6 bottles, a waved oval salver and 2 associated glasses, 10½in (26.5cm) wide.
£650-750 *C*

A Tunbridgeware sewing box, the interior with removable tray with later divisions, 19thC, 9½in (24cm).
◁ **£250-300** *L*

A George III mahogany knife box.
£250-300 *CEd*

A tortoiseshell sewing box, inlaid with mother-of-pearl, 19thC, 9½in (24cm).
£350-400 *L*

An Anglo-Indian ivory work box, a fitted interior with various lidded compartments, late 18thC, 19in (48cm).
£1,000-1,200 *C*

An Anglo-Indian ivory sewing box, shaped as a cottage, the hinged roof, with chimney finial, enclosing a fitted interior, with one drawer to the side, early 19thC, 6in (15cm) wide.
£3,200-3,600   C

An Anglo-Indian coromandel wood sewing box, fitted with compartments, smothered in ivory and various rare East Indian woods, c1830.
£1,000-1,200   EA

A tortoiseshell tea caddy, the front inlaid with mother-of-pearl floral design, the interior with lidded compartments, 19thC, 8½in (21.5cm).
£450-500   L

A tortoiseshell tea caddy, the interior with 2 compartments, 19thC, 7½in (19cm).
£350-400   L

A tortoiseshell veneered tea caddy, the interior divided into 2 sections, each with tortoiseshell veneered cover, mid-19thC, 6½in (16cm) high.
£350-400   WIL

A William IV tea caddy, with inlaid mother-of-pearl foliated scroll decoration, fitted with 2 lift out compartments, 12in (30cm).
£170-200   AG

A George III japanned tea caddy, the interior with 3 tôle peinte cannisters, 14in (25cm) wide.
£450-500   P

A George III satinwood, rosewood and fruitwood tea caddy, with 3 lidded detachable compartments, the central circular one a mixing bowl, with silver plaques, lettered G, I and B from left to right, 12½in (31.5cm) wide.
£1,400-1,600   C

A Georgian kingwood crossbanded satinwood tea caddy, 9in (23cm).
£350-400   LBP

A George III pear tea caddy, with steel furniture, 7in (18cm) high.
£900-1,000   P

A marquetry tea caddy, the interior with the initials EJ within a cartouche supported by angels, the twin cannisters with lids labelled H and B, 18thC, 9in (22.5cm).
£2,000-2,500   P

A tortoiseshell tea caddy, the interior with 2 lidded compartments, 19thC, 7in (18cm).
£300-350   L

A George III applewood tea caddy, late 18thC, 4in (10.5cm) high.
£700-900   CNY

A Regency paper filigree tea caddy, 6½in (17cm), in original fitted box with documentation.
£2,200-2,500   P

An early George II laburnum wood tea caddy, the interior with 3 large and 4 small compartments, 2nd quarter 18thC, 11in (27cm) wide.
£1,200-1,600   *CNY*

A rare Oriental lacquer writing box, with European mounts, 15½ by 12in (40 by 31cm).
£550-650   *P*

An English writing set, comprising 2 glass bottles, a gold mounted glass seal, 3 gold nibs, a propelling pencil and a steel blade in gold mounted shagreen box, c1770.
£700-800   *P*

A Regency penwork tea caddy, c1820.
£200-300   *RdeR*

A Victorian burr walnut portable writing box, with well fitted interior and stationery compartment, flanked by drawers and fold-out writing slope, 17in (43cm) wide.
£250-300   *TW*

A Regency brass inlaid mahogany writing box, the fitted interior with leather lined sloping writing surface, the 2 glass bottles with silver plate caps, with Bramah lock, 20in (51cm) wide.
£500-600   *C*

A Dutch tobacco box, 18thC, 5½in (13.5cm).
£70-100   *P*

A Regency tortoiseshell tea caddy with silver mounts, c1820, 6in (15cm) high.
£300-450   *RdeR*

A Dutch tobacco box, the base engraved with St. Anthony of Padua, 18thC, 4½in (11cm).
£120-160   *P*

A snuff box, with an engraving of a monk taking snuff, 19thC, 4½in (11cm) diam.
£100-150   *RdeR*

A George IV rosewood and satinwood writing box, with a partly fitted interior, 15½in (39cm) wide.
£300-400   *C*

A burr walnut fitted stationery box, 19thC, 16in (41cm) wide.
£350-400   *JMW*

A Continental kingwood strongbox, fitted with secret drawers, with screw mechanism enabling the box to be screwed to the surface.
£2,200-2,500   *EA*

A lacquered gilt decorated and mother-of-pearl inlaid writing box, 19thC, 14in (35cm).
£180-240   *CW*

An early Victorian mahogany artist's box, by Winsor & Newton Ltd, with a well fitted interior, including cut glass ink and mixing bottles, 15in (38cm) wide.
£800-900 *CEd*

An Anglo-Indian Regency calamanderwood box, 15½in (39cm) wide.
£750-850 *C*

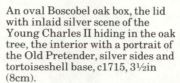

An oval Boscobel oak box, the lid with inlaid silver scene of the Young Charles II hiding in the oak tree, the interior with a portrait of the Old Pretender, silver sides and tortoiseshell base, c1715, 3½in (8cm).
£900-1,100 *WW*

A Charles II ebony and marquetry lace box, 22in (56cm) wide, on a later stand with square tapered legs.
£900-1,100 *Bon*

A good Sinhalese coromandel wood box, the interior of the lid inlaid in ivory, ebony and other woods, 17½in (44.5cm).
£250-300 *PWC*

An oak cased letter box, late 19thC, 14in (35.5cm) high.
£300-350 *WIL*

An ebony and enamel miniature casket, 19thC, 6in (15cm) high.
£600-700 *P*

A walnut casket, with double locking mechanism, pine lined interior with candle box, the top with concealed sliding compartment enclosing keyholes, probably Southern European, 18thC, 23in (58cm) wide.
£350-450 *Re*

An Anglo-Indian Vizagapatam casket, 18thC, 17in (43cm) wide.
£2,000-2,300 *C*

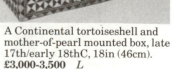

A Continental tortoiseshell and mother-of-pearl mounted box, late 17th/early 18thC, 18in (46cm).
£3,000-3,500 *L*

An Indo-Portuguese tortoiseshell and mother-of-pearl portable box, late 17th/early 18thC, 16in (40.5cm).
£1,400-1,800 *L*

A sailor's valentine, c1840-50, 10in (25cm) diam.
£300-500 *RdeR*

Love tokens from the South Sea Islands that sailors gave their sweethearts.

Enamel

A Bilston enamel combined bonbonniere and patch box, 2in (5cm).
£800-900   *L*

An enamel leopard's head bonbonniere, enriched in tones of brown, yellow, puce and pale blue, Battersea, c1780, 3in (8cm) long.
£1,600-2,000   *CNY*

An enamel bear's head bonbonniere, in tones of brown and red, some repair to enamel, Battersea, c1775, 2in (6cm) long.
£800-900   *CNY*

An English enamel gilt metal mounted apple snuff box, enriched in tones of red, green, yellow and puce, some repair to enamel, Battersea c1780, 2½in (6cm) wide.
£400-500   *CNY*

A Continental enamel cigarette case, with English import marks.
£500-600   *P*

A Continental engine turned cigarette case with concealed enamelled cover, depicting a harem scene, also a vesta case enamelled with the monogram of the Maharajah of Patiala who is reputed to have presented both items to Roy Kilner of Yorkshire County Cricket Club.
£800-1,000   *P*

An enamelled box, in two shades of blue and green, embossed with angels, probably Greek, 19thC.
£150-180   *P*

A South Staffordshire enamel on copper patch box, with interior mirror, late 18thC, 2.5in (7cm).
£200-250   *HSS*

A Bilston type enamel patch box, damaged.
£70-100   *HSS*

A Viennese enamel vinaigrette, the engraved glass sphere supported by a pelican, 19thC, 5in (13cm) high.
£1,000-1,200   *P*

RADIOS

★ in 1894 Branly and Lodge transmitted signals by Hertzian waves and the 'wireless' was born
★ Morse and speech transmitters were developed during the First World War
★ commercial broadcasting began in the U.S.A. in 1920 and Britain in 1922
★ the first mains radio set (the Radiola 17) was produced in America in 1925
★ this is a fascinating field for the collector and has increased in popularity over the past few years. Sets should be in full working order. Novelty shapes are highly collectable as are any of the very early experimental sets

Electrical – Radios

A set of 4 Continental gilt bronze and enamel foliate wall appliqués, 14½in (36cm) wide.
£12,000-14,000   *P*

A bakelite 'Ekco' radio, in working order, c1936.
£120-150   *COB*

A Selector radio set, c1928.
£60-70 *MGM*

A Baird Televisor, No. 204, in arched brown-painted aluminium case with disc, valve and plaque on front.
£1,500-1,700 *CSK*

A souvenir of the International Radio-telegraphic Conference, London, 1912, being a model of 'Marconi's Disc Discharger', in original case.
£130-160 *P*

A magnetic detector, by Marconi's Wireless Telegraph Co Ltd, No. 89598.
£2,200-2,500 *CSK*

Typewriters

A Hall typewriter, with defective rubber type sheet.
£200-250 *CSK*

A Lambert typewriter, No. 2908, by The Lambert Typewriter Co, New York.
£200-250 *CSK*

A Merritt typewriter, the linear index mechanism on wood base board with cover and instructions pasted in.
£400-450 *CSK*

Miscellaneous

A Walmore crystal set in oak case with BBC transfer, glazed cover and two pairs of headphones.
£60-70 *CSK*

A chrome microphone, c1940, 11in (29cm) high.
£60-70 *COB*

A Marconiphone V-2, 2-valve receiver with BBC transfer, two wavelength plates and regenerator unit.
£400-450 *CSK*

Miller's is a price Guide not a price List

The price ranges given reflect the average price a purchaser should pay for similar items. Condition, rarity of design or pattern, size, colour, provenance, restoration and many other factors must be taken into account when assessing values.
When buying or selling, it must always be remembered that prices can be greatly affected by the condition of any piece. Unless otherwise stated, all goods shown in Miller's are of good merchantable quality, and the valuations given reflect this fact. Pieces offered for sale in exceptionally fine condition or in poor condition may reasonably be expected to be priced considerably higher or lower respectively than the estimates given herein.

Transport

A 1924 Rolls-Royce Silver Ghost 40/50 HP 4-seat convertible limousine, coachwork by Barker, Reg. No. XR 3080, chassis No. 69EM, engine; 6-cylinder side valve, 7428 cc, 40/50 hp, 4-speed right-hand change sliding mesh gearbox, mechanical servo 4-wheel brakes, suspension semi-elliptic front and cantilever rear, wire wheels with dual sidemounted spares.
£37,000-40,000   *CSK*

A Morris Cowley Six saloon, first registered January 19th, 1934, in midnight blue and black.
£1,700-2,000   *Re*

A 1930 Riley Nine Monaco 4-door saloon, Reg. No. EO.4810, chassis No. 60/5426, engine No. 60/5426.
£3,500-4,000   *CSK*

A 1946 SS Jaguar 2½ litre sports saloon, Reg. No. HXK 465, chassis No. 510370, engine No. P385.
£2,500-3,000   *ONS*

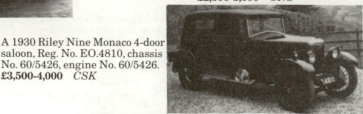

A 1934 Alvis Speed Twenty 4-seat tourer, coachwork by Vanden Plas, chassis No. 15797, engine No. 12474, engine; 6-cylinder, overhead valve, dual ignition, triple SU carburettors, 2511 cc, 87 bhp.
£16,000-18,000   *CSK*

A 1935 Standard 'Nine' saloon, engine No. A.52971, chassis No. 312792, capacity 1056 cc, date of original registration November 23rd, 1935.
£1,300-1,800   *P*

A 1930 Austin Seven 'Chummy', painted in primrose yellow and black, Reg. No. KR4012.
£3,500-4,000   *O*

A 1938 Railton Straight Eight Fairmile drophead coupé, Reg. No. MG.5981, chassis No. 745447, engine No. 31747, engine; Hudson 8-cylinder in line, side valve, 4.2 litres, 100 bhp, three forward speed gearbox, 4-wheel hydraulic brakes, semi-elliptic suspension.
£5,500-6,000   *CSK*

A 1937 Leyland open fire appliance, Reg. No. XS.4860, engine No. 3609, engine; 6 cylinder, overhead valve, 4.9 litre, 30 hp, manual sliding mesh gearbox, 4-wheel brakes, semi-elliptic suspension.
£5,500-6,000   *CSK*

The interesting registration number is one of a batch issued to University Motors and more often seen on the MGs that they sold.

A 1951 Singer Nine roadster, chassis No. 4AB 7159.
£2,000-2,500   *ONS*

A 1953 Bristol Type-403 2-door sports saloon, chassis No. 403/1444, engine No. 1542.
£1,500-2,000   *ONS*

A 1954 Bentley R-type Continental sports saloon, coachwork by H.J. Mulliner, chassis No. BC11C, engine No. BCD7, engine; 6-cylinder, inlet over exhaust valve, 4875 cc, power output undisclosed, independent coil spring front and semi-elliptic rear suspension with adjustable dampers.
£33,000-36,000 *CSK*

A 1955 Sunbeam Talbot MK.III drophead coupé, chassis No. A.3502211/9/HCO, engine No. A.350261/ODH50.
£1,000-1,400 *ONS*

A 1964 Sunbeam Alpine Mk.IV sports saloon convertible, chassis and engine No. B.9402783 H.R.O.
£500-600 *ONS*

A 1958 Bedford H.C.B. Angus Short Tender, ex Dumfries & Gallow Fire Service, Reg. No. LCS 149.
£600-700 *AG*

A 1960 MGA 1600 sports 2-seater, chassis No. GHN/82765, engine No. 14057, engine; 4-cylinder, overhead valve, 1588 cc, gearbox, four-speed synchromesh, brakes, disc front drum rear, suspension, independent coil spring front, semi-elliptic rear.
£3,500-4,000 *CSK*

A 1962 Alvis TD21 foursome drophead coupé, chassis and engine No. 26733.
£2,700-3,000 *ONS*

This is one of 1,067 chassis of the TD21 series built between 1959 and 1962.

A 1907 Triumph 3½ HP solo motorcycle, engine No. 1203, frame No. 108056, Reg. No. XN 9022.
£1,800-2,400 *ONS*

A 1968 Aston Martin DB.6. Superleggera grand touring 4-seater, Reg. No. WGU 957G, chassis No. DB6.3485, engine No. 4003773.
£3,000-3,500 *ONS*

A 1909 Triumph 3½ HP solo motorcycle, engine No. 5658, frame No. 139731, Reg. No. AH 2226.
£1,500-1,800 *ONS*

A 1968 Jensen Interceptor Mk.I 2-door fixed head coupé, Reg. No. EDL 725F, chassis No. 115/2759, engine No. 752/15.B.
£1,500-2,000 *ONS*

A 1924 Excelsior 2½ HP standard solo motorcycle, engine No. J2169, frame No. J2197, Reg. No. KL 964.
£1,300-1,600 *ONS*

A Douglas model B 2¾ HP solo motorcycle, engine No. 038, frame No. 562730, Reg. No. P5524, c1910.
£2,000-2,200 *ONS*

A 1937 Brough superior 11-50 special 1150 cc motorcycle combination, engine No. LT2. F55863.5N, frame No. M81805, Reg. No. DKA 255.
£4,200-5,000 *ONS*

A 1926 Norton 16-H 490 cc solo motorcycle, engine No. 45357, frame No. 38987, Reg. No. PP 7097.
£1,600-1,800 *ONS*

A bicycle, with 54½in 136cm) diam. wheel with radial spokes, adjustable pedals mounted on the axle, and with iron backbone with mounting step, c1880.
£900-1,200 *Bea*

A nickel-plated brass mascot modelled as Charles Lindberg's Spirit of St. Louis, 6in (15cm) wingspan, on turned wood stand.
£600-700 *ONS*

l. A child's antique Penny Farthing bicycle with Dunlop saddle.
£300-350

r. A similar child's Penny Farthing bicycle.
£300-350 *FR*

A West Country jingle.
£400-500 *MIL*

A plated Rolls Royce 'Kneeling Lady' mascot, fitted to correct radiator cap, for the 'Silver Wraith/Silver Dawn' range of cars, display base mounted.
£130-180 *P*

A twenty-two man manual horse-drawn fire appliance, by Shand Mason & Co, London, c1871, 126in (320cm) long overall.
£4,000-6,000 *CSK*

A small sized 'Old Bill' mascot with original nickel plating, the helmet signed 'Bruce Bairnsfather', 2½in (6cm) high, display base mounted.
£50-60 *P*

A Jaguar SS100 'Leaping Cat' mascot, the rocky base stamped 'Desmo' and 'Copyright', original chrome plating on brass, on correct radiator cap, the cat 7½in (19cm) long.
£100-150 *P*

A rare Lincoln-Imp silver plated brass motor car mascot, with blue beads for eyes, mounted to a radiator cap, 5½in (13.5cm) high.
£100-150 *P*

A Lalique clear glass mascot, moulded 'R. Lalique' and 'France' markings, damaged, 8in (20cm) high, 2½in (6cm) diam. base.
£180-240 *P*

A nickel plated 'Safety First' vintage accessory mascot, 5in (13cm) high, display base mounted.
£50-60 *P*

Use the Index!

Because certain items might fit easily into any of a number of categories, the quickest and surest method of locating any entry is by reference to the index at the back of the book.
This has been fully cross-referenced for absolute simplicity.

A G.W.R. 4-6-0 4000 Star Class 'Knight of the Grand Cross' cast brass number plate 4018.
£450-500 *ONS*

A pair of chromium plated Auterroche oil sidelights, with blue glass filters, inscribed D173, 7in (18cm) high.
£300-350 *ONS*

A pair of plated brass car lamps by C.A.V., early 20thC.
£200-250 *B*

A rare nickel plated brass veteran bicycle candle headlamp, by Herm Riemann, 'The Germania Laterne', 9½in (25cm).
£120-175 *P*

A bronze stylised motor tyre, with a figure seated inside in flowing robes, the base inscribed AEL. R/D, 4in (10cm) high.
£600-800 *ONS*

A vintage 'Coracle-London' motoring picnic set, with large black leatherette-covered case.
£300-400 *P*

Fishing

A miniature brass creel, maker unknown, 2½ by 1½in (6 by 4cm) with hinged lid.
£30-40 *JMG*

An enamel tinplate pictorial sign, 'Cunard Line', 6½ by 9½in (17 by 24cm).
£150-170 *ONS*

An early padded leather flying helmet, c1909.
£200-250 *ONS*

A chrome jet petrol lighter, early 1950s, 9in (23cm) long.
£100-150 *COB*

A rare Scottish vintage fishing tackle dealer, c. 1924, with a deep knowledge of old reels, grey beard, ruddy-ish patina, and a most generous nature towards owners of fine tackle; buys up to £300 *JMG*

Monaco Grand Prix 1959, Jack Brabham in the winning Cooper Climax at the Station Hairpin chased by Phil Hill in the Ferrari, signed, on board, 12 by 18in (31 by 46 cm).
£350-400 *ONS*

An unnamed angler's knife, with four tools.
£10-15 *JMG*

A 'Helical' line drier, by the Helical Co of Redditch, with four wooden arms, fixable into centre wooden holder and clamp.
£10-20 *JMG*

A Hardy 'Uniqua' trout fly reel, with ivorine handle, 1910 style check, 3in (8cm).
£25-35 *JMG*

A rare casting reel, the 'Kitchen's Patent', dated 1920, 4¾ by 3in (12 by 7.5cm).
£200-300 *JMG*

The only known example of a belt-driven multiplier.

A Brown Robertson lock-joint tool of aluminium, with 9 recesses for gripping jammed rod joints, 5 by 1in (12.5 by 2.5cm).
£5-10 *JMG*

An Arthur Allan spinet fixed spool reel, with half bail arm and open cogs, c1920, 2in (5cm) diam.
£10-20 *JMG*

◁

A Malloch 'Sun and Planet' reel, designed for harling on the Tay, sizes 2½ to 5in (6 to 12cm).
£80-100 *JMG*

Sport

A rare Hardy salmon size Spintac tackle box, of fine oak with five internal compartments and lift-out trace carrier, c1940-50, 8½ by 4½in (21 by 11cm).
£30-40 *JMG*

A Victorian archery target.
£60-100 *CPT*

A set of lignum vitae bowls.
£75-100 *CPT*

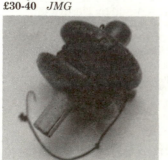

A pike trimmer from Lake Windermere, the red and white cork bearing owner's name, J. Wrigley, c1880, 4in (10cm).
£20-30 *JMG*

A good quality table croquet set.
£150-200 *CPT*

A late Victorian silver vesta case, moulded as a footballers leg and ball, 2in (5cm).
£400-500 *P*

A silverplate vesta case, enamelled in colours with a footballer before a goal, 1½in (4cm).
£100-150 *P*

A silverplate and enamel vesta case, inscribed 'Colman's Mustard', 2in (5cm).
£50-100 *P*

A silvered metal striker/lighter modelled as football boot and ball, 2¼in (5.5cm).
£50-60 *P*

A pair of copper-coloured spelter figures of a footballer and a goalkeeper, damage to goalkeeper's arm, 20in (50cm).
£150-200 *P*

A gold-coloured spelter group depicting four footballers, inscribed 'Un Match Interessant', some restoration, 13½in (34cm).
£350-400 *P*

A silver table lighter in the form of a football, upon circular foot, 2½in (6cm).
£60-80 *P*

A Football League Champions Southern Section Division 3 gold medal.
£130-160 *P*

A Scottish League Championship winners gold medal for 1922-23, won by Glasgow Rangers Football Club, and inscribed 'W. Robb'.
£250-300 *P*

▷ A canvas pigeon decoy.
£15-30 *CPT*

A Liverpool Cup winners gold medal for 1885, the reverse inscribed 'Everton F.C.– J. McG.'.
£100-130 *P*

Jack McGill was the first professional that Everton F.C. ever signed.

A Victorian 'Bussey' table tennis set.
£100-130 *CPT*

A Victorian sledge, 32in (80cm) long.
£60-100 *CPT*

A mahogany tennis racket press, c1900.
£100-130 *CPT*

Golfing

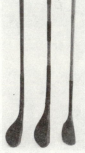

A pair of rare F.H. Ayres table tennis rackets, c1890, 17in (43cm) long.
£150-170   *CPT*

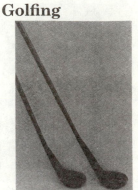

Two scarred head golf clubs, c1895.
£100-130 each   *CPT*

1. A Forgan putter, c1875.
£400-450

2. A McEwan spoon, c1870.
£1,500-2,000

3. A scarred head L.T. putter, c1890-1900.
£100-150   *CPT*

A Forgan putter, c1875.
£400-450

A feathery golf ball, c1840.
£1,300-1,400   *CPT*

A 'hole in one' adjustable golf club, c1925.
£75-125   *CPT*

A golfing mug.
£70-90   *CPT*

A Royal Doulton 'Kingsware' oviform golfing mug, in green and amber, pink and yellow against a green and dark brown ground, c.m.l. & c., 5½in (14cm).
£300-400   *P*

A brown glazed oviform single-handled jug, modelled with golfers in blue, green and brown, printed Royal Doulton marks, 9in (23cm).
£250-400   *CSK*

A golfing mug, 'From Kirkstone Pass Inn, 1,500ft altitude'.
£70-90   *CPT*

A Royal Doulton teapot, sugar bowl and milk jug with silver rim, dated 1910.
£175-200   *SAR*

A Copeland Spode teapot in royal blue.
£125-175   *SAR*

A golf trophy of Pam Barton, spelterware, 6in (15cm).
£100-140   *CPT*

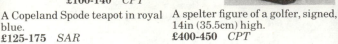

A spelter figure of a golfer, signed, 14in (35.5cm) high.
£400-450   *CPT*

l. A colourful metal golfer.
£20-40

r. A Strauss mechanical toy, USA, c1930s, in original box.
£70-100 SAR

Crafts

l. A silver 'hole in one' trophy.
£40-60

c. A silver toast rack.
£120-150

r. A silver golfing figure, 2in (5cm) high.
£45-70 SAR

A silver match striker case, 2in (5cm).
£70-100

A selection of spoons.
£30-45 SAR

A Royal Doulton ceramic trophy, 11½in (29cm).
£300-350 SAR

A rare earthenware bowl, by Sir Frank Brangwyn, in rich russet with patches of iron-black on a yellow underglaze, 10in (25cm) diam.
£100-150 C

A set of four two-handled bowls, by Michael Cardew, covered in a rich dark brown glaze, impressed MC and Wenford Bridge seals, small rim chips, c1970, 5½in (13.5cm) average diam.
£200-300 C

An earthenware mustard-coloured slip decorated rhyme tankard, by Michael Cardew, with strap handle, inscribed between incised borders, 'Brandy & Gin Swell out the Skin & Make A Man Feel Very Queer & Whenever I Puts Them Into My Guts I Always Wish They were Beer', impressed MC and Winchcombe Pottery seals, c1926, 5½in (13.5cm) high.
£350-400 C

A black stoneware bulbous vase, by John Leach, the saggar-fired matt black body with sandy and smooth textures, impressed JL seal and Muchelney, 8½in (22cm) high.
£180-250 C

A porcelain cut-sided bottle, by Shigeyoshi Ichino, covered in a pale celadon glaze, impressed Shige and St. Ives seal, c1968, 11in (28cm) high.
£150-180 C

A large stoneware lidded jar, by Michael Cardew, covered in a rich dark brown glaze, impressed MC and Wenford Bridge seals, c1970, 13in (33cm) high.
£400-500 C

A tall stoneware vase, by Joanna Constantinidis, with burnished texture revealing manganese beneath a buff slip, impressed C seal, 1971, 26½in (66.5cm).
£400-450 C

A stoneware cut-decorated bottle, by Janet Leach, with dark brown body with blackish-green glaze trails and splashes, impressed JL and St. Ives seals, c1958, 10in (25cm) high.
£250-350 C

A large shaped stoneware rectangular dish, 'Gothic', by John Maltby, on a cream ground crackled with red veining and decorated in red slip, blue enamels, and blue-black abstract panels, signed 'Maltby', 16in (41cm) wide.
£100-150 *C*

A large stoneware grain jar and cover, by Audu Mugu Sokoto, the semi-matt black streaked brown glaze with deep sgraffito markings, impressed seals including Abuja partially obscured by glaze, c1960, 23½in (60cm) high.
£350-450 *C*

A stoneware thrown perimeter slab built vase, by Colin Pearson, covered in grey buff glaze with running areas of green oxide, impressed seal, 12in (30cm) high.
£250-300 *C*

A porcelain flask form vase, by William Marshall, covered in a white slip splashed with green and brushed with iron-brown plant motifs, impressed and incised WM, c1983, 10½in (26cm).
£300-350 *C*

A stoneware bottle, by Katherine Pleydell-Bouverie, covered in a cinnamon-brown glaze, decorated with cream, brown and brownish-black, impressed KPB seal, slight restoration to rim, c1950, 12½in (32cm) high.
£700-900 *C*

A stoneware bowl with cut sides, by Margaret Rey, inlaid with pale blue slip and covered in a shaded olive-green and turquoise glaze, impressed seal, c1930, 6½in (16cm) high.
£150-200 *C*

A large stoneware footed bowl, by Margaret Rey, covered in a specked buff glaze with bold iron-brown decoration, impressed seal, c1930, 13in (33cm).
£400-500 *C*

A porcelain sgraffito bottle, by Lucie Rie, covered in a bronze manganese glaze, with matt cobalt blue on the inner rim and shoulders, impressed LR seal, c1980, 10in (25cm) high.
£950-1,000 *C*

An earthenware handbuilt coiled amphora, by Fiona Salazar, decorated in burnished black, brick-red and amber slips, painted 'Fiona Salazar', c1984, 11in (28cm).
£250-300 *C*

A porcelain sgraffito bowl, by Lucie Rie, with a matt manganese glaze, impressed LR seal, c1978, 8½in (21cm) diam.
£3,000-3,200 *C*

A stoneware beaker-shaped vase, by William Staite Murray, covered in a creamy-buff glaze with charcoal grey decoration, impressed M seal, c1930, 5½in (14cm).
£200-300 *C*

A raku deep circular bowl, by Martin Smith, decorated in grey and pink, minor chips to rim, c1977, 9½in (24cm) diam.
£400-500 *C*

Tribal Art

An Eastern European native silver belt, applied with coral, silver floral bosses and blue and green champlevé enamels.
£150-200 *P*

A Benin wood box, ornately carved, a good patina overall, 19 by 4in (48.5 by 10.5cm).
£300-350 *P*

A fur ivory bracelet, with stained circular motifs between 2 engraved linear bands, 3in (7.5cm) diam, and 2 other ivory items.
£50-70 *P*

A Tlingit wool fringed blanket, Chilkat, dyed in yellow, turquoise and white on a black field, 66 by 33½in (166 by 85cm).
£4,000-4,200 *P*

A Rajasthan cloth, in purple and browns on a red ground, attached khaki border, 58½in (146cm) square.
£400-500 *CSK*

A Bambara wood horseman, the rider carved with the arms free of the body, crusty to glossy dark brown patina, 17in (43cm) high.
£300-500 *CSK*

A Poto knife, metal bound hilt with large wood double knob finial, 27in (68cm) long.
£150-200 *CSK*

A guro wood mask, with pierced slit eyes, incised raised brows, surmounted by two horns, serrated border, glossy dark brown patina, 12½in (32cm) high.
£300-350 *CSK*

A Plains feather war bonnet, comprising 28 eagle feathers with green stroud binding, and polychrome beaded headband, with red, white and blue ribbons attached.
£350-400 *P*

A pair of Yoruba female Ibeji figures, with a string of blue beads around the necks, well patinated elongated faces with ridged tripartite coiffures, 11½in (29cm) high.
£300-350 *P*

An African carved wood fertility god, a kneeling female figure with tall head-dress, an infant on her back, with covered cooking pot supported by 2 small kneeling figures on circular base, 26in (65cm) high.
£5,000-5,500 *DSH*

A pair of Great Lakes beaded skin moccasins, with black velvet flaps and panels sewn with coloured beads, dark brown tanned skin, 7in (18cm) long.
£60-100 *CSK*

An Akan wood maternity figure, the mother crouching holding the suckling child to her lap, beaded ornaments, black patina, 18in (46cm).
£350-500 *CSK*

A Jalisco pottery kneeling female figure, the body modelled with skirt, tunic and headgear, 13in (33cm) high.
£350-450 *CSK*

A fine and rare Yoruba bronze group, for the Ogboni cult, of a seated male figure, probably a priest, the male attendant holding a pair of edan Ogboni, the female her breasts, probably from Ilorin, c1900, 8½in (22cm).
£700-800 *CSK*

A Bambara wood marionette figure, comprising a highly stylised 4-legged female, surmounted by tiers of elongated heads decreasing in size, decorated overall with pierced and punched panels of brass, copper and white metal, 67in (168cm).
£500-600 *P*

A Yaka wood female figure, with abdominal fetish cavity, traces of yellow about the eyes and white to the ears, glossy brown patina, 18½in (47cm) high.
£200-250 *CSK*

A large Watam canoe prow, carved in the form of a crocodile with incised curvilinear decoration, 48½in (121cm) long.
£100-150 *P*

A Loango ivory tusk, spirally carved in relief with native figures, some wearing European clothing, 11½in (29cm) long.
£60-90 *P*

A Cameroon circular wood stool, the support pierced and carved with 3 tiers of bat heads, scorched ornament, Tikar/Babanki-Kijem, 16½in (41.5cm).
£300-500 *CSK*

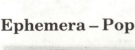

A Loango hippopotamus tooth, finely carved in low relief on one side, and in the Chinese manner on the other, creamy yellow patina, 13½in (34cm) long.
£300-400

A Loango ivory tusk, spirally carved with figures, most of whom are fighting, seated female figure finial, cracks, 9½in (24cm) long.
£300-400 *CSK*

A Southern Plains hide quiver, decorated at each end with beadwork in blue, yellow and red on a green ground, a wood bow and two arrows, 34in (86cm).
£350-450 *P*

Ephemera – Pop

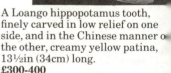

The Beatles – 'One & One is Two', a Dick James Music single-sided demo disc, 1964, in (?) original sleeve.
£300-450 *CSK*

A coloured aquatint of Buddy Holly and others, No. 7 of 10 artist's proofs, numbered, titled, signed and dated by the artist, David Oxtoby, 1977, plate area 27 by 21in (68 by 53cm), framed and glazed.
£150-200 *CSK*

A colour transparency collection, comprising approx. 5,000 labelled transparencies, 2¼in (5.5cm) square, protected by transparent bags and protecting card mounts, in twelve card index drawers.
£7,000-8,000 *P*

Cigarette Cards

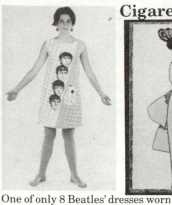

Jung Nickel, No. 328, No. 329 and No. 331, women in hats and costume, G to F.
£180-220 *P*

One of only 8 Beatles' dresses worn by usherettes for the Royal Premiere of 'Help' in July 1965, sleeveless with pink and white polka dots, with ink signatures of all 4 members, Ringo Starr signing twice, and those of Cynthia Lennon and Brian Epstein.
£1,500-2,000 *P*

Mela Koehler, No. 310, No. 312 and No. 315, women in costume, G to F.
£120-130 *P*

Mela Koehler, No. 375 and No. 589, women in hats and costume, G to F.
£100-120 *P*

Maria Likarz, No. 722, No. 777 and No. 781, women in hats and costume, G to F.
£120-150 *P*

Mela Koehler, Nos 519-523, women in costume with dogs before patterned backgrounds, G to F.
£300-320 *P*

Wills, Cricketers 1896, a complete set of 50.
£700-1,200 *CSK*

Baker, Beauties of All Nations 1899, a set of 25.
£70-100 *CSK*

Wills, Cricketers Series 1901, a complete set of 50.
£100-150 *CSK*

Gallaher, Royalty Series, a complete set.
£100-150 *CSK*

Carreras, Women on War Work, a set of 50.
£70-100 *CSK*

Arnold Nechanski, No. 891 and No.898, theatrical designs, G to F.
£70-100 *P*

Cope, Dickens Gallery, a complete set of 50.
£100-120 *CSK*

Postcards & Posters

Raphael Tuck, Celebrated Posters
No. 1501, Ogden's Guinea Gold
Cigarettes and A Country Girl at
Daly's Theatre.
£40-60 *CSK*

Raphael Tuck, Celebrated Posters
No. 1501, Rowntree's Elect Cocoa,
No. 1501, Dewar's and No. 1506,
Mazawattee Cocoa.
£60-100 *CSK*

Marilyn Monroe, 'The Seven Year
Itch', a polychrome film poster,
1955, small clean tear at folds, 30
by 40in (76 by 100cm).
£100-120 *CSK*

A postcard showing flooding in
Southsea High St, and others (about
1,000) in one album.
£200-250 *CSK*

Louis Wain, The Meeting Between a
Puppy and a Kitten, signed,
watercolour heightened with white,
7½ by 11½in (19 by 29cm).
£200-500 *CSK*

A signed photograph of Vivien
Leigh.
£150-175 *N*

George Ernest Studdy, I'm Much
Slicker When There Aint A Moon!,
signed and inscribed, pencil, pen,
black ink and watercolour
heightened with white, unframed,
10½ by 15in (26.5 by 38cm).
£300-500 *CSK*

George Ernest Studdy, Can't We
Think of Anything Nice To Do?,
signed, inscribed, pencil, pen, black
ink and watercolour, heightened
with white, unframed, 10½ by 15in
(26.5 by 38cm).
£100-120 *CSK*

Louis Wain, Ginger Tomcat, signed,
pencil and coloured chalks, pastel,
unframed, 9 by 7in (23 by 18cm).
£700-900 *CSK*

William Henry ▷
Walker, A Fairy
Bower, signed, pen,
black ink and
watercolour,
unframed, 10 by
5in (25 by 12.5cm).
£800-900 *CSK*

◁
Ethel Larcombe, Gathering Roses,
signed with monogram, pencil and
watercolour heightened with white,
unframed, 20 by 15in (50 by 38cm).
£400-450 *CSK*

Cecil Aldin, In Disgrace; A
Welcome Surprise; The Favoured
One; and Dutch Boys Fishing,
signed, with inscriptions on reverse,
pencil and watercolour heightened
with white, unframed, 11½ by 9in
(29 by 23cm).
£800-900 *CSK*

English School: There was an Old Woman who lived in a Shoe, pen and black ink, 9 by 13in (23 by 33cm).
£50-100 *CSK*

Ethel Larcombe, The Mistress with her Page, signed with monogram, watercolour, unframed, 20 by 15in (50 by 38cm).
£300-350 *CSK*

Ernest Howard Shepard, Adversaries in The Bad Old Days, signed with initials and inscribed, pen and black ink, unframed, 14 by 10in (35 by 25cm).
£450-500 *CSK*

Ronald Searle, Alls Well that ends Well, signed and inscribed, pen, brown and red ink, brown washes, published Punch, September 30th, 1953, 11 by 14in (28 by 35cm).
£200-400 *CSK*

Ethel Larcombe, The Blue of Heaven is larger than the Cloud, signed with monogram and inscribed, pencil and watercolour, unframed, 9½ by 6in (24 by 15cm), and another unframed watercolour by the same artist.
£200-250 *CSK*

William Henry Walker, Pan, signed, pen, black ink and watercolour, unframed, 10 by 7in (25 by 18cm).
£700-800 *CSK*

Edward Jeffrey Irving Ardizzone, The Fight on its Bridge, inscribed, further inscribed 'Milldale, Chapt. XIV', No. 2, pencil and pen and black ink, 7 by 10½in (18 by 26cm).
£100-300 *CSK*

Ronald Searle, Twelfth Night, signed, inscribed and dated 1954, further inscribed 'Punch Theatre', brush, pen, brown ink and brown washes, published Punch, January 13th, 1954, 11 by 14in (28 by 35cm).
£100-300 *CSK*

A German magic poster of one of the most famous magicians, c1930.
£100-150 *JIL*

A 'Player's Weights' poster, signed 'Winks', 19½ by 29½in (49 by 74cm).
£15-30 *JIL*

Osbert Lancaster, 'Personally I don't believe a word of this thin man stuff – I know damn well just what the old Gauguin of Fleet St is up to', signed twice, inscribed, further inscribed 'Specially Commissioned . . .', brush, pen, brown ink and blue crayon, on three sheets, 9½ by 22in (24 by 55cm).
£120-180 *CSK*

Disneyalia

Snow White and the Seven Dwarfs, eight polychrome moulded plaster figures, bases stamped or printed 'G. Leonardi by Permission of Walt Disney Mickey Mouse Ltd', some chipped, one repaired, c1937, 12 and 7-8in (31 and 18-20cm) high.
£150-200   *CSK*

Snow White and the Seven Dwarfs, with an EPNS souvenir spoon, Snow White possibly repainted, 1939.
£100-150   *P*

Vulture from Robin Hood, gouache on full celluloid, 12 by 15½in (31 by 39cm).
£100-200   *CSK*

Hen, from Robin Hood, gouache on full celluloid, 12 by 15½in (31 by 39cm).
£100-200   *CSK*

Penny, from The Rescuers, gouache on full celluloid, 12 by 15in (31 by 38cm).
£100-200   *CSK*

Scripophily

National Bank: £1 specimen 1870, GVF.
£110-130   *P*

Barclays Bank: 1924 (c) original artwork in brown and blue on light card for £1 note, view of Douglas harbour on reverse, VF.
£300-500   *P*

£10 proof on paper for Belfast 1830 (c), VF.
£100-120   *P* ▷

Lincoln and Lindsey Banking Company: £5 proof on card (G.S369A) plus a letter from the Bank dated 1839 and instructing Perkins, Bacon and Petch to print and deliver 4,000 £5 notes, GVF.
£70-80   *P*

£1 and £3 1881, plus £1 1882, all proofs on paper with the signature area cut out, VF-EF.
£140-160   *P*

1819 – 10 roubles State Assignat (P.A18), V.G.
£90-100   *P*

USA: Bank of the United States of America 1832 share certificate signed by 'Biddle', slight stains on fold, small tears, and repaired badly with sellotape, scarce, F.
£150-180   *P* ▷

◁

Newmarket Bank: £5 1899 (G.2061c) overstamped 'Cancelled' twice, VF.
£50-60   *P*

1862 $2 (p.129), F.
£70-90   P

Argentina: 1880 Banco Otero & Ca.
20 pesos proof (P.–), engraved by
Bradbury Wilkinson, EF.
£120-140   P

Channel Tubular Railway
Preliminary Co Ltd, 1892 five
bearer shares, VF-EF.
£125-150   P

Trinidad: 1 March 1939 Barclays
Bank $5 (P.S102), pinholes top left
corner, otherwise crisp, GVF.
£160-190   P

Azores: 1905 5 milreis prata
VG.
£90-100   P

Oriental – Bamboo

A carved bamboo incense stick
holder, densely carved and pierced
with entwined 'chilong' dragons,
the hardwood ends with cylindrical
stoppers, mid Qing Dynasty, 9in
(23cm) long.
£1,100-1,400   C

A carved bamboo group of Shoulao,
surrounded by seven young
attendants, 17th/18thC, 13in
(32.5cm) high.
£500-600   C

A pair of Japanese cloisonné
vases, decorated on a yellow
ground, thumbnail chip to
one vase, 19thC,
46in (115cm).
£5,500-6,000   CRY

A pair of cloisonné enamel vases
and covers, on a pale blue ground,
5in (15cm).
£350-400   L

A pair of Chinese cloisonné vases
with sky blue ground, on a highly
decorated ground of red and pale
pink, late 19thC, 12in (31cm) high.
£300-350   Nes

Cloisonné & Enamel

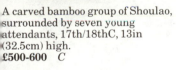

A Cantonese enamel scalloped
bowl, decorated in imitation lapis
lazuli and filled with ivory balls,
11½in (29cm) diam.
£2,900-3,100   C

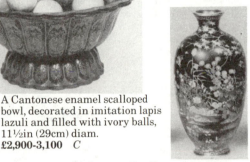

A fine small oviform cloisonné
enamel vase, decorated in colours
and aventurine on a dark blue
ground, with silver rims, slightly
bruised, signed on the base 'Murase
seizo', Meiji period, 5in (12cm) high.
£800-900   C

Make the most of Miller's

*Price ranges in this book
reflect what one should
expect to pay for a similar
example. When selling one
can obviously expect a
figure below. This will
fluctuate according to a
dealer's stock, saleability
at a particular time, etc. It
is always advisable to
approach a reputable
specialist dealer or an
auction house which has
specialist sales.*

A pair of cloisonné enamel censers
and detachable covers, with
turquoise bodies, red crests and
multi-coloured wings, standing on
fixed gilt bronze stands, minor
damage, 18th/19thC, 11½in
(28.5cm) high overall.
£1,700-1,900   C

Furniture

A pair of cloisonné enamel figures of hawks standing on turquoise rockwork, with black, white and mottled grey feather markings and lime-green eyes, minor pitting, 18in (45cm) wide.
£2,000-3,000 *C*

A Japanese black lacquer table cabinet, the interior with an arrangement of drawers, c1870, 19½in (48cm) wide.
£500-600 *Bon*

A Japanese cherrywood display cabinet, 19thC, 50in (125cm).
£1,200-1,400 *JMW*

A pair of Japanese lacquer cabinets on stands, 19in (47cm).
£600-700 *JD*

A carved padoukwood three-piece suite.
£600-700 *PC*

A composite suite of Chinese carved pierced hardwood furniture, each piece profusely pierced and carved, the arms in the form of dragons, raised on carved legs with animals masks and feet, 7 pieces.
£2,000-2,500 *AGr*

A Japanese bronze miniature four-fold screen, the panels decorated with inset enamel, gold and silver, together with a wooden stand, 19thC, 9in (23cm) wide, fully extended.
£500-600 *BS*

A Huali altar table, the top inset with three burr-wood panels, Qing Dynasty, 33in (83cm).
£1,100-1,300 *C*

A Chinese hardwood whatnot, with six cleated shelves on curvilinear supports, 26in (65cm) wide.
£600-750 *Bea*

A Japanese lacquer four-tier whatnot, with 2 pairs of doors, brass mounts and gilt foliate decoration, 38in (95cm).
£1,100-1,300 *JD*

Glass

A hair crystal bottle with irregularly scattered black rutile needles, stopper.
£350-400   *C*

A Beijing red overlay glass flattened bottle, carved with 3 'qilong' forming a continuous pattern of irregular circles, the clear body with snowstorm inclusions, with stopper.
£300-350   *C*

An inside-painted glass bottle, painted on both sides, inscribed and signed 'Ye Zhongsan', with stopper.
£400-500   *C*

A pair of Beijing overlay violet-blue milk-ground glass baluster vases, late Qing Dynasty, 10½in (26cm) high.
£600-1,000   *C*

A Chinese reverse painted glass panel, colourfully decorated, 19thC, 20 by 14in (50 by 35cm), wooden frame.
£300-350   *Bon*

A smoked crystal figure of a hawk, perched on a rocky outcrop, 9in (23cm) high.
£250-300   *L*

Ivory

A fine Tokyo school ivory carving of a lady dressed in a kimono, a little boy climbing on her back, age cracks, signed 'Koraku', 19thC, 10in (25.5cm) high.
£900-1,100   *C*

Horn

A horn bottle, carved in low relief, minor repair, stopper.
£450-500   *C*

Inros

A Japanese five-case inro, decorated with various coloured lacquer, with attached ojime Netsuke, late 19thC, 3¼in (8cm).
£250-300   *BS*

A three-case gold sprinkled roironuri inro, decorated in hiramakie and kinji, with a tasselled Chinese style fan, signed in gold hiramakie on a gyobu ground, Kyoto Kokaku ke (family), okuru (gift to) Kimura Shozaburo, slightly scratched, tiny chips, early 19thC, with attached pink coral bead ojime.
£900-950   *C*

A wood and ivory carving of a drum seller, with roped sandals on his feet, stained hair and eye detail, signed on a rectangular red tablet Kazuyuki, late 19thC, 10½in (26cm).
£1,100-1,200   *C*

A sectional ivory okimono of a basket weaver and his wife, signed on an oval red tablet, Eitoku, late 19thC, 4in (10cm) high.
£600-700   *C*

A fine ivory carving of Kannon, engraved and stained detail, base of figure slightly cracked, signed Shunyosai Nobuyuki to, late 19thC, 5½in (14cm).
£600-700   *C*

A Japanese carved ivory rectangular plaque, in pierced hardwood frame and stand, red lacquer seal, c1900, 16in (40.5cm) wide.
£600-700   *Bon*

An ivory medical figure of a maiden lying naked except for a pair of shoes, signed, hardwood stand, 7in (19cm) long.
£600-700   *L*

A stained ivory censer and fluted cover, the details inlaid in shell and other materials, signed on the reverse of the cover Tamayuki, Meiji period, wood stand, 11½in (29cm) high.
£1,000-1,500   *C*

A carved ivory figure of a fisherman on natural base, 15½in (39cm) high.
£1,100-1,500   *Re*

An ivory tusk carving of a barge, with a shi-shi mask and a phoenix, signed on a red lacquer tablet, carved wood stand, 16in (40.5cm) long.
£500-600   *L*

A set of 5 ivory groups, each group of musicians playing various instruments, on carved hardwood stands, 6in (15cm) high.
£600-700   *Re*

A pair of ivory tusk vases, with Shibayama decoration, metal mounts and carved wood bases, 12in (30.5cm) high.
£1,500-1,700   *LT*

Jade

A white jade bottle, carved in low relief on both sides with grazing horses, rose quartz domed stopper, 3in (7.5cm).
£300-350   *Bon*

An unusual jade boulder, carved as a Daoist cave, with Daoist Immortals and 'lehan' grouped around Budai seated on a plinth behind a smoking censer, late Qing Dynasty, 13½in (34cm) wide.
£3,200-3,700   *C*

A carnelian oval box and cover, carved in the form of a cicada, 2½in (6.5cm) long, and a carnelian pendant, pierced for suspension, 2½in (6cm), 19thC.
£400-450   *C*

Lacquer

A rare pair of Chinese Cinnabar lacquer boxes, each surmounted with a Dog of Fo, in red lacquer on a black lacquer diaper ground, each containing 3 stacking boxes, late 18thC, 10½in (26.5cm).
£3,300-3,500   *DWB*

A massive dark green 'new jade' carving of Shoulao, wearing a simple cap and long flowing robes, 32½in (83cm) high.
£900-1,200   *C*

A pair of massive North European bronze lions, on oblong bases, greenish patina, original pitting, late 17th/early 18thC, 54in (136cm).
£45,000-55,000   *C*

Ajax Committing Suicide, late 17th C.
£25,000-30,000   *C*

A French statuette of a dancing putto, some damage, late 16thC, 10in (24.5cm).
£35,000-40,000   *C*

An unsigned bronze group of an 18thC scientist seated on a rococo style chair, beside plate electrical machine, marble base, 19thC, 12in (30cm) wide.
£1,200-1,500   *CSK*

An Italian gilt-bronze hunting group, in the style of the Master of the Bull Hunt, late 17th/early 18thC, 19in (48cm).
£2,500-3,000   *C*

An Italian bronze door-knocker in the form of a
pouncing lion, late 16th/early 17thC, 13in (34cm)
long.
£4,000-6,000   *C*

A French gilt-bronze group of the Three
Graces, on rosso antico plinth, early 19thC,
17in (43cm) high.
£7,000-8,000   *C*

A gold snuff box with miniature
of Napoleon, 1810.
£20,000-25,000   *C*

Above: A French copper-
gilt crozier, with velvet
covered wooden stand,
gilding rubbed, some losses,
15thC, 65in (163cm)
overall.
£3,000-4,000   *C*

An English bronze bust of
Gracie Doncaster, known
as the 'Age of Innocence',
cast from a model by
Alfred Drury, integrally
cast flared base on shaped
marble plinth, greenish
patina to bronze, fine
casting crack running
round base, dated 1897,
26in (66cm) high
excluding plinth.
£8,000-10,000   *C*

Right: A George II silver-
gilt two-handled cup and
cover engraved with coat-
of-arms and crest, by
Benjamin Godfrey, 1738,
12¼in (31cm), 81oz.
£7,000-8,000   *C*

A William and Mary double quart lidded tankard engraved with a contemporary coat-of-arms within a cartouche, the moulded cover with cast wing thumbpiece, cast cut card front, scroll handle, maker's mark F.S. with pellet above and below, London 1689, 8½in (21cm) high, 48oz.
£15,000-18,000   *WW*

A pair of large Louis XV candlesticks, the bases with accolé coats-of-arms, Nicholas Besnier, Paris, sockets possibly English 18thC replacements, 10¼in (26cm), 72oz.   **£15,000-20,000**   *CNY*

The arms are those of Bateman àccolé with Spencer

A fine tureen and cover designed by Georg Jensen, stamped Georg Jensen 337B, 52in (132cm) wide, 63oz 16dwt. **£18,000-25,000**   *C*

Apprentices were required to make a similar version of this tureen, known as the Rosenbonbonnière, before they could become master silversmiths at Georg Jensen

A Victorian pilgrim bottle, the shoulders applied with female masks with scrolls and acanthus and hung with a chain, the front engraved with the Royal arms of Edward, Prince of Wales, maker's mark TWD, London, 1894, 21½in (53cm), 152oz.
£8,000-12,000   *CNY*

A pair of Victorian six-light candelabra by Barnard Brothers in the style of Paul Storr, the shaped circular bases cast and chased in high relief with lions' masks, flowers and foliate scrolls on matted ground, bases stamped 'Thomas, 153 New Bond St' fully marked, London 1872, 28in (70cm) high, 430oz.
£20,000-25,000   *CNY*

A pair of George IV wine coolers by Paul Storr, plain removable collars and plated liners, marked on bases and collars, London, 1826, 11in (29cm) high, 150oz.
£10,000-15,000   *CNY*
The arms are those of Robyns of Staffordshire and Worcestershire. The crest of two dolphins, forms the design for the handles.

A Regency four-piece tea and coffee service by Paul Storr, later engraved crest, fully marked London 1809-11, 121oz.
£12,000-15,000   *CNY*

A George IV soup tureen, cover and stand, top of stand engraved with Royal coat-of-arms, Ed. Farrell, London 1823, 17in (43cm), 203oz.
£30,000-40,000   *CNY*

A large tazza designed by Georg Jensen, stamped marks Georg Jensen G1925, 264, 10½in (28cm) high, 35oz 12dwt.
£3,000-5,000   *C*

A George III silver-gilt tea tray by John Crouch and Thomas Hannam, later armorials in the style of Walter Jackson, London, 1784, 29½in (74cm) long, 173oz.
£14,000-18,000   *CNY*

A set of 24 silver-gilt dinner plates by Martin-Guillaume Biennais, Paris, 1809-19, 9½in (24cm), 442oz.
£16,000-18,000   *CNY*

A pair of Roman busts, after the antique, with fiorito alabaster shoulders, 17thC, 36in (91cm).
£35,000-40,000 *C*

An Italian marble bust of a Roman Emperor, the shoulders of variegated marble on a cement core, minor damage, 17thC, 36in (92cm).
£16,000-20,000 *C*

A Florentine marble bust of the Infant Christ, unfinished, by Mino da Fiesole, late 15thC, 8½in (21cm).
£6,000-8,000 *C*

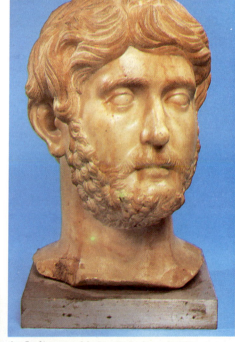

An Italian marble head of a bearded Roman, possibly Geta, 17thC, some damage, 13in (33.5cm).
£1,500-2,000 *C*

Left: An Italian marble statue of Paolina Borghese Bonaparte as Venus Victrix, reclining on a painted wooden chaise longue, attributed to Adamo Tadolini, minor repairs, early 19thC, 36in (90cm) long.
£10,000-14,000 *C*

A pair of Roman black marble and pietra dura pedestals, late 16th/early 17thC, 48½in (121cm) high.
£3,000-4,000   *C*

A Hereford sandstone statue of a seated knight wearing chain mail, with a seated dog at his side, the back flat and unworked, slightly weathered and with consequent losses, 13thC, 55in (137cm), and another, left, his hand on his heart, a medallion around his neck, the back flat and unworked, slightly weathered.
£28,000-30,000each   *C*

A marble head of a Maenad, her wavy hair entwined with ivy tendrils and berries, a lock escaping below the nape of the neck, the eyes with unarticulated pupils, a Roman copy after a Greek original of 4th Century B.C., 10in (26cm) high.
£22,000-25,000   *C*

A George III ormolu-mounted blue john pot pourri vase, with foliate handles, the pierced domed cover cast with foliage and with berried finial, on spreading socle with laurel leaf collar, on a square plinth outlined with black and white marble, 19½in (48cm) high.
£8,000-9,000   *C*

An Attic black-figure amphora, near
the Antimenes group, domed lid
repaired, late 6th Century B.C., 13¾in
(34cm) high.
£8,000-10,000   *C*

l. A bronze figure of Anubis, the jackal-headed god, on marble
stand, 6th/4th Century B.C.
£2,000-3,000

r. A bronze figure of Harpocrates, on marble base, 4th/2nd
Century B.C., 5¾in (15cm) high.
£3,000-4,000   *C*

An inscribed bronze measuring jar, inscribed 'the good god,
Menkheperre, beloved of Amen-re, given life', 1490-
1436B.C., 6in (15cm) high.
£9,000-12,000   *C*

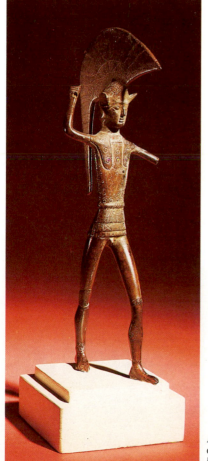

An Etruscan bronze figure of a striding warrior, with incised
decoration, right arm raised in striking position, spear missing,
5th Century B.C., 10in (25cm) high.
£95,000-100,000   *C*

A serpentine royal shabti of King Senkamenisken, bearing 6 lines from Ch.6 of the Book of the Dead, 643-623B.C., 7½in (18cm) high.
£6,000-7,000   *C*

Senkamenisken was the grandson of King Taharqa and was buried at Nuri

An Egyptian bronze figure of a seated cat, modern gold hooped earrings, on marble base, 5th/4th Century B.C., 7¼in (18cm) high.
£45,000-50,000   *C*

A Hellenistic hollow gold bracelet with central Herakles knot motif, 3rd Century B.C., 2¾in (7cm) diam. 55gm.
£8,000-12,000   *C*

Right An Egyptian bronze figure of Horus the falcon, with finely chased wings and one eye encircled with gold, on hollow rectangular base, 6th-4th Century B.C., 5¾in (15cm) high.
£3,000-3,500   *C*

Below An Egyptian turquoise-glazed model of hippopotamus and baby, (14cm) long, Dynasty XII, 1991-1778 B.C.
£12,000-15,000   *C*

A silk and cotton Heriz carpet, very slight overall wear, 203in (515cm).
£30,000-32,000 *C*

A silk Heriz rug, the ivory field with a waisted and cusped brick-red palmette medallion, a shaded steel-blue vine border, excellent condition, 72 by 53in (180 by 133cm).
£14,000-16,000 *C*

A Hamadan carpet, the field with columns of flowerheads, dated AH 1304 (AD1886), 124 by 80in (314 by 204cm).
£4,000-5,000 *C*

An Isfahan carpet, the ivory field with palmettes and floral sprays around a blood-red and beige cusped floral medallion with pendants, the blue spandrels with arabesques and palmettes, in a blood-red palmette and vine border between ivory and blue floral stripes, slightly stained, 172 by 126in (436 by 320cm).
£14,000-16,000 *C*

Right A silk Khotan saph, the field with 8 alternating blood-red and light blue prayer arches with plants with floral mihrabs, 161 by 32in (408 by 110cm).
£5,000-6,000 *C*

An Aubusson rug, 119 by 77in (300 by 195cm).
£3,000-4,000 *C*

A Bidjar rug, 80 by 53in (202 by 134cm).
£2,500-3,500 *C*

Left A Talish runner, 142 by 35in (360 by 88cm).
£2,500-3,000 *C*

Right A Chinese embossed carpet, 151 by 141in (383 by 358cm).
£4,000-5,000 *C*

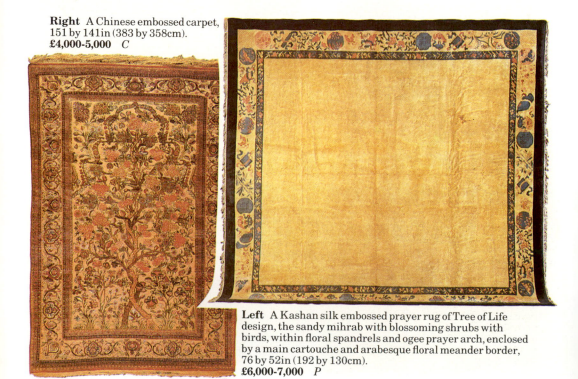

Left A Kashan silk embossed prayer rug of Tree of Life design, the sandy mihrab with blossoming shrubs with birds, within floral spandrels and ogee prayer arch, enclosed by a main cartouche and arabesque floral meander border, 76 by 52in (192 by 130cm).
£6,000-7,000 *P*

Right A Ziegler carpet, the ivory field with an open floral medallion in a blue-grey similar border, 200 by 149in (508 by 379cm).
£13,000-15,000 *C*

Left A Bessarabian kilim carpet, in the Empire style, the sky blue ground covered by an ivory spoke-like centre medallion and graduated ivory spheres, with surrounding grape wreath and flaming torchere and caduceus spandrels, with a brown primary border, backed, 163 by 156in (414 by 396cm).
£25,000-30,000 *CNY*

Below A part silk Isfahan carpet, tomato red field with indigo and ivory concentric roundels, 128 by 82in (314 by 208cm).
£25,000-30,000 *C*

Above A Ziegler carpet, the blood-red field with palmettes and floral sprays around floral medallions, in a blue flowering vine border between floral stripes, 173 by 150in (440 by 320cm).
£4,500-5,500 *C*

A Donegal carpet, the ivory field with a broad white border of floral sprays and scrolls, 158 by 114in (401 by 289cm).
£5,000-6,500 *C*

A silk and metal thread Kum Kapu prayer rug, signed Zare Agha, excellent condition, 72 by 48in (180 by 120cm).
£50,000-60,000 *C*

Below A Meshed part silk carpet, the burgundy field with large flowering trees with a variety of birds in an indigo palmette and vine border between yellow flowering vine stripes, 116 by 93in (294 by 241cm).
£11,000-12,000 *C*

An Ushak carpet, 177 by 146in (450 by 370cm).
£600-1,000 *C*

A Greek Kilim woven in 2 parts, the royal blue field with columns of large floral roundels in a large open floral spray border, 169 by 150in (429 by 382cm).
£2,500-3,000 *C*

A Kirman pictorial rug, the beige field and crimson border with rows of 101 portrait oval medallions of Kings of Persia with inscriptions, 84 by 55in (213 by 138cm).
£3,000-3,500 *P*

A silk Souf Kashan prayer rug, with royal blue mihrab, vertical crease line of wear, 79 by 51in (200 by 128cm).
£5,000-6,000 *C*

Left A Qum silk carpet, with ivory field, blood-red panel and blue medallion, and boteh border, 155 by 115in (394 by 290cm).
£15,000-17,000 *C*

Right A silk Tabriz carpet, the blood-red field with a centre column of blue scalloped palmettes, with ivory medallions, in an indigo border, 72 by 50in (180 by 125cm).
£13,000-15,000 *C*

Left An Axminster carpet with flower heads, floral swags and ribbons around a yellow central roundel, in an outer mottled purple floral frame, with a broad brown floral border, areas of slight wear and repair, 324 by 197in (822 by 500cm).
£6,500-7,500   *C*

Below A silk Tabriz prayer rug, the brick-red field with 2 flower vases, in an ivory palmette frame, an indigo floral arcade above, in an indigo boteh border between stripes, repaired, 96 by 65in (242 by 162cm).
£9,000-10,000   *C*

A Ziegler carpet, 230 by 165in (584 by 419cm).
£3,000-3,500   *C*

Right A fine Sileh, the blood-red field with 2 columns of indigo and ivory stylised dragon motifs surrounded by stylised floral motifs, in a reciprocal skittle pattern border, 92 by 80in (232 by 202cm).
£5,000-6,000   *C*

Left A verdure tapestry,
18thC, 154in (390cm).
£7,000-8,000 *P*

Right A Brussels tapestry woven in silk and
wool in well preserved tones with the family of
Darius prostrate before Alexander the Great,169
by 271in (404 by 628cm).
£5,000-7,000 *C*

*There is a similar but smaller panel of this subject
at Hampton Court woven by Judocus de Vos after
Le Brun.*

Left A Flemish verdure tapestry
woven with various scenes in a
forest, the fruiting borders with
masks and various animals and
birds on a sunlit pool, seated figures
beneath drapery, possible
Oudenarde, reduced, a little re-
weaving, late 16thC, 101 by 263in
(255 by 668cm).
£18,000-19,000 *C*

Right A pair of
tapestries, woven in
silk and wool showing
statues in trellis-work
pagodas, beside rivers,
possibly Berlin, late
18thC, lacking borders
126 by 92in (320 by
232cm).
£2,500-3,500 *C*

A pair of Aubusson entre fenêtres, cord-bound edges, backed, 151 by 49in (384 by 124cm).
£1,000-2,000   *C*

A Dutch tapestry woven in silks and wool with Christ and the woman caught in adultery, mid-16thC, 94in (236cm) high.
£12,000-15,000   *C*

Right: A French composite needlework panel, 96 by 59in (244 by 150cm).
£2,000-3,000   *C*

Below: A sampler by Catherine Fitz-simone, dated 1807, 18in (45cm).
£400-500   *MA*

Right: A sampler by Peggy Kelbrick, in excellent condition, dated 1836, maple frame, 28in (70cm) square.
£1,300-1,500   *MA*

An undated sampler by Ann Davies
aged 11, with French knots, cross stitch
and satin stitch worked in coloured
wools, c1810, 14 by 10in (35 by 25cm).
£200-300 *MA*

A silk map sampler of
England by I Toghill, dated
1787 in original gilt frame,
12in (30cm).
£100-150 *MA*

A Scottish sampler by Marion Weir, dated 1842 in rosewood frame, 20
by 24in (50 by 60cm).
£700-800 *MA*

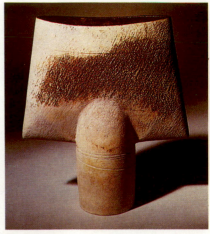

An earthenware footed bowl by Michael Cardew, impressed marks, c1935, 10in (26cm) diam.
£800-1,200 *C*

A buff stoneware spade form by Hans Coper, the interior revealing amber beneath manganese glaze, HC seal, 1973, 11in (28cm) high.
£4,000-5,000 *C*

Two stoneware vases and a bottle by Hans Coper:-
l. A vase, impressed HC seal, c1965, 13in (33cm) high.
£6,000-7,000

c. A vase, impressed HC seal, c1952, 10in (26cm) high.
£9,000-12,000

r. A bottle, impressed HC seal, c1965, 11in (29.5cm).
£6,000-8,000 *C*

A glass sculpture in 2 sections, 'Split Triangle', each section engraved Colin Read 1985 R 140 A&B, 36in (90cm) long.
£3,500-5,000 *C*

Above: Two bowls by Lucie Rie:

l. A stoneware bowl, impressed LR seal, c1980, 13in (32cm).
£4,500-5,000

r. A porcelain sgraffito footed bowl, impressed LR seal, c1966, 13in (33cm).
£3,000-4,000 *C*

Right: A rectangular stoneware slab bottle by Bernard Leach, impressed BL and St Ives seals, c 1955, 8in (19cm) high.
£400-500 *C*

Above: A massive 'famille rose' Canton enamel dish, the reverse with flowers, foliage, rockwork and an inscription with the date 'jiwei' year (1739), 31in (77cm) diam.
£6,000-7,000 *C*

A large cloisonné oviform vase on wooden stand, late 19thC, 37in (92cm).
£1,800-2,200 *C*

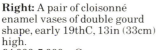

Right: A pair of cloisonné enamel vases of double gourd shape, early 19thC, 13in (33cm) high.
£4,000-5,000 *C*

An Ando cloisonné and plique-à-jour bowl, late Meiji/Taisho period, 7½in (18.5cm) square, with wood stand and fitted wooden box.
£2,000-3,000 *C*

l. An Ando cloisonné vase, signed in seal form, factory mark, 12in (33cm). **£12,000-15,000**
r. An Ando cloisonné vase, late Meiji period, 15in (37cm). **£1,500-2,500** *CNY*

A German sporting crossbow with steel bow, worn and damaged, the crossbow early 17thC, the cranequin late 16thC.
£5,000-6,000 *C*

A carved nephrite figure by Fabergé, in fitted case stamped Wartski, London, 11.5cm.
£55,000-60,000 *CG*

A hardstone figure of John Bull, signed Fabergé, workmaster Henrik Wigström, St. Petersburg, 1896-1908, repair to right boot, 12cm, in original fitted case with Imperial Warrant mark.
£55,000-60,000 *CG*

A George III satinwood and tulipwood tea caddy, crossbanded lid with foliate ormolu handle and cavetto border, the interior with 3 chinoiserie painted tôle canisters, the front, sides and back crossbanded in tulipwood, c1790, 6in (15cm) high.
£3,500-4,000 *CNY*

Left A George III Pontypool or Usk scarlet hot water kettle and brazier, c1800, 18in (46cm). **£1,000-1,200**
And a similar coal scuttle, 14in (36cm). **£1,400-1,600** *CNY*

Right above A rare ivory recorder, by Thomas Stanesby Junior, branded Stanesby/Junior/6, 12in (31cm) long.
£26,000-30,000 *C*

A Greek icon of Saint Paraskeva, depicted half-length, holding a cross in her right hand and wearing a dark brown maphorion on a gilt ground, the lower border depicting 3 scenes from her martyrdom, early 16thC, 24 by 16½in (60 by 41cm).
£4,000-6,000 *C*

A pair of Royal doors, depicting the Annunciation and Four Doctors of the Church, Northern Greek or Balkan, 17thC, 49½ by 15in (125 by 38cm).
£5,000-7,000 *C*

Above A Bwa wood cock mask, 30in (76cm).
£4,000-5,000 *CNY*

Right A rare kaka wood paternity figure, with child on father's back, thick crusty patina, 28in (70cm).
£7,000-8,000 *CNY*

A Tibetan gilt copper repoussé figure of Padmasambhava on separate lotus base, Khatvanga missing, late 18thC, 28in (71cm).
£4,500-5,500 *C*

Left A large Ming cloisonné enamel deep dish, decorated with red and yellow 5-clawed dragons, minor pitting, integral cloisonné enamel mark at the base centre, 20in (50cm) diam.
£17,000-18,000   *C*

Below A large late Ming gilt-lacquered bronze figure of Guandi, seated wearing flowing robes over his armour, holding his belt in his right hand, supported on a base with a tortoise and snake, areas of gilding remaining, old damage, 16th/early 17thC, 28in (70cm) high.
£2,000-2,500   *C*

A pine base, with 4 glazed doors at the front with 4 shelves (not shown), the back open, also with 4 shelves, probably English, superb carving with intricate woodwork and joints, c1850.
£800-900   *AL*

A large Korean inlaid silver-flecked brown lacquer box and cover, the top and sides inset in mother-of-pearl and wire, minor damage, 18thC, 13½ by 26½in (33 by 65.5cm).
£3,000-3,500   *C*

A27 ANTIQUES COMPLEX

CHAUCER TRADING ESTATE
DITTONS ROAD
(A27 TRUNK ROAD).
POLEGATE, EAST SUSSEX
Tel: (03212) 7167/5301 ■ (0435) 882553 (OUT OF HOURS)

**4 DEALERS OCCUPYING 26,000 SQUARE
FEET OFFERING QUALITY MERCHANDISE
FOR ALL MARKETS.**

GRAHAM PRICE ANTIQUES LIMITED

Antique wholesalers, importers and exporters

Specialists in quality stripped pine from UK, Ireland and Europe Country French and decorative items Georgian, Victorian and later furniture Container packing – restoration workshops – courier service

JOHN BOTTING ANTIQUES

Wholesale export specialist in Period, Victorian, Edwardian furniture and accessories.
Good call for all Overseas and UK buyers

MONARCH ANTIQUES (JOHN KING)

Specialising in quality Victorian, Edwardian and later oak mahogany and walnut furniture and accessories. Comprehensive and varied selection of furniture changing frequently

BBC ANTIQUES (BOBBY MORLEY)

English country wood and grass seated chairs, 19th Century Pine and Oak country furniture

**The most comprehensive call in Southern England
Open Mon-Fri 9am-6pm.
Weekends by appointment.
Clients met from airports or station – friendly, efficient service.
Visit us on your next buying trip.**

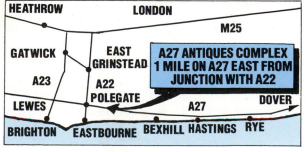

HEATHROW   LONDON
M25
GATWICK   EAST GRINSTEAD   A27 ANTIQUES COMPLEX 1 MILE ON A27 EAST FROM JUNCTION WITH A22
A23   A22
POLEGATE
LEWES   A27   DOVER
BRIGHTON   EASTBOURNE   BEXHILL HASTINGS   RYE

A large contemporary wood netsuke, boldly carved as a foreigner carrying a stag across his shoulders, with stained ivory and lacquer inlay, signed 'Seihosai Meikei'.
£10,000-15,000   *CNY*

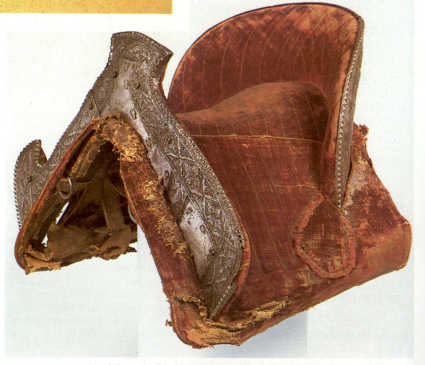

A silver-inlaid bronze shroud weight, Han Dynasty, 3in (7cm) wide.
£45,000-50,000   *CNY*

A steel-mounted saddle etched in the manner of Jörg Sorg of Augsburg, wood and leather frame, Augsburg, c1550. **£4,000-5,000**   *C*

A rectangular Roironuri cabinet, decorated in gold, silver, red, brown and black hiramakie, takamakie, nashiji and heidatsu, some old wear and damage, one carrying handle missing, 19thC, 17½ by 11in (45 by 28cm).
£1,500-2,000 *C*

A Momoyama period rectangular black lacquered wood casket with hinged cover, decorated in gold lacquer and shell inlay, original Kanagu with possible hasp replacement, normal old damage due to wear, c1600.
£1,800-2,100 *C*

A rectangular tabako-bon decorated in gold and silver hiramakie, hirame and heidatsu on a yasuriko ground, with nashiji interiors, the top incorporating two silvered metal liners with silver covers decorated en suite to the box, silvered metal carrying handle, slightly chipped and cracked, late 19thC, 8in (20cm) wide.
£750-850 *C*

Metal

A fine bronze figure of Ebisu, his kimono decorated in gilt nikubori, unsigned but probably by Miyao, late 19thC, wood stand, 23in (58.5cm) high.
£1,800-2,000 *C*

A Japanese bronze figure of a Samurai in armour, the dress highlighted in gold, standing on a shaped wooden plinth, late 19thC, 13in (32cm).
£900-1,000 *BS*

A bronze of a temple dog, 7in (18cm).
£200-250 *LRG*

A bronze group of toads, naturalistically cast and chased, 3½in (9cm) long.
£400-450 *L*

l. A good Japanese inlaid and onlaid bronze baluster vase, signed on a panel, 18in (46cm).
£500-550

c. A large Japanese bronze baluster vase, table lamp conversion available, 21½in (54.5cm) high.
£200-250

r. A Chinese porcelain vase, decorated in coloured enamels within green key patterned borders, basal hairline crack, 17in (43cm) high.
£200-250 *PWC*

A bronze conservatory fountain, the body cast in the form of a knarled old tree trunk with entwined fiery dragon surmounting, 19thC, 35 by 26in (89 by 66cm), standing on an oak table with heavily carved cabriole supports and pad feet.
£5,000-6,000 *Re*

A Japanese bronze of a trumpeting elephant with ivory tusks, on stand, 9in (23cm) overall.
£200-250 *DWB*

An important large Chinese silver water carrier in the form of a winged dragon, the whole with alternate plain and punched scales, standing upon scaled bird's clawed feet with 3 front and one rear toe, 19in (48cm) high, 152oz approx.
£14,000-15,000 *BS*

Netsuke

A fine Chinese gold splashed bronze vase, 17thC.
£3,000-3,500 *DWB*

A finely patinated ivory netsuke, of a professional sneezer seated tickling himself with a stick, age cracks, signed Ryuko, and kao, early/mid-19thC.
£500-550 *C*

An ivory netsuke of an ape, his arms holding a section of bamboo across his back, his fur engraved with stained detail, tiny chip, unsigned, Kyoto School, early 19thC.
£300-400 *C*

An ivory netsuke of Hotei, holding an uchiwa with a karako climbing on his back, inscribed Okakoto, early 19thC.
£200-250 *C*

An okimono-style ivory netsuke, of the Annamese tribute elephant richly caparisoned in Shibayama-style inlay, signed on a gilt tablet Shibayama, 19thC.
£1,000-1,200 *C*

An ivory netsuke of a coiled snake, eyes inset in dark horn, inscribed Toshitsugu, late 19thC.
£500-600 *C*

A well carved ivory netsuke of a large rat, eyes inset in dark horn, a smaller rat on his back, small chips, inscribed Okatomo, 19thC.
£800-1,000 *C*

An ivory netsuke of Daikoku, his kimono and hat inlaid in Shibayama style, stained hair and eye details, signed on a rectangular red tablet Masatamo, late 19thC.
£250-350 *C*

An ivory netsuke of a catfish, its eyes inlaid in coloured horn and metal foil, inscribed on a raised oval panel Masanao, probably Meiji-Taisho period.
£800-900 *C*

A well carved boxwood netsuke of a snail, crawling over a well-bucket bound with rope, the material bearing a three-tone effect, signed Shigemasa, early 19thC.
£1,500-2,000 *C*

A finely detailed wood netsuke of a cicada on half a walnut, unsigned, 19thC.
£400-500 *C*

Yoshichika; a carved boxwood netsuke of a bell-shaped flowerhead, the underside enclosing 7 ebonised free carved seed pods, signed in panel, 4cm, and a carved boxwood netsuke in the form of numerous interwoven fruits, unsigned, some stalks cracked, 4cm wide.
£250-300 *Bon*

Tsuba

A large presentation tsuba, signed Nemoto, the word on the flag held by the child says 'Hanamiren', the edge with cloisonné inlay, the faces with mother-of-pearl Shibayama decoration, gilt grounds, signatures, 4½ by 4in (11 by 10cm).
£1,300-1,600 *LT*

Miscellaneous

Wood

A painted wood 'No' mask of Kumasaka, his eyes applied with gilt metal, slightly damaged, signed on the reverse Deme Eiman, 19thC, 8in (20.5cm).
£600-700 *C*

A boxwood case of Napiers bones, containing 9 four-sided rods engraved on all sides, and an end triple rod engraved on 2 sides only, the whole sliding into a case decorated with geometrical lines, 3½in (9cm).
£300-400 *L*

A set of 3 oriental silk screen panels, floral and bird decoration, late 19thC, 30 by 17in (76 by 43cm).
£700-750 *CRY*

A Cantonese densely carved tortoiseshell circular box and cover, 19thC, 5½in (14.5cm).
£700-750 *C*

A Japanese hardwood circular plaque, finely decorated and inlaid with carved ivory, mother-of-pearl and gilt-decorated lacquer.
£400-450 *JRB*

Russian – Works of Art

A Russian porcelain octafoil dish for the Order of St. Andrew, mock Meissen mark, mid-19thC, 11in (29cm) diam.
£300-400 *C*

A Russian Imperial dish, with later Soviet motifs, painted with a commissar standing before the Petrograd Palace Square, the borders painted with red and black Cyrillic inscription 'Petrograd, Uritsky Square', painted after a dish 'the Commissar' by A. Shchkotina-Pototskaya, with over-glaze Imperial Factory mark, Period of Nicholas II and later Soviet marks, with minor chip, 1922.
£900-1,000 *C*

A Russian Imperial dish, with later Soviet motifs, brightly painted, with motto 'In the hands, hammer, scythe, book' painted after a dish 'The Literacy' by A. Shchkotina-Pototskaya, with underglaze Imperial Factory mark, Period of Nicholas II and later Soviet marks, 1921.
£800-850 *C*

A pair of Imperial porcelain dinner plates from the Kremlin Service, by the Imperial Porcelain Factory, Period of Nicholas I, 1825-1855, each with the blue underglaze cypher of Nicholas I, gilt worn, 9in (24cm) diam.
£600-900 *C*

A silver niello crucifix, centred by the Saviour on the Cross flanked by oval panels nielloed with the half-length figures of the Virgin and Saint John, God the Father above, and Jerusalem below, maker's mark A.B., Moscow, 1791, 16½in (42cm) high, 27oz 10dwt.
£950-1,100 *C*

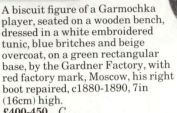

A biscuit figure of a peasant, wearing a white blouse over a printed blue tunic, by the Gardner Factory, Moscow, with impressed and stamped red factory mark, repair to bench and base repainted, late 19thC, 5½in (14cm) high.
£400-450 *C*

A biscuit figure of a Garmochka player, seated on a wooden bench, dressed in a white embroidered tunic, blue britches and beige overcoat, on a green rectangular base, by the Gardner Factory, with red factory mark, Moscow, his right boot repaired, c1880-1890, 7in (16cm) high.
£400-450 *C*

A parcel-gilt niello kovsh, the exterior of the bowl overall nielloed with Italianate landscape, with gilt interior, Vologda 1816, assay-master Semen Klishin, with unrecorded maker's mark Cyrillic (?) G, split to rim, 7½in (18.5cm) long, 8oz 8dwt.
£1,900-2,100 *C*

A parcel-gilt covered beaker on 3 ball feet, with bulbous panels repoussé and chased with rocaille on matte ground, signed with the initials of Andrei Kostrinsky, Moscow, feet repaired, c1750, 6¼in (16cm) high, 7oz 10dwt.
£900-1,500 *C*

A pair of tapering cylindrical silver beakers, the body engraved with a wide band of arabesques below a reeded rim signed with initials of Timofei Silianov and Andrei Kostrinsky, Moscow, 1751, 4oz 17dwt.
£900-1,200 *C*

A silver-gilt sugar sack, chased to simulate a hessian sack, the top folded down, signed with the Imperial Warrant Mark of Sazikov, Moscow, 1860, 2½in (5.5cm) high, 8oz 2dwt.
£1,200-1,500 *C*

A circular silver niello sugar bowl, depicting views of the Kremlin, on stippled ground, with swing handle, by M. Sokolov, Moscow, c1890, 4in (10cm) diam., 8oz.
£300-400 *C*

A silver tea glass holder, chased with a troika scene on spreading base and with C-scroll handle, with gilt interior, by Fabergé, Moscow, 1899-1908, 4½in (11.5cm) high, 4oz 15dwt.
£350-450 *C*

A small jewelled Continental or Russian metal-gilt mounted coconut cup, on spreading foot, the coconut body carved and set with 6 coloured stones at intervals, within a beaded border further decorated with green enamel rosettes, coral and coloured stones, 17thC, 3in (6.5cm) diam.
£600-700 *C*

A shaped triangular silver-gilt picture frame, signed 'Fabergé Moscow 1894', with wooden back and easel strut, 7½in (19cm) high.
£3,800-4,500 *C*

An unusual Russian lacquered purse, the side painted with a peasant couple conversing by a wicket fence, 3in (7.5cm).
£200-250 *P*

A Russian cloisonné enamel egg cup, decorated in red, green, white, mauve and three shades of blue, stamped twice apparently with the mark of August Hollming, the foot with the mark of Pavel Ovchinnikov, c1910, 3½in (9cm) high.
£300-450 *P*

A pair of Russian cloisonné spoons enamelled in pastel shades of pink, blue, mauve and green on a frosted background with white enamel bead borders, maker's mark VA, Cyrillic, c1900, 8in (20cm) long.
£500-600   *P*

A Russian spice box of customary form.
£300-350   *Bon*

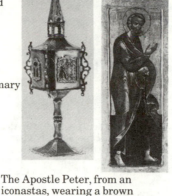

The Smolensk Mother of God, painted with dark brown, green, ochre and gilt highlights on a tan ground within red borders, 18thC, 12 by 10in (31 by 26cm).
£900-1,100   *C*

The Apostle Peter, from an iconastas, wearing a brown himation over a dark green chiton, with gilt halo, on ivory ground, Northern, 17thC, 31½ by 12½in (80 by 32cm).
£1,500-1,800   *C*

A diptych of the Virgin of the Sign and Saint Nicholas, naturalistically painted within a metal case enamelled with blue, green, yellow and white within white pellet borders, with suspension ring and clasp, 18thC, 3½in (8.5cm) wide extended.
£1,000-1,200   *C*

A Greek triptych, painted in cinnabar and dark green on gilt grounds, Greek Islands, 18thC, 15¼in (38cm) wide extended.
£1,300-1,500   *C*

The Virgin Smolenskaya, finely painted and covered with a repoussé and chased riza, with ornately designed haloes, the lower border applied with two inscribed nielloed plaques, signed with initials of Vasili Iakovlev, Moscow, 1803, 14½ by 12in (36 by 31cm).
£1,200-1,500   *C*

The Vladimir Mother of God, painted in brown with gilt highlights, on an ivory ground, the borders depicting a guardian angel and a Chosen Saint, covered with a repoussé and chased parcel-gilt riza, 19thC, the riza probably Riga, 1857, 12 by 10½in (31 by 26cm).
£1,500-1,800   *C*

A miniature parcel-gilt triptych, maker's mark Cyrillic G S, Moscow, c1880, 3½in (8.5cm) wide extended.
£700-800   *C*

The Vernicle, naturalistically painted, covered with a parcel-gilt riza chased to simulate cloth, 19thC, maker's mark Cyrillic E L, the riza c1880, 12 by 10in (31 by 25cm).
£400-500   *C*

The Tikhvin Mother of God, naturalistically painted and covered with a finely chased and repoussé parcel-gilt riza, maker's mark Cyrillic S G, in wooden kiot, Moscow, c1880, 11 by 9in (28 by 23cm).
£1,200-1,400   *C*

The Virgin Bogolubskaya, brightly painted before a monastery, with applied vari-colour cloisonné enamel halo and champlevé enamel plaque, 19thC, the riza signed with the initials of Ivan Alekseev, Moscow, c1890, 10½ by 9in (26 by 23cm).
£1,200-1,500   *C*

A small silver rectangular Panagia (icon pendant) of Saint George slaying the Dragon, with raised borders, Odessa, 1908–17, 2½in (6cm) high.
£500-700   *C*

Christ Pantocrator, naturalistically painted and covered with a parcel-gilt repoussé and chased riza, 19thC, the riza by the 28th Artel, Moscow, 1908–17, 9 by 7in (22 by 18cm).
£700-800   *C*

The Tikhvin Mother of God, naturalistically painted and applied with vari-coloured cloisonné enamel haloes, 19thC, the riza Moscow, 1908–17, maker's mark Cyrillic S G, 9 by 7in (22 by 18cm).
£1,000-1,300   *C*

The Head of Saint John the Baptist, finely painted, depicting the Saint's severed head in a silver repoussé bowl, late 19thC, 12 by 10½in (31 by 26cm).
£500-600   *C*

A Russian icon of St. Basil, signed and dated, painted by I.G. Myator, Koetroma, 1909, 14 by 12½in (35.5 by 31cm).
£500-600   *P*

A Russian icon, probably the sainted Prince Vladimir – 'Equal of the Apostles', silver gilt Oklad and cross, silver gilt key pattern frame, Petersburg 1888, maker I. Sofronov, 12 by 10½in (31 by 26cm).
£300-400   *PWC*

A Nantgarw Masonic tumbler, ex. Wells collection, unmarked, c1819.
£600-750   *BRE*

Masonicalia

A Masonic Lodge medallion, finely engraved with Masonic emblems, and mottos relating to Prescot Lodge number 86 ('Lod no.86'), 18thC.
£200-300   *P*

A George II unusual Masonic mahogany armchair, decorated with Masonic arms above a pierced vase shaped splat.
£1,200-1,500   *AG*

Price

Prices vary from auction to auction – from dealer to dealer. The price paid in a dealer's shop will depend on:
1) *what he paid for the item*
2) *what he thinks he can get for it*
3) *the extent of his knowledge*
4) *awareness of market trends*

It is a mistake to think that you will automatically pay more in a specialist dealer's shop. He is more likely to know the 'right' price for a piece. A general dealer may undercharge but he could also overcharge.

One half-litre Tokaj Eszencia – Vintage 1848 – Tokaj Hegyaljai Bortermeld, the intact label states 'Very Sweet King of Kings of Old Tokaj Wine' and '30° proof.
£300-400   *CNY*

Wine

Two bottles: Château Lafite – Vintage 1874 – Pauillac, 1er cru classé, recorked by Whitwham & Co. 18 July 1980, reference numbers 432 and 434, original labels intact, bin-soiled and tattered but legible, wax capsules, the bottles have the vintage embossed in a glass button attached to the shoulder, original corks attached to the necks, both bottles appear to have excellent colour, one bottle with neck level, one with top-shoulder level.
£2,200-2,400   *CNY*

One magnum: Château Mouton Rothschild – Vintage 1878, Pauillac, 1er cru classé, recorked by Whitwham & Co. 18th July 1980, reference number 448, original label bin-soiled but intact and legible, wax capsule, appears to have excellent deep colour, neck level, very rare.
£2,500-2,700   *CNY*

Clos de Gamont – Vintage 1914 – Cahors, Jouffreau et Fils, Prayssac, excellent general appearance with good colour and neck level.
£200-250   *CNY*

Two bottles: Simi Sonoma County Cabernet Sauvignon – Vintage 1935 – perfect neck levels.
£500-550   *CNY*

One bottle: Château d'Yquem – Vintage 1929 – Sauternes, 1er grand cru classé, excellent general appearance, with high-shoulder level, normal for age, typical dark-tea colour.
£400-450   *CNY*

One bottle: Beaulieu Vineyard Cabernet Sauvignon – Vintage 1956 – private reserve, Georges de Latour, excellent general appearance with neck level and good mature colour.
£400-450   *CNY*

One bottle: Château Pétrus –
Vintage 1948 – Pomerol,
excellent general appearance with
high-shoulder level, normal for age.
£450-500   *CNY*

Five bottles: Heitz
Cellar Martha's
Vineyard
Cabernet
Sauvignon –
Vintage 1968,
excellent general
appearance with
perfect neck
levels.
£900-950   *CNY*

Lighting

A Regency giltmetal hanging
lantern, fitted for electricity, 42in
(196cm) high.
£6,000-7,000   *C*

A pair of Venetian parcel-gilt and
black-painted lanterns, fitted for
electricity, 18thC, 35in (89cm) high.
£2,600-3,100   *C*

A giltmetal hall lantern, fitted for
electricity, 19thC, 37in (94cm) high.
£1,200-1,500   *C*

A wrought iron and glass ceiling
light, the ironwork in the style of
Edgar Brandt, the shade attributed
to Daum, the shade in mottled
amber, purple and cloudy glass,
23in (58cm) high.
£1,100-1,500   *C*

A pair of swivelling telescopic rise-
and-fall wall lights, with milk glass
shades, 1895, backplate 8 by 4in (20
by 10cm).
£450-500   *FF*

A Venetian cut glass triple
chandelier, hung with cut glass
drops, 31in (77cm) high.
£600-650   *Wor*

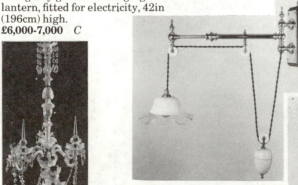

An Art Nouveau electric table
lamp, with vaseline shade, c1900,
16in (40cm) high.
£200-250   *FF*

▷

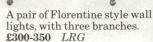

A pair of Florentine style wall
lights, with three branches.
£300-350   *LRG*

A plated two-branch student's oil lamp, with green tinted shades.
£200-250   *WIL*

A bronze candelabrum, with two tôle shades and domed base stamped 'VR' below a crown, fitted for electricity, 24in (61cm) high.
£1,200-1,400   *C*

A Regency bronze candlestick, fitted for electricity, with pleated green silk shade, 30½in (78cm) high including shade.
£1,200-1,400   *C*

A late Georgian silver-plated Corinthian column lamp with stepped base and card shade, 30½in (78cm) high including shade.
£1,200-1,400   *C*

A Restauration bronze and ormolu candlestick, fitted for electricity, with pleated and fringed green silk shade, 21in (54cm) high including shade.
£600-700   *C*

A Tiffany bronze table lamp, with mottled palm tree style telescopic stem and three-light shade, both impressed Tiffany Studios, New York, 1651, 35in (88cm) high, fully extended, shade 19in (48cm) diam.
£2,000-2,500   *GSP*

A tôle urn decorated in lacquer, fitted for electricity, with coffee-coloured silk shade, 27½in (69cm) high including shade.
£1,300-1,500   *C*

An electroplate Corinthian column table lamp, formerly a spirit lamp, c1900–10, 28in (70cm) high to lamp-holder, with later lamp fitting and shade.
£350-400   *TW*

An electroplated Corinthian column table lamp, formerly a spirit lamp, late 19thC, 25in (63cm) high to lamp-holder, with later lamp fitting and shade.
£400-450   *TW*

A Regency ormolu column lamp base, with fluted shaft, 21in (54cm) high.
£1,400-1,600   *C*

A pair of Chinese cream crackle glazed lamps, applied with biscuit lion's mask handles, the chinoiserie giltmetal mounts signed 'F. Barbedienne', the oil lamps now converted to electricity, 17in (43cm) high.
£600-700   *L*

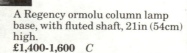

A silver-plated Corinthian column table lamp, with opaque glass shade.
£150-200   *LRG*

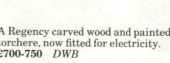
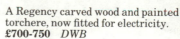

A Regency carved wood and painted torchere, now fitted for electricity.
£700-750   *DWB*

A heavy cast Victorian standard lamp, with original oil, telescopic, with painted shade, 1891, 21in (53cm) across base.
£450-550 *FF*

A good quality Victorian brass telescopic standard lamp.
£200-250 *FR*

A silvered brass Corinthian column lamp, with stepped base, 19thC, fitted for electricity, 31½in (79cm) high.
£1,100-1,200 *C*

A particularly fine Palissy-ware model of an elephant forming the base of an oil lamp, the elephant fully draped with howdah and mahoot, with original shade, 16½in (41cm) high excluding lamp and shade.
£2,000-2,500 *LT*

So called Majolica wares which are decorated in transparent coloured glazes should perhaps be more correctly termed Palissy-ware. True majolica employs an overglaze painting in opaque colours.

A pair of Louis XVI ormolu mounted candelabra, on dove grey marble bases.
£2,500-3,000 *EA*

A pair of French giltmetal candelabra, with blue porcelain bodies, late 19thC, 32in (80cm) high.
£2,500-3,000 *DWB*

A pair of English candelabra, on red marble bases, with bronze putti, c1830.
£600-700 *EA*

A pair of Swedish candlesticks, 18thC, 7½in (19cm) high.
£250-300 *KEY*

A German ceramic oil lamp, in the form of an owl with acorns, late 19thC.
£500-700 *RdeR*

Papier Mâché

A pair of papier mâché wine coasters, the red grounds decorated in red on black between black and gilt bands, 5in (13cm) diam.
£800-900 *Bon*

A single wine coaster, decorated in green and gilt on a black ground, rim chip, 5½in (13cm) diam.
£200-250 *Bon*

A heavy cast French ormolu three-branch floor standing candelabrum, with basket-work shelf and ornate tripod base.
£500-550 *FR*

A pair of black papier mâché wine coasters, 5in (13cm) diam.
£400-450 *Bon*

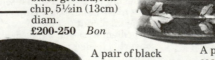

A pair of papier mâché wine coasters, the red grounds embellished in gilt and black with a band of oak leaves, the sides moulded in relief with a slender rib, 5in (12.5cm) diam.
£400-450 *Bon*

A Victorian large papier mâché tray, decorated in gilt, enriched with mother-of-pearl on a black ground and on a folding stand with splayed supports, 31½in (80cm) wide.
£500-600   *L*

A papier mâché tray, the reverse bearing the label T. Simpson & Co., early 19thC, 30½in (76cm) wide.
£900-1,000   *P*

A set of three graduated papier mâché trays, decorated on a black ground, 19thC, 30in (75cm) largest.
£1,000-1,200   *DWB*

A good black lacquered papier mâché tray, painted in enamel colours, slight damage, mid-19thC, 31½in (80cm).
£700-800   *Bea*

A set of three graduated Victorian papier mâché trays, the turned borders of each decorated with gilt foliate scrolls and mother-of-pearl inlay, the largest 30in (75cm) wide.
£400-600   *CSK*

A papier mâché tray, with raised rim, the whole decorated on a black ground, 19thC, 30½in (76cm) wide.
£1,800-2,000   *L*

◁ A papier mâché tray, of extended octagonal form, stamped Clay, King ST. Covt Garden, 19thC.
£1,000-1,500   *P*

A papier mâché tray, painted with a rustic scene, after George Morland, on later supports, early 19thC, 31½in (79cm).
£700-750   *P*

A Victorian papier mâché bread tray, 16½in (41cm) wide, and a rectangular Victorian papier mâché inkstand, fitted with two glass bottles and a pen tray, standing on four bun feet, stamped Jennens & Bettridge, London, 12½in (32cm) wide.
£200-250   *CSK*

A Victorian papier mâché tray, 31in (77cm) wide.
£400-450   *CSK*

A Victorian papier mâché tray, the centre decorated with a painted and mother-of-pearl inlay, the reverse stamped Jennens & Bettridge, 2nd Quality, 31in (77cm) wide.
£400-450   *CSK*

Two Victorian papier mâché tea trays.
£800-900 each   *RBB*

A papier mâché tray, early 19thC, 30in (75cm) wide.
£600-700 *CSK*

A good Continental painted papier mâché box, decorated on a gold ground, 19thC, 8½in (22cm) wide.
£600-700 *P*

A fine papier mâché games box, the lid inlaid with mother-of-pearl and set above an interior fitted with four similarly decorated small boxes and a larger central one, the base of the exterior stamped Jennens & Bettridge Patent Pearl, mid-19thC, 11 by 10in (27.5 by 25cm).
£1,200-1,500 *CSK*

A Victorian papier mâché tea caddy, decorated with painted and gilt flowers and foliage, above a compartmented interior, 7in (18cm) wide.
£150-200 *CSK*

A pair of oval papier mâché dishes, signed 'D. Cox', the scalloped borders of each heightened with gilt foliate scrolls, 10½in (26cm) wide.
£500-600 *CSK*

A pair of black papier mâché decanter stands, with oval gilt painted panel decoration, late 18thC.
£750-850 *WW*

A pair of Victorian papier mâché hand screens, on giltwood and ebonised handles, 9½in (24cm) wide.
£100-120 *CSK*

◁

A pair of Victorian papier mâché hand screens, each painted with an Oriental landscape and heightened in gilt, on turned giltwood handles, 9in (22cm) wide.
£400-600 *CSK*

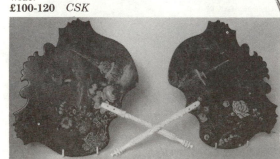

A pair of papier mâché Wolverhampton face screens, with ivory handles, c1840, 14in (35cm) long.
£250-400 *RdeR*

A pair of Victorian papier mâché hand screens, on turned giltwood handles, 9in (22.5cm) wide.
£150-200 *CSK*

Sewing

A Palais Royal lemon-wood sewing casket, complete, c1820, 6½in (16cm) wide.
£500-700 *RdeR*

A Patent Friction Taylor hand lockstitch sewing machine, with separate bobbin-winder.
£200-250 *CSK*

A Grover & Baker hand sewing machine, on mahogany base board with brass Patent plaque, with patents to 1863.
£1,200-1,500 *CSK*

'La Populaire, système Avrial' sewing machine, in carrying case, with wooden treadle and associated clamps, together with set of instructions.
£1,200-1,500 *P*

'The Challenge' sewing machine manufactured by Joseph Harris of Oriel House, Bull Street, Birmingham, with gilt decoration, registration mark 12th Feb. 1871, on wood base, with wooden carrying case.
£150-200 *P*

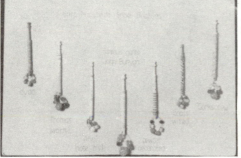

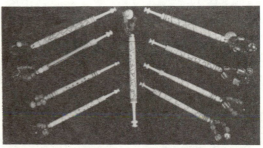

A carved and stained turned bone bobbin inscribed 'A gift from my brother George Mark', another 'John Bunyan', two named 'Thomas' and 'Ann' and three others, mounted.
£80-100 *P*

Nine carved and stained turned bone bobbins, inscribed, three named 'Sarah', 'John' and 'Richard', each with spangles.
£350-400 *P*

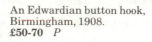

An Edwardian pin cushion, Birmingham, 1908.
£200-220 *P*

An Edwardian button hook, Birmingham, 1908.
£50-70 *P*

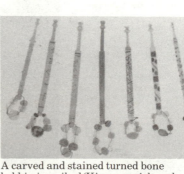

A carved and stained turned bone bobbin inscribed 'Kiss me quick and don't look shy'; one 'Diana Freeman'; one 'King Richard'; one 'George Gren'; and four others, each with spangles.
£150-200 *P*

Miniatures

An oval miniature, indian ink on vellum, by James Ferguson of a young lady, c1750, 2½in (6cm), in a turned wooden frame.
£250-300 P

An oval miniature, by Richard Cosway of a gentleman, with blue eyes and brown hair, wearing a blue cloak with lace jabot, c1765, 3cm, in a gold slide frame.
£200-300 P

An oval miniature, by Richard Crosse of a gentleman, c1770, 3.5cm, in a gold slide frame.
£500-600 P

A miniature portrait of Soloman Dayrolles, French, c1780, 3in (7.5cm), in a tooled red morocco case.
£300-400 L

'Lovers strolling in a country park', English School, c1790, 2 by 1½in (5 by 3.5cm), in a gold pendant frame with hairwork reverse.
£200-250 CSK

A portrait of a gentleman, in a gold enamel frame, set with hair on reverse, c1800.
£400-450 SHP

Empress Marie Louise, by Peter Mayr, signed and dated 1810, giltmetal mounts, 7cm high, in rectangular gilt wood frame.
£2,300-2,500 C

A circular miniature by Kolfmann of Mlle Tassin, wearing a lace inset red décolleté frock, signed and dated 1820, 5.5cm, in wooden frame.
£250-300 P

A miniature of Margaret Campbell, wife of Robert Dun Eglington, c1840, 6in (15cm) high.
£300-350 SA

A rectangular miniature by Charles Foot Taylor of a seated lady, holding an open miniature case in one hand, c1845, 4½ by 3in (11 by 8cm), cased.
£200-250 P

An oval portrait miniature of a young man, the reverse set with a seed pearl and gilt thread mounted hair locket panel, in gold mount, 19thC, 7 by 6cm.
£300-400 Re

An oval miniature by N.H. of a young girl, wearing a white frock with floral and 'gothic' background, signed with the initials and dated 1900, 4½in (11cm), in gilt metal surround.
£100-120 P

A pair of silhouette paintings 'On the Road to the Races 1830' and 'Returning from the Races', black painted on glass, 15 by 11in (38 by 28cm).
£900-1,000   P

An oval enamel miniature after Lampi, of the Empress Catherine II, wearing a pink jacket over a white frock and ermine cloak with the sash of St. Andrews and the Imperial Crown, 3in (7.5cm), in chased silver frame with paste surround, the surmount in the form of the Imperial Crown.
£500-600   P

A miniature portrait, said to be of Hersey, Marchioness of Linlithgow as a child, in a gold and blue enamel frame, in leather folding case.
£200-250   L

A wax profile portrait relief of George III, wearing ceremonial garments, within gilt surround, glazed and within turned wood frame, 8½in (21.5cm) diam.
£200-300   Bon

A gentleman by Heinrich Schoedl, signed, gilt metal frame, 3in (7.5cm) high.
£350-400   C

A gentleman, said to be John Miller, facing left, wearing a black coat and spotted waistcoat, 2½ by 2in (6 by 5cm).
£200-250   CSK

Coins

Norwich, Dunham & Yallop, Goldsmiths, 1793 (last figure of date over-cut on a 2), obv. arms of Norwich, rev. shop front, (D & H 29).
£500-600   C

Lady Byron by F. Read, wearing a black dress with lace collar, a red stole and holding a posy of flowers, 3½ by 2in (9 by 5.5cm), in a fitted tooled leather case.
£300-350   CSK

An oval miniature by George Engleheart of Mrs Herries, wearing a lace-trimmed lilac décolleté frock, 4cm, in a gilt metal surround.
£700-1,000   P

A pair of glazed wax octagonal reliefs, one of Robert Adam after Tassie, 6 by 4½in (15 by 11.5cm).
£1,000-1,300   C

A pair of Victorian wax reliefs of Queen Victoria and Prince Albert, in mahogany frame, 6 by 8½in (15 by 21.5cm).
£200-300   C

Suffolk, Ipswich, Penny, 1796, but of Cardinal Wolsey left, rev. Conder's Drapery Warehouse, etc. (D & H 11; Schw.ll(i)).
£300-350   C

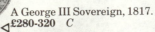

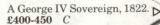

Suffolk, Ipswich, Penny, 1797, view of Wolsey Gate, rev. cypher IMC (D & H 14).
£250-300 *C*

A George IV Sovereign, 1822.
£400-450 *C* ▷

A George III Sovereign, 1817.
▷**£280-320** *C*

Norwich, Skidmore's Globe Series, Penny, 1797, obv. Norwich Castle, rev. globe on stand (D & H Middlesex 130).
£120-150 *C*

Cornwall, West Wheal Mine, Penny, view of St. Michael's Mount rev. West Wheel Fortune – One Penny Token, Prince of Wales' feathers issuing from coronet, (D.15).
£450-500 *C*

Austrian, Salzburg, Wolf Dietrich ▷ von Raitenau, Klippe Double-thaler, 1593, St. Rudbert seated, shield of arms before, rev. four winds blowing at tower.
£240-280 *C*

Brazil, John V, 10,000-Reis, 1725, Minas Gerais (V. 39; F.34).
£600-700 *C*
◁

Norwich, Dinmore & Son, obv. bottle, rev. Hope standing, plain edge, gilt-proof, (D & H 24c).
£200-250 *C*

Germany, Saxony, Johann Georg I, Double-thaler, 1617, half-figure right, rev. helmeted arms (Dav. 7590a).
£350-400 *C*

◁

Germany, Hesse-Darmstadt, Ludwig X, Thaler, 1793, civilian bust right, rev. crowned and supported arms, (Dav. 2337).
£1,000-1,200 *C*

Germany, Hamburg, Admiralty Portugalöser, on the launch of a new convoy ship, 1736, gold, by D. Haesling, (Gaedechens 1815; Forrer Vol II, p.375).
£2,200-2,500 *C*

Italy, Subalpine Republic, 20-Francs, L'AN 10 (=1801), on the victory of Marengo (F.1172).
£500-600 *C*

Norway, Carl XIV Johann, Half-speciedaler, 1824, (NM.19B).
£350-400 *C*

Puerto Rico, Alfonso XIII (of Spain), Peso, 1895, (C & C 16036).
£650-700 *C*

Malta, Emmanuel Pinto, 20-Scudi, 1764, crowned arms of the Order and Grand Master, rev. St. John holding banner, Paschal lamb at his feet (R & S 22; F35).
£500-550 *C*

Spain, Charles III, 8-Escudos, 1773 PJ, Madrid (C & C. 11550; F.137).
£1,200-1,600 *C*

Sarawak, Charles J. Brooke, Proof 20-Cents, 1906 H (Pr.5; Y.11).
◁ **£200-250** *C*

Roman Republic, Janus/Prow series, c250-225 B.C., as (T & V pl.35,51).
£400-500 *C*

U.S.A., Half-Dollar, 1807, Heraldic Eagle reverse.
£400-450 *C*

Sweden, Oscar I, Riksdaler, 1853 (SM.33; Dav.354).
◁ **£250-300** *C*

Malta, Emmanuel de Rohan, 20-Scudi, 1778, cuirassed bust right, rev. arms of the Order and of the de Rohan family on oval shields, edge decorated with leaves (R & S.3; F.43).
£500-550 *C*

U.S.A., 3-Dollars, 1854.
£600-700 *C*

Switzerland, Lucerne, 4-Franken, 1814 (Dav 364).
◁ **£250-300** *C*

Pine Furniture –
Beds

A bedstead with high ships sides, 19thC, 72in (180cm) long.
£175-200 *AF*

A two-door Irish bed cupboard, with panelled sides, c1840, 48 by 78in (120 by 197.5cm).
£550-600 *LC*

A German bed, c1890, 75½in (191cm) long.
£150-200 *Sca*

An Irish settle bed, which opens out to a bed, c1840, 72in (182.5cm) long.
£250-300 *LC*

Bookcases

A stripped pine bookcase on cupboard, 84in (212.5cm) high.
£650-700 *Wor*

A European blind top bureau bookcase, with plain interior indicating provincial construction, c1800, 42in (105cm).
£750-850 *PIN*

A Victorian glazed secretaire bookcase, etched glass doors, fitted interior, c1820.
£1,000-1,150 *PIN*

Chairs

A pine chair with new cane seat, 31½in (78cm) high.
£70-100 *AL*

A rocking chair, c1860, 34in (85cm) high.
£100-130 *AL*

An 'American' action beech rocking chair, all woodwork and metalwork original, re-upholstered, c1850.
£250-350 *PIN*

A pine high chair which converts to a play pen, c1920.
£70-125 *AL*

A set of 4 pine chairs, 32in (80cm).
£150-180 *AL*

An American pine and bleached mahogany rocking chair, on original casters, c1900, 42in (105cm) high.
£150-170 *LAM*

An elm, ash and oak Yorkshire spindle-back rocking chair, 42in (105cm) high.
£250-300 *SSD* ▷

Chests

A Victorian chest of drawers with shaped gallery back, 33in (82.5cm).
£65-95 *AF*

A selection of traditional Orkney chairs with original straw backs,

l ladies chair with drawer.
£175-225

c gentleman's chair with hood, very rare.
£400-500

r child's chair.
£150-195 *STE*

A Georgian chest of drawers, c1790, 48 by 42in (120 by 105cm).
£165-185 *STW*

A pine coffer dated 1715, carved 'In this chest are the books and maps belonging to the Commission of Severs for the Eastern park of the County of Kent, 1715', with original escutcheons, feet replaced, 19 by 78in (47.5 by 197.5cm).
£400-450 *LAM*

An original bow-fronted chest, with graduated drawers, 18thC, 36in (90cm).
£500-700 *RdeR*

An Irish astragal glazed two-part planner chest, c1850, 72 by 48in (180 by 120cm).
£850-900 *LC*

A Georgian chest of drawers, with high bracket feet and original brass handles, 39in (97.5cm) high.
£225-260 *AF*

A 3 piece bedroom suite, comprising chest of drawers, 45 by 46in (112.5 by 115cm), wardrobe, 89 by 49 (225 by 122.5cm) and a dressing table, 64 by 50in (160 by 125cm).
£1,000-1,500 *Sca*

A two-drawer mule chest, c1860.
£175-200 *PIN*

A Welsh mule chest, c1820, 22 by 35in (55 by 87.5cm).
£170-190 *HG*

A chemist's shop flight of drawers, with original knobs, 19thC.
£150-225 *AF*

Cupboards

A rustic Irish food cupboard, with oak frame and pine, early 18thC, 51in (127.5cm).
£500-600 *PIN*

A German chest of drawers with turned columns, original handles and fittings, c1850, 34 by 43in (85 by 108cm).
£400-450 *Sca*

A Northern Irish panelled food cupboard, c1800, 78 by 58in (197.5 by 145cm).
£600-750   *HG*

An Irish 4-door cupboard with arched and decorated interior, c1780, 94 by 50in (237.5 by 125cm).
£1,600-1,800   *HG*

An Irish 4-door astragal glazed cupboard, with carved interior, c1830, 78 by 48in (197.5 by 120cm).
£850-900   *LC*

A large Victorian housekeeper's cupboard, on unusual 9-drawer base, c1840, 78in (197.5cm).
£750-850   *PIN*

A large Irish 4-door cupboard, with panelled sides and rope-twist frame, c1840–50, 78 by 54in (197.5 by 135cm).
£1,150-1,250   *LC*

A Dutch linen press, with pin hinged doors, mahogany carved pelmet and original fittings, c1790, 87 by 57in (220 by 142.5cm).
£2,500-3,000   *Sca*

A linen press with panelled doors and beading, 46in (115cm), and base with original dark stained handles, c1820.
£500-600   *PIN*

A corner cupboard, made up from old wood, 63 by 30in (157.5 by 75cm).
£200-250 *LAM*

A Dutch bowfront corner cabinet, the broken pediment above a pair of cupboard doors, the lower section with 5 frieze drawers and 2 cupboard doors below, on bracket feet, 18thC, 40in (101cm).
£350-400 *Bon*

A drum pot cupboard with marble top, c1840, 15½in (38cm) diam.
£200-250 *LAM*

A bedside cabinet with gallery top, c1900, 31 by 14in (77.5 by 35cm).
£70-120 *LAM*

A pot cupboard, 29 by 16½in (72.5 by 40cm).
£100-120 *AL*

Desks

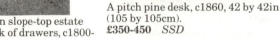

A Georgian pine bureau, the top drawer acts as a support for the writing leaf, oak interior, c1800.
£600-750 *PIN*

A late Georgian slope-top estate desk, with bank of drawers, c1800-30.
£250-300 *PIN*

A pitch pine desk, c1860, 42 by 42in (105 by 105cm).
£350-450 *SSD*

Dressers

A pine bureau. 24in (60cm).
£250-300 *AL*

A North Wales pot-board dresser, c1780, 78 by 68in (197.5 by 170cm).
£1,150-1,350 *HG*

An Irish dresser, with rope-twist shelves, c1840, 75 by 66in (190 by 165cm).
£650-700 *LC*

A Welsh breakfront dresser, Anglesey, c1830, 80 by 63in (202.5 by 157.5cm).
£1,150-1,300 *HG*

A small chiffonier, c1820, 45 by 38in (112.5 by 95cm).
£300-350 *AL*

> **Use the Index!**
> *Because certain items might fit easily into any of a number of categories, the quickest and surest method of locating any entry is by reference to the index at the back of the book.*
> *This has been fully cross-referenced for absolute simplicity.*

A Welsh chiffonier, c1830, 68 by 55in (170 by 137.5cm).
£900-1,000 *Sca*

A large Irish arched base dresser, c1840, 78 by 60in (198 by 150cm).
£650-700 *LC*

A Yorkshire serpentine front dresser, c1850, 50 by 54in (125 by 135cm).
£600-650 *SSD*

An Irish dog kennel dresser, c1850, 78 by 60in (198 by 150cm).
£650-700 *LC*

▷

A Lancashire pine dresser, with 3 bowfront drawers, c1860, 59 by 57½in (147.5 by 143cm).
£500-550 *Sca*

An Irish fiddle front dresser with 3 drawers, c1840, 78 by 66in (198 by 165cm).
£750-800 *LC*

A narrow cottage spice dresser, c1860, 34in (85cm).
£350-400 *PIN*

An Irish hanging dresser rack with bevelled drawers, c1850, 66 by 60in (165 by 150cm).
£350-400   *LC*

A North Country enclosed dresser, 19thC.
£550-600   *JMW*

A one-piece Irish dresser with plate rack, c1860, 54in (135cm).
£520-650   *PIN*

Dressing Tables

A William IV chiffonier, with two drawers and side pillars.
£275-325   *AF*

A Victorian dressing chest, c1880, 62 by 42in (155 by 105cm).
£280-320   *Sca*

A dressing chest, with original handles and fittings, c1840, 44 by 41in (110 by 102.5cm).
£300-350   *Sca*

A hand stripped 'satinwood' dressing chest, c1890, 63 by 36in (157.5 by 90cm).
£250-300   *SSD*

Mirrors

A pine and elm dressing table mirror, c1860, 24 by 22in (60 by 55cm).
£100-120   *SSD*

A carved mirror, 34½ by 30in (86 by 75cm).
£150-170   *AL*

Settles

A church pew, c1850, 33 by 64in (82.5 by 160cm).
£200-225   *Sca*

A Dutch settle, c1880, 44½ by 40in (111 by 100cm).
£200-250   *Sca*

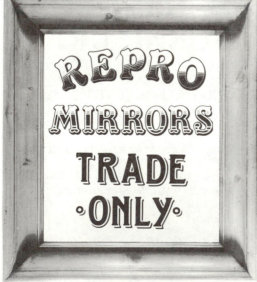

A carved mirror, 27 by 23in (67.5 by 57.5cm).
£100-130   *AL*

A Georgian bowfronted settle, 69in (172.5cm) wide.
£450-500   *JMW*

Sideboards

A North Country sideboard, c1880, 36 by 58in (90 by 145cm).
£400-450 *Sca*

Stools

A pine stool, 19½ by 18in (48 by 45cm).
£30-50 *AL*

A pine stool, 27in (67.5cm) high.
£40-70 *AL*

Tables

A Georgian sycamore topped carving table with 2 drawers and 6 legs, c1810.
£700-800 *PIN*

A Georgian cricket table, c1820, 29in (72.5cm) diam.
£160-200 *PIN*

A sloping desk stool, 29½ by 16in (73 by 40cm).
£40-70 *AL*

An English pine table, c1860, 30 by 96in (75 by 242.5cm).
£600-700 *Sca*

A bed table, c1860, 28½in (71cm).
£40-80 *AL*

An octagonal table, 47½in (118cm) diam.
£400-450 *AL*

A Regency side table with original handles, 29½ by 32in (74 by 80cm).
£100-150 *AL*

Wardrobes

A hand stripped 'satinwood' wardrobe, c1890, 79 by 48in (200 by 120cm).
£300-350 *SSD*

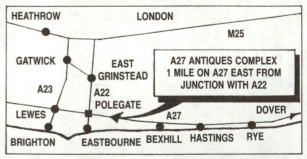

A carved Austrian double wardrobe with one full width drawer, c1860, 42in (105cm).
£425-525 *PIN*

An arched door wardrobe, with shelves on one side, 54in (135cm).
£375-450 *AF*

A wine cupboard, with 2 raised and fielded panelled doors, on bracket feet, 18thC, 48in (120cm) wide.
£475-550 *AF*

Washstands

A marble topped washstand with cupboard, c1850, 49 by 42in (122.5 by 105cm).
£250-300 *Sca*

A double washstand, c1860, 39 by 45in (97.5 by 112.5cm).
£120-150 *LAM*

A marble topped washstand, with green tiles, c1860, 46½ by 36½in (116 by 90cm).
£175-200 *Sca*

A washstand, c1860, 30 by 36in (75 by 90cm).
£100-150 *SSD*

Miscellaneous

A Georgian lady's work box fitted with a sliding shelf, 30½ by 20½in (76 by 51cm).
£150-200   *LAM*

A blanket box fitted with candle box and 2 drawers, c1860, 21½ by 43in (53 by 107.5cm).
£120-150   *Sca*

An Irish panelled grain bin with 3 secret compartments, c1800, 60 by 48cm (160 by 120cm).
£300-500   *LC*

An Irish cheese press, with 4 doors and 2 drawers, c1850, 78 by 66in (197.5 by 165cm).
£650-700   *LC*

A pine box, 11 by 20in (27.5 by 50cm).
£40-60   *AL*

A large dough bin, with scrubbed top used for a work surface, c1820, 34 by 50½in (85 by 126cm).
£300-325   *AL*

Pine shelves, c1860. 48 by 33in (120 by 82.5cm).
£125-150   *AL*

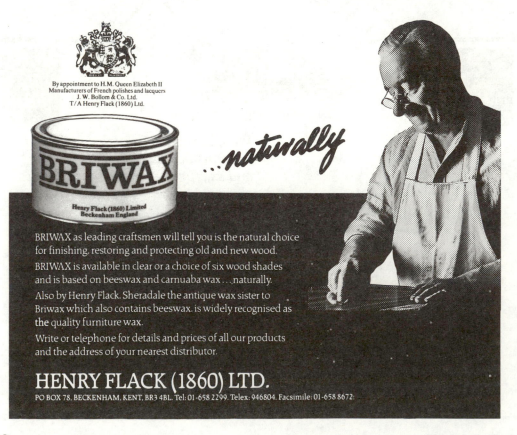

Pine steps, 49in (122.5cm) high.
£40-50 *AL*

A pine mystery object, 31 by 24in (77.5 by 60cm).
£50-70 *AL*

A pine Liberty shelf, 31 by 20in (77.5 by 50cm).
£50-75 *AL*

A towel rail, 35 by 22in (87.5 by 55cm).
£30-50 *AL*

A George III pine fireplace with gesso applications.
£700-750 *EA*

An adjustable easel, on a trestle base, with casters, 92 by 29in (232.5 by 72.5cm).
£950-1,000 *CNY*

A rare pine longcase clock, Scandinavian, Swiss origin, c1810, 79½in (201cm) high.
£1,000-1,200 *SBA*

A Flemish painted pine cabinet, the sides with linen-fold panels and the front decorated in high relief with a central fall-front flanked by cupboards, 19thC, 47 by 55½in (118 by 138cm).
£800-900 *L*

A glazed drapers display unit, with original handles and escutcheons, 63 by 75½in (157.5 by 191cm).
£400-450 *LAM*

A pine cradle, 35 by 34in (87.5 by 85cm).
£200-220 *WHA*

A Victorian two-fold screen, restored, c1870.
£240-300 *PIN*

Kitchenalia

A sycamore flour scoop, 18thC, 10in
(25cm) long.
£35-40 *HL*

A small sycamore spoon, 18thC, 7in
(17.5cm).
£20-30 *HL*

An English seal top spoon with
maker's mark, c1600, 6in (15cm)
long.
£150-175 *HL*

A sycamore measure or water
dipper, 18thC, 5in (12.5cm) diam.
£45-50 *HL*

An ice cream wafer maker as used
before the War.
£10-20 *WHA*

A sycamore ladle, 18thC, 14½in
(35cm) long.
£35-40 *HL*

A wooden scoop for flour, etc.
£20-25 *WHA*

A German ladle, the bowl made
from a shell, c1800, 15in (37.5cm)
long.
£70-90 *WHA*

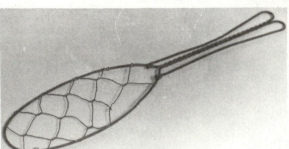

A handmade wire utensil suitable
for many purposes; whisk, fish slice,
server, made from wire netting and
wire.
£5-10 *WHA*

A metal whisk with collar for
altering span of whisk.
£5-10 *WHA*

A Danish wooden flour scoop.
£25-30 *WHA*

Two eel forks, with wooden handles.
£50-70 each *WHA*

Two Yorkshire pottery jelly moulds.
£15-20 *WHA*

A toasting fork, blacksmith made.
£10-15 WHA

A wooden pestle and mortar.
£20-30 WHA

A walnut pestle and mortar, c1800,
6½in (16cm) high.
£500-550 CAS

An unusual Danish mortar, with
heavy steel ball for crushing herbs,
etc. 14in (35cm) diam.
£80-100 WHA

An oatmeal roller, 19thC, 26in
(65cm) long.
£30-40 HL

A tôle-ware coffee pot, early 19thC,
10in (25cm) high.
£200-250 HL

A Virol jar, 'a preparation of bone
marrow, an ideal fat food for
children and invalids'.
£10-15 WHA

A good walnut platter, late 18thC,
11in (29cm) diam.
£200-250 HL

A treen round pierced bowl, with a
central brass inlaid panel, early
19thC, 10in (25cm).
£300-350 CW

A sycamore skimmer, 6in (15cm)
diam.
£30-35 HL

A treen wooden bowl, 10in (25cm)
diam.
£50-70 WHA

A 'Lazy Susan' oak cheese board,
carved with acorns, 22in (55cm)
diam.
£200-240 WHA

Make the most of Miller's

*Every care has been taken
to ensure the accuracy of
descriptions and
estimated valuations.
Where an attribution is
made within inverted
commas (e.g.
'Chippendale') or is
followed by the word
'style' (e.g. early Georgian
style) it is intended to
convey that, in the opinion
of the publishers, the piece
concerned is a later –
though probably still
antique – reproduction of
the style so designated.
Unless otherwise stated,
any description which
refers to 'a set', or 'a pair'
includes a valuation for
the entire set or the pair,
even though the
illustration may show only
a single item.*

A Miele geared butter churn, c1895, 15in (38cm) high, 14in (35cm) diam.
£100-120 *WHA*

A pitch pine base with oak butter churn, made in Leeds, c1860, 48in (120cm) high.
£130-160 *LAM*

A German steam-sponge mould, with lid.
£30-40 *WHA*

A pine plate rack, 31 by 24½in (78 by 61cm).
£80-100 *AL*

A painted pine spoon rack, c1780, with 17thC and 19thC brass and pewter spoons.
rack **£250**
spoons **£20-120 each** *KEY*

Two German icing sugar moulds for wedding cakes.
£30-60 each *WHA*

A pair of plaster moulds depicting hunting scenes, c1820, 14½in (36cm) long.
£600-650 *CAS*

An egg timer, 3½in (8.5cm) high.
£40-50 *WHA*

A German egg box.
£50-70 *WHA*

A set of Art Nouveau style scales, by Salter.
£25-30 *WHA*

A treen string box.
£60-80 *WHA*

A German cherry-pipper, 10in (25cm) high.
£20-25 *WHA*

A wooden darning mushroom.
£8-10 *WHA*

A wooden clamp.
£10-12 *WHA*

A Danish wooden meat press, 14in (35cm) long.
£30-35 *WHA*

An African wooden mixing bowl on legs, 13in (33cm) high, 15in (38cm) diam.
£50-70 *WHA*

An Irish wrought iron rushlight candleholder, c1780.
£150-200 *KEY*

A late Victorian Maypole Tea tin, 6 by 5 by 7in (15 by 12.5 by 17.5cm).
£40-50 *COB*

A wooden money box shaped like a pail, an early souvenir marked 'Present from Blackpool', made in the Lake District, Bobbin Mills.
£20-25 *WHA*

Three English wooden based rushlight holders, c1760, approx. 9in (22.5cm) high.
£130-150 each *KEY*

A French wrought iron candleholder, c1760, 8in (20cm) high.
£150-160 *KEY*

A pair of flat irons.
£5-7 each *WHA*

A wrought iron oat-cake spit stand.
£100-125 *McC*

An English iron and wood rushlight holder, c1760, 7in (17.5cm) high.
£170-180 *KEY*

A Yorkshire brass and metal fire-front trivet.
£50-70 *WHA*

Tools

1. A beechwood compass plane with concentric top, adjustable steel sole and Mathieson iron.
£40-80

2. A Dutch beechwood brace with eleven bits in pads.
£180-200

3. A Dutch plough with iron bow-nuts and carved date 1785 in a panel.
£300-400

4. A Dutch plough with wing nuts, the toe stamped 'I†R, Ryke' and 'KP', dated 1790 in shaped panel.
£350-450 *CSK*

Two hogscraper iron candlesticks, c1820, 7 and 8in (17.5 and 20cm) high.
£30-55 *KEY*

A rosewood box plane, with cast brass sole plate and steel blade by Hearnshaw Bros., 7½in (19cm) long.
£80-100 *DSH*

An A1 dovetailed steel panel plane, by Norris, with Patent Adjustment, 15½in (39cm) long.
£350-400 *CSK*

An unusual cast iron jack plane with beechwood wedge and handle, with adjustable front sole, 14¼in (35.5cm) long.
£30-60 *CSK*

A panel-raising plane, by Gabriel (zb), with adjustable fence and depth-stop and iron by Green.
£100-120 *CSK*

Make the most of Miller's

Price ranges in this book reflect what one should expect to pay for a similar example. When selling one can obviously expect a figure below. This will fluctuate according to a dealer's stock, saleability at a particular time, etc. It is always advisable to approach a reputable specialist dealer or an auction house which has specialist sales.

A rare ogee plane, by Richard Mealing, (Zb), early 18thC, 10½in (26cm) long.
£400-500 *CSK*

A fielding plane, by Wm. Toone, (-1740-), the stock rebated on both sides.
£350-450 *CSK*

A brass block plane with ebony infill and wedge, the sole 7in (17cm) long.
£100-130 *CSK*

A bronze chariot plane with mahogany foregrip and wedge, the sole 5in (13cm) long.
£120-150 *CSK*

A beechwood double-bound octagon lever pad brace, by Robert Marples, with brass baluster and ebony head with inlaid ivory ring.
£250-300 *CSK*

A brass framed ebony ultimatum brace, by Robert Marples, Sheffield, 13in (33cm) long.
£120-140 *DSH*

A handled bridle plough by Mathieson, Edinburgh, with steel bridle and original varnish finish, and an off-the-bench wedge-stem sash fillister by the same maker, in similar condition, c1930.
£500-550 *CSK*

A Norris 50G coffin-sided gunmetal smoother with steel sole, Patent adjustment and walnut closed handle.
£500-550 *CSK*

A small draw-knife, by Maw & Staley, with mahogany handles, the blade 5in (13cm) long.
£30-60 *CSK*

A gentleman's tool kit by Holtzapffel of London, c1850.
£1,250-1,750 *NP*

Sundry Trades

A tin hanging shoe-cleaning box, 7in (17.5cm) wide.
£7-10 *WHA*

A five-inch centre lathe, by Holtzapffel & Deyerlein, No.1048, complete with accessories and reconstructed treadle, the bed 44½in (111cm) long overall.
£500-600 *CSK*

A shoemaker's pattern.
£20-25 *WHA*

A shoemaker's pattern.
£20-22 *WHA*

Two Victorian hat-maker's blocks.
£60-70 *CPT*

Thomas Clark's Patented crimping machine, composed of a green painted cast iron frame, supporting two brass rollers, 9½in (24cm) high.
£70-100 *WIL*

Agriculture

A hop measure, 35in (88cm) high.
£40-45 *AL*

A Scandinavian painted flax-cutter.
£25-30 *HL*

A teasing panel of nails for combing wool, 24in (60cm) long.
£25-30 *WHA*

A German wool-winder, 27in (68cm) high.
£50-55 *WHA*

A hop scuppett, 23in (58cm) wide.
£60-65 *AL*

A flax-basher, 24in (60cm) long.
£15-20 *HL*

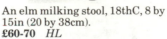

An elm milking stool, 18thC, 8 by 15in (20 by 38cm).
£60-70 *HL*

An oak bushel measure, complete with Orkney Customs & Excise stamp on every stave, 19thC.
£55-75 *STE*

Drinking Vessels

A Scandinavian fruitwood skala, the rim painted with the initials 'W J W' and dated '1871', 11½in (29cm).
£350-370 *Bea*

A coconut treen cup, 6in (15cm) high.
£50-55 *WHA*

A horn beaker.
£15-20 *WHA*

The Dining Room

A rosewood salt, c1820, 3½in (9cm) high.
£100-120 *CAS*

A good Georgian mahogany wine coaster, 6½in (15cm) diam.
£180-200 *CAS*

A pair of fruitwood wine coasters, c1780, 3in (7.5cm) high.
£180-200 *CAS*

A pepper box, 5½in (14cm) high.
£35-40 *HL*

A pair of carved bellows, probably Scandinavian, 18th/19thC, 25½in (64cm).
£90-110 *P*

Miscellaneous

A mahogany smoker's compendium, with snuff pot in the top, pipe rack in the middle and tobacco jar in the base, c1860, 15½in (39cm) high.
£900-1,000 *CAS*

A treen watch stand on circular base, with ivory mounts on turned pillars and stretchers, mid-19thC.
£50-60 *WIL*

A Gledhill Brook time recorder for 'clocking on for work', 9in (22.5cm) high, 14in (35cm) wide.
£170-200 *WHA*

Arms & Armour – Armour

A rare left-hand tilting gauntlet, late 16thC, 13in (33cm).
£1,800-2,000 *C*

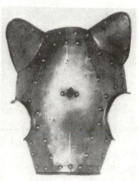

An Italian half-chanfron of bright steel, shaped to the upper part of the horse's head and boxed above and below the flanged eye-openings, slight surface cracking in places, late 16thC, 15in (37cm) high.
£750-800 *C*

A copy of a suit of German Gothic style armour, 19thC, helmet of later date, 69in (173cm) high.
£2,500-3,000 *CBD*

An Italian comb morion of one piece, the skull with a row of lining rivets with brass rosette washers, the whole surface etched with trophies of arms against a granular ground and within gilt borders, probably Milanese, the skull with old internal patch, c1570, 12in (30cm) high.
£1,600-1,800 *C*

A pair of crane-neck rowel spurs of iron, with figure-eight terminals, large rowel of sixteen points, original buckles and hooks, incomplete on one spur, and with considerable remains of gilding throughout, probably German, early 17thC, 6in (15cm).
£700-800 *C* ▷

A Commonwealth steel lobster tail helmet, with adjustable nose guard and pointed peak, one ear flap missing, 17thC, 10½in (26cm), with wood stand.
£450-550 *Bea*

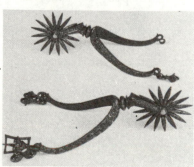

A very rare French model armour, manufactured by Granger of Paris, c1870, 12in (30cm) overall.
£900-1,000   *WD*

A close helmet of blued steel, plume-holder missing, pivoted chin-piece with turned and roped upper border, retaining nuts replaced, neck-guard of two plates front and rear, both the lower plates replaced, retaining much original blued finish, probably French, late 16thC, 12½in (32cm) high.
£4,500-5,500   *C*

A composite cuirassier half-armour of bright steel, comprising close helmet, gorget, breast-plate struck with London Armourers' Company mark at the neck, full arm defences including fingered gauntlets, back-plate and tassets extending to below the knee, many rivets replaced by nuts and bolts throughout, some plates loose, basically mid-17thC.
£2,800-3,200   *C*

A Persian chiselled and damascened steel kulah khud and dhai, the former fitted with two plume-holders, central spike, the latter with four steel bosses, 19thC, 11in (29cm) high and 18in (45cm) diam.
£3,000-4,000   *C*

A mace, the head with seven flanges, the points of two slightly damaged, probably German, 16thC, 24½in (61cm).
£1,500-2,000   *C*

Cannon

A pair of iron ship's cannon, the tapered ringed barrels with the initials B.P. with crown above, each mounted with rope rings and stays, barrels 43in (107.5cm).
£1,500-2,000   *BS*

The initials B.P. are probably for Bailey-Pegg, makers to the Crown.

An English cannon, 18thC, 80in (200cm) wide.
£1,000-1,500   *MIL*

A rare brace of Spanish brass ship's cannon barrels, the vent plane of one bearing the Royal Cypher of Charles IV, 1788-1808, the trunnion ends of one marked no.399, the other CORBRE DE RIO TINTO & P.129, the barrel weighing approx. 130 lbs, dark age patina, a near pair, late 18thC, bores 3in (7.5cm) diam., 31in (78cm) overall.
£2,000-2,500   *WD*

Crossbows

A large Flemish crossbow with steel bow struck with a mark, a unicorn's head, string replaced, the handles both inset with a Spanish (?) coin, the claws struck with a mark, rubbed, 17thC, 45in (113cm).
£2,700-3,200   *C*

Bayonets, Daggers & Knives

A huntsman's plug bayonet, probably Spanish, the grip with brass pommel, in its original brass mounted green leather sheath, minor blade rust, tip of point broken, 19thC, blade 7in (18cm).
£30-40   *WD*

Make the most of Miller's

Unless otherwise stated, any description which refers to 'a set' or 'a pair' includes a valuation for the entire set or the pair, even though the illustration may show only a single item.

A German left-hand dagger, with original indented grip bound with steel wire and with two Turks' heads, probably late 16thC, 16in (40cm).
£1,000-1,200   *C*

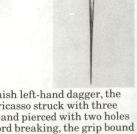

A Spanish left-hand dagger, the broad ricasso struck with three marks and pierced with two holes for sword breaking, the grip bound with copper wire, probably by Francisco Perez of Toledo, late 17thC, 22½in (56cm).
£2,000-2,200   *C*

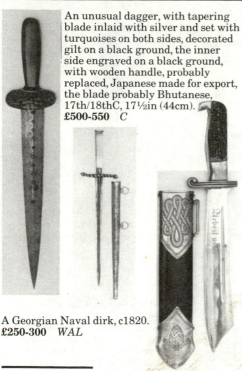

An unusual dagger, with tapering blade inlaid with silver and set with turquoises on both sides, decorated gilt on a black ground, the inner side engraved on a black ground, with wooden handle, probably replaced, Japanese made for export, the blade probably Bhutanese, 17th/18thC, 17½in (44cm).
£500-550 *C*

A Georgian Naval dirk, c1820.
£250-300 *WAL*

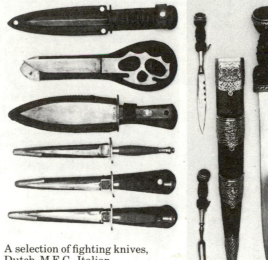

A selection of fighting knives, Dutch, M.E.C., Italian, Commandos.
1 **£45-50**
2 **£90-100**
3 **£200-250**
4 **£250-300**
5 **£250-300**
6 **£350-400** *WW*

A Scottish Officer's dirk set of the Argyll and Sutherland Highlanders.
£700-750 *WW*

Swords – European

A Nazi R.A.D. Mans Dagger, by 'AXT und Hauerfabrik Solingen', also marked 'R.A.J.D.', plated mounts, staghorn grip, stamped on lower grip mount 'R.166', in its steel sheath with plated mounts, stamped on throat mount 'BG 1230', GC, minor sheath painted finish wear.
£200-250 *WAL*

A Nazi S.A. dagger, by 'E.P.&S', blade retaining virtually all original polish, GS mounts, in its metal sheath with single hanging strap and belt clip, some minor wear to painted sheath finish, tip of chape dented.
£150-200 *WAL*

◁ A Viking sword, in excavated condition, retaining fragments of its wooden scabbard, pommel missing, late 9th/10thC, blade 28in (70cm).
£1,200-1,500 *C*

A mediaeval sword in excavated ▷ condition, with bold wheel pommel of latten, later leather-covered grip, late 13th/early 14thC, blade 34in (85cm).
£3,000-3,500 *C*

A swept hilt rapier, the blade of flattened diamond section with twin central fullers and struck each side with a mark, the faceted hilt chiselled with scallop shells on the outer face, wire bound grip with Turks' heads, probably French, one hilt bar cracked and one Turk's head lacking, late 16thC, blade 45in (112.5cm).
£900-1,000 *P*

A Nazi Kriegsmarine Officer's dirk, by Eickhorn Original, Solingen, with brass plated hilt, in its brassed scabbard, some damage to portepee, blade 10in (25cm).
£150-170 *WD*

A mediaeval sword with flat tapering double-edged shortened blade, with a series of marks inlaid in brass, brass incomplete, one side with running wolf mark, also inscription in Naskhi script, 14thC, with later wooden grips, blade 30in (75cm).
£9,000-11,000 *C*

A Charles II hunting hanger, c1680.
£600-700 *Sei*

An English silver smallsword with etched 31½in (80cm) colichemarde blade, lion passant mark.
£700-750 *CSK*

A silver-mounted hanger with straight tapering double-edged blade, struck under one quillon a mark, 'W.C' in a shield, in later leather scabbard with original silver mouth-locket decorated en suite, probably English or Dutch, late 17thC, 21in (52cm).
£600-800   *C*

A Grenadier Guards Officer's sword, 1822.
£300-350   *WW*

A court sword, with silver ribbed wire handle and hand guards, the triangular channelled blade inscribed 'Hunniball', the silver scabbard mount inscribed 'Callum Kings Cutler, Charing Cross', late 18thC.
£500-600   *WW*

A French smallsword, with slender blade of flattened hexagonal section etched and gilt over its entire length and inscribed 'Frederico Pichinio' within each of the two narrow fullers on both sides at the forte, the lightly chiselled russet steel hilt decorated throughout with a symmetrical design involving gilt military trophies and flowers, framed by garlands and scrolls, including double shell-guard, original steel and brass wire bound grip, and retaining much original gilt finish, c1775, blade 28in (71cm).
£600-800   *C*

An Hungarian dress sabre with fullered 29in (73.5cm) blade, with foliate chased silver gilt hilt and scabbard mounts decorated with raised bosses set with garnets, turquoise and blister pearls.
£1,200-1,500   *CSK*

A rare Victorian presentation sword, probably for a senior Police Officer or civic dignatory, made by Reeves, Birmingham, the hilt and mounts retaining most original gilding, blade 34½in (87.5cm).
£450-550   *WD*

Swords – Eastern inc. Japanese

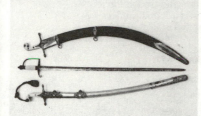

t A Mameluke sabre, blade 33in (84cm) long, housed in brass mounted hide-covered scabbard with inscription.
£900-1,000

c A George III court sword.
£75-100

b A Victorian General Officer's Mameluke sabre, by Hawkes & Co. Ltd., 30½in (77cm) blade inscribed: 'To F.D.B. from H.C.S. on appointment to the 18th Hussars, 6th Nov. 1883'.
£900-1,000 *FHF*

A Persian jambiya, with carved ivory hilt, inscribed 'Osno', with Persian inscriptions above and below, in original cloth-covered wooden scabbard, cloth worn, with chased silver mounts, early 19thC, 14in (35.5cm).
£900-1,100 *C*

An Arab shamshir with curved watered Persian blade, silver hilt with applied gold decoration, silver pommel replaced, in leather covered scabbard with gold and silver mounts, the blade probably 18thC, blade 31in (79cm).
£1,300-1,500 *C*

A Turkish kindjal, with foliate brass inlay, in a purple cloth-covered wooden sheath with 2 large pierced silver chapes, 21½in (55cm) long overall.
£450-500 *HSS*

An Arab jambiya, the hilt entirely sheathed in gold decorated and applied with 2 small stones, contained in gold covered scabbard decorated en suite, slight damage to hilt, blade 6in (15cm).
£650-700 *P*

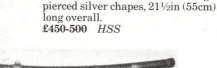

A court tachi, with suguba hamon signed 'Inouye Izumi no Kami Kunisada' and dated 1668, blade 25½in (64.5cm).
£1,300-1,500 *P*

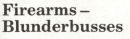

A Japanese short sword, the hilt with applied parcel gilt bronze mounts, the lacquered scabbard with parcel gilt bronze mounts and brass hilted knife, 14in (35.5cm) long overall.
£200-250 *Re*

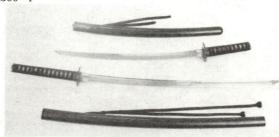

A Daisho, the katana with copper tsuba inlaid with engraved gold panels, with brown mottled lacquered scabbard, late 19thC, blade 28½in (72.5cm).
£1,200-1,250 *O*

Firearms – Blunderbusses

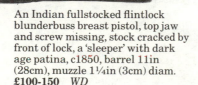

An Indian fullstocked flintlock blunderbuss breast pistol, top jaw and screw missing, stock cracked by front of lock, a 'sleeper' with dark age patina, c1850, barrel 11in (28cm), muzzle 1¼in (3cm) diam.
£100-150 *WD*

A flintlock blunderbuss by Bunney, 14in (35.5cm) brass barrel.
£700-750 *BD*

An Irish over-and-under double barrelled percussion blunderbuss, by 'Kavanagh Dublin', c1850, barrel 13½in (34cm), muzzle 2⅛in (6cm) diam.
£1,200-1,500 *WD*

Muskets & Sporting Guns

A matchlock musket, signed, barrel with moulded muzzle inlaid in silver, replacement steel ramrod, 38½in (98cm).
£700-750 *P*

A German wheel-lock sporting gun, with slender octagonal sighted barrel struck on the breech with 3 acorn marks and with a further mark, 'HE' conjoined (New Støckel 2821), unsigned, late 17thC, 35½in (90cm).
£3,000-3,500 *C*

An English 16 bore fullstocked flintlock fowling piece, some pitting, c1780, 39in (99cm) barrel.
£400-450 *WD*

A South American (Mexican) fullstocked matchlock carbine, the octagonal steel barrel with a brass trumpet muzzle to give the impression of being a blunderbuss, the serpentine and pan cover replaced, some rust and pitting, stock bruised, c1800, 25½in (64.5cm) barrel.
£300-400 *WD*

A dog lock musket, with 2 stage 42½in (106cm) barrel, octagonal at the breech, the plain lock with dog catch, later wood ramrod, some defects, 59in (147cm) long overall.
£700-750 *L*

A French D.B. flintlock sporting gun with gold damascened barrels engraved 'Canon Tordu' along the gilt rib, with maker's marks on the breech and retaining much original blue, by Brunon l'âiné à Caen, c1790, 30in (76cm) barrel.
£2,200-2,500 *C*

A 12 bore fullstocked flintlock sporting carbine, by Newton, Grantham, with silver foresight, the breech flat struck with maker's mark WN and crowned P mark of a private Birmingham Proof House, requires restoration, c1780, 25in (63.5cm) barrel.
£400-500 *WD*

A Birmingham proved 7 bore halfstocked percussion wildfowling gun, by Robert Gill, c1830, the patent breech with platinum safety plug and inlaid platinum band, barrel 31½in (80cm).
£400-450 *WD*

A 12 bore 2¾in (7cm), boxlock ejector gun by Charles Hellis & Sons, No. 2978, in leather case with accessories and a wooden bird carrier.
£800-900 *CSK*

A Herzegovenian Miquelet.
£500-520

A Persian blunderbuss.
£320-350 *WW*

Rifles

A composite wheel-lock sporting rifle, the breech struck with a mark, New Støckel 1044, and retaining traces of engraving and maker's signature, by Johann Stifter of Prague, some repairs, late 17thC, 32½in (82.5cm) barrel.
£2,100-2,200 *C*

A Turkish flintlock rifle, decorated with gold, the butt inlaid with green and white horn and brass pellets and rosettes, the fore-end with green horn cap, ramrod missing, c1800, 36½in (92.5cm) barrel.
£800-900 *C*

A rare London proved 16 bore fullstocked Manton Patent percussion tube lock sporting rifle, converted from flintlock, marked Jam.s Wilkinson London, the lockplate engraved John Manton & Son, some damage, c1820, 21in (53cm) barrel.
£500-600 *WD*

A 12 bore D.B. percussion 'cape' rifle, engraved steel mounts including rectangular patchbox cover engraved with a lion, and original brass-mounted ramrod, signed Deans, London, Birmingham proof marks, c1860, 30in (76cm) barrel.
£900-1,000 *C*

A good double barrelled 40 bore percussion express rifle, damascus barrels signed on the rib J. Purdey, 314 Oxford Street, London, complete with brass tipped wooden ramrod, Serial No. 5194 for 1856, retaining some original colour overall, 30½in (77.5cm) barrel.
£1,700-1,800 *P*

An Irish 40 bore over-and-under percussion sporting rifle, with original horn-tipped ramrods, by Wm. & Jn. Rigby, Dublin, No.8715, some rust pitting, c1841, 30in (76cm) barrel.
£900-1,000 *C*

Pistols

A military wheel lock pistol, with some restoration, 23½in (59cm) overall length.
£1,600-1,700 *L*

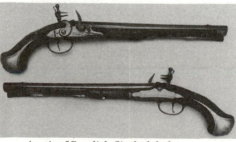

A pair of Swedish flintlock holster pistols, with long barrels signed 'Felix Meier in Wienn' on the sighting flats, with pierced silver escutcheons with coronet above, horn fore-end caps, and original horn-tipped ramrods, one fore-end an old replacement, some wear throughout, early 18thC, 21in (53.5cm).
£2,600-2,700 *C*

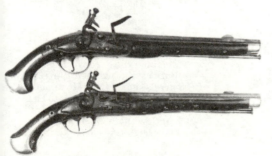

A brace of Continental military holster pistols, barrels with large brass blade fore sights, plain locks, full stocked with plain brass mounts and complete with their steel ramrods, probably Danish or Norwegian, both butts drilled through and one fore-end with contemporary repair, c1750, 13in (33cm) barrel.
£1,000-1,100 *P*

A pair of silver mounted flintlock holster pistols, by John Brazier, London, London silver hallmarks for 1751, maker's mark of James Brooker, one cock associated, the other repaired, ramrods replaced, 13½in (34cm).
£2,300-2,400 *C*

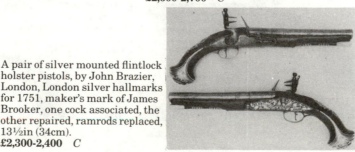

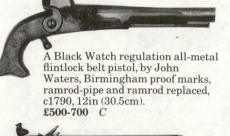

A Scottish all steel flintlock belt pistol, with signed lock by Thomas Murdoch, London proof marks, steel and trigger associated, ramrod later, late 18thC, 12½in (32cm).
£650-700 *C*

A Black Watch regulation all-metal flintlock belt pistol, by John Waters, Birmingham proof marks, ramrod-pipe and ramrod replaced, c1790, 12in (30.5cm).
£500-700 *C*

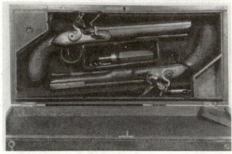

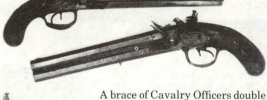

A pair of flintlock holster pistols, sighted octagonal barrels signed Towler, Dublin, contained in baize-lined mahogany case with brass swing handle complete with copper flask and cleaning rod, one fore-end damaged, one cock repaired and cock retaining screw missing, 9½in (23.5cm) barrel.
£750-800 *P*

A brace of Cavalry Officers double barrelled flintlock holster pistols, by D. Egg.
£3,000-3,500 *WAL*

An unusual pair of Irish small flintlock pistols, with engraved case-hardened patent breeches with gold lines and platinum vent, signed engraved bolted locks with rollers, and 'French' cocks, one missing, by William Dempsey, Dublin, much original finish, c1820, 6in (14.5cm).
£3,000-3,500 *C*

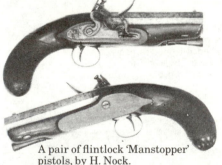

A pair of flintlock 'Manstopper' pistols, by H. Nock.
£900-1,000 *WAL*

A Danish Lobnitz percussion pistol.
£900-1,000 *WAL*

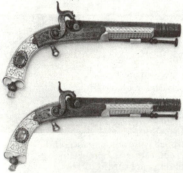

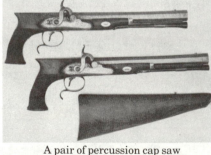

A pair of Scottish percussion belt pistols, signed Campbell, steel parts re-blued and one ramrod replaced, 6½in (17cm) barrel.
£1,700-1,800 *P*

A pair of percussion cap saw handled target pistols by H.W. Mortimer & Co., converted from flintlock, the browned 10in (25.5cm) barrels signed H.W. Mortimer & Co. London, Gun Makers to His Majesty, 15½in (39.5cm) overall length without extension, with some accessories in a later fitted case.
£1,900-2,000 *L*

A pair of Officer's double barrelled percussion belt pistols by Staudenmayer.
£1,200-1,500 *WAL*

A fine pair of percussion pistols, by John Dickson & Son, proof marks, Nos. 4070/1, late 19thC, 16in (40.5cm).
£1,700-1,800 *C*

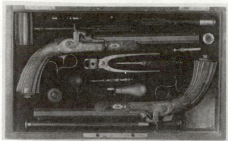

A pair of Belgian percussion rifle target pistols, in original lined and fitted mahogany case with accessories, corner lid missing, Liège proof, c1850, 15in (38cm).
£2,100-2,200 *C*

A Colt five-shot percussion pocket revolver, Serial No. 8154 on all parts, contained in red lined mahogany case complete with all accessories, 5in (12.5cm) barrel.
£1,800-1,900 *P*

The pistol retains nearly all its blueing and colour hardening.

Medals

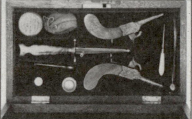

A pair of cased percussion pistols with dagger, by Fenton.
£600-700 *WAL*

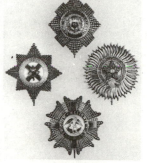

An important group of four 'reduced size' stars':

1. The Most Ancient and Most Noble Order of the Thistle (K.T.), pierced silver cross with gold centre and gold brooch fittings, elliptical, 6.2 by 5.5cm.

2. The Most Illustrious Order of St. Patrick (K.P.) pierced silver star with gold centre, slight green enamel damage to trefoil, 6cm.

3. The Most Exalted Order of the Star of India, Knight Grand Commander (G.C.S.I.) the star worked entirely in gold, 6cm.

4. The Most Distinguished Order of St. Michael and St. George, Knight Grand Cross (G.C.M.G.) silver, silver gilt, gold centre and enamels, with gold brooch fittings, 6cm.
£8,000-9,000 *C*

Pair: Sepy Sundar Singh, 36th Bengal Infantry, Indian Order of Merit, 3rd Class, Military Division, lacking its silver riband buckle, reverse inscribed '352 Lce. Naick Sundar Singh Indian Contingent British Central Africa' and officially engraved '3rd. Class Order of Merit', Central Africa, one clasp, light contact marks, 1894-98.
£1,300-1,500 *C*

Six: M.B.E. 2nd type mil., 1939-45 star, Atlantic star, Burma star with Pacific bar, War, N.G.S. 1915 1 bar S.E. Asia 1945-46 (Sen. Gd. Gnr. J. M. Bell M.B.E. R.N.) GVF, mounted as worn, together with set of miniatures Palestine, 1945-48 bar replaces S.E. Asia.
£170-200 *WAL*

An Indian Mutiny medal, Defence of Lucknow 32nd Lt. Infantry.
£850-900 *WAL*

A Waterloo medal, 79th Regt.
£1,000-1,100 *WAL*

A Crimea medal 4th Dragoons Light Brigade Charge Survivor.
£1,900-2,000 *WW*

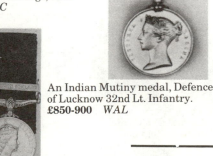

Pair: Guardsman I. Glendenning, Coldstream Guards, Military Medal, E.II.R., 2nd type, General Service Medal, 1962, one clasp, Northern Ireland, an edge bruise to each medal.
£800-1,000 *C*

Drums

A 16th/5th Queens Lancers side drum.
£350-400 *WW*

Helmets

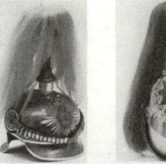

Saxony, Heavy Cavalry Troopers helmet.
£1,300-1,500 *WW*

A Victorian Officers helmet, Royal Horse Artillery.
£1,500-1,700 *WAL*

6th Dragoon Guards, The Carabiniers, Officer's gilt helmet, with chin chain.
£600-900 *CSK*

A Yeomanry Cavalry Officers metal helmet to the Fife Light Horse.
£800-850 *AR*

17th Duke of Cambridge's Own Lancers Officers chapka, lance cap, with white swan's feather plume, gold bullion boss bears embroidered George V cypher, corded gilt plume socket modified, and chin chain lined with white leather.
£1,000-1,400 *CSK*

A Prussian Infantry Reservist Officer's Pickelhaube, gilt brass HP, brass leather backed chinscales, both cockades, original silk and leather lining, GC, some stitching of neck and peak mounts damaged, some wear to patent leather finish.
£200-250 *WAL*

A Prussian Infantryman's NCO's Pickelhaube, gilt brass HP, brass leather backed chinscales, brass spike and mounts, leather lining, state cockade GC, some wear to patent leather finish, neck and peak guard leather age congealed.
£100-150 *WAL*

French Dragoons of the Line, Trumpeter's brass helmet of 1830 pattern with correct red chenille, but some non-regulation features, including the white poupette.
£400-550 *CSK*

French Cuirassiers Trooper's helmet of heavy polished steel, with brass mounts, red hair tuft and a red hackle-plume, helmet impressed beneath mane, A. Godillot and 83 and 57.
£400-450 *CSK*

Militaria – Badges/Plates

A gilt shako badge and a belt plate, the 10th North Lincoln Regiment, 19thC.
£300-350 *Nes*

A good officer's silvered 1869 pattern shako plate, universal Militia Pattern, near VGC.
£40-70 *WAL*

A Victorian Officers helmet plate, the Border Regt.
£350-400 *WAL*

A Victorian Officers Home Service helmet to the Royal Irish, 1878 Pattern.
£350-400 *AR*

Uniforms

An Officers Glengarry badge, 72nd
Highlanders.
£400-450 *WAL*

An Officers busby badge, Bengal
Artillery.
£150-200 *WAL*

An Officers silver bonnet badge, A
& S Highlanders.
£150-200 *WAL*

Powder Flasks

A German carved staghorn powder-
flask, with forked body of natural
horn the outer face carved with a
Resurrection scene, cracked,
retaining traces of original blue,
some pitting, late 16th/early 17thC,
9½in (24.5cm) high.
£600-650 *C*

A scarce and complete post 1902
Trooper's full dress blue uniform of
the City of London Yeomanry,
Rough Riders, comprising lance
cap, tunic, peaked cap and a pair of
overalls with double purple stripe,
items named to H.F. Stephens, GC
very minor service wear, repair and
surface moth traces.
£700-800 *WAL*

A rare American Colonial cow-horn
powder-flask, original turned
wooden base plate and later owner's
name, c1760, 12in (30.5cm).
£1,300-1,500 *C*

A Caucasian silver mounted
powder-flask, with L-shaped horn
body and ivory base plate, the top
and bottom mount each with beaded
border, 18th/19thC, 8in (20cm).
£400-450 *C*

Tinder Lighters

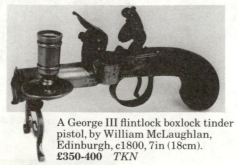

A George III flintlock boxlock tinder
pistol, by William McLaughlan,
Edinburgh, c1800, 7in (18cm).
£350-400 *TKN*

An English steel and wood tinder
pistol, c1780, 5in (12.5cm) long.
£450-500 *KEY*

On the whole, during the past twelve months, jewellery prices have remained steady, with occasional ripples of excitement in the trade, when a rare, authenticated piece came onto the market, and an astronomical price was paid. This often bears no relation to the actual intrinsic value of the item, but rather to the fact that there are many people who have a strong desire to own a rare item, and can afford to go on bidding far beyond its actual market value. Nevertheless, there are still many pieces of good secondhand as well as Antique and Victorian jewellery which are excellent value. Quality of workmanship, together with excellent condition are the main criteria on which to judge an item's value; shoddy workmanship, obvious damage, and poor quality repair work can drastically reduce the value of all items of jewellery.

A turquoise and white enamel and split seed pearl brooch/pendant set in gold.
£425-450 *PVH*

Any damage would reduce a similar item to a fraction of this price.

An Art Deco period pendant, with pavé set diamonds, and a fine 'fancy' yellow diamond in the centre of the flower motif.
£4,250-4,500 *PVH*

Good examples of this period are especially sought after, but still extremely good value, due to the quality of the stones which were used.

A Victorian period 15ct gold black enamel Mourning brooch, set with diamonds in perfect condition.
£500-550 *PVH*

Mourning jewellery had been worn for very many years before the death of Queen Victoria's beloved Prince Albert, but after his death, the fashion for wearing black jewellery to commemorate the death of a loved one almost overwhelmed the jewellery craftsmen of the day. Rings, necklaces, brooches and earrings were made in their thousands, from Whitby Jet, French Jet (black glass), black enamel and black onyx. Often the details of the deceased were engraved on the back of the item, together with a lock of hair placed within a specially made recess covered by a tiny piece of closely fitting glass. A large quantity of this type of jewellery has survived until the present day, and can still be bought very reasonably, primarily because it does not enjoy a wide appeal, due to what some feel to be its 'morbid' associations.

Oriental baroque pearls set in decorated gold 'wirework' on gold neck chain, c1920.
£100-150 *PVH*

A 15ct. gold brooch set with freshwater seed pearl, requires restoration.
£80-100 *PVH*

The above in perfect condition.
£225-250

A turquoise, gold and seed pearl bracelet, c1880.
£500-550 *PVH*

Many examples of this style of bracelet are to be found and, according to age, condition and the stone set within them, prices range from £100 for gold and about £30 for silver. Victorian gilded base metal examples even cheaper.

A Victorian gold necklace set with various coloured agates, interlinked by short lengths of gold chain.
£175-225

A Victorian agate brooch set in gilded metal.
£25-50 *PVH*

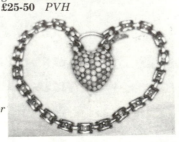

An exceptionally fine Florentine mosaic brooch, in gold Castellani style mount.
£375-425 *PVH*

A heavy quality Victorian silver locket and collarette, Registered Design Mark.
£140-175 *PVH*

A Victorian diamond-set gold hinged half-hoop bangle.
£800-900 *C*

A 15ct gold, diamond and seed pearl mounted hinged bangle, with applied foliate decoration and safety chain.
£350-400 *Bea*

A snake bracelet, 18ct with diamonds, and ruby eyes, 1860, in original box.
£4,500-4,800 *MAK*

An Edwardian diamond, onyx and pearl bracelet, by Dussaussoy, Paris.
£7,000-7,500 *TRI*

A diamond mounted bracelet of tapering rectangular links, millegrain and pavé-set with brilliant cut stones.
£2,700-3,000 *Bea*

A gold ram's head hinged bangle, decorated all over with granulation and wirework, maker's mark C.B., c1865.
£800-900 *Bea*

A gold, ruby and diamond bracelet, set with circular and rose cut diamonds and calibré cut rubies on a gold bracelet.
£700-750 *Bea*

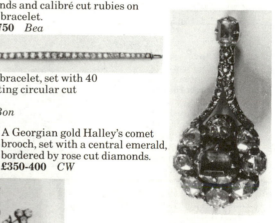

A Victorian gold hinged bangle, set with diagonal rows of coral and half pearls, interspersed with rose diamonds.
£600-700 *WW*

A diamond line bracelet, set with 40 slightly graduating circular cut diamonds.
£1,100-1,300 *Bon*

A Georgian gold Halley's comet brooch, set with a central emerald, bordered by rose cut diamonds.
£350-400 *CW*

A gold, opal and diamond brooch, pavé set with brilliant and rose cut diamonds, oval and circular opals.
£550-700 *Bea*

A gold brooch, by Castellani, set with a grey agate scarab, signed, small chips, 19thC.
£550-600 *WW*

A Victorian gold and shell cameo bracelet.
£800-900 *Bon*

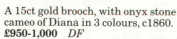

A 15ct gold brooch, with onyx stone cameo of Diana in 3 colours, c1860.
£950-1,000 *DF*

A Victorian diamond feather brooch.
£1,900-2,000 *Cre*

A gold brooch with rose diamonds, 19thC.
£450-500 *DWB*

A carved shell cameo, 19thC, 2¼in (6cm).
£130-160 *DWB*

A Victorian diamond frog brooch, set with cushion and rose diamonds.
£500-550 *Bon*

A Victorian gold, white and dark blue enamelled knot brooch with 17 diamonds, and a pair of similar earrings.
£600-650 *DWB*

A Victorian diamond and sapphire bee brooch.
£2,650-2,750 *DWB*

A Victorian mosaic demi parure, consisting of a brooch/pendant, earrings and two buttons, in original fitted case, Italian, c1870.
£1,700-2,000 *VP*

PEARLS

★ pearls have been a favourite form of adornment since the earliest recorded times. Whether they are the beautiful natural oriental pearls taken from the oyster beds of the Far East, or the exquisite little fresh water seed pearls found in profusion in our British rivers since early Roman times, or the cultured pearl, which has been imported and sold in this country since the 1920's, all are highly desirable and all are found inside a shell fish or mollusc

★ the only difference between a natural pearl and a cultured pearl is that in a cultured pearl, the nucleus has been introduced by hand to the oyster, and with a natural pearl it has been formed by accident

★ all pearls from shell fish will feel slightly 'gritty' when rubbed gently along your natural teeth, whilst any artificial variety will feel smooth

★ the only method of identifying natural pearls from the cultured variety is by x-ray or with an endiscope in a gem testing laboratory

A Victorian rose diamond, sapphire, ruby and half pearl butterfly brooch, mounted in silver and gold.
£600-650 *C*

A late Victorian gold, silver, and diamond flower brooch, pavé set with brilliant and rose cut stones.
£1,900-2,000 *Bea*

A 15ct Victorian snake bracelet, with emerald eyes, cabochon garnet, boxed.
£900-950 *AGA*

A Victorian diamond set bee brooch, with ruby eyes.
£600-650 *WW*

◁ An enamelled and diamond mounted regimental brooch, of the Royal Poona Horse Regiment, decorated with red enamel and pavé set with rose diamonds.
£250-300 *Bea*

A diamond and blue enamel lapel brooch, with rose diamond and blue enamel oval brooch with central initial and coronet.
£350-400 *C*

A Victorian diamond and pearl brooch.
£1,000-1,100 *DWB*

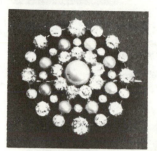

A diamond brooch, set with 10 varying sized collet set circular cut diamonds within pavé set diamond scrollwork.
£2,500-3,500 *Bon*

A pearl and diamond target brooch/pendant.
£1,000-1,100 *WW*

A modern 9ct gold diamond and ruby bar brooch, in the form of a diamond set fox mask with ruby eyes set on a riding crop.
£200-250 *L*

A diamond and ruby brooch, with central ruby flanked by two rows of full cut brilliant diamonds.
£2,200-2,500 *FHF*

◁ A piece of silver cocktail jewellery.
£200-250 *Rev*

A fine quality aquamarine and diamond brooch, with 5 central graduated emerald-cut aquamarines flanked by full brilliant diamonds, terminating at either end with lozenge shaped aquamarines, by Cartier, London.
£2,500-3,000 *FHF*

A platinum and diamond bow.
£2,000-2,500 *AGA*

A pair of Victorian gold carbuncle and diamond fly pendant earrings, inscribed and dated 1871, in original fitted case.
£600-650 *Bon*

A pair of Victorian gold earrings.
£300-350 *L*

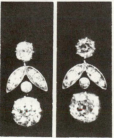

◁ A pair of diamond flower pendant earrings.
£1,700-1,900 *WW*

A pair of sapphire earclips, each approx. 5 carats with 10 stone diamond surrounds.
£4,100-4,300 *GSP*

A pair of 18ct amethyst and diamond earrings.
£700-750

And a 15ct amethyst brooch.
£550-600   *PU*

A Turkoman Afghanistan necklace, 19thC.
£450-500   *TAL*

A topaz necklace and cruciform pendant with earrings en suite, possibly Italian.
£900-1,000   *L*

A pair of diamond pendant earrings, each with a line of square set brilliants, suspending a single pear shaped diamond in millegrain setting.
£4,500-6,000   *Bea*

An 18ct gold and diamond snake necklace, c1940's.
£5,000-5,500   *VP*

An 18ct ruby and diamond necklace, c1940's.
£2,500-3,000   *RR*

A late Victorian diamond necklace.
£3,500-4,000   *Gil*

A late Victorian gold and diamond rivière with 62 graduated 'old mine' brilliants in silver collet settings.
£3,500-4,000   *Bea*

An unusual German 'angel' pendant necklace, by Paul Wunderlich, with a central formalised and headless female form with hinged outspread wings on wirework collar, with original receipt for 1979, and fitted case.
£250-300   *P*

A gold enamel and pearl pendant cross by Carlo Giulliano, c1860.
£2,500-3,000   *DF*

A French 18ct gold enamel and red pearl frame stone cameo, c1850.
£2,500-3,000   *DF*

A Victorian 29 stone diamond circular target pendant suspended on a diamond set knife edge bar, with detachable brooch pin.
£1,500-2,000   *FHF*

A gold and enamel pendant, set with diamonds and pearls, by Arthur Phillips, c1860.
£1,250-1,500   *DF*

A gold enamel and pearl pendant cross by Carlo Giulliano, c1860.
£2,200-2,500   *DF*

An Edwardian style silver and gold mounted diamond open work pendant, with centre heart shaped opal and opal drop, on silver neckchain.
£450-500 *FHF*

A gold, silver and diamond circular locket pendant, pavé set with 'old mine' brilliant cut stones, the reverse with glazed cover, late 19thC.
£1,100-1,200 *Bea*

An Edwardian gold, peridot and diamond pendant, of openwork scroll design, pavé and millegrain set with brilliant and rose cut diamonds, key-stone, octagonal and marquise-cut peridots.
£750-850 *Bea*

A diamond set yoke pendant, the 2 drops each with 2 diamonds, on a fine link necklet.
£1,100-1,200 *WW*

A gold pendant with enamel portrait of a gypsy, set with rose diamonds, with black enamel and rose diamond surround, the whole mounted on a diamond set pendant with non-contemporary decoration and chain loop.
£800-900 *FHF*

A single stone diamond ring, the circular cut diamond in yellow and white 18ct gold mount.
£2,600-3,000 *Bon*

A gold and half stone shell-shaped pendant, with pierced textured gold mount, applied with diamond set scrollwork.
£300-400 *Bon*

A Victorian diamond and enamel pendant, centred by a 6 pointed rose diamond star within a blue enamel surround, all on a shaped raised panel with white enamel beading, and similar pendant ring.
£600-700 *L*

An emerald and diamond pendant, pavé set with brilliant cut diamonds, calibré and cushion shaped emeralds, on a fine chain.
£1,700-2,000 *Bea*

A diamond footballer charm, set with baguette diamonds, emeralds, sapphires and rubies.
£500-600 *Bon*

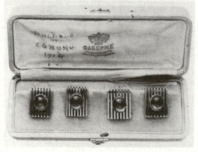

A Faberge set of 4 gold, platinum and sapphire buttons, each with a single oval cabochon sapphire, millegrain set on a cagework frame with bolt rings to convert to a pair of cuff-links, workmaster August Holming, in fitted case.
£4,500-5,000 *Bea*

A single stone diamond ring, the circular cut diamond with pierced diamond shoulders, plain hoop.
£2,300-2,500 *Bon*

757

An early Victorian French silver brooch, set with miniature portrait and coloured pastes.
£125-150 *PVH*

A golden brown amber necklace, restrung in the 'flapper style' of the 1920/30s.
£120-150

A matching pair of earrings with 9ct screw fittings.
£45-65 *PVH*

Amber is the fossilized resin of prehistoric pine trees originating in the Baltic regions. Much of the amber used in Victorian jewellery came from Sicily, whilst quite large amounts have been picked up on the beaches of Norfolk, washed down over a period of time. Always cut 'en cabochon' and often containing the remains of prehistoric insects, vegetation and even fish scales.

Many substances have been produced to simulate precious stones, but in Victorian and Edwardian times great use was made of 'paste' stones, often originating in France. They are made from a very soft lead glass, which when new will pass very well for the 'real thing' in artificial light, but because of its softness will very soon become scratched and lose its original lustre. Often the presence of distinctive 'glass bubbles' will confirm that these stones are artificial.

A Victorian 15ct gold locket, decorated with coloured enamel star design, inset with split seed pearls.
£475-500

A 15ct belcher link neck chain.
£250-300 *PVH*

This must be the most popular design of Victorian locket ever made, and many have stood the test of time by surviving in mint condition, comparing very favourably in price to their modern counterpart. Price will be drastically reduced by any damage or missing stones, etc.

A Boucheron diamond bow.
£2,000-2,500 *AGA*

A very fine 15ct gold citrine intaglio carved seal ring, depicting a slave in prayer with motto in French carved around the edge, 19thC.
£475-500 *PVH*

Seal rings have been a popular form of jewellery since ancient times and have been made in a variety of metals both precious and base, and set with all manner of real and imitation stones including glass. Seal rings can be purchased for as little as £75.

A 15ct gold Victorian brooch/pendant, set with split seed pearls and peridot, in perfect condition.
£375-450 *PVH*

If damaged this item could be bought for about £40 upwards.

This type of brooch was considered highly suitable for a young lady of the Victorian period. It was considered very unladylike for an unmarried woman to wear diamonds, and even if married, it was considered vulgar and ostentatious to wear diamonds in the day time!

DIAMONDS

The 'brilliant cut' for diamonds was invented in the 17th century by a Venetian lapidary named Vincenzo Peruzzi and remained basically much the same for the next 200 years. Most of the diamonds found in Georgian and Victorian jewellery are cut in this way, or if not, the 'rose cut' was used. This is a semi-spherical dome shape of triangular facets (usually 24 or 12 in all) culminating in a point. (Even tiny off-cuts of diamonds were made use of, and were commonly known as 'chips'.) Size was considered of much more importance than colour or quality, and most of the diamonds used in antique jewellery originated in East India or South America. (The stones mined in Brazil sometimes had a definite yellow tinge, and were commonly known as 'Whisky' diamonds for obvious reasons.) With the discovery of diamonds in South Africa in the mid-19th century there was a shift in the whole world market, and to this day the majority of diamonds come from there.

An Italian gold and Roman mosaic pendant cross, with central circular panel with dove motif.
£300-400 *Bea*

An emerald and diamond cluster ring, the cushion shaped emerald in a surround of 16 rose diamonds, 18ct gold shank, c1800, the emerald approx. 1.5ct.
£2,100-2,500   *WW*

An Arts and Crafts pendant, in the manner of Sybil Dunlop, set with cabochons of green stained chalcedony and amethyst, in a mount of vine leaves and grapes, 9cm long.
£200-250   *P*

A five stone diamond half hoop ring, with 8 small brilliant cut diamonds, in a pierced foliate claw setting, with foliate shoulders and 18ct gold shank.
£1,700-2,000   *HSS*

A three stone diamond half hoop ring, claw set with platinum shank.
£1,400-1,600   *HSS*

Auctioneers
in the South of England

AUCTIONEERS

JULIAN DAWSON

LEWES AUCTION ROOMS

Regular sales of
ANTIQUE FURNITURE AND EFFECTS

Weekly sales of
GENERAL FURNITURE, BRIC-A-BRAC etc,
every Monday at 11 am

Auction Offices, 56 High Street. Lewes. Tel. Lewes 478221
Salerooms, Garden Street, Lewes, Sussex.

John Hogbin & Son

Fine Art Salerooms

at

53 High Street
Tenterden
Kent
Tel: (05806) 2241

15 Cattle Market
Sandwich
Kent
Tel: (0304) 611044
(The Drill Hall, The Quay
Sandwich)

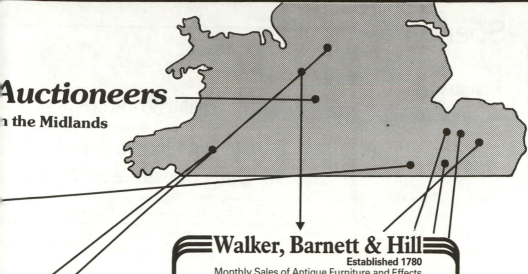

Auctioneers
n the Midlands

Walker, Barnett & Hill
Established 1780

Monthly Sales of Antique Furniture and Effects
in Town Centre Salerooms
Free Inspection and Advice Given
Transport and Storage Arranged
Complete House Clearances
Valuations for Insurance, Probate and Family Division
Specialists in Country House Sales No Buyers' Premium

3-5 WATERLOO ROAD, WOLVERHAMPTON
Wolverhampton (0902) 773531
Offices also at Bridgnorth, Newport and Market Drayton

Sworders
stablished 1782

**Chequers, 19 North Street,
Bishop's Stortford,
Hertfordshire CM23 2LF
Telephone: (0279) 52441 (10 lines)**

G.E. Sworder & Sons

*f you wish to realise the value of your possessions please
elephone David Fletcher, A.R.I.C.S., for free advice.
Ve are ideally located less than one hour from London. We
re proud not to charge a buyers premium and are pleased to
ndertake valuations for all purposes.*

Three weekly Sales of Antiques, Silver and Paintings held on
Tuesdays at 10 a.m.

General Sales are held on Saturday mornings fortnightly.
NO BUYERS PREMIUM

Estate Agents, Surveyors,
Valuers, Auctioneers.
Mortgages and Insurance.

Incorporating Ekins, Dilley & Handley

Prudential
Property Services
FINE ARTS & CHATTELS
The Salesroom, Market Square, St. Ives.
Tel: (0480) 68144

Januarys

*REGULAR AUCTIONS — ANTIQUES, OBJETS D'ART,
JEWELLERY, PAINTINGS, SPORTING ITEMS,
FURNITURE, SPECIALIST EQUESTRIAN SALES.*

Rothsay House Galleries
124 High Street
Newmarket
Tel: 668679

Auctioneers
n the Midlands

Warner
Sheppard & Wade
Fine Art Auctioneers and Valuers

THE WARNER AUCTION ROOMS
16-18 HALFORD STREET · LEICESTER LE1 1JB
Telephone (0533) 21613

COLLIERS BIGWOOD & BEWLAY

WEEKLY SALES OF Victorian, Edwardian and Later Household Goods and Shipping Furniture, Ceramics and Glassware
SPECIALISED MONTHLY SALES OF Period Furniture and Works of Art, Textiles, Rugs, Silver Jewellery, Coins and Oil Paintings
WELL ESTABLISHED SPECIALIST SALES four times a year of Wines, Spirits and Collectors items
PERIODIC SALES OF Veteran, Vintage and Classic Cars, Motorbikes, Bicycles and Memorabilia
VALUATIONS undertaken for all purposes, distance immaterial
SALES on the premises and conducted throughout the U.K.
OPEN 5½ days per week

Fine Art Auctioneers & Valuers
Fine Art Saleroom, The Old School, Tiddington, Stratford-upon-Avon
Warwickshire CV37 7AW
Tel: 0789 69415
Also at London, Birmingham Banbury & Oxford

Aylsham Salerooms

PICTURES · PICTURES · PICTUR

Our modern Saleroom centre caters for all types of Sales. ANTIQUES inc. furniture, porcelain, silver etc. held every 3 weeks.
PICTURE SALES bi monthly.
Book Sales periodically.
"Visiting Norfolk, interested in Auctions, then we shall be pleased to see you".
Weekly Sales of household and shipping furniture and effects.
Sales Calendar and further details from

G.A.KEY
FINE ART AUCTIONEERS
MARKET PLACE
AYLSHAM 733195

AUCTIONEERS

Loves
of Perth · *est. 1869*

Auctioneers and Valuers

The Auction "Centre" of Scotland

Regular Sales of Antique and Decorative Items

Weekly (every Friday) Sales of Victoriana, Household and Collectors' Items

We do not charge a buyers premium

Valuations undertaken for all purposes including Insurance, Probate and Family Division

For further information please contact:–
**The Auction Galleries
52 Canal Street, Perth
Tel: (0738) 24111
Telex: 76224**

Tiffen King Nicholson
Fine Art & Antiques Saleroom

*Regular Catalogue Sales of
Antiques and Works of Art*

*Illustrated Catalogues — £9 per annum
Weekly Sales of Household
Furniture and Effects*

**12 Lowther Street · CARLISLE · CA3 8DA
Telephone: (0228) 25259**

 Wright-Manley

Beeston Sales Centre, Near Tarporley, Cheshire

Regular Furniture and Fine Art Sales

Fortnightly Collective Sales of Antique and Modern Furniture

Information: Mr. William T. Witter
Tel: (08293) 2151

Boulton & Cooper Ltd

 Fine Art Auctioneers
Estate Agents
Auctioneers

Founded in 1801

**St. Michael's House, Market Place
Malton, North Yorkshire
Tel: (0653) 2151**

STANILAND'S
WILLIAM H. BROWN

CHARTERED SURVEYORS ★ AUCTIONEERS ★ VALUERS ★ ESTATE AGENTS

Regular Sales of Antiques and Works of Art

**STANILANDS WM. H. BROWN
28 NETHER HALL ROAD, DONCASTER, YORKSHIRE
TEL. (0302) 67766 & 27121**

H.C.CHAPMAN & SON
Chartered Surveyors   Established 1903
MEMBERS OF THE SOCIETY   OF FINE ART AUCTIONEERS

**MONTHLY COLLECTIVE
ANTIQUE SALES**

**SPECIALIST
SALES OF FINE ART
SILVER, PLATE & JEWELLERY**

**MONTHLY SALES OF
VICTORIAN AND LATER
SHIPPING FURNITURE & BRIC-A-BRAC**

Weekly Sales of Modern Household Furnishings

Illustrated Antique & Special Sale Catalogues available on annual subscription

Also mailing list for Specialist Requirements

Town Centre Saleroom next to the Multi-storey Car-park

H.C.CHAPMAN & SON
Estate Office & Salerooms:
The Auction Mart, North St.

Tel: Scarborough (0723) 372424

Auctioneers

Scotland and the North of England

AUCTIONEERS

Tennant's of Yorkshire

ANTIQUE AND FINE ART AUCTIONEERS

ESTATE AGENTS · SURVEYORS · VALUERS

Head office: 26-27 Market Place · Leyburn
North Yorkshire DL8 5AS
Telephone: Wensleydale (0969) 23451

Thomas Watson & Son

Est 1840

General Antique Sales - Monthly (Cat. Sub. £10.00)
House Contents Sales - Twice Weekly

Auctioneers & Valuers
NORTHUMBERLAND STREET,
DARLINGTON DL3 7HJ

J R Parkinson Son and Hamer Auctions

Auctioneers
Fine Art, Antique & Modern Furnishings

**THE AUCTION ROOMS, ROCHDALE ROAD
(KERSHAW STREET), BURY
Tel: (061) 761 1612 & 761 7372**

Dacre, Son & Hartley

At the entrance to the Yorkshire Dales
AUCTIONEERS OF FURNITURE AND FINE ARTS
SINCE THE REIGN OF GEORGE IV.
Regular Specialist and General Shipping Sales at Victoria
Hall Salerooms, Little Lane, Ilkley.

NO BUYERS PREMIUM

Offices:– 1-5 The Grove, Ilkley, tel. (0943) 600655

771

DIRECTORY OF AUCTIONEERS

This directory is by no means complete. Any auctioneer who holds frequent sales should contact us for inclusion in the 1988 Edition. Entries must be received by April 1987. There is, of course, no charge for this listing.

LONDON

Allen of Lee Ltd.,
165 Lee High Road, SE13
Tel: 01-852 3145

Bonhams, Montpelier Galleries,
Montpelier Street, Knightsbridge,
SW7
Tel: 01-584 9161

Camden Auctions,
The Saleroom, Hoppers Road,
Winchmore Hill, N21
Tel: 01-886 1550

Christie Manson & Woods Ltd.,
8 King Street, St. James's, SW1
Tel: 01-839 9060

Christie's Robson Lowe,
47 Duke Street, London, SW1
Tel: 01-839 4034/5

Christie's South Kensington Ltd.,
85 Old Brompton Road, SW7
Tel: 01-581 7611

Colney Hatch Auctions,
54/56 High Street, Hornsey, N8
Tel: 01-340 5334

Forrest & Co.,
79-85 Cobbold Road, Leytonstone,
E11
Tel: 01-534 2931

Stanley Gibbons Auctions Ltd.,
399 Strand, WC2
Tel: 01-836 8444

Glending & Co.,
Blenstock House, 7 Blenheim
Street, New Bond Street, W1
Tel: 01-493 2445

Harmers of London Stamp
Auctioneers Ltd.,
91 New Bond Street, W1
Tel: 01-629 0218

Harvey's Auctions Ltd.,
14, 16 and 18 Neal Street, WC2
Tel: 01-240 1464/5/6/7

Jackson-Stops & Staff,
14 Curzon Street, W1
Tel: 01-499 6291

Lefevre & Partners (Auctioneers)
Ltd.,
The Persian Carpet Galleries, 152
Brompton Road, SW3
Tel: 01-584 5516

London Bridge Auction,
6/8 Park Street, London Bridge,
SE1
Tel: 01-407 9577

Lots Road Chelsea Auction
Galleries,
71 Lots Road, Worlds End,
Chelsea, SW10
Tel: 01-351 7771/01-352 2349

Newington Green Auctions,
55 Green Lanes, N16
Tel: 01-226 4442 & 0368

Phillips,
Blenstock House,
7 Blenheim Street, New Bond
Street, W1
Tel: 01-629 6602

Rippon Boswell & Co.,
The Arcade, Sth. Kensington
Station, SW7
Tel: 01-589 4242

Sotheby's,
34-35 New Bond Street, W1
Tel: 01-493 8080

Southgate Antique Auction
Rooms,
Rear of Southgate Town Hall,
Green Lanes, Palmers Green, N13
Tel: 01-886 7888

Waltham Forest Auctions,
101 Hoe Street, E17
Tel: 01-520 2998

GREATER LONDON

Bonsor Penningtons,
82 Eden Street, Kingston, Surrey
Tel: 01-546 0022

Croydon Auctions Rooms (Rosan &
Co.),
144-150 London Road, Croydon
Tel: 01-688 1123/4/5

Parkins,
18 Malden Road, Cheam, Surrey
Tel: 01-644 6633 & 6127

AVON

Aldridges, Bath,
The Auction Galleries, 130-132
Walcot Street, Bath
Tel: (0225) 62830 & 62839

Blessley Davis,
Chartered Surveyors, 42 High
Street, Chipping Sodbury, Bristol
Tel: (0454) 312848/313033

Hoddell Pritchard,
Sixways, Clevedon
Tel: (0272) 876699

Lalonde Bros. & Parham,
71 Oakfield Road, Clifton, Bristol
Tel: (0272) 734052
also at:
Station Road, Weston-super-Mare
Tel: (0934) 33174

Osmond Tricks,
Regent Street Auction Rooms,
Clifton, Bristol
Tel: (0272) 737201

Phillips Auction Rooms of Bath,
1 Old King Street, Bath
Tel: (0225) 310609 & 319709

Taviner's Auction Rooms,
Prewett Street, Redcliffe, Bristol
Tel: (0272) 25996

Woodspring Auction Rooms,
Churchill Road, Weston-super-
Mare
Tel: (0934) 28419

BEDFORDSHIRE

Peacock,
The Auction Centre, 26 Newnham
Street, Bedford
Tel: (0234) 66366

BERKSHIRE

Chancellors Hollingsworths,
31 High Street, Ascot
Tel: (0990 27101

Dreweatts,
Donnington Priory, Donnington,
Newbury
Tel: (0635) 31234

Holloway's,
12 High Street, Streatley, Reading
Tel: (0491) 872318

Martin & Pole (incorporating
Watts & Son Estd. 1846),
Chartered Surveyors, 5a & 7
Broad Street, Wokingham
Tel: (0734) 780777

Neates,
108 High Street, Hungerford
Tel: (0488) 82808

Thimbleby & Shorland,
31 Great Knollys Street, Reading
Tel: (0734) 508611

Duncan Vincent Fine Art &
Chattel Auctioneers,
105 London Street, Reading
Tel: (0734) 594748

BUCKINGHAMSHIRE

Hetheringtons, Pretty & Ellis,
The Amersham Auction Rooms,
Turret House,
125 Station Road, Amersham
Tel: (02403) 29292/3

Geo. Wigley & Sons,
Winslow Sale Room, Market
Square, Winslow
Tel: (029 671) 2717

CAMBRIDGESHIRE

Cheffins Grain & Chalk,
2 Clifton Road and 49-53 Regent
Street, Cambridge
Tel: (0223) 358721

Comins,
25 Market Place, Ely
Tel: (0353) 2265

Ekins Dilley & Handley
(Prudential Property Services),
The Saleroom, Market Square, St.
Ives, Huntingdon
Tel: (0480) 68144

Grounds & Co.,
2 Nene Quay, Wisbech
Tel: (0945) 585041

Hammond & Co.,
Cambridge Place, off Hills Road,
Cambridge
Tel: (0223) 356067

Maxey & Son,
1-3 South Brink, Wisbech
Tel: (0945) 583123/4

CHESHIRE

Andrew, Hilditch & Son,
19 The Square, Sandbach
Tel: (0270) 762048/767246

Bridgfords Ltd,
The Alderley Saleroom, 1 Heyes
Lane, Alderley Edge
Tel: (0625) 585347

Brocklehurst,
King Edward Street, Macclesfield
Tel: (0625) 29236

Burling Morrison,
St. Mary's Saleroom, Buxton Old
Road, Disley
Tel: (06632) 4854

Jackson-Stops & Staff,
25 Nicholas Street, Chester
Tel: (0244) 28361

Frank R. Marshall & Co.,
Marshall House, Church Hill,
Knutsford
Tel: (0565) 53284/53461

Phillips in Chester,
New House, 150 Christleton Road,
Chester
Tel: (0244) 313936

Reeds Rains,
Antiques & Fine Art Auctioneers,
Trinity House, 114 Northenden
Road, Sale, Manchester
Tel: (061 962) 9237 & (061 969)
7173

Sotheby's,
Booth Mansion, 28-30 Watergate
Street, Chester
Tel: (0244) 315531

Peter Wilson,
Victoria Gallery, Market Street,
Nantwich
Tel: (0270) 623878

Wright Manley,
Beeston Sales Centre, 63 High
Street, Tarporley
Tel: (0829) 260318

CLEVELAND

Norman Hope & Partners,
2 South Road, Hartlepool
Tel: (0429) 267828

Lithgow Sons & Partners,
The Auction Houses, Station Road,
Stokesley, Middlesborough
Tel: (0642) 710158 & 710326

Thomas Watson & Son,
North Ormesby Road,
Middlesbrough
Tel: (0642) 242979

CORNWALL

W. H. Cornish,
Central Auction Rooms, Castle
Street, Truro
Tel: (0872) 72968

Eric Distin & Dolton,
58 Fore Street, Saltash
Tel: (07555) 2355
also at:
7 New Road, Callington
Tel: (0579) 83322
also at:
18 Dean Street, Liskeard
Tel: (0579) 44366

W. H. Lane & Son,
Fine Art Auctioneers & Valuers,
St. Mary's Auction Rooms,
64 Morrab Road, Penzance
Tel: (0736) 61447

David Lay, A.S.V.A.,
7 Morrab Road, Penzance
Tel: (0736) 61414

Miller & Co.,
Antique & Fine Art Auctioneers,
Lemon Quay Auction Rooms,
Lemon Quay, Truro
Tel: (0872) 74211

Phillips Cornwall,
Cornubia Hall, Par
Tel: (072 681) 4047

Rowse Jeffery & Watkins,
5 Fore Street, Lostwithiel
Tel: (0208) 872245

Western Galleries t/as Old Town
Hall Auctions,
High Street, Falmouth
Tel: (0326) 319437

CUMBRIA

Mitchells,
Fairfield House, Cockermouth
Tel: (0900) 822016

Alfred Mossops & Co.,
Loughrigg Villa, Kelsick Road,
Ambleside
Tel: (09663) 3015

James Thompson,
64 Main Street, Kirkby Lonsdale
Tel: (0468) 71555

Thomson, Roddick & Laurie,
24 Lowther Street, Carlisle
Tel: (0228) 28939 & 39636

Tiffen, King & Nicholson,
12 Lowther Street, Carlisle
Tel: (0228) 25259

DERBYSHIRE

Noel Wheatcroft & Son,
The Matlock Auction Gallery,
39 Dale Road, Matlock
Tel: (0629) 4591

DEVON

Bearnes,
Rainbow, Avenue Road, Torquay
Tel: (0803) 26277

Eric Distin & Dolton,
2 Bretonside, Plymouth
Tel: (0752) 663046

Peter J. Eley,
Western House, 98-100 High
Street, Sidmouth
Tel: (03955) 2552

Robin A. Fenner & Co.,
51 Bannawell Street, Tavistock
Tel: (0822) 4974

Gribble, Booth & Taylor,
West Street, Axminster
Tel: (0297) 32323

Charles Head & Son,
113 Fore Street, Kingsbridge
Tel: (0548) 2352

Michael G. Matthews,
Devon Fine Art Auction House,
Dowell Street, Honiton
Tel: (0404) 41872/3137

Michael Newman,
The Central Auction Rooms,
Kinterbury House, St. Andrew's
Cross, Plymouth
Tel: (0752) 669298

Phillips,
Alphin Brook Road, Alphington,
Exeter
Tel: (0392) 39025/6

Rendells,
Stone Park, Ashburton
Tel: (0364) 53017

G. S. Shobrook & Co.,
20 Western Approach, Plymouth
Tel: (0752) 663341

John Smale & Co.,
Chartered Surveyors &
Auctioneers,
19 Cross Street, Barnstaple
Tel: (0271) 42000/42916

Spencer-Thomas & Woolland,
Harbour Road Salerooms, Seaton
Tel: (0297) 22453

David Symonds, F.S.V.A.,
The Estate Office, High Street,
Crediton
Tel: (03632) 2700/4100

Taylors,
Honiton Galleries, 205 High
Street, Honiton
Tel: (0404) 2404

Taylor, Lane & Creber,
The Western Auction Rooms,
38 North Hill, Plymouth
Tel: (0752) 670700

Ward & Chowen,
1 Church Lane, Tavistock
Tel: (0822) 2458

Whitton & Laing,
32 Okehampton Street, Exeter
Tel: (0392) 52621

DORSET
S. W. Cottee & Son,
The Market, East Street,
Wareham
Tel: (09295) 2826

Hy. Duke & Son,
Fine Art Salerooms, Weymouth
Ave., Dorchester
Tel: (0305) 65080
also at:
The Weymouth Saleroom, St.
Nicholas Street, Weymouth
Tel: (0305) 783488

House & Son,
Lansdowne House, Christchurch
Road, Bournemouth
Tel: (0202) 26232

John Jeffery & Son,
Auctioneers, Minster House, The
Commons, Shaftesbury
Tel: (0747) 3331

Morey & Sons,
50 East Street, Bridport
Tel: (0308) 22078

Riddetts of Bournemouth,
Richmond Hill, Bournemouth
Square, Bournemouth
Tel: (0202) 25686

COUNTY DURHAM
G. H. Edkins & Son,
122 Newgate Street, Bishop
Auckland
Tel: (0388) 603095

Thomas Watson & Son,
Northumberland Street,
Darlington
Tel: (0325) 462559

ESSEX
Abridge Auction Rooms,
Market Place, Abridge
Tel: (037881) 2107/3113

Ambrose,
149 High Road, Loughton
Tel: 01-508 2121

Cooper Hirst,
Goldlay House, Parkway,
Chelmsford
Tel: (0245) 58141

Spurgeon & Gilchrist,
1st Floor, Tokenhouse Chambers,
Rosemary Road, Clacton-on-Sea
Tel: (0255) 422472

John Stacey & Sons,
Leigh Auction Rooms, 86-90 Pall
Mall, Leigh-on-Sea
Tel: (0702) 77051

Vosts' Fine Art Auctioneers,
Layer Marney, Colchester
Tel: (0206) 331005

Edwin Watson & Son,
1 Mark Street, Saffron Walden
Tel: (0799) 22058

J. M. Welch & Son,
Old Town Hall, Great Dunmow
Tel: (0371) 2117/8

GLOUCESTERSHIRE
Bruton, Knowles & Co.,
111 Eastgate Street, Gloucester
Tel: (0452) 21267

Fraser Glennie & Partners,
The Old Rectory, Siddington, Nr.
Cirencester
Tel: (0285) 3938

Hobbs & Chambers,
Market Place, Cirencester
Tel: (0285) 4736
also at:
15 Royal Crescent, Cheltenham
Tel: (0242) 513722

Jackson-Stops & Staff,
Dollar Street House, Cirencester
Tel: (0285) 3334

Ken Lawson t/as Specialised
Postcard Auctions,
25 Gloucester Street, Cirencester
Tel: (0285) 69057

Mallams,
26 Grosvenor Street, Cheltenham
Tel: (0242) 35712

Moore, Allen & Innocent,
33 Castle Street, Cirencester
Tel: (0285) 61831

Sandoe Luce Panes,
The Wotton Auction Rooms,
Tabernacle Road, Wotton-under-
Edge
Tel: (0453) 844733

HAMPSHIRE
Andover Saleroom,
41A London Street, Andover
Tel: (0264) 64820

Austin & Wyatt,
79 High Street, Fareham
Tel: (0329) 234211/4

Michael G. Baker, F.S.V.A.,
Beales Furniture & Fine Art
Dept.,
13a The Hundred, Romsey
Tel: (0794) 513331

Elliott & Green,
The Salerooms, Emsworth Road,
Lymington
Tel: (0590) 77225

Fox & Sons,
5 & 7 Salisbury Street,
Fordingbridge
Tel: (0425) 52121

Stanley Gibbons Auctions Ltd.,
5 Parkside, Christchurch Road,
Ringwood
Tel: (04254) 77107

Hants & Berks Auctions,
40 George Street, Kingsclere
Tel: (0635) 298181
also at:
Heckfield Village Hall, Heckfield,
Berks

Jacobs & Hunt,
Lavant Street, Petersfield
Tel: (0730) 62744/5

Martin & Stratford,
The Auction Mart, Market Square,
Alton
Tel: (0420) 84402

May & Son,
18 Bridge Street, Andover
Tel: (0264) 23417

D. M. Nesbit & Co.,
7 Clarendon Road, Southsea
Tel: (0705) 864321

Onslow Auctioneers
Tel: (0962) 75411

Pearsons (a subsidiary of
Prudential Property Services
Ltd.),
54 Southampton Road, Ringwood
Tel: (04254) 3333
also at:
Walcote Chambers, High Street,
Winchester
Tel: (0962) 64444

HEREFORD &
WORCESTER
Banks & Silvers,
66 Foregate Street, Worcester
Tel: (0905) 23456

Blinkhourn & Co.,
41-43 High Street, Broadway
Tel: (0386) 852456

Coles, Knapp & Kennedy,
Georgian Rooms & Tudor House,
Ross-on-Wye, Hereford
Tel: (0989) 62227/63553/4

Maurice Fellows,
6 The Tything, Worcester
Tel: (0905) 27755

Andrew Grant, F.R.I.C.S.,
59/60 Foregate Street, Worcester
Tel: (0905) 52310

Arthur G. Griffiths & Son,
57 Foregate Street, Worcester
Tel: (0905) 26464

Philip Laney & Jolly,
12a Worcester Road, Gt. Malvern
Tel: (06845) 63121/2

Lear & Lear,
71 Church Street, Malvern
Tel: (06845) 61767/8
also at:
46 Foregate Street, Worcester
Tel: (0905) 25184/25194/25494

Phipps & Pritchard,
Bank Buildings, Kidderminster
Tel: (0562) 2244/6 & 2187

Russell, Baldwin & Bright,
Fine Art Saleroom, Ryelands
Road, Leominster
Tel: (0568) 3897

Stooke, Hill & Co.,
Antiques & Fine Art Auctioneers,
Imperial Chambers,
24 Windemarsh Street, Hereford
Tel: (0432) 272413

HERTFORDSHIRE
George Jackson & Son,
Paynes Park House, Paynes Park,
Hitchin
Tel: (0462) 55212

M. & B. Nesbitt,
The Antique Centre, 23 Hydeway,
Welwyn Garden City
Tel: (07073) 34901

Norris & Duvall,
106 The Fore Street, Hertford
Tel: (0992) 52249

Pamela & Barry Auctions,
The Village Hall, High Street,
Sandridge, St. Albans
Tel: (0727) 61180

G. E. Sworder & Sons,
Chequers, 19 North Street,
Bishops Stortford
Tel: (0279) 52441

Watsons,
Water Lane, Bishops Stortford
Tel: (0279) 52361/4

HUMBERSIDE
NORTH
Gilbert Baitson, F.S.V.A.,
The Edwardian Auction Galleries,
194 Anlaby Road, Hull
Tel: (0482) 223355/645241/865831

Broader & Spencer,
18 Quay Road, Bridlington
Tel: (0262) 70355/6

Dee & Atkinson,
The Exchange, Driffield
Tel: (0377) 43151

H. Evans & sons,
1 Parliament Street, Hull
Tel: (0482) 23033

F. A. Larard & Sons,
18 Wednesday Market, Beverley
Tel: (0482) 868555

HUMBERSIDE
NORTH
Dickinson, Davy & Markham,
10 Wrawby Street, Brigg
Tel: (0652) 53666

ISLE OF MAN
Chrystals Auctions,
St. James Chambers, Athol Street,
Douglas
Tel: (0624) 73986

ISLE OF WIGHT
Sir Francis Pittis & Son,
Cross Street Salerooms, Newport
Tel: (0983) 523812

Way, Riddett & Co.,
Town Hall Chambers, Lind Street,
Ryde
Tel: (0983) 62255

KENT
Albert Andrews Auctions & Sales,
Maiden Lane, Crayford, Dartford
Tel: (0322) 528868

Bracketts,
27-29 High Street, Tunbridge
Wells
Tel: (0892) 33733

Butler & Hatch Waterman,
102 High Street, Tenterden
Tel: (05806) 2083/3233

Cobbs, Burrows & Day,
39/41 Bank Street, Ashford
Tel: (0233) 24321

Geering & Colyer,
22-24 High Street, Tunbridge
Wells
Tel: (0892) 25136

Stewart Gore,
100-102 Northdown Road,
Margate
Tel: (0843) 221528/9

Hobbs Parker,
Romney House, Ashford Market,
Elwick Road, Ashford
Tel: (0233) 22222

John Hogbin & Son,
53 High Street, Tenterden
Tel: (05806) 3200
also at:
The Sandwich Sale Room, The
Drill Hall, The Quay, Sandwich
Tel: (0304) 611044

Ibbett Mosely,
125 High Street, Sevenoaks
Tel: (0732) 452246

Kent Sales,
'Giffords', Holmesdale Road, South
Darenth
Tel: (0322) 864919

Lawrence Butler & Co.
(incorporating F. W. Butler & Co.),
Fine Art Salerooms, Butler House,
86 High Street, Hythe, Kent
Tel: (0303) 66022/3

One One Five Auctioneers,
R. B. Lloyd, 115 Main Road,
Sutton-at-Hone, Dartford
Tel: (0322) 862112

Parsons, Welch & Cowell,
49 London Road, Sevenoaks
Tel: (0732) 451211/4

Phillips,
Folkestone, Bayle Place, 11 Bayle
Parade, Folkestone
Tel: (0303) 45555

James B. Terson & Son,
27-29 Castle Street, Dover
Tel: (0304) 202173

Ward & Partners,
16 High Street, Hythe
Tel: (0303) 67473

Peter S. Williams, F.S.V.A.,
Auctioneer & Valuer, Orchard
End, Sutton Valence, Maidstone
Tel: (9622) 842350

Worsfolds,
40 Station Road West, Canterbury
Tel: (0227) 68984

LANCASHIRE
Artingstall & Hind,
378-380 Deansgate, Knott Mill,
Manchester
Tel: (061 834) 4559

Capes Dunn & Co.,
The Auction Galleries, 38 Charles
Street, Manchester
Tel: (061 273) 6060

Entwistle Green,
The Galleries, Kingsway, Ansdell,
Lytham St. Annes
Tel: (0253) 735442

Johnson Kelly,
33 Bradshawgate, Bolton
Tel: (0204) 384384

Mckennas, formerly Hothersall,
Forrest, McKenna & Sons,
Bank Salerooms, Harris Court,
Clitheroe
Tel: (0200) 25446/22695

J. R. Parkinson Son & Hamer
Auctions,
The Auction Rooms, Rochdale
Road, Bury
Tel: (061 761) 1612/7372

John E. Pinder & Son,
Stone Bridge, Longridge, Preston
Tel: (077478) 2282

Smythe, Son & Walker,
174 Victoria Road West, Cleveleys
Tel: (0253) 852184 & 854084

LEICESTERSHIRE
Gilding (Fine Arts),
Gumley, Market Harborough
Tel: (053753) 2847

Oadby Auctions,
The Churchgate Saleroom,
25 Churchgate
Tel: (0533) 21416

Snushall Auctions,
The Saleroom, Wordsworth Road
Tel: (0533) 702801

David Stanley Auctions,
Stordon Grange, Osgathorpe,
Loughborough
Tel: (0530) 222320

Walker Walton Hanson,
4 Market Place, Oakham
Tel: (0572) 3377

Warner, Sheppard & Wade,
The Warner Auction Rooms,
16/18 Halford Street, Leicester
Tel: (0533) 21613

LINCOLNSHIRE
Brogden & Co.,
38/39 Silver Street, Lincoln
Tel: (0522) 31321

William H. Brown,
Fine Art Dept., Westgate Hall,
Westgate, Grantham
Tel: (0476) 68861

Earl & Lawrence,
55 Northgate, Sleaford
Tel: (0529) 302946

James Eley & Son,
1 Main Ridge West, Boston
Tel: (0205) 61687

Henry Spencer & Sons,
38 St. Mary's Street, Stamford
Tel: (0780) 52136

Lyall & Co.,
Auction Salerooms, Spalding
Road, Bourne
Tel: (0788) 422686

Thomas Mawer & Son,
63 Monks Road, Lincoln
Tel: (0522) 24984

Wright & Hodgkinson,
Abbey Road, Bourne
Tel: (07782) 2567

MERSEYSIDE
Ball & Percival,
132 Lord Street and 21 Hoghton
Street, Southport
Tel: (0704) 36900

Kingsley Galleries,
3-4 The Quadrant, Hoylake,
Wirral
Tel: (051 632) 5821

Lavelle and Lavelle,
St. Helens Auction Rooms, The
Galleries, 3 George Street, St.
Helens
Tel: (0744) 59258

Mills & Radcliffe,
101 Union Street, Oldham
Tel: (051 624) 1072

Outhwaite & Litherland,
Kingsway Galleries, Fontenoy
Street, Liverpool
Tel: (051 236) 6561/3

Talbot Wilson & Co. Ltd.,
Tynwald Road, West Kirby, Wirral
Tel: (051 625) 6491

Eldon E. Worrall,
15 Seel Street, Liverpool
Tel: (051 709) 2950

NORFOLK
Noel D. Abel,
32 Norwich Road, Watton
Tel: (0953) 881204

Ewings,
Market Place, Reepham, Norwich
Tel: (0603) 870473

Thos. Wm. Gaze & Son,
10 Market Hill, Diss
Tel: (0379) 51931

Hanbury Williams,
34 Church Street, Cromer
Tel: (0263) 513247

Charles Hawkins & Sons,
Lynn Road, Downham Market
Tel: (0366) 382112

Nigel F. Hedge,
28B Market Place, North
Walsham
Tel: (0692) 402881

Hilhams,
Baker Street, Gorleston, Great
Yarmouth
Tel: (0493) 662152 & 600700

James Norwich Auctions Ltd.,
33 Timberhill, Norwich
Tel: (0603) 624817/625369

G. A. Key,
8 Market Place, Aylsham
Tel: (026373) 3195

Long & Beck,
2 Oak Street, Fakenham
Tel: (0328) 2231

NORTHAMPTON-SHIRE
M. B. Carney, F.S.V.A.,
Brackley Auction Rooms, Hill
Street, Brackley
Tel: (0280) 701124

T. W. Arnold Corby & Co.,
30-32 Brook Street, Raunds
Tel: (0933) 623722

Goldsmith & Bass,
15 Market Place, Oundle
Tel: (0832) 72349

Heathcote Ball & Co.,
Albion Auction Rooms,
Commercial Street
Tel: (0604) 22735

R. L. Lowery & Partners,
24 Bridge Street, Northampton
Tel: (0604) 21561

Southam & Sons,
Corn Exchange, Thrapston,
Kettering
Tel: (08012) 4486

H. Wilford Ltd.,
Midland Road, Wellingborough
Tel: (0933) 222760 & 222762

NOTTINGHAMSHIRE
Edward Bailey & Son,
17 Northgate, Newark
Tel: (0636) 7013141 & 77154

Arthur Johnson & Sons Ltd.,
The Nottingham Auction Rooms,
The Cattle Market, London Road
Tel: (0602) 869128

Neales of Nottingham,
192 Mansfield Road, Nottingham
Tel: (0602) 624141

John Pye & Sons,
Corn Exchange, Cattle Market,
London Road, Nottingham
Tel: (0602) 866261

C. B. Sheppard & Son,
The Auction Galleries,
Chatsworth Street, Sutton-in-
Ashfield
Tel: (0773) 872419

Henry Spencer & Sons Ltd.,
20 The Square, Retford
Tel: (0777) 706767

Walker Walton Hanson
(Auctions),
The Nottingham Auction Mart,
Byard Lane, Bridlesmith Gate,
Nottingham
Tel: (0602) 54272

OXFORDSHIRE
Green & Co.,
33 Market Place, Wantage
Tel: (02357) 3561/2

Holloways,
49 Parsons Street, Banbury
Tel: (0295) 53197/8

Mallams,
Fine Art Auctioneers, 24 St.
Michael's Street, Oxford
Tel: (0865) 241358

Messengers Salerooms,
27 Sheep Street, Bicester
Tel: (0869) 252901

Phillips Inc. Brooks,
39 Park End Street, Oxford
Tel: (0865) 723524

Simmons & Lawrence,
32 Bell Street, Henley-on-Thames
Tel: (0491) 571111

SHROPSHIRE
Bowen Son & Watson,
The Oswestry Auction Rooms,
35 Bailey Street, Oswestry
Tel: (0691) 652367
also at:
Ellesmere
Tel: (0691) 712534

Cooper & Green,
3 Barker Street, Shrewsbury
Tel: (0743) 50081

John German,
43 High Street, Shrewsbury
Tel: (0743) 69661/4

Hall, Wateridge & Owen,
Welsh Bridge Salerooms,
Shrewsbury
Tel: (0743) 60212

McCartneys,
25 Corve Street, Ludlow
Tel: (0584) 2636

Nock, Deighton & Son,
10 Broad Street, Ludlow
Tel: (0584) 2364/3760

Perry & Phillips,
Newmarket Salerooms,
Newmarket Buildings, Listley
Street, Bridgnorth
Tel: (07462) 2248

SOMERSET
Cooper & Tarrant Ltd.,
44a Commercial Road, Shepton
Mallet
Tel: (0749) 2607 & 2624

Dores,
The Auction Mart, Vicarage
Street, Frome
Tel: (0373) 62257

W. R. J. Greenslade Co.,
13 Hamet Street, Taunton
Tel: (0823) 77121
also at:
Priory Saleroom, Winchester
Street, Taunton

King Miles,
25 Market Place, Wells
Tel: (0749) 73002

Lawrence Fine Art of Crewkerne,
South Street, Crewkerne
Tel: (0460) 73041

The London Cigarette Card Co.
Ltd.,
Sutton Road, Somerton
Tel: (0458) 73452

Nuttall Richards & Co.,
The Square, Axbridge
Tel: (0934) 723969

Phillips, Sanders & Stubbs,
32 The Avenue, Minehead
Tel: (0643) 2281/3

Wellington Salerooms, Mantle
Street, Wellington
Tel: (082347) 4815

STAFFORDSHIRE
Bagshaws,
17 High Street, Uttoxeter
Tel: (08893) 2811

Hall & Lloyd,
Auctioneers, South Street Auction
Rooms, Stafford
Tel: (0785) 58176

Louis Taylor & Sons,
Percy Street, Hanley, Stoke-on-
Trent
Tel: (0782) 260222

Wintertons,
St. Mary's Chambers, Lichfield
Tel: (0543) 263256

SUFFOLK
Abbotts (East Anglia) Ltd.,
The Hill, Wickham Market,
Woodbridge
Tel: (0728) 746321

Boardman Fine Art Auctioneers,
Station Road Corner, Haverhill
Tel: (0440) 703784

Diamond, Mills & Co.,
117 Hamilton Road, Felixstowe
Tel: (0394) 282281

Durrant's,
10 New Market, Beccles
Tel: (0502) 712122

Flick & Son,
Ashford House, Saxmundham
Tel: (0728) 3232/4

Charles Hawkins,
Royal Thoroughfare, Lowestoft
Tel: (0502) 2024

James-in Suffolk,
31 St. John's Street, Bury St.
Edmunds
Tel: (0284) 702415

January,
Rothsay Sale Rooms, 124 High
Street, Newmarket
Tel: (0638) 668679

Lacy Scott,
Fine Art Department, The Auction
Centre, 10 Risbygate Street, Bury
St. Edmunds
Tel: (0284) 63531

Neal Sons & Fletcher,
26 Church Street, Woodbridge
Tel: (03943) 2263/4

Olivers,
23-24 Market Hill, Sudbury
Tel: (0787) 72247

Oxborrows, Arnott & Calver,
14 Church Street, Woodbridge
Tel: (03943) 2244/5

Phillips,
Dover House, Wilsey Street,
Ipswich
Tel: (0473) 55137

Tuohy & Son,
Denmark House, 18 High Street,
Aldeburgh
Tel: (072885) 2066

H. C. Wolton & Son,
6 Whiting Street, Bury St.
Edmunds
Tel: (0284) 61336

SURREY

Clarke Gammon,
The Guildford Auction Rooms,
Bedford Road, Guildford
Tel: (0483) 66458

Cubitt & West,
Millmead, Guildford
Tel: (0483) 504030

Lawrences,
Fine Art Auctioneers, Norfolk
House, 80 High Street,
Bletchingley
Tel: (0883) 843323

Messenger May Baverstock,
93 High Street, Godalming
Tel: (04868) 23567

Stephen R. Thomas,
15 Milton Road, Egham
Tel: (0784) 31122

Wentworth Auction Galleries,
21 Station Approach, Virginia
Water
Tel: (09904) 3711

White & Sons,
Vernon Smith, 104 High Street,
Dorking
Tel: (0306) 887654

Harold Williams Bennett &
Partners,
2-3 South Parade, Merstham,
Redhill
Tel: (07374) 2234/5

P. F. Windibank,
18-20 Reigate Road, Dorking
Tel: (0306) 884556

SUSSEX-EAST

Burstow & Hewett,
Abbey Auction Galleries and
Granary Sale Rooms, Battle
Tel: (04246) 2374

Gorringes Auction Galleries,
15 North Street, Lewes
Tel: (0273) 472503

Graves, Son & Pilcher,
Fine Arts, 71 Church Road, Hove
Tel: (0273) 735266

Edgar Horn,
46-50 South Street, Eastbourne
Tel: (0323) 22801

Raymond P. Inman,
Auction Galleries, 35 & 40 Temple
Street, Brighton
Tel: (0273) 774777

Lewes Auction Rooms (Julian
Dawson),
56 High Street, Lewes
Tel: (0273) 478221

Meads of Brighton,
St. Nicholas Road, Brighton
Tel: (0273) 202997

Vidler & Co.,
Rye Auction Galleries, Cinque
Ports Street, Rye
Tel: (0797) 222124

Wallis & Wallis,
West Street Auction Galleries,
Lewes
Tel: (0273) 473137

E. Watson & Sons,
Heathfield Furniture Salerooms,
The Market, Burwash Road,
Heathfield
Tel: (04352) 2132

SUSSEX-WEST

T. Bannister & Co.,
Market Place, Haywards Heath
Tel: (0444) 412402

Peter Cheney,
Western Road Auction Rooms,
Western Road, Littlehampton
Tel: (0903) 722264 & 713418

R. H. Ellis & Sons,
44-46 High Street, Worthing
Tel: (0903) 38999

Fox & Sons,
31 Chatsworth Road, Worthing
Tel: (0903) 205565

Horsham Auction Galleries,
31 The Carfax, Horsham
Tel: (0403) 53837

G. Knight & Son,
West Street, Midhurst
Tel: (073081) 2456

Sotheby's in Sussex,
Summers Place, Billinghurst
Tel: (040381) 3933

Stride & Son,
Southdown House, St. John's
Street, Chichester
Tel: (0243) 780207

Sussex Auction Galleries,
59 Perrymouth Road, Haywards
Heath
Tel: (0444) 414935

Turner, Rudge & Turner,
29 High Street, East Grinstead
Tel: (0342) 313022

Wyatt & Son,
Baffins Hall, Baffins Lane,
Chichester
Tel: (0243) 787548

TYNE & WEAR

Anderson & Garland,
Fine Art Salerooms, Anderson
House, Market Street, Newcastle-
upon-Tyne
Tel: (091) 232 6278

Boldon Auction Galleries,
24a Front Street, East Boldon
Tel: (0783) 372630

Thomas N. Miller,
18-22 Gallowgate, Newcastle-
upon-Tyne
Tel: (091) 232 5617

WARWICKSHIRE

John Briggs & Calder,
133 Long Street, Atherstone
Tel: (08277) 68911

Colliers, Bigwood & Bewlay,
The Old School, Tiddington,
Stratford-upon-Avon
Tel: (0789) 69415

Locke & England,
18 Guy Street, Leamington Spa
Tel: (0926) 27988

Seaman of Rugby,
Auction House, 132 Railway
Terrace, Rugby
Tel: (0788) 2367

WEST MIDLANDS

Allsop Sellers,
8 Hagley Road, Stourbridge
Tel: (0384) 392122

Biddle & Webb,
Icknield Square, Ladywood
Middleway, Birmingham
Tel: 021-455 8042

Cariss Residential,
20-22 High Street, Kings Heath,
Birmingham 14
Tel: 021-444 5311

Ronald E. Clare,
Clare's Auction Rooms, 70 Park
Street, Birmingham
Tel: 021-643 0226

Codsall,
Codsall Village Hall, Codsall,
Wolverhampton
Tel: (0902) 66728

Collins, Son & Harvey North,
42/44 High Street, Erdington,
Birmingham
Tel: 021-382 8870

Frank H. Fellows & Sons,
Bedford House, 88 Hagley Road,
Edgbaston, Birmingham
Tel: 021-454 1261 & 1219

Giles Haywood,
The Auction House, St. Johns
Road, Stourbridge
Tel: (0384) 370891

Henley-in-Arden Auction Sales
Ltd.,
The Estate Office, Warwick Road,
Henley-in-Arden, Solihull
Tel: (05642) 3211

James & Lister Lea,
11 Newhall Street, Birmingham
Tel: 021-236 1751

Adrian Keefe & Partners,
The Auction Room, Trinity Road,
Dudley
Tel: (0384) 73181

Midland Auctions,
14 Lowwood Road, Erdington,
Birmingham
Tel: 021-373 0212

Phillips,
The Old House, Station Road,
Knowle, Solihull
Tel: (05645) 6151

K. Stuart Swash FSVA,
Stamford House,
2 Waterloo Road, Wolverhampton
Tel: (0902) 710626

Walker Barnett & Hill,
3 Waterloo Road, Wolverhampton
Tel: (0902) 773531

Weller & Dufty Ltd.,
141 Bromsgrove Street,
Birmingham
Tel: 021-692 1414

WILTSHIRE

Allen & Harris,
Saleroom & Auctioneers Dept.,
The Planks (off The Square),
Old Town, Swindon
Tel: (0793) 615915

Berry, Powell & Shackell,
46 Market Place, Chippenham
Tel: (0249) 653361

Dennis Pocock & Drewett,
20 High Street, Marlborough
Tel: (0672) 53471

Farrant & Wightman,
Blagrove House, 2/3 Newport
Street, Old Town, Swindon
Tel: (0793) 33301

Geoffrey Taylor & Co.,
13 Market Place, Devizes
Tel: (0380) 2321

Woolley & Wallis,
The Castle Auction Mart, Castle
Street, Salisbury
Tel: (0722) 21711

YORKSHIRE-NORTH

Boulton & Cooper Ltd.,
Forsyth House, Market Place,
Malton
Tel: (0653) 2151

H. C. Chapman & Son,
The Auction Mart, North Street,
Scarborough
Tel: (0723) 372424

Dee & Atkinson,
The Exchange, Driffield
Tel: (0377) 43151

Lawson, Larg,
St. Trinity House, King's Square,
York
Tel: (0904) 21532

Morphets of Harrogate,
4-6 Albert Street, Harrogate
Tel: (0423) 502282

M. Philip H. Scott,
Church Wynd, Burneston, Bedale
Tel: (0677) 23325

Renton & Renton,
16 Albert Street, Harrogate
Tel: (0423) 61531

Stephenson & Son,
43 Gowthorpe, Selby
Tel: (0757) 706707

G. A. Suffield & Co.,
27 Flowergate, Whitby
Tel: (0947) 603433

Geoffrey Summersgill, A.S.V.A.,
8 Front Street, Acomb, York
Tel: (0904) 791131

Tennant's,
26-27 Market Place, Leyburn
Tel: (0969) 23451

Ward Price & Co.,
Royal Auction Rooms, Queen
Street, Scarborough
Tel: (0723) 365455

D. Wombell & Son,
Bell Hall, Escrick, York
Tel: (090 487) 531

YORKSHIRE-SOUTH

Eadon Lockwood & Riddle,
2 St. James' Street, Sheffield
Tel: (0742) 71277

Stanilands, William H. Brown,
28 Nether Hall Road, Doncaster
Tel: (0302) 67766 & 27121

Wilbys,
Regent Street South, Barnsley
Tel: (0266) 206871

YORKSHIRE-WEST

Dacre, Son & Hartley,
1-5 The Grove, Ilkley
Tel: (0943) 600655

de Rome,
12 New John Street, Bradford
Tel: (0274) 734116

Eddisons,
Auction Rooms, 4-6 High Street,
Huddersfield
Tel: (0484) 533151

Laidlaws,
Crown Court Salerooms (off Wood Street), Wakefield
Tel: (0924) 375301

W. Mackay Audsley, F.R.V.A.,
11 Morris Lane, Kirkstall, Leeds 5
Tel: (0532) 758787

Phillips,
17a East Parade, Leeds
Tel: (0532) 448011

John H. Raby & Son,
Salem Auction Rooms, 21 St. Mary's Road, Bradford
Tel: (0274) 491121

Chas E. H. Yates & Son,
The Salerooms, Otley Road, Guiseley
Tel: (0943) 74165

CHANNEL ISLANDS

Langlois Ltd.,
Don Street, St. Helier, Jersey
Tel: (0534) 22441
also at:
St. Peter Port, Guernsey
Tel: (0481) 23421

F. Le Gallais & Sons,
Bath Street, St. Helier, Jersey
Tel: (0534) 30202

Martel, Maides & Le Pelley,
The Property Centre, 50 High Street, St. Peter Port, Guernsey
Tel: (0481) 21203

SCOTLAND

John Anderson,
Auctioneers, 33 Cross Street, Fraserburgh, Aberdeenshire
Tel: (0346) 28878

Christie's Scotland,
164-166 Bath Street, Glasgow
Tel: (041 332) 8134

B. L. Fenton & Sons,
Forebank Auction Halls, 84 Victoria Road, Dundee
Tel: (0382) 26227

Frasers (Auctioneers),
28-30 Church Street, Inverness
Tel: (0463) 232395

J. & J. Howe,
24 Commercial Street, Alyth, Perthshire
Tel: (08283) 2594

Thomas Love & Sons Ltd.,
The Auction Galleries, 52 Canal Street, Perth
Registered Office: St. John's Place, Perth
Tel: (0738) 24111

McTears (Robert McTear & Co.),
Royal Exchange Showrooms, Glasgow
Tel: (041 221) 4456

John Milne,
9 North Silver Street, Aberdeen
Tel: (0224) 639336

Robert Paterson & Son,
8 Orchard Street, Paisley, Renfrewshire
Tel: (041 889) 2435

Phillips in Scotland,
207 Bath Street, Glasgow
Tel: (041 332) 3386
also at:
65 George Street, Edinburgh
Tel: (031 225) 2266

L. S. Smellie & Sons Ltd.,
Within the Furniture Market, Lower Auchingramont Road, Hamilton
Tel: (0698) 282007

WALES

T. Brackstone & Co.,
19 Princes Drive, Colwyn Bay, Clwyd
Tel: (0492) 30481

Dodds Property World,
K. Hugh Dodd & Partners, Victoria Auction Galleries, Chester Street, Mold, Clwyd
Tel: (0352) 2552

Graham H. Evans, F.R.I.C.S., F.R.V.A.,
Auction Sales Centre, The Market Place, Kilgetty, Dyfed
Tel: (0834) 812793 & 811151

John Francis,
Curiosity Salerooms, King Street, Carmarthen
Tel: (0267) 233456

King Thomas,
Lloyd Jones & Company, Bangor House, High Street, Lampeter, Dyfed
Tel: (0570) 422550

Rennies,
1 Agincourt Street, Monmouth
Tel: (0600) 2916

Wingett's Auction Gallery,
29 Holt Street, Wrexham, Clwyd
Tel: (0978) 353553

INDEX TO ADVERTISERS

When on business or holiday in Great Britain and Ireland, consult

EGON RONAY'S GUIDES

Appearing in November 1986

EGON RONAY'S CELLNET GUIDE 1987
to Hotels, Restaurants & Inns

This is the 28th edition of this best-selling annual Guide.
Covering some 2,500 of the best hotels and restaurants and including budget hotels and economy evening meals in London, bed and breakfast for under £32 for two, bargain weekends, hotels with sport facilities, executive hotels and country house hotels.
Contains over 800 pages, including 56 pages of maps.

Appearing in February 1987

JUST A BITE, EGON RONAY'S GUIDE 1987
for Gourmets on a Family Budget

This is the eighth annual edition.
Most useful for the best snacks, teas, light lunches and dinners, etc., at modest prices in restaurants, wine bars, tearooms, cafés, snack bars, etc.

Appearing in March 1987

EGON RONAY'S PUB GUIDE 1987
to Food and Accommodation

The seventh annual edition, with around 1,000 pubs offering excellent bar food and homely, clean and pleasant bedrooms—also marvellous breakfasts.

Egon Ronay's Guides are annually researched and written, with a large number of new recommendations replacing old ones after reappraisal.

Available from AA Centres and booksellers everywhere

DIRECTORY OF SPECIALISTS

This directory is in no way complete. If you wish to be included in next year's directory or you have a change of address or telephone number, please could you inform us before April 1st 1987. Finally we would advise readers to make contact by telephone before a visit, therefore avoiding a wasted journey, which nowadays is both time consuming and expensive.
Any entry followed by (R) denotes a specialist who undertakes restoration work.

ARCHITECTURAL ANTIQUES

LONDON
Nigel Bartlett,
67 St. Thomas Street, SE1
Tel: 01-378 7895

AVON
Walcot Reclamation,
108 Walcot Street, Bath
Tel: (0225) 66291/2

DEVON
Ashburton Marbles,
Englands Antique Fireplaces,
6 West Street, Ashburton
Tel: (0364) 53189

DORSET
Talisman Antiques,
The Old Brewery, Wyke,
Gillingham
Tel: (074 76) 4423

GLOS.
Hayes & Newby,
The Pit, 70 Hare Lane
Tel: (0452) 31145

GT. MANCHESTER
Antique Fireplaces,
1090 Stockport Road,
Levenshulme
Tel: 061-431 8075

HANTS
Glover & Stacey Ltd.,
Malthouse Premises, Kingsley,
Nr. Bordon
Tel: (042 03) 5754 or evenings
(0420) 89067

LANCASHIRE
Susan & James Cook,
Dixon's Farm, Wigan Road,
Cuerden, Preston
Tel: (0772) 321390

WALES
M. & A. Main Architectural
Antiques (R),
The Old Smithy, Cerrig-y-
Drudion, Corwen
Tel: (049 082) 491

ARMS & MILITARIA

LONDON
The Armoury of St. James's,
17 Piccadilly Arcade, SW1
Tel: 01-493 5082

Michael C. German,
38b Kensington Church Street,
W8
Tel: 01-937 2771

Tradition,
5a Shepherd Street, W1
Tel: 01-493 7452

GLOS.
H.Q. 84,
82-84 Southgate Street, Gloucester
Tel: (0452) 27716

HANTS
Romsey Medal Centre,
112 The Hundred, Romsey
Tel: (0794) 512069

SURREY
Casque & Gauntlet Antiques,
55/59 Badshot Lea Road, Badshot
Lea, Farnham
Tel: (0252) 20745

SUSSEX
J. R. Barrett,
63 Spences Lane, Lewes
Tel: (0273) 473268

Military Antiques (by
appointment only),
42 Janes Lane, Burgess Hill
Tel: (044 46) 3516 & 43088

YORKS
The Antique Shop,
226 Harrogate Road, Leeds
Tel: (0532) 681785

Andrew Spencer Bottomley (by
appointment only),
32 Rotcher Hill, Holmfirth
Tel: (0484) 685234

WALES
Hermitage Antiques,
10 West Street, Fishguard
Tel: (0348) 873037

ART DECO & ART NOUVEAU

LONDON
Baptista Arts,
Stand D3/4, Chenil Galleries,
183 King's Road, SW3
Tel: 01-352 2123

Butler & Wilson,
189 Fulham Road, SW3
Tel: 01-352 3045

Chilton,
Stand A11/12, Chenil Galleries,
181-183 King's Road, SW3
No Tel.

T. Coakley,
Stand D13, Chenil Galleries, 181-
183 King's Road, SW3
Tel: 01-351 2914

Cobra & Bellamy,
149 Sloane Street, SW1
Tel: 01-730 2823

Ebury,
20 Brook Drive, SE11
Tel: 01-735 6160

Editions Graphiques Gallery,
3 Clifford Street, W1
Tel: 01-734 3944

The Facade,
196 Westbourne Grove, W11
Tel: 01-727 2159

Galerie 1900,
267 Camden High Street, NW1
Tel: 01-485 1001

Galerie Moderne, Le Style
Lalique,
10 Halkin Arcade, Motcomb
Street, SW1
Tel: 01-245 6907

Gallery '25,
4 Halkin Arcade, Motcomb Street,
SW1
Tel: 01-235 5178

David Gill (appointment only),
25 Palace Gate, W8
Tel: 01-584 9184

Patrick & Susan Gould
L17, Grays Mews, Davies Mews, W1
Tel: 01-408 0129

John Jesse and Irina Laski Ltd.,
160 Kensington Church Street, W8
Tel: 01-229 0312

Lewis M. Kaplan Associates Ltd.,
50 Fulham Road, SW3
Tel: 01-589 3108

John & Diana Lyons Gallery,
47-49 Mill Lane, West Hampstead,
NW6
Tel: 01-794 3537

P. & J.,
K13-J28 Grays Mews, Davies
Mews, W1
Tel: 01-499 2719

Pruskin Gallery,
73 Kensington Church Street, W8
Tel: 01-937 1994
also at:
183 King's Road, SW3
Tel: 01-352 9095

BERKS
Lupin Antiques,
134 Peascod Street, Windsor
Tel: (0753) 856244

GT. MANCHESTER
A. S. Antiques,
26 Broad Street, Salford
Tel: 061-737 5938

LEICS
Birches Antique Shop,
15 Francis Street, Stoneygate,
Leicester
Tel: (0533) 703235

MERSEYSIDE
Osiris,
24 Princes Street, Southport
Tel: (0704) 60418

Galerie 39,
39 Kew Road, Richmond
Tel: 01-948 1633 & 3337

Peter & Debbie Gooday,
20 Richmond Hill, Richmond
Tel: 01-940 8652

SUSSEX
Armstrong-Davis Gallery,
The Square, Arundel
Tel: (0903) 882752

YORKS
Dragon Antiques,
10 Dragon Road, Harrogate
Tel: (0423) 62037

Mr. Muir Hewitt,
Halifax Antiques Centre, Queens
Road/Gibbet Street, Halifax
Tel: (0422) 66657

SCOTLAND
The Rendezvous Gallery,
100 Forest Avenue, Aberdeen
Tel: (0224) 323247

BOXES, TREEN & WOODEN OBJECTS

LONDON
Simon Castle,
38B Kensington Church Street,
W8
Tel: 01-937 2268

Halcyon Days,
14 Brook Street, W1
Tel: 01-629 8811

Gerald Mathias (R),
R5/6 Antiquarius, 135 King's
Road, SW3
Tel: 01-351 0484

Alistair Sampson Antiques,
156 Brompton Road, SW3
Tel: 01-589 5272

BERKS
Charles Toller,
Hall House, 20 High Street,
Datchet
Tel: (0753) 42903

BUCKS
A. & E. Foster (by appointment
only),
Little Heysham, Forge Road,
Naphill
Tel: (024 024) 2024

HANTS
Gerald Austin Antiques,
2A Andover Road, Winchester
Tel: (0962) 69824 Ext. 2

House of Antiques,
4 College Street, Petersfield
Tel: (0730) 62172

LEICS
Stable Antiques,
14 Loughborough Road, Horton,
Nr. Loughborough
Tel: (0509) 880208

OXON
Key Antiques,
11 Horsefair, Chipping Norton
Tel: (0608) 3777

SUSSEX
Michael Wakelin & Helen
Linfield,
10 New Street, Petworth
Tel: (0798) 42417

CAMERAS

LONDON
Sean Sexton,
Stand 606, Alfie's Antique Market,
13-25 Church Street, NW8
Tel: 01-723 1370

Vintage Cameras Ltd.,
254/256 Kirkdale, Sydenham
Tel: 01-778 5416 & 5841

CARPETS

LONDON
Robert Bailey (by appointment
only),
51-53 Rivington Street
Tel: 01-550 5435

David Black Oriental Carpets,
96 Portland Road, Holland Park,
W11
Tel: 01-727 2566

Hindustan Carpets Ltd.,
B Block, 53/79 Highgate Road,
NW5
Tel: 01-485 7766

Lefevre & Partners,
57/61 Mortimer Street, W1
Tel: 01-584 5516

Mayfair Carpet Gallery,
6-8 Old Bond Street, W1
Tel: 01-493 0126/7

Swillet Rug Restorations (R),
(Warehouse), 8 Albert Wharf,
17 New Wharf Road, N1
Tel: 01-833 3529

Vigo Carpet Gallery,
6a Vigo Street, W1
Tel: 01-439 6971

Vigo Sternberg Galleries,
37 South Audley Street, W1
Tel: 01-629 8307

BUCKS
Swillet Rug Restorations (R),
22 Lodge Lane, Chalfont-St-Giles
Tel: (024 04) 4776

DORSET
J. L. Arditti (Old Oriental Rugs),
88 Bargates, Christchurch
Tel: (0202) 485414

GLOS
Thornborough Galleries,
28 Gloucester Street, Cirencester
Tel: (0285) 2055

SOMERSET
M. & A. Lewis,
Oriental Carpets & Rugs, 8 North
Street, Wellington
Tel: (082 347) 7430

SUSSEX
Lindfield Galleries,
59 High Street, Lindfield
Tel: (04447) 3817

YORKS
Omar (Harrogate) Ltd.,
8 Crescent Road, Harrogate
Tel: (0423) 503675

SCOTLAND
Whytock & Reid,
Sunbury House, Belford Mews,
Edinburgh
Tel: (031) 226 4911

TEXTILES
LONDON
Matthew Adams,
A1 Rogers Antique Galleries,
65 Portobello Road, W11
Tel: 01-579 5560

Gallery of Antique Costume &
Textiles,
2 Church Street, Marylebone,
NW8
Tel: 01-723 9981

Linda Wrigglesworth,
Grays Inn, The Mews, 1-7 Davies
Mews, W1
Tel: 01-408 0177

NORWICH
Mrs. Woolston,
Design House, 29 St. Georges
Street
Tel: (0603) 623181
also at:
Long Melford Antique Centre

SUSSEX
Celia Charlotte's Antiques,
7 Malling Street, Lewes
Tel: (0273) 473303

CLOCKS, WATCHES & BAROMETERS
LONDON
Asprey PLC,
165-169 New Bond Street, W1
Tel: 01-493 6767

Bobinet Ltd.,
102 Mount Street, W1
Tel: 01-408 0333/4

Aubrey Brocklehurst,
124 Cromwell Road, SW7
Tel: 01-373 0319

Camerer Cuss & Co.,
17 Ryder Street, St. James's, SW1
Tel: 01-930 1941

J. Carlton-Smith,
17 Ryder Street, St. James's, SW1
Tel: 01-930 6622

Chelsea Clocks,
479 Fulham Road
Tel: 01-731 5704
Also at:
69 Portobello Road
Tel: 01-727 5417

Antiquarius,
135/141 King's Road, SW3
Tel: 01-352 8646

The Clock Clinic Ltd.,
85 Lower Richmond Road, SW15
Tel: 01-788 1407

John Craggs Ltd.,
15/17 King Street, St. James's, SW1
Tel: 01-930 3817

Philip & Bernard Dombey,
174 Kensington Church Street,
W8
Tel: 01-229 7100

Garner & Marney Ltd.,
41/43 Southgate Road, N1
Tel: 01-226 1535

Keith Harding, F.B.H.I., (R),
93 Hornsey Road, N7
Tel: 01-607 6181 & 2672

E. Hollander Ltd.,
80 Fulham Road, SW3
Tel: 01-589 7239

Gerald Mathias (R),
R5/6 Antiquarius, 135 King's
Road, SW3
Tel: 01-351 0484

North London Clock Shop Ltd. (R),
72 Highbury Park, N5
Tel: 01-226 1609

R. E. Rose, F.B.H.I.,
731 Sidcup Road, Eltham, SE9
Tel: 01-859 4754

Strike One (Islington) Ltd.,
51 Camden Passage
Tel: 01-226 9709

Temple Brooks,
12 Mill Lane, NW6
Tel: 01-452 9696

Volpone,
12 Wynyatt Street, Clerkenwell,
EC1
Tel: 01-837 5686

AVON
Smith & Bottrill,
The Clock House, 17 George
Street, Bath
Tel: (0225) 22809

BERKS
Medalcrest Ltd.,
Charnham House, Charnham
Street, Hungerford
Tel: (0488) 84157

Times Past Antiques Ltd.,
59 High Street, Eton
Tel: (0753) 857018

BUCKS
The Guild Room,
The Lee, Great Missenden
Tel: (024 020) 463

CAMBS
Rodney T. Firmin,
16 Magdalene Street, Cambridge
Tel: (0223) 67372

CHESHIRE
Peter Bosson Antiques,
10B Swan Street, Wilmslow
Tel: (0625) 525250 & 527857

Coppelia Antiques,
Holford Lodge, Plumley Moor
Road, Plumley
Tel: (056 581) 2197

Derek Rayment Antiques (R),
Orchard House, Barton Road,
Barton, Nr. Farndon
Tel: (0829) 270429

CORNWALL
Ian Tuck (R),
The Friary, Trethurgy, St. Austell
Tel: (0726) 850039

CUMBRIA
Don Burns,
The Square, Ireby, Carlisle
Tel: (096 57) 477

DERBYS
Derby Clocks,
974 London Road, Derby
Tel: (0332) 74996

D. J. Mitchell,
Temple Antiques, Glenwood
Lodge, Temple Walk, Matlock Bath
Tel: (0629) 4253

DORSET
Good Hope Antiques,
2 Hogshill Street, Beaminster
Tel: (0308) 862119

Tom Tribe & Son,
Bridge Street, Sturminster
Newton
Tel: (0258) 72311

ESSEX
It's About Time (R),
863 London Road, Westcliff-on-Sea
Tel: (0702) 72574 & 205204

Littlebury Antiques,
58/60 Fairycroft Road, Saffron
Walden
Tel: (0799) 27961

Simpson Antiques,
44 Lower Street, Stanstead
Montfichet
Tel: (0279) 813388

Tempus Fugit (appointment only),
c/o Trinity House, Trinity Street,
Halstead
Tel: (0787) 475409

Trinity Clocks,
26 Trinity Street, Colchester
Tel: (0206) 46458

GLOS
J. & M. Bristow Antiques,
28 Long Street, Tetbury
Tel: (0666) 52222

George Curtis,
13 Montpellier Retreat,
Cheltenham
Tel: (0242) 42178

Colin Elliott,
4 Great Norwood Street,
Cheltenham
Tel: (0242) 528590

Saxton House Gallery,
High Street, Chipping Camden
Tel: (0386) 840278

Southbar Antiques,
Digbeth Street, Stow-on-the-Wold
Tel: (0451) 30236

HANTS
Charles Antiques,
101 The Hundred, Romsey
Tel: (0794) 512885

Evans & Evans,
40 West Street, Alresford
Tel: (096 273) 2170

Gerald E. Marsh,
32A The Square, Winchester
Tel: (0962) 54505

HEREFORD
G. & V. Taylor Antiques,
Winforton Court, Winforton
Tel: (054 46) 226

HERTS
Country Clocks (R),
3 Pendley Bridge Cottages, Tring
Station, Tring
Tel: (044 282) 5090

John de Haan,
12A Seaforth Drive, Waltham
Cross
Tel: (0992) 763111 & (0920) 2534

ISLE OF WIGHT
Museum of Clocks,
Alum Bay
Tel: (0983) 754193

KENT
John Chawner Antiques,
44 Chatham Hill, Chatham
Tel: (0634) 811411 & (0843) 43309

Hadlow Antiques,
No. 1 The Pantiles, Tunbridge
Wells
Tel: (0892) 29858

Henry Hall Antique Clocks,
19 Market Square, Westerham
Tel: (0959) 62200

The Old Clock Shop,
63 High Street, West Malling
Tel: (0732) 843246

Derek Roberts Antiques,
24/25 Shipbourne Road, Tonbridge
Tel: (0732) 358986

Malcolm G. Styles (R),
Tunbridge Wells
Tel: (0892) 30699

Anthony Woodburn,
Orchard House, Leigh, Nr.
Tonbridge
Tel: (0732) 832258

LANCS
Kenneth Weigh,
Signwriting & Numbering,
9 Links Road, Blackpool
Tel: (0253) 52097

LEICS
Clock Replacements (R),
239 Welford Road
Tel: (0533) 706190

G. K. Hadfield (R),
Blackbrook Hill House, Tickow
Lane, Shepshed
Tel: (0509) 503014

C. Lowe & Sons Ltd. (R),
37-40 Churchgate, Loughborough
Tel: (0509) 217876

MERSEYSIDE
T. Brown Horological Restorers
(R),
12 London Road, Liverpool 3
Tel: 051-709 4048

MIDDX
Court House Antiques,
19 Market Place, Brentford
Tel: 01-560 7074 & (093 22) 27186

Onslow Clocks,
48 King Street, Twickenham
Tel: 01-892 7632

NORFOLK
Delawood Antiques & Clock
Restoration (R),
10 Westgate, Hunstanton
Tel: (048 53) 2903

OXON
Peter Fell of Thame,
81 High Street, Thame
Tel: (084 421) 4487

Laurie Leigh Antiques,
36 High Street, Oxford
Tel: (0865) 244197

Telling Time,
57 North Street, Thame
Tel: (084 421) 3007

Witney Antiques,
96-98 Corn Street, Witney
Tel: (0993) 3902

SOMERSET
Bernard G. House,
Mitre Antiques, 13 Market Place,
Wells
Tel: (0749) 72607

Edward A. Nowell,
21-23 Market Place, Wells
Tel: (0749) 72415

Matthew Willis,
Antique Clocks, 3 Wells Road,
Glastonbury
Tel: (0458) 32103

SUFFOLK
Billinghurst Antiques (R),
White Gates, Elmswell Road,
Great Ashfield
Tel: (0359) 40040

SURREY
B.S. Antiques,
39 Bridge Road, East Molesey
Tel: 01-941 1812

The Clock Shop,
64 Church Street, Weybridge
Tel: (0932) 4047 & 55503

Roger A. Davis,
Antiquarian Horologist,
19 Dorking Road, Great Bookham
Tel: (0372) 57655 & 53167

Hampton Court Antiques,
75 Bridge Road, East Molesey
Tel: 01-941 6398

Horological Workshops,
204 Worplesdon Road, Guildford
Tel: (0483) 576496

Geoffrey Stevens,
26-28 Church Road, Guildford
Tel: (0483) 504075

Surrey Clock Centre,
3 Lower Street, Haslemere
Tel: (0428) 4547

SUSSEX
Adrian Alan Ltd.,
4 Frederick Place, Brighton
Tel: (0273) 25277

Bay Tree House Ltd.,
19 Middle Street, Brighton
Tel: (0273) 24688

Dean House Antiques,
Bepton Road, Midhurst
Tel: (073 081) 2277

Sam Orr and Magnus Broe,
36 High Street, Hurstpierpoint
Tel: (0273) 832081

David & Sarah Pullen,
29/31 Sea Road, Bexhill-on-Sea
Tel: (0424) 222035

TYNE AND WEAR
T. P. Rooney, Grad. B.H.I. (R),
191 Sunderland Road, Harton
Village, South Shields
Tel: 091-456 2950

WEST MIDLANDS
Osborne's (R),
91 Chester Road, New Oscott,
Sutton Coldfield
Tel: 021-355 6667

WILTSHIRE
Avon Antiques,
26-27 Market Street, Bradford-on-
Avon
Tel: (022 16) 2052

P. A. Oxley,
The Old Rectory, Cherhill, Nr.
Calne
Tel: (0249) 816227

YORKS
Brian Loomes,
Calf Haugh Farm, Pateley Bridge
Tel: (0423) 711163

The Clock Shop,
Hilltop House, Bellerby, Nr.
Leyburn
Tel: (0969) 22596

Haworth Antiques (R),
Harrogate Road, Huby, Nr. Leeds
Tel: (0423) 74293
Also at:
West Park Antiques Pavilion,
20 West Park, Harrogate
Tel: (0423) 61758

SCOTLAND
Browns Clocks Ltd.,
203 Bath Street, Glasgow
Tel: 041-248 6760

Christopher Wood (appointment
only),
Harlaw House, Kelso
Tel: (057 37) 321

DOLLS, TOYS & GAMES
LONDON
Dr. Colin Baddiel,
Stand B24/B25, Grays Mews, 1-
7 Davies Mews, W1
Tel: 01-408 1239

Jilliana Ranicar-Breese,
Martin Breese Ltd., 7A Jones
Arcade, Westborne Grove (Sats.
only)
Tel: 01-727 9378

Stuart Cropper,
Gray's Mews, 1-7 Davies Mews,
W1
Tel: 01-499 6600

Donay Antiques,
12 Pierrepont Row, N1
Tel: 01-359 1880

Engine 'n' Tender,
19 Spring Lane, Woodside, SE25
Tel: 01-654 0386

Pete McAskie,
Stand D10-12 Basement, Grays
Mews Antiques, 1-7 Davies Mews,
W1
Tel: 01-629 2813

The Dolls House Toys Ltd.,
29 The Market, Covent Garden,
WC2
Tel: 01-379 7243

The Singing Tree,
69 New King's Road, SW6
Tel: 01-736 4527

CORNWALL
Mrs. Margaret Chesterton,
33 Pentewan Road, St. Austell
Tel: (0726) 72926

DORSET
Hobby Horse Antiques,
29 West Allington, Bridport
Tel: (0308) 22801

GLOS
Lilian Middleton's Antique Dolls'
Shop & Dolls' Hospital,
Days Stable, Sheep Street, Stow-
on-the-Wold
Tel: (0451) 30381

China Doll,
31 Suffolk Parade, Cheltenham
Tel: (0242) 33164

KENT
Hadlow Antiques,
1 The Pantiles, Tunbridge Wells
Tel: (0892) 29858

STAFFS
Multro Ltd.,
10 Madeley Street, Tunstall,
Stoke-on-Trent
Tel: (0782) 813621

SURREY
Heather & Clifford Bond,
Victoriana Dolls
Tel: (073 72) 49525

Curiosity Shop,
72 Stafford Road, Wallington
Tel: 01-647 5267

Doll Shop (appointment only),
18 Richmond Hill, Richmond
Tel: 01-940 6774

Elizabeth Gant,
52 High Street, Thames Ditton
Tel: 01-398 0962

Doll & Teddy Bear Restorer (R),
Wendy Foster, Minto, Codmore
Hill, Pulborough
Tel: (079 82) 2707

WEST MIDLANDS
Woodsetton Antiques,
65 Sedgley Road, Woodsetton,
Dudley
Tel: (0384) 277918

YORKSHIRE
Andrew Clark,
12 Ingfield, Oakenshaw, Bradford
Tel: (0274) 675342

Mr. Haley,
2 Lanehead Road, Soyland,
Sowery Bridge
Tel: (0422) 822148

SCOTLAND
The Workshop,
88 Union Place, Dundee
Tel: (0382) 633950

WALES
Museum of Childhood Toys & Gift
Shop,
1 Castle Street, Beaumaris,
Anglesey, Gwynedd
Tel: (0248) 712498

EPHEMERA
LONDON
Bayly's Gallery,
8 Princes Arcade, Piccadilly, W1
Tel: 01-734 0180

Jilliana Ranicar-Breese,
Martin Breese Ltd.,
164 Kensington Park Road,
Notting Hill Gate, W11
Tel: 01-727 9378 (by appointment
only)
Also at:
7A Jones Arcade, Westbourne
Grove (Sats. only)
Also at:
Roger's Arcade, 65 Portobello Road
(Sats. only)

Gilda Conrich Antiques,
12 The Mall, 359 Upper Street,
Camden Passage, N1
Tel: 01-226 5319

M. & R. Glendale,
Antiquarian Booksellers, 9A New
Cavendish Street, W1
Tel: 01-487 5348

David Godfrey's Old Newspaper
Shop,
37 Kinnerton Street, SW1
Tel: 01-235 7788

Jubilee,
10 Pierrepont Row, Camden
Passage, N1
Tel: 01-607 5462

Pleasures of Past Times,
11 Cecil Court, Charing Cross
Road, WC2
Tel: 01-836 1142

Danny Posner,
The Vintage Magazine Shop,
39/41 Brewer Street, W1
Tel: 01-439 8525

Peter Stockham at Images,
16 Cecil Court, Charing Cross
Road, WC2
Tel: 01-836 8661

AVON
Paul Finch,
Hampton House, 2 Hampton Road,
Bristol
Tel: (0272) 745320

BUCKS
Omniphil Ltd.,
Germains Lodge, Fullers Hill,
Chesham
Tel: (0494) 771851
Also at:
Stand 110, Gray's Antique
Market, 58 Davies Street, W1
Tel: 01-629 3223

KENT
Mike Sturge,
17 Market Buildings Arcade,
Maidstone
Tel: (0622) 54702

SURREY
Richmond Antiquary,
28 Hill Rise, Richmond
Tel: 01-938 0583

FISHING TACKLE
DORSET
Yesterday Tackle & Books,
67 Jumpers Road, Christchurch
Tel: (0202) 476586

KENT
Alan Clout,
36 Nunnery Fields, Canterbury
Tel: (0227) 455162

SURREY
Gary Brooker,
Wintershall, Dunsfold
Tel: (048 649) 478

SUSSEX
N. Marchant-Lane,
Willow Court, Middle Street,
Petworth
Tel: (0798) 43443

SCOTLAND
Jamie Maxtone Graham,
Nithside, Closeburn, Thornhill,
Dumfries
Tel: (0848) 31382

FURNITURE
LONDON
Asprey PLC,
165-169 New Bond Street, W1
Tel: 01-493 6767

F. E. A. Briggs Ltd.,
73 Ledbury Road, W1
Tel: 01-727 0909 & 01-221 4950

C. W. Buckingham,
301-303 Munster Road, SW6
Tel: 01-385 2657

John Creed Antiques Ltd.,
3 & 5A Camden Passage, N1
Tel: 01-226 8867

Eldridge,
99-101 Farringdon Road, EC1
Tel: 01-837 0379 & 0370

John Keil Ltd.,
154 Brompton Road, SW3
Tel: 01-589 6454

C. H. Major (Antiques) Ltd.,
154 Kensington Church Street,
W8
Tel: 01-229 1162

Mallett & Son (Antiques) Ltd.,
40 New Bond Street, W1
Tel: 01-499 7411

M. & D. Seligmann,
37 Kensington Church Street, W8
Tel: 01-937 0400

Michael Marriott Ltd.,
588 Fulham Road, SW6
Tel: 01-736 3110

Murray Thomson Ltd.,
141 Kensington Church Street,
W8
Tel: 01-727 1727

Oola Boola Antiques,
166 Tower Bridge Road, SE1
Tel: 01-403 0794

Phelps Ltd.,
133-135 St. Margaret's Road,
E. Twickenham
Tel: 01-892 1778 & 7129

Alistair Sampson Antiques,
156 Brompton Road, SW3
Tel: 01-589 5272

Arthur Seager Ltd.,
25a Holland Street, Kensington,
W8
Tel: 01-937 3262

Stair & Co.,
120 Mount Street, W1
Tel: 01-499 1784/5

William Tillman,
30 St. James's Street, SW1
Tel: 01-839 2500

O. F. Wilson Ltd.,
Queen's Elm Parade, Old Church
Street, SW3
Tel: 01-352 9554

Robert Young Antiques,
68 Battersea Bridge Road, SW11
Tel: 01-228 7847

Zal Davar Antiques,
26a Munster Road, SW6
Tel: 01-736 1405 & 2559

AVON
Cottage Antiques,
The Old Post Office, Langford
Place, Langford, Nr. Bristol
Tel: (0934) 862597

BERKS

Mary Bells Antiques,
Charnham Close, Hungerford
Tel: (0488) 82620

Biggs of Maidenhead,
Hare Hatch Grange, Twyford
Tel: (073 522) 3281

The Old Malthouse,
Hungerford
Tel: (0488) 82209

Medalcrest Ltd.,
Charnham House, Charnham
Street, Hungerford
Tel: (0488) 84157

Charles Toller,
Hall House, 20 High Street,
Datchet
Tel: (0753) 42903

BUCKS

Jeanne Temple Antiques,
Stockwell House, 1 Stockwell
Lane, Wavendon, Milton Keynes
Tel: (0908) 583597

A. & E. Foster (by appointment
only),
Little Heysham, Forge Road,
Naphill
Tel: (024 024) 2024

CHESHIRE

Coppelia Antiques,
Holford Lodge, Plumley Moor
Road, Plumley
Tel: (056 581) 2197

Derbyshire Antiques Ltd.,
157-159 London Road South,
Poynton
Tel: (0625) 873110

Townwell House Antiques,
52 Welsh Row, Nantwich
Tel: (0270) 625953

CUMBRIA

Haughey Antiques,
Market Street, Kirkby Stephen
Tel: (0930) 71302

Fenwick Pattison,
Bowmanstead, Coniston
Tel: (0966) 41235

Townhead Antiques,
Newby Bridge
Tel: (0448) 31321

Jonathan Wood Antiques,
Broughton Hall, Cartmel, Grange-
over-Sands
Tel: (044 854) 234

DERBYS

Maurice Goldstone & Son,
Avenel Court, Bakewell
Tel: (062 981) 2487

Spurrier-Smith Antiques,
28B & 41 Church Street,
Ashbourne
Tel: (0335) 43669 and (home)
(077 389) 368

Yesterday Antiques,
6 Commercial Road, Tideswell, Nr.
Buxton
Tel: (0298) 871932

DORSET

Johnsons of Sherborne Ltd.,
South Street, Sherborne
Tel: (0935) 812585

Stone Hall Antiques,
Down Hall Road, Matching Green,
Harlow
Tel: (0279) 731440

Talisman Antiques,
The Old Brewery, Wyke,
Gillingham
Tel: (074 76) 4423

GLOS

Baggott Church Street Ltd.,
Church Street, Stow-on-the-Wold
Tel: (0451) 30370

W. R. Cambridge & Son,
14 Rotunda Terrace, Cheltenham
Tel: (0242) 314502

Country Life Antiques,
Sheep Street, Stow-on-the-Wold
Tel: (0451) 30776
Also at:
Grey House, The Square, Stow-on-
the-Wold
Tel: (0451) 31564

Gloucester House Antiques,
Market Place, Fairford
Tel: (0285) 712790

Huntington Antiques Ltd.,
The Old Forge, Church Street,
Stow-on-the-Wold
Tel: (0451) 30842

Painswick Antiques & Interiors,
Beacon House, Painswick
Tel: (0452) 812578

Antony Preston Antiques Ltd.,
The Square, Stow-on-the-Wold
Tel: (0451) 31586

Studio Antiques Ltd.,
Bourton-on-the-Water
Tel: (0451) 20352

HANTS

C. W. Buckingham,
Twin Firs, Southampton Road,
Cadnam
Tel: (0703) 812122

Cedar Antiques,
High Street, Hartley Wintney
Tel: (025 126) 3252

Mark Collier Antiques,
24 The High Street, Fordingbridge
Tel: (0425) 52555

House of Antiques,
4 College Street, Petersfield
Tel: (0730) 62172

Lita Kay of Lyndhurst,
13 High Street, Lyndhurst
Tel: (042 128) 2337

HEREFORD & WORCESTER

Great Brampton House Antiques
Ltd.,
Madley
Tel: (0981) 250244

Jean Hodge-Antiques,
Peachley Manor, Lower
Broadheath, Worcester
Tel: (0905) 640255

HERTS

C. Bellinger Antiques,
91 Wood Street, Barnet
Tel: 01-449 3467

Phillips of Hitchin (Antiques) Ltd.,
The Manor House, Hitchin
Tel: (0462) 32067

HUMBERSIDE

Geoffrey Mole,
400 Wincolmlee, Hull
Tel: (0482) 27858

KENT

Chislehurst Antiques,
7 Royal Parade, Chislehurst
Tel: 01-467 1530

Nigel Coleman Antiques,
High Street, Brasted
Tel: (0959) 64042

John McMaster,
5 Sayers Square, Sayers Lane,
Tenterden
Tel: (058 06) 2941

Steppes Hill Farm Antiques,
Stockbury, Sittingbourne
Tel: (0795) 842205

Sutton Valence Antiques,
Sutton Valence, Maidstone
Tel: (0622) 843333 & 843499

LANCS

De Molen Ltd.,
Moss Hey Garages, Chapel Road,
Marton Moss, Blackpool
Tel: (0253) 696324

West Lancs. Exports,
Black Horse Farm, 123 Liverpool
Road, South Burscough, Nr.
Ormskirk
Tel: (0704) 894634

LEICS

Lowe of Loughborough,
37-40 Church Gate, Loughborough
Tel: (0509) 217876

LINCS

Kirkby Antiques Ltd.,
Kirkby-on-Bain, Woodhall Spa
Tel: (0526) 52119 & 53461

Geoff Parker Antiques Ltd.,
Haltoft End, Freiston, Nr. Boston
Tel: (0205) 760444

MIDDLESEX

Binstead Antiques,
21 Middle Lane, Teddington
Tel: 01-943 0626

J. W. Crisp Antiques,
166 High Street, Teddington
Tel: 01-977 4309

Phelps Ltd.,
133-135 St. Margaret's Road,
E. Twickenham
Tel: 01-892 1778

NORFOLK

Arthur Brett & Sons Ltd.,
40-44 St. Giles Street, Norwich
Tel: (0603) 628171

Peter Howkins Antiques,
39, 40 & 135 King Street, Great
Yarmouth
Tel: (0493) 851180

Pearse Lukies,
Bayfield House, White Hart
Street, Aylesham
Tel: (026 373) 4137

NORTHANTS

Paul Hopwell Antiques,
30 High Street, West Haddon
Tel: (078 887) 636

NOTTS

Matsell Antiques Ltd.,
2 & 4 Derby Street, off Derby
Road, Nottingham
Tel: (0602) 472691 & 288267

OXON

David John Ceramics,
11 Acre End Street, Eynsham
Tel: (0865) 880786

Elizabethan House Antiques,
28 & 55 High Street, Dorchester-
on-Thames
Tel: (0865) 340079

Key Antiques,
11 Horsefair, Chipping Norton
Tel: (0608) 3777

Peter Norden Antiques,
High Street, Burford
Tel: (099 382) 2121

Manfred Schotten Antiques,
The Crypt, High Street, Burford
Tel: (099 382) 2302

Telling Time,
57 North Street, Thame
Tel: (084 421) 3007

Zene Walker,
The Bull House, High Street,
Burford
Tel: (099 382) 3284

Witney Antiques,
96-98 Corn Street, Witney
Tel: (0993) 3902

SHROPSHIRE

Castle Lodge,
Ludlow
Tel: (0584) 2838

Castle Gate Antiques,
15 Castle Gate, Shrewsbury
Tel: (0743) 61011 (evenings)

R. G. Cave & Sons Ltd.,
17 Broad Street, Ludlow
Tel: (0584) 3568

Doveridge House of Neachley,
Long Lane, Nr. Shifnal
Tel: (090 722) 3131/2

Paul Smith,
The Old Chapel, Old Street,
Ludlow
Tel: (0584) 2666

M. & R. Taylor (Antiques),
53 Broad Street, Ludlow
Tel: (0584) 4169

White Cottage Antiques,
Tern Hill, Nr. Market Drayton
Tel: (063 083) 222

Stanley Woolston,
29 Broad Street, Ludlow
Tel: (0584) 3554

SOMERSET

Colin Dyte Antiques,
Huntspill Road, Highbridge
Tel: (0278) 788590

Grange Court Antiques,
Corfe, Nr. Taunton
Tel: (082 342) 498

Trevor Micklem Antiques Ltd.,
Gateway House, North Street,
Milverton
Tel: (0823) 400404

Edward A. Nowell,
21-23 Market Place, Wells
Tel: (0749) 72415

SUFFOLK

David Gibbins Antiques,
21 Market Hill, Woodbridge
Tel: (039 43) 3531

Michael Moore Antiques,
The Old Court, Nethergate Street,
Clare
Tel: (0787) 277510

Peppers Period Pieces (R),
22-24 Churchgate Street, Bury St.
Edmonds
Tel: (0284) 68786

Randolph,
97 & 99 High Street, Hadleigh
Tel: (0473) 823789

SURREY

Keith Atkinson,
59 Brighton Road, South Croydon
Tel: 01-688 5559

Dorking Desk Shop,
41 West Street, Dorking
Tel: (0306) 883327 & 880535

Dovetail Antique Restoration (R),
Riverdale Farm, Broadmead Road,
Old Woking
Tel: (048 62) 22925

Hampshires of Dorking,
48-52 West Street, Dorking
Tel: (0306) 887076

J. Hartley Antiques,
186 High Street, Ripley
Tel: (0483) 224318

Heath-Bullock,
3 Meadrow, Godalming
Tel: (048 68) 22562

Ripley Antiques,
67 High Street, Ripley
Tel: (0483) 224981

Swan Antiques,
62a West Street, Dorking
Tel: (0306) 881217

Anthony Welling Antiques,
Broadway Barn, High Street,
Ripley
Tel: (0483) 225384

Wych House Antiques,
Wych Hill, Woking
Tel: (048 62) 64636

SUSSEX

A27 Antiques Warehouses,
Chaucer Industrial Estate, Dittons
Road, Polegate
Tel: (032 12) 7167 & 5301

Bursig of Arundel,
The Old Candle Factory, Tarrant
Street, Arundel
Tel: (0903) 883456

Humphry Antiques,
East Street, Petworth
Tel: (0798) 43053

Richard Davidson,
Lombard Street, Petworth
Tel: (0798) 42508

The Grange Antiques,
High Street, Robertsbridge
Tel: (0580) 880577

Lakeside Antiques,
The Old Cement Works, South
Heighton, Newhaven
Tel: (0273) 513326

John G. Morris Ltd.,
Market Square, Petworth
Tel: (0798) 42305

The Old Mint House,
High Street, Pevensey,
Eastbourne
Tel: (0323) 762337

Village Antiques,
2 & 4 Cooden Sea Road, Little
Common, Bexhill-on-Sea
Tel: (042 43) 5214

WARKS
Colliers, Bigwood & Bewlay,
The Old School, Tiddington,
Stratford-upon-Avon
Tel: (0789) 69415

WEST MIDLANDS
John Hubbard Antiques,
224-226 Court Oak Road,
Harborne, Birmingham
Tel: 021-426 1694

Rock House Antiques & Collectors
Centre,
Rock House, The Rock, Tettenhall,
Wolverhampton
Tel: (0902) 754995

WILTS
Avon Antiques,
26-27 Market Street, Bradford-
upon-Avon
Tel: (022 16) 2052

Robert Bradley,
71 Brown Street, Salisbury
Tel: (0722) 333677

Combe Cottage Antiques,
Castle Combe, Nr. Chippenham
Tel: (0249) 782250

Ian G. Hastie, BADA,
46 St. Ann Street, Salisbury
Tel: (0722) 22957

Robert Kime Antiques,
Dene House, Lockeridge
Tel: (067 286) 250

Monkton Galleries,
Hindon
Tel: (074 789) 235

Paul Wansbrough,
Seend Lodge, Seend, Nr.
Melksham
Tel: (038 082) 213

K. & A. Welch,
1a Church Street, Warminster
Tel: (0985) 214687 & 213433
(evenings)

WORCS
Gavina Ewart,
60-62 High Street, Broadway
Tel: (0386) 853371

YORKS
Robert Aagaard Ltd.,
Frogmire House, Stockwell Road,
Knaresborough
Tel: (0423) 864805
(Specialises in fireplaces)

Barmouth Court Antiques,
Abbeydale House, Barmouth
Road, Sheffield
Tel: (0742) 582160 & 582672

Bernard Dickinson,
88 High Street, Gargave
Tel: (075 678) 285

Jeremy A. Fearn,
The Old Rectory, Winksley, Ripon
Tel: (076 583) 625

W. F. Greenwood & Sons Ltd.,
2 & 3 Crown Place, Harrogate
Tel: (0423) 504467

Old Rectory Antiques,
The Old Rectory, West Heslerton,
Malton
Tel: (094 45) 364

R. M. S. Precious,
King William House, High Street,
Settle
Tel: (072 92) 3946

SCOTLAND
John Bell of Aberdeen Ltd.,
Balbrogie, By Blackburn,
Kinellar, Aberdeenshire
Tel: (0224) 79209

Paul Couts Ltd.,
101-107 West Bow, Edinburgh
Tel: 031-225 3238

Letham Antiques,
20 Dundas Street, Edinburgh
Tel: 031-556 6565

Roy Sim Antiques,
21 Allan Street, Blairgowrie,
Perthshire
Tel: (0250) 3860 & 3700

Unicorn Antiques,
54 Dundas Street, Edinburgh
Tel: 031-556 7176

FURNITURE – PINE
LONDON
Adams Antiques,
47 Chalk Farm Road, NW1
Tel: 01-267 9241

The Barewood Company,
58 Mill Lane, West Hampstead,
NW6
Tel: 01-435 7244

Olwen Carthew,
109 Kirkdale, SW26
Tel: 01-699 1363

Princedale Antiques,
70 Princedale Road, W11
Tel: 01-727 0868

Scallywag,
187-191 Clapham Road, Stockwell,
London, SW9
Tel: 01-274 0300

This & That (Furniture),
50 & 51 Chalk Farm Road, NW1
Tel: 01-267 5433

AVON
Abbas Combe Pine,
4 Upper Maudlin Street, Bristol
Tel: (0272) 299023

BEDS
Country Primitives,
Ampthill Antiques Centre,
Ampthill
Tel: (0296) 668294

BUCKS
The Pine Merchants,
52 High Street, Gt. Missenden
Tel: (024 06) 2002

CO. DURHAM
Horsemarket Antiques,
27 Horsemarket, Barnard Castle
Tel: (0833) 37881

CUMBRIA
Cumberland Pine,
Cromwell Road, Penrith
Tel: (0768) 66940

DERBYS
Old Farm Furniture
Parwick Lees Farm, Ashbourne
Tel: (0335) 25473

DEVON
County Cottage Furniture,
The Old Smithy, Back Street,
Modbury
Tel: (0548) 830888

Fine Pine,
Woodland Road, Harbertonford
Tel: (080 423) 465

GLOS.
Bed of Roses Antiques
12 Prestbury Road, Cheltenham
Tel: (0242) 31918

Denzil Verey Antiques,
The Close, Barnsley House,
Barnsley, Nr. Cirencester
Tel: (028 574) 402

Gloucester House Antiques,
Market Place, Fairford
Tel: (0285) 712790

The Pine Dealer,
High Street, Fairford
Tel: (0285) 712502

HANTS
C. W. Buckingham
Twin Firs, Southampton Road,
Cadnam
Tel: (0703) 812122

The Pine Cellars,
38 Jewry Street, Winchester
Tel: (0962) 67014

The Pine Co.,
104 Christchurch Road, Ringwood
Tel: (042 54) 3932

HEREFORD &
WORCESTER
The Hay Galleries Ltd.,
4 High Town, Hay-on-Wye
Tel: (0497) 820356

Paul Somers Interiors
incorporating Woodstock Interiors,
Unicorn Yard, Belle Vue Terrace,
Malvern, Worcester
Tel: (068 45) 60297

HERTS
Out of Town,
21 Ware Road, Hertford
Tel: (0992) 52848

Romic,
4 Evron Place (off Market Place),
Hertford
Tel: (0992) 552880

HUMBERSIDE
Bell Antiques,
68 Harold Street, Grimsby
Tel: (0472) 695110

The Hull Pine Co.,
253 Anlaby Road, Hull
Tel: (0482) 227169

Paul Wilson Pine Furniture,
Perth Street West, Hull
Tel: (0482) 447923 & 448607

KENT
Penny Lampard,
Rectory Farm, Langley, Maidstone
Tel: (0622) 861377

Sissinghurst Antiques,
Hazelhurst Cottage, The Street,
Sissinghurst,
Nr. Cranbrook
Tel: (0580) 713893

Traditional Furniture,
248 Seabrook Road, Seabrook,
Hythe
Tel: (0303) 39931

LANCS
Robert Sheriff,
Moss Hey Garages, Chapel Road,
Marton Moss, Blackpool
Tel: (0253) 696324

Cottage Furniture,
Farnworth Park Industrial Estate,
Queen Street, Farnworth, Bolton
Tel: (0204) 700853

Enloc Antiques,
Old Corporation Yard, Knotts
Lane, Colne
Tel: (0282) 861417

Utopia Pine,
Holme Mills, Carnforth
Tel: (0524) 781739

LEICS
Richard Kimbell Antiques,
Riverside, Market Harborough
Tel: (0858) 33444

LINCS
Allens antiques,
Moor Farm, Stapleford
Tel: (052 285) 392

J. & J. Palmer Ltd.,
42/44 Swinegate, Grantham
Tel: (0476) 70093

Stowaway (UK) Ltd.,
2 Langton Hill, Horncastle
Tel: (065 82) 7445

NORTHANTS
Acorn Antiques,
The Old Mill, Moat Lane,
Towcester
Tel: (0327) 52788

OXON
Market Place Antiques,
35 Market Place, Henley-on-
Thames
Tel: (0491) 57287

SOMERSET
Domus,
Woodcock Street, Castle Cary
Tel: (0963) 50912

Herald House Antiques,
Herald House, North Street,
Langport
Tel: (0458) 250587

Grange Court Antiques,
Corfe, Taunton
Tel: (0823) 42498

Pennard House,
East Pennard, Shepton Mallet
Tel: (074 986) 266

STAFFS
Anvil Antiques Ltd.,
Cross Mills, Cross Street, Leek
Tel: (0538) 371657

Aspleys Antiques,
Compton Mill, Compton, Leek
Tel: (0538) 373396 & 373346

Gemini Trading,
Limes Mill, Abbotts Road, Leek
Tel: (0538) 387834

Stone-wares,
The Stripped Pine Shop, 24
Radford Street, Stone
Tel: (0785) 815000

SUFFOLK
Michael Moore Antiques,
The Old Court, Nethergate Street,
Clare
Tel: (0787) 277510

SURREY
Odiham Antiques,
High Street, Compton, Guildford
Tel: (0483) 810215

F. & L. Warren,
The Sawmills, Firgrove Hill,
Farnham
Tel: (0252) 726713

Wych House Antiques,
Wych Hill, Woking
Tel: (048 62) 64636

Pine Warehouse at:-
34 London Road, Staines (off The
Crooked Billet roundabout A30)
Tel: (0784) 65331

SUSSEX
Hillside Antiques,
Units 12-13, Lindfield Enterprise
Park, Lewes Road, Lindfield
Tel: (044 47) 3042

Ann Lingard,
Ropewalk Antiques, Ropewalk,
Rye
Tel: (0797) 223486

Peppers Antique Pine,
Crouch Lane, Seaford
Tel: (0323) 891400

Graham Price Antiques Ltd.,
A27 Antiques Complex, Unit 4,
Chaucer Industrial Estate, Dittons
Road, Polegate
Tel: (032 12) 7167 & 7681

Touchwood (Mervyn & Sue),
The Square, Herstmonceux
Tel: (0323) 832020

Michael Wakelin & Helen
Lindfield,
10 New Street, Petworth
Tel: (0798) 42417

YORKS
Daleside Antiques,
St. Peter's Square, Cold Bath
Road, Harrogate
Tel: (0423) 60286

Early Days,
7 Kings Court, Pately Bridge,
Harrogate
Tel: (0423) 711661

Manor Barn Pine,
Burnside Mill, Main Street,
Addinsham, Ilkley
Tel: (0943) 830176

Pine Finds,
The Old Corn Mill, Bishop
Monkton, Harrogate
Tel: (0765) 87159

IRELAND
Albert Forsythe,
Mill Hall, 66 Carsonstown Road,
Saintfield, Co. Down, Northern
Ireland
Tel: (0238) 510398

Luckpenny Antiques,
Kilmurray House, Shinrone, Birr,
Co. Offaly, Southern Ireland
Tel: (010 353 505) 47134

W. J. Somerville,
Shamrock Antiques Ltd.,
Killanley, Ballina, Co. Mayo
Tel: (096) 36275

SCOTLAND
A. & P. Steadman,
Unit 1, Hatston Industrial Estate,
Kirkwall, Orkney
Tel: (0856) 5040

WALES
Heritage Restorations,
Maes y Glydfa, Llanfair,
Caereinion, Welshpool, Powys
Tel: (0938) 810384

GLASS
LONDON
Asprey PLC,
165-169 New Bond Street, W1
Tel: 01-493 6767

Phyllis Bedford Antiques,
3 The Galleries, Camden Passage,
N1
Tel: 01-354 1332;
home 01-882 3189

Christine Bridge Antiques,
K10-12 Grays Mews, 1-7 Davies
Mews, W1
Tel: 01-499 3562

W. G. T. Burne (Antique Glass)
Ltd.,
11 Elystan Street, SW3
Tel: 01-589 6074

Delomosne & Son Ltd.,
4 Campden Hill Road, W8
Tel: 01-937 1804

Eila Grahame,
97C Kensington Church Street,
W8
Tel: 01-727 4132

Lloyds of Westminster,
5A Motcomb Street, SW1
Tel: 01-235 1010

S. W. Parry (Old Glass),
Stand A4-A5 Westbourne Antique
Arcade, 113 Portobello Road, W11
(Sat. only)
Tel: 01-740 0248 (Sun to Fri)

J. F. Poore,
5 Wellington Terrace, W2
Tel: 01-229 4166

Gerald Sattin Ltd.,
25 Burlington Arcade, Piccadilly,
W1
Tel: 01-493 6557

R. Wilkinson & Son (R),
43-45 Wastdale Road, Forest Hill,
SE23
Tel: 01-699 4420

AVON
Somervale Antiques,
6 Radstock Road, Midsomer
Norton, Bath
Tel: (0761) 412686

DORSET
A & D Antiques
21 East Street, Blandford Forum
Tel: (0258) 55643

Quarter Jack Antiques,
The Quarter Jack, Bridge Street,
Sturminster Newton
Tel: (0258) 72558

HANTS
Todd & Austin Antiques& Fine
Art,
2 Andover Road, Winchester
Tel: (0962) 69824

SOMERSET
Abbey Antiques,
51 High Street, Glastonbury
Tel: (0458) 31694

SUFFOLK
Maureen Thompson,
Sun House, Long Melford
Tel: (0787) 78252

SURREY
Shirley Warren
(by appointment only),
42 Kingswood Avenue,
Sanderstead
Tel: 01-657 1751

SUSSEX
Rusthall Antiques,
Chauteaubriand Antique Centre,
High Street, Burwash
Tel: (0435) 882535 &
(0892) 20668 (evenings)

SCOTLAND
Janet Lumsden,
51A George Street, Edinburgh
Tel: 031-225 2911

William MacAdam (appointment
only),
86 Pilrig Street, Edinburgh
Tel: 031-553 1364

GRAMOPHONES,
PHONOGRAPHS &
RADIOS
LONDON
Keith Harding,
93 Hornsey Road, N7
Tel: 01-607 6181 & 2672

AVON
The Vintage Wireless Co.,
Tudor House, Cossham Street,
Mangotsfield, Bristol
Tel: (0272) 565474

SOMERSET
Philip Knighton (R),
The Wellington Workshop,
14 South Street, Wellington
Tel: (082 347) 7332

WEST MIDLANDS
Woodsetton Antiques,
65 Sedgley Road, Woodsetton,
Dudley
Tel: (0384) 277918

ICONS
LONDON
Mark Gallery,
9 Porchester Place, Marble Arch,
W2
Tel: 01-262 4906

JEWELLERY
NORFOLK
Peter & Valerie Howkins,
39, 40 & 135 King Street, Great
Yarmouth
Tel: (0493) 844639

SOMERSET
Edward A. Nowell,
21-23 Market Place, Wells
Tel: (0749) 72415

SUSSEX
Rusthall Antiques,
Chateaubriand Antique Centre,
High Street, Burwash
Tel: (0435) 882535
(0892) 20668 (evenings)

LIGHTING
LONDON
Judy Jones,
194 Westbourne Grove, W11
Tel: 01-229 6866

HEREFORD
Fritz Fryer,
27 Gloucester Road, Ross-on-Wye,
Hereford
Tel: (0989) 64738 & 84512

MARINE
ANTIQUES
ESSEX
Littlebury Antiques,
58/60 Fairycroft Road, Saffron
Walden
Tel: (0799) 27961

METALWARE
LONDON
Christopher Bangs
(by appointment only)
Tel: 01-352 3384

Jack Casimir Ltd.,
The Brass Shop, 23 Pembridge
Road, W11
Tel: 01-727 8643

Arthur Davidson Ltd.,
78-79 Jermyn Street, SW1
Tel: 01-930 6687

Robert Preston,
1 Campden Street, W8
Tel: 01-727 4872

Alistair Sampson Antiques,
156 Brompton Road, SW3
Tel: 01-589 5272

AVON
Cottage Antiques,
The Old Post Office, Langfor'
Place, Langford, Nr. Bristol
Tel: (0934) 862597

BEDS
Christopher Sykes Antiques,
The Old Parsonage, Woburn,
Milton Keynes
Tel: (052 525) 259/467

BERKS
Rye Galleries,
60-61 High Street, Eton
Tel: (0753) 862637

BUCKS
Albert Bartram,
177 Hivings Hill, Chesham
Tel: (0494) 783271

CUMBRIA
Stable Antiques,
Oakdene Country Hotel, Garsdale
Road, Sedbergh
Tel: (0587) 20280

GLOS
Country Life Antiques,
Sheep Street, Stow-on-the-Wold
Tel: (0451) 30776
Also at:
Grey House, The Square, Stow-on-
the-Wold
Tel: (0451) 31564

OXON
Robin Bellamy Ltd.,
97 Corn Street, Witney
Tel: (0993) 4793

Elizabethan House Antiques,
28 & 55 High Street, Dorchester-
on-Thames
Tel: (0865) 340079

Key Antiques,
11 Horsefair, Chipping Norton
Tel: (0608) 377

Lloyd & Greenwood Antiques,
Chapel House, High Street,
Burford
Tel: (099 382) 2359

SUFFOLK
Brookes Forge Flempton (R),
Flempton, Bury St. Edmunds,
Suffolk
Tel: (028 484) 473 business
(0449) 781376 home

SUSSEX
Michael Wakelin & Helen
Linfield,
10 New Street, Petworth
Tel: (0798) 42417

WILTS
Avon Antiques,
26-27 Market Street, Bradford-
upon-Avon
Tel: (022 16) 2052

Combe Cottage Antiques,
Castle Combe, Chippenham
Tel: (0249) 782250

Rupert Gentle Antiques,
The Manor House, Milton
Lilbourne, Nr. Pewsey
Tel: (0672) 63344

YORKS
Windsor House Antiques (Leeds)
Ltd.,
18-20 Benson Street, Leeds
Tel: (0532) 444666

MUSICAL
INSTRUMENTS
LONDON
Mayflower Antiques,
117 Portobello Road, W11
Tel: 01-727 0381
(Sats. only 7am-3pm)

ESSEX
Mayflower Antiques,
2 Una Road, Parkeston, Harwich
Tel: (0255) 504079

KENT
David Bailey Pianos Warehouse,
Ramsgate Road, Sandwich
Tel: (0304) 613948

SUFFOLK
The Suffolk Piano Workshop,
The Snape, Maltings
Tel: (072 888) 677

SUSSEX
Sound Instruments,
Lower Barn Farm, Horsted Green,
Nr. Uckfield
Tel: (0825) 61594

OXON
Laurie Leigh Antiques,
36 High Street, Oxford
Tel: (0865) 244197

PORCELAIN
LONDON
Albert Amor Ltd.,
37 Bury Street, St. James's, SW1
Tel: 01-930 2444
Antique Porcelain Co. Ltd.,
149 New Bond Stret, W1
Tel: 01-629 1254
Susan Becker,
18 Lower Richmond Road, SW15
Tel: 01-788 9082
David Brower Antiques,
113 Kensington Church Street,
W8
Tel: 01-221 4155

Cale Antiques,
24 Cale Street, Chelsea Green,
SW3
Tel: 01-589 6146

Cathay Antiques,
12 Thackeray Street, W8
Tel: 01-937 6066

Craven Antiques,
17 Garson House, Gloucester
Terrace, W2
Tel: 01-262 4176

Marilyn Delion,
Wyllie Gallery, 12 Needham Road,
W11
Tel: 01-727 0606

Delomosne & Son Ltd.,
4 Campden Hill Road, W8
Tel: 01-937 1804

H. & W. Deutsch Antiques,
111 Kensington Church Street,
W8
Tel: 01-727 5984

Miss Fowler,
1A Duke Street, Manchester
Square, W1
Tel: 01-935 5187

Graham & Oxley (Antiques) Ltd.,
101 Kensington Church Street,
W8
Tel: 01-229 1850

Grosvenor Antiques Ltd.,
27 Holland Street, Kensington,
W8
Tel: 01-937 8649

Harcourt Antiques,
5 Harcourt Street, W1
Tel: 01-723 5919

Heirloom & Howard Ltd.,
1 Hay Hill, Berkeley Square, W1
Tel: 01-493 5868

Hoff Antiques Ltd.,
66A Kensington Church Street,
W8
Tel: 01-229 5516

Klaber & Klaber,
2A Bedford Gardens, Kensington
Church Street, W8
Tel: 01-727 4573

D. M. & P. Manheim Ltd.,
69 Upper Berkeley Street,
Portman Square, W1
Tel: 01-723 6595

Mayfair Gallery,
97 Mount Street, W1
Tel: 01-499 5315

Mercury Antiques,
1 Ladbroke Road, W11
Tel: 01-727 5106

St. Jude's Antiques,
107 Kensington Church Street,
W8
Tel: 01-727 8737

Edward Salti,
43 Davies Street, W1
Tel: 01-629 2141

Gerald Sattin Ltd.,
25 Burlington Arcade, Piccadilly,
W1
Tel: 01-493 6557

Jean Sewell (Antiques) Ltd.,
3 Campden Street, Kensington
Church Street, W8
Tel: 01-727 3122

Simon Spero,
109 Kensington Church Street,
W8
Tel: 01-727 7413

Aubrey Spiers Antiques,
Shop C5, Chenil Galleries,
183 King's Road, SW3
Tel: 01-352 7384

Constance Stobo,
31 Holland Street, W8
Tel: 01-937 6282

Earle D. Vandekar of
Knightsbridge Ltd.,
138 Brompton Road, SW3
Tel: 01-589 8481/3398

Venner's Antiques,
7 New Cavendish Street, W1
Tel: 01-935 0184

Winifred Williams,
3 Bury Street, St. James's, SW1
Tel: 01-930 4732

AVON
Andrew Dando,
4 Wood Street, Queen Square,
Bath
Tel: (0225) 22702

BERKS
Len's Crested China,
Twyford Antiques Centre, Nr.
Reading
Tel: (0753) 35162

The Old School Antiques,
Dorney, Windsor
Tel: (062 86) 3247

CORNWALL
Mrs. Margaret Chesterton,
33 Pentewan Road, St. Austell
Tel: (0726) 72926

London Apprentice Antiques,
Pentewan House, St. Austell
Tel: (0726) 63780

DERBYS
C. B. Sheppard Antiques
(appointment only),
Hurst Lodge, Chesterfield Road,
Tibshelf
Tel: (0773) 872419

DEVON
David J. Thorn,
2 High Street, Budleigh Salterton
Tel: (039 54) 2448

GLOS
Gloucester House Antiques,
Market Place, Fairford
Tel: (0285) 712790

Hamand Antiques,
Friday Street, Painswick
Tel: (0452) 812310

Pamela Rowan,
High Street, Blockley, Nr.
Moreton-in-Marsh
Tel: (0386) 700280

Studio Antiques Ltd.,
Bourton-on-the-Water
Tel: (0451) 20352

Wain Antiques,
45 Long Street, Tetbury
Tel: (0666) 52440

HANTS
Gerald Austin Antiques,
2A Andover Road, Winchester
Tel: (0962) 69824 Ext. 2

Goss & Crested China Ltd.,
62 Murray Road, Horndean
Tel: (0705) 597440

HEREFORD &
WORCS
Sabina Jennings,
Newcourt Park, Lugwardine
Tel: (0432) 850752

M. Lees & Sons,
Tower House, Severn Street,
Worcester
Tel: (0905) 26620

KENT
Bygones,
Peirce Cottage, Charing, Ashford
Tel: (023371) 2494

Dunsdale Lodge Antiques,
Brasted Road, Westerham
Tel: (0959) 62160

The History in Porcelain Collector,
High Street, Shoreham Village,
Nr. Sevenoaks
Tel: (095 92) 3416

Steppes Hill Farm Antiques,
Stockbury, Sittingbourne
Tel: (0795) 842205

W. W. Warner (Antiques) Ltd.,
The Green, Brasted
Tel: (0959) 63698

LANCS
Burnley Antiques & Fine Arts
Ltd.,
336A Colne Road, Burnley
Tel: (0282) 20143/65172

LEICS
Charnwood Antiques,
54 Sparrow Hill, Loughborough
Tel: (0509) 231750

NORFOLK
T. C. S. Brooke,
The Grange, Wroxham
Tel: (060 53) 2644

Margaret Corson,
Irstead Manor, Neatishead
Tel: (0692) 630274

OXON
Castle Antiques,
Lamb Arcade, Wallingford, Oxon
Tel: (0491) 35166

David John Ceramics,
11 Acre End Street, Eynsham,
Oxford
Tel: (0865) 880786

SHROPS
Castle Gate Antiques,
15 Castle Gate, Shrewsbury
Tel: (0743) 61011 evenings

Teme Valley Antiques,
1 The Bull Ring, Ludlow
Tel: (0584) 4686

Tudor House Antiques,
33 High Street, Ironbridge
Tel: (095 245) 3237

SURREY
Elias Clark Antiques Ltd.,
1 The Cobbles, Bletchingley
Tel: (0883) 843714

J. P. Raison (by appointment only),
Heathcroft, Walton Heath,
Tadworth
Tel: (073 781) 3557

Whittington Galleries,
22 Woodend, Sutton
Tel: 01-644 9327

SUSSEX
Barclay Antiques,
7 Village Mews, Little Common,
Bexhill-on-Sea
Tel: (0797) 222734 home

Ron Beech L.A.P.A.D.A.,
150 Portland Road, Hove
Tel: (0273) 724477

Geoffrey Godden,
Chinaman, 17-19 Crescent Road,
Worthing
Tel: (0903) 35958

William Hockley Antiques,
East Street, Petworth
Tel: (0798) 43172

Leonard Russell,
21 King's Avenue, Newhaven
Tel: (0273) 515153

WILTS
The China Hen,
9 Woolley Street, Bradford-on-
Avon
Tel: (022 16) 3369

Mark Collier Antiques,
High Street, Downton
Tel: (0725) 21068

WORCS
Gavina Ewart,
60-62 High Street, Broadway
Tel: (0386) 853371

YORKS
Brian Bowden,
199 Carr House Road, Doncaster
Tel: (0302) 65353

David Love,
10 Royal Parade, Harrogate
Tel: (0423) 65797

Nanbooks,
Undercliffe Cottage, Duke Street,
Settle
Tel: (072 92) 3324

WALES
Brenin Porcelain & Pottery,
Old Wool Barn, Verity's Court,
Cowbridge, South Glamorgan
Tel: (044 63) 3893

Gwalia Antiques,
Main Street, Goodwick,
Fishguard, Dyfed
Tel: (0348) 872634

POTTERY
LONDON
Britannia,
Stand 101, Gray's Market,
58 Davies Street, W1
Tel: 01-629 6772

Cale Antiques,
24 Cale Street, Chelsea Green,
SW3
Tel: 01-589 6146

Gerald Clark Antiques,
1 High Street, Mill Hill Village,
NW7
Tel: 01-906 0342

Marilyn Delion,
Wyllie Gallery, 12 Needham Road,
W11
Tel: 01-727 0606

Richard Dennis,
144 Kensington Church Street,
W8
Tel: 01-727 2061

Graham & Oxley (Antiques) Ltd.,
101 Kensington Church Street,
W8
Tel: 01-229 1850

Jonathan Horne,
66C Kensington Church Street,
W8
Tel: 01-221 5658

D. M. & P. Manheim Ltd.,
69 Upper Berkeley Street,
Portman Square, W1
Tel: 01-723 6595

J. & J. May,
40 Kensington Church Street, W8
Tel: 01-937 3575

Mercury Antiques,
1 Ladbroke Road, W11
Tel: 01-727 5106

Oliver-Sutton Antiques,
34C Kensington Church Street,
W8
Tel: 01-937 0633

Rogers de Rin,
76 Royal Hospital Road, SW3
Tel: 01-352 9007

St. Jude's Antiques,
107 Kensington Church Street,
W8
Tel: 01-727 8737

Alistair Sampson Antiques,
156 Brompton Road, SW3
Tel: 01-589 5272

Constance Stobo,
31 Holland Street, W8
Tel: 01-937 6282

Earle D. Vandekar of
Knightsbridge Ltd.,
138 Brompton Road, SW3
Tel: 01-589 8481 & 3398

CORNWALL
Mrs. Margaret Chesterton,
33 Pentewan Road, St. Austell
Tel: (0726) 72926

CUMBRIA
Kendal Studio Pottery,
2-3 Wildman Street, Kendal
Tel: (0539) 23291

DEVON
David J. Thorn,
2 High Street, Budleigh Salterton
Tel: (039 54) 2448

GLOS.
Wain Antiques,
45 Long Street, Tetbury
Tel: (0666) 52440

KENT
Bygones,
Peirce Cottage, Charing, Ashford
Tel: (0233) 712494

A. C. Scott,
Dunsdale Lodge Antiques, Brasted
Road, Westerham
Tel: (0959) 62160

W. W. Warner (Antiques) Ltd.,
The Green, Brasted
Tel: (0959) 63698

LANCS
Burnely Antiques & Fine Arts
Ltd.,
336A Colne Road, Burnley
Tel: (0282) 20143/65172

NORFOLK
Margaret Corson,
Irstead Manor, Neatishead
Tel: (0692) 630274

SURREY
Elias Clark Antiques Ltd.,
1 The Cobbles, Bletchingley
Tel: (0883) 843714

Whittington Galleries,
22 Woodend, Sutton
Tel: 01-644 9327

SUSSEX
Leonard Russell,
21 King's Avenue, Newhaven
Tel: (0273) 515153

WILTS
Bratton Antiques,
Market Place, Westbury
Tel: (0373) 823021

YORKS
Nanbooks,
Undercliffe Cottage, Duke Street,
Settle
Tel: (072 92) 3324

WALES
Brenin Porcelain & Pottery,
Old Wool Barn, Verity's Court,
Cowbridge, South Glamorgan
Tel: (044 63) 3893

SCIENTIFIC INSTRUMENTS
LONDON
Jilliana Ranicar-Breese,
Martin Breese Ltd.,
164 Kensington Park Road,
Notting Hill Gate, W11
Tel: 01-727 9378
(Optical Toys/Illusion)

Arthur Davidson Ltd.,
78-79 Jermyn Street, SW1
Tel: 01-930 6687

Mariner Antiques Ltd.,
55 Curzon Street, W1
Tel: 01-499 0171

Mayfair Microscopes Ltd.,
64 Burlington Arcade, W1
Tel: 01-629 2616

Mayflower Antiques,
117 Portobello Road, W11
Tel: 01-727 0381
(Sats. only 7am-3pm)

Arthur Middleton Ltd.,
12 New Row, Covent Garden, WC2
Tel: 01-836 7042/7062

Trevor Philip & Sons Ltd.,
75A Jermyn Street, St. James's,
SW1
Tel: 01-930 2954/5

Harriet Wynter Ltd. (by
appointment only),
50 Redcliffe Road, SW10
Tel: 01-352 6494

BEDS
Christopher Sykes Antiques,
The Old Parsonage, Woburn,
Milton Keynes
Tel: (052 525) 259/467

DEVON
Galaxy Arts,
38 New Street, Barbican,
Plymouth
Tel: (0752) 667842

ESSEX
Mayflower Antiques,
2 Una Road, Parkeston, Harwich
Tel: (0255) 504079

GLOS
Country Life Antiques,
Sheep Street, Stow-on-the-Wold
Tel: (0451) 30776
Also at:
Grey House, The Square, Stow-on-
the-Wold
Tel: (0451) 31564

Wain Antiques,
45 Long Street, Tetbury
Tel: (0666) 52440

KENT
Hadlow Antiques,
No. 1 The Pantile, Tunbridge
Wells
Tel: (0892) 29858

NORFOLK
Margaret Corson,
Irstead Manor, Neatishead
Tel: (0692) 630274

Humbleyard Fine Art,
Waterfall Cottage, Mill Street,
Swanton Morley
Tel: (036 283) 793
Also at:
Coltishall Antiques Centre,
Coltishall, Norfolk

Turret House (Dr. D. H. Morgan),
27 Middleton Street, Wymondham
Tel: (0953) 603462

SURREY
Whittington Galleries,
22 Woodend, Sutton
Tel: 01-644 9327

WALES
Brenin Porcelain & Pottery,
Old Wool Barn, Verity's Court,
Cowbridge, South Glamorgan
Tel: (044 63) 3893

SILVER
LONDON
Asprey PLC,
165-169 New Bond Street, W1
Tel: 01-493 6767

N. Bloom & Son (Antiques) Ltd.,
40-41 Conduit Street, W1
Tel: 01-629 5060

Bond Street Galleries,
111-112 New Bond Street, W1
Tel: 01-493 6180

J. H. Bourdon-Smith,
24 Mason's Yard, Duke Street, St.
James's SW1
Tel: 01-839 4714

H. & W. Deutsch Antiques,
111 Kensington Church Street,
W8
Tel: 01-727 5984

Howard Jones,
43 Kensington Church Street, W8
Tel: 01-937 4359

London International Silver Co.,
82 Portobello Road, W11
Tel: 01-979 6523

S. J. Phillips Ltd.,
139 New Bond Street, W1
Tel: 01-629 6261/2

Gerald Sattin Ltd.,
25 Burlington Arcade, Piccadilly,
W1
Tel: 01-493 6557

S. J. Shrubsole Ltd.,
43 Museum Street, WC1
Tel: 01-405 2712

KENT
Bygones,
Peirce Cottage, Charing, Ashford
Tel: (0233) 712494

Ralph Antiques,
40A Sandwich Industrial Estate,
Sandwich
Tel: (0304) 611949/612882

Steppes Hill Farm Antiques,
Stockbury, Sittingbourne
Tel: (0795) 842205

OXON
Thames Gallery,
Thameside, Henley-on-Thames
Tel: (0491) 572449

SOMERSET
Edward A. Nowell,
21-23 Market Place, Wells
Tel: (0749) 72415

YORKS
Georgian House,
88 Main Street, Bingley
Tel: (0274) 568883

WINE ANTIQUES
LONDON
Brian Beat,
36 Burlington Gardens, W1
Tel: 01-437 4975

Graham Bell,
177/8 Grays Antique Market,
58 Davies Street, W1
Tel: 01-493 1148

Eximious Ltd.,
10 West Halkin Street, W1
Tel: 01-627 2888

Richard Kihl,
164 Regent's Park Road, NW1
Tel: 01-586 3838

AVON
Robin Butler,
9 St. Stephen's Street, Bristol
Tel: (0272) 276586

BEDS
Christopher Sykes Antiques,
The Old Parsonage, Woburn,
Milton Keynes
Tel: (052 525) 259 & 467

CHESHIRE
Bacchus Antiques,
27 Grange Avenue, Hale, Nr.
Altrincham
Tel: 061-980 4747

WARWICKSHIRE
Colliers, Bigwood & Bewlay
Auctioneers,
The Old School, Tiddington,
Stratford-upon-Avon
Tel: (0789) 69415

FAIR ORGANISERS
LONDON
K.M. Fairs,
58 Mill Lane, NW6
Tel: 01-794 3551

Penman Antique Fairs,
Cockhaise Mill, Lindfield,
Haywards Heath
Tel: (044 47) 2514

Philbeach Events Ltd.,
Earl's Court Exhibition Centre,
Warwick Road, SW5
Tel: 01-385 1200

BERKS
Bridget Fraser,
Granny's Attic Antique Fairs,
Dean House, Cookham Dean
Tel: (062 84) 3658

Silhouette Fairs (inc. Newbury
Antique & Collectors' Fairs),
25 Donnington Square, Newbury
Tel: (0635) 44338

CHESHIRE
Susan Brownson,
Antique Fairs North West,
Brownslow House, Gt. Budworth,
Northwich
Tel: (0606) 891267 & (061962)
5629

Pamela Robertson,
8 St. George's Crescent, Queen's
Park, Chester
Tel: (0244) 678106

CORNWALL
West Country Antiques &
Collectors' Fairs (Gerry Mosdell),
Hillside, St. Issey, Wadebridge
Tel: (084 14) 666

ESSEX
Robert Bailey Antiques Fairs,
1 Roll Gardens, Gants Hill
Tel: 01-550 5435

Stephen Charles Fairs,
3 Leigh Hill, Leigh-on-Sea
Tel: (0702) 714649/556745 and
(0268) 774977

Emporium Fairs,
Longlands, Kedington, Haverhill
Tel: (0440) 704632

Heirloom Markets,
11 Wellfields, Writtle, Chelmsford
Tel: (0245) 422208

HERTS
Bartholomew Fayres,
Executive House, The Maltings,
Station Road, Sawbridgeworth
Tel: (0279) 725809
Also in: Essex

Camfair (Ros Coltman),
Longlands, Kedington, Haverhill
Tel: (0440) 704632

HUMBERSIDE
Seaclef Fairs,
78 Humberston Avenue,
Humberston, Grimsby
Tel: (0472) 813858

KENT
Darent Fairs,
Whitestacks Cottage, Crockenhill
Lane, Eynsford
Tel: (0474) 63992

Tudor Fairs,
59 Rafford Way, Bromley
Tel: 01-460 2670

NOTTS
Top Hat Exhibitions Ltd.,
66-72 Derby Road, Nottingham
Tel: (0602) 419143

OXON
Portcullis Fairs,
6 St. Peter's Street, Wallingford
Tel: (0491) 39345

SURREY
Antiques & Collectors' Club,
No. 1 Warehouse, Horley Row,
Horley
Tel: (0293) 772206

Joan Braganza,
76 Holmesdale Road, Reigate
Tel: (073 72) 45587

Cultural Exhibitions Ltd.,
8 Meadrow, Godalming
Tel: (048 68) 22562

Historic and Heritage Fayres
Tel: 01-398 5324

SUSSEX
Brenda Lay,
Dyke Farm, West Chiltington
Road, Pulborough
Tel: (079 82) 2447

Penman Antique Fairs,
Cockhaise Mill, Lindfield,
Haywards Heath
Tel: (044 47) 2514

YORKS
Bowman Antique Fairs,
P.O. Box 37, Otley
Tel: (0532) 843333
Also in:
Cheshire, Cleveland, Lincs, Staffs
and Yorks

SHIPPERS
LONDON
Featherston Shipping Ltd.,
24 Hampton House, 15-17 Ingate
Place, SW8
Tel: 01-720 0422

Lockson Services Ltd.,
29 Broomfield Street, E14
Tel: 01-452 3454

Stephen Morris Shipping,
89 Upper Street, N1
Tel: 01-359 3159

Phelps Ltd.,
133-135 St. Margaret's Road,
E. Twickenham
Tel: 01-892 1778/7129

Pitt & Scott Ltd.,
20/24 Eden Grove, N7
Tel: 01-607 7321

DORSET
Alan Franklin Transport,
Unit 8, 27 Black Moor Road,
Ebblake Industrial Estate,
Verwood
Tel: (0202) 826539 & 826394 &
827092

HANTS
Colin Macleod's Antiques
Warehouse,
139 Goldsmith Avenue, Hants
Tel: (0705) 816278

HUMBERSIDE
Geoffrey Mole,
400 Wincolmlee, Hull
Tel: (0482) 27858

LANCS
G. G. Antique Wholesalers,
25 Middleton Road, Middleton,
Morecambe
Tel: (0524) 51565

West Lancs. Antique Exports,
Black Horse Farm, 123 Liverpool
Road, South Burscough, Nr.
Ormskirk
Tel: (0704) 894634/35720

SOMERSET
Colin Dyte Antiques,
Huntspill Road, Highbridge
Tel: (0278) 788590

STAFFS
Aspleys Antiques,
Compton Mill, Compton, Leek
Tel: (0538) 373396

SUSSEX
British Antiques Exporters Ltd.,
Queen Elizabeth Avenue, Burgess
Hill
Tel: (044 46) 45577

Graham Price Antiques Ltd.,
A27 Antiques Complex, Unit 4,
Chaucer Industrial Estate, Dittons
Road, Polegate
Tel: (032 12) 7167 & 7681

Lou Lewis,
Avis Way, Newhaven
Tel: (0273) 513091

Peter Semus Antiques,
The Warehouse, Gladstone Road,
Portslade
Tel: (0273) 420154/202989

S.J.B. Shipping,
Chewton High Street, Angmering
Tel: (0903) 770198/785560

SCOTLAND
Mini-Move Maxi-Move (Euro)
Ltd.,
27 Jock's Lodge, London Road,
Edinburgh
Tel: 031-652 1255

TRADE SUPPLIERS
Air Improvement Centre Ltd.,
23 Denbigh Street, London, SW1
Tel: 01-834 2834

Green & Stone of Chelsea,
259 King's Road, London, SW3
Tel: 01-352 6521/0837

C. & A. J. Barmby,
Fine Art Accessories, 68 Judd
Road, Tonbridge, Kent
Tel: (0732) 356479

G. G. Antique Wholesalers,
25 Middleton Road, Middleton,
Morecambe
Tel: (0524) 51565

Stanley Tools Ltd.,
Woodside, Sheffield, S. Yorkshire
Tel: (0742) 78678

Westham Desk Leathers,
High Street, Westham, Pevensey
Tel: (0323) 766483

ANTIQUE CENTRES AND MARKETS
LONDON
A.B.C. Antique Centres,
15 Flood Street, SW3
Tel: 01-351 5353

Alfies Antique Market,
13-25 Church Street, NW8
Tel: 01-723 6066

Antiquarius Antique Market,
135/141 King's Road, Chelsea,
SW3
Tel: 01-351 5353

Bermondsey Antique Market &
Warehouse,
173 Bermondsey Street, SE1
Tel: 01-407 2040

Bond Street Antique Centre,
124 New Bond Street, W1

Chenil Galleries,
181-183 King's Road, SW3
Tel: 01-351 5353

Grays,
1-7 Davies Mews, 58 Davies
Street, W1
Tel: 01-629 7034

Hampstead Antique Emporium,
12 Heath Street, NW3
Tel: 01-794 3297

London Silver Vaults,
Chancery House, 53-65 Chancery
Lane, WC2
Tel: 01-242 3844

AVON
Bath Antique Market,
Guinea Lane, Paragon, Bath
Tel: (0225) 22510

Clifton Antiques Market,
26/28 The Mall, Clifton
Tel: (0272) 741627

Great Western Antique Centre,
Bartlett Street, Bath
Tel: (0225) 24243

BEDS
Woburn Abbey Antiques Centre,
Woburn Abbey
Tel: (052 525) 350

BERKS
Twyford Antiques Centre,
1 High Street, Twyford
Tel: (0734) 342161

BUCKS
Great Missenden Antique Arcade,
76 High Street, Gt. Missenden
Tel: (024 06) 2819 & 2330

CAMBS
Collectors' Market,
Dales Brewery, Gwydir Street (off
Mill Road), Cambridge

CHESHIRE
Antique & Collectors Fair,
The Guildhall, Watergate Street,
Chester
(no number)
Chester Antique Centre,
(Antique Forum Ltd.),
41 Lower Bridge Street, Chester
Tel: (0244) 314991

CLEVELAND
Mother Hubbard's Antiques
Arcade,
140 Norton Road, Stockton-on-
Tees
Tel: (0642) 615603

CUMBRIA
Cockermouth Antiques Market,
Main Street, Cockermouth
Tel: (0900) 824346
J. W. Thornton Antiques,
Supermarket, North Terrace,
Bowness-on-Windermere
Tel: (0229) 88745
(0966) 22930 & 25183

DEVONSHIRE
Barbican Antiques Market,
82-84 Vauxhall Street, Barbican,
Plymouth
Tel: (0752) 266927

New Street Antique Centre,
27 New Street, The Barbican,
Plymouth
Tel: (0752) 661165

Torquay Antique Centre,
177 Union Street, Torquay
Tel: (0803) 26621

DORSET
Antique Market,
Town Hall/Corn Exchange,
Dorchester
Tel: (0963) 62478

Antique Market,
Digby Hall, Sherborne
Tel: (0963) 62478

Antiques Trade Warehouse,
28 Lorne Park Road, Bournemouth
Tel: (0202) 292944

Barnes House Antiques Centre,
West Row, Wimborne Minster
Tel: (0202) 886275

ESSEX
Antique Centre,
Doubleday Corner, Coggeshall
Tel: (0376) 62646

Baddow Antiques & Craft Centre,
The Bringy, Church Street, Great
Baddow
Tel: (0245) 71137 & 76159

Boston Hall Antiques Fair,
Boston Hall Hotel, The Leas,
Westcliff-on-Sea
Tel: (0702) 714649

Maldon Antiques & Collectors'
Market,
United Reformed Church Hall,
Market Hill, Maldon
Tel: (078 75) 2826

Orsett Antiques Fair,
Orsett Hall, Prince Charles
Avenue, Orsett
Tel: (0702) 714649

Trinity Antiques Centre,
7 Trinity Street, Colchester
Tel: (0206) 577775

GLOS
Antique Centre,
London House, High Street,
Moreton-in-Marsh
Tel: (0608) 51084

Cheltenham Antique Market,
54 Suffolk Road, Cheltenham
Tel: (0242) 29812/32615/20139

Cirencester Antique Market,
Market Place (Antique Forum
Ltd.), Cirencester
Tel: 01-262 1168 &
01-263 4045

Gloucester Antique Centre,
1 Severn Road, Gloucester
Tel: (0452) 29716

Tewkesbury Antique Centre,
78 Church Street, Tewkesbury
Tel: (0684) 294091

HAMPSHIRE
Winchester Craft & Antique
Market,
King's Walk, Winchester
Tel: (0962) 62277

HEREFORD & WORCESTER
Leominster Antiques Market,
14 Broad Street, Leominster
Tel: (0568) 2189/2155

HERTS
The Herts. & Essex Antiques
Centre,
The Maltings, Station Road,
Sawbridgeworth
Tel: (0279) 722044

St. Albans Antique Market,
Town Hall, Chequer Street, St.
Albans
Tel: (0727) 66100 & 50427

KENT
The Antiques Centre,
120 London Road, Sevenoaks
Tel: (0732) 452104

Canterbury Antique Centre,
Latimers, Ivy Lane (Nr. Coach
Park), Canterbury
Tel: (0227) 60378

Canterbury Weekly Antique
Market,
Sidney Cooper Centre, Canterbury
(No telephone no.)

Hoodeners Antiques & Collectors's
Market,
Red Cross Centre, Lower Chantry
Lane, Canterbury
Tel: (022 770) 437

Hythe Antique Centre,
The Old Post Office, 5 High Street,
Hythe
Tel: (0303) 69643

Noah's Ark Antique Centre,
King Street, Sandwich
Tel: (0304) 611144

The Old Rose Gallery (Antique
Market),
152 High Street, Sandgate
Tel: (0303) 39173

Rochester Antiques & Flea
Market,
Rochester Market, Corporation
Street, Rochester
Tel: 01-262 1168 &
01-263 4045

Sandgate Antiques Centre,
61-63 Sandgate High Street,
Sandgate (Nr. Folkestone)
Tel: (0303) 38987

Westerham Antique Centre,
18 Market Square, Westerham
Tel: (0959) 62080

LANCS
Bolton Thursday Antique Market,
St. Paul's Parochial Hall
Tel: (0204) 51257 (Thurs. only)

Castle Antiques,
Moore Lane, Clitheroe
Tel: (0254) 35820

Eccles Used Furniture & Antique
Centre,
325/7 Liverpool Road, Patricroft
Bridge, Eccles
Tel: 061-789 4467

Manchester Antique
Hypermarket,
Levenshulme Town Hall, 965
Stockport Road, Levenshulme
Tel: 061-224 2410

North Western Antique Centre,
New Preston Mill (Horrockses
Yard), New Hall Lane, Preston
Tel: (0772) 798159

LEICS
The Kibworth Antique Centre,
5 Weir Road, Kibworth
Tel: (053 753) 2761

Leicester Antique Centre Ltd.,
16-26 Oxford Street, Leicester
Tel: (0533) 553006

LINCS
The Antique Centre,
1 Spilsby Road, Wainfleet
Tel: (0754) 880489

NORFOLK
Coltishall Antiques Centre,
High Street, Coltishall
Tel: (0603) 738306

Holt Antiques Centre,
Albert Hall, Albert Street, Holt
Tel: (0362) 5509 &
(0263) 733301

The Old Granary Antique &
Collectors' Centre,
King Staithe Lane, off Queen's
Street, King's Lynn
Tel: (0553) 5509

Norwich Antique & Collectors'
Centre,
Quayside, Fye Bridge, Norwich
Tel: (0603) 612582

NORTHANTS
Finedon Antiques Centre,
3 Church Street, Finedon
Tel: (0933) 680316

The Village Antique Market,
62 High Street, Weedon
Tel: (0327) 42015

NORTHUMBD
Colmans of Hexham,
(Saleroom & Antique Fair), 15 St.
Mary's Chare, Hexham
Tel: (0434) 603812/605522

NOTTS
East Bridgford Antiques Centre,
Main Street, East Bridgford
Tel: (0949) 20540 & 20741

Newark Art & Antiques Centre,
The Market Place, Chain Lane,
Newark
Tel: (0636) 703959

Nottingham Antique Centre,
British Rail Goods Yard, London
Road, Nottingham
Tel: (0602) 54504/55548

Top Hat Antiques Centre,
66-72 Derby Road, Nottingham
Tel: (0602) 419143

OXFORDSHIRE
The Antique Centre,
Laurel House, Bull Ring, Market
Place, Deddington
Tel: (0869) 38968

SHROPSHIRE
Ironbridge Antique Centre,
Dale End, Ironbridge
Tel: (095 245) 3784

Ludlow Antiques Centre,
29 Corve Street, Ludlow
Tel: (0584) 5157

Shrewsbury Antique Market,
Frankwell Quay Warehouse
(Vintagevale Ltd.), Shrewsbury
Tel: (0734) 50916

SOMERSET
Taunton Antiques Centre,
27/29 Silver Street, Taunton
Tel: (0823) 89327

STAFFS
The Antique Centre,
Royal Hotel, Walsall
Tel: (0922) 24555

Bridge House Antiques &
Collectors' Centre,
56 Newcastle Road, Stone
Tel: (0785) 818218

Rugeley Antique Centre,
161/3 Main Road, Rugeley
Tel: (088 94) 77166

SUFFOLK
Old Town Hall Antique Centre,
High Street, Needham Market
Tel: (0449) 720773

St. John's Antique Centre,
31-32 St. John's Street, Bury St.
Edmunds
Tel: (0284) 3024

Waveney Antique Centre,
The Old School, Peddars Lane,
Beccles
Tel: (0502) 716147

SURREY
Antique Centre,
22 Haydon Place, Corner of Martyr
Road, Guildford
Tel: (0483) 67817

Andrew Cottrell Galleries,
7/9 Church Street, Godalming
Tel: (048 68) 7570

Farnham Antique Centre,
27 South Street, Farnham
Tel: (0252) 724475

Maltings Market,
Bridge Square (Farnham Maltings
Association Ltd.)
Tel: (0252) 726234

The Old Forge Antiques Centre,
The Green, Godstone
Tel: (0883) 843230

The Old Smithy Antique Centre,
7 High Street, Merstham
Tel: (073 74) 2306

Victoria & Edward Antiques,
61 West Street, Dorking
Tel: (0306) 889645

SUSSEX-EAST
Antique Market,
Leaf Hall, Seaside, Eastbourne
Tel: (0323) 27530

Heathfield Antiques Centre,
Heathfield Market, Heathfield
Tel: (042 482) 387

Lewes Antiques Centre,
20 Cliffe High Street, Lewes
Tel: (0273) 476148

Newhaven Flea Market,
28 South Way, Newhaven
Tel: (0273) 517207

Seaford's 'Barn Collectors'
Market',
The Barn, Church Lane, Seaford
Tel: (0323) 890010

Strand Antiques,
Strand House, Rye
Tel: (0797) 222653

SUSSEX-WEST
Antiques Market,
Parish Hall, South Street, Lancing
Tel: (0903) 32414

Arundel Antiques Market,
5 River Road, Arundel
Tel: (0903) 882012

Midhurst Antiques Market,
Knockhundred Row, Midhurst
Tel: (073 081) 4231

Mostyns Antiques Centre,
64 Brighton Road, Lancing
Tel: (0903) 752961

Petworth Antiques Market,
East Street, Petworth
Tel: (0798) 42073

Snoopers Paradise Bric-a-Brac
Market,
over 5, 7, 9 South Farm Road
Robert Warner & Son Ltd.,
South Farm Road, Worthing
Tel: (0903) 32710

Treasure House Antiques Market,
Rear of High Street, in Crown
Yard, Arundel
Tel: (0903) 883101

TYNE & WEAR
Newcastle Antiques Centre,
64-80 Newgate Street, Newcastle-
upon-Tyne
Tel: (0632) 614577

WARWICKSHIRE
Antiques Etc.,
22 Railway Terrace, Rugby
Tel: (0788) 62837

Bidford-on-Avon Antiques Centre,
High Street, Bidford-on-Avon
Tel: (0789) 773680

Kenilworth Monthly Antique
Market,
Greville Suite, De Montfort Hotel,
Kenilworth
Tel: (0926) 55253

Vintage Antique Market,
36 Market Place, Warwick
Tel: (0926) 491527

Warwick Antique Centre,
16-18 High Street, Warwick
Tel: (0962) 492482

WEST MIDLANDS
Birmingham Thursday Antique
Centre,
141 Bromsgrove Street,
Birmingham
Tel: 021-692 1414

The City of Birmingham Antique
Market,
St. Martins Market, Edgbaston
Street
Tel: 021-267 4636

Rock House Antiques & Collectors
Centre,
Rock House, The Rock, Tettenhall,
Wolverhampton
Tel: (0902) 754995

N. YORKS
Grove Collectors' Centre,
Grove Road, Harrogate
Tel: (0423) 61680

West Park Antiques Pavilion,
20 West Park, Harrogate
Tel: (0423) 61758

S. YORKS
Treasure House Antiques and
Antique Centre,
8-10 Swan Street, Bawtry
Tel: (0302) 710621

W. YORKS
Halifax Antique Centre,
Queen's Road/Gibbet Street,
Halifax
Tel: (0422) 66657

SCOTLAND
Bath Street Antique Centre,
203 Bath Street, Glasgow
Tel: 041-248 4220

Corner House Antiques,
217 St. Vincent Street, Glasgow
Tel: 041-221 1000

The Victorian Village,
57 West Regent Street, Glasgow
Tel: 041-332 0808

**GRAYS
IN
DAVIES
STREET**

INDEX